Handbook of Unethical Work Behavior

Handbook of Unethical Work Behavior

Implications for Individual Well-Being

Edited by
Robert A. Giacalone and Mark D. Promislo

M.E.Sharpe
Armonk, New York
London, England

The EuroSlavic fonts used to create this work are © 1986–2012 Payne Loving Trust.
EuroSlavic is available from Linguist's Software, Inc.,
www.linguistsoftware.com, P.O. Box 580, Edmonds, WA 98020-0580 USA
tel (425) 775-1130.

Library of Congress Cataloging-in-Publication Data

Handbook of unethical work behavior : implications for individual well-being / edited by Robert A. Giacalone,
and Mark D. Promislo.
    p. cm.
  Includes bibliographical references and index.
  ISBN 978-0-7656-3255-5 (hardcover : alk. paper) — ISBN 978-0-7656-3256-2 (pbk. : alk paper)
1. Harassment. 2. Work environment. 3. Leadership—Moral and ethical aspects. I. Giacalone, Robert A.
II. Promislo, Mark D., 1964–

  HM1116.H36 2013
  323.4′9—dc23   2012003925

Printed in the United States of America

The paper used in this publication meets the minimum requirements of
American National Standard for Information Sciences
Permanence of Paper for Printed Library Materials,
ANSI Z 39.48-1984.

IBT (c)   10   9   8   7   6   5   4   3   2   1
IBT (p)   10   9   8   7   6   5   4   3   2   1

We dedicate this book to our families, who make life worth living

Bob — *Karen, Drew, Liz, and Josh*

Mark — *Susan, Alexa, and Carly*

CONTENTS

Part III. Individual Differences, Justice, and Moral Emotions

Part IV. Organizational and Societal Perspectives

FOREWORD

Diane L. Swanson

The point of an edited volume is to bring together experts who can advance knowledge in a particular area of inquiry. In this respect, the *Handbook of Unethical Work Behavior: Implications for Individual Well-Being* will not disappoint. Edited by Robert A. Giacalone and Mark D. Promislo, this volume follows in the tradition of a humanistic inquiry into the quality of worklife. In this tradition, the *Handbook* delivers what undoubtedly will come to be known as a groundbreaking statement that will spur further research on unethical work behavior and individual well-being. The volume will influence teaching, research, and management practice for years to come.

The genesis of the *Handbook* can be found in an article by Giacalone and Promislo (2010) in which they note an important limitation of research on ethics and social responsibility. Specifically, they hold that this inquiry is usually tethered to an organization-centered worldview, which focuses on investigating an organization's relationships with various stakeholders and the impact of its conduct on society (and frequently the issue of firms' profitability). According to the authors, the problem is that when organizations are the foci of analysis, individuals get lost in the translation. In contrast, organizational scholars from various areas, such as industrial psychology and human resource management, have examined specific behaviors in organizations that diminish the quality of life for individuals, These behaviors include abusive supervision, bullying, discrimination, incivility, and others forms of injustice. Taken together, the focus on organizational and societal outcomes (in ethics and social responsibility inquiry) and the emphasis on individual outcomes (in organizational research) demonstrate a considerable interest in how organizations can function as vehicles for societal and individual well-being. Even so, Giacalone and Promislo view this cumulative scholarship as incomplete. As visionaries who insist on a human-centered approach to what is quintessentially a human-impacted area of life, they call for research into unethical workplace behavior that is both deeper and broader than the current body of knowledge conveys. In terms of depth, they call for more attention to the harm that unethical behavior can cause to individual well-being on physical, psychological, and emotional levels. In terms of breadth, they advocate for further research into the negative effects of unethical conduct not only on the victim but on the entire network of people associated with the target of undesirable behavior, including witnesses, friends, coworkers, family members, and even the perpetrators themselves.

The appeal for breadth is especially significant. The effects of unethical behavior at work will be vastly understated if the human-centered approach advocated by Giacalone and Promislo is not extended to those who are indirectly affected by the toxicity of such behavior. In fact, this approach can bridge the two veins of scholarship mentioned earlier—ethics and social responsibility on the one hand, and organizational behavior on the other (see Swanson and Niehoff, 2001). That is, a deeper grasp of the impact of unethical behavior on the individual can help scholars and practitioners comprehend the ripple effects in social networks that add up to significant harm for society at large. Authored by Promislo, Giacalone, and Jurkiewicz, the *Handbook*'s introductory chapter provides this depth and breadth with a systematic approach to the diminished psychological and physical well-being of those harmed by unethical workplace behavior. This method could ultimately influence management practice and public policy, since a decline in well-being typically translates into lost productivity and money spent for medical and psychological treatments. Nevertheless, as conveyed in the introductory chapter, the human-centered approach does not take financial considerations as the primary reason to understand and promote ethics in the workplace (Giacalone and Thompson, 2006). Something more existential is at stake—the dark side of unethical behavior in organizations—an experience from which few in contemporary life can escape. The message is that we need to understand this dark matter in order to envision and promote well-being in the workplace and society at large. For, if organizations cannot function as vehicles for individual and societal well-being, then their justification for existence should be called to account, a point on which the human-focused and organization-centered scholars seem to agree.

Readers will find depth and breadth of research represented in the four sections of this volume: (1) Attacking Others: Revenge, Aggression, Bullying, and Abuse; (2) Harmful Behaviors and Work Stress; (3) Individual Differences, Justice, and Moral Emotions; and (4) Organizational and Societal Perspectives. The chapters in these sections add up to a think tank of multidisciplinary scholarship rarely found in one outlet. As a result, the *Handbook of Unethical Work Behavior: Implications for Individual Well-Being* is destined to provoke exciting new channels of inquiry into an area of great import in human affairs.

REFERENCES

Giacalone, R.A., and Promislo, M.D. 2010. Unethical and unwell: Decrements in well-being and unethical activity at work. *Journal of Business Ethics,* 91, 275–297.
Giacalone, R.A., and Thompson, K.R. 2006. Business ethics and social responsibility education: Shifting the worldview. *Academy of Management Learning and Education*, 5, 266–277.
Swanson, D.L., and Niehoff, B. 2001. Business citizenship outside and inside organizations: An emergent synthesis of corporate responsibility and employee citizenship. In *Perspectives on Corporate Citizenship*, ed. J. Andriof and M. McIntosh, 104–116. Sheffield, UK: Greenleaf.

PREFACE

We have all seen the ongoing reports of disturbing unethical behavior at workplaces across the globe. Often it feels as if we are witnessing scandal after scandal, with only a small respite in between. Ethical debacles have undermined corporations both in the United States (e.g., Enron, Tyco, Adelphia, and WorldCom) and internationally (e.g., Sumitomo, Parmalat, Toyota, and Ahold). And just as often, it seems that a host of journalists and academics focus on the damaging economic impact of these scandals—reflected in depressed stock prices, ruined company reputations, and individuals' finances.

But what receives less attention is that these financial ramifications are not the only negative effects of unethical behavior, and in fact may not even be the most significant to us personally. A few years ago, in our paper, "Unethical and Unwell" (Giacalone and Promislo, 2010), we proposed that unethical behavior at work is damaging to individual well-being at physical, psychological, and emotional levels. Further, we highlighted that these negative effects can be seen not just in the direct victims of immoral acts. Indeed, an entire web of people can be harmed, including witnesses to the acts, perpetrators themselves, and people associated with a victim, witness, or perpetrator (such as friends, coworkers, or family members).

This book illustrates our hypothesis that unethical workplace behaviors have a significant impact on people's well-being. This impact can be seen in mental health problems like depression and anxiety, as well as serious and life-threatening physical conditions such as heart disease. The net effect of the unethical actions described in this book is frightening, and we believe that these issues should receive more research attention. To that end, most chapters conclude with suggestions for future research and new directions to explore.

We believe that specific types of unethical workplace activity can be identified, and their impact measured on individual well-being both inside and outside the organization. The volume builds on an interdisciplinary view of ethics that taps the literature in organizational behavior, human resource management, psychology, sociology, traumatology, and medicine. It provides a burgeoning scientific interest and investigation into the role that ethics plays in well-being, with each chapter approaching the theme from the authors' areas of expertise. Collectively, these chapters provide a framework for inquiry and an impetus for further study on how the unethical workplace behaviors we read about in the press can have a very personal impact on people's lives. We hope that this book will spur scientific work to further explore this connection and that more scholars will choose to advance this new ethics frontier.

We would like first to thank the authors for their considerable efforts toward developing this volume. We are honored that they were willing to lend their expertise to this endeavor. We would also like to recognize Harry Briggs, our editor, who remains one of the nicest, most supportive, and honest people in the publishing business. Thanks to Temple University for its summer research grant and sabbatical to the lead editor, and to Rider University for its summer fellowship and encouragement to the second editor. Additional thanks to the MERI Institute of the Graduate Management Admissions Council for a generous Faculty Fellowship that helped to advance the ideas in this book, and to the Institute for Ethical Awareness for their support of this research area. Finally, we wish to express our gratitude and love to our families, friends, and colleagues for their support.

REFERENCE

Giacalone, R.A., and M.D. Promislo. 2010. Unethical and unwell: Decrements in well-being and unethical activity at work. *Journal of Business Ethics,* 91, 275–297.

Robert A. Giacalone
and
Mark D. Promislo

Handbook of Unethical Work Behavior

1

ETHICAL IMPACT THEORY (EIT)

Unethical Work Behavior and Well-Being

Mark D. Promislo, Robert A. Giacalone, and
Carole L. Jurkiewicz

If there was any doubt that ethical standards can have a significant impact on work life, research has shown that such doubt is unwarranted. A multitude of research has demonstrated that ethics is related to a variety of important job-related outcomes. For example, studies have shown that a higher ethical work climate (Mulki, Jaramillo, and Locander, 2008) and top leadership support for ethics (Viswesvaran, Deshpande, and Joseph, 1998) are both positively related to job satisfaction. Ethics codes (Valentine and Fleischman, 2008), ethics training, and perceived corporate social responsibility are also linked to job satisfaction.

Meanwhile, organizational commitment appears to be enhanced by a higher ethical climate, ethics institutionalization (the degree to which an organization incorporates ethics into its decision-making processes) (Singhapakdi and Vitell, 2007), and the existence of an ethics code (Valentine and Barnett, 2002). Employee retention is associated with ethics as well, as perceptions of a high ethical climate are negatively related to turnover intentions (Stewart et al. 2011). Schwepker's (1999) research has shown that ethical conflict resulting from a lack of fit between a manager's and employee's values results in greater intention to leave the organization. Further, ethical climate influences both turnover intention (Mulki, Jaramillo, and Locander, 2008) and conflict with coworkers (Babin, Boles, and Robin, 2000).

Research has also shown the relationship of ethics to other aspects of organizational life. Corporate ethical values are positively related to person–organization fit (Valentine, Godkin, and Lucero, 2002), while ethical climate is associated with decreased individual misconduct (Andreoli and Lefkowitz, 2009), and a heightened degree to which employees identify with their organizations. Ethical practices can also reduce work-related conflict (Jaramillo, Mulki, and Solomon, 2006). A company's ability to foster an ethical corporate culture is linked to an increased ability to attract employees (Sims and Kroeck, 1994) and to enhance job performance (Jaramillo, Mulki, and Solomon, 2006). Perhaps most interestingly, the perception of corporate ethical values is positively related to group creativity (Valentine et al., 2011).

While this research highlights the importance of ethics in creating valuable organizational outcomes, this chapter examines the other side of the coin and in a more personal domain. What are the effects on individual well-being when workers and organizations act *unethically?* Who gets hurt, and what are the negative outcomes of such behavior? Further, what processes (mediators) account for any harm to well-being? In this chapter we argue that the damage caused by unethical behavior needs to be examined holistically. To accomplish this, we adopt a human-centered

3

approach advocated by Giacalone and Thompson (2006). This perspective targets the individual, nonfinancial effects of unethical behavior on employee well-being.

While evidence for the relationship between unethical actions and well-being has been documented (Agervold and Mikkelsen, 2004; Zapf, 1999), its scope has been circumscribed in a triangular fashion. One perimeter is constrained by a focus on discrete relationships between *particular* actions and well-being without connecting them to the broader domain of unethical work behavior. A second boundary is imposed by the lack of a conceptual link to theory; in other words, there is no framework within which to place this research. The third border limits research to those directly victimized by unethical actions, generally ignoring the wider number of individuals who are also harmed by unethical events. In this chapter, we transcend these limitations by advancing a theoretical approach to the relationship between unethical behavior and well-being, building on and expanding the work of Giacalone and Promislo (2010).

THE CONNECTION BETWEEN UNETHICAL BEHAVIOR AND WELL-BEING

Unethical behavior at work ranges from minor acts of deviance to immoral decisions that result in catastrophes such as the BP oil disaster in 2010 (National Commission on the BP Deepwater Horizon Oil Spill and Offshore Drilling, 2011). Three fields of research provide especially clear data on the connection between unethical workplace acts and well-being: discrimination, bullying, and injustice. Discrimination is conceptualized as either individual-level actions, such as biased personnel assessments (Landrine and Klonoff, 1996), or systemic conditions, such as segregation or glass ceilings (Krieger, 1999). Researchers have linked discrimination to detrimental effects on both psychological and physical well-being (Landrine et al., 2006). Individuals subjected to discrimination are likely to show symptoms such as cardiovascular reactivity (Guyll, Matthews, and Bromberger, 2001), sleep problems (Thomas et al., 2006), anxiety (Klonoff, Landrine, and Ullman, 1999), and mental health troubles (Schneider, Hitlan, and Radhakrishnan, 2000).

Arguably, the sturdiest evidence of the link between unethical activity and well-being is the body of research on bullying by peers (Lyons, Tivey, and Ball, 1995) and by supervisors, which Tepper (2000) labels "abusive supervision." Bullying is defined as threatening and/or humiliating behavior that is unrelenting and malevolent toward another person (Lyons, Tivey, and Ball, 1995). Specific bullying behaviors encompass public humiliation, verbal abuse, isolation of workers, and physical intimidation (Mikkelsen and Einarsen, 2001). Research in this area has grown in tandem with the scope of the problem in modern organizations (Vega and Comer, 2005). Victims of bullying suffer from a host of problems such as depression (Niedl, 1996), low self-esteem (Zapf, Knorz, and Kulla, 1996), anxiety (Mikkelsen and Einarsen, 2001), job-induced stress (Agervold and Mikkelsen, 2004), insomnia (Vega and Comer, 2005), and even suicide (Rayner and Hoel, 1997). Bullying victims are also likely to hold pessimistic outlooks on life in general. Research suggests that the effects of bullying can persist over a long period of time and may even be permanent (Hoel, Faragher, and Cooper, 2004).

The literature on organizational injustice provides a third research domain linking unethical behavior to well-being. Repeated episodes of procedural, distributive, and interactional injustices can trigger stress that is linked to increased morbidity and mortality (Geronimus, 1992). Injustice has been connected to coronary heart disease (Kivimäki et al., 2005), sleep disorders (Elovainio et al., 2003), and sickness-related absenteeism (Elovainio, Kivimäki, and Vahtera, 2002).

> Proposition 1:   Unethical behavior at work will be associated with diminished psychological and physical well-being in those victimized by the behavior.

OTHERS HARMED BY UNETHICAL BEHAVIOR

In studying the outcomes of unethical workplace behavior, researchers typically focus on its direct victims (Giacalone and Promislo, 2010). This tendency is understandable; after all, victims are the most visible and the easiest to identify. If a manager discriminates against a worker based on race, people feel outraged and sympathize with the employee. Still, despite these emotions, a focus only on victims provides a myopic view of the potential people who can be harmed by unethical actions. We argue that unethical behavior can also lead to diminished well-being for perpetrators themselves, witnesses to the act, and others indirectly involved, such as coworkers, family, and friends (Evans et al., 2007).

Perpetrators of Unethical Behavior

Those who commit unethical acts are generally held in disdain and thus it is not surprising that the impact on the perpetrators themselves has been little studied. But this disregard for the perpetrator fails to appreciate that situational contexts can exert a powerful influence on individual behavior, leading some to act in violation of their own moral precepts. Milgram's (1975) renowned experiments on obedience to authority first brought this behavioral pattern to light. Further, cultures characterized by extreme competitiveness (Kohn, 1986) or large power disparities (Zimbardo, 2007) can goad individuals into committing unethical acts.

Notably, some research indicates that perpetrators *can* be harmed by their own actions. Some individuals may behave unethically yet be uncomfortable with what they have done; perhaps the social and professional pressures they face to behave wrongly are too strong to resist, yet the cognitive dissonance remains (Evans et al., 2007). In the face of such pressures, some individuals willfully violate their own moral standards. Then, stressed by personal guilt, fear of being caught, or anxiety about the shame they may face, people may experience harm to their well-being (Byrne, 2003).

> Proposition 2:   Engaging in unethical behavior that violates one's personal ethical standards will be associated with diminished psychological and physical well-being.

Witnesses to Unethical Behavior

Beyond the perpetrators and victims, individuals who witness unethical acts, or those who are connected with a perpetrator, witness, or victim, may also show diminished well-being. This can be the result of experiencing the shock of witnessing an immoral act (Bloom, 1995) or vicarious harm by virtue of an empathic attachment to someone cared about (Sexton, 1999).

Those who witness unethical behavior can be harmed in one of three ways (Bloom, 1995): they can be affected because of their empathy for the victim or perpetrator (Pearlman, 1995); they can also be affected by viewing the act through the lens of their own fears (Grunberg, Moore, and Greenberg, 2001), feeling that they, too, could be similarly victimized or forced to engage in unethical acts; and finally, they can witness behavior that shatters their worldview, their conception of organizational systems, or the character of society (Janoff-Bulman, 1989).

The negative impact of unethical behavior can also extend to those who simply hear about a disturbing incident. For example, people experience distress over reports of societal harms or family victimizations, although they have not directly witnessed these acts (Bell and Jenkins, 1993). In the same vein, those who work in a group with a high level of ambient sexual harassment can experience distress even if they are not directly subjected to the abuse (Glomb et al., 1997).

Proposition 3:	Employees who are aware of, or witness, unethical acts that violate their personal ethical standards will suffer diminished psychological and physical well-being.

"Associated persons," those with connections to the perpetrator, victim, or witness (such as family members or coworkers) can also experience reduced well-being. For example, a husband who knows his wife is bullied at work can, through his empathy for her, experience distress. To be affected, an associated person must have a strong connection to the perpetrator, victim, or witness, such that either: (1) they are emotionally connected to the distress those persons exhibit and can empathize with their situation (Pearlman, 1995); or (2) the unethical act violates their own moral standards and causes a shift in their worldview (for example, if a wife learns about her husband's unethical activities at work) (Janoff-Bulman, 1989).

Evidence suggests that the negative impact of unethical behavior on associated persons is substantial. For example, mental health workers are at risk of developing depression, anxiety, and obsessive-compulsive disorders (Collins and Long, 2003). This phenomenon has also been reported in spouses of war veterans (Bramsen, van der Ploeg, and Twisk, 2002) and in the children of parents who are crime victims (Dulmus and Wodarski, 2000).

Proposition 4a:	Persons associated with the perpetrators of unethical acts will suffer diminished psychological and physical well-being.
Proposition 4b:	Persons associated with the victims of unethical acts will suffer diminished psychological and physical well-being.
Proposition 4c:	Persons associated with the witnesses to unethical acts will suffer diminished psychological and physical well-being.

THE MECHANISMS OF DIMINISHED WELL-BEING

Unethical behavior can cause diminished well-being that is immediate and visible, such as with the victims of workplace violence. However, usually the impact of unethical acts is less noticeable, such as when a target of bullying suffers from anxiety and insomnia. A review of the literature reveals three primary mechanisms linking unethical behavior to reductions in well-being: stress, trauma, and poor health behaviors. This interdisciplinary body of research includes psychology (Adler and Matthews, 1994), social psychology (Ormel and Wohlfarth, 1991), criminology (Britt, 2000), traumatology (Schnurr, Friedman, and Bernardy, 2002), and medicine (Scherwitz et al., 1992).

The Stress Mechanism

Work stress remains one of the most extensively researched variables in organizational studies (Jovanovic, Lazaridis, and Stefanovic, 2006). Stress occurs when someone feels they cannot effectively cope with the demands being made of them (Lazarus and Folkman, 1984: 15). Work stress is a key factor both as an outcome of work and life pressures and as a predictor of damaging cardiovascular effects (Theorell and Karasek, 1996) and reduced quality of life (Aneshensel, 1992). Potential sources of work stress include ineffective leadership, environmental hazards, and office politics (Barling, Kelloway, and Frone, 2005).

We assert that unethical behavior is a key work stressor as well. Three aspects of the literature on work stress offer support for this view. First, from a sociological perspective, unhealthy or ethically dysfunctional work environments can lead to stress (Taylor, Repetti, and Seeman, 1997). These environments can include skewed workplace mores (Hammer et al., 2004) and biased cultural and belief systems (Peterson and Wilson, 2004).

Second, the psychological perspective focuses upon individual-level cognitive processing of work events and the consequent appraisals that affect a response (Lazarus and Folkman, 1984). In this framework, the individual's perception of unethical actions, rather than the actions themselves, shape stress and consequent diminished well-being (Jackson, Kubzansky, and Wright, 2006).

Stress responses comprise cognitive, emotional, and motivational changes (Jackson, Kubzansky, and Wright, 2006). In the context of unethical behavior, we theorize that the "role" the individual plays (i.e., perpetrator, victim, witness, or associated person) is a critical part of these changes (Bloom, 1995). Because the perception and appraisal of unethical actions can lead to negative emotions (Lazarus, 1999), which in turn are linked to stress and diminished well-being (Suinn, 2001), one's emotional reactions likely depend on one's connection to the unethical act. Perpetrators may feel guilt in connection with their actions (Byrne, 2003), victims can become enraged (Riggs et al., 1992), and witnesses may be shocked and confused (Janoff-Bulman, 1989). Associated persons can experience a range of emotional responses, depending upon the type of relationship; for example, people associated with the perpetrator can experience shame (Pollock, 1999), while those affiliated with the victim will likely feel empathy (Pearlman, 1995).

Finally, individuals can experience stress due to violation of the basic ethical standards that guide them on a daily basis (Hobfoll, 1988). Such a violation of core beliefs can damage self-worth (Janoff-Bulman, 1989) and individual identity (Tajfel, 1982), leading to feelings of vulnerability and stress (Mikkelsen and Einarsen, 2002). The stress-vulnerability (or "accumulation") model posits that being repeatedly subjected to harmful events takes a heavy toll on coping resources, eventually depleting the individual (Zapf, Knorz, and Kulla, 1996).

The Trauma Mechanism

Trauma is another mechanism by which individuals can suffer diminished well-being as a result of unethical behavior. Such an association is justified for several reasons. First, ethical violations can destroy the assumptions one holds about the world and how it functions (Koltko-Rivera, 2004). Second, ethical violations at work can erode the trust that we place in people or institutions that we depend upon. For example, capricious downsizing can lead to trauma by destroying employee trust while at the same time endangering the employee's livelihood (Moore, Grunberg, and Greenberg, 2004).

Research has even established that certain forms of unethical workplace behavior are associated with posttraumatic stress disorder (PTSD). Most research on PTSD to date has focused on war veterans (Schnurr, Friedman, and Bernardy, 2002) and victims of natural disasters (Joseph, Williams, and Yule, 1993) or violent acts (Kubany et al., 2000). However, PTSD can result from nonlethal events as well, such as bullying (Zapf, Knorz, and Kulla, 1996), corporate downsizing (Moore, Grunberg, and Greenberg, 2004), and sexual harassment (Avina and O'Donohue, 2002; Bowling and Beehr, 2006). Conceptualizing unethical behavior as a precursor to trauma is thus a natural extension of the literature.

Collectively, decades of research have demonstrated that individuals who are traumatized suffer disproportionately from serious psychological and physical effects (Friedman and Schnurr, 1995) that result in significant morbidity and mortality (Schnurr, Friedman, and Bernardy, 2002). These effects are not limited solely to victims of unethical acts. Research shows that perpetrators can be traumatized by their own behavior and ultimately suffer from PTSD (Byrne, 2003; Pollock, 1999). One's breach of values can lead to extreme guilt, anxiety, and reductions in physical and psychological well-being (Evans et al., 2007).

The research is even more expansive regarding both witnesses and associated persons. Such individuals can experience *secondary (or vicarious) trauma,* defined as "the transfer of trauma symptoms from those who have been traumatized to those who have close and extended contact with trauma victims" (Motta et al., 1999: 997). Studies show that individuals who witness a traumatic event, or hear graphic details of it (Collins and Long, 2003), can experience long-term, debilitating stress (Lerias and Byrne, 2003). This secondary trauma can also impact the well-being of those affiliated with trauma victims, such as spouses (Lev-Wiesel and Amir, 2001) or children (Dulmus and Wodarski, 2000). The effects of such secondary trauma are very similar to those experienced by direct victims (Figley, 1995).

Proposition 5a: Perpetrators of unethical acts that violate their personal ethical standards will experience stress or trauma as a result.

Proposition 5b: Victims of unethical acts that violate their personal ethical standards will experience stress or trauma as a result.

Proposition 5c: Witnesses of unethical acts that violate their personal ethical standards will experience stress or trauma as a result.

Proposition 5d: Individuals associated with the perpetrator, victim, or witness to an unethical act that violates their personal ethical standards will experience stress or trauma as a result.

The Health Behaviors Mechanism

While stress and trauma can impact well-being directly, the effects of unethical behavior on well-being can also occur due to negative changes in health behaviors. Such changes refer to an increase in unhealthy habits and activities (e.g., smoking), or to a decrease of beneficial health habits and activities (e.g., exercise). Negative health behaviors are strongly connected to the development of illnesses (Hemingway and Marmot, 1999) and increases in mortality (Adler and Matthews, 1994).

Thus, stress may affect well-being due to unhealthy habits such as excessive alcohol consumption, poor diet, smoking, disturbed sleep patterns, poor compliance with medical regimes, and distrust of physicians (Lee et al., 1992; Leiker and Hailey, 1988).

Meanwhile, the evidence linking trauma to poor health behaviors is also clear (Kilpatrick et al., 1997), with trauma victims found likely to engage in risky behaviors (Felitti et al., 1998) and to abuse alcohol (Stewart, 1996). Within the context of unethical behavior, research shows connections between acts of discrimination (Landrine and Klonoff, 1996) and bullying (Zapf, Knorz, and Kulla, 1996) and poor health behaviors.

Proposition 6:	The stress or trauma resulting from committing, being victimized by, witnessing, or being associated with unethical behavior will lead to poor health behaviors, which in turn contribute to diminished psychological and physical well-being.

MODERATORS OF DECLINES IN WELL-BEING

The literature demonstrates that the relationship between unethical behavior and well-being can depend on a number of factors (Penninx et al., 1996). Thus, not everyone who engages in, is victimized by, witnesses, or is associated with unethical behavior suffers diminished well-being. Moreover, even among those who do show a decline in well-being, not all will experience it to the same degree.

Detailing all potential moderators is beyond the scope of this chapter, but highlighting a few of them is key to understanding the range of research in this area. In general, these moderators can be separated into three key clusters: perceptual variables; sociodemographic variables; and coping behaviors. In the model we introduced previously, moderators can influence both: (1) whether unethical behavior leads to stress/trauma in individuals (which we label "Moderator Path 1"); and (2) whether stress/trauma leads to diminished well-being (which we label "Moderator Path 2"). Here we theorize about which variables are likely to be involved in each of these paths.

Perceptual Variable Cluster: Moderator Path 1

Jackson, Kubzanksy, and Wright (2006) argued that the extent to which an event is perceived as unjust is critical to whether it will produce an impact on well-being. Similarly, in order for an unethical act to negatively impact one's well-being, that person must perceive it as unethical and determine the act to be of sufficient magnitude to have an impact on them (Magley et al., 1999). If this perception does not occur, the individual will experience neither stress nor trauma.

Unethical acts at work may not be perceived as unjust for a number of reasons. First, people may rationalize unethical behaviors as part of the job (e.g., fulfilling a superior's order) (Anand, Ashforth, and Joshi, 2005). Also, individuals may simply be unaware that something unethical has occurred if it happened behind closed doors or was couched in palliative terms (Landau and Freeman-Longo, 1990). The second reason that some may fail to perceive an unethical act as such can be due to self-protection; recognizing an act as unethical can undermine social relationships and organizational life (Contrada et al., 2000). Third, if the unethical act is sufficiently ambiguous, individuals can try to maintain a sense of personal control by diminishing their recognition of its immorality (Landau and Freeman-Longo, 1990).

Even when an action *is* recognized as unethical, individuals' responses are influenced by their prior experiences with immoral actions as well as their attitudes toward particular types of behaviors (Fitzgerald, Swan, and Magley, 1997). For example, some targets of bullying internalize the experience and suffer greatly, while others more readily ignore or downplay the abuse (Parzefall and Salin, 2010). The literature details three types of variables that can impact perceptions of unethical behavior: personality variables, perceived magnitude, and centrality to one's worldview or identity.

Personality Variables

A general disposition to experience anxiety, anger, sadness, guilt, irritability, and other negative emotions (Watson and Pennebaker, 1989), commonly referred to as negative affectivity (NA), can affect how unethical behaviors are perceived. Because individuals high in NA tend to hold negative views of themselves, others, and the world (Watson and Clark, 1984), they may be more liable to perceive an action, event, or working environment as unethical and experience stress as a result. At the same time, such individuals are also more likely to engender social wrath due to their expressed negativity, anger, and dissatisfaction with others (Einarsen, Raknes, and Matthiesen, 1994). Thus, to some extent they may perceive greater levels of unethical behavior because they brought such reactions upon themselves.

Perceived Magnitude

Just as perceptions can vary concerning whether an unethical act has occurred, so too does the perceived magnitude of the event. An individual's perception of the scale of the transgression can be exacerbated if one's possessions or social conditions (e.g., money, relationships, or job environment) are thought to be threatened or lost (Hobfoll, 1988). Likewise, the dose-response model hypothesizes that negative outcomes worsen as the perceived magnitude of the transgression increases (March, 1993). This magnitude can be influenced by the duration of an unethical act (Shrubsole, 1999), the number of times it occurred, or the extent of the injury or life disruption it is perceived to have caused (Bolin, 1985).

Centrality to One's Worldview or Identity

Centrality is the degree to which individuals perceive that an action or event affects their goals, views of the world, or personal/social identity. The more that an unethical act is perceived as central, the more intense the response (i.e., stress or trauma) will be (Lazarus and Smith, 1988). Jackson, Kubzansky, and Wright (2006: 25) theorize that "social group relevance" is a key factor in perceptions of unfairness, asserting that, "because the perceiver imagines the impact of the unfairness not just for the self, but also for all those for whom the perceiver has positive regard in the group, effects may be amplified."

Sociodemographic Variable Cluster: Moderator Path 2

A number of sociodemographic variables have been linked to health outcomes, and it is likely that such factors moderate the relationship between stress/trauma and well-being. Gender is an important variable in that women tend to report lower psychological well-being and poorer health than men (Jick and Mitz, 1985), and are more likely to suffer from depression and anxiety (Kessler, 1995). When combined with other variables such as race, gender appears to be an even more important factor in predicting declines in well-being. For example, African American women experience more rapid deterioration in health relative to other races, which is believed to be caused by multiple stressors that have a cumulative impact (Geronimus, 1992).

Socioeconomic status (SES) is another key moderator, with research revealing an association between lower SES and negative health outcomes (Adler et al., 1993). Lower SES is related to increased rates of chronic and infectious disorders, major causes of morbidity, and mortality (Williams and Collins, 1995). Research is needed regarding how these SES-related outcomes interact with the broader environmental context including factors such as crime, crowding, and inadequate resources (e.g., food and housing).

Coping Behaviors Cluster: Moderator Path 2

When individuals are faced with unethical behavior, the potential impact to their well-being depends upon their ability to access resources (e.g., problem-solving skills, social networks, and financial and physical assets) to help them cope (Folkman, 1984). Coping behaviors, particularly in the form of social support, are inversely associated with a variety of psychological and physical disorders, as well as mortality (Aneshensel and Stone, 1982; Turner, 1981). Conversely, individuals who perceive unethical actions as uncontrollable and unpredictable experience sustained elevations of stress hormones (Baum, Cohen, and Hall, 1993), making them more susceptible to harmful health consequences (Gallo and Matthews, 2003; Lepore, Evans, and Palsane, 1991).

The sufficiency of coping resources also depends in part upon which coping tactics are used. For example, in research on married couples, "optimistic comparisons"—comparing one's situation to the past or to one's peers—were shown to be effective both in reducing existing distress and in avoiding problems later (Menaghan, 1982). On the other hand, "selective ignoring"—paying attention to positive aspects of the relationship while attempting to ignore the unpleasant parts—was unsuccessful.

Personality Variables: Moderator Path 2

We have already highlighted that personality variables can determine the extent to which unethical behaviors create stress or trauma (Moderator Path 1). However, personality factors can also affect the extent to which stress/trauma leads to declines in well-being. High trait neuroticism, which predisposes individuals to undergo psychological distress (Ormel and Wohlfarth, 1991), is known to be a powerful predictor of traumatic stress (McFarlane, 1989). Likewise, those with an external locus of control are more likely to experience depression and somatic symptoms (Fusilier, Ganster, and Mayes, 1987). Additionally, factors such as optimism have been linked to more positive moods, coping abilities, and better immune function (Segerstrom et al., 1998).

NA provides one of the most robust links to well-being. Individuals high in NA interpret ambiguous, benign bodily sensations to be symptomatic of actual physical illness (Watson and Pennebaker, 1989). Studies using factor analysis have found that psychological problems (depression, anger, anxiety) all load on the NA dimension (Costa and McCrae, 1992), However, although NA is associated with somatic self-reports, it is not necessarily connected to actual physical illness (Costa and McCrae, 1987) and may actually serve as a buffer against some ailments (Watson and Pennebaker, 1989).

Proposition 7a:	The relationship between unethical behavior and responses of stress/trauma will be moderated by perceptual variables, including personality, perceived magnitude, and centrality.
Proposition 7b:	The relationship between stress/trauma and diminished well-being will be moderated by sociodemographic variables, coping behaviors, and personality variables.

ASPECTS OF WELL-BEING AFFECTED BY UNETHICAL BEHAVIOR

A wide range of well-being outcomes are related to unethical behavior, many of which we have already highlighted in our discussions of discrimination, bullying, and injustice. These indicators of well-being are obtained via both self-report (e.g., psychosomatic complaints) and objective sources (e.g., medical records and professional diagnoses). Overall, these outcomes can be placed in three broad categories of well-being: (1) psychological disorders; (2) physical health; and (3) physiological measures.

Psychological Disorders

The most frequently studied impact of unethical actions has been psychological disorders, such as anxiety, depression, burnout, and PTSD. For example, sexism (Moradi and Subich, 2004), sexual harassment (Schneider, Swan, and Fitzgerald, 1997), and injustice are associated with a higher risk of psychiatric morbidity (Elovainio, Kivimäki, and Vahtera, 2002). Meanwhile, depression, anxiety, and occupational strain have all been linked to a number of unethical activities, including bullying (Mikkelsen and Einarsen, 2001), workplace harassment (Bowling and Beehr, 2006), and discrimination (Noh et al., 1999). Occupational strain, which is a measure of depression, nervousness, and difficulty in concentrating, was found to be associated with workplace harassment (Bowling and Beehr, 2006) and perceptions of an unfair workplace (Francis and Barling, 2005).

Physical Health

Variables related to physical health reflect a mix of (mostly) self-reported health measures as well as clinical diagnoses such as coronary heart disease (CHD). A host of unethical behaviors such as bullying (Leymann and Gustafsson, 1996), injustice (Elovainio et al., 2003), criminal victimization (Britt, 2000), workplace harassment (Bowling and Beehr, 2006), and discrimination (Pavalko, Mossakowski, and Hamilton, 2003) have all been associated with psychosomatic complaints. Meanwhile, sleep difficulties were related to perceived discrimination (Thomas et al., 2006), and CHD was linked to low procedural and relational justice (Elovainio et al., 2003).

Physiological Measures

While self-report measures are most common in studies of well-being, some research provides physiological measures that are not subject to self-report biases. Many of these studies have focused on cardiovascular health. For example, African Americans who perceived they were treated unfairly were found to have greater carotid intima-media thickness (Troxel et al., 2003). Further, race-based discrimination has been connected to increases in blood pressure (Din-Dzietham et al., 2004) that were similar to those seen in women with posttraumatic stress (Newton, Parker, and Ho, 2005).

But the relationship of unethical activity to physiological health measures is not limited to cardiovascular effects. For example, individuals who experienced greater levels of justice were found to have lower body mass indexes (Kivimäki et al., 2005), while women who reported high levels of racial discrimination were more likely to deliver preterm or low birth weight babies (Mustillo et al., 2004).

ETHICAL IMPACT THEORY: A MODEL OF UNETHICAL BEHAVIOR AND WELL-BEING

Figure 1.1 provides a summary model of how unethical behaviors in the workplace can lead to diminished psychological and/or physical well-being. The process begins with unethical behaviors carried out by one or more individuals in an organization. Various individuals, including perpetrators, victims, witnesses, and associated persons, are affected by these unethical acts. This impact is mediated by three mechanisms—stress, trauma, and poor health behaviors due to stress or trauma—through which unethical behavior ultimately leads to diminished physiological and psychological well-being. As discussed, a number of variables may function as moderators at two places in the model: the relationship between unethical behavior and individual responses of stress/trauma (Moderator Path 1); and the relationship between stress/trauma and reductions in well-being (Moderator Path 2).

CONCLUSION AND SUGGESTIONS FOR FUTURE RESEARCH

As we have shown in this chapter, abundant interdisciplinary evidence demonstrates a relationship between unethical behavior and diminished well-being. However, because specific unethical actions have never been linked together as a superordinate category of unethical behavior, it is not surprising that the literature has not proposed a coherent model to illustrate this relationship. By linking these various unethical behaviors into a comprehensive framework, we hope to spur additional research that can explore the consequences of unethical activity in a more holistic fashion. In particular, future research should encompass the wider range of individuals (beyond the direct victims) who are affected by unethical behavior

Further, the complexity and potential span of the many possible relationships between diverse forms of unethical behavior and well-being required us to limit the scope of this chapter. For example, we recognize that the connections we discuss can be extended beyond the individual level. When individual well-being is diminished in any way, its impact is likely to include group, organizational, and societal effects as well. These broader effects should be one focus of future research efforts.

Similarly, we excluded certain variables from our model, such as organizational culture and ethical climate, that likely have significant roles as either antecedents or moderators of unethical behavior and diminished well-being. The general economic environment is another factor that was beyond the purview of this chapter, yet it too probably has a considerable impact on stress and resulting negative well-being. For example, the recent U.S. recession created stressors that depleted individuals' coping resources and left them extremely vulnerable to attacks on their well-being.

Finally, Ethical Impact Theory has public policy implications that we have not touched upon. First, because the deleterious impact of unethical behavior is not restricted to internal stakeholders alone; external stakeholders such as investors, customers, and local communities are all negatively affected by such behavior. Second, since our model enlarges the scope of individuals whose well-being is impacted by unethical behavior (such as associated persons), it has ramifications regarding public health. We have proposed that the stress/trauma associated with unethical behavior can affect the well-being of others through a process of secondary traumatization. Thus, we see our model as the impetus to connect unethical behavior to a wide array of public policy concerns.

14

Figure 1.1 Ethical Impact Theory (EIT) of Unethical Behavior

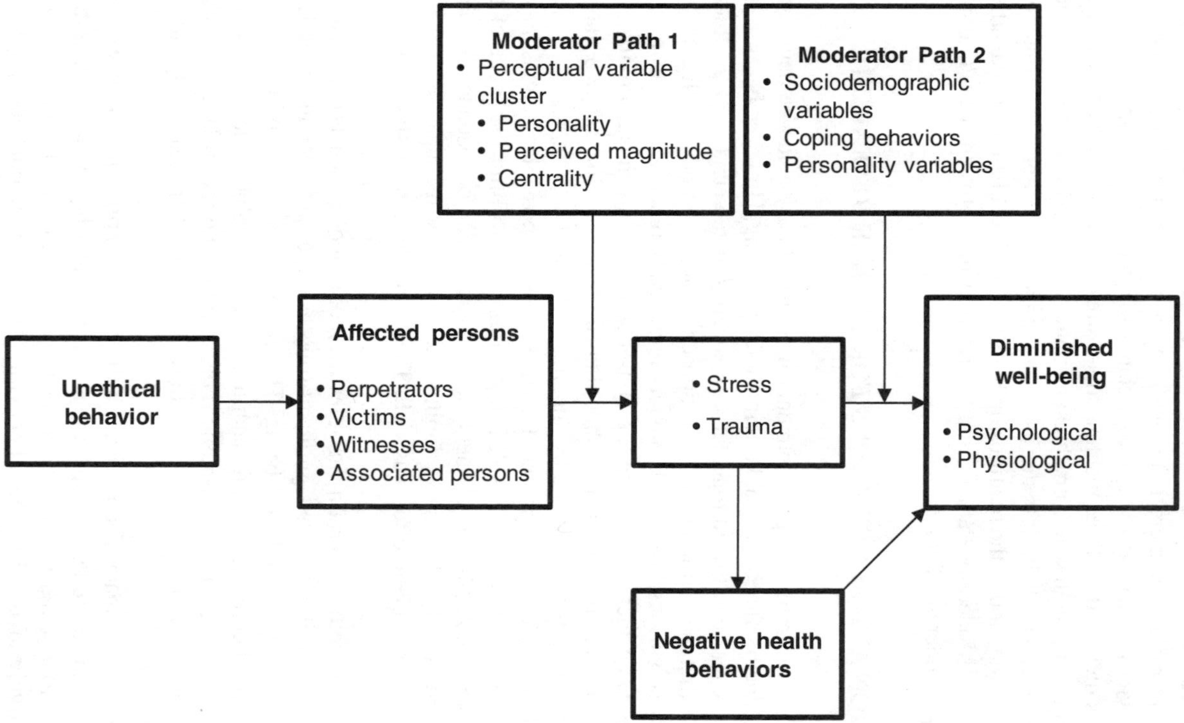

REFERENCES

Adler, N., and Matthews, K. 1994. Health psychology: Why do some people get sick and some stay well? *Annual Review of Psychology*, 45, 229–259.

Adler, N.E.; Boyce, W.T.; Chesney, M.A.; Folkman, S.; and Syme, S.L. 1993. Socioeconomic inequalities in health: No easy solution. *Journal of the American Medical Association*, 269, 3140–3145.

Agervold, M., and Mikkelsen, E.G. 2004. Relationships between bullying, psychosocial work environment and individual stress reactions. *Work and Stress*, 18, 4, 336–351.

Anand, V.; Ashforth, B.E.; and Joshi, M. 2005. Business as usual: The acceptance and perpetuation of corruption in organizations. *Academy of Management Executive,* 19, 4, 9–23.

Andreoli, N., and Lefkowitz, J. 2009. Individual and organizational antecedents of misconduct in organizations. *Journal of Business Ethics,* 85, 3, 309–332.

Aneshensel, C.S. 1992. Social stress: Theory and research. *Annual Review of Sociology,* 18, 15–38.

Aneshensel, C.S., and Stone, J.D. 1982. Stress and depression: A test of the buffering model of social support. *Archives of General Psychiatry,* 39, 12, 1392–1396.

Avina, C., and O'Donohue, W. 2002. Sexual harassment and PTSD: Is sexual harassment diagnosable trauma? *Journal of Traumatic Stress,* 15, 69–75.

Babin, B.J.; Boles, J.S.; and Robin, D.P. 2000. Representing the perceived ethical work climate among marketing employees. *Journal of the Academy of Marketing Science,* 28, 3, 345–358.

Barling, J.; Kelloway, E.K.; and Frone, M.R. (eds.). 2005. *Handbook of Work Stress.* Thousand Oaks, CA: Sage.

Baum, A.; Cohen, L.; and Hall, M. 1993. Control and intrusive memories as possible determinants of chronic stress. *Psychosomatic Medicine,* 55, 274–286.

Bell, C.C., and Jenkins, E.J. 1993. Community violence and children on Chicago's Southside. *Psychiatry: Interpersonal and Biological Processes,* 56, 1, 46–54.

Bloom, S.L. 1995. The germ theory of trauma: The impossibility of ethical neutrality. In *Secondary Traumatic Stress: Self-care Issues for Clinicians, Researchers and Educators,* ed. B. Stamm, 257–276. Lutherville, MD: Sidran Press.

Bolin, R. 1985. Disaster characteristics and psychosocial impacts. In *Disasters and Mental Health: Selected Contemporary Perspectives,* ed. B.J. Sowder, 3–28. Rockville, MD: National Institute of Mental Health.

Bowling, N.A., and Beehr, T.A. 2006. Workplace harassment from the victim's perspective: A theoretical model and meta-analysis. *Journal of Applied Psychology,* 91, 5, 998–1012.

Bramsen, I.; van der Ploeg, H.M.; and Twisk, J.W.R. 2002. Secondary traumatization in Dutch couples of World War II survivors. *Journal of Consulting and Clinical Psychology,* 70, 1, 241–245.

Britt, C.L. 2000. Health consequences of criminal victimization. *International Review of Victimology,* 8, 1, 63–73.

Byrne, M.K. 2003. Trauma reactions in the offender. *International Journal of Forensic Psychology,* 1, 1, 59–70.

Collins, S., and Long, A. 2003. Working with the psychological effects of trauma: Consequences for mental health-care workers—a literature review. *Journal of Psychiatric and Mental Health Nursing,* 10, 4, 417–424.

Contrada, R.J.; Ashmore, R.D.; Gary, M.L.; Coups, E.; Egeth, J.D.; Sewell, A.; Ewell, K.; Goyal, T.M.; and Chasse, V. 2000. Ethnicity-related sources of stress and their effects on well-being. *Current Directions in Psychological Science,* 9, 4, 136–139.

Costa, P.T. Jr., and McCrae, R.R. 1987. Neuroticism, somatic complaints, and disease: Is the bark worse than the bite? *Journal of Personality,* 55, 2, 299–316.

———. 1992. *Revised NEO Personality Inventory , NEO–PI–r and NEO Five-factor Inventory , NEO–FFI: Professional Manual.* Odessa, FL: Psychological Assessment Resources.

Din-Dzietham, R.; Nembhard, W.N.; Collins, R.; and Davis, S.K. 2004. Perceived stress following race-based discrimination at work is associated with hypertension in African-Americans: The metro Atlanta heart disease study, 1999–2001. *Social Science and Medicine,* 58, 3, 449–461.

Dulmus, C.N., and Wodarski, J.S. 2000. Trauma-related symptomatology among children of parents victimized by urban community violence. *American Journal of Orthopsychiatry,* 70, 2, 272–277.

Einarsen, S.; Raknes, B.I.; and Matthiesen, S.B. 1994. Bullying and harassment at work and their relationships to work environment quality: An exploratory study. *European Work and Organizational Psychologist,* 4, 4, 381–401.

Elovainio, M.; Kivimäki, M.; and Vahtera, J. 2002. Organizational justice: Evidence of a new psychosocial predictor of health. *American Journal of Public Health,* 92, 1, 105–108.

Elovainio, M.; Kivimäki, M.; Vahtera, J.; Keltikangas-Jarvinen, L.; and Virtanen, M. 2003. Sleeping problems and health behaviors as mediators between organizational justice and health. *Health Psychology,* 22, 3, 287–293.

Evans, C.; Ehlers, A.; Mezey, G.; and Clark, D.M. 2007. Intrusive memories in perpetrators of violent crime: Emotions and cognitions. *Journal of Consulting and Clinical Psychology,* 75, 1, 134–144.

Felitti, V.J.; Anda, R.F.; Nordenberg, D.; Williamson, D.F.; Spitz, A.M.; and Edwards, V. 1998. Relationship of childhood abuse and household dysfunction to many of the leading causes of death in adults: The Adverse Childhood Experiences (ACE) Study. *American Journal of Preventive Medicine,* 14, 245–258.

Figley, C.R. 1995. Compassion fatigue as secondary traumatic stress disorder: An overview. In *Compassion Fatigue: Coping with Secondary Traumatic Stress Disorder in Those Who Treat the Traumatized,* ed. Figley, 1–21. New York: Brunner/Mazel.

Fitzgerald, L.F.; Swan, S.; and Magley, V.J. 1997. But was it really sexual harassment? Legal, behavioral, and psychological definitions of the workplace victimization of women. In *Sexual Harassment: Theory, Research and Treatment,* ed. W. O'Donohue, 5–28. Boston: Allyn and Bacon.

Folkman, S. 1984. Personal control and stress and coping processes: A theoretical analysis. *Journal of Personality and Social Psychology,* 46, 4, 839–852.

Francis, L., and Barling, J. 2005. Organizational injustice and psychological strain. *Canadian Journal of Behavioural Science,* 37, 4, 250–261.

Friedman, M.J., and Schnurr, P.P. (eds.). 1995. *The Relationship Between Trauma, Post-Traumatic Stress Disorder, and Physical Health.* Philadelphia, PA: Lippincott Williams and Wilkins.

Fusilier, M.R.; Ganster, D.C.; and Mayes, B.T. 1987. Effects of social support, role stress, and locus of control on health. *Journal of Management,* 13, 3, 517–528.

Gallo, L.C., and Matthews, K.A. 2003. Understanding the association between socioeconomic status and physical health: Do negative emotions play a role? *Psychological Bulletin,* 129, 1, 10–51.

Geronimus, A.T. 1992. The weathering hypothesis and the health of African-American women and infants: Evidence and speculations. *Ethnicity and Disease,* 2, 207–221.

Giacalone, R.A., and Promislo, M.D. 2010. Unethical and unwell: Decrements in well-being and unethical activity at work. *Journal of Business Ethics,* 91, 275–297.

Giacalone, R.A., and Thompson, K.R. 2006. Business ethics and social responsibility education: Shifting the worldview. *Academy of Management Learning and Education,* 5, 3, 266–277.

Glomb, T.M.; Richman, W.L.; Hulin, C.L.; Drasgow, F.; Schneider, K.T.; and Fitzgerald, L.F. 1997. Ambient sexual harassment: An integrated model of antecedents and consequences. *Organizational Behavior and Human Decision Processes,* 71, 3, 309–328.

Grunberg, L.; Moore, S.Y.; and Greenberg, E. 2001. Differences in psychological and physical health among layoff survivors: The effect of layoff contact. *Journal of Occupational Health Psychology,* 6, 1, 15–25.

Guyll, M.; Matthews, K.A.; and Bromberger, J.T. 2001. Discrimination and unfair treatment: Relationship to cardiovascular reactivity among African American and European American women. *Health Psychology,* 20, 5, 315–325.

Hammer, T.H.; Saksvik, P.O.; Nytro, K.; Torvatn, H.; and Bayazit, M. 2004. Expanding the psychosocial work environment: Workplace norms and work-family conflict as correlates of stress and health. *Journal of Occupational Health Psychology,* 9, 1, 83–97.

Hemingway, H., and Marmot, M. 1999. Psychosocial factors in the aetiology and prognosis of coronary heart disease: Systematic review of prospective cohort studies. *British Medical Journal,* 318, 1460–1467.

Hobfoll, S.E. 1988. *The Ecology of Stress.* Washington, DC: Hemisphere.

Hoel, H.; Faragher, B.; and Cooper, C.L. 2004. Bullying is detrimental to health, but all bullying behaviours are not necessarily equally damaging. *British Journal of Guidance and Counselling,* 32, 3, 367–387.

Jackson, B.; Kubzansky, L.D.; and Wright, R.J. 2006. Linking perceived unfairness to physical health: The perceived unfairness model. *Review of General Psychology,* 10, 1, 21–40.

Janoff-Bulman, R. 1989. Assumptive worlds and the stress of traumatic events: Applications of the schema construct. *Social Cognition,* 7, 2, 113–136.

Jaramillo, F.; Mulki, J.P.; and Solomon, P. 2006. The role of ethical climate on salesperson's role stress, job attitudes, turnover intention, and job performance. *Journal of Personal Selling and Sales Management,* 26, 3, 271–282.

Jick, T.D.; and Mitz, L.F. 1985. Sex differences in work stress. *Academy of Management Review,* 10, 3, 408–420.

Joseph, S.; Williams, R.; and Yule, W. 1993. Changes in outlook following disaster: The preliminary development of a measure to assess positive and negative responses. *Journal of Traumatic Stress,* 6, 2, 271–279.

Jovanovic, J.; Lazaridis, K.; and Stefanovic, V. 2006. Theoretical approaches to problem of occupational stress. *ACTA FAC MED NAISS,* 23, 3, 163–169.

Kessler, R.C. 1995. The national comorbidity survey: Preliminary results and future directions. *International Journal of Methods in Psychiatric Research,* 5, 2, 139–151.

Kilpatrick, D.G.; Acierno, R.; Resnick, H.; Saunders, B.; and Best, C. 1997. A two-year longitudinal analysis of the relationships among violent assault and substance use in women. *Journal of Consulting and Clinical Psychology,* 65, 834–847.

Kivimäki, M.; Ferrie, J.E.; Brunner, E.; Head, J.; Shipley, M.J.; Vahtera, J.; and Marmot, M.G. 2005. Justice at work and reduced risk of coronary heart disease among employees: The Whitehall II Study. *Archives of Internal Medicine,* 165, 2245–2251.

Klonoff, E.A.; Landrine, H.; and Ullman, J.B. 1999. Racial discrimination and psychiatric symptoms among blacks. *Cultural Diversity and Ethnic Minority Psychology,* 5, 4, 329–339.

Kohn, A. 1986. *No Contest: The Case Against Competition.* Boston: Houghton Mifflin.

Koltko-Rivera, M.E. 2004. The psychology of worldviews. *Review of General Psychology,* 8, 1, 3–58.

Krieger, N. 1999. Embodying inequality: A review of concepts, measures, and methods for studying health consequences of discrimination. *International Journal of Health Services,* 29, 2, 295–352.

Kubany, E.S.; Leisen, M.B.; Kaplan, A.S.; and Kelly, M.P. 2000. Validation of a brief measure of posttraumatic stress disorder: The Distressing Event Questionnaire , DEQ. *Psychological Assessment,* 12, 2, 197–209.

Landau, S.F., and Freeman-Longo, R.E. 1990. Classifying victims: A proposed multidimensional victimological typology. *International Review of Victimology,* 1, 267–286.

Landrine, H., and Klonoff, E.A. 1996. The schedule of racist events: A measure of racial discrimination and a study of its negative physical and mental health consequences. *Journal of Black Psychology,* 22, 144–168.

Landrine, H.; Klonoff, E.A.; Corral, I.; Fernandez, S.; and Roesch, S. 2006. Conceptualizing and measuring ethnic discrimination in health research. *Journal of Behavioral Medicine,* 29, 1, 79–94.

Lazarus, R.S. 1999. *Stress and Emotion: A New Synthesis.* New York: Springer.

Lazarus, R.S., and Folkman, S. 1984. *Stress, Appraisal, and Coping.* New York: Springer.

Lazarus, R.S., and Smith, C. A. 1988. Knowledge and appraisal in the cognition-emotion relationship. *Cognition and Emotion,* 2, 4, 281–300.

Lee, D.J.; Mendes de Leon, C.F.; Jenkins, C.D.; and Croog, S.H. 1992. Relation of hostility to medication adherence, symptom complaints, and blood pressure reduction in a clinical field trial of antihypertensive medication. *Journal of Psychosomatic Research,* 36, 2, 181–190.

Leiker, M., and Hailey, B.J. 1988. A link between hostility and disease: Poor health habits? *Behavioral Medicine,* 14, 3, 129–133.

Lepore, S.J.; Evans, G.W.; and Palsane, M.N. 1991. Social hassles and psychological health in the context of chronic crowding. *Journal of Health and Social Behavior,* 32, 4, 357–367.

Lerias, D., and Byrne, M.K. 2003. Vicarious traumatization: Symptoms and predictors. *Stress and Health,* 19, 129–138.

Lev-Wiesel, R., and Amir, M. 2001. Secondary traumatic stress, psychological distress, sharing of traumatic reminisces, and marital quality among spouses of holocaust child survivors. *Journal of Marital and Family Therapy,* 27, 4, 433–444.

Leymann, H., and Gustafsson, A. 1996. Mobbing at work and the development of post-traumatic stress disorders. *European Journal of Work and Organizational Psychology,* 5, 2, 251–275.

Lyons, R.; Tivey, H.; and Ball, M. 1995. *Bullying at Work: How to Tackle It. A Guide for MSF Representatives and Members.* London: Manufacturing Science Finance.

Magley, V.J.; Hulin, C.L.; Fitzgerald, L.F.; and DeNardo, M. 1999. Outcomes of self-labeling sexual harassment. *Journal of Applied Psychology,* 84, 3, 390–402.

March, J.S. 1993. What constitutes a stressor? The "Criterion A" issue. In *Posttraumatic Stress Disorder: DSM-IV and Beyond,* ed. J. Davidson and E. Foa, 37–54. Washington, DC: American Psychiatric Press.

McFarlane, A.C. 1989. The aetiology of post-traumatic morbidity: Predisposing, precipitating and perpetuating factors. *British Journal of Psychiatry,* 154, 221–228.

Menaghan, E.G. 1982. Measuring coping effectiveness: A panel analysis of marital problems and coping efforts. *Journal of Health and Social Behavior,* 23, 3, 220–234.

Mikkelsen, E.G., and Einarsen, S. 2001. Bullying in Danish work-life: Prevalence and health correlates. *European Journal of Work and Organizational Psychology,* 10, 4, 393–413.

———. 2002. Basic assumptions and symptoms of post-traumatic stress among victims of bullying at work. *European Journal of Work and Organizational Psychology,* 11, 1, 87–111.

Milgram, S. 1975. *Obedience to Authority: An Experimental View.* New York: Harper and Row.

Moore, S.; Grunberg, L.; and Greenberg, E. 2004. Repeated downsizing contact: The effects of similar and dissimilar layoff experiences on work and well-being outcomes. *Journal of Occupational Health Psychology,* 9, 3, 247–257.

Moradi, B., and Subich, L.M. 2004. Examining the moderating role of self-esteem in the link between experiences of perceived sexist events and psychological distress. *Journal of Counseling Psychology,* 51, 1, 50–56.

Motta, R.W.; Kefer, J.M.; Hertz, M.D.; and Hafeez, S. 1999. Initial evaluation of the secondary trauma questionnaire. *Psychological Reports,* 85, 997–1002.

Mulki, J.; Jaramillo, J.; and Locander, W. 2008. Effect of ethical climate on turnover intention: Linking attitudinal- and stress theory. *Journal of Business Ethics,* 78, 4, 559–574.

Mustillo, S.; Krieger, N.; Gunderson, E.P.; Sidney, S.; McCreath, H.; and Kiefe, C.I. 2004. Self-reported experiences of racial discrimination and Black-White differences in preterm and low-birthweight deliveries: The CARDIA Study. *American Journal of Public Health,* 94, 12, 2125–2131.

National Commission on the BP Deepwater Horizon Oil Spill and Offshore Drilling. 2011. *Deep Water: The Gulf Oil Disaster and the Future of Offshore Drilling.* Report to the President, January 11. Washington, DC: Government Printing Office.

Newton, T.L.; Parker, B.C.; and Ho, I.K. 2005. Ambulatory cardiovascular functioning in healthy postmenopausal women with victimization histories. *Biological Psychology,* 70, 2, 121–130.

Niedl, K. 1996. Mobbing and well-being: Economic and personnel development implications. *European Journal of Work and Organizational Psychology,* 5, 2, 239–249.

Noh, S.; Beiser, M.; Kaspar, V.; Hou, F.; and Rummens, J. 1999. Perceived racial discrimination, depression, and coping: A study of southeast Asian refugees in Canada. *Journal of Health and Social Behavior,* 40, 3, 193–207.

Ormel, J., and Wohlfarth, T. 1991. How neuroticism, long-term difficulties, and life situation change influence psychological distress: A longitudinal model. *Journal of Personality and Social Psychology,* 60, 5, 744–755.

Parzefall, M.-R., and Salin, D.M. 2010. Perceptions of and reactions to workplace bullying: A social exchange perspective. *Human Relations,* 63, 6, 761–780.

Pavalko, E.K.; Mossakowski, K.N.; and Hamilton, V.J. 2003. Does perceived discrimination affect health? Longitudinal relationships between work discrimination and women's physical and emotional health. *Journal of Health and Social Behavior,* 44, 1, 18–33.

Pearlman, L.A. 1995. Notes from the field: What is vicarious traumatization? In *Secondary Traumatic Stress: Self-care Issues for Clinicians, Researchers and Educators,* ed. B. Stamm. Lutherville, MD: Sidran Press.

Penninx, B.W.J.H.; Kriegsman, D.M.W.; van Eijk, J.T.M.; Boeke, A.J.P.; and Deeg, D.J.H. 1996. Differential effect of social support on the course of chronic disease: A criteria-based literature study. *Families, Systems, and Health,* 14, 2, 223–244.

Peterson, M., and Wilson, J.F. 2004. Work stress in America. *International Journal of Stress Management,* 11, 2, 91–113.

Pollock, P.H. 1999. When the killer suffers: Post-traumatic stress reactions following homicide. *Legal and Criminological Psychology,* 4, 2, 185–202.

Rayner, C., and Hoel, H. 1997. A summary review of literature relating to workplace bullying. *Journal of Community and Applied Social Psychology,* 7, 3, 181–191.

Riggs, D.S.; Dancu, C.V.; Gershuny, B.S.; Greenberg, D.; and Foa, E.B. 1992. Anger and post-traumatic stress disorder in female crime victims. *Journal of Traumatic Stress,* 5, 4, 613–625.

Scherwitz, L.; Perkins, L.; Chesney, M.; Hughes, G.; Sidney, S.; and Manolio, T. 1992. Hostility and health behaviors in young adults: The CARDIA Study. *American Journal of Epidemiology,* 136, 136–145.

Schneider, K.T.; Hitlan, R.T.; and Radhakrishnan, P. 2000. An examination of the nature and correlates of ethnic harassment experiences in multiple contexts. *Journal of Applied Psychology,* 85, 1, 3–12.

Schneider, K.T.; Swan, S.; and Fitzgerald, L.F. 1997. Job-related and psychological effects of sexual harassment in the workplace: Empirical evidence from two organizations. *Journal of Applied Psychology,* 82, 3, 401–415.

Schnurr, P.P.; Friedman, M.J.; and Bernardy, N.C. 2002. Research on posttraumatic stress disorder: Epidemiology, pathophysiology, and assessment. *Journal of Clinical Psychology,* 58, 8, 877–889.

Schwepker, C.H. Jr. 1999. Research note: The relationship between ethical conflict, organizational commitment and turnover intentions in the salesforce. *Journal of Personal Selling and Sales Management,* 19, 1, 43–49.

Segerstrom, S.C.; Taylor, S.E.; Kemeny, M.E.; and Fahey, J.L. 1998. Optimism is associated with mood, coping and immune change in response to stress. *Journal of Personality and Social Psychology,* 74, 6, 1646–1655.

Sexton, L. 1999. Vicarious traumatisation of counsellors and effects on their workplaces. *British Journal of Guidance and Counselling,* 27, 3, 393–403.

Shrubsole, D. 1999. *Natural Disasters and Public Health Issues: A Review of the Literature with a Focus on the Recovery Period.* Toronto: Institute for Catastrophic Loss Reduction.

Sims, R.L., and Kroeck, K.G. 1994. The influence of ethical fit on employee satisfaction, commitment and turnover. *Journal of Business Ethics,* 13, 12, 939–947.

Singhapakdi, A., and Vitell, S.J. 2007. Institutionalization of ethics and its consequences: A survey of marketing professionals. *Journal of the Academy of Marketing Science,* 35, 2, 284–294.

Stewart, R.; Volpone, S.; Avery, D.; and McKay, P. 2011. You support diversity, but are you ethical? Examining the interactive effects of diversity and ethical climate perceptions on turnover intentions. *Journal of Business Ethics,* 100, 4, 581–593.

Stewart, S.H. 1996. Alcohol abuse in individuals exposed to trauma: A critical review. *Psychological Bulletin,* 120, 1, 83–112.

Suinn, R.M. 2001. The terrible twos—anger and anxiety: Hazardous to your health. *American Psychologist,* 56, 1, 27–36.

Tajfel, H. 1982. Social psychology of intergroup relations. *Annual Review of Psychology,* 33, 1–39.

Taylor, S.E.; Repetti, R.L.; and Seeman, T. 1997. Health psychology: What is an unhealthy environment and how does it get under the skin? *Annual Review of Psychology,* 48, 411–447.

Tepper, B.J. 2000. Consequences of abusive supervision. *Academy of Management Journal,* 43, 2, 178–190.

Theorell, T., and Karasek, R.A. 1996. Current issues relating to psychosocial job strain and cardiovascular disease research. *Journal of Occupational Health Psychology,* 1, 1, 9–26.

Thomas, K.S.; Bardwell, W.A.; Ancoli-Israel, S.; and Dimsdale, J.E. 2006. The toll of ethnic discrimination on sleep architecture and fatigue. *Health Psychology,* 25, 5, 635–642.

Troxel, W.M.; Matthews, K.A.; Bromberger, J.T.; and Sutton-Tyrrell, K. 2003. Chronic stress burden, discrimination, and subclinical carotid artery disease in African American and Caucasian women. *Health Psychology,* 22, 3, 300–309.

Turner, R.J. 1981. Social support as a contingency in psychological well-being. *Journal of Health and Social Behavior,* 22, 4, 357–367.

Valentine, S., and Barnett, T. 2002. Ethics codes and sales professionals' perceptions of their organizations' ethical values. *Journal of Business Ethics,* 40, 3, 191–200.

Valentine, S., and Fleischman, G. 2008. Ethics programs, perceived corporate social responsibility and job satisfaction. *Journal of Business Ethics,* 77, 2, 159–172.

Valentine, S., Godkin, L., and Lucero, M. 2002. Ethical context, organizational commitment, and person-organization fit. *Journal of Business Ethics,* 41, 4, 349–360.

Valentine, S.; Godkin, L.; Fleischman, G.; and Kidwell, R. 2011. Corporate ethical values, group creativity, job satisfaction and turnover intention: The impact of work context on work response. *Journal of Business Ethics,* 98, 3, 353–372.

Vega, G., and Comer, D.R. 2005. Sticks and stones may break your bones, but words can break your spirit: Bullying in the workplace. *Journal of Business Ethics,* 58, 101–109.

Viswesvaran, C.; Deshpande, S.P.; and Joseph, J. 1998. Job satisfaction as a function of top management support for ethical behavior: A study of Indian managers. *Journal of Business Ethics,* 17, 4, 365–371.

Watson, D., and Clark, L.A. 1984. Negative affectivity: The disposition to experience aversive emotional states. *Psychological Bulletin,* 96, 3, 465–490.

Watson, D., and Pennebaker, J.W. 1989. Health complaints, stress, and distress: Exploring the central role of negative affectivity. *Psychological Review,* 96, 2, 234–254.

Williams, D.R., and Collins, C. 1995. U.S. socioeconomic and racial differences in health: Patterns and explanations. *Annual Review of Sociology,* 21, 1, 349–386.

Zapf, D. 1999. Organisational, work group related and personal causes of mobbing/bullying at work. *International Journal of Manpower,* 20, 1/2, 70–85.

Zapf, D.; Knorz, C.; and Kulla, M. 1996. On the relationship between mobbing factors, and job content, social work environment, and health outcomes. *European Journal of Work and Organizational Psychology,* 5, 2, 215–237.

Zimbardo, P.G. 2007. *The Lucifer Effect: Understanding How Good People Turn Evil.* New York: Random House.

PART I

ATTACKING OTHERS

Revenge, Aggression, Bullying, and Abuse

2

BEYOND THE CONSEQUENCES TO THE VICTIM

The Impact of Abusive Supervision on Third-Party Observers

MARIE S. MITCHELL, RYAN M. VOGEL, AND ROBERT FOLGER

Over the past decade, there has been a rise in research on the topic of abusive supervisors (cf. Tepper, 2007) or supervisors who yell at, ridicule, harass, intimidate, and undermine their employees (Keashly, 1998). Abusive supervision is defined as subordinates' perceptions of persistent verbal and nonverbal hostilities against them by their supervisors (Tepper, 2000). An important aspect of this definition is that abusive supervision is a subjective phenomenon, based on the subordinate's perception of the supervisor's behavior. To be sure, some supervisors may have no intention of harming their subordinates; some may even think that treating a subordinate in a harsh fashion is a type of "tough love," intended to help the subordinate improve. Regardless of the supervisor's intention, what matters is how subordinates perceive the supervisor's behavior. Additionally, abusive supervision is perceived as sustained behavior. Subordinates do not perceive the abuse as a one-time event or passive mood swing; instead, subordinates believe that their supervisors purposefully target and perpetrate hostile acts against victims over an extended period of time (Tepper, 2000).

Research shows that abusive supervision produces a host of detrimental outcomes to its victims, such as decreased psychological well-being and heightened tension, psychological distress, and problem drinking (e.g., Bamberger and Bacharach, 2006; Duffy, Ganster, and Pagon, 2002; Harvey et al., 2007; Tepper, 2000). Abusive supervision is also harmful to organizations and their members; it decreases productive work behavior (e.g., Harris, Kacmar, and Zivnuska, 2007; Zellars, Tepper, and Duffy, 2002) and increases destructive and counterproductive behavior (e.g., Mitchell and Ambrose, 2007; Tepper et al., 2008; Thau et al., 2009). Abusive supervision is also financially draining to organizations through its impact on absenteeism, health-care costs, and the expense of defending actionable claims (Tepper et al., 2006).

The consequences of abusive supervision are considerable. Yet, much of the research in this area has focused on understanding the impact of abusive supervision on its victims and/or the organization; less research gives focus to its consequences on third-party observers (see Tepper, 2007, for a review). This is surprising given the fact that research shows employees often witness abusive interpersonal behavior at work (Pearson and Porath, 2005). The research on observer reactions to such behavior suggests that being a third-party observer of supervisor abuse would produce detrimental outcomes, such as diminished well-being and nonproductive work behavior (e.g., Giacalone and Promislo, 2010; Lim, Cortina, and Magley, 2008; Miner-Rubino and Cortina, 2007). We do not counter these arguments, but suggest that not all third-party observers view the supervisor's behavior as inappropriate and, thus, such negative consequences may not occur. We propose that the extent to which observers of supervisor abuse experience negative outcomes depends on whether or not they believe the supervisor's behavior is justified. These beliefs will also impact third-party observers' reactions to the supervisor's behavior and their behavior toward the target of the supervisor's abuse.

The purpose of this chapter is to consider the consequences of being a third-party observer of abusive supervision. We draw from a deontic perspective of justice (Folger, 2001, 2011). The word *deontic* stems from the Greek word *deon,* which means duty or obligation; hence, the emphasis is not only on justice as a deserved state of affairs but also on circumstances under which one or more parties has some form of obligation or duty to respond in an appropriate way relative to that state of affairs (e.g., to see that it comes to pass, to give people what they deserve, or to make sure institutions are designed to increase the likelihood people will get what they deserve). For instance, a third-party observer might feel a duty to act differently toward an abusive supervisor than toward other supervisors who seem to be treating their subordinates fairly.

We also draw from *scope of justice* principles (Deutsch, 1974; Opotow, 1990, 1995). Scope of justice theory suggests that all individuals hold a psychological boundary, called the "scope of justice," under which they gauge whether people are deserving (or not) of treatment for which moral rules apply. In particular, individuals who are excluded from one's scope of justice are characterized as highly dissimilar, or are considered a threat to the observer or the observer's social group (Opotow, 1995). Consequently, these excluded individuals are perceived as not worthy of just and fair treatment. In contrast, individuals within one's scope of justice are regarded as approximate equals to the observer and, as such, should be given every consideration of moral values, rules, and fairness. We argue that third-party observers' reactions, specifically *deontic reactions* (those charged by an obligation to maintain or restore what is just), depend on observers' scope of justice beliefs. How observers respond to abusive supervision should depend on their scope of justice beliefs about the employee who is the target of abuse and about the supervisor, the perpetrator.

To highlight these ideas, we discuss potential deontic behavioral reactions of third-party observers of abusive supervision. Folger's theory of deonance (e.g., 2001), when applied to justice issues, suggests that observers of interpersonal mistreatment seek to regulate their conduct within the bounds of what they believe is just and morally appropriate. Accordingly, we developed a typology identifying four categories of observer responses, which differ according to observers' scope of justice beliefs about the target of abuse. We then elaborate on these potential deontic reactions based on observers' scope of justice beliefs about the supervisor. Below, we expand on these ideas and discuss the implications of being a third-party observer of abusive supervision. We begin by providing a formal definition of what we mean by third-party observers and outline the general consequences based on third parties' observations of abusive supervision.

WHO ARE THIRD-PARTY OBSERVERS OF ABUSIVE SUPERVISION?

Third-party observers are individuals who take an interest in the abusive supervisory treatment imposed upon an employee targeted with abuse. Within the work environment, third-party observers include individuals who directly witness the supervisor's behavior, such as coworkers, peers, or other organizational members (e.g., other supervisors). They may also include individuals who are not directly employed by the organization but who witnessed the supervisor mistreat the employee, such as a client, customer, or other visiting organizational outsider (e.g., delivery person, building personnel).

However, we do not limit the term "third-party observer" only to those able to directly witness the supervisor's abusive treatment against the employee. Rather, and consistent with previous theorizing (Skarlicki and Kulik, 2005; Treviño, 1992), a third-party observer can become aware of the supervisor's treatment through less direct means. For example, an observer may learn about the abuse by word of mouth from other observers or from the target of abuse. To be classified as an observer, the third party's "awareness must be high enough to instigate a cognitive appraisal" of the event (Treviño, 1992, p. 650). This means third-party observers can include any individual who directly witnesses or is privy to the supervisor's hostile treatment of the employee. Expanding the term in this way means that third-party observers include direct witnesses (e.g., other employees, clients, managers) and anyone who is aware of the abuse (e.g., the target's family members, friends).

THE CONSEQUENCES OF ABUSIVE SUPERVISION TO THIRD-PARTY OBSERVERS

The impact of third-party observers of abusive supervision should not be taken lightly by organizational decision makers. Research shows that supervisor abuse can significantly impact the psychological and physical well-being of third-party observers (e.g., Glomb et al., 1997; Miner-Rubino and Cortina, 2007). Furthermore, research shows that third-party observers can exert a strong influence on employees' reactions to being mistreated by their supervisor (see Table 2.1 for a summary of empirical research). For instance, observers can assist employees in realizing that the supervisor's behavior is not accidental and, instead, is a human rights violation (Barley, 1991). Third-party observer reactions have also affected organizations' bottom line (i.e., significant drop in stock price) when public reports highlight specific incidents of supervisor abuse against employees (Saporito, 1998). Moreover, recent research suggests that some observers take action into their own hands to rectify supervisors' wrongs (Umphress et al., 2012). Still, not all observers necessarily feel that the supervisor's behavior is inappropriate. This too has negative implications for organizations, particularly if the abuse then goes unreported or if observers emulate the supervisor and cause interpersonally abusive behavior to spiral throughout the work group and, potentially, throughout the organization (Andersson and Pearson, 1999).

We believe that deontic principles of justice (Folger, 2001, 2011) can provide a foundation for understanding the consequences of abusive supervision to third-party observers. Deonance theory suggests that individuals feel an obligation to abide by their sense of what is right and fair interpersonal treatment (Folger, 2001). Deonance motivates individuals to act according to their view of what is just and motivates them to try to make others act according to their view as well. Thus, deonance motivates individuals to react to perceived interpersonal injustices (e.g., abusive supervision) in an attempt to rectify wrongs against the person who is considered *the perpetrator of injustice*. Yet, who the perpetrator of injustice is depends on the observer's belief of what is just. That is, what is considered just lies "in the eye of the beholder" (Folger, 2011, p. 123). Rawls (1971) suggested that justice perceptions are defined by social expectations. What is considered to be unfair or unjust, therefore, breaches the observer's expectations of appropriate behavior within the social environment. Hence, understanding how third-party observers conceptualize the meaning of what is just is important because it has implications for their thinking and reactions (Folger, 2011; Heider, 1958).

We analyze how third-party observers think and react by bringing together deontic principles of justice and principles from a scope of justice perspective (Deutsch, 1974; Opotow, 1990, 1995). First, we comment on the scope of justice perspective in general, providing a brief overview that indicates how we conceptualize its applicability to third-party reactions. Next, we focus on reactions to a target of abuse that observers consider to be *included within* their scope of justice. We

Table 2.1

Empirical Studies Examining the Consequences of Observing Abusive Supervision or Supervisor Mistreatment

Study	Type of supervisor behavior	Consequences	Mediators (M) or Moderators (Z)	Overall findings
Atwater et al. (2001)	Supervisor disciplining a subordinate	• Vicarious learning • Attitude toward supervisor	• Fairness of discipline^Z	Mistreatment enhanced vicarious learning, even if observers felt the discipline was unfair; observers held more favorable attitudes toward the supervisor and emotions were less negative when they felt the discipline was fair rather than unfair.
Glomb et al. (1997)	Ambient sexual harassment by supervisors and coworkers	• Work withdrawal • Job withdrawal • Health conditions • Health satisfaction	• Job satisfaction^M • Psychological distress^M	Occupational context related to ambient sexual harassment, which negatively related to job satisfaction and positively to psychological distress; job satisfaction mediated effects to work and job withdrawal; psychological distress mediated effects to health conditions and health satisfaction.
Hegtvedt et al. (2009)	Supervisor procedural injustice	• Persuade supervisor to provide the victim benefits • Persuade others to talk to supervisor to provide the victim benefits	• Group identification^Z • Endorsement of supervisor^Z • Distributive justice^M	Outcome viewed most fair when supervisor endorsed and used fair procedures; viewed as least fair when supervisor used unfair procedures; observer most likely to try to engage in persuasive discussions when group identity was high rather than low; distributive justice mediated the effects.
Miner-Rubino and Cortina (2007)	Supervisor hostility	• Job burnout • Physical well-being • Job withdrawal • Organizational commitment	• Psychological well-being^M • Occupational well-being^M • Gender^Z	Hostility negatively affected psychological and occupational well-being; psychological and occupational well-being mediated the effects of hostility to physical well-being, job burnout, organizational commitment, and job withdrawal; the effects were greater for women than men.
Porath and Erez (2009)	Supervisor rudeness	• Task performance • Citizenship behavior • Dysfunctional ideation (i.e., want to hurt or hit someone)	• Negative affect^M • Competitive versus cooperative tasks^Z	Supervisor rudeness diminishes observer performance and citizenship behaviors; negative affect mediates these effects; the effects are greater when observers are involved in cooperative versus competitive tasks with victims.

Raver and Gelfand (2005)	Ambient sexual harassment by supervisors and coworkers	• Team citizenship behavior • Team financial performance	• Team conflict[M] • Team cohesion[M]	Mistreatment enhanced team conflict and weakened team cohesion, citizenship behavior, and financial performance; team conflict and cohesion mediated effects on financial performance.
Saporito (1998)	Reports of supervisor mistreatment in financial records	• Stock prices		Companies with reported incidents of supervisor mistreatment of employees experienced a drop in stock prices.
Skarlicki and Rupp (2010)	Supervisor mistreatment (interpersonal injustice)	• Retribution tendencies	• Experiential (i.e., emotional) versus rational processing[Z] • Moral identity[Z]	Mistreatment enhanced retribution tendencies; these effects are stronger for experiential versus rational processing; for observers with a weak rather than strong moral identity, the interactive effects of experiential processing were even greater; observers with a strong rather than weak moral identity reacted strongly, regardless of whether they used experiential or rational processing.
Turillo et al. (2002, Study 4)	Authority member verbal abuse to a subordinate	• Perceived offensiveness of behavior • Willingness to help the perpetrator • Anger toward the perpetrator	• Group identification[Z] • Perceived perpetrator's intent to harm the victim[Z]	The more observers rated mistreatment as more offensive, the less willing they were to help the perpetrator and the more angry they felt toward the perpetrator; these effects were stronger when perceived intent to harm was high rather than low; group identification did not moderate effects.
Umphress et al. (2012)	Supervisor injustice	• Anger toward supervisor • Desire to punish the supervisor	• Perceived intent of supervisor to cause harm[Z]	Injustice strengthened anger toward supervisor and desire to punish supervisor, and these effects were stronger when intentions to harm were high rather than low.

then address the case of targets *excluded from* the observers' scope of justice. With those discussions as background, we return to deontic principles and outline how they can be integrated with our analysis of third-party reactions from the scope of justice perspective.

Scope of Justice as a Perspective on Third-Party Reactions to Targets of Abuse

Scope of justice principles suggest that individuals' behavior toward another depends on whether or not they regard that focal person as worthy of fair and moral treatment. If an individual is included within an observer's scope of justice, then the observer feels that the observed person should be treated in a manner similar to that of the observer. Because the observed employee is considered worthy, he or she should be treated with a high degree of fairness and respect. If an individual is excluded from an observer's scope of justice, then that person is not worthy of moral and just treatment because he or she holds characteristics or has exhibited behaviors that breach the observer's expectations of what is considered just. Excluded individuals "are perceived as nonentities, expendable, or undeserving; consequently, harming them appears acceptable, appropriate, or just" (Opotow, 1990, p. 1). To be sure, scope of justice principles have been invoked to explain discriminatory behavior against people with divergent ideology, skin color, religious beliefs, and other differences. This research shows that individuals outside an observer's scope of justice are often treated with extreme exclusionary behavior, such as preventing the target of abuse from attaining any community privileges and protections (see Opotow, 1995, for a review).

We, therefore, contend that an important factor to consider in determining how third-party observers react to abusive supervision is observers' scope of justice beliefs. For example, third-party observers who consider the observed employee (i.e., the target of abuse) to be included within their scope of justice should view the supervisor's abusive behavior as unfair and inappropriate because they believe the observed employee should be treated with the same respect and dignity that should be offered to the observer. Witnessing or being aware of the abuse against someone who is within observers' scope of justice will not sit well with these observers. In contrast, third-party observers who regard the observed employee as excluded from their scope of justice will view the abuse as warranted because the observed employee is viewed as someone who holds unfavorable characteristics and/or is a threat to the observer and the observer's work group. As a result, the abusive supervisor will be viewed as being fair and behaving in a way to maintain what the observer believes is just interpersonal treatment. This line of reasoning suggests that observers' scope of justice beliefs influence the consequences of abusive supervision on third-party observers.

The Consequences When Targets of Abuse Are Within Observers' Scope of Justice

When individuals are within observers' scope of justice, observers believe these individuals should be treated morally and fairly. Much of the theorizing on third-party observer reactions to mistreatment adopts a "within scope of justice" perspective about targets of mistreatment and suggests that observing abusive supervision against them invokes strong, negative consequences (for reviews, see Giacalone and Promislo, 2010; Skarlicki and Kulik, 2005). Justice as deonance and scope of justice principles suggest that the reason why third-party observers experience negative reactions to witnessing or being privy to abuse is because they believe that the observed employee is being treated unfairly. The observed employee is perceived to be an individual worthy of fair treatment, like the observer, and this association can bring with it a sense of concern and empathy (Bar-On, 2001; Staub, 1996). Knowing about or watching the employee being abused can arouse strong emotional reactions (e.g., moral outrage) and negative behavioral reactions (Folger, 2001).

Research supports these ideas. Studies show that being a third-party observer to mistreatment enhances felt stress (Jenkins and Baird, 2002; Lutgen-Sandvik, Tracy, and Alberts, 2007; Vartia, 2001), emotional labor (Spencer and Rupp, 2009), and job burnout (Jenkins and Baird, 2002; Miner-Rubino and Cortina, 2007). Being an observer to abuse also diminishes observers' overall well-being (Vartia, 2001). In particular, observing abusive interpersonal work behavior negatively impacts observers' psychological well-being (Glomb et al., 1997; Miner-Rubino and Cortina, 2007; Pearlman and MacIan, 1995), mental health (Lim, Cortina, and Magley, 2008), and physical health (Glomb et al., 1997; Lim, Cortina, and Magley, 2008; Miner-Rubino and Cortina, 2007). Furthermore, research shows that being a third-party observer of abuse negatively impacts productive work behavior (e.g., performance and citizenship behavior [Porath and Erez, 2009]; team relationship and task conflict [Raver and Gelfand, 2005]) and promotes withdrawal (e.g., job withdrawal [Miner-Rubino and Cortina, 2007]; work withdrawal [Glomb et al., 1997]). In some cases, victims of supervisor abuse take out their frustration aggressively on the third-party observers (e.g., family members [Hoobler and Brass, 2006]).

Additionally, theorists suggest that some third-party individuals take a more active stand against observed abusive interpersonal behaviors (e.g., Folger, 2001; Goldberg, Clark, and Henley, 2011; Skarlicki and Kulik, 2005). That is, some observers seek to rectify the perpetrator's behavior and restore justice in some way, even if doing so is at a sacrifice to the observer (Folger, 2001; Opotow, 1993, 1994). Goldberg, Clark, and Henley (2011) theorized that observers of unfair interpersonal treatment who regarded the target as being within their scope of justice, would express resentment about the mistreatment and voice their concerns to authorities. Whistle-blowing research supports their arguments and shows that some third-party observers report abusive behavior (e.g., Miceli and Near, 1992; Near and Miceli, 1996). Further, Hegtvedt et al. (2009) found that observers who believed the observed employee was treated unfairly were more inclined to try to change the situation.

Emerging work in the organizational sciences also shows that some third-party observers of supervisor mistreatment take matters into their own hands and retaliate on behalf of the observed employee. Studies show that some witnesses of another's mistreatment regard the mistreatment as unfair and, consequently, these observers seek to punish the perpetrator—even if doing so incurs personal costs to the observer (Kahneman, Knetsch, and Thaler, 1986; Turillo et al., 2002; Umphress et al., 2012). Rupp and Bell (2010) extended this work and found that these third-party observers seek to punish perpetrators because they are driven by retributive motives; these observers felt the abusers deserved their "just deserts" for mistreating the victim.

Notwithstanding the importance of this research, ample evidence shows that many individuals who observe others being mistreated do nothing (e.g., Bar-On, 2001; Kärnä et al., 2010; Oh and Hazler, 2009; Zapf, 1999). There are reasons why third-party observers may choose not to help a target of abuse; they may not care, or they may feel that the abuse "is not their problem." Additionally, observers may choose to do nothing because they fear being victimized themselves or retaliated against by the supervisor or other organizational authorities (Bar-On, 2001; Koss et al., 1994; Rayner, 1999). Indeed, a recent study shows that third-party observers of mistreatment who weigh the costs of engaging in retributive reactions are far less likely to retaliate against the transgressor compared to observers who are driven by their outrage (Skarlicki and Rupp, 2010).

Still, these ideas assume that the observer *cares* about what happens to the observed employee and that the observed employee is someone considered worthy of just treatment. Yet, research shows that not all observers may care about another's mistreatment (Rayner, 1999). We contend that another possibility exists: that some observers may not perceive the supervisor's behavior toward the observed employee as unfair. Indeed, research shows that observers sometimes believe a supervisor's abusive behavior is appropriate to maintain accountability for firm performance (cf. Bond et al., 1985; Den Hartog et al., 1999; Tyler, Lind, and Huo, 2000). Such observers, then, would not be compelled to intervene and stop the supervisor's behavior and, alternatively, might instead be inclined to act similarly (Bar-On, 2001; Opotow, 1990). This would be the case if observers see the observed employee as someone excluded from their scope of justice.

The Consequences When Targets of Abuse Are Excluded from Observers' Scope of Justice

Individuals who are not given fair and just attention are morally excluded from one's scope of justice (Opotow, 1990). Theorists contend that perceived differences among group members explain why individuals can be morally excluded (Crosby, 1976; Folger, 1986; Opotow, 1990; Staub, 1989, 1999). As Leary (2001, p. 13) notes, "people seek those with whom they can share rewarding experiences and ignore, avoid, or reject those whose proclivities are markedly different." Specifically, scope of justice research suggests that individuals give little to no moral consideration to another when the other person offers more harm than benefits to the overall group or culture, when they are dissimilar, or when they are a threat to the observer or the observer's in-group (see Opotow, 1995, for a review).

When third-party observers witness or know about an excluded person's mistreatment, observers' allegiance to in-group members heightens and action is mobilized against that excluded member (see Eidelson and Eidelson, 2003, for a review). Although some observers may innocuously respond to the excluded person (e.g., ignore or avoid them; Leary, 2001), others may take a more active approach (Bar-On, 2001; Opotow and Weiss, 2000). For instance, some observers trivialize any victimization experienced by excluded members, treat them with disdain, and sometimes even disparage and denigrate them (Opotow and Weiss, 2000). Research also shows that some observers perversely and pathologically enjoy watching the mistreatment of excluded members (Bagby, 2000; Bar-On, 2001). These ideas have been used to explain why seemingly good people torture others in times of war (Fiske, Harris, and Cuddy, 2004) and why soldiers kill without remorse and may even take pride in ending another person's life (Grossman, 1995; Kelman, 1973).

We believe that the principles of moral exclusion also apply to third-party observers of abusive supervision. That is, supervisors' mistreatment of individuals who are excluded from observers' scope of justice would be thought appropriate, justified, and the right thing to do. The observed employee would likely be an outcast—someone who is perceived as markedly different, who is a potential threat, and/or who behaves in a way that is not consistent with the group's norms and standards. The observed employee, therefore, would be unworthy of moral treatment and deserving of the supervisor's abusive treatment. Instead of abusive supervision evoking moral outrage from the observers (cf. Folger, 2001), it could induce moral delectation and contentment (Bagby, 2000 ; Bar-On, 2001). Consequently, third-party observers who exclude the observed employee from their scope of justice would support the supervisor's behavior and might even engage in exclusionary behavior against that employee.

Some studies provide suggestive evidence to support these ideas in work settings. For instance, research shows that observers of unethical work behavior were far less likely to report the transgressor if they felt that the transgressor was acting in ways consistent with in-group norms (e.g., Greenberg and Scott, 1996; Schmidtke, 2007). Further, third-party observers are more likely to believe in-group perpetrators of unethical acts have done nothing wrong (Payne, 1989). Accordingly, we believe third-party observers of abusive supervision will be less likely to see the supervisor's behavior as unfair or wrongful when the supervisor is abusing an employee who is excluded from the observers' scope of justice.

Additionally, research suggests that observers may personally act against targets of abuse who are morally excluded. For example, research on workplace discrimination shows that individuals who are dissimilar from the majority are treated in an exclusionary fashion (e.g., Blakemore et al., 1997; Maranto and Griffin, 2011). Similarly, team members are more likely to engage in exclusionary behavior against dissimilar team members; excluded members are not included in group communications and are discouraged from participating in group activities (Panipucci, 2003). Research also shows that employees become very angry with and exclude coworkers who are not performing up to group norms and standards, and they even promote strong punishments by the supervisor against the poorly performing outcast (Niehoff, Paul, and Bunch, 1998; Tagger and Neubert, 2008). Further, research shows that coworkers tend to feel mistreatment is more appropriate for coworkers who are competing against them because these competitors pose a potential threat to the observer. For instance, Porath and Erez (2009) found that observers performed better and experienced less negative affect after witnessing an authority member abuse an employee when that employee was competing versus cooperating with them. Further, DeCremer and Hiel (2010) found that observers became very angry and frustrated with authority members who treated their competitors fairly—so much so that the observers intentionally tried to sabotage the competitor's productivity.

In sum, third-party observers' reactions to abusive supervision depend on whether they believe the supervisor's treatment is just. What is considered "just" involves "treating others as they *should* or *deserve* to be treated by adhering to standards of right and wrong" (Cropanzano, Goldman, and Folger, 2003, p. 1019). Third-party observers consider their standard of treatment based on a priori value-system beliefs about how human beings should be treated within a particular context (Bar-On, 2001; Opotow and Weiss, 2000). Our review suggests that the outcomes of being a third-party observer to abusive supervision can be detrimental to observers (e.g., enhanced felt stress, emotional labor, job burnout; decreased well-being) and the organization when the observed employee is considered to be included within the observer's scope of justice. The nature of the outcomes is quite different, however, when observers see the observed employee as morally excluded. Morally excluded employees (i.e., employees who pose a threat to the observer and/ or the observer's work group, or employees who do not conform to group norms) are not given the same, empathic regard as is afforded to employees who are within their scope of justice. The nature of third-party observers' reactions then depends on observers' scope of justice. We elaborate on these ideas below.

DEONTIC REACTIONS OF THIRD-PARTY OBSERVERS TO ABUSIVE SUPERVISION

Traditionally, deontic principles have provided a basis to understand one type of reaction of third-party observers: retaliation against the transgressor (see Skarlicki and Kulik, 2005, for a review). Notwithstanding the importance of this research, we suggest that deontic reactions extend beyond retributive motives. We define deontic reactions as behaviors engaged in by third-party observers either to restore or to maintain their sense of justice. Thus, deontic reactions are actions performed to maintain observers' adherence to what they believe is right and constitutes fair interpersonal treatment. Deonance not only creates an obligation to govern one's own behavior in accordance with a sense of fairness but also motivates observers to ensure that others act in ways consistent with their justice beliefs (Folger, 2001). Yet, we contend, deontic reactions depend on observers' scope of justice beliefs and, specifically, beliefs about the observed employee and the supervisor. We first review deontic reactions that are motivated by scope of justice beliefs about the observed employee and then take observers' scope of justice beliefs about the supervisor into consideration with respect to these reactions.

Deontic Reactions Based on Observers' Scope of Justice Beliefs about the Observed Employee

We developed a typology that identifies potential behavioral reactions by third-party observers of abusive supervision that involve the observer's scope of justice beliefs about the target of the supervisor's behavior (the observed employee). Third-party observers who regard the target as someone within their scope of justice will likely view the supervisor's abusive behavior as inappropriate and unfair. Consequently, these observers might be motivated to restore justice on behalf of the target of abuse. In contrast, third-party observers who regard the target of abuse as falling more outside their scope of justice are more likely to view the supervisor's behavior as justified and appropriate. Because they do not see the supervisor's abusive treatment as unfair, and instead see it as warranted, these observers are more likely to be motivated to maintain what they believe is just interpersonal treatment against the target of the supervisor's abusive behavior (and if they do not actively engage in behaviors to maintain the abusive conditions, they will tend to think and act in ways generally consistent with the perception that abuse is justified—by essentially not even considering it to be "abuse" in the first place).

Further, we suggest that observers' responses also depend on whether the observer attempts to resolve the situation directly or indirectly. With respect to "direct" deontic reactions, these are acts that are targeted directly at the perpetrator of injustice. With respect to "indirect" deontic reactions, these are acts that attempt to restore or maintain justice, but they do so without directly addressing the issue with the perpetrator of injustice. For observers who regard the observed employee as within their scope of justice, the perpetrator of injustice would likely be the supervisor because the supervisor's behavior would be regarded as unfair and inappropriate. For observers who regard the observed employee as excluded from their scope of justice, it would be as if the observed employee has become a type of "perpetrator"—and as such, this employee is deserving of the supervisor's abuse. Stated differently, the observed employee who is perceived to be an "as if perpetrator" is someone who holds unfavorable characteristics or has engaged in behaviors that are considered to be inappropriate to the observer (e.g., threatening behavior to the observer and/or the work group).

The typology depicted in Figure 2.1 illustrates the types of deontic reactions of third-party observers of abusive supervision. The typology comprises two dimensions: the third-party observer's scope of justice beliefs (whether the observed employee is included within or excluded from the observer's scope of justice) and the form of the third-party observer's deontic reaction (whether it is directly or indirectly targeted toward the perpetrator of injustice). These two dimensions produce four types of third-party responders that we have labeled: (1) the Avenger, (2) the Protagonist, (3) the Copycat, and (4) the Collaborator. We describe each in more detail below.

The *Avenger* is a category of third-party observers who regard the observed employee as someone *included within their scope of justice*. Consequently, they believe the observed employee is

Figure 2.1   **A Typology of Deontic Reactions to Abusive Supervision About the Observed Employee**

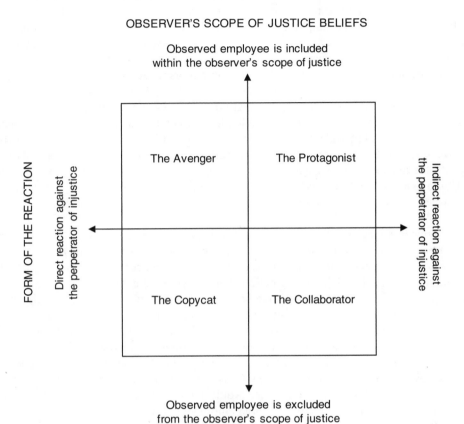

OBSERVER'S SCOPE OF JUSTICE BELIEFS

Observed employee is included
within the observer's scope of justice

FORM OF THE REACTION

Direct reaction against
the perpetrator of injustice

Indirect reaction against
the perpetrator of injustice

The Avenger   The Protagonist

The Copycat   The Collaborator

Observed employee is excluded
from the observer's scope of justice

being treated unfairly. Avengers also seek to target their reaction *directly* toward the perpetrator of injustice or the abusive supervisor. Accordingly, Avengers seek to restore just interpersonal behavior and do so through actions directed at the supervisor. Generally speaking, Avengers are individuals who take vengeance for and on behalf of the individual who is harmed (i.e., the observed employee). Given this, it is very possible for Avengers to harm or retaliate against the supervisor for abusing the observed employee (e.g., withhold needed information, insult the supervisor). Indeed, research supports these arguments and shows that third-party observers of another's mistreatment seek to retaliate against the perpetrator of injustice (e.g., Kahneman, Knetsch, and Thaler, 1986; Rupp and Bell, 2010; Turillo et al., 2002; Umphress et al., 2012). It is also possible, however, for Avengers to address the injustice constructively with the supervisor. For example, research has shown that some observers may go to the source of mistreatment (the supervisor) and try to change the observed employee's situation for the better (Hegtvedt et al., 2009). These reactions are not retaliatory per se, but are nonetheless directed toward the perpetrator of injustice and seek to benefit the observed employee.

The *Protagonist* is a category of third-party observers who also regard the observed employee as someone *included within their scope of justice;* the observed employee is thus deserving of fair treatment and the supervisor is considered to be the perpetrator of injustice. Protagonists, however, *indirectly* try to deal with the supervisor's behavior. Unlike Avengers, Protagonists do not feel comfortable dealing directly with the offending supervisor and, instead, seek to resolve and champion the observed employee's situation indirectly (cf. Shelton and Stewart, 2004). For example, Protagonists may report the supervisor's abusive behavior to other organizational authority members (e.g., a human resources representative, office ombudsman or ethics officer, their boss, the supervisor's boss) or may utilize within-organizational complaint procedures to report the supervisor's wrongdoings (e.g., telephone reporting or hotlines, anonymous reporting procedures). Alternatively, the Protagonist might try to support the victim in some way. For example, Nadisic (2008) contends that some individuals may take resources from the organization (or the supervisor) and provide it to the victim as a way of restoring justice, which he calls the *Robin Hood effect*. Protagonists might also counsel the victim of the supervisor's abuse to report the mistreatment and/or seek legal remedies (e.g., retain an attorney or report the behavior to the Equal Employment Opportunity Commission, U.S. Sentencing Commission). Indeed, research has shown that third-party observers can convince a mistreated employee to seek legal recourse (Barley, 1991).

The *Copycat* is a category of third-party observers who see the observed employee as *excluded from their scope of justice*. Consequently, the observed employee is considered to be someone who is deserving of the supervisor's treatment—someone who has done something or is holding characteristics that foster beliefs that the observed employee has done something wrong to deserve the supervisor's abusive behavior. Scope of justice principles stipulate that people become excluded when they engage in behavior and/or hold characteristics that are threatening to the observer and/or the observer's work group (Bar-On, 2001; Opotow, 1995). Therefore, when the observed employee is excluded from the observer's scope of justice, it is the observed employee who is considered the "perpetrator" of injustice (not the supervisor). Further, Copycats target their reactions *directly* at such observed employees (i.e., treating them "as if" perpetrators of injustice). Deonance would then motivate Copycats to restore justice directly against that perpetrator (the observed employee). Thus, mistreating the observed employee (copying or imitating the abusive supervisor) would be considered the right thing to do because the observed employee is seen as a threat. Although researchers have not explored these ideas directly, evidence suggests Copycat behavior occurs. For example, research shows that employees are more likely to copy others' aggressive behavior at work (Glomb and Liao, 2003; Robinson and O'Leary-Kelly, 1998). More consistent with the moral-exclusion motive, however, observers studied by De Cremer and Hiel (2010) tried to sabotage group members who were seen as a threat. Additionally, Ferguson and Barry (2011) found that third-party observers who either directly witnessed or learned indirectly about another's mistreatment were more likely to mistreat the observed employee when that employee was not seen as a cohesive work group member. We believe that these results are consistent with scope of justice principles and suggest that the more someone is viewed as an outcast by group members, the more likely mistreatment will be seen as warranted. Research on workplace mobbing supports this reasoning as well and shows that individuals become targets of abusive interpersonal behavior by group members when they are seen as being different from the rest of their work group (see Zapf and Einarsen, 2005, for a review).

Finally, the *Collaborator* is a category of third-party observers who see the observed employee as *excluded from their scope of justice*. Like the Copycat, they view the observed employee as the perpetrator of injustice—someone who is undeserving of fair treatment—so they believe such abusive treatment is appropriate toward the observed employee. Unlike Copycats, however, Collaborators attempt to *indirectly* maintain exclusionary behavior against the ob-served employee. We call these observers Collaborators because, like Copycats, they believe the supervisor's behavior is justified and they too engage in behaviors that further exclude the observed employee. They do so, however, without directing their behavior at that employee. For example, Opotow (1995) suggests that individuals who are morally excluded (i.e., the observed employee) are often monitored because their behavior poses a potential threat to the observer and the observer's in-group. Any behavior considered threatening, different, or a violation of group norms engaged in by the excluded member would, then, be reported. Thus, we believe it is very likely for Collaborators to report the excluded employee's questionable behavior to the supervisor in an effort to maintain the standing of the work group. Consistent with these ideas, research shows that individuals report others' inappropriate behavior to their supervisors be-cause it allows them to feel as if they are doing something that appropriately facilitates effective group functioning (Heck, 1992; Kowalski, 1999, 2002; Treviño, 1992). It is also possible for Collaborators to exclude the observed employee, but to do so indirectly, such as by distancing themselves from the excluded employee (Kowalski, 1996), by convincing others to mistreat the observed employee (Zapf, 1999), or by disrupting something that the observed employee cares about (e.g., work schedule, resources). Although these acts are not directed specifically at the excluded member, they still serve the overall goal of rectifying or maintaining just interpersonal treatment within the work group.

Extending Deontic Reactions to also Consider Scope of Justice Beliefs about the Supervisor

Our theorizing so far has focused on observers' scope of justice beliefs about the observed em-ployee or the target of the supervisor's abusive behavior. Yet, we believe that observers' reactions may also depend on whether the supervisor is perceived as deserving of moral consideration. That is, observers' reactions should depend not only on whether the observed employee is included within or excluded from observers' scope of justice beliefs but also on whether the supervisor is included within or excluded from the observers' scope of justice beliefs. Considering both parties, we find that four types of situations can emerge: (1) observers who regard the observed employee as included within their scope of justice but regard the supervisor as excluded from their scope of justice, (2) observers who regard the observed employee as excluded from their scope of justice but regard the supervisor as included within their scope of justice, (3) observers who regard both the observed employee and the supervisor as included within their scope of justice, and (4) observers who regard both the observed employee and the supervisor as excluded from their scope of justice (see Figure 2.2). Each of these situations has implications for third-party observers' deontic reactions.

The first two situations (Situations 1 and 2) are depicted in our Figure 2.1 typology. Specifically, the first situation (observers who regard the observed employee as included within their scope of justice but regard the supervisor as excluded from their scope of justice) is represented on the top half of our typology, above the "form of reaction" line. These observers will be motivated to try to maximize beneficial outcomes for the observed employee and maximize penalties to the supervisor because the observed employee is considered worthy of fair treatment and the supervisor is not. As such, these observers will likely depict Avenger and Protagonist behaviors.

The second situation (observers who regard the observed employee as excluded from their scope of justice but regard the supervisor as included within their scope of justice) is represented on the bottom half of our typology, below the "form of the reaction" line. These observers will be

Figure 2.2 **Observers Scope of Justice Beliefs and the Observed Employee and the Supervisor**

Scope of justice beliefs
about the observed employee

	Included	Excluded
Excluded	**Situation 1** Maximize benefits to the employee and harm to the supervisor *(Avengers and Protagonists)*	**Situation 4** Maximize harm to the employee and the supervisor
Included	**Situation 3** Maximize benefits to the employee and the supervisor	**Situation 2** Maximize harm to the employee and benefits to the supervisor *(Copycats and Collaborators)*

Scope of justice beliefs about the observed supervisor

motivated to try to maximize benefits to the supervisor and maximize penalties to the observed employee; the supervisor's behavior is considered to be appropriate and just because the observed employee is viewed as deserving of punishment. Accordingly, these observers will likely depict Copycat and Collaborator behaviors.

The last two types of situations (Situations 3 and 4) depict extremes of the observer's level of consideration for the parties and, therefore, observers' reactions may differ from those depicted in our proposed typology. When both parties are considered to be included within observers' scope of justice, observers will not want to penalize either person and, instead, will be motivated to maximize benefits for both parties (Situation 3). Consequently, these observers may talk to the supervisor directly to try to benefit the observed employee and to get the supervisor to stop being abusive (i.e., Avenger behavior). They may also go directly to the observed employee and convince that employee to see the supervisor's point of view and try to help the observed employee adapt his/her behavior to avoid future abuse. Alternatively, these observers might ask someone else (e.g., a coworker, human resource representative, office manager) to resolve the situation so that the observer can maintain impartiality and not be viewed as taking sides.

At the other extreme are observers who regard both parties as excluded from their scope of justice (Situation 4). These observers would feel motivated to maximize penalties and harm to both parties because both the observed employee and the supervisor are considered unworthy of just or moral treatment and instead deserve retributive actions directed at them. Observers would likely see the situation as a disruption to the work environment and, therefore, might report the situation to upper management to try to get both parties in trouble and/or removed from the work group. Alternatively, these observers might try to fuel the abusiveness because it will likely result in harm to both parties.

IMPLICATIONS OF THIRD-PARTY OBSERVERS' DEONTIC
REACTIONS TO ABUSIVE SUPERVISION

Our chapter has outlined extant research regarding the effects that abusive supervision has on third-party observers. Additionally, we theorized why the consequences for observers differ depending on their scope of justice beliefs (or whether they consider the supervisor's abusive behavior to be warranted or inappropriate). Doing so is a departure from the existing literature, which has primarily considered only the detrimental effects of abusive supervision to third-party observers. We concede that observing and knowing about abusive supervision can produce harmful outcomes for third parties because these observers believe the supervisor's treatment is morally outrageous and inappropriate. However, we also contend that these consequences may not befall all observers. Some may actually be quite content in witnessing or knowing about the supervisor's abusiveness (Bagby, 2000; Bar-On, 2001). In the end, observers' reactions to abusive supervision depend on whether the observed employee (the target of abusive supervision) and the abusing supervisor are considered to be within or excluded from the observer's scope of justice beliefs. Individuals who are morally excluded are not considered worthy of just interpersonal behavior (or to put it another way, harsh interpersonal treatment of them is considered appropriately fair); instead, these individuals are considered a threat to the observer and/or the observer's work group. Consequently, these morally excluded employees are not given the same sympathetic regard.

Expanding the consequences of abusive supervision to third-party observers in this way—and specifically by looking at different types of deontic reactions—suggests fruitful areas for research in the organizational sciences. To date, much of the theorizing and research on third-party observers of mistreatment (for reviews, see Giacalone and Promislo, 2010; Skarlicki and Kulik, 2005) interprets abusive supervision as a source of perceived unfairness for observers. Clearly, some of the research outlined in this chapter supports those contentions. Nonetheless, these ideas should be expanded to consider observers who do not see the supervisor's abuse as unfair and who instead view it as justified, warranted, and, perhaps, "tough love." Not all targets of abusive supervision are seen as victims. Consequently, we believe our proposed deontic reactions offer a starting point for future research. Although we outlined potential direct and indirect deontic reactions, more research and theorizing is needed to understand why and how targets of abusive supervision are differentially viewed by third-party observers and which personality and situational factors impact their scope of justice beliefs and their reactions.

Additionally, our chapter highlights the need to examine the impact of abusive supervision on third-party observers' well-being. Research on third-party observer mistreatment shows that being witness to or knowing about another's mistreatment can negatively affect observers' well-being (e.g., Jenkins and Baird, 2002; Lutgen-Sandvik et al., 2007; Spencer and Rupp, 2009). Still, only two studies have examined the effects of *supervisor* mistreatment on well-being outcomes of third-party observers (Glomb et al., 1997; Miner-Rubino and Cortina, 2007), and these studies have examined specific forms of supervisor mistreatment—sexual harassment and misogynistic behavior—as opposed to the range of downward hostilities generally regarded as abusive supervision (see Tepper, 2007, for a review). Consequently, much more research is needed to understand the impact of abusive supervision on third-party observers. To this end, we offer some areas for consideration.

We expect that observing abusive supervision will negatively impact observers' psychological and physical well-being, in a manner consistent with the literature on third-party observers of mistreatment, when the observed employee is someone included within the observer's scope of justice (i.e., Avengers, Protagonists). Research shows that when third-party observers believe the supervisor's behavior against another employee is unfair, observers develop negative attitudes about the supervisor and about the organization more generally (Atwater et al., 2001). Theoretically, this makes sense—and in terms of observers' well-being, workplace stress principles might apply. Witnessing or knowing about another person being mistreated, who is an employee like the observer, causes stress; such stress negatively impacts the psychological and physical well-being of observers (Glomb et al., 1997; Miner-Rubino and Cortina, 2007). Part of the stress is a consequence of the level of empathy and regard the observer has for the observed employee. Another part of the stress may emerge simply knowing that a supervisor (someone who may interact with the observer and control important resources over the observer's work life) is abusing an employee in the work environment, heightening concern that the same behavior may occur to the observer. In a way, being a third-party observer of abusive supervision serves as a form of vicarious abuse, evoked by the stress of observing a fellow employee being abused (cf. Glomb et al., 1997).

We also believe that abusive supervision may have implications for the well-being of observers who do not regard the observed employee as being within their scope of justice (i.e., Copycats and Collaborators). On the one hand, being a Copycat or Collaborator may be beneficial for the observer, as both of those deontic ways of responding provide the observer with opportunities for keeping the observed employee in line and for expressing the observer's outrage about the offending employee. Engaging in Copycat and Collaborator behaviors may feel good to the observer (e.g., Knutson, 2004 ; Tripp and Bies, 1997). Consequently, observers might feel a sense of contentment from engaging in Copycat or Collaborator behaviors, which may positively affect their well-being. On the other hand, engaging in Copycat and Collaborator behaviors might prove overly taxing to observers and, ultimately, may negatively impact observers' well-being. For one thing, engaging in tit-for-tat negative exchanges takes effort and drains needed self-resources (cf. Thau and Mitchell, 2010). Further, not all observers might feel so comfortable engaging in hostile behavior, even if it is against an individual the observer believes deserves it. Aquino and Reed (2002) suggest that this might be the case for individuals who have a strong moral identity or for individuals who define their sense of self according to principles of morality (e.g., being a caring, compassionate, and generous person). A strong moral identity is said to help individuals maintain ethical behavior and refrain from engaging in wrongful behavior against others. For example, individuals with a strong moral identity are less likely to punish or retaliate against transgressors (see Shao, Aquino, and Freeman, 2008, for a review). It is reasonable, then, that having to maintain appropriate, nonhostile behavior against an individual whom an observer (with a high moral identity) believes is deserving might be taxing and may negatively impact the overall well-being of the observer. We leave these ideas for future research to explore.

So far, we have considered the situations in which observers include the observed employee but exclude the supervisor from their scope of justice (Situation 1 in Figure 2.2) and situations in which observers exclude the observed employee but include the supervisor within their scope of justice (Situation 2 in Figure 2.2). We believe that investigating the extreme situations, in which both the observed employee and the supervisor are included within observers' scope of justice and excluded from observers' scope of justice (Situations 3 and 4 of Figure 2.2), might also reveal effects on observers' well-being. Either of these extremes represents a challenging work environment for the observer. For observers who consider both parties to be within their scope of justice, their sense of care for both the employee and supervisor would make it uncomfortable and likely heighten stress reactions, which generally affect well-being negatively. Conversely, working in an environment in which observers consider both parties to be excluded from their scope of justice would also be stressful, as the abusive environment would prove taxing to work in day by day—particularly if the parties engage in hostilities against each other.

Although our chapter's focus has been on the consequences of abusive supervision for third-party observers, our review also sheds light on outcomes that can befall the target of abuse, the supervisor, and the organization more generally. In particular, observers can be a source of social support for or further harm to the target of abuse. For example, Avengers and Protagonists may assist the target of abuse in stopping the supervisor's behavior. Copycats and Collaborators, in contrast, may make the target's work life more miserable and potentially dangerous. Consequently, targets of abusive supervision may be in an even more volatile situation if observers do not believe that they are worthy of fair treatment and, therefore, decide to engage in Copycat or Collaborator behaviors.

For supervisors, our discussion suggests that observers' scope of justice beliefs can be either helpful or harmful to them. Supervisors may not even realize that their interactions with a particular subordinate are perceived as abusive. Abusive supervision is a subjective phenomenon (Tepper, 2000). Accordingly, employees are the judge of which behaviors are abusive and which are not. Supervisors who seemingly engage in hostilities against their subordinates may not be trying to "abuse" them, but, in fact, are perceived as such. Our review suggests that such behaviors affect more than the target of the supervisor's behavior. How supervisors treat their subordinates also affects how others respond to the target of the supervisor's behavior and the supervisor. If observers feel the supervisor's behavior is warranted, observers will likely support the supervisor and be motivated to act similarly. Copycat and Collaborator behaviors attempt to help supervisors to keep the offending employee "in line" with group norms and expected behaviors. What our review also suggests, however, is that observers may engage in hostile behavior—by acting directly against the observed employee or by instigating hostilities against the observed employee from other coworkers. Either way, the reality is a sad one and suggests that observers can help abusive supervisors foster an environment of tyranny and fear, which can be highly detrimental to organizations (Morrison and Milliken, 2000).

Finally, we believe our chapter offers some practical implications for organizational decision makers. Our chapter suggests that abusive supervision can spark hostility that spreads throughout the work group and organization. Researchers have estimated the costs of abusive supervision to organizations to be billions of dollars annually (Tepper et al., 2006). These estimates are based on the financial burden associated with the rise in health-care and litigation costs and the counter-productivity in which victims engage. Such cost estimates, however, do not consider the impact of abusive supervision beyond the victim—to those who know about or witness the supervisor abusing an employee. Thus, the consequences of abusive supervision extend far beyond these estimates, which is quite troublesome for organizations.

In short, abusive supervision presents a significant social problem that not only warrants scholarly inquiry but also demands managerial attention (Tepper, 2007). Seemingly, these bosses are allowed to continue their tyranny within organizations and to potentially create a toxic environment. Our review suggests that abusive supervision may also cause bystanders to act similarly and/or in other ways that are detrimental to organizations. Because of it, organizational decision makers should seek to identify potential abusers and rectify their behavior. Moreover, training is needed to ensure that supervisors (and other organizational members) understand how to manage themselves and their employees in an interpersonally effective and fair manner. To be sure, some employees will test the patience of supervisors, but it does not give them cause to abuse the employee—and, potentially, doing so will bring far more harm to the organization than to the target of abuse.

REFERENCES

Andersson, L.M., and Pearson, C.M. 1999. Tit for tat? The spiraling effect of incivility in the workplace. *Academy of Management Review,* 24, 452–471.

Aquino, K., and Reed, A. II. 2002. The self-importance of moral identity. *Journal of Personality and Social Psychology,* 83, 1423–1440.

Atwater, L.E.; Waldman, D.A.; Carey, J.A.; and Cartier, P. 2001. Recipient and observer reactions to discipline: Are managers experiencing wishful thinking? *Journal of Organizational Behavior,* 22, 249–270.

Bagby, J. 2000. Justifications for state bystander intervention statutes: Why crime witnesses should be required to call for help. *Indiana Law Review,* 33, 571–591.

Bamberger, P.A., and Bacharach, S.B. 2006. Abusive supervision and subordinate problem drinking: Taking resistance, stress and subordinate personality into account. *Human Relations,* 59, 723–752.

Barley, S.R. 1991. Contextualizing conflict: Notes on the anthropology of disputes and negotiations. In *Research on Negotiation in Organizations,* vol. 3, ed. M. Bazerman, R. Lewicki, and B.H. Sheppard, 165–202. Greenwich, CT: JAI Press.

Bar-On, D. 2001. The bystander in relation to the victim and the perpetrator: Today and during the holocaust. *Social Justice Research,* 14, 125–148.

Blakemore, J.; Switzer, J.Y.; DiLorio, J.; and Fairchild, D. 1997. Exploring the campus climate for women faculty. In *Subtle Sexism: Current Practice and Prospects for Change,* ed. N. Benokraitis, 54–71. Thousand Oaks, CA: Sage.

Bond, M.H.; Wan, K.C.; Leung, K.; and Giacalone, R.A. 1985. How are responses to verbal insult related to cultural collectivism and power distance? *Journal of Cross-Cultural Psychology,* 16, 111–127.

Cropanzano, R.; Goldman, B.; and Folger, R. 2003. Deontic justice: The role of moral principles in workplace fairness. *Journal of Organizational Behavior,* 24, 1019–1024.

Crosby, F. 1976. A model of egoistic relative deprivation. *Psychological Review,* 83, 85–113.

De Cremer, D., and Hiel, A.V. 2010. Becoming angry when another is treated fairly: On understanding when own and other's fair treatment influences negative reactions. *British Journal of Management,* 21, 280–298.

Den Hartog, D.N.; House, R.J.; Hanges, P.J.; Ruiz-Quintanilla, S.A.; and Dorfman, P.W. 1999. Culturally specific and cross-culturally generalizable implicit leadership theories: Are attributes of charismatic/transformational leadership universally endorsed? *Leadership Quarterly,* 10, 219–256.

Deutsch, M. 1974. Awaking the sense of injustice. In *The Quest for Justice: Myth, Reality, Ideal,* ed. M. Lerner and M. Ross, 19–42. Toronto: Holt, Rinehart and Winston.

Duffy, M.K.; Ganster, D.; and Pagon, M. 2002. Social undermining in the workplace. *Academy of Management Journal,* 45, 331–351.

Eidelson, R.J., and Eidelson, J.I. 2003. Dangerous ideas: Five beliefs that propel groups toward conflict. *American Psychologist,* 58, 182–192.

Ferguson, M., and Barry, B. 2011. I know what you did: The effects of interpersonal deviance of bystanders. *Journal of Occupational Health Psychology,* 16, 80–94.

Fiske, S.T.; Harris, L.T.; and Cuddy, A.J.C. 2004. Why ordinary people torture enemy prisoners. *Science,* 306, 1482–1483.

Folger, R. 1986. A referent cognitions theory of relative deprivation. In *Relative Deprivation and Social Comparison,* ed. J.M. Olson, C.P. Herman, and M.P. Zanna, 33–55. Hillsdale, NJ: LEA.

———. 2001. Fairness as deonance. In *Theoretical and Cultural Perspectives on Organizational Justice,* ed. S. Gilliland, D. Steiner, and D. Skarlicki, 3–33. Greenwich, CT: Information Age.

———. 2011. Deonance: Behavioral ethics and moral obligation. In *Behavioral Business Ethics: Ideas on an Emerging Field,* ed. D. De Cremer and A. Tenbrunsel, 123–142. London: Taylor and Francis.

Giacalone, R.A., and Promislo, M.D. 2010. Unethical and unwell: Decrements in well-being and unethical activity at work. *Journal of Business Ethics,* 91, 275–297.

Glomb, T.M., and Liao, H. 2003. Interpersonal aggression in work groups: Social influence, reciprocal, and individual effects. *Academy of Management Journal,* 46, 486–496.

Glomb, T.M.; Richman, W.L.; Hulin, C.L.; Drasgow, F.; Schneider, K.T.; and Fitzgerald, L.F. 1997. Ambient sexual harassment: An integrated model of antecedents and consequences. *Organizational Behavior and Human Decision Processes,* 71, 309–328.

Goldberg, C.B.; Clark, M.A.; and Henley, A.B. 2011. Speaking up: A conceptual model of voice responses following unfair treatment of others in non-union settings. *Human Resource Management,* 50, 75–94.

Greenberg, J., and Scott, K. 1996. Why do workers bite the hands that feed them? Employee theft as a social exchange process. *Research in Organizational Behavior,* 18, 111–156.

Grossman, D. 1995. *On Killing.* New York: Little, Brown.

Harris, K.J.; Kacmar, K.M.; and Zivnuska, S. 2007. An investigation of abusive supervision as a predictor of performance and the meaning of work as a moderator of the relationship. *Leadership Quarterly,* 18, 252–263.

Harvey, P.; Stoner, J.; Hochwater, W.; and Kacmar, C. 2007. Coping with abusive supervision: The neutralizing effects of ingratiation and positive affect on negative employee outcomes. *Leadership Quarterly,* 18, 264–280.

Heck, W.P. 1992. Police who snitch: Deviant actors in a secret society. *Deviant Behavior,* 13, 253–270.

Hegtvedt, K.A.; Johnson, C.; Ganem, N.M.; Waldron, K.W.; and Brody, L.M. 2009. When will the unaffected seek justice for others? Perceptions of and responses to another's injustice. *Australian Journal of Psychology*, 61, 22–31.

Heider, F. 1958. *The Psychology of Interpersonal Relations.* New York: Wiley.

Hoobler, J. M., and Brass, D. J. 2006. Abusive supervision and family undermining as displaced aggression. *Journal of Applied Psychology*, 91, 1125–1133.

Jenkins, S.R., and Baird, S. 2002. Secondary traumatic stress and vicarious trauma: A validational study. *Journal of Traumatic Stress,* 15, 423–432.

Kahneman, D.; Knetsch, J.L.; and Thaler, R.H. 1986. Fairness and the assumptions of economics. *Journal of Business,* 59, 101–116.

Kärnä, A.; Voeten, M.; Poskiparta, E.; and Salmivalli, C. 2010. Vulnerable children in varying classroom contexts: Bystanders' behaviors moderate the effects of risk factors on victimization. *Merrill-Palmer Quarterly,* 56, 261–282.

Keashly, L. 1998. Emotional abuse in the workplace: Conceptual and empirical issues. *Journal of Emotional Abuse,* 1, 85–117.

Kelman, H.C. 1973. Violence without moral restraint: Reflections on the dehumanization of victims and victimizers. *Journal of Social Issues,* 29, 25–61.

Koss, M.P.; Goodman, L.A.; Browne, A.; Fitzgerald, L.F.; Keita, G.P.; and Russo, N.F. 1994. Responses to sexual harassment. In *No Safe Haven: Male Violence Toward Women at Home, at Work, and in the Community*, ed. M.P. Koss and L.A. Goodman, 133–148. Washington, DC: American Psychological Association.

Kowalski, R.M. 1996. Complaints and complaining: Antecedents, functions, and consequences. *Psychological Bulletin,* 119, 179–196.

———. 1999. Speaking the unspeakable: Self-disclosure and mental health. In *The Social Psychology of Emotional and Behavioral Problems*, ed. R.M. Kowalski and M.R. Leary, 225–247. Washington, DC: American Psychological Association.

———. 2002. Whining, griping, and complaining: Positive in the negativity. *Journal of Clinical Psychology,* 58, 1023–1035.

Knutson, B. 2004. Sweet revenge? *Science,* 305, 1246–1247.

Leary, M.R. 2001. Toward a conceptualization of interpersonal rejection. In *Interpersonal Rejection,* ed. Leary, 3–20. Oxford: Oxford University Press.

Lim, S.; Cortina, L.M.; and Magley, V.J. 2008. Personal and workgroup incivility: Impact on work and health outcomes. *Journal of Applied Psychology,* 93, 95–107.

Lutgen-Sandvik, P.; Tracy, S.J.; and Alberts, J.K. 2007. Burned by bullying in the American workplace: Prevalence, perception, degree and impact. *Journal of Management Studies,* 44, 6, 837–862.

Maranto, C.L., and Griffin, A.E.C. 2011. The antecedents of a "chilly climate" for women faculty in higher education. *Human Relations,* 64, 139–159.

Miceli, M.P., and Near, J.P. 1992. *Blowing the Whistle.* New York: Lexington.

Miner-Rubino, K., and Cortina, L.M. 2007. Beyond targets: Consequences of vicarious exposure to misogyny at work. *Journal of Applied Psychology,* 92, 1254–1269.

Mitchell, M.S., and Ambrose, M.L. 2007. Abusive supervision and workplace deviance and the moderating effects of negative reciprocity beliefs. *Journal of Applied Psychology,* 92, 1159–1168.

Morrison, E.W., and Milliken, F.J. 2000. Organizational silence: A barrier to change and development in a pluralistic world. *Academy of Management Review,* 25, 706–725.

Nadisic, T. 2008. The Robin Hood effect: Antecedents and consequences of managers using invisible remedies to correct workplace injustice. In *Justice, Morality and Social Responsibility,* ed. S.W. Gilliland, D.D. Steiner, and D.P. Skarlicki, 125–153. Greenwich, CT: Information Age Publishing.

Near, J.P., and Miceli, M.P. 1996. Whistle-blowing: Myth or reality. *Journal of Management,* 22, 507–526.

Niehoff, B.; Paul, R.; and Bunch, J. 1998. The social effects of punishment events: The influence of violator past performance record and severity of the punishment on observers' justice perceptions and attitudes. *Journal of Organizational Behavior,* 19, 589–602.

Oh, I., and Hazler, R. 2009. Contributions of personal and situational factors to bystanders' reactions to school bullying. *School Psychology International,* 30, 291–310.

Opotow, S. 1990. Moral exclusion and injustice: An introduction. *Journal of Social Issues,* 46, 1–20.

———. 1993. Animals and the scope of justice. *Journal of Social Issues,* 49, 71–85.

———. 1994. Predicting protection: Scope of justice and the natural world. *Journal of Social Issues,* 50, 49–63.

———. 1995. Drawing the line: Social categorization, moral exclusion, and scope of justice. In *Conflict, Cooperation, and Justice*, ed. M. Deutsch, 347–369. San Francisco, CA: Jossey-Bass.

Opotow, S., and Weiss, L. 2000. Denial and the process of moral exclusion in environmental conflict. *Journal of Social Issues,* 56, 475–490.

Panipucci, D. 2003. When teams devalue diversity. Paper presented at the Academy of Management, Seattle, WA.

Payne, S. 1989. Self-presentational tactics and employee theft. In *Impression Management in Organizations,* ed. R. Giacalone and P. Rosenfeld, 397–410. Hillsdale, NJ: Erlbaum.

Pearlman, L.A., and MacIan, P.S. 1995. Vicarious traumatization: An empirical study of the effects of trauma work on trauma therapists. *Professional Psychology: Research and Practice,* 26, 558–565.

Pearson, C.M., and Porath, C.L. 2005. On the nature, consequences and remedies of workplace incivility: No time for "nice"? Think again. *Academy of Management Executive,* 19, 7–18.

Porath, C.L., and Erez, A. 2009. Overlooked but not untouched: How rudeness reduces onlookers' performance on routine and creative tasks. *Organizational Behavior and Human Decision Processes,* 109, 29–44.

Raver, J.L., and Gelfand, M.J. 2005. Beyond the individual victim: Linking sexual harassment, team processes, and team performance. *Academy of Management Journal,* 48, 387–400.

Rawls, J. 1971. *A Theory of Justice.* Cambridge, MA: Harvard University Press.

Rayner, C. 1999. Workplace bullying. PhD diss. University of Manchester Institute of Science and Technology.

Robinson, S.L., and O'Leary-Kelly, A.M. 1998. Monkey see, monkey do: The influence of work groups on the antisocial behavior of employees. *Academy of Management Journal,* 41, 658–672.

Rupp, D.E., and Bell, C.M. 2010. Extending the deontic model of justice: Moral self-regulation in third-party responses to injustice. *Business Ethics Quarterly,* 20, 89–106.

Saporito, B. 1998. Taking a look inside Nike's factories. *Time,* 15, 52.

Schmidtke, J.M. 2007. The relationship between social norm consensus, perceived similarity, and observer reactions to coworker theft. *Human Resource Management,* 46, 561–582.

Shao, R.; Aquino, K.; and Freeman, D. 2008. Beyond moral reasoning: A review of moral identity research and its implications for business ethics. *Business Ethics Quarterly,* 18, 513–540.

Shelton, J.N., and Stewart, R.E. 2004. Confronting perpetrators of prejudice: The inhibitory effects of social costs. *Psychology of Women Quarterly*, 28, 215–223.

Skarlicki, D.P., and Kulik, C.T. 2005. Third-party reactions to employee (mis)treatment: A justice perspective. *Research in Organizational Behavior,* 26, 183–229.

Skarlicki, D.P., and Rupp, D.E. 2010. Dual processing and organizational justice: The role of rational versus experiential processing in third-party reactions to workplace mistreatment. *Journal of Applied Psychology,* 95, 944–952.

Staub, E. 1989. *The roots of evil: The origins of genocide and other group violence.* NY: Cambridge University Press.

Spencer, S., and Rupp, D.E. (2009). Angry, guilty, and conflicted: Injustice toward coworkers heightens emotional labor through cognitive and emotional mechanisms. *Journal of Applied Psychology,* 94, 429–444.

———. 1996. Preventing genocide: Activating bystanders, helping victims, and the creation of caring. *Peace and Conflict: Journal of Peace Psychology*, 2, 189–200.

———. 1999. The roots of evil: Social conditions, culture, personality, and basic human needs. *Personality and Social Psychology Review,* 3, 179–192.

Taggar, S., and Neubert, M.J. 2008. A cognitive (attributions)-emotion model of observer reactions to free-riding poor performers. *Journal of Business Psychology,* 22, 167–177.

Tepper, B.J. 2000. Consequences of abusive supervision. *Academy of Management Journal,* 43, 178–190.

———. 2007. Abusive supervision in work organizations: Review, synthesis, and research agenda. *Journal of Management,* 33, 261–289.

Tepper, B.J.; Duffy, M.K.; Henle, C.A.; and Lambert, L.S. 2006. Procedural injustice, victim precipitation, and abusive supervision. *Personnel Psychology,* 59, 101–123.

Tepper, B.J.; Henle, C.; Lambert, L.S.; Giacalone, R.J.; and Duffy, M.K. 2008. Abusive supervision and subordinates' organization deviance. *Journal of Applied Psychology,* 92, 721–732.

Thau, S., and Mitchell, M.S. 2010. Self-gain or self-regulation impairment? Tests of competing explanations of the supervisor abuse and employee deviance relationships through perceptions of distributive justice. *Journal of Applied Psychology,* 95, 1009–1031.

Thau, S.; Bennett, R.J.; Mitchell, M.S.; and Maars, M. 2009. How management style moderates the relationship between abusive supervision and workplace deviance: An uncertainty management theory perspective. *Organizational Behavior and Human Decision Processes,* 108, 79–92.

Treviño, L.K. 1992. The social effects of punishment in organizations: A justice perspective. *Academy of Management Review,* 17, 647–676.

Tripp, T.M., and Bies, R.J. 1997. What's good about revenge? The avenger's perspective. In *Research on Negotiation in Organizations,* ed. R.J. Lewicki, R.J. Bies, and B.H. Sheppard, 145–160. Greenwich, CT: JAI Press.

Turillo, C.J.; Folger, R.; Lavelle, J.J.; Umphress, E.E.; and Gee, J.O. 2002. Is virtue its own reward? Self-sacrificial decisions for the sake of fairness. *Organizational Behavior and Human Decision Processes,* 89, 839–865.

Tyler, T.R.; Lind, E.A.; and Huo, Y.J. 2000. Cultural values and authority relations: The psychology of conflict resolution across cultures. *Psychology, Public Policy, and Law,* 6, 1138–1163.

Umphress, E.E.; Simmons, A.; Folger, R.; Ren, R.; and Bobocel, R. 2012. Observer reactions to interpersonal injustice: The roles of perpetrator intent and victim perception. *Journal of Organizational Behavior.* DOI 10.1002/10b.1801.

Vartia, M. 2001. Consequences of workplace bullying with respect to the well-being of its targets and observers of bullying. *Scandinavian Journal of Work Environment and Health,* 27, 63–69.

Zapf, D. 1999. Organizational, work group related and personal causes of mobbing and bullying at work. *International Journal of Manpower,* 20, 70–85.

Zapf, D., and Einarsen, S. 2005. Mobbing at work: Escalated conflict in organizations. In *Counterproductive Work Behavior: Investigations of Actors and Targets,* ed. S. Fox and P. Spector, 237–270. Washington, DC: American Psychological Association.

Zellars, K.L.; Tepper, B.J.; and Duffy, M.K. 2002. Abusive supervision and subordinates' organizational citizenship behavior. *Journal of Applied Psychology,* 87, 1068–1076.

3

COPING WITH UNETHICAL BEHAVIOR

Forgoing the Sweetness of Revenge for the Healthy Choice of Forgiveness

REBECCA J. BENNETT AND SUSIE S. COX

When employees experience unethical acts such as betrayal, breach of trust, or other forms of injustice at work, they are likely to experience both psychological and physical distress, which can have both short- and long-term consequences on their health and well-being.[1] Our chapter takes a somewhat different perspective from the others in this volume by focusing on the recipients of such acts of unethical behavior and their use of forgiveness as a positive coping response. Forgiveness of unethical acts is presented as a coping response that can moderate the harmful effects of offenses on well-being. This chapter offers a model of how unethical behaviors result in negative emotions and broken relationships, which harms individual well-being. To develop this model we begin by explaining how forgiveness intentions and behaviors are different from forgiveness disposition or tendency. We then review the relevant literature on forgiveness and well-being, and extrapolate from the research on forgiveness and wellness in other settings to predict how forgiveness may affect well-being in the workplace. Finally, we describe recent research on forgiveness motives and forgiveness climate in the workplace and suggest some future research directions.

UNETHICAL BEHAVIORS AS GRIEVANCES IN INTERDEPENDENT RELATIONSHIPS

Organizations are defined as people working together to achieve a common objective. Therefore, interdependent relationships are vital to organizational life and success. Individuals are often required to spend many of their working hours communicating and interacting with one another. They may be required to share resources, office space, and assignments. In light of this, as with all interdependent relationships, there is always a risk that one party's actions may be perceived to be unethical and hence have the potential to offend the other party. Being treated in an unethical manner (e.g., enduring sexual harassment or ostracism) results in a sense of injustice or even moral outrage (Bies, 1987; Bies and Moag, 1986). Such a serious breach of trust or sense of great injustice has been labeled a grievance (Luskin, 2002) or hurt (Leary et al., 1998; Worthington, 2006). Grievances are likely to occur when individuals work closely together in the workplace. When faced with an unethical behavior that has caused a hurt or grievance, the offended must find a way to cope with the offense. There are multiple coping behaviors that can be enacted.

For example, the offended may choose to avoid the offender; however, this is not feasible if the offended must work with the offender to accomplish work tasks. Another method of coping is to seek revenge. Although this method of coping may help the offended feel that justice has been served, it may not help advance organizational objectives and, furthermore, may promote retaliation. The offended may try to pretend the offense did not happen, but this self-delusion is difficult to maintain, especially if coworker witnesses confirmed the offense. This chapter focuses on how one particular coping response, forgiveness, can affect individuals' well-being as they react to unethical offenses of their coworkers.

FORGIVENESS AS A COPING RESPONSE

Throughout time, forgiveness has played a vital part in spiritual and interpersonal relationships. Forgiveness plays a prominent role in all major world religions and is universally accepted (Denton and Martin, 1998). The role of forgiveness has been explored in counseling, philosophy, psychiatry, and theology (Enright, 1991); however, its role has been relatively overlooked in the workplace (Bradfield and Aquino, 1999). Forgiveness is identified as a psychological phenomenon that may include accommodation, willingness to sacrifice, and willingness to forgo immediate self-interest, thus contributing to the welfare of another person and engaging in positive relationship interactions (McCullough, 2000). Since interaction with coworkers is a requirement of most jobs, the long-term quality of one's relationships is an essential factor affecting individual well-being (Aquino et al., 2003). Hence, forgiveness may play a crucial role in relationships and attachments in the workplace, especially since coworkers must often continue to interact with those who have offended them.

Defining Forgiveness and Reconciliation

While many studies have attempted to define forgiveness, currently there is no consensus on an operational definition among scholars (Denton and Martin, 1998; Witvliet, Ludwig, and Vander Lann, 2001; Younger et al., 2004). There appears to be more agreement among scholars regarding what forgiveness is *not* rather than what it is (McCullough, Pargament, and Thoresen, 2000). Forgiveness is not pardoning (legal term), condoning (justifying of the offense), excusing, forgetting, or denying (McCullough and Witvliet, 2002). Forgiveness is also distinct from reconciliation. Forgiveness is intrapersonal—the individual acting to change his or her own emotions and thoughts—while reconciliation is interpersonal—two people coming together to restore their relationship (Aquino, Tripp, and Bies, 2001, 2006; Subkoviak et al., 1995). A review of the psychology literature suggests a general consensus that: (1) forgiveness occurs after an individual has suffered a wrongdoing by another person and (2) forgiveness is a voluntary, active choice to forgo anger or revenge (Kaminer et al., 2000). Researchers generally agree that forgiveness embodies a choice of letting go of negative emotions (e.g., resentment, anger, and hostility) toward the offender; however, not all agree on what (if anything) should replace the anger and desire for revenge. Denton and Martin (1998) asked clinicians to define forgiveness. Respondents who viewed forgiveness as therapeutic defined forgiveness as "an inner process, central to psychotherapy, where the injured person no longer seeks to return hurt, and the process has physical, psychological, and emotional benefits" (Denton and Martin, 1998, p. 288). In general, findings from this study support the idea that the forgiveness process could free the offended to engage in less negative and more positive feelings. Nevertheless, the debate remains concerning whether forgiveness mandates positive responses toward the offender as well as a release of the negative feelings, cognitions, and behavior (Rye et al., 2001).

With respect to well-being of the individual, research supports the claim that both releasing negative responses and substituting positive responses improve outcomes (Cox and Bennett, 2006; Finkel et al., 2002; Toussaint and Webb, 2005; Worthington and Scherer, 2004). Cox and Bennett (2006) found that not all individuals claiming to have forgiven a workplace offense experience positive well-being outcomes. Their study examined the releasing of negative affect, cognitions, and behaviors such as not ruminating over the offense or seeking revenge and replacing the negative with positive affect, cognitions, and behaviors such as feeling at peace about the individual and having compassion. They found that those respondents who reported the absence of negative affect, cognitions, and behaviors also reported significantly fewer health problems. However, they also found that those respondents who reported the absence of negative affect, cognitions, and behaviors and the presence of positive affect, cognitions, and behavior toward the offender also reported higher job satisfaction. Hence, it appears that it is necessary to release the negative and replace the negative with positive feelings, thoughts, and behaviors in order to fully experience well-being benefits from forgiveness. This research supports the belief that forgiveness is a process of both letting go and moving past the negative emotions. Letting go includes the release of the negative feelings, thoughts, and behaviors, and moving on includes the presence of positive feelings, thoughts, and behaviors. Embracing the positive aspects of forgiveness may further promote reconciliation of the relationship when reconciliation is appropriate. Hence, it appears that forgiveness and reconciliation may add benefits beyond forgiveness's effect on a victim's well-being.[2]

Within the context of the workplace, the need for continuance of interdependent relationships may be critical. Therefore, we must note that forgiveness within ongoing relationships differs from forgiveness of a stranger's one-time offense. Forgiveness within an ongoing working relationship needs some form of reconciliation to restore the relationship to a functional level. Worthington et al. (2005) note that forgiveness is either decisional or emotional; however, reconciliation is relational. Therefore, reconciliation is important in interdependent relationships where individuals must work together to accomplish organizational objectives. However, reconciliation is not a requirement for forgiveness. Worthington et al. (2005) noted that researchers examining forgiveness within the context of ongoing relationships view forgiveness as an elimination of unforgiveness by replacing the negative with the positive. The general population shares the perspective that restoring the relationship is often a critical aspect of forgiveness. Kantz (2000) as well as Zechmeister and Romero (2002) found that a majority of those they surveyed believed that reconciliation was a necessary part of forgiveness. Fehr, Gelfand, and Nag (2010), in their meta-analysis of forgiveness, also included the behavioral aspect of relationship restoration in their definition: forgiveness is a prosocial motivation of the offended to reconcile differences, cooperate on interdependent tasks, and forgo ill will. Because we are concerned with relationship reconciliation as an important aspect of well-being, we build on Fehr, Gelfand, and Nag's (2010) definition of forgiveness in this chapter.

Forgiveness as a Trait

Researchers have examined forgiveness through several lenses. For example, forgiveness has been viewed as both a trait and a state. Therefore, it is necessary to differentiate between forgiveness as a state and forgiveness as a trait (i.e., forgivingness). State forgiveness is forgiveness granted for a specific offense or a specific offender. For some individuals, forgiveness comes much more easily than for others. These people are likely to possess the tendency to forgive or a forgiving personality. Worthington et al. (2007) call this "forgivingness." The personality trait of forgivingness may be influenced by personality traits such as Machiavellianism (see chapter 12 in this book by Dahling, Kuyumcu, and Librizzi), agreeableness and neuroticism (McCullough and Witvliet, 2002), as well as age (Enright, Santos, and Al-Mabuk, 1989; Mullet and Girard, 2000) and the stage of cognitive moral development an individual has attained (Enright, Santos, and Al-Mabuk, 1989).

Research has discovered that those with the tendency to forgive report better well-being than those without this tendency (Lawler-Row and Piferi, 2006; Toussaint et al., 2001). Lawler et al. (2003), for instance, found that trait forgiveness was associated with lower levels of blood pressure. Lawler-Row and Piferi (2006) reported that individuals with a forgiving personality reported lower stress, higher subjective and psychological well-being, and less depression. Thus, research shows that possessing the trait of forgiveness propensity directly affects well-being. On the other hand, what about the role of state forgiveness on one's well-being? When an employee's unethical behavior affects another employee, how does the act of forgiving affect the well-being of the forgiver?

MODEL OF UNETHICAL BEHAVIOR AND WELL-BEING

Thus far we have noted that unethical behaviors can and do occur in workplaces and the offended party has to determine how he or she will cope with the grievance. In response to this need to cope, we have offered the notion that forgiveness is one option and that forgiveness has the potential to engender positive effects on the offended party's well-being. To elaborate further on this idea, we offer a model of how forgiveness may play an intervening role in the relationship between unethical behaviors and well-being that builds on the concept of forgiveness as a restorative coping mechanism (see Figure 3.1).

When an individual experiences a hurt or grievance, negative emotions transpire such as resentment, bitterness, hostility, hatred, anger, and fear (Exline et al., 2003; Leary et al., 1998; Tripp and Bies, 2009; Worthington, 2006; Worthington and Scherer, 2004). According to research by Leary et al. (1998), the common denominator in all instances of hurt feelings is the perception of relational devaluation—the perception that the offending partner does not value the relationship. This perception is influenced by the frequency and/or severity of the unethical behavior. For instance, enduring repeated demeaning remarks may result in greater damage to the relationship than having a coworker steal one's last Diet Coke or lunch from the office refrigerator. This negative affect causes a rift or break in the attachment associated with the relationship. In one study, Leary et al. (1998) reported two-thirds of respondents claimed that the relationship was weakened after the offense. Hence, this segment of our model proposes that hurt (negative affect) results in severed relationships.

The third portion of our model is based on the premise that positive relationships are essential for well-being. Anthropological, sociological, biological, and psychological perspectives on human motives and desire for connections all suggest that "interpersonal connection is essential to human thriving" (Ryff and Singer, 2000, p. 31). It is a fundamental human need to form social attachments. Humans have evolved to have a need to belong, to form lasting relationships, and to cooperate to achieve mutually beneficial outcomes (Baumeister and Leary, 1995). Once these attachments are established, individuals are reluctant to dissolve them for to do so is likely to negatively impact survival (Axelrod and Hamilton, 1981; Buss, 1991). Indeed, research suggests that breaks in attachment or weaker attachments are linked to poorer health and well-being than are strong intact attachments (Baumeister and Leary, 1995; Heaphy and Dutton, 2008).

48

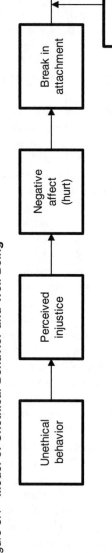

Figure 3.1 **Model of Unethical Behavior and Well-Being**

COPING STRATEGIES FOR GRIEVANCES/HURTS

Individuals experiencing a break in attachment of a valued relationship will look for a method to cope with the break. Since positive interpersonal relationships at work have positive effects on individual well-being (Heaphy and Dutton, 2008; Reich and Hershcovis, 2011), we conclude that coping responses that maintain the relationship (forgiveness and reconciliation) will result in improved well-being. On the other hand, coping with an offense by dissolving the relationship through revenge or avoidance (Aquino, Tripp, and Bies, 2006) has been referred to as "unforgiveness" (Worthington et al., 2007), and we expect that the severed workplace relationships that result from unforgiveness of hurts will harm employees' health and well-being. Worthington et al. (2005, p. 269) suggest that the presence of unforgiveness "takes a toll on a person's physical, mental, relational, and sometimes spiritual well-being." Thus, as a final component of our model, we propose a moderating effect for the differing coping responses individuals choose as a response to hurts experienced in the workplace, in particular, forgiveness versus nonforgiveness.

The Act of Forgiveness and Its Effect on Well-Being

"When people forgive, they become less avoidant, less vengeful, and more benevolent toward the people who have hurt them" (McCullough, Root, and Cohen, 2006, p. 887). There are several direct benefits of forgiveness at the individual, dyadic, and social level, including the reduction of stress, the possibility of reestablishing/repairing the relationship, and the enforcing of the social status quo or norms (Droll, 1984). To understand the value of forgiveness of workplace offenses and to appreciate the potential benefit to well-being, there must be an understanding of how forgiveness can have a positive impact on the individual offended, the relationship between the individuals, and the organization. Several studies have produced glimpses of how this might occur.

Benefits of Forgiveness at the Individual Level

With respect to the well-being of the offended, there is ample empirical evidence that forgiveness can impact psychological and physical well-being. Worthington and Scherer (2004) proposed that forgiveness might reduce hostility in the victim. Hostility remains a key component of unforgiveness. Other researchers have found support for the idea that forgiveness is associated with a reduction of negative emotions (Hebl and Enright, 1993; Kearns and Fincham, 2004) and the healing of relationships (McCullough, 2000; McCullough and Worthington, 1995). Worthington et al. (2007) proposed that forgiveness could have benefits on health by affecting the immune system at a cellular level and a neuroendocrine level. State forgiveness has been found to directly affect physiological outcomes such as heart rate, blood pressure, and cortisol levels. For instance, Witvliet, Ludwig, and Vander Laan (2001) found that when study participants rehearsed hurtful memories (i.e., unforgiving), they experienced increased heart rate, blood pressure changes, and more negative emotions. Those participants who recalled a memory of when they forgave a transgression perceived having greater control and lower physiological stress responses. Lawler and her colleagues (2003) interviewed 168 college students concerning interpersonal conflict and found that trait and state forgiveness were associated with lower blood pressure levels. State forgiveness was also related to a reduced heart rate. Lawler et al. (2005) also found that health was affected by both trait and state forgiveness levels. State forgiveness was positively related to reports of fewer symptom complaints, fewer medicines taken, better sleep quality, reduced fatigue, and fewer somatic complaints. Trait forgiveness was also related to these outcomes; however, it accounted for less variance explained.

The empirical evidence on forgiveness in intimate and ongoing relationships appears to clearly demonstrate that forgiveness of offenses results in better individual well-being than unforgiveness does. However, the research on outcomes of forgiveness has largely been conducted in non-work settings. We see no reason to believe that forgiveness in the workplace will yield different outcomes than that in intimate friendship or marital relationships; however, we do believe that not all forgiveness is equal, and this is perhaps truer in the workplace than in other settings. We mentioned earlier that the workplace environment may demand that one continue working with someone who has offended you with their unethical behavior (e.g., a supplier or coworker who makes harassing comments or a boss who takes credit for subordinate's ideas). These individuals may claim that they have forgiven the offense, yet their motives for doing so can vary considerably. Cox et al. (2012) conducted an exploratory study to examine why individuals forgive workplace offenses. Five distinct motives of forgiveness were revealed through factor analysis. Motives of forgiveness identified were apology ("She apologized for what she did"), lack of alternatives ("I had to forgive"), moral ("Forgiving was the morally right thing to do"), religious ("God expects me to forgive"), and relationship ("The relationship is important to me"). They found, indeed, that some individuals who claimed forgiveness of a workplace offense reported higher levels of perceived stress and poorer general health. They explained this surprising outcome by demonstrating a correlation with negative outcomes and certain forgiveness motives. Their findings suggest that those forgiving because they felt there was no other alternative or that God required forgiveness reported lower well-being than those who were motivated to forgive because they believed forgiveness was the morally correct action.

Benefits of Forgiveness Occur at Multiple Levels of Analysis

Droll (1984) acknowledged that forgiveness could not only benefit the individual granting forgiveness but also could actually have effects at three different levels. First, as we have discussed thus far in this chapter, the offended individual is relieved of the stress of maintaining negative feelings and emotions. Second, the interpersonal relationship may be restored toward harmony and trust (Exline and Baumeister, 2000) and both members of the dyad will benefit from the return of positive affect, cognitions, and behaviors. Third, the context in which the individual and the offended party operate (i.e., the workplace) also benefits.

While there is a growing cluster of studies at the individual and dyadic level of analysis, at an organizational level much less research has been reported. One unique study (Cox 2008) reports the effects of a forgiveness climate on organizational behaviors, employee satisfaction, job stress, and organizational performance. The forgiveness climate is defined as a climate where employees perceive that the members of the group are willing to forgo grudges and work through problems as they arise. Findings from this study reported that individuals who reported having a more forgiving climate in the workplace also reported engaging in organizational citizenship behaviors, having higher job satisfaction, and having lower job stress. However, organizations where individuals reported a more forgiving climate at work had lower performance scores. This counterintuitive finding may be because climates that are "too" forgiving may not hold offenders accountable.

MANAGERIAL IMPLICATIONS

Although forgiveness in organizations has not been widely studied, there is increased interest in this positive coping mechanism for hurts resulting from others' unethical actions. Forgiveness is a crucial part of restoring relationships and enhancing well-being. On the other hand, unforgiveness causes the continuation of strained relationships and negative effects on physical and emotional well-being. Several implications can be gleaned from previous research. First, the benefits of practicing forgiveness have been well documented. For example, forgiveness has been linked with lower stress and systolic blood pressure. Hence, managers may choose to train employees in conflict resolution—specifically, forgiveness techniques—in order to benefit individual health. Furthermore, when individuals are dealt an interpersonal injustice in the workplace, there is a psychological need to deal with the hurt that is felt. These individuals may decide to avoid the perpetrator, to seek revenge, or to ruminate on the offense. It is likely that these negative coping mechanisms will *not* benefit the victim or the relationship between the offender and the offended party. However, reduction of the unforgiveness, by letting go of the negative and replacing those feelings, thoughts, and behaviors with the positive, can benefit both the relationship and the well-being of the offended individual. One way previous forgiveness intervention research has shown to increase the positive thoughts, feelings, and actions is through perspective-taking exercises (Enright, 2001; Smedes, 1996).

A second managerial implication, therefore, is that managers might develop perspective-taking exercises in order to enhance intrinsic forgiveness in interpersonal relationships at work. Third, since forgiveness mends relationships and hence positively affects social well-being among co-workers (Keyes, 1998), managers should facilitate team-building opportunities in the workplace to build strong relationships between organizational members, which may engender further intrinsic forgiveness and better well-being. Finally, research suggests that the organization as a whole can benefit from a forgiveness climate. Managers may choose to establish a workplace climate that encourages forgiveness and hence positively affects employee well-being. However, in order to avoid the potential negative performance implications of a forgiveness climate, managers may be called on to be advocates for forgiveness while holding the offender accountable for his/her un-ethical actions. Worthington et al. (2005) noted that although forgiveness does not oppose holding offenders accountable, forgiveness has the potential to "erode the justice motive if people allow it" (p. 281). A pattern of forgiveness may lead offenders to feel free to offend again by removing unwanted consequences for their behavior (e.g., anger, criticism, rejection, loneliness) that would otherwise discourage reoffending. Understanding that forgiveness is a process that does not nec-essary release the offender from accountability may aid individuals in their willingness to let go of the negative affect, cognitions, and behaviors, replacing them with positive affect, cognitions, and behaviors. Furthermore, as the body of research continues to grow in support of the benefits of forgiveness, employees should be made aware of these benefits as well as the importance of an accountability culture.

RESEARCH IMPLICATIONS

Research on forgiveness of unethical offenses' impact on well-being is in its infancy and thus offers much potential for continued research in this area. In this chapter, we have taken the per-spective of forgiveness as a positive effect on the victim's well-being, but perpetrators and wit-nesses to the offense, as well as more peripheral actors (family members, work group members not directly witnessing the offense, customers) may also be impacted. Giacalone and Promislo (2010) reviewed a wide variety of literatures in providing evidence of the far-reaching scope of unethical behavior on those linked to the victim such as spouses and children. Of course, those associated with the perpetrator of the unethical offenses may be affected as well. Research on abusive supervision has demonstrated that those who are abusive toward their subordinates at work are also abusive to their families at home (Hoobler and Brass, 2006), thus extending the ripple effect of the original injustice on cumulative societal well-being. It may be that perpetrators are also harmed in unanticipated ways by their own unethical actions. Raskolnikov, the murderer in Dostoevsky's literary masterpiece *Crime and Punishment*, gets away with the "perfect" crime, yet his own guilt and anxiety lead to a substantial decline in his own personal well-being. Beyond this literary evidence, Giacalone and Promislo (2010) cite research (Pollock, 1999) suggesting that those engaging in criminal and unethical acts can themselves be traumatized when they commit an act they know is wrong. Such a breach of one's own values (guilty conscience?) can lead to extreme guilt, anxiety, and associated declines in physical and psychological well-being (Byrne, 2003; Evans et al., 2007 as cited by Giacalone and Promislo, 2010). These research findings and literary insight prompt us to question whether unethical behaviors have more far-reaching implications not only for the well-being of victims, bystanders, and those close to them but also for the perpetrators themselves. Future research might investigate whether abusive supervisors experience poorer personal well-being than nonabusive supervisors do. Perhaps self-forgiveness training (as well as ethical management skills training) could result in better health for the unethical manager/employee.

NOTES

1. Defining well-being, Bono, McCullough, and Root (2007) measured well-being by physical systems, satisfaction with life, a more positive mood, and a less negative mood.
2. We acknowledge that reconciliation is not always safe or advisable for victims (e.g., sexual or physical assault). Extremely serious offenses would likely lead to a severed workplace relationship anyway through the firing or arrest of the offender, thereby making reconciliation of the workplace relationship impossible.

REFERENCES

Aquino, K.; Tripp, T.M., and Bies, R.J. 2001. How employees respond to personal offense: The effects of blame attribution, victim status, and offender status on revenge and reconciliation in the workplace. *Journal of Applied Psychology,* 86, 52–59.
———. 2006. Getting even or moving on? Power, procedural justice, and types of offense as predictors of revenge, forgiveness, reconciliation, and avoidance in organizations. *Journal of Applied Psychology,* 91, 653–668.
Aquino, K.; Grover, S.L.; Goldman, B.; and Folger, R. 2003. When push doesn't come to shove: Interpersonal forgiveness in workplace relationships. *Journal of Management Inquiry,* 12, 209–216.
Axelrod, R., and Hamilton, W.D. 1981. The evolution of cooperation. *Science,* 211, 1390–1386.
Baumeister, R.F., and Leary, M.R. 1995. The need to belong: Desire for interpersonal attachments as a fundamental human motivation. *Psychological Bulletin,* 117, 497–529.
Bies, R.J. 1987. The predicament of injustice: The management of moral outrage. In *Research in Organizational Behavior,* vol. 9, ed. L.L. Cummings and B.M. Staw, 289–319. Greenwich, CT: JAI Press.
Bies, R.J., and Moag, J. 1986. Interactional justice: Communication criteria of fairness. In *Research on Negotiation in Organizations,* vol.1, ed. R.J. Lewicki, B.H. Sheppard, and M.H. Bazerman, 43–55. Greenwich, CT: JAI Press.
Bono, G.; McCullough, M.E.; and Root, L.M. 2007. Forgiveness, feeling connected to others, and wellbeing: Two longitudinal studies. *Personality and Social Psychology Bulletin,* 34, 182–195.
Bradfield, M., and Aquino, K. 1999. The effects of blame attribution and offender likableness on forgiveness and revenge in the workplace. *Journal of Management,* 25, 607–631.
Buss, D.M. 1991. Evolutionary personality psychology. *Annual Review of Psychology,* 45, 459–491.
Byrne, M. K. 2003. Trauma reactions in the offender, *International Journal of Forensic Psychology,* 1, 59–70.

Cox, S.S. 2008. A forgiving workplace: An investigation of forgiveness climate, individual differences and workplace outcomes. PhD diss. Louisiana Tech University, Ruston.

Cox, S.S., and Bennett, R.J. 2006. Is letting go enough? The influence of forgiveness on health and job satisfaction. In *Proceedings from Southern Management Association 2006 Meeting*, 529–534. Clearwater Beach, FL, October 25–28.

Cox, S.S.; Bennett, R.J.; Tripp, T.M.; and Aquino, K. 2012. An empirical test of forgiveness motives' effects on employees' health and well-being. *Journal of Occupational Health Psychology,* 17(3). 330–340. Charles, LA.

Denton, R.T., and Martin, M.W. 1998. Defining forgiveness: An empirical exploration of process and role. *American Journal of Family Therapy,* 28, 281–292.

Droll, D.M. 1984. Forgiveness: Theory and research. PhD diss. University of Nevada-Reno.

Enright, R.D. 1991. The moral development of forgiveness. In *Handbook of Moral Behavior and Development,* vol. 1, ed. W. Kurtines and J. Gewritz, 123–152. Hillsdale, NJ: Erlbaum.

———. 2001. *Forgiveness Is a Choice.* Washington, DC: APA Life Tools.

Enright, R.D.; Santos, M.J.; and Al-Mabuk, R. 1989. The adolescent as forgiver. *Journal of Adolescence,* 12, 95–110.

Exline, J.J., and Baumeister, R.F. 2000. Expressing forgiveness and repentance: Benefits and barriers. In *Forgiveness: Theory, Research and Practice,* ed. M.E. McCullough, K.I. Pargament, and C.E. Thoresen, 133–155. New York: Guilford Press.

Exline, J.J., Worthington, E.L., Jr., Hill, P., and McCullough, M.E. 2003. Forgiveness and justice: A research agenda for social and personality psychology. *Personality and Social Psychology Review,* 7, 337–348.

Fehr, R.; Gelfand, M.; and Nag, M. 2010. The road to forgiveness: A meta-analytic synthesis of its situational and dispositional correlates. *Psychological Bulletin,* 136, 894–914.

Finkel, E.J.; Rusult, C.E.; Kumashiro, M.; and Hannon, P.A. 2002. Dealing with betrayal in close relationships: Does commitment promote forgiveness? *Journal of Personality and Social Psychology,* 82, 956–974.

Giacalone, Robert A., and Promislo, Mark D. 2010. Unethical and unwell: Decrements in well-being and unethical activity at work. *Journal of Business Ethics* 91 (2): 275–297.

Heaphy, E.D., and Dutton, J.E. 2008. Positive social interactions and the human body at work: Linking organizations and physiology. *Academy of Management Review,* 33, 137–162.

Hebl, J.H., and Enright, R.D. 1993. Forgiveness as a psychotherapeutic goal with elderly females. *Psychotherapy,* 30, 658–667.

Hoobler, J.M., and Brass, D.J. 2006. Abusive supervision and family undermining as displaced aggression. *Journal of Applied Psychology,* 91, 1125–1133.

Kaminer, D.; Stein, D.J.; Mbanga, I.; and Zungu-Dirwayi, N. 2000. Forgiveness: Toward an integration of theoretical models. *Psychiatry: Interpersonal and Biological Processes,* 63, 344–357.

Kantz, J.E. 2000. How do people conceptualize and use forgiveness? The forgiveness attitudes questionnaire. *Counseling and Values,* 44, 174–186.

Kearns, J.N., and Fincham, F.D. 2004. A prototype analysis of forgiveness. *Personality and Social Psychology Bulletin,* 30, 838–855.

Keyes, C.L.M. 1998. Social well-being. *Social Psychology Quarterly,* 61, 121–140.

Lawler-Row, K.A., and Piferi, R.L. 2006. The forgiving personality: Describing a life well lived? *Personality and Individual Differences,* 41, 1009–1020.

Lawler, K.A.; Younger, J.W.; Piferi, R.L.; Jobe, R.; Edmondson, K.A.; and Jones, W.H. 2005. The unique effects of forgiveness on health: An exploration of pathways. *Journal of Behavioral Medicine,* 28, 157–167.

Lawler, K.A.; Younger, J.W.; Piferi, R.L.; Billington, E.; Jobe, R.; Edmondson, K.; Jones, W.H. 2003. A change of heart: Cardiovascular correlates of forgiveness in response to interpersonal conflict. *Journal of Behavioral Medicine,* 26, 373–393.

Leary, M.R.; Springer, C.; Negel, L.; Ansell, E.; and Evans, K. 1998. The causes, phenomenology and consequences of hurt feelings. *Journal of Personality and Social Psychology,* 74, 1225–1237.

Luskin, F. 2002. *Forgive for Good: A Proven Prescription for Health and Happiness.* New York: HarperCollins.

McCullough, M.E. 2000. Forgiveness as human strength: Theory, measurement, and links to well-being. *Journal of Social and Clinical Psychology,* 19, 43–55.

McCullough, M.E., and Witvliet, C.V. 2002. The psychology of forgiveness. In *Handbook of Positive Psychology,* ed. C.R. Snyder and S.J. Lopez, 446–458. New York: Oxford University Press.

McCullough, M.E., and Worthington, E.L. 1995. Promoting forgiveness: A comparison of two brief psychoeducational group interventions with a waiting-list control. *Counseling and Values,* 40, 55–68.

McCullough, M.E.; Pargament, K.I.; and Thoresen, C.E. 2000. The psychology of forgiveness: History, conceptual issues, and overview. In *Forgiveness: Theory, Research, and Practice,* ed. McCullough, Pargament, and Thoresen, 1–14. New York: Guilford Press.

McCullough, M.E.; Root, L.M.; and Cohen, A.D. 2006. Writing about the benefits of an interpersonal transgression facilitates forgiveness. *Journal of Counseling and Clinical Psychology,* 74, 887–897.

Mullet, E., and Girard, M. 2000. Developmental and cognitive points of view on forgiveness. In *Forgiveness: Theory, Research and Practice*, ed. M.E. McCullough, K.I. Pargament, and C.E. Thoresen, 111–132. New York: Guilford.

Pollock, P. H. 1999, When the killer suffers: Post-traumatic stress reactions following homicide, *Legal and Criminological Psychology* 4, 185–202.

Reich, T.C., and Hershcovis, M.S. 2011. Interpersonal relationships at work. In *APA Handbook of Industrial and Organizational Psychology,* Vol. 3: *Maintaining, Expanding, and Contracting the Organization*, ed. Sheldon Zedeck, 223–248. Washington, DC: American Psychological Association.

Rye, M.S.; Loiacono, D.M.; Folck, C.D.; Olszewski, B.T.; Heim, T.A.; and Madia, B.P. 2001. Evaluation of the psychometric properties of two forgiveness scales. *Current Psychology: Developmental, Learning, Personality, and Social,* 20, 260–277.

Ryff, C.D., and Singer, B. 2000. Interpersonal Flourishing: A positive health agenda for the new millennium. *Personality and Social Psychology Review,* 4, 30–44.

Smedes, L.B. 1996. *The Art of Forgiving.* New York: Ballantine Books.

Subkoviak, M.J., Enright, R.D., Wu, C., Gassin, E.A., Freedman, S., Olson, L.M., and Sarinopoulos, I. 1995. Measuring interpersonal forgiveness in late adolescence and middle adulthood. *Journal of Adolescence,* 18, 641–655.

Toussaint, L., and Webb, J.R. 2005. Theoretical and empirical connections between forgiveness, mental health, and well-being. In *Handbook of Forgiveness*, ed. E.L. Worthington Jr., 207–226. New York: Brunner–Routledge.

Toussaint, L.L., Williams, D.R., Musick, M.A., and Everson, S.A. 2001. Forgiveness and health: Age differences in a U.S. probability sample. *Journey of Adult Development,* 8, 249–257.

Tripp, T.M., and Bies, R.J. 2009. *Getting Even: The Truth About Workplace Revenge—and How to Stop It.* San Francisco, CA: Jossey-Bass.

Witvliet, C.V.; Ludwig, T.E.; and Vander Laan, K.L. 2001. Granting forgiveness or harboring grudges: Implications for emotion, physiology, and health. *Psychological Science,* 12, 117–123.

Worthington, E.L. 2006. *Forgiveness and Reconciliation: Theory and Application.* New York: Routledge.

Worthington, E.L., and Scherer, M. 2004. Forgiveness is an emotion-focused coping strategy that can reduce health risks and promote health resilience: Theory, review, and hypothesis. *Psychology and Health,* 19, 385–405.

Worthington, E.L.; Berry, J.W.; Shivy, V.A.; and Browstein, E. 2005. Forgiveness and positive psychology in business ethics and corporate social responsibility. In *Positive Psychology in Business Ethics and Corporate Responsibility,* ed. R.A. Giacalone, C.L. Jurkiewicz, and C. Dunn, 265–284. Greenwich, CT: Information Age.

Worthington, E.L.; Witvliet, C.V.; Pietrini, P.; and Miller, A.J. 2007. Forgiveness, health, and well-being: A review of evidence for emotional versus decisional forgiveness, dispositional forgiveness, and reduced unforgiveness. *Journal of Behavior Medicine,* 30, 291–302.

Younger, J.W.; Piferi, R.L.; Jobe, R.L.; and Lawler, K.A. 2004. Dimensions of forgiveness: The views of laypersons. *Journal of Social and Personal Relationships,* 21, 837–855.

Zechmeister, J.S., and Romero, C. 2002. Victim and offender accounts of interpersonal conflict: Autobiographical narratives of forgiveness and unforgiveness. *Journal of Personality and Social Psychology,* 82, 675–686.

4

THE MORALITY AND ETHICS OF WORKPLACE REVENGE

Avengers' Moral Considerations and the Consequences of Revenge for Stakeholder Well-Being

DAVID A. JONES

To some observers, revenge in the workplace is simply immoral: it is rooted in an avenger's desire to inflict harm that is disguised under a false cloak of justice, can damage relationships among coworkers, and reflects an avenger's morally corrupt character. However, to other observers—including most avengers—there is a rationality and morality underlying revenge, such as when it serves to restore justice and deter future abuse (Tripp and Bies, 2009).

In this chapter I explore the morality and ethics of revenge in the workplace. I review theory and research through the lens of a process model that delineates key aspects of a typical revenge episode as experienced from an avenger's perspective, starting with a perceived offense and culminating in revenge behavior. While describing this model, I highlight moral-based considerations that can affect avengers throughout a revenge episode, explore consequences for avenger well-being, and identify avenues for future scholarly inquiry.

After describing the revenge episode model, I then consider the ethics of workplace revenge more broadly. Is it right or wrong to engage in revenge at work? In answering this question, I consider the consequences of revenge for the well-being of all major stakeholders, and conclude by offering suggestions for organizational practice.

FROM PERCEIVED OFFENSE TO REVENGE BEHAVIOR: A REVENGE EPISODE PROCESS MODEL

Revenge refers to actions that are intended to inflict harm on a party deemed responsible for an offense (Stuckless and Goranson, 1992). The desire for revenge reflects the endorsement of the "eye for an eye" principle in the pursuit of justice (Tripp and Bies, 2009). The primary stakeholders of a revenge episode in the workplace are the offender—the individual or group who is believed to have committed some offense; third-parties—employees or customers who are potentially affected by the revenge episode; and the avenger—the individual seeking revenge.

Figure 4.1 displays a process model of a typical revenge episode as experienced from the avenger's perspective. In response to an offense that is often perceived as an undeserved injustice, avengers attribute blame and experience intense anger, which fuel their desires for revenge, ultimately leading them to commit actions intended to harm the offender.

The processes illustrated in Figure 4.1 commence once an avenger has experienced or learned of an offense,[1] which often involves some type of perceived injustice (Jones, 2009, 2010). These offenses tend to fall within one of three categories (Tripp and Bies, 2009): goal obstruction (e.g., an offender blocks the pursuit of a career objective), rule and social norm violation (e.g., an offender shows favoritism in his or her decisions about promotion or takes credit for another's ideas), and reputation damage (e.g., an offender makes an unfair accusation or publically insults someone in a disrespectful manner). As seen in Figure 4.1, an avenger first appraises the severity of the offense and makes attributions about who or what is responsible.

Appraisal of Offense Severity

> *And where the offense is, let the great axe fall.*
> —William Shakespeare

What makes an offense sufficiently offensive to warrant revenge? Drawing upon the multiple-needs model of justice (Cropanzano et al., 2001), Jones (2010) asserted that offenses are more severe, and hence more likely to trigger desires for revenge, to the extent they violate or threaten people's core psychological needs (control, belonging, self-esteem, and moral purpose), thereby arousing associated motives for justice (instrumental, uncertainty management, relational, and deontic). Through revenge, individuals attempt to repair damaged needs and address the justice motives aroused by the offense. For example, desires for revenge can be triggered by offenses perceived as an unjust attack on the victims' identity and standing within their work group, thereby damaging their needs for self-esteem and belonging. Such offenses arouse relational justice motives because people want to maintain positive self-images and social identities, which motivates would-be avengers to defend against the threat posed by the offense (Aquino and Douglas, 2003). Through revenge, people can restore their self-esteem and status within the group (Bies and Tripp, 1996; Tripp and Bies, 1997). Thus, avengers' desire to restore or protect aspects of their psychological well-being that were damaged or threatened by an offense acts as a motivating force that compels them to seek vengeance.

Moral Considerations During Appraisals of Offense Severity

To provide moral legitimacy for their impending revenge, avengers often frame the triggering offense as an undeserved act of injustice (Bies and Tripp, 1996; Tripp and Bies, 2010). Consistent with this notion, research has shown that relationships between employees' perceptions of injustice and counterproductive behaviors, such as theft or ignoring supervisors' instructions, are mediated by desires for revenge (Jones, 2009). Moreover, people involved in a conflict episode tend to view the other party as the initial offender, thereby helping would-be avengers frame the offender's actions as unprovoked and, hence, unjust (Bies, Tripp, and Kramer, 1997).

Some offenses, such as sexual harassment or discrimination, may be so morally repugnant that people feel obliged to seek revenge. Consistent with some avengers' descriptions of their revenge episodes (Jones, 2010), theory on the "deontic response" suggests that offenses that violate moral norms can trigger intense emotional responses, fueling a sense of duty to strike back at harmdoers who *deserve* to be punished (Folger, Cropanzano, and Goldman, 2005). Studies suggest that people can experience moral outrage upon learning of an injustice, prompting them to punish the offender even at the expense of their self-interest (Turillo et al., 2002).

The deontic response is presumably more likely to occur among individuals who hold values about the importance of justice, thereby making injustices particularly salient, which is reflected

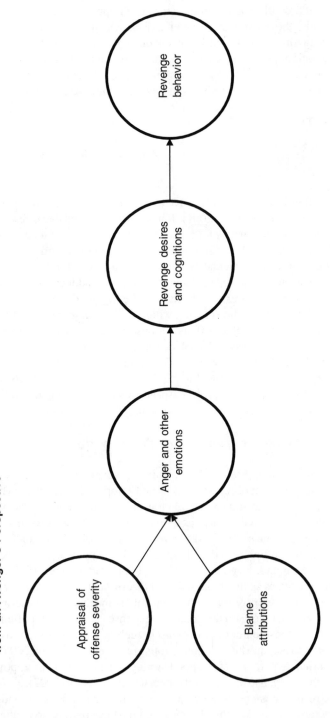

Figure 4.1. **From Perceived Offense to Revenge Behavior: A Revenge Episode Process Model from an Avenger's Perspective**

in their justice orientation (Holtz and Harold, in press; Liao and Rupp, 2005; Rupp, Byrne, and Wadlington, 2003). For these would-be avengers, not only might morally repugnant offenses have especially negative effects on their well-being in ways described next, but the motivating power of such offenses ultimately increases the likelihood that they expose themselves to the risks associated with enacting revenge, a topic to which I return later.

Appraisals of Offense Severity and Avenger Well-Being

Other than studies described later showing that revenge is fueled by negative emotions like anger that follow from perceived injustice (e.g., Barclay, Skarlicki, and Pugh, 2005), little empirical evidence directly addresses the effects of a revenge-triggering offense on avenger well-being or, for that matter, the effects of any aspect of a revenge episode on the well-being of the affected stakeholders. To promote research on this important but neglected topic, I consider how each aspect of a revenge episode might affect avenger well-being. These assertions, derived largely from qualitative research on workplace revenge and empirical studies in other literatures, are intended to serve as propositions for future research, and I start with the possible effects of the initial offense.

Some workplace avengers claim to have suffered considerable psychological distress and anxiety from being the target of an offense that ultimately triggered their revenge (Jones, 2010; Tripp and Bies, 2009). These retrospective accounts are consistent with empirical research outside of the workplace revenge literature, suggesting that some offenses have the potential to damage avengers' well-being, which refers to their subjective happiness, psychological well-being, and physical well-being as reflected by physiological health-related outcomes (Giacalone and Promislo, 2010). For instance, the victims of bullying and discrimination tend to experience poorer psychological well-being (e.g., depression, lower self-esteem), as well as diminished physical well-being (e.g., stress and insomnia; see Giacalone and Promislo, 2010).

In a recent review of evidence in the organizational justice literature, Greenberg (2010) concluded that, "individuals who perceive injustice in the workplace are inclined to suffer mental and physical illness" (p. 206). For instance, employees who perceive greater injustice at work (e.g., about the fairness of their pay, decision-making procedures, or interpersonal treatment from managers) are more likely to suffer negative psychological outcomes like depression (e.g., Kivimäki et al., 2003; Tepper, 2001). Perceived injustice is also associated with several negative health-related outcomes, such as those described in Chapter 13 of this volume. For example, in one study of over 6,000 British civil-service employees, perceived injustice at work was associated with several indicators of coronary heart disease (CHD) measured nine years later, including nonfatal myocardial infarctions, self-reported angina confirmed by medical records, abnormalities observed in coronary angiograms, and fatalities due to CHD (Kivimäki et al., 2005).

While compelling, the link between perceived injustice and well-being presumably reflects, at least to some degree, persistent levels of perceived injustice that can plague employees for considerable lengths of time. As such, these effects found on well-being may not generalize to the context of a single offense that triggers a revenge response; however, they might for some revenge episodes. In one interview-based study, most avengers claimed that the offense that led to their revenge occurred after a history of mistreatment from the offender, and they often characterized the offense as "the straw that broke the camel's back" (Jones, 2010). Moreover, an examination of why these offenses triggered revenge when prior offenses did not suggested that the revenge-triggering offenses tended to involve a threat or damage to avengers' core psychological needs. Accordingly, research is needed to test the possibility that offenses have increasingly negative effects on avenger well-being to the extent that they threaten or damage important psychological needs (control, belonging, self-esteem, and moral purpose), especially when the offenses follow prior mistreatment by the offender. Moreover, other aspects of a revenge episode that are subsequently described likely heighten these effects, such as the degree that avengers experience anger and blame an offender whose motives are attributed to malicious and immoral intent.

Negative effects on avengers' well-being might also occur when they spend considerable time obsessing about the offense. Some workplace avengers report repeatedly reviewing and ruminating over the offense, which for the avengers in one sample lasted for an average of three weeks before they engaged in revenge (Jones, 2010). Interview-based findings suggest that ruminating over the offense can maintain or heighten avengers' anger (Bies and Tripp, 1996; Tripp and Bies, 1997), and I later explore the consequences of this anger for avenger well-being. Research also suggests that ruminating about the offense is nonadaptive and can inhibit forgiveness (Berry et al., 2005), thereby increasing the likelihood that would-be avengers will expose themselves to the risks associated with enacting their revenge. Ruminating about the offense may have relatively strong effects on avenger well-being when the experience lowers their self-esteem and sense of belonging, both of which are unpleasant mental states.

Other studies have linked workplace injustice to sleep difficulties, including quasi-experimental research in which levels of insomnia were reduced among nurses whose managers were trained to provide interpersonally just treatment (Greenberg, 2006). One study of several thousand Finnish hospital workers showed that perceived injustice was associated with poorer self-reported health, and this relationship was explained through the effects of injustice on insomnia (Elovaini et al., 2003). These findings are suggestive of an intriguing possibility: avengers who ruminate over the perceived offense may suffer from its interfering with their sleep, in turn leading to negative health outcomes. As recognized by Greenberg (2010), negative health outcomes may also occur through the effects of perceived injustice on negative emotional experiences and unhealthy behaviors (e.g., excessive alcohol consumption).

Blame Attributions

> *It is impossible to suffer without making someone pay for it.*
> —Friedrich Nietzsche

Because avengers seek to make someone pay for their suffering, their attributions about who or what is to blame play a critical role in revenge. As portrayed in Figure 4.1, upon experiencing an offense, in addition to appraising the severity of the offense, would-be avengers seek to impute responsibility through attributions of blame. People are motivated to understand why an injustice occurred to gain some degree of psychological control over the event (Folger and Cropanzano, 2001). When an offense is deemed to have been under the offender's volitional control, victims hold the offender responsible for their pain, often perceiving the offense as a personal attack (Folger and Cropanzano, 2001). Interview-based studies consistently highlight the importance of blaming in the revenge process (e.g., Bies and Tripp, 1996; Jones, 2010), and empirical research shows that blame attributions relate positively to revenge (Allred, 1999; Aquino, Tripp, and Bies, 2001; Barclay, Skarlicki, and Pugh, 2005; Bradfield and Aquino, 1999).

Moral Considerations During Blaming

The effects of blame attributions on desires for revenge are likely magnified when the offense is viewed as morally reprehensible. Fairness theory (Folger and Cropanzano, 2001) proposes that when individuals experience an injustice they mentally compare the event to imagined alternatives to determine whether the event *could* have happened differently (i.e., attributions about the offender's intentionality), and whether a different event *should* have occurred instead (i.e., assessments about whether the event violated norms for moral conduct). When individuals conclude that the offender should have acted differently yet chose otherwise, anger and resentment swell, fostering a deep-seated desire for revenge. Folger and Skarlicki (1998) stress that the degree of harm on its own is not what motivates revenge; rather, revenge is motivated by the belief that an offender's actions are both intentional and morally repugnant. Consistent with this notion, a study of rejection letters sent to job applicants found that explanations for the rejections designed to minimize thoughts about what "could" and "should" have occurred led to responses that were more favorable than the additive effects of each explanation on its own (Gilliland et al., 2001).

The assignment of blame frames individuals' beliefs about the morality of revenge (Tripp and Bies, 2009). Most often, avengers attribute the offender's motives to selfishness (e.g., to personally profit or steal ideas) and malevolence (i.e., intentional harm; Bies and Tripp, 1996), both of which have immoral undertones that likely facilitate the decision to punish the offender. The so-called sinister attribution error refers to the tendency for people to overattribute malevolent intent on the part of an offender, resulting in intensified anger and heightened desires for revenge (Bies, Tripp, and Kramer, 1997). By attributing malicious intent, avengers cast an offender as an "evil" person who must be punished, thereby conferring moral justification for their revenge. Reflecting this notion, one avenger working in a veterinary clinic stated, "They don't deserve to make money because they are bad people. I felt very justified" (Jones, 2010, p. 132).

An offender's past behavior likely affects avengers' attributions and conclusions about the immorality of the offender and the offense. Because the intent underlying an offense is often ambiguous (Bies, Tripp, and Kramer, 1997), avengers likely draw upon information about the offender's past behavior to judge his or her moral character and, hence, the underlying intentions for the offense (Jones, 2010). Would-be avengers who believe that an offender has a history of mistreating others may view this as evidence that the latest offense was controllable and committed by an immoral person, which provides a moral justification for their revenge.

Blame Attributions and Avenger Well-Being

Theory and research suggest that victims of workplace injustice sometimes infer from it that they are not valued or respected members of a work group (Cropanzano et al., 2001). Extending this notion to attribution processes in a revenge episode, when avengers conclude that the offense occurred because the offender wanted to harm them specifically, their psychological well-being likely suffers from the damage caused to their sense of belonging and positive self-worth.

In some cases, avengers' attributions about the offense might induce sustained levels of stress and anxiety, which may eventually affect avengers' physical well-being given that both are risk factors for cardiovascular disease (Suls and Bunde, 2005). Attributions of blame are also known to influence the degree to which injustice is perceived (Folger and Cropanzano, 2001), and perceived injustice is linked to stress-related outcomes such as burnout (Moliner et al., 2008). Some avengers report obsessing over the initial offense (e.g., Bies and Tripp, 1996), and they may devote some of this cognitive attention to thinking about who is responsible for the offense and why it occurred. When avengers attribute the offender's motives to malicious intent as they often do, they may obsess over the possibility of suffering from willful mistreatment in the future, which is likely stressful and anxiety-provoking, especially when the offender is a manager who has control over the allocation of important resources such as their compensation. Theory and accounts from avengers (Jones, 2010) suggest that such conditions trigger revenge responses because they arouse instrumental-based mo-tives to restore justice (Tyler, 1987) and avengers engage in revenge to gain psychological control (Bies, Tripp, and Kramer, 1997) and defend their interests (Bies and Tripp, 1998).

Anger and Other Emotions

> *Revenge is a confession of pain.*
> —Latin Proverb

Avengers consistently report feeling intense anger and other negative emotions in response to the offense that precipitated their revenge (e.g., Jones, 2010; Tripp and Bies, 2009; Tripp, Bies, and Aquino, 2002, Study 1). Although anger can occur as an immediate reaction to an offense, especially one that is morally charged (Folger, Cropanzano, and Goldman, 2005), research on revenge sug-gests that anger tends to occur after an offense is perceived as highly unjust and some party is held accountable, as reflected in Figure 4.1 (Allred, 1999; Bies and Tripp, 1996). For instance, Barclay, Skarlicki, and Pugh (2005) found that perceived injustice was associated with emotions like anger and hostility when a party was blamed for it, which ultimately predicted the degree of retaliation.

Moral Considerations During Emotional Responses

When an injustice is deemed to be morally reprehensible, anger is intensified (Folger and Skarlicki, 1998). Tripp and Bies (2010) characterize avengers' anger as a *righteous* anger, visceral and mor-ally loaded, and driven by a sense of violation. Righteous anger is intense and often long-lasting, creating a moral foundation that feeds an obsessive desire to see that justice is served.

Emotional Responses and Avenger Well-Being

The negative emotions avengers experience in response to an offense represent a negative outcome relating to their subjective happiness and well-being. Negative effects on their physical well-being may also occur when their anger persists over time, as it often does (Jones, 2010), given that chronic anger is implicated as a risk factor for cardiovascular disease (Suls and Bunde, 2005). Anger in response to perceived injustice has been associated with increased heart rates (Vrijkotte, van Doornan, and de Geus, 2000), leading Greenberg (2010) to suggest that anger may mediate the relationship between perceived injustice and coronary heart disease. Research is needed to examine whether the anger that follows a revenge-triggering offense can ultimately result in detrimental effects on avengers' physiological well-being. Some avengers report experiencing other negative emotional reactions, such as shock and humiliation, to an offense (Bies and Tripp, 2002; Jones, 2010), and their potential effects on avenger well-being are also in need of research attention.

The Desire for Revenge and Other Revenge Cognitions

> *This is certain, that a man that studieth revenge keeps his own wounds green,*
> *which otherwise would heal, and do well.*
> —Francis Bacon

As reflected in Figure 4.1, the most proximal precursor of revenge behavior is the desire for revenge, which is often accompanied by other thoughts about getting even (Aquino, Tripp, and

Bies, 2001; Bradfield and Aquino, 1999; Jones, 2009; Jones and Carroll, 2007). Most avengers do not immediately "strike back" in the heat of the moment when an injustice is experienced in the workplace; instead, they often ruminate about the offense and think about getting even for some time, often several weeks or more, before they act (Bies and Tripp, 2001).

Jones and Carroll (2007) used avengers' descriptions of what they thought about before seeking revenge to develop measures of revenge cognitions, which comprised thoughts about different options for their revenge, consideration of the consequences, and mental planning of acts of revenge. The authors found that these revenge cognitions were associated with revenge attitudes, negative reciprocity endorsement, and retaliatory intentions. Thus, rather than revenge being a thoughtless "knee jerk" response to an offense, individuals often "coolly calculate the costs and benefits of their actions" before seeking revenge (Bies and Tripp, 2001, p. 206).

Moral Considerations in Revenge Cognitions

According to the cognitive model of justice-related aggression (Beugré, 2005), individuals' values and ethical standards affect whether they act upon their retributive cognitions. Individuals who consider engaging in revenge typically think about it as a righteous pursuit of justice because their actions would "right a wrong" (Bies and Tripp, 1998; Jones, 2010; McLean Parks, 1997; Tripp and Bies, 1997). Such thoughts reflect a retributive justice philosophy: an offender who commits an injustice deserves to be punished so that justice is served (Carlsmith, Darley, and Robinson, 2002). This "just deserts" principle not only motivates revenge, but helps avengers legitimize their intent to punish the offender on moral grounds (Tripp and Bies, 2009).

In contrast, other people are less likely to engage in revenge because doing so violates values that they hold deeply. Paradoxically, some of the values that make injustice more salient and important to people, such as the values captured by their justice orientation, appear to lessen the likelihood of ultimately seeking revenge despite wanting to do so (Liao and Rupp, 2005; Rupp, Byrne, and Wadlington, 2003). Holtz and Harold (in press), for example, found that employees who more strongly valued respectful and dignified treatment (Study 1) and who were higher on justice orientation (Study 2) were less likely to engage in deviant behavior in response to perceived injustice. Another study of service employees showed that those who had stronger identities as moral people were less likely to engage in customer-related sabotage in the face of perceived injustice (Skarlicki, van Jaarsveld, and Walker, 2008). However, it is unknown whether these findings reflect avengers' cognitions about the morality of revenge, but it is plausible that they do.

People can hold conflicting values about the importance of justice and the morality of revenge. Rupp and Bell (2010) drew upon Bandura's (1991) theorizing on moral self-regulation and proposed that victims of an offense sometimes weigh different moral standards until a dominant standard emerges to guide their decision about seeking revenge, doing so in an attempt to avoid any self-condemnation that would follow from engaging in regrettable behavior. If, for instance, a principle of "justice should be served but not if it harms innocent parties" emerges as dominant, the victim of an offense may forgo any acts of revenge that might harm other people beyond the offender. Reflecting such processes, Turillo et al. (2002) found that individuals were willing to punish an unjust offender, but this willingness was reduced if their punishment would also affect an innocent party.

Revenge Cognitions and Avenger Well-Being

Some avengers report that they had elaborate fantasies about enacting their revenge, which apparently lessened their desire for vengeance and helped them vent their anger (Tripp and Bies, 2009). But desires for revenge cannot always be placated by fantasies. It is likely quite functional in workplace settings for avengers to consider the consequences of their revenge and carefully plan one or more acts, because of power differences among the parties involved and the implications of their revenge for their continued employment (Jones and Carroll, 2007). In this way, revenge cognitions may promote avengers' psychological well-being by lessening any post-revenge anxiety or stress that would follow from making poor or unsafe choices about how to enact their revenge. Alternatively, avengers who do not spend much time plotting the perfect—and perhaps safest—revenge, who instead strike back in the heat of the moment or when opportunity arises, may suffer from the risks and negative consequences associated with workplace revenge that are reviewed later.

On the other hand, evidence suggests that ruminating about enacting revenge may create a barrier to thinking about forgiveness (Bradfield and Aquino, 1999), thereby increasing the likelihood that would-be avengers are exposed to the risks inherent in revenge. Thinking about revenge may also be accompanied by a continued obsession over the offense that occurred, and the potential impact of this on well-being was previously reviewed. This possibility is reflected in the quote from Bacon at the opening of this section: by thinking about revenge, one "keeps his own wounds green, which otherwise would heal, and do well."

Revenge Behavior

> *And if you wrong us, shall we not revenge!*
> —William Shakespeare

As reflected in Figure 4.1, when an offense is deemed to be a severe injustice for which some party is held accountable, the resulting anger leads to a desire for revenge and other thoughts about seeking vengeance. Individuals are particularly apt to enact their revenge when they believe it is morally justified and that they can perform acts of revenge that might repair or protect the psychological needs affected by the offense, or accomplish other goals in a relatively safe manner. Sometimes the desire for revenge manifests itself more subtly, such as through "freezing" out an offender from social interactions, withdrawing effort at work to get even with a manager, or sullying the offender's reputation; at other times, vengeance is more severe, such as when avengers steal from their employer, damage equipment, take steps to have an offender's employment terminated, pursue litigation, or even commit acts of violence (Jones, 2010; Tripp and Bies, 2009). Some avengers perform multiple acts of revenge over long periods of time (e.g., for six months, on average, in one study; Jones, 2010).

Moral Considerations When Choosing an Act of Revenge

Research shows that third-party observers view acts of revenge as justified when, as the saying goes, the "punishment fits the crime" (Tripp, Bies, and Aquino, 2002). Most avengers, too, probably aim to achieve equivalency between the severity of the offense and their revenge, which presumably shapes the types and frequency of revenge behavior that they feel is morally justified. However, these assertions need to be tested in future studies. Individual differences likely play a role in avengers' beliefs about the moral justification for a given revenge response, but this too needs to be tested in future research. One study, while not necessarily reflecting revenge motives, found that people at higher stages of moral development were less likely to steal money in response to perceived injustice (Greenberg, 2002). Research is needed to determine whether such people are also apt to refrain from less morally questionable acts of revenge, such as badmouthing an offender.

Thus far, I have described a process model of workplace revenge and highlighted that avengers can be affected by a variety of moral-based considerations that occur throughout a revenge episode, and I have explored potential consequences for avenger well-being that should be tested in future studies. Moving beyond the moral considerations among those who seek revenge, I now consider the ethics of workplace revenge more broadly: Is it right or wrong to seek revenge?

THE ETHICS OF WORKPLACE REVENGE AND CONSEQUENCES FOR STAKEHOLDER WELL-BEING

> *Don't get mad, get even.*
> —Robert F. Kennedy

> *To err is human, to forgive divine.*
> —Alexander Pope

From a moral standpoint, how *should* employees respond to injustice? Should injustice be avenged, as suggested by the quote from Kennedy, or should it be forgiven as suggested by the quote from Pope? To answer this question, I begin by posing another: Is it better to judge the morality of revenge using a moral precept (i.e., a deontological approach) or by considering the consequences for those who are affected (i.e., a teleological approach)?

Grounded in philosophies of ethics, deontological perspectives suggest that acts of revenge can be judged, a priori, as either moral or immoral. However, reliance on a deontological approach can be dissatisfying because how does one decide which principle offers the best barometer for judging the morality of revenge? A retributive justice principle demands vengeance, while a "do no harm" rule calls for the opposite. Moreover, many ethical principles seem incapable of addressing the complexities inherent in most revenge episodes in the workplace. For instance, at first glance, adherence to a "do no harm" rule suggests that revenge should not occur; however, in some cases, by choosing not to seek revenge some stakeholders will suffer harm, such as when the absence of revenge leaves little else to deter an abusive manager from continuing his or her dubious ways.

In contrast to deontological approaches, teleological perspectives on ethics suggest that the morality of revenge depends on its consequences. For instance, utilitarianism approaches generally suggest that the morally superior action is the one that produces the "greatest good for the greatest number" (or, as it may be in the case of revenge, the least harm for the greatest number). However, teleological perspectives also have their drawbacks. For instance, if the goal is to provide the most benefit and least harm to stakeholders, it raises the question of whether the interests of an offender who committed a serious injustice should be given the same moral weight as the interests of the victim of the offense, or of an innocent third-party observer. Moreover, the consequences of revenge can be difficult to predict, or even observe after the fact.

Despite the shortcomings of teleological approaches, the complexity of the social context surrounding revenge episodes in the workplace perhaps likely requires "moral judges" to reject a reliance on any blanket moral precepts and to adopt an episode-specific focus on the likely consequences of revenge for stakeholder well-being. As other scholars have recognized (Skarlicki and Folger, 2004), an act of revenge often defies easy categorization as right or wrong because, as I aim to show, it can have both negative and positive consequences for the well-being of all major stakeholders affected by revenge in the workplace.

CONSEQUENCES OF REVENGE BEHAVIOR FOR OFFENDER WELL-BEING

Presumably, revenge behavior has few positive consequences for the target, other than the possibility that it may serve as a "wake-up call" that ultimately leads to career-enhancing behavior change. The consequences of revenge for offender well-being are more negative when the revenge is severe (i.e., violating core psychological needs) and frequent in its occurrence, and offenders are likely subject to the same negative effects that their offenses can have on avenger well-being. Some people also report feeling upset about being the target of revenge, and even bewildered when they were unaware they had committed an offense (Tripp and Bies, 2009). Moreover, the target of revenge may respond in-kind, potentially embroiling the two parties in an escalating cycle of tit for tat (Andersson and Pearson, 1999) in which the offender can suffer from the same negative effects on well-being that I now describe for avengers.

Consequences of Revenge Behavior for Avenger Well-Being

Positive Effects of Revenge on Avenger Well-Being

In some cases, revenge can have positive effects on avengers' psychological well-being. Revenge can restore justice and moral balance (Tripp and Bies, 2009), which presumably brings a degree of psychological peace to the victims of the offense. Avengers sometimes feel vindicated and empowered after enacting their revenge (ibid.) and can experience satisfaction and joy from seeing that offenders received the punishment they deserve (Carlsmith, Darley, and Robinson, 2002). Avengers also benefit when their revenge repairs the psychological needs that were damaged by an offense (Jones, 2010), such as when the revenge bolsters their self-esteem and reaffirms their social status (Aquino and Douglas, 2003), or when it restores their sense of power and control (Bies and Tripp, 1996; Vidmar, 2000).

Revenge can also fulfill an important social control function by deterring future mistreatment from a "repeat offender," thereby protecting avengers' economic, psychological, and social interests at work (Carlsmith, Darley, and Robinson, 2002; Vidmar, 2000). Some workplace avengers claim their revenge was simultaneously motivated by an intent to harm and to deter the offender from committing additional abuse, so they performed acts of revenge to signal that such behavior will not be tolerated (Jones, 2010). Other avengers claim that they sought to deter future mistreatment by "tattling on" and even lying about the offender in an effort to convince managers to terminate the offender's employment (Jones, 2010). Avengers often characterize offenders as being guilty of committing multiple offenses prior to the offense that triggered their revenge (Jones, 2010), and employees who are the victims of ongoing bullying (Hoel, Rayner, and Cooper, 1999) and repeated interpersonal incivility (Lim and Cortina, 2005) are more likely to suffer from negative physical and psychological health outcomes, such as depression. As such, the deterrence function of revenge has important positive effects on avenger well-being.

Negative Effects of Revenge on Avenger Well-Being

Of course, revenge comes with considerable risk to those who engage in it. The moral self-regulation processes described by Rupp and Bell (2010) suggest that when avengers contemplate whether to seek revenge, if the "wrong" values or principles come to dominate their decision, their psychological well-being may suffer from experiencing regret and guilt over their actions. Consistent with this possibility, some avengers report regretting their revenge behavior because they felt unprofessional for letting their emotions "get the best of them," and that they experienced guilt because their revenge caused disproportionate harm (Tripp and Bies, 1997).

By engaging in revenge, avengers also forgo the potential benefits of forgiveness. Forgiveness is the "moral antithesis of revenge" (Tripp and Bies, 2009, p. 172), and some people believe it is a dominant moral principle over retributive justice. Forgiveness—the foreswearing of anger, resentment, and the desire to harm an offender—represents an alternative to revenge for coping with an offense (Aquino, Tripp, and Bies, 2006), and it reduces anger and the resulting negative effects on health and physical well-being (Worthington and Scherer, 2004).

Other negative effects on well-being are suggested by avengers who report that they suffered from stress and anxiety caused by the unpredictable and risky nature of revenge (Tripp and Bies, 1997). Avengers may fret over the possibility that their actions might sully their reputation or damage their relationships with coworkers who disapprove of their vengeance, or lead to a formal reprimand by their employer. The psychological burden of carrying such risks could potentially last for a considerable amount of time after engaging in revenge. Anxiety or feelings of regret may be especially strong when avengers have little to show in return for their burden of risk, such as when their actions fail to achieve their intended aims and their motives for revenge remain unfulfilled. In such cases, avengers may experience guilt due to the harm they caused to someone with little to show for it. Consistent with these speculations, some avengers claim to regret their revenge because it was ineffectual in addressing the precipitating problem (Tripp and Bies, 1997).

Among the most potentially negative consequences of revenge is the risk of invoking a counter-retaliatory response from the target of revenge. Avengers may experience fear and stress over the possibility that the offender will strike back for the revenge. If they persist over time, this fear and stress may lead to negative physiological outcomes such as coronary heart disease, heightened heart rates, and the release of stress hormones. Moreover, given the intense emotions that accompany experienced injustice—which the offender, now the target of revenge, may experience in much the same fashion as the avenger initially did—the conflict can quickly spiral into a long-lasting feud that is difficult to resolve (Tripp and Bies, 2010). Over time, the psychological costs of holding a grudge will accrue for both parties (Tripp and Bies, 2009). Even if the target of revenge responds by subsequently avoiding the avenging coworker, rather than through counter-retaliation, cooperation and information sharing among interdependent coworkers can suffer, thereby hampering their job performance. For these reasons, it may behoove avengers to heed the advice of Publilius Syrus: "It is folly to punish your neighbor by fire when you live next door."

Consequences of Revenge Behavior for Third-Party Well-Being

Revenge can sometimes have positive effects on the well-being of coworkers who were not the direct targets of the initial offense or the intended beneficiaries of the revenge response, such as when the revenge ultimately deters an offender from mistreating others in the future, or when it results in terminating the employment of a "toxic" manager or coworker who had been sapping the morale from an otherwise functional work group. In addition to "accidentally" contributing to third-party well-being through revenge, some avengers claim that their revenge was also motivated by prosocial concerns, such as to protect the interests of their coworkers who are likewise harmed by the offender's actions (Bies and Tripp, 1996; Jones, 2010; Tripp and Bies, 1997). Even employees who are not directly harmed by an offender sometimes seek to avenge the harm the offender has wrought upon their coworkers (Jones, 2010; O'Reilly and Aquino, 2011). Such prosocial motives also extend to customers: avengers have described giving unauthorized discounts to customers who were systematically overcharged by a less scrupulous manager, and taking other actions to prevent the exploitation of clients (Jones, 2010). If avengers' post hoc accounts of their motives for revenge—which are subject to impression management motives and desires to justify their revenge—are accepted at face value, the co-occurrence of prosocial motives with intentions to harm an offender is by no means a rare occurrence (Jones, 2010).

Revenge can also have negative effects on the well-being of third-party observers of a revenge episode. For instance, when revenge occurs in the context of a long-lasting cycle of tit-for-tat exchanges (Andersson and Pearson, 1999), third-party observers can find the tension awkward and uncomfortable (Tripp and Bies, 2009). Even worse, third-parties are sometimes harmed accidentally or through willful indifference by avengers' actions, such as when avengers intentionally quit without advance notice at an especially busy time, thereby burdening their former coworkers with unexpectedly larger workloads (Jones, 2010). It is also possible that misplaced blame attributions result in the avenger striking back against an innocent third-party.

Moreover, a conflict between two parties who work on the same team or within the same unit may consume the time and energy of uninvolved coworkers who are nonetheless drawn into conversations about or with the conflicting coworkers, casting a cloud of negative energy over the group. Work environments in which aggressive, deviant, or counterproductive behaviors occur frequently are not particularly pleasant for anyone, and are associated with lower morale and higher turnover (Robinson and Greenberg, 1999). Research also suggests that the act of witnessing unethical behavior can affect third parties negatively because they can experience emotional distress when they empathize with the victim (in the case of a revenge episode, the offender), and fear from the realization that they too may be targeted in the future (Giacalone and Promislo, 2010).

IMPLICATIONS FOR ORGANIZATIONAL PRACTICE

Given the negative and positive consequences of revenge for stakeholder well-being, it is not necessarily so that revenge will always, or even usually, produce more harm than good. Nonetheless, acts of revenge have the potential to cause considerable harm so it behooves organizations and their managers to minimize this harm by reducing the occurrence of revenge-triggering offenses and by providing alternatives for restoring justice when offenses occur.

Reducing the Occurrence of Offenses that Motivate Revenge

Employees who seek revenge most often do so in response to offenses that are perpetrated by the organization or its managers (e.g., Jones, 2010). As such, managers should be trained in the principles of organizational justice, which have been shown to increase perceptions of fairness among employees (Skarlicki and Latham, 2005). Managers should avoid committing offenses that are known to provoke revenge, such as when an employee is treated disrespectfully in front of coworkers, or when promises are broken (Tripp and Bies, 2009). Managers also need to manage employees' attributions of blame when delivering potentially bad news, as has been described in other research on workplace revenge (Jones, 2010; Tripp and Bies, 2009).

Revenge episodes in the workplace also occur among coworkers and team members, whose decisions to seek revenge are often less constrained by power differences that exist, for example, when an employee "gets even" with a manager (Tripp and Bies, 2009). Thus, organizational leaders should seek to create and reinforce a culture of respectful treatment among all employees because offenses that are perceived as indicative of disrespect are especially strong triggers of revenge (e.g., Jones, 2009). Organizations might also benefit from using employee socialization programs to shape and reinforce a culture that highly values dignified and respectful treatment of all organizational members (Holtz and Harold, in press).

Promoting Alternatives to Revenge for Restoring Justice

Research shows that employees are more likely to seek revenge when their organization lacks formal mechanisms through which justice can be served (Aquino, Tripp, and Bies, 2006). As Tripp and Bies (2009) describe, employees expect their workplace to be fair and just, so they want to see that those who commit offenses are punished. The presence of organizational mechanisms through which justice can be restored lessens avengers' desire to pursue vigilante justice outside of the official channels. Through such mechanisms, avengers' needs may be satisfactorily met while avoiding the potential harm cause by revenge for their own and other stakeholders' well-being.

Official grievance channels (e.g., an ombudsperson) should be created and communicated, as should systems and policies that specify how offenders who act unjustly will be judged and, if deemed culpable, punished. Organizations should create and communicate whistle-blower policies that protect individuals who "speak out." When managers are cast in the role of the offender, they need to possess effective communication skills to adequately apologize for the offense while demonstrating a degree of self-punishment and attempting to "fix what's broken" (see Jones, 2010). Managers should work to foster a sense of mutual respect and trust with their employees to minimize the perceived risks associated with coming to a manager with a serious concern about some offense. Complaints about offenses need to be investigated promptly to avoid creating a false belief among the victims of an injustice that they need to take matters into their own hands in order to see that justice is served (Tripp and Bies, 2009).

NOTES

I thank the editors and Christine O'Neill for feedback on earlier versions of this chapter.

1. In addition to avengers who were harmed by an offense, this model applies to third-party avengers who were not directly harmed but nonetheless seek to avenge those who were (Jones, 2010; O'Reilly and Aquino, 2011). To facilitate a parsimonious description of this model, I focus on avengers who were directly harmed by the offense.

REFERENCES

Allred, K.G. 1999. Anger driven retaliation: Toward an understanding of impassioned conflict in organizations. In *Research on Negotiations in Organizations*, vol. 7, ed. R.J. Bies, R.J. Lewicki, and B.H. Sheppard, 27–51. Greenwich, CT: JAI Press.

Andersson, L.M., and Pearson, C.M. 1999. Tit for tat? The spiraling effect of incivility in the workplace. *Academy of Management Review,* 24, 3, 452–471.

Aquino, K., and Douglas, S. 2003. Identity threat and antisocial behavior in organizations: The moderating effects of individual differences, aggressive modeling, and hierarchical status. *Organizational Behavior and Human Decision Processes,* 90, 195–208.

Aquino, K.; Tripp, T.M.; and Bies, R.J. 2001. How employees respond to personal offense: The effects of blame, attribution, victim status, and offender status on revenge and reconciliation in the workplace. *Journal of Applied Psychology,* 86, 52–59.

———. 2006. Getting even or moving on? Power, procedural justice, and types of offense as predictors of revenge, forgiveness, reconciliation, and avoidance in organizations. *Journal of Applied Psychology,* 91, 653–668.

Bandura, A. 1991. Social cognitive theory of moral thought and action. In *Handbook of Moral Behavior and Development: Theory, Research and Applications,* vol. 1, ed. W.M. Kurtines and J.L. Gewirtz, 71–129. Hillsdale, NJ: Erlbaum.

Barclay, L.J.; Skarlicki, D.P.; and Pugh, S.D. 2005. Exploring the role of emotions in injustice perceptions and retaliation. *Journal of Applied Psychology,* 90, 629–643.

Berry, J.W.; Worthington, E.L.; O'Connor, L.E.; Parrott, L. III; and Wade, N.G. 2005. Forgiveness, vengeful rumination, and affective traits. *Journal of Personality,* 73, 183–225.

Beugré, C.D. 2005. Reacting aggressively to injustice at work: A cognitive stage model. *Journal of Business and Psychology,* 20, 291–301.

Bies, R.J., and Tripp, T. 1996. Beyond distrust: "Getting even" and the need for revenge. In *Trust in Organizations,* ed. R.M. Kramer and T. Tyler, 246–260. Thousand Oaks, CA: Sage.

———. 1998. Revenge in organizations: The good, the bad, and the ugly. In *Dysfunctional Behavior in Organizations,* vol. 1: *Violent Behaviors in Organizations,* ed. R.W. Griffin, A. O'Leary-Kelly, and J. Collins, 49–68. Greenwich, CT: JAI Press.

———. 2001. A passion for justice: The rationality and morality of revenge. In *Justice in the Workplace: From Theory to Practice*, vol. 2, ed. R. Cropanzano, 197–208. Mahwah, NJ: Erlbaum.

———. 2002. Hot flashes, open wounds: Injustice and the tyranny of its emotions. In *Emerging Perspectives on Managing Organizational Justice,* ed. S. Gilliland, D. Steiner, and D. Skarlicki, 203–223. Greenwich, CT: JAI Press.

Bies, R.J.; Tripp, T.M.; and Kramer, R.M. 1997. At the breaking point: Cognitive and social dynamics of revenge in organizations. In *Antisocial Behavior in Organizations*, ed. R.A. Giacalone and J. Greenberg, 18–36. Thousand Oaks, CA: Sage.

Bradfield, M., and Aquino, K. 1999. The effects of blame attributions and offender likeableness on forgiveness and revenge in the workplace. *Journal of Management,* 25, 607–631.

Carlsmith, K.M.; Darley, J.M.; and Robinson, P.H. 2002. Why do we punish? Deterrence and just deserts as motives for punishment. *Journal of Personality and Social Psychology,* 83, 284–299.

Cropanzano, R.; Byrne, Z.S.; Bobocel, D.R.; and Rupp, D.E. 2001. Moral virtues, fairness heuristics, social entities, and other denizens of organizational justice. *Journal of Vocational Behavior,* 58, 164–201.

Elovainio, M.; Kivimäki, M.; Vahtera, J.; Keltikangas-Jjärvinen, L.; and Virtanen, M. 2003. Sleeping problems and health behavior as mediators between organizational justice and health. *Health Psychology,* 22, 287–293.

Folger, R., and Cropanzano, R. 2001. Fairness theory: Justice as accountability. In *Advances in Organizational Behavior,* ed. J. Greenberg and R. Cropanzano, 1–55. Palo Alto, CA: Stanford University Press.

Folger, R., Cropanzano, R., and Goldman, B. 2005. What is the relationship between justice and morality? In *Handbook of Organizational Justice*, ed. J. Greenberg and J.A. Colquitt, 215–245. Mahwah, NJ: Erlbaum.

Folger, R., and Skarlicki, D.P. 1998. A popcorn metaphor for employee aggression. In *Dysfunctional Behavior in Organizations*, vol. 1: *Violent and Deviant Behavior*, ed. R.W. Griffin, A. O'Leary-Kelly, and J.M. Collins, 43–81. Greenwich, CT: JAI Press.

Giacalone, R.A., and Promislo, M.D. 2010. Unethical and unwell: Decrements in well-being and unethical activity at work. *Journal of Business Ethics,* 91, 275–397.

Gilliland, S.W.; Groth, M.; Baker, R.C., Dew, A.F.; Polly, L.M.; and Langdon, J.C. 2001. Improving applicants' reactions to rejection letters: An application of fairness theory. *Personnel Psychology,* 54, 669–703.

Greenberg, J. 2002. Who stole the money and when? Individual and situational determinants of employee theft. *Organizational Behavior and Human Decision Processes,* 89, 985–1003.

———. 2006. Losing sleep over organizational injustice: Attenuating insomniac reactions to underpayment inequity with supervisory training in interactional justice. *Journal of Applied Psychology,* 91, 58–69.

———. 2010. Organizational justice as an occupational health risk. *Academy of Management Annals,* 4, 205–243.

Hoel, H.; Rayner, C.; and Cooper, C.L. 1999. Workplace bullying. In *International Review of Industrial and Organizational Psychology,* vol. 14, ed. C.L. Cooper and I.T. Robertson, 195–230. New York: Wiley.

Holtz, B.C., and Harold, C.M. In press. Interpersonal justice and deviance: The moderating effects of interpersonal justice values and justice orientation. *Journal of Management.* http://jom.sagepub.com/content/early/2010/12/18/0149206310390049.full.pdf+html.

Jones, D.A. 2004. Counterproductive work behavior toward supervisors and organizations: Injustice, revenge, and context. In *Paper Proceedings of the Sixty-Fourth Annual Meeting of the Academy of Management,* ed. D.H. Nagao, (CD), ISSN 1543–8643.

———. 2009. Getting even with one's supervisor and one's organization: Relationships among types of injustice, desires for revenge, and counterproductive work behaviors. *Journal of Organizational Behavior,* 30, 525–542.

———. 2010. Getting even for interpersonal mistreatment in the workplace: Triggers of revenge motives and behavior. In *Insidious Workplace Behavior*, ed. J. Greenberg, 101–148. New York: Routledge.

Jones, D.A., and Carroll, S.A. 2007. Revenge is a dish best served cold: Avengers' accounts of calculated revenge cognitions and assessment of a proposed measure. Paper presented at the Twentieth Annual Meeting of the International Association of Conflict Management, Budapest, Hungary. July 1–4, 2007.

Kivimäki, M.; Elovainio, M.; Vahetera, J.; Virtanen, M.; and Stansfield, S.A. 2003. Association between organizational inequity and incidence of psychiatric disorders in female employees. *Psychological Medicine*, 33, 319–326.

Kivimäki, M.; Ferrie, J.E.; Brunner, E.; Head, J.; Shipley, M.J.; Vahtera, J.; and Marmot, M.G. 2005. Justice at work and reduced risk of coronary heart disease among employees. *Archives of Internal Medicine*, 165, 2245–2251.

Liao, H., and Rupp, D.E. 2005. The impact of justice climate and justice orientation on work outcomes: A cross-level multifoci framework. *Journal of Applied Psychology*, 90, 242–256.

Lim, S., and Cortina, L.M. 2005. Interpersonal mistreatment in the workplace: The interface and impact of general incivility and sexual harassment. *Journal of Applied Psychology*, 90, 483–496.

McLean Parks, J.M. 1997. The fourth arm of justice: The art and science of revenge. In *Research on Negotiation in Organizations*, vol. 6, ed. R.J. Lewicki, R.J. Bies, and B.H. Sheppard, 113–144. Greenwich, CT: JAI Press.

Moliner, C.; Martínez-Tur, V.; Ramos, J.; Peiró, J.; Cropanzano, R. 2008. Organizational justice and extrarole customer service: The mediating role of well-being at work. *European Journal of Work and Organizational Psychology*, 17, 327–348.

O'Reilly, J., and Aquino, K. 2011. A model of third parties' morally motivated responses to mistreatment in organizations. *Academy of Management Review*, 36, 526–543.

Robinson, S.L., and Greenberg, J. 1999. Employees behaving badly: Dimensions, determinants and dilemmas in the study of workplace deviance. In *Trends in Organizational Behavior*, vol. 5, ed. C.L. Cooper and D.M. Rousseau, 1–23. New York: Wiley.

Rupp, D.E., and Bell, C.M. 2010. Extending the deontic model of justice: Moral self-regulation in third-party responses to injustice. *Business Ethics Quarterly*, 20, 89–106.

Rupp, D.E.; Byrne, Z.S.; and Wadlington, P. 2003. Justice orientation and its measurement: Extending the deontological model. Paper presented at the Eighteenth Annual Conference of the Society for Industrial and Organizational Psychology, Orlando, FL. April 11–13, 2003.

Skarlicki, D.P., and Folger, R. 2004. Deepening our understanding of organizational retaliatory behavior. In *The Dark Side of Organizational Behavior*, ed. R. Griffin and A. O'Leary-Kelly, 373–403. San Francisco, CA: Jossey-Bass.

Skarlicki, D.P., and Latham, G.P. 2005. How can training be used to foster organizational justice? In *Handbook of Organizational Justice*, ed. J. Greenberg and J.A. Colquitt, 499–522. Mahwah, NJ: Erlbaum.

Skarlicki, D.P.; van Jaarsveld, D.D.; and Walker, D.D. 2008. Getting even for customer mistreatment: The role of moral identity in the relationship between customer interpersonal injustice and employee sabotage. *Journal of Applied Psychology*, 93, 1335–1347.

Stuckless, N., and Goranson, R. 1992. The Vengeance Scale: Development of a measure of attitudes toward revenge. *Journal of Social Behavior and Personality*, 7, 25–42.

Suls, J., and Bunde, J. 2005. Anger, anxiety and depression as risk factors for cardiovascular disease: The problems and implications for overlapping affective dispositions. *Psychological Bulletin*, 131, 260–300.

Tepper, B.J. 2001. Health consequences of organizational injustice: Tests of main and interactive effects. *Organizational Behavior and Human Decision Processes*, 86, 197–215.

Tripp, T.M., and Bies, R.J. 1997. What's good about revenge? The avenger's perspective. In *Research on Negotiation in Organizations*, vol. 6, ed. R.J. Lewicki, R.J. Bies, and B.H. Sheppard, 145–160. Greenwich, CT: JAI Press.

———. 2009. *Getting Even: The Truth About Workplace Revenge—And How to Stop It*. San Francisco, CA: Jossey-Bass.

———. 2010. "Righteous" anger and revenge in the workplace: The fantasies, the feuds, the forgiveness. In *International Handbook of Anger: Biological, Psychological, and Social Processes*, ed. M. Potegal, G. Stemmler, and C. Spielberger, 413–431. Amsterdam: Springer.

Tripp, T.M.; Bies, R.J.; and Aquino, K. 2002. Poetic justice or petty jealousy? The aesthetics of revenge. *Organizational Behavior and Human Decision Processes*, 89, 966–984.

Turillo, C.J.; Folger, R.; Lavelle, J.J.; Umphress, E.E.; and Gee, J.O. 2002. Is virtue its own reward? Self-sacrificial decisions for the sake of fairness. *Organizational Behavior and Human Decisions Processes,* 89, 839–865.

Tyler, T.R. 1987. Conditions leading to value-expressive effects in judgments of procedural justice: A test of four models. *Journal of Personality and Social Psychology,* 52, 333–344.

Vidmar, N. 2000. Retribution and revenge. In *Handbook of Justice Research in Law*, ed. J. Sanders and V.L. Hamilton, 31–63. New York: Kluwer Academic.

Vrijkotte, T.G.; van Doornan, L.J.; and de Geus, E.J. 2000. Effects of work stress on ambulatory blood pressure, heart rate, and heart rate variability. *Hypertension,* 35, 880–886.

Worthington, E., and Scherer, M. 2004. Forgiveness is an emotion-focused coping strategy that can reduce health risks and promote health resilience: Theory, review, and hypotheses. *Psychology and Health,* 19, 385–405.

5

BULLYING AND WELL-BEING

Denise Salin

Workplace bullying is about repeated and prolonged exposure to various forms of predominantly psychological mistreatment (Einarsen, et al., 2011; Hauge, Skogstad, and Einarsen, 2010). It can take many different forms, from direct actions such as verbal abuse, accusations, and public humiliation, to acts of a more subtle and disguised nature in the form of gossiping, spreading of rumors, and social exclusion. Often it is a gradually evolving process, where the target over time ends up in an inferior position, not having the possibilities or resources to retaliate in kind (cf. Einarsen et al., 2011).

Workplace bullying is a form of unethical behavior that violates generally accepted norms about appropriate workplace behavior. Unethical behavior has been defined as behavior that brings harm to others and that is either illegal or morally unacceptable to the larger community (Jones, 1991). Bullying would generally be seen as unfair and inhumane and it creates destructive impacts for those concerned. A number of European countries and some regions in Australia and Canada have even passed explicit laws against bullying, signaling a strong condemnation of such behaviors. The aim of this chapter is to provide an overview of how this form of unethical behavior affects well-being for targets, bystanders, and others indirectly involved. However, before proceeding to the effects of bullying on well-being, some general information about bullying is presented.

Large surveys conducted in the United States indicate that approximately 10 percent of the working population report being bullied in their current jobs. In an online survey, Lutgen-Sandvik, Tracy, and Alberts (2007) found that 9.4 percent self-labeled as bullied. In large national surveys undertaken by the Workplace Bullying Institute and Zogby International in 2007 and 2010, 12.6 percent and 8.8 percent, respectively, of those responding reported that they had been subjected to any or all of the following types of repeated mistreatment: sabotage by others that prevented work from getting done, verbal abuse, threatening conduct, intimidation, or humiliation (Namie, 2007, 2010). When counting also those who had experienced bullying at a previous point in time, the number rose to approximately one-third of the respondents, and when including also those who had witnessed bullying, the results showed that half had some experience with bullying.

Those subjected to bullying indicated superiors as bullies in approximately 80 percent of the cases (Namie, 2007), a trend found also in studies from the United Kingdom (e.g., Hoel, Cooper, and Faragher, 2001; Rayner, 1997). In the Anglo-American context, the focus thus often seems to be on bullying as abusive supervision. In contrast, in the Scandinavian countries (i.e., Norway, Sweden, and Denmark), where much of the research on bullying has originated, targets seem to indicate superiors and coworkers as bullies in almost equal proportions, indicating a higher prevalence of peer-to-peer bullying (see Zapf et al., 2011).

Many different explanations for the occurrence of bullying have been put forward. Some of these have focused on the characteristics of victims and perpetrators. There is some support for the idea that employees who are higher in neuroticism, those who are seen as "outsiders" in a particular work context and therefore in a particularly salient position, those who have low self-esteem and therefore are particularly vulnerable, and those who are aggressive themselves or very strict (and therefore seen as provocative), are somewhat more at risk for being targets of bullying (for a summary, see Zapf and Einarsen, 2011). Then again, Norwegian research has demonstrated that most bullying victims do not differ from nonvictims with respect to personality, indicating that although personality should not be overlooked, other factors seem to be of even higher importance (Glasø, Nielsen and Einarsen, 2009; Glasø et al., 2007). While we generally know fairly little about the perpetrators—partly due to methodological difficulties in contacting and surveying perpetrators—some hypotheses have been put forward. For example, it has been argued that bullies may have high, but unstable, self-esteem, or low emotional control and low social competencies (Zapf and Einarsen, 2011).

Other studies have sought to test the "work environment hypothesis" (Hauge, Skogstad, and Einarsen, 2007), which highlights different aspects of the job context and organization as risk factors for bullying. Overall, there has been considerable support for this perspective (see Salin, 2003; Salin and Hoel, 2011, for summaries). Role conflict, role ambiguity, lack of clear goals, and a culture that "permits" bullying have been presented as particular risk factors (Hauge, Skogstad, and Einarsen, 2007; Salin and Hoel, 2011). Also leadership styles have been examined, showing that, on the one hand, highly autocratic leadership and noncontingent punishment (i.e., unpredictable leadership) are risk factors; on the other hand, laissez-faire leadership, where leaders abdicate responsibility, also constitutes a risk (Hoel et al., 2010; Salin and Hoel, 2011).

WORKPLACE BULLYING AND EFFECTS ON WELL-BEING

As shown above, many different factors may contribute to bullying, and data on the relative importance of different risk factors are largely missing. However, there seems to be strong agreement among researchers that workplace bullying has severe detrimental effects. In attempts to persuade managers and organizational representatives to take action, the financial costs of bullying are often highlighted. For example, in a report commissioned by the International Labor Organization (ILO), the researchers undertaking the study estimated that absence and replacement costs because of bullying amount to £2 billion annually in Great Britain alone (Hoel, Sparks, and Cooper, 2001). Bullying can also lead to costs, or loss of income, in more indirect ways—for example, through decreases in productivity, motivation, and creativity, and bad publicity. Internal investigations or litigation are other possible costs (Hoel et al., 2011). These arguments are often put forward to encourage organizations to act in a more ethical and socially responsible way with respect to bullying.

However, a human-centered perspective of ethical and social responsibility looks beyond financial outcomes and considers the impact that unethical behavior has on the well-being of stakeholders more broadly (e.g., Giacalone and Promislo, 2010; Giacalone and Thompson, 2006). This is also the approach taken in this chapter. In this chapter, I use the definition suggested by Giacalone and Promislo (2010, p. 276), that well-being is "the extent to which an individual is satisfied with his/her life, experiences a preponderance of positive affect, and possesses a healthy body and mind."

A vast amount of research has been undertaken to study the effects of bullying, and the results are highly consistent—bullying has severe effects on well-being (e.g., Hogh, Mikkelsen, and Hansen, 2011). In this chapter, I start by presenting empirical findings on bullying and psychological and physical health and by discussing why bullying results in decreased health. This is followed by an overview of how bullying affects self-esteem, job satisfaction, and employability. Subsequently, I discuss how individual factors moderate the relationship between bullying and well-being, and what we know about the effects of bullying for those other than the ones directly targeted (e.g., bystanders, perpetrators, and family members). I end the chapter by discussing how framing bullying as a form of unethical behavior can help us understand the relationship between bullying and well-being even better, and how emphasizing ethical leadership and an ethical climate may reduce the prevalence of bullying.

Effects on Psychological and Physical Health

The relationship between bullying and physical and mental health has been extensively researched. Studies have shown that bullying can lead to a vast range of negative effects on the psychological and physical health of those subjected to this systematic mistreatment. Typical symptoms associated with bullying are anxiety (Bilgel, Aytac, and Bayram, 2006; Hauge, Skogstad, and Einarsen, 2010; Mikkelsen and Einarsen, 2001), disturbed sleep (Niedhammer et al., 2009; Notelaers et al., 2006), and different psychosomatic symptoms (Hallberg and Strandmark, 2006; Mikkelsen and Einarsen, 2001).

Hallberg and Strandmark (2006) interviewed victims of bullying and found that victims often started experiencing symptoms early on, only months after the bullying had commenced. In the beginning the symptoms were present only at work, but over time they became more or less chronic. Victims typically reported emotional reactions, inability to concentrate, memory problems, mood swings, anxiety, sleep problems, fear, and despair. Different psychosomatic symptoms were common among the victims. These symptoms included headaches, respiratory or cardiac complaints, hypertension, and hypersensitivity to sounds. Hallberg and Strandmark (2006) also reported that symptoms of chronic diseases, such as diabetes, asthma, and hypertension, worsened as a result of bullying.

Depressive symptoms have also been reported in a large number of studies on bullying (Bilgel, Aytac, and Bayram, 2006; Hallberg and Strandmark, 2006; Hauge, Skogstad, and Einarsen, 2010; Kivimäki et al., 2003; Leymann and Gustafsson, 1996; Mikkelsen and Einarsen, 2001; Moreno-Jiménez et al., 2007). Kivimäki et al. (2003) showed that the longer the bullying, the more severe the depressive symptoms were. Bullying has further been linked to burnout (Einarsen, Matthiesen, and Skogstad, 1998; Mathisen, Einarsen, and Mykletun, 2008) and even suicide (Leymann, 1987; Pompili et al., 2008).

Overall, studies indicate that the effects of bullying on health are highly significant. For instance, in a recent Norwegian study, exposure to bullying behaviors alone accounted for 27 percent of the variance in psychological health complaints and 10 percent of the variance in psychosomatic complaints (Vie, Glasø, and Einarsen, 2011). Similarly, in a Danish study, exposure to bullying behavior explained 27 percent of the variance in psychological health complaints (Mikkelsen and Einarsen, 2002). This shows that the effects of bullying are by no means marginal, and that bullying, in fact, is a very significant work-related predictor of different health complaints.

While most studies on workplace bullying and health outcomes have been cross-sectional, thus not strictly allowing for conclusions about causality, an exception is a longitudinal study by Kivimäki et al. (2003) conducted among Finnish hospital employees. More than 5,000 employees took part in the survey and responded to the questions at two different times. Bullying at time 1 predicted both subsequent depression and cardiovascular disease. Moreover, depression also predicted subsequent bullying, indicating a vicious circle where mental problems are a result of bullying, but also make employees more susceptible to becoming victims of bullying. Similar results have also been reported in two recent Norwegian studies, which both found that psychological distress was a predictor as well as a consequence of bullying (Finne, Knardahl, and Lau, 2011; Nielsen et al., 2012).

Studies on workplace bullying and health typically ask respondents themselves to judge their own health. However, when measuring effects on health by looking at sick leave, a similar pattern emerges, with victims reporting higher levels of sickness absence than nonvictims (Hoel and Cooper, 2000; Kivimäki, Elovainio, and Vahtera, 2000; Voss, Floderus, and Diderichsen, 2004). These studies thus offer additional evidence for the relationship between bullying and decreases in physical and mental health and also remind us that individual suffering and financial costs in this case go hand in hand.

Explanatory Models

Unethical behavior may result in decreased physical and mental health for those concerned through different routes. Giacalone and Promislo (2010) discuss three different mechanisms: *stress, trauma,* and *changes in health behavior,* which are discussed below in relation to bullying.

A stress theoretical perspective may be useful in trying to understand and explain the relationship between bullying and decreases in well-being. *Stress* arises when an individual perceives that he or she cannot effectively cope with the demands being made on him or her (Lazarus and Folkman, 1984). In the literature, bullying has been described as a severe social stressor (e.g., Hauge, Skogstad, and Einarsen, 2010). In fact, Hauge, Skogstad, and Einarsen (2010) concluded that workplace bullying is indeed a potent social stressor with consequences similar to, or even more severe than, the effects of other stressors frequently encountered within organizations, such as high job demands, low decision authority, role ambiguity, and role conflict. Further, they found that bullying has a considerable effect on exposed individuals also when controlling for the effects of other job stressors. Several other studies have also reported a clear link between bullying and general and mental stress (Bilgel, Aytac, and Bayram, 2006; Vartia, 2001).

The second mechanism argued to play a role in the relationship between unethical behavior and decreased well-being is *trauma* (Giacalone and Promislo, 2010). Individuals who are traumatized suffer disproportionately from various mental and physical effects (Friedman and Schnurr, 1995). "Scarring or remaining scarred for life" are themes that have emerged in qualitative research of bullying (Hallberg and Strandmark, 2006; Lewis, 2004). Targets report that bullying leaves an internal scar or vulnerability, which never heals completely and which can easily reopen whenever reminded of the events (Hallberg and Strandmark, 2006). Targets often perceive bullying as a psychic trauma, a traumatic life event, or a life crisis. Other research has confirmed that victims of bullying seem to suffer from symptoms similar to those of people diagnosed with posttraumatic stress syndrome (Leymann and Gustafsson, 1996; Matthiesen and Einarsen, 2004).

Besides effects linked to stress and trauma, *unethical behavior* may also result in detrimental health through *changes in health behavior*. In a large-scale UK study, Hoel (2002) analyzed the relationship between bullying and different health outcomes. He found a significant correlation between exposure to bullying behavior and daily cigarette consumption. In the same study he also analyzed the association between alcohol consumption and bullying. However, here the numbers were less clear. It seemed that the correlations between exposure to bullying behavior and alcohol consumption varied strongly for different forms of bullying: "managerial bullying," that is, work-related bullying instigated by superiors, was the form with the highest correlation with alcohol consumption. While this study seems to indicate that bullying affects health behavior negatively, not all studies support this. In a longitudinal study among Finnish hospital employees, exposure to bullying at time 1 did not predict smoking or drinking habits at time 2 (Kivimäki et al., 2003), so the findings are inconclusive.

Not only changes in health behavior but also changes in sleep and *sleep disturbances* may help to explain the relationship between bullying and decreased well-being. Sleep deprivation may be regarded as a neurobiological and physiological stressor, and sleep disturbances may negatively affect daytime functioning and overall well-being (Hansen et al., 2011). Studies demonstrate that targets of bullying are more likely to have sleep difficulties and impaired sleep quality (Hansen et al., 2011; Notelaers et al., 2006), and to use more sleep-inducing drugs and sedatives (Vartia, 2001). A recent French study found that the more frequent the exposure to bullying, the higher the risk of experiencing sleep disturbances. Not only did those currently exposed to bullying report more sleep disturbances, but also past exposure to bullying and observing someone else being bullied in the workplace were associated with increased sleep disturbances (Niedhammer et al., 2009). Sleep disturbances thus appear to be an additional important mechanism that contributes to the relationship between bullying and decreased health.

Effects on Self-Esteem, Job Satisfaction, and Employability

As discussed earlier, the concept of well-being extends beyond actual health issues and incorporates perceptions of happiness and general satisfaction with different aspects of life (Giacalone and Promislo, 2010). Bullying has been shown to have detrimental effects on general self-esteem and job satisfaction; for some, it has even resulted in expulsion from work life.

Targets of bullying often experience self-blame, guilt, and diminished self-esteem when trying to make sense of what is happening. Interviews with targets have shown that when targets feel they are less valued this feeling easily becomes internalized over time and grows within the victim. Also, feelings of guilt and shame develop as bullies blame the victims for the conflicts and for a lack of comfort at the workplace, and some targets start to doubt their own adequacy when they are portrayed as the scapegoat (Hallberg and Strandmark, 2006). In interviews with college and university lecturers who had been bullied, interviewees described feelings of powerlessness, humiliation, inferiority, and withdrawal (Lewis, 2004). Admitting to being bullied was associated with high levels of shame for many of the interviewees. Overall, these processes had detrimental effects on the targets' self-image, and targets started questioning their own worth. Quantitative studies have also confirmed the relationship between bullying and decreased self-confidence (Vartia, 2001).

Furthermore, bullying has a negative impact on many targets' social lives. In a Canadian study, targets spoke of feeling isolated and feeling that they had no one to talk to and nowhere to turn (MacIntosh, 2005). Several participants felt unable to discuss the bullying experience with spouses or partners because they feared further misunderstanding and further isolation. Similarly, Hallberg and Strandmark (2006) described how many targets over time withdrew from social contacts because of their constant fear of the bullies and because of negative rumors that had been spread about them. Some targets thus retreated and isolated themselves and tried to avoid interaction with other people, which also affected the families of the targets. For example, some targets experiencing high anxiety reported that they invited no one over to their house and even feared answering the phone.

Not surprisingly, being subjected to bullying is associated with decreased job satisfaction (Hauge, Skogstad, and Einarsen, 2010; Mathisen, Einarsen, and Mylketun, 2008; Quine, 1999). Qualitative interviews undertaken with bullied women in Canada have shown that bullying changed the way that the interviewees worked as well as the meaning of work for them (MacIntosh et al. 2010a, 2010b). The women interviewed could not continue working in a business-as-usual way after experiencing bullying, because it interfered with their health and their usual work practices.

The interviewees felt that the quality of their work suffered, they were depleted of energy, their productivity declined, and their thoughts were consumed by the interference of bullying. Overall, many felt that they were not able to use their abilities and competencies (MacIntosh et al., 2010a). Similarly, interviews with female nurses who had been bullied showed that their perceptions of and feelings toward work, colleagues, and careers changed. This change manifested as a loss in meaning derived from work, which in turn resulted in diminished work satisfaction. It also challenged the value placed on work, interfered with providing care for the patients, and, sometimes, undermined self-confidence (MacIntosh et al., 2010b).

Given the nature of bullying it is understandable that many victims consider leaving their jobs, and many studies have established a link between bullying and intention to leave (e.g., Bowling and Beehr, 2006; Djurkovic, McCormack, and Casimir, 2004; Hauge, Skogstad, and Einarsen, 2010; Hoel and Cooper, 2000; Mathisen, Einarsen, and Mykletun, 2008; Quine, 1999). However, the decision to actually change jobs is also affected by ease of movement and perceptions of the availability of other jobs (cf. Hoel et al., 2011), meaning that many feel forced to stay despite the mistreatment. As bullying itself is typically a highly stressful and draining experience, it can wear the victim down and negatively affect self-confidence and employability. Consequently, taking the initiative required to actually change jobs may become more and more difficult as the coping resources are depleted. Gossip and rumors spread about the victim may also reach other organizations, making it more difficult for the target to find another job. Moreover, victims themselves may feel reluctant to leave before they have achieved redress and justice (Kile, 1990).

In a Canadian study, interviewees in a rural and small city context raised concerns relating to financial and career impacts, and for some participants financial risk compounded the bullying experience (MacIntosh, 2005). Participants who felt they had no choice but to leave their workplaces incurred financial stress and loss. They further felt that having to leave their workplace jeopardized their careers in that field, and they feared that the bullying experience might damage their reputation and future employability in the local community. Another source of financial stress was counseling, on which many targets spent money in order to try to cope with the bullying experience.

Heinz Leymann (1996), a pioneer of bullying research, argued that bullying often is a process, consisting of several phases. A "normal" conflict can be the critical incident that triggers the negative behavior. Over time, the behavior becomes systematic and the victim becomes stigmatized. As a following step, the victim becomes regarded as "a case for personnel management to take care of." Due to previous stigmatization, the victim alone is often blamed for the problems. Finally, the process is likely to end in expulsion of the victim from the workplace. Other researchers have also confirmed that bullying is associated with a risk of early retirement (Matthiesen, Raknes, and Rokkum, 1989) and a risk of unemployment (Einarsen, Matthiesen, and Mikkelsen, 1999). A study of home-care workers in Sweden found that bullying was a significant predictor of permanent work disability and disability pension five years later (Dellve, Lagerström, and Hagberg, 2003). There seems to be a real risk that bullying may lead to expulsion from work life altogether, which is likely to be accompanied by further decreases in self-esteem, in well-being, and potentially in living conditions due to loss of income.

Individual Differences and Contextual Factors

So far, we have established that workplace bullying is associated with negative effects on the target's health, self-esteem, and job satisfaction. However, as discussed below, not all targets react in the same way or to the same degree, and both the nature of the acts and the characteristics of the targets appear to be important. This is in line with general research showing that personality differences affect both stress exposure and stress reactivity (cf. Vie, Glasø, and Einarsen, 2011).

Individual characteristics appear to be especially important for low levels of exposure to negative acts. Nielsen, Matthiesen, and Einarsen (2008) showed that sense of coherence, which is an individual disposition to view the world and the environment as comprehensible, manageable, and meaningful, offered protective benefits to targets exposed to low levels of bullying, whereas these benefits diminished as bullying became more severe. Similarly, self-labeling appears to be an important determinant in the bullying–health relationship, with targets who label their exposure to negative acts as bullying reporting more health effects than those who do not (Vie, Glasø, and Einarsen, 2011). This may be because labeling oneself as a victim influences the target's self-schema and identity and highlights one's vulnerability, thereby leading to elevated levels of distress. Alternatively, it may affect the interpretation of future negative acts and affect target reactions, making the target appear either more vulnerable or more aggressive in the eyes of others, thereby increasing the risk of further victimization (cf. Vie, Glasø, and Einarsen, 2011). However, moderator analyses seem to indicate that self-labeling acts as moderator only in cases of low exposure (Vie, Glasø, and Einarsen, 2011). Persistent exposure to workplace bullying seems to have considerable harmful effects on the target's health, independently of whether the experience is labeled as bullying or not. Similarly, at high levels of bullying, employees with a high sense of coherence in fact reported even stronger health effects (Nielsen, Matthiesen, and Einarsen, 2008).

Other individual characteristics that have been studied include self-efficacy and social anxiety. The concept of self-efficacy refers to people's beliefs about their capacity to exercise control over events that affect their lives. Individuals with a higher degree of generalized self-efficacy report somewhat fewer psychological health complaints following exposure to bullying behaviors (Mikkelsen and Einarsen, 2002). Moreover, targets scoring high on social anxiety report more depression and more psychosomatic symptoms (Einarsen et al., 1996; Moreno-Jiménez et al., 2007).

Gender has often been hypothesized to affect the relationship between bullying and health effects. However, the evidence is contradictory. While Vartia (2001) found no gender differences in health effects, Moreno-Jiménez et al. (2007) found stronger effects on women. How we measure bullying also seems to be relevant for gender differences in health effects. In a large UK survey, Hoel, Faragher, and Cooper (2004) found that when measuring bullying by asking about exposure to negative acts, the correlations were slightly higher for women. However, when measuring bullying through self-labeling, in contrast, the correlations between bullying and health effects were slightly stronger for men. This seems to support the general finding that men have a somewhat higher threshold for negative acts and are less likely to label themselves as bullied, but when they do, this process appears to take a heavier toll on men (Salin and Hoel, in press).

A Turkish study in the public sector highlighted the importance of social support, showing that victims with low social support reported the poorest health (Bilgel, Aytac, and Bayram, 2006). Similarly, a UK study among health-service employees showed that a supportive work environment moderated the relationship between bullying and job satisfaction, propensity to leave, and depression (Quine, 1999). A Danish study confirmed the importance of support and showed that support from a supervisor weakened the effects of bullying on victim health (Hansen et al., 2006). The authors also reported a relationship between witnessing bullying and anxiety, but noted that low support from a supervisor mediated the relationship between witnesses of bullying and anxiety, indicating that it may not be so much the observed bullying as the lack of support that explains the association between witnessing bullying and the symptoms (Hansen et al., 2006). Also, more generally, the level of perceived organizational support has been hypothesized to moderate the relationship between bullying and adverse outcomes (Parzefall and Salin, 2010).

Effects on Bystanders, Perpetrators and Significant Others

Most of the research on the effects of workplace bullying has been carried out among victims. However, there are strong reasons to assume that the effects reach beyond those directly affected.

Also those affected indirectly by unethical acts, for example, those who witness unethical behavior or are associated with the victims, may show reductions in well-being. This may be because they feel empathy for the victim, because they fear becoming the next victim, or because the incidents shatter the third party's worldview or beliefs in a just world (cf. Giacalone and Promislo, 2010).

Research on bystanders of bullying supports this. Bystanders report significantly more general stress and mental stress reactions than employees from workplaces without bullying (Vartia, 2001). In a British survey of a public sector trade union, 73 percent of the witnesses of bullying reported increased stress levels, while 44 percent worried about becoming a target of bullying (Rayner, 1999a). Only 16 percent of the witnesses claimed not to be affected in any way. Other findings also suggest that those who have witnessed bullying report worse health than those not affected, but better health than those currently or previously bullied themselves (Hoel and Cooper, 2000). However, while targets of bullying report decreased self-confidence, this does not seem to be the case for observers (Vartia, 2001). Witnessing bullying also has an effect on work-related attitudes and has also been reported to be negatively correlated with job satisfaction and commitment (Mathisen, Einarsen, and Mykletun, 2008). A general climate of fear at the workplace, resulting from bullies "getting away with it," has also been noted in studies of bullying (cf. Hoel et al., 2011). It thus seems clear that the effects of bullying extend clearly beyond those directly affected.

In some cases bystanders also see themselves as friends of the target, thus complicating the picture even further. D'Cruz and Noronha (2011), who interviewed targets of bullying and bystanders at Indian call centers, reported how bystanders who considered themselves friends of the targets at first tried to help, both by providing support and by trying to bring up the issues with management. However, many bystanders censored their support over time as they learned that dissent was not tolerated. Many reported a pervasive sense of helplessness and emotional turmoil, as their own interests conflicted with their concern for the target and their ethical and moral positions. Further, many reported being haunted by guilt and remorse, feeling that that they had betrayed not only their friends but also their principles.

We need to remember that the number of employees indirectly affected is high, due to high numbers of those who have witnessed bullying in their workplaces (e.g., Namie, 2007). Because a typical coping mechanism among victims is to seek social support and discuss the problem with colleagues (Hoel and Cooper, 2000), it becomes even more difficult for bystanders and colleagues to remain uninvolved or neutral (cf. Einarsen, 1996).

So far we know surprisingly little about the perpetrators of bullying. This is largely because of the methodological and ethical issues involved in getting data from alleged perpetrators. Few employees admit to being bullies. A representative study of bullies would require us to first ask third parties and victims to name bullies and then ask these alleged bullies to participate in the study. This means we could not guarantee anonymity in the data collection process, and since bullies would be unlikely to take part if informed why they were invited, it would most likely also require some level of deceit about the purpose of the study. Although some research has been undertaken to study whether the personality of self-labeled perpetrators differs from that of other employees (Glasø, Nielsen, and Einarsen, 2009), we still know little about the reasons why some employees/superiors bully. While thoughtlessness and lack of empathy and social skills are often put forward as reasons (see, e.g., Zapf and Einarsen, 2011), we cannot rule out the possibility that some people resort to bullying behavior, even though it conflicts with their own ethical norms (cf. Giacalone and Promislo, 2010). Certain social situations, for example, involving extreme power, powerful pressure, or expectations of obedience (cf. Giacalone and Promislo, 2010; Milgram, 1975; Zimbardo, 2007) have been shown to influence individuals to commit immoral acts. This might be the case, for example, when a victim is bullied by a group of colleagues and some join in simply to avoid becoming the next victim. There might also be cases where managers who are under high pressure themselves resort to bullying because they see no other options to reach the targets set for their departments. Under such circumstances, it is reasonable to expect that the mismatch between the perpetrator's own values and his or her behavior would be likely to produce extreme guilt, anxiety, and stress, which could significantly affect well-being (Giacalone and Promislo, 2010). For instance, research on criminal offenders shows that perpetrators may become traumatized themselves and even suffer from post-traumatic stress disorder (PTSD) (e.g., Byrne, 2003), and we can expect to see similar processes among perpetrators of bullying.

Moreover, a perpetrator may be aware of being seen as a "bully" and experience stress because of this stigma. Jenkins, Winefield, and Sarris (2011) interviewed twenty-four Australian employees in managerial/supervisory positions who had been accused of bullying, and found that the allegations had had significant effects on their well-being. The interviewees had experienced high levels of anxiety, depression, and stress, and over half of the interviewees had taken sick leave because of the symptoms. The interviewees had also experienced a number of difficulties in returning to their roles as managers following the allegations. Loss of confidence and trust were themes that strongly emerged in the interviews, and several of the interviewees had left the organization afterward. However, both those who were later found guilty and those who were acquitted experienced very similar symptoms, which suggests that the allegations rather than the act of engaging in bullying behavior caused the distress.

In a study on workplace aggression, Haines, Marchand, and Harvey (2006) found crossover effects within the family—that is, not only those experiencing workplace aggression themselves but also their spouses exhibited increased levels of stress. The study used responses from more than 2,900 dual-earner couples who responded to questions concerning psychological distress, experiences of workplace aggression, their job situation, and other possible stressors. Although their study included only questions related to intimidation, violence, and sexual harassment it is highly likely that similar crossover effects within the family may also be relevant for couples where one partner has been subject to bullying. Qualitative research has also given support for the idea that there might be spillover effects on other family members. For example, in an interview study, some interviewees themselves recognized that they had become more aggressive toward their spouse as a result of being bullied at work (MacIntosh, 2005).

DISCUSSION AND IMPLICATIONS FOR MANAGERS

This overview of findings on bullying and well-being has demonstrated that bullying is a severe stressor at work and poses serious threats to employee well-being. As discussed in this chapter, bullying has the potential to negatively affect many dimensions of well-being: mental and physical health, self-esteem and social life, job satisfaction, and even the financial situation of targets. Not only targets but also bystanders and family members are affected. All of these are important reasons why managers, labor unions, and labor organizations (such as the ILO), policymakers, and politicians need to take this form of unethical behavior very seriously.

For those concerned only with the bottom line, it is important to remember that the effects of bullying as discussed above also translate into high financial costs both for organizations and society as a whole (cf. Hoel et al., 2011). As discussed earlier, bullying leads to increased absence due to sickness, increased turnover of personnel for the "wrong" reasons, increased health-care costs, possible expulsion from work life, higher risk of early retirement, and a general lack of well-being in society.

A number of European countries and some regions in Canada and Australia have passed explicit laws against bullying, requiring employers to take action to stop such mistreatment. This development may raise general awareness and send an important signal about the unacceptability of the phenomenon. Still, some research indicates that such laws and ordinances, while raising employee expectations, may be ridden with different shortcomings, which makes it difficult to truly implement them (cf. Hoel and Einarsen, 2010). While legal regulation may be one step in the attempt to combat bullying, it also requires true commitment from managers and other organizational representatives.

Organizational policies on workplace bullying often require targets to bring the case to the attention of managers, and in addition to confront the perpetrator him or herself first (Salin, 2008). However, we know that many targets never confront the perpetrator or make informal/formal complaints to their managers (Namie, 2007; Rayner, 1997). We can assume that there are several reasons for this. First of all, targets may fear repercussions and negative effects on their careers. Because research shows that employees reporting mistreatment often face retaliation from both superiors and colleagues, this fear is not unwarranted (Cortina and Magley, 2003). Second, targets may question whether filing a complaint will actually have any positive effects. Unfortunately, empirical findings indicate that targets who approach human resources representatives and organizational representatives often get little help (D'Cruz and Noronha, 2011). Third, as discussed earlier, bullying has negative effects on employee self-confidence and also leads to depletion of energy (cf. Hallberg and Strandmark, 2006). As such, it may be fairly naive to expect victims to have the confidence and strength to actually bring about change themselves. The points above demonstrate how difficult it is for targets to successfully address bullying themselves. Therefore, it is important that organizations address bullying proactively, even if targets do not make formal complaints.

Today we have extensive knowledge about organizational risk factors (Hauge, Skogstad, and Einarsen, 2010; Salin and Hoel, 2011), which, at least to some extent, can be controlled through management action. This means that we also have improved possibilities, if not totally to prevent bullying, at least to significantly reduce the risk. By reducing role conflict, clarifying goals, and undertaking organizational changes in ways that minimize the perceived degree of insecurity and unfairness, we can significantly lower the risk of bullying (cf. Salin and Hoel, 2011). Similarly, leadership training is important and above all, highlighting the risks of destructive forms of leadership, such as autocratic, noncontingent or laissez-faire styles of leadership (cf. Hoel et al., 2010). We also need to ensure that employees and managers alike are aware of and understand the destructive impacts of bullying.

All too often targets report that they are the ones forced to leave the organization, not the perpetrators (e.g., Namie, 2007). Also human resource professionals themselves report that it is equally often the targets as it is the perpetrators who are transferred when organizational representatives see no alternative but to separate target and perpetrator (Salin, 2009). While there undoubtedly are cases where it is in the best interest of the target to get a chance to start fresh in a new organization or new work context, this approach is clearly risky. First of all, it means that the targets may feel that they never got redress. In addition, and perhaps even more important, it also sends the wrong signals to bystanders and potential future bullies. If we want to prevent bullying and the negative effects on well-being discussed in this chapter, it is imperative that organizations take a clear stance against bullying and also stand behind this decision when bullying behavior is discovered. When employees are asked about why bullying exists in their organization, one of the most typical replies is because "bullies get away with it" (Rayner, 1999b: p. 31). This insightful comment says a lot about why bullying continues to flourish in organizations.

Studies show that both social and organizational support help to reduce the negative impacts of bullying (Bilgel, Aytac, and Bayram, 2006; Hansen et al., 2006; Quine, 1999). Again, this, too, points to the importance for organizations of taking a clear stance against bullying and supporting targets. Furthermore, some studies indicate that contrary to common belief men and women seem to report similar levels of symptoms in response to bullying (Hoel, Faragher, and Cooper, 2004; Vartia, 2001). It is thus important that organizational representatives ensure that men, too, get access to rehabilitation and support and that they are not misled by the common myth that male targets do not need help (cf. Salin and Hoel, in press).

BULLYING AS UNETHICAL BEHAVIOR: DIRECTIONS FOR FUTURE RESEARCH

As illustrated in this chapter, much research has been undertaken to increase our understanding of workplace bullying. Bullying has typically been studied as an escalated conflict (e.g., Leymann, 1996), as a major stressor in the workplace (Hauge, Skogstad, and Einarsen, 2010), or as a form of counterproductive work behavior (Fox and Spector, 2005). In contrast, despite the highly unethical nature of bullying behavior, only a few studies have explicitly discussed bullying from an ethical perspective (e.g., Bulutlar and Öz, 2009; Giacalone and Promislo, 2010; Stouten et al., 2010). Still, thinking of bullying from an ethical perspective raises many new and relevant questions.

First of all, research on ethical and unethical behavior has long studied factors that affect individuals' moral choices. While many studies have sought to identify individual characteristics of moral exemplars, there is strong evidence for an interaction between personal variables and situational cues in determining individual responses to ethical dilemmas (e.g., Aquino et al., 2009). As discussed earlier, we know little about the personality and motives of perpetrators of bullying, and this is an important area for future research. Research on other forms of unethical and immoral behavior can give us valuable ideas to explore. For example, research on unethical behavior has found the concept of "moral identity" to be a significant predictor of (un)ethical behavior (Aquino et al., 2009; O'Reilly and Aquino, 2011). Moral identity refers to the extent to which individuals see being a moral person as central to their self-concept (Blasi, 1984; O'Reilly and Aquino, 2011). However, situational cues can also temporarily affect the current accessibility of the moral self-schema, thereby affecting the individual's actual behavior. For example, in a series of experiments, Aquino et al. (2009) demonstrated that when thinking of the Ten Commandments before completing an assignment individuals behaved more ethically, but when presented with cues signaling competition, financial incentives, or selfishness among other participants they behaved less ethically. These findings are of potential interest to bullying researchers. An important avenue for further research would be to study the importance of moral identity as a predictor of bullying behavior and also to study how situational cues interact with this. In other words, this would mean studying which factors in the work environment either activate or deactivate the centrality of a potential bully's moral identity and thus make bullying more or less likely to take place. Time pressure, ethical norms within the organization, and the possibility to rationalize the negative acts are some examples of such situational cues identified in earlier research on (un)ethical behavior (Aquino et al., 2009).

Moreover, moral identity and the centrality of moral identity in particular situations also have the potential to affect third-party reactions. O'Reilly and Aquino (2011) have hypothesized that moral identity, alongside situational factors, predicts third-party responses to mistreatment in the workplace. When becoming aware of bullying in the organization, third parties may try to help or support the victim, punish the perpetrator, or simply ignore the situation and avoid action. O'Reilly and Aquino (2011) argue that individuals whose moral identity is highly central to their self-concept are more likely to perceive injustices as a moral violation, to experience moral anger, and to take action. A central argument in their reasoning is that third parties make their decision not only based on instrumental self-interest (i.e., cost-benefit analysis of what they personally have to gain), but also because they feel "it is the right thing to do" (i.e., a deontic emotion). Research on third parties in bullying cases has typically focused more on how bullying affects their well-being and less on how the actions of third parties can increase or decrease the risk of continued bullying behavior. A better understanding of the role of third parties and factors that affect their reasoning and behavior can be an important step in the prevention of bullying. Third-party reactions and moral reasoning among third parties are therefore important areas for further research.

In line with the arguments above, we can also expect employees with a strong moral identity to experience more dissonance when they see colleagues being bullied. As such, we could expect moral identity to moderate the relationship between bullying and well-being so that employees with a high moral identity experience higher levels of stress when they either witness bullying or feel pressured to engage in such behavior themselves. The literature on unethical behavior also draws attention to the perceived magnitude of an event and the centrality of the unethical action to one's worldview and identity as potentially moderating variables between unethical acts and diminished well-being in victims, third parties, and perpetrators (Giacalone and Promislo, 2010; Magley et al., 1999). All of these topics remain to be empirically tested by bullying researchers.

As discussed above, situational factors are important predictors of moral behavior. We can also expect ethical leadership and the ethical climate to influence the likelihood of bullying behavior among organizational members. Stouten et al. (2010) confirmed that ethical leadership was associated with lower levels of bullying. Ethical leaders appear to set an example by communicating and rewarding ethical behavior, by acting as role models, and by investing in a good work environment. Ethical climate, which is related to ethical leadership, has been defined as "the shared perceptions of what is ethically correct behavior and how ethical issues should be handled" (Victor and Cullen, 1987, pp. 51–52). A small-scale study conducted in Turkey provides preliminary support for the impact of the ethical climate (Bulutlar and Öz, 2009). An instrumental climate, where norms enforce ethical decision making from an egoistic perspective, was associated with higher levels of bullying. In contrast, principle-driven climates based on laws, codes, and rules seemed to decrease the risk of bullying. Moreover, caring climates, characterized by benevolence, and independence climates, based on personal morality and the employees' deeply held values, were negatively associated with some forms of bullying behaviors, such as underestimation and social isolation. We should thus encourage additional studies to try to replicate the findings of Bulutlar and Öz (2009) in larger and more diverse samples, and if they corroborate the functioning of ethical climate as a protective mechanism, we should encourage studies on how to change or strengthen the ethical climate in organizations.

As this chapter has demonstrated, bullying can have severe effects on the physical and psychological health of those concerned. Most of the research on bullying and well-being to date has focused on the private forms of well-being and personal functioning. However, with the concept of social well-being, Keyes (1998) draws attention to the social features of well-being, which involve the appraisal of one's circumstance and functioning in society. Although there is scarce empirical evidence so far, we can expect bullying to affect different dimensions of social well-being as well. For example, bullied individuals may end up feeling they are no longer part of and connected with the larger society (lack of social integration), that their social values have decreased (lack of social contribution), that they have difficulty making sense of the world around them (lack of social coherence), and that they may lose trust in others (lack of social acceptance). Interview studies with victims indirectly support this (e.g., Hallberg and Strandmark, 2006; MacIntosh, 2005; MacIntosh et al., 2010a, 2010b), but more systematic analyses of bullying and social well-being still remain to be undertaken.

CONCLUSION

As shown in this chapter, bullying can have severe consequences for employee health and well-being. On the positive side, today we have extensive knowledge of the phenomenon of bullying, which increases our chances of early detection and prevention. Framing bullying as a form of unethical behavior also draws our attention to concepts such as moral identity, ethical climates, and ethical leadership. All of these appear to be highly important in our endeavor to prevent workplace bullying. Central challenges thus appear to be to make managers and other organizational representatives aware of the importance of the issue of workplace bullying and inform them of what they can do to minimize the risk of bullying in their own organizations.

REFERENCES

Aquino, K.; Freeman, D.; Reed, A.; Lim, V.; and Felps, W. 2009. Testing a social-cognitive model of moral behavior: The interactive influence of situations and moral identity centrality. *Journal of Personality and Social Psychology,* 97, 1, 123–141.

Bilgel, N.; Aytac, S.; and Bayram, N. 2006. Bullying in Turkish white-collar workers. *Occupational Medicine,* 56, 4, 226–231.

Blasi, A. 1984. Moral identity: Its role in moral functioning. In *Morality, Moral Behavior and Moral Development,* ed. W. Kurtines and J. Gewirtz, 128–139. New York: Wiley.

Bowling, N.A., and Beehr, T.A. 2006. Workplace harassment from the victim's perspective: A theoretical model and meta-analysis. *Journal of Applied Psychology,* 91, 5, 998–1012.

Bulutlar, F., and Öz, E.Ü. 2009. The effects of ethical climate on bullying behaviour in the workplace. *Journal of Business Ethics,* 86, 3, 273–295.

Byrne, M.K. 2003. Trauma reactions in the offender. *International Journal of Forensic Psychology,* 1, 1, 59–70.

Cortina, L., and Magley, V. 2003. Raising voice, risking retaliation: Events following interpersonal mistreatment in the workplace. *Journal of Occupational Health Psychology,* 8, 4, 247–265.

D'Cruz, P., and Noronha, E. 2011. The limits to workplace friendship: Managerialist HRM and bystander behaviour in the context of workplace bullying. *Employee Relations,* 33, 3, 269–288.

Dellve, L.; Lagerström, M.; and Hagberg, M. 2003. Work-system risk factors for permanent work disability among home-care workers: A case-control study. *International Archives of Occupational and Environmental Health,* 76, 3, 216–224.

Djurkovic, N.; McCormack, D.; and Casimir, G. 2004. The physical and psychological effects of workplace bullying and their relationship to intention to leave: A test of the psychosomatic and disability hypotheses. *International Journal of Organization Theory and Behavior,* 7, 4, 469–497.

Einarsen, S. 1996. Bullying and harassment at work: Epidemiological and psychosocial aspects. PhD diss. Bergen, Norway: University of Bergen.

Einarsen, S.; Matthiesen, S.B.; and Mikkelsen, E. 1999. *Tiden leger alle sår? Senvirkningerav mobbing iarbetslivet* [Time heals all wounds? Late effects of bullying at work]. Bergen, Norway: Institut for Samfunnspsykologi, University of Bergen.

Einarsen, S.; Matthiesen, S.; and Skogstad, A. 1998. Bullying, burnout, and well-being among assistant nurses. *Journal of Occupational Health Safety,* 14, 563–568.

Einarsen, S.; Hoel, H.; Zapf, D.; and Cooper, C., 2011. *Bullying and Harassment in the Workplace: Developments in Theory, Research and Practice.* London: Taylor and Francis.

Einarsen, S.; Raknes, B.I.; Matthiesen, S.B.; and Hellesøy, O. 1996. Bullying at work and its relationships with health complaints: Moderating effects of social support and personality. *Nordisk Psykologi,* 48, 2, 116–137.

Finne, L.B.; Knardahl, S.; and Lau, B. 2011. Workplace bullying and mental distress: A prospective study of Norwegian employees. *Scandinavian Journal of Work, Environment and Health,* 37, 4, 276–286.

Fox, S., and Spector, P. 2005. *Counterproductive Work Behavior: Investigations of Actors and Targets.* Washington, DC: American Psychological Association.

Friedman, M., and Schnurr, P. 1995. *The Relationship Between Trauma, Post-traumatic Stress Disorder and Physical Health.* Philadelphia: Lippincott Williams and Wilkins.

Giacalone, R., and Promislo, M. 2010. Unethical and unwell: Decrements in well-being and unethical activity at work. *Journal of Business Ethics,* 91, 2, 275–297.

Giacalone, R., and Thompson, K.R. 2006. Business ethics and social responsibility education: Shifting the worldview. *Academy of Management Learning and Education,* 5, 3, 266–277.

Glasø, L.; Nielsen, M.; and Einarsen, S. 2009. Interpersonal problems among targets and perpetrators of workplace bullying. *Journal of Applied Social Psychology,* 39, 6, 1316–1333.

Glasø, L.; Matthiesen, S.B.; Nielsen, M.; and Einarsen, S. 2007. Do targets of workplace bullying portray a general victim personality profile? *Scandinavian Journal of Psychology,* 48, 4, 313–319.

Haines, V.Y.; Marchand A.; and Harvey, S. 2006. Crossover of workplace aggression experiences in dual-earner couples. *Journal of Occupational Health Psychology,* 11, 4, 305–314.

Hallberg, L., and Strandmark, M. 2006. Health consequences of workplace bullying: Experiences from the perspective of bully victims. *International Journal of Qualitative Studies on Health and Well-being,* 1, 109–119.

Hansen, Å-M., and the Nordic Bullying Network Group. 2011. State of the art report on bullying at the workplace in the Nordic countries. TemaNord: 515. Copenhagen: Nordic Council of Ministers.

Hansen, Å.-M.; Hogh, A.; Persson, R.; Karlson, B.; Garde, A.H.; and Ørbaek, P. 2006. Bullying at work, health outcomes, and physiological stress response. *Journal of Psychosomatic Research,* 60, 1, 63–72.

Hauge, L.J.; Skogstad, A.; and Einarsen, S. 2007. Relationships between stressful work environments and workplace bullying: Results of a large representative study. *Work and Stress,* 21, 3, 220–242.

———. 2010. The relative impact of workplace bullying as a social stressor at work. *Scandinavian Journal of Psychology,* 51, 5, 426–433.

Hoel, H. 2002. Workplace bullying in Great Britain. PhD diss. Manchester: University of Manchester Institute of Science and Technology.

Hoel, H., and Cooper, C. 2000. *Destructive Conflict and Bullying at Work.* Report produced by the Manchester School of Management. Manchester: University of Manchester, Institute of Science and Technology.

Hoel, H., and Einarsen, S. 2010. The Swedish ordinance against victimization: A critical assessment. *Comparative Labor Law and Policy Journal,* 32, 101–125.

Hoel, H.; Cooper, C.; and Faragher, B. 2001. The experience of bullying in Great Britain: The impact of organizational status. *European Journal of Work and Organizational Psychology,* 10, 4, 443–465.

Hoel, H.; Faragher, B.; and Cooper, C. 2004. Bullying is detrimental to health, but all bullying behaviours are not necessarily equally damaging. *British Journal of Guidance and Counselling,* 32, 3, 367–387.

Hoel, H.; Sparks, K.; and Cooper, C. 2001. *The Cost of Violence/Stress at Work and the Benefits of a Violence/Stress-free Working Environment.* Geneva: International Labour Organisation.

Hoel, H.; Sheehan, M.; Cooper, C.; and Einarsen, S. 2011. Organisational effects of workplace bullying. In *Bullying and Harassment in the Workplace: Developments in Theory, Research and Practice,* ed. S. Einarsen, H. Hoel, D. Zapf, and C. Cooper, 129–147. London: Taylor and Francis.

Hoel, H.; Glasø, L.; Hetland, J.; Cooper, C.; and Einarsen, S. 2010. Leadership as predictor of self-reported and observed workplace bullying. *British Journal of Management,* 21, 2, 453–468.

Hogh, A.; Mikkelsen, E.; and Hansen, Å-M. 2011. Individual consequences of workplace bullying/mobbing. In *Bullying and Harassment in the Workplace: Developments in Theory, Research and Practice,* ed. S. Einarsen, H. Hoel, D. Zapf, and C. Cooper, 107–128. London: Taylor and Francis.

Jenkins, M.; Winefield, H.; and Sarris, A. 2011. Consequences of being accused of workplace bullying. An exploratory study. *International Journal of Workplace Health Management,* 4, 1, 33–47.

Jones, T.M. 1991. Ethical decision-making by individuals in organizations: An issue-contingent model. *Academy of Management Review,* 16, 2, 366–395.

Keyes, C.L.M. 1998. Social well-being. *Social Psychology Quarterly,* 61, 2, 121–140.

Kile, S.M. 1990. *Helsefarleg leierskap: ein explorerande studie* [Leadership with negative health implications: An exploratory study]. Bergen: Report to the Norwegian General Science Council.

Kivimäki, M.; Elovainio, M.; and Vahtera, J. 2000. Workplace bullying and sickness absence in hospital staff. *Occupational and Environmental Medicine,* 57, 10, 656–660.

Kivimäki, M.; Virtanen, M.; Vartia, M.; Elovainio, M.; Vahtera, J.; and Keltikangas-Järvinen, L. 2003. Workplace bullying and the risk of cardiovascular disease and depression. *Occupational and Environmental Medicine,* 60, 10, 779–783.

Lazarus, R.S., and Folkman, S. 1984. *Stress, Appraisal and Coping.* New York: Springer.

Lewis, D. 2004. Bullying at work: The impact of shame among university and college lecturers. *British Journal of Guidance and Counselling,* 32, 3, 281–299.

Leymann, H. 1987. Självmord till följd av förhållanden i arbetsmiljön [Suicide and conditions at the workplace]. *Arbete, människa, miljö,* 3, 155–160.

———. 1996. The content and development of mobbing at work. *European Journal of Work and Organizational Psychology,* 5, 2, 164–185.

Leymann, H., and Gustafsson, A. 1996. Mobbing at work and the development of post-traumatic stress disorders. *European Journal of Work and Organizational Psychology,* 5, 2, 251–275.

Lutgen-Sandvik, P.; Tracy, S.J.; and Alberts, J.K. 2007. Burned by bullying in the American workplace: Prevalence, perception, degree and impact. *Journal of Management Studies,* 44, 6, 837–862.

MacIntosh, J. 2005. Experiences of workplace bullying in a rural area. *Issues in Mental Health Nursing,* 26, 9, 893–910.

MacIntosh, J.; Wuest, J.; Gray, M.M.; and Aldous, S. 2010a. Effects of workplace bullying on how women work. *Western Journal of Nursing Research,* 32, 7, 910–931.

MacIntosh, J.; Wuest, J.; Gray, M.M.; and Cronkhite, M. 2010b. Workplace bullying in health care affects the meaning of work. *Qualitative Health Research,* 20, 8, 1128–1141.

Magley, V.; Hulin, C.L.; Fitzgerald, L.F.; and DeNardo, M. 1999. Outcomes of self-labeling sexual harassment. *Journal of Applied Psychology,* 84, 3, 390–402.

Mathisen, G.E.; Einarsen, S.; and Mykletun, R. 2008. The occurrences and correlates of bullying and harassment in the restaurant sector. *Scandinavian Journal of Psychology,* 49, 1, 59–68.

Matthiesen, S.B., and Einarsen, S. 2004. Psychiatric distress and symptoms of PTSD among victims of bullying at work. *British Journal of Guidance and Counselling,* 32, 3, 335–356.

Matthiesen, S.B.; Raknes, B.I.; and Rokkum, O. 1989. Mobbing på arbeidsplassen [Bullying at work]. *Tidskrift for Norsk Psykologforening,* 26, 761–784.

Mikkelsen, E., and Einarsen, S. 2001. Bullying in Danish work-life: Prevalence and health correlates. *European Journal of Work and Organizational Psychology,* 10, 4, 393–413.

———. 2002. Relationships between exposure to bullying at work and psychological and psychosomatic health complaints: the role of state negative affectivity and generalized self-efficacy. *Scandinavian Journal of Psychology,* 43, 5, 397–405.

Milgram, S. 1975. *Obedience to Authority: An Experimental View.* New York: Harper and Row.

Moreno-Jiménez, B.; Rodríguez-Muñoz, A.; Moreno, Y.; and Garrosa, E. 2007. The moderating role of assertiveness and social anxiety in workplace bullying: Two empirical studies. *Psychology in Spain,* 11, 1, 85–94.

Namie, G. 2007. *U.S. Workplace Bullying Survey September 2007.* Bellingham, WA: Workplace Bullying Institute and Zogby International. Available at http://workplacebullying.org/multi/pdf/WBIsurvey2007.pdf

———. 2010. *Results of the 2010 WBI U.S. Workplace Bullying Survey.* Bellingham, WA: Workplace Bullying Institute and Zogby International. Available at http://workplacebullying.org/multi/pdf/WBI_2010_Natl_Survey.pdf

Niedhammer, I.; David, S.; Degioanni S.; Drummond A.; and Philip, P. 2009. Workplace bullying and sleep disturbances: Findings from a large scale cross-sectional survey in the French working population. *Sleep,* 32, 9, 1211–1219.

Nielsen, M.; Matthiesen, S.B.; and Einarsen, S. 2008. Sense of coherence as a protective mechanism among targets of workplace bullying. *Journal of Occupational Health Psychology,* 13, 2, 128–136.

Nielsen, M.B.; Hetland, J.; Matthiesen S.B.; and Einarsen, S. 2012. Longitudinal relationships between workplace bullying and psychological distress. *Scandinavian Journal of Work, Environment and Health.* 38, 1, 38–46.

Notelaers, G.; Einarsen, S.; De Witte, H.; and Vermunt, J. 2006. Measuring exposure to bullying at work: The validity and advantages of the latent class cluster approach. *Work and Stress,* 20, 4, 288–301.

O'Reilly, J., and Aquino, K. 2011. A model of third parties' morally motivated responses to mistreatment in organizations. *Academy of Management Review,* 36, 3, 526–543.

Parzefall, M., and Salin, D. 2010. Perceptions of and reactions to workplace bullying: A social exchange perspective. *Human Relations,* 63, 6, 761–780.

Pompili, M.; Lester, D.; Innamorati, M.; De Pisa, E.; Iliceto, P.; Puccinno, M.; Nastro, P.F.; Tatarelli R.; and Girardi, P. 2008. Suicide risk and exposure to mobbing. *Work,* 31, 2, 237–243.

Quine, L. 1999. Workplace bullying in the NHS community trust: Staff questionnaire survey. *British Medical Journal,* 318, 7178, 228–232.

Rayner, C. 1997. The incidence of workplace bullying. *Journal of Community and Applied Social Psychology,* 7, 199–208.

———. 1999a. Workplace bullying. PhD diss. Manchester: University of Manchester Institute of Science and Technology.

———. 1999b. From research to implementation: Finding leverage for prevention. *International Journal of Manpower,* 20, 1, 28–38.

Salin, D. 2003. Ways of explaining workplace bullying: A review of enabling, motivating and precipitating structures and processes in the work environment. *Human Relations,* 56, 10, 1213–1232.

———. 2008. The prevention of workplace bullying as a question of human resource management: Measures adopted and underlying organizational factors. *Scandinavian Journal of Management,* 24, 3, 221–231.

———. 2009. Organisational responses to workplace harassment: An exploratory study. *Personnel Review,* 38, 1, 26–44.

Salin, D., and Hoel, H. 2011. Organizational causes of bullying. In *Bullying and Harassment in the Workplace: Developments in Theory, Research and Practice,* ed. S. Einarsen, H. Hoel, D. Zapf, and C. Cooper, 227–243. London: Taylor and Francis.

———. In press. Workplace bullying as a gendered phenomenon: A review of the literature, theoretical explanations and directions for further research. Forthcoming in *Journal of Managerial Psychology.*

Stouten, J.; Baillien, E.; Van den Broeck, A.; Camps, J.; DeWitte, H.; and Euwema, M. 2010. Discouraging bullying: The role of ethical leadership and its effects on the work environment. *Journal of Business Ethics,* 95, S1, 17–27.

Vartia, M. 2001. Consequences of workplace bullying with respect to the well-being of its targets and the observers of bullying. *Scandinavian Journal of Work and Environmental Health,* 27, 1, 63–69.

Victor, B., and Cullen, J.B. 1987. A theory and measure of ethical clime in organizations. In *Research in Corporate Social Performance and Policy,* 9, ed. W.C. Frederick and L.E. Preston, 51–71. Greenwich, CT: JAI Press.

Vie, T.L.; Glasø, L.; and Einarsen, S. 2011. Health outcomes and self-labeling as a victim of workplace bullying. *Journal of Psychosomatic Research,* 70, 11, 37–43.

Voss, M.; Floderus, B.; and Diderichsen, F. 2004. Physical, psychosocial, and organizational factors relative to sickness absence: a study based on Sweden post. *Occupational and Environmental Medicine,* 58, 3, 178–184.

Zapf, D., and Einarsen, S. 2011. Individual antecedents of bullying: victims and perpetrators. In *Bullying and Harassment in the Workplace: Developments in Theory, Research and Practice,* ed. S. Einarsen, H. Hoel, D. Zapf, and C. Cooper, 177–200. London: Taylor and Francis.

Zapf, D.; Escartín, J.; Einarsen, S.; Hoel, H.; and Vartia, M. 2011. Empirical findings on prevalence and risk groups of bullying in the workplace. In *Bullying and Harassment in the Workplace: Developments in Theory, Research and Practice,* ed. S. Einarsen, H. Hoel, D. Zapf, and C. Cooper, 75–105. London: Taylor and Francis.

Zimbardo, P.G. 2007. *The Lucifer Effect: Understanding How Good People Turn Evil.* New York: Random House.

6

WORKPLACE AGGRESSION, UNETHICAL BEHAVIOR, AND EMPLOYEE WELL-BEING

An "Aggressive" Examination of the Issues

JOEL H. NEUMAN

At the extremes, the relationships between aggression, unethical behavior, and well-being seem fairly obvious. For example, in a case of workplace violence, in which a current employee takes the life of a coworker or superior, that would most certainly represent an instance of unethical behavior—assuming that the homicide was not an act of self-defense (i.e., justifiable homicide). In this example, the impact on the well-being of the victim is equally apparent—assuming, as I do, that death is incompatible with well-being. Less obvious is the impact of homicide on witnesses, other employees not physically present during the incident, family and friends of the perpetrator or victim, as well as the potential impact on customers and clients—especially those who have had (or continue to have) an ongoing relationship with the organization. Related to this, what about the impact of these acts on perpetrators? While little attention (or compassion) is typically focused on the well-being of aggressors, there are serious consequences to those individuals and, potentially, to their friends and family members. In fact, one might easily make the case that there are "victims" at both ends of a shooting—especially when such incidents involve acts of self-defense, or involve actions resulting from years of persecution, untreated mental illness, or other extenuating (mitigating) circumstances.

In addition to lethal assaults (with and without weapons), interpersonal aggression includes nonlethal physical attacks (e.g., sexual and nonsexual assaults, fistfights, property damage, physical intimidation), verbal assaults (e.g., yelling, harsh criticism, demeaning/disrespectful comments, epithets related to a target's gender, ethnicity, race, and/or sexual orientation), temper tantrums (throwing things, slamming doors, intimidating gestures), and covert (subtle/insidious) instances of harm-doing (gossip, passive aggression, social exclusion, withholding resources or support).

Many of the behaviors that may be subsumed, in whole or in part, under the heading of aggression will be covered in other chapters of this book (e.g., bullying, abusive supervision, ostracism, revenge, discrimination). Consequently, I will focus my attention extensively (but not exclusively) on physical forms of aggression.

DEFINITIONAL AND CONCEPTUAL ISSUES

The terms "aggression," "unethical behavior," and "well-being" are employed in everyday discourse. Thus, before proceeding further, I address some important definitional and conceptual issues.

Aggression and Violence

As employed in the subtitle of this chapter, the word "aggressive" suggests a "forceful" or "uncompromising" investigation of the focal issues under examination. In a similar vein, when characterizing a salesperson as "aggressive," one might picture a highly energetic and motivated employee—a real "go-getter." While most employers would no doubt value an "aggressive" salesperson, they might be less sanguine about employing an "aggressive" customer service representative. As these examples suggest, the word "aggressive" is commonly used to characterize both assertive and hostile forms of behavior. Contrary to this everyday usage of the term, social scientists generally view aggression as "any form of behavior directed toward the goal of harming or injuring another living being who is motivated to avoid such treatment" (Baron and Richardson, 1994, p. 7). In other words, aggression involves behavior that is intended to harm others—whether or not that objective is achieved.

The inclusion of perpetrator intent as a defining characteristic of aggression has received a good deal of attention over the years (Baron and Richardson, 1994; Berkowitz, 1993; Geen, 1991). Clearly, it may be difficult, if not impossible, to know what is in the "heart" or mind of another person. However, failure to include intent in a definition poses difficulties, too. If we merely judge an act on the outcome (for example, whether or not physical or psychological pain is inflicted by an actor), being subjected to an agonizing medical procedure by a health-care professional would be defined as an aggressive act. Conversely, if someone fires a gun at you but the bullet misses its intended mark, the attempt would not be considered an act of aggression if the definition relies solely on the successful delivery of harm to the target. Because of such issues, a majority of aggression researchers consider the actual underlying intent (as opposed to perceived intent as judged by targets or witnesses) as an important defining feature of aggression. I will revisit this discussion below when talking about the role of intent in unethical behavior.

Extending the preceding definition of aggression to organizational settings, *workplace aggression* involves efforts by individuals to harm others in work settings (Neuman and Baron, 1997, 2011). Obviously, the array of behaviors subsumed under this definition is limited only by one's imagination and resources. As relates to aggression in all social contexts, Buss (1961) noted that harm-doing may be described using three dichotomies: (1) physical/verbal, (2) active/passive, and (3) direct/indirect. The physical/verbal category involves harming others with deeds or words, respectively. Active aggression involves doing something to harm another individual, while passive aggression involves withholding something valued or needed by the target. Finally, direct aggression involves face-to-face incidents, while indirect aggression involves harming the target by more circuitous means—for example, harming something or someone that the target values (refer to Table 6.1 for other examples). As noted previously, the primary focus of this chapter is on behavior that is physical, active, and direct in nature.

A number of other issues are relevant to the current discussion. First, consistent with other aggression researchers (e.g., Baron and Richardson, 1994; Huesmann, 1994), I reserve the term "violence" for extreme acts of aggression involving direct physical assault. Second, social scientists make a distinction between proactive (instrumental) and reactive (hostile) forms of aggression (Feshbach, 1964; Poulin and Boivin, 2000; Raine et al., 2006). With respect to instrumental forms of aggression, the harm done to a target may be incidental to obtaining some other objective— as in the case of a victim being harmed during an armed robbery or, possibly, some military or peacekeeping action. In the case of reactive or hostile aggression, the primary objective is to harm the target. Of course, people may be driven by multiple/mixed motives, both hostile and instrumental in nature.

Table 6.1

Examples of Eight Types of Workplace Aggression Categorized According to the Buss (1961) Typology

Physical/verbal dimension	Active/passive dimension	Direct/indirect dimension	
		Direct	Indirect
Physical	Active	Homicide, physical/sexual assault	Theft, sabotage
		Dirty looks, obscene gestures	Consuming/hiding needed resources
		Interrupting others	Defacing property
	Passive	Intentional work slowdowns	Showing up late for meetings
		Refusal to provide needed resources	Delay work making target look bad
		Leave area when target enters	Fail to protect the target's welfare
		Prevent target from expressing self	Causing others to delay important action
Verbal	Active	Yelling, threats, sexual harassment	Spreading rumors, whistle-blowing
		Insults, sarcasm, flaunting status	Transmitting damaging information
		Unfair performance evaluations	Belittling opinions, attacking protégé
	Passive	Fail to return phone calls	Fail to transmit information or defend target
		Silent treatment, damn with faint praise	Fail to deny false rumors
		Refusing target's request	Fail to warn of impending danger

Third, aggression varies in terms of its obviousness and severity. Some forms of aggression are overt in operation, severe in both immediacy and consequences, easily observed by targets and witnesses (e.g., physical assaults, verbal threats, physical gestures, etc.). Covert aggression falls at the other end of the continuum and involves behavior that may not be directly visible to the target or witnesses—often subtle and insidious in nature (Greenberg, 2010). Some violent behaviors may be "covert" in the sense that they are visible to targets but not third parties.

Fourth, in this chapter, I will discuss aggression and violence in both traditional and nontraditional "work" settings; consequently, I employ a rather expansive conceptualization of the term "employee," broadly referring to individuals who are paid to engage in some activity.

Finally, aggressive/violent acts may occur in situations in which the actor lacks the capacity to form the requisite intent to harm. This would include situations in which the actor is suffering from some form of mental illness or acting under the influence of alcohol or a mind-altering substance. As relates to sublethal forms of aggression, actors may not be aware that their behaviors are being perceived as aggressive or may not consider the possibility that their actions are potentially harmful. This might be the case in terms of behaviors that are perceived as rude or disrespectful even when they are not intended as such. In these instances, the behavior would not be intentional (not aggressive) but still be potentially damaging to targets and third parties. This distinction is important to my discussion of unethical behavior, to which I now turn my attention.

Unethical Behavior

With respect to unethical behavior, following Jones (1991), I consider the terms "immoral" and "unethical" to be equivalent and adopt the position that an immoral issue is present when a person's *intentional actions* may harm one or more other individuals. In short, both unethical behavior and aggression involve intentional behavior that is potentially harmful to others. Employing this definition, all instances of aggression, as previously defined, involve immoral/unethical behavior—as they are intended to inflict harm on one or more targets. Certainly, one can postulate that an aggressive act might be employed in the service of accomplishing some "greater good." For example, ethicists discuss such moral dilemmas in their attempts to distinguish between "just" and "unjust" wars (Walzer, 1977). In distinguishing between moral and immoral actions, Walzer (1977) identifies humanitarian *intent* as an important criterion—as in the case of a military intervention launched to save lives or serve as a "just" response to, or deterrence of, aggression by others. I apply a similar criterion when distinguishing between aggressive and nonaggressive acts. Specifically, I consider the presence or absence of intent and, in the case of motivated behavior, whether or not the underlying intention was prosocial or antisocial in nature. In work settings, this consideration comes into play when attempting to distinguish between "tough" and "abusive" leadership. For example, if I assign a difficult job to a subordinate in the hope that it will help this individual develop as a manager, but the employee fails at the task—resulting in damage to his/her career—is that aggression? If my intention was to help and not harm, I would not consider this an act of aggression. On the other hand, the act would be classified as aggressive if my actions were designed to damage the person professionally.

Extending this discussion, one might consider that revenge might be employed to restore justice and discourage future transgressions (Bies and Tripp, 1998; Tripp and Bies, 1997). Again, I believe that the underlying intent of the actor(s) must be considered in defining the action as aggressive or nonaggressive. As in many ethical dilemmas, there may be few answers in absolute terms and one must consider prevailing norms of behavior when attempting to characterize a particular action.

Again, quoting from Jones, "an *unethical act* is defined as either illegal or morally unacceptable to *the larger community*" (1991, p. 367; emphasis added).

While the preceding discussion has focused on questions of moral justice, many acts of aggression are defined as unethical on legal grounds, as codified by laws enacted by the society at large. This would be the case as relates to criminal activities involving fatal and nonfatal physical assault, armed robberies, sexual harassment, and sexual assault. Finally, there are instances of violence that might be considered legal but, nevertheless, immoral/unethical. As I will discuss below, there are people who are employed by "the state," in whole or in part, to kill other people.

Finally, there are other connections between unethical behavior and aggression. Moral/ethical conduct is defined in terms of nonjudicial standards of right and wrong, and this is closely related to well-known antecedents and consequences of aggression—injustice perceptions (Greenberg and Alge, 1998; Neuman, 2004). Specifically, the sense of anger and moral outrage that occurs when actions are viewed as violating important societal norms often triggers aggressive behavior, and, conversely, acts of aggression are typically perceived as unjust and immoral by targets (Harris, 1993)—a form of self-serving bias. "Research has shown that the strongest reactions to organizational injustice occur when an employee perceives both unfair outcomes (distributive injustice) and unfair and unethical procedures and treatment" (Kickul, 2001, p. 289).

In sum, four classes of variables are central to both theories of social justice and theories of human aggression: situations that (1) violate social norms, (2) produce frustration and stress, (3) induce negative affect, and (4) assault individual dignity and self-worth (Neuman and Baron, 1998). These factors are also related to individual well-being.

Well-Being

Well-being is viewed as "the extent to which an individual is satisfied with his/her life, experiences a preponderance of positive affect, and possesses a healthy body and mind" (Giacalone and Promislo, 2010, p. 276). As captured by this definition, well-being is a broad construct encompassing psychological, physiological, and emotional components. As noted by Danna and Griffin:

> While definitions and measures of health and well-being vary, there tend to be two salient person-related concepts that are often combined with a more societal-level perspective. The first is that *health and well-being* can refer to the actual physical health of workers, as defined by physical symptomatology and epidemiological rates of physical illnesses and diseases. The second is that *health and well-being* can refer to the mental, psychological, or emotional aspects of workers as indicated by emotional states and epidemiological rates of mental illnesses and diseases. Adding to these two person-related dimensions are the societal dimensions of health and well-being, such as alcoholism and drug abuse rates and their consequences encompassing both work and non-work factors. (Danna and Griffin, 1999, p. 361; original emphasis)

Although the primary focus of this chapter is on employment-related issues, there is a significant spillover effect between work and nonwork domains. Parenthetically, alcohol and drug abuse are often associated with the causes and consequences of workplace aggression (Barling, 1996; Bennett and Lehman, 1996; McFarlin et al., 2001). Finally, as noted above, the violation of important social norms and the production of negative affect are strongly associated with interpersonal aggression and unethical behavior and incompatible with individual well-being, as discussed below.

THE RELATIONSHIP BETWEEN AGGRESSION AND WELL-BEING

In the section that follows, I examine some of the consequences of aggression on the well-being of primary and secondary victims (direct targets and those individuals witnessing or vicariously exposed to aggression, respectively). Following this, I discuss the impact of engaging in aggression on the well-being of the perpetrators of these actions.

The Impact of Aggression on Primary and Secondary Victims

The most severe and consequential forms of aggression involve acts of violence resulting in death or serious physical injury to one or more primary victims (direct outcomes) as well as psychological and emotional damage to secondary victims (indirect outcomes). In the case of nonfatal physical assault, primary victims suffer both direct and indirect outcomes.

An examination of the trends in workplace homicide between 1993 and 2002 reveals the following. Over that period of time, there were 8,148 workplace homicides. Contrary to the popular conception of workplace violence as involving employees "going postal," 6,682 homicides (81.5 percent) occurred during the course of robberies and other crimes and 669 (8.2 percent) involved current or former employees (Hendricks, Jenkins, and Anderson, 2007). According to the most recent data available (U.S. Bureau of Labor Statistics, 2011), an additional 3,993 workplace homicides occurred between 2003 and 2009. In short, a total of 13,308 homicides occurred between 1992 (the first year that such data were recorded by the Bureau of Labor Statistics) and 2009 ($M = 739$, $SD = 204$). The only good news to report is that workplace homicide rates have generally declined from a high of 1,080 in 1994 to a low of 526 in 2008. According to the most recent preliminary data available, there were 506 homicides in 2010.

In discussing the impact of fatal and nonfatal physical assault on primary and secondary victims of aggression, it is important to understand the nature of the relationship between these individuals, as this has a bearing on the severity of the consequences to individual well-being (Hershcovis and Barling, 2010). As relates to workplace violence, research suggests that perpetrator–victim relationships fall into four categories (State of California/OSHA, 1995; University of Iowa Injury Prevention Research Center, 2001).

Type I violence involves assaults in which the perpetrator is a criminal intruder or organizational outsider. This category includes assailants who have no legitimate relationship with the organization and enter the work location to commit a criminal act. More employees are killed as a result of this type of violence than all of the other types of violence combined. Typically the motive is robbery; consequently, any occupation that involves exchanging money with the public or guarding valuable property or possessions puts employees at increased risk. This would include, but is not limited to, bank employees, bartenders, store owners, stock handlers, security guards, hotel clerks, and taxicab drivers.

Type II violence involves perpetrators who have a relationship with the organization based on the exchange of goods/services (e.g., customers, clients, students, patients) or, as in the case of the criminal justice system, some jurisdictional nexus (violations of civil or criminal law). Data suggest that more than 50 percent of nonfatal assaults occur within this category (LeBlanc and Barling, 2005; Peek-Asa and Howard, 1999). For example, individuals employed in the service sector are at greatest risk and this includes health-care workers, social workers, and retail employees. As relates to health-care workers, violence is most likely to occur in psychiatric settings, geriatric facilities, emergency/trauma centers, and waiting rooms (Kingma, 2001; Lanza, 2006; Lehmann, McCormick, and Kizer, 1999; Merecz et al., 2006). In fact, violence in the health-care sector may constitute almost a quarter of all violence at work (Di Martino, 2002). With respect to social-service workers, they are often put in the position of having to deny service to members of the public or in the extremely dangerous position of removing children from the home.

As one might suspect, psychiatric conditions, alcohol or substance abuse, physical pain, stress, and frustration often play a role in the health-care or social-service sectors, and these are well known antecedents of aggression and violence. As relates to the definitions employed in this chapter, individuals lashing out against others as a result of some underlying psychiatric condition or alcohol/substance-induced impairment of their judgment process and impulse control would not qualify as aggressive or unethical. While these conditions might serve as mitigating factors on theoretical, judicial, and moral grounds, the consequences to the well-being of primary and secondary victims are palpable.

Type III violence involves organizational insiders—current or former employees. This category subsumes the prototypical examples of workplace violence captured by the expression, "going postal." The important defining characteristic associated with this category is that the violence is motivated (or at least triggered) by factors occurring within an organization (Baron and Neuman, 1996; O'Leary-Kelly, Griffin, and Glew, 1996; Spector, 1975).

Type IV violence involves instances in which the perpetrators and victims of an incident have some personal relationship (e.g., domestic violence that spills over into the workplace). As noted by LeBlanc and Barling (2005), the issue of domestic violence has received little attention from workplace violence researchers. In the case of Type IV violence, the perpetrators have no relationship with the organization but have a personal relationship with the victim—or intended victim. In those instances in which perpetrators follow their targets into the workplace, many people—including the intended victim—are at risk. In 1997, 5 percent of workplace homicides were the result of domestic violence, and a more recent study estimated that 2 percent of nonfatal violence was associated with partner violence (LeBlanc and Barling, 2005). In 1990, the Bureau of National Affairs estimated that domestic violence resulted in $3–5 billion annually due to turnover, absenteeism, health-care costs, and lowered productivity (White et al., 2002). In addition, research also suggests that batterers often make harassing phone calls to their victims and their supervisors (LeBlanc and Barling, 2005).

The impact on individual well-being will vary in severity, depending upon (a) the nature and severity of the violence (extending from threats and intimidation, through nonfatal physical/sexual assaults, to homicide), (b) the nature of the relationship between the perpetrator and the victim, (c) the proximity of the individual to the incident, (d) the frequency of violence in particular work settings or occupations, and (e) the likelihood/predictability of future incidents.

Beyond the obvious impact of homicide on primary victims, research demonstrates that fatal assaults result in indirect harm to secondary victims. These individuals are likely to suffer from fear of future violence, generalized anxiety, depression, and a range of other emotional reactions, such as anger and survivor guilt (Baron, 1993; Mantell and Albrecht, 1994). For those in close proximity to the violence, post-traumatic stress reactions are common, along with a range of psychosomatic disorders (Høgh and Viitasara, 2005; Miller, 2005; Rippon, 2000). The impact of workplace violence on employee well-being is further evidenced by the number of disability and workers' compensation claims, decreased levels of productivity, and employee turnover, associated with the aftermath of workplace violence (Mannila, 2008; Mueller and Tschan, 2011). The impact of violence may spread beyond the workplace as customers and clients become fearful of dealing with the organization (Neuman, 2012).

Also, as relates to secondary victims, workplace violence affects the well-being of immediate family members, other relatives, and friends of the victims and perpetrators of workplace shootings. Obviously, family members must deal with the sudden loss of a loved one and, along with other relatives and friends, deal with shock and grief. Sometimes these individuals have to deal with their grief in public ways, for example, when dealing with reporters pursuing the story. In the case of the families of perpetrators, they have to deal with the stigma and their failure to prevent the tragedy.

People employed by an organization in which violence has occurred, but not actually present during the incident, may be affected in numerous ways. In many instances, people may have missed work the day of the incident, for a variety of reasons. Often, they relive their near-death experience and revisit the random events that apparently saved their lives. This begins a process of ruminating in which these individuals consider what might have happened had fate not intervened. Left untreated, this can result in long-term psychological damage.

Whether talking about fatal or nonfatal forms of physical aggression or nonphysical (psychological) forms of aggression, most research examining the impact of aggression on well-being employs a stressor–stress–strain model. According to this perspective, all forms of aggression and violence serve as potential stressors that may elicit stress reactions, often leading to strain—in the form of psychological (e.g., frustration, dissatisfaction), emotional (e.g., fear, anxiety, depression), physical (e.g., headaches, dizziness, gastrointestinal distress, increased blood pressure), and behavioral (e.g., turnover, accidents, substances abuse) reactions. This relationship has been demonstrated on an array of harmful behaviors including workplace bullying, mobbing, abusive supervision, sexual harassment, incivility, counterproductive work behavior, social undermining, and emotional abuse. For example, psychologically abusive workplace behavior has been associated with increases in ambulatory blood pressure (Wager, Fieldman, and Hussey, 2001, 2003), sleep disturbances (Niedhammer et al., 2009), gastrointestinal disturbances and suicidal thoughts (Leymann, 1990; Roland, 2002). These consequences extend to bystanders who witness such workplace harassment. Research demonstrates that witnesses are at increased risk for depression, fear and anxiety, guilt, and insecurity (Vartia, 2001). As the consequences of many of these nonphysical forms of aggression will be discussed in other chapters of this book, I now turn my attention to something that has received little attention—the impact of aggression on perpetrators.

The Impact of Aggression on the Well-Being of Perpetrators

A good deal of literature in the area of interpersonal aggression has focused on the antecedents of aggression—why, and under what circumstances, individuals engage in aggression against others. That is why aggression researchers have tended to focus their attention on actor intent. However, little empirical work has focused on the well-being of the actors initiating aggression against others. Consequently, some of the ideas I propose in the sections that follow should be considered speculative in nature.

The Actors/Perpetrators

When individuals observe others engaged in aggressive interactions, they tend to believe that the aggression they are observing is caused by the personalities of the people involved in the altercation. In part, this may relate to the actor–observer effect, in which observers tend to discount the role of situational factors and attribute the cause of others' behavior to characteristics of the actor (Jones and Nisbett, 1971; Nisbett et al., 1973, 1982). Of course, it is certainly true that aggression may, in fact, be related to individual difference characteristics. These would include, but are not limited to, antisocial personality disorder/psychopathic behavior (Lykken, 1995), narcissism (Wu and Lebreton, 2011), Machiavellianism (Christie and Geis, 1970), type-A behavior pattern (Baron, Neuman, and Geddes, 1999; Edguer and Janisse, 1994), low impulse control (Hynan and Grush, 1986), negative affectivity (Barling, Dupré, and Kelloway, 2009), trait anger (Douglas and Martinko, 2001), disagreeableness (Tepper, Duffy, and Shaw, 2001), hostile attributional bias (Lanza et al., 1996), and high self-esteem (Baumeister, 2001; Baumeister, Smart, and Boden, 1996).

In light of all these personal antecedents to aggression, it is easy to believe that many people "enjoy" or are "indifferent" to the harm that they inflict on others. However, as is the case with most human behavior, aggression is determined by the interplay of an assortment of personal, social, and situational factors. Consequently, the majority of people who engage in aggression are not likely to be dispassionate and detached about the process or outcomes. In fact, reactive aggression characterizes a large proportion of workplace aggression and bullying (Neuman and Baron, 2011). Therefore, contemporary models of reactive aggression may prove useful in understanding the potential impact of aggression on aggressors.

The general affective aggression model (GAAM) (Anderson, 1997; Anderson, Anderson, and Deuser, 1996; Neuman and Baron, 2005) is a well-established model of reactive aggression that demonstrates how personal (dispositional) and situational (e.g., stress, frustration, injustice perceptions, and norm violations) factors may trigger a process that leads to aggression. Central to this model is the finding that the following three critical internal states serve as important antecedents to aggression: (1) physiological arousal, (2) negative affect, and (3) hostile cognitions. Any stimulus that triggers one or more of these internal states may increase the likelihood of an aggressive response. Key to the current discussion, each of these three internal states has the ability to elicit the other two. For example, increased physiological arousal may elicit negative affect and hostile cognitions. Similarly, the process may begin with either negative affect or hostility-related cognitions. In short, there may be a physiological, psychological, and emotional price to be paid for engaging in aggressive behavior—especially over time. As in the case of the type-A behavior pattern, it is well established that the hostility component of this dispositional characteristic is related to coronary heart disease and other adverse consequences to well-being (Edguer and Janisse, 1994; Evans, Palsane, and Carrere, 1987; Friedman and Rosenman, 1974; Spector and O'Connell, 1994). Furthermore, as defined earlier, the experience of negative affect, dissonant cognitions, and unpleasant physiological arousal are associated with a state of diminished well-being—regardless of the expression of these states in actual acts of aggression. That is, anger does not have to be expressed for it to have an adverse impact on individual well-being (Martin et al., 1999). In fact, anger has been identified as a psychological/emotional strain (Jex and Beehr, 1991).

Assuming, as the evidence suggests, that the majority of people find interpersonal confrontations unpleasant, I suspect that engaging in such activities (even when justified, from the actor's perspective) requires a substantial amount of "emotional labor." This would be especially true in situations in which people see their own aggression against others as a necessary job requirement (e.g., the need to project power and avoid the appearance of weakness) but feel that such behavior is inherently coercive and unethical. As suggested by Greenberg (1997), as relates to theft, people may believe that stealing is wrong but steal for prosocial reasons (e.g., adherence to supervisory or group norms condoning or encouraging theft). Similarly, individuals may engage in aggressive or deviant tactics even when they find the behavior unethical or distasteful (Bennett et al., 2005).

Of course, there are more direct ways in which aggression against others leads to adverse consequences to well-being. As demonstrated in the reciprocity and revenge literatures, people often look for ways to even the score. As a result, aggressors must weigh the consequences of their actions on their own well-being. As noted by Björkqvist, Osterman, and Lagerspetz:

The effect/danger ratio is an expression of the subjective estimation of the likely consequences of an aggressive act. The aggressor assesses the relation between a) the effect of the intended strategy, and b) the dangers involved, physical, psychological or social, for him/herself, and for people important to him/her. The objective is to find a technique that will be effective and at the same time, incur as little danger as possible. The aggressor tries to maximize the effect, and to minimize the risks involved. For example, physical aggression is effective but also risky, and if unsuccessful, the aggressor is likely to get hurt him/herself. (1994, pp. 28–29)

As described in the revenge literature, this fear is quite justified (Bies and Tripp, 1996; Bies, Tripp, and Kramer, 1997; Lee, 1989; Tripp and Bies, 1997). A review of Table 6.1 clearly suggests that aggressors have an array of tactics they can employ to harm their targets, and many of these strategies are covert in operation. For this and other reasons, no accurate data exist on the nature and number of "paybacks" that may be dished out by targets on perpetrators. Readers are encouraged to review the possibilities in the privacy of their own thoughts (and revenge fantasies).

Type V Violence

At this point, I introduce another category into the four-factor typology of violence presented earlier. I believe that we might consider instances of "state-sanctioned" violence against others. These incidents occur in nontraditional work settings—for example, the case of executioners employed in various state correctional facilities charged with carrying out sentences for capital crimes. As of September 2011, thirty-four states in the United States sanctioned the death penalty. Since 1976, there have been 1,276 executions in this country, including 734 (58 percent of the total) in the preceding twelve years (Death Penalty Information Center, 2011). Between January and September 2011, 37 people were executed, and other condemned prisoners await their fate.

Regardless of your position on the death penalty, there are certainly consequences for the people being executed as well as the people doing the executing. In the song, "A Hard Rain's A-Gonna Fall," Bob Dylan observes that "The executioner's face is always hidden." This speaks to the stigma attached to the job as well as fear of retribution for carrying out the act. In addition, to mitigate the psychological and emotional consequences attached to executions, society has endeavored to make the process as mechanical, anonymous, and impersonal as possible. Gone are the days when one person would pull the lever (hanging), the trigger (firing squads), or the switch (electrocution). Now, in the case of lethal injection, a mechanical device actually "pushes" the plunger delivering the lethal cocktail. But, someone has to give that order. Someone has to set up and activate the device. Individuals have to escort the condemned prisoner to the death chamber, strap that individual to a gurney, insert the needle, observe the deed, and pick up the corpse. The Devil truly is in the details. Recently, five retired wardens and one senior-level correction official sent a letter to the Georgia Department of Corrections requesting a stay of execution. In this letter (which, by the way, was unsuccessful), these officials focused attention on the toll that executions take on the individuals charged with imposing the penalty. In part, the letter said:

Living with the nightmares is something that we know from experience. No one has the right to ask a public servant to take on a lifelong sentence of nagging doubt, and for some of us, shame and guilt. Should our justice system be causing so much harm to so many people when there is an alternative? (Savali, 2011, paragraph 5)

Similarly, Lifton and Mitchell (2000) describe a retired executioner's years of physical, psychological, and emotional suffering resulting from his "job." In the words of this person, an execution is like "being in a car wreck that's going on forever" (Lifton and Mitchell, 2000, p. 89). This is consistent with clinical psychological research demonstrating that criminal offenders experience an assortment of traumatic responses in the aftermath of committing violence (Byrne, 2003; Evans et al., 2007). Finally, some executioners have committed suicide rather than continue to live with the lingering trauma (Gonnerman, 2005).

Another nontraditional "job" setting involves our military and peacekeeping forces engaged around the globe. Even in those instances in which people are highly trained and carefully selected for service, killing may take a toll. Not all the targets of lethal force are reviled, as in the case of the mastermind of 9/11. While the members of our elite and famed SEAL Team 6 have the support of a nation and a sense of moral justification for their actions, what about combat soldiers and peacekeepers who are called on to employ lethal force in more ambiguous and ethically questionable circumstances? While these may not fit your prototypical image of a "job," these individuals are employed to engage in legally sanctioned violence, which has significant short- and long-term consequences for their well-being (Inness and Barling, 2006).

CONCLUDING COMMENTS

In this chapter, I have discussed the interrelationships of aggression, unethical behavior, and employee well-being. While this discussion has been necessarily brief, it should be clear that all forms of aggression have the potential to adversely affect the well-being of primary and secondary victims. To a large degree, the impact of aggression on well-being relates to the relationship between actors and targets, the nature and severity of the aggression, the frequency of occurrence, and the likelihood and predictability of future incidents. The outcomes can range from death or nonfatal physical injury through an assortment of psychological, emotional, and physiological consequences.

In addition, I have discussed the effect of engaging in violence on the well-being of aggressors, as relates to executioners and peacekeepers. I realize that these are extreme examples and not typical of most work-related contexts. However, these are paid jobs in which people are employed to harm (or must be prepared to harm) others. Currently, these professions have received little or no attention in the workplace violence literature (for an exception, see Inness and Barling, 2006). Also, I have suggested that contemporary theories of aggression (which include stressor–stress–strain components) suggest that there may be psychological, emotional, and physiological consequences for contemplating and engaging in aggression against others. This is especially true in a wide variety of situations in which actors engage in reactive aggression or feel compelled or "encouraged" to engage in instrumental aggression, as a function of their jobs. While it is customary for people to assign individual blame for the aggression they witness, the research literature is replete with examples of social/relational, situational, and environmental antecedents to aggression. Consequently, I think it is important to explore the impact of aggression on the well-being of the actors as well as targets.

Considering that this chapter has focused on the dark side of human behavior, I would like to end on a positive note. While it is true that aggression is all too common in work and other social settings, there are indications that violence has been declining in the American workplace. While there may be no clear reason for this relatively short-term trend, Steven Pinker (2011) presents intriguing and counterintuitive data showing a decline in violence throughout history. Believe it or not, we are living in a much less violent world than has historically been the case—a trend, I am sure, that each of us hopes will continue.

REFERENCES

Anderson, C.A. 1997. Effects of violent movies and trait hostility on hostile feelings and aggressive thoughts. *Aggressive Behavior,* 23, 161–178.

Anderson, C.A.; Anderson, K.B.; and Deuser, W.E. 1996. Examining an affective aggression framework: Weapon and temperature effects on aggressive thoughts, affect, and attitudes. *Personality and Social Psychology Bulletin,* 22, 366–376.

Barling, J. 1996. The prediction, experience, and consequences of workplace violence. In *Violence on the Job: Identifying Risks and Developing Solutions*, ed. G.R. VandenBos and E.Q. Bulatao, 29–49. Washington, DC: American Psychological Association.

Barling, J.; Dupré, K.E.; and Kelloway, E.K. 2009. Predicting workplace aggression and violence. *Annual Review of Psychology,* 60, 671–692.

Baron, R.A., and Neuman, J.H. 1996. Workplace violence and workplace aggression: Evidence on their relative frequency and potential causes. *Aggressive Behavior,* 22, 161–173.

Baron, R.A.; Neuman, J.H.; and Geddes, D. 1999. Social and personal determinants of workplace aggression: Evidence for the impact of perceived injustice and the Type A Behavior Pattern. *Aggressive Behavior,* 25, 281–296.

Baron, R.A., and Richardson, D.R. 1994. *Human Aggression.* 2nd ed. New York: Plenum.

Baron, S.A. 1993. *Violence in the Workplace: A Prevention and Management Guide for Business.* Ventura, CA: Pathfinder.

Baumeister, R.F. 2001. Violent pride: Do people turn violent because of self-hate, or self-love? *Scientific American,* 284, 4, 96, 98–101.

Baumeister, R.F.; Smart, L.; and Boden, J.M. 1996. Relation of threatened egotism to violence and aggression: The dark side of high self-esteem. *Psychological Review,* 103, 5–33.

Bennett, J.B., and Lehman, W.E.K. 1996. Alcohol, antagonism, and witnessing violence in the workplace: Drinking climates and social alienation—integration. In *Violence on the Job: Identifying Risks and Developing Solutions,* ed. G.R. VandenBos and E.Q. Bulatao, 105–152. Washington, DC: American Psychological Association.

Bennett, R.J.; Aquino, K.; Reed II, A.; and Thau, S. 2005. The normative nature of employee deviance and the impact of moral identity. In *Counterproductive Work Behavior: Investigations of Actors and Targets,* ed. S. Fox and P.E. Spector, 107–125. Washington, DC: American Psychological Association.

Berkowitz, L. 1993. *Aggression: Its Causes, Consequences, and Control.* Philadelphia, PA: Temple University Press.

Bies, R.J., and Tripp, T.M. 1996. Beyond distrust: Getting even and the need for revenge. In *Trust in Organizations,* ed. R.M. Kramerand and R. Tyler, 246–260. Thousand Oaks, CA: Sage.

———. 1998. Doing justice: The motivational dynamics of revenge. In *Advances in Organizational Justice Theories: The Motivation to Engage in Dysfunctional Behavior,* ed. A.M. O'Leary-Kelly and D.P. Skarlicki. Symposium conducted at the meeting of the Academy of Management, San Diego, CA, August 20, 1998.

Bies, R.J.; Tripp, T.M.; and Kramer, R.M. 1997. At the breaking point: Cognitive and social dynamics of revenge in organizations. In *Antisocial Behavior in Organizations*, ed. R.A. Giacalone and J. Greenberg, 18–36. Thousand Oaks, CA: Sage.

Björkqvist, K.; Osterman, K.; and Lagerspetz, K.M.J. 1994. Sex differences in covert aggression among adults. *Aggressive Behavior,* 20, 27–33.

Buss, A.H. 1961. *The Psychology of Aggression.* New York: Wiley.

Byrne, M.K. 2003. Trauma reactions in the offender. *International Journal of Forensic Psychology,* 1, 59–70.

Christie, R., and Geis, F.L. 1970. *Studies in Machiavellianism.* New York: Academic Press.

Danna, K., and Griffin, R.W. 1999. Health and well-being in the workplace: A review and synthesis of the literature. *Journal of Management,* 25, 357–384.

Death Penalty Information Center. 2011. Facts about the death penalty. www. deathpenaltyinfo. org/documents/FactSheet. pdf (accessed September 29, 2011).

Di Martino, V. 2002. Workplace violence in the health sector: Country case studies Brazil, Bulgaria, Lebanon, Portugal, South Africa, Thailand, plus an additional Australian study. Synthesis report. www. who. int/violence_injury_prevention/violence/activities/workplace/WVsynthesisreport.pdf (accessed October 9, 2009).

Douglas, S.C., and Martinko, M.J. 2001. Exploring the role of individual differences in the prediction of workplace aggression. *Journal of Applied Psychology,* 86, 547–559.

Edguer, N., and Janisse, M.P. 1994. Type A behaviour and aggression: Provocation, conflict and cardio-vascular responsivity in the Buss teacher-learner paradigm. *Personality and Individual Differences,* 17, 377–393.

Evans, C.; Ehlers, A.; Mezey, G.; and Clark, D.M. 2007. Intrusive memories in perpetrators of violent crime: Emotions and cognitions. *Journal of Consulting and Clinical Psychology,* 75, 134–144.

Evans, G.W.; Palsane, M.N.; and Carrere, S. 1987. Type A behavior and occupational stress: A cross-cultural study of blue-collar workers. *Journal of Personality and Social Psychology,* 52, 1002–1007.

Feshbach, S. 1964. The function of aggression and the regulation of aggressive drive. *Psychological Review,* 71, 257–272.

Friedman, M., and Rosenman, R.H. 1974. *Type A Behavior and Your Heart.* New York: Knopf.

Geen, R.G. 1991. *Human Aggression.* Pacific Grove, CA: Brooks/Cole.

Giacalone, R.A., and Promislo, M.D. 2010. Unethical and unwell: Decrements in well-being and unethical activity at work. *Journal of Business Ethics,* 91, 275–297.

Gonnerman, J. 2005. The last executioner. *Village Voice,* 50, 4 (January 26), 28–31.

Greenberg, J. 1997. The STEAL motive: Managing the social determinants of employee theft. In *Antisocial Behavior in Organizations,* ed. R.A. Giacalone and J. Greenberg, 85–108. Thousand Oaks, CA: Sage.

———. (ed.). 2010. *Insidious Workplace Behavior.* Hillsdale, NJ: Routledge Academic.

Greenberg, J., and Alge, B.J. 1998. Aggressive reactions to workplace injustice. In *Dysfunctional Behavior in Organizations: Violent and Deviant Behavior.* Vol. 23, part A, ed. R.W. Griffin, A.M. O'Leary-Kelly, and J.M. Collins, 83–117. Stamford, CT: JAI Press.

Harris, M.B. 1993. How provoking! What makes men and women angry? *Aggressive Behavior,* 19, 199–211.

Hendricks, S.A.; Jenkins, L.E.; and Anderson, K.R. 2007. Trends in workplace homicides in the U.S., 1993–2002: A decade of decline. *American Journal of Industrial Medicine,* 50, 316–325.

Hershcovis, M.S., and Barling, J. 2010. Towards a multi-foci approach to workplace aggression: A meta-analytic review of outcomes from different perpetrators. *Journal of Organizational Behavior,* 31, 24–44.

Høgh, A., and Viitasara, E. 2005. A systematic review of longitudinal studies of nonfatal workplace violence. *European Journal of Work and Organizational Psychology,* 14, 291–313.

Huesmann, L.R. (ed.). 1994. *Aggression: Current Perspectives.* New York: Plenum.

Hynan, D.J., and Grush, J.E. 1986. Effects of impulsivity, depression, provocation, and time on aggressive behavior. *Journal of Research in Personality,* 20, 158–171.

Inness, M., and Barling, J. 2006. Violence in peacekeeping. In *Handbook of Workplace Violence,* ed. E.K. Kelloway, J. Barling, and J.J. Hurrell Jr., 309–329. Thousand Oaks, CA: Sage.

Jex, S.M., and Beehr, T.A. 1991. Emerging theoretical and methodological issues in the study of work-related stress. *Research in Personnel and Human Resources Management,* 9, 311–365.

Jones, E.E., and Nisbett, R.E. 1971. *The Actor and the Observer: Divergent Perceptions of the Causes of Behavior.* Morristown, NJ: General Learning Press.

Jones, T.M. 1991. Ethical decision making by individuals in organizations: An issue-contingent model. *Academy of Management Review,* 16, 366–395.

Kickul, J. 2001. When organizations break their promises: Employee reactions to unfair processes and treatment. *Journal of Business Ethics,* 29, 289–307.

Kingma, M. 2001. Workplace violence in the health sector: A problem of epidemic proportion. *International Nursing Review,* 48, 129–130.

Lanza, M.L. 2006. Violence in nursing. In *Handbook of Workplace Violence,* ed. E.K. Kelloway, J. Barling, and J.J. Hurrell Jr., 147–167. Thousand Oaks, CA: Sage.

Lanza, M.L.; Kayne, H.L.; Pattison, I.; Hicks, C.; Islam, S.; Bradshaw, J.; et al. 1996. The relationship of behavioral cues to assaultive behavior. *Clinical Nursing Research,* 5, 6–26.

LeBlanc, M.M., and Barling, J. 2005. Understanding the many faces of workplace violence. In *Counterproductive Work Behavior: Investigations of Actors and Targets,* ed. S. Fox and P.E. Spector, 41–63. Washington, DC: American Psychological Association.

Lee, E.L. 1989. Violent avengers. *Security Management,* 33, 38–41.

Lehmann, L.S.; McCormick, R.A.; and Kizer, K.W. 1999. A survey of assaultive behavior in Veterans Health Administration Facilities. *Psychiatric Services,* 50, 384–389.

Leymann, H. 1990. Mobbing and psychological terror at workplaces. *Violence and Victims,* 5, 119–126.

Lifton, R.J., and Mitchell, G. 2000. *Who Owns Death? Capital Punishment, the American Conscience, and the End of Execution*. New York: HarperCollins.

Lykken, D.T. 1995. *The Antisocial Personalities*. Hillsdale, NJ: Erlbaum.

Mannila, C. 2008. How to avoid becoming a workplace violence statistic. *Training and Development*, 62, 7, 60–65.

Mantell, M., and Albrecht, S. 1994. *Ticking Bombs: Defusing Violence in the Workplace*. Burr Ridge, IL: Irwin Professional.

Martin, R.; Wan, C.K.; David, J.P.; Wegner, E.L.; Olson, B.D.; and Watson, D. 1999. Style of anger expression: Relation to expressivity, personality, and health. *Personality and Social Psychology Bulletin*, 25, 1196–1207.

McFarlin, S.K.; Fals-Stewart, W.; Major, D.A.; and Justice, E.M. 2001. Alcohol use and workplace aggression: An examination of perpetration and victimization. *Journal of Substance Abuse*, 13, 303–321.

Merecz, D.; Rymaszewska, J.; Mościcka, A.; Kiejna, A.; and Jarosz-Nowak, J. 2006. Violence at the workplace: A questionnaire survey of nurses. *European Psychiatry*, 21, 442–450.

Miller, L. 2005. Workplace violence and psychological trauma: Clinical disability, legal liability, and corporate policy. www.doereport.com/article_workplaceviolence.php (accessed January 26, 2006).

Mueller, S., and Tschan, F. 2011. Consequences of client-initiated workplace violence: The role of fear and perceived prevention. *Journal of Occupational Health Psychology*, January 17. Advance online publication. doi: 10.1037/a0021723.

Neuman, J.H. 2004. Injustice, stress, and aggression in organizations. In *The Dark Side of Organizational Behavior*, ed. R.W. Griffin and A.M. O'Leary-Kelly, 62–102. San Francisco, CA: Jossey-Bass.

———. 2012. Workplace violence and aggression: When you do not want your company on the news. In *Work and Quality of Life: Ethical Practices in Organizations*, ed. N.P. Reilly, M.J. Sirgy, and C.A. Gorman, 343–373. New York: Springer.

Neuman, J.H., and Baron, R.A. 1997. Aggression in the workplace. In *Antisocial Behavior in Organizations*, ed. R. Giacalone and J. Greenberg, 37–67. Thousand Oaks, CA: Sage.

———. 1998. Perceived injustice as a cause of—and justification for—workplace aggression and violence. In *Advances in Organizational Justice Theories: The Motivation to Engage in Dysfunctional Behavior*, ed. A.M. O'Leary-Kelly and D.P. Skarlicki. Symposium conducted at the meeting of the Academy of Management, San Diego, CA, August 20, 1998.

———. 2005. Aggression in the workplace: A social psychological perspective. In *Counterproductive Work Behavior: Investigations of Actors and Targets*, ed. S. Fox and P.E. Spector, 13–40. Washington, DC: American Psychological Association.

———. 2011. Social antecedents of bullying: A social interactionist perspective. In *Bullying and Harassment in the Workplace: Developments in Theory, Research, and Practice*, 2d ed., ed. S. Einarsen, H. Hoel, D. Zapf, and D.L. Cooper, 201–225. London: CRC Press.

Niedhammer, I.; David, S.; Degioanni, S.; Drummond, A.; and Philip, P. 2009. Workplace bullying and sleep disturbances: Findings from a large scale cross-sectional survey in the French working population. *Sleep*, 32, 1211–1219.

Nisbett, R.E.; Caputo, C.; Legant, P.; and Marecek, J. 1973. Behavior as seen by the actor and as seen by the observer. *Journal of Personality and Social Psychology*, 27, 154–164.

———. 1982. Behavior as seen by the actor and as seen by the observer. In *Contemporary Issues in Social Psychology*, 4th ed., ed. J.C. Brigham and L.S. Wrightsman, 288–300. Monterey, CA: Brooks/Cole.

O'Leary-Kelly, A.M.; Griffin, R.W.; and Glew, D.J. 1996. Organization-motivated aggression: A research framework. *Academy of Management Review*, 21, 225–253.

Peek-Asa, C., and Howard, J. 1999. Workplace-violence investigations by the California Division of Occupational Safety and Health, 1993–1996. *Journal of Occupational and Environmental Medicine*, 41, 647–653.

Pinker, S. 2011. *The Better Angels of Our Nature: Why Violence Has Declined*. New York: Viking.

Poulin, F., and Boivin, M. 2000. Reactive and proactive aggression: Evidence of a two-factor model. *Psychological Assessment*, 12, 115–122.

Raine, A.; Dodge, K.; Loeber, R.; Gatzke-Kopp, L.; Lynam, D.; Reynolds, C.; et al. 2006. The reactive-proactive aggression questionnaire: Differential correlates of reactive and proactive aggression in adolescent boys. *Aggressive Behavior*, 32, 159–171.

Rippon, T.J. 2000. Aggression and violence in health care professions. *Journal of Advanced Nursing*, 31, 452–460.

Roland, E. 2002. Bullying, depressive symptoms and suicidal thoughts. *Educational Research,* 44, 55–68.

Savali, K.W. 2011. Breaking news: Warden of prison where Troy Davis is held asks for stay of execution. *Your Black World,* September 22. http://yourblackworld.com/2011/09/22/breaking-news-warden-of-prison-where-troy-davis-is-held-asks-for-stay-of-execution/ (accessed September 22, 2011).

Spector, P.E. 1975. Relationship of organizational frustration with reported behavioral reactions of employees. *Journal of Applied Psychology,* 60, 635–637.

Spector, P.E., and O'Connell, B.J. 1994. The contribution of personality traits, negative affectivity, locus of control and type A to the subsequent reports of job stressors and job strains. *Journal of Occupational and Organizational Psychology,* 67, 1–11.

State of California, Division of Occupational Safety and Health (Cal/OSHA). 1995. *Guidelines for Workplace Security.* March 30. www.dir.ca.gov/dosh/dosh%5Fpublications/worksecurity.html (accessed March 30, 1995).

Tepper, B.J.; Duffy, M.K.; and Shaw, J.D. 2001. Personality moderators of the relationship between abusive supervision and subordinates' resistance. *Journal of Applied Psychology,* 86, 974–983.

Tripp, T.M., and Bies, R.J. 1997. What's good about revenge? The avenger's perspective. In *Research on Negotiation in Organizations,* vol. 6, ed. R.J. Lewicki, R.J. Bies, and B.H. Sheppard, 145–160. Greenwich, CT: JAI Press.

University of Iowa Injury Prevention Research Center. 2001. *Workplace Violence: A Report to the Nation.* February. www.nyspef.org/stopworkplaceviolence/files/report_to_the_nation.pdf (accessed February 2001).

U.S. Bureau of Labor Statistics. 2011. Number of fatal work injuries, 1992–2009. Table. www.bls.gov/iif/oshwc/cfoi/cfch0008.pdf (accessed August 12, 2011).

Vartia, M. 2001. Consequences of workplace bullying with respect to the well-being of its targets and the observers of bullying. *Scandinavian Journal of Work, Environment and Health,* 27, 63–69.

Wager, N.; Fieldman, G.; and Hussey, T. 2001. The impact of perceptions of supervisor style upon employees' blood pressure. *Consciousness and Experiential Psychology,* 6, 5–11.

———. 2003. The effect on ambulatory blood pressure of working under favorably and unfavorably perceived supervisors. *Occupational and Environmental Medicine,* 60, 468–474.

Walzer, M. 1977. *Just and Unjust Wars: A Moral Argument with Historical Illustrations.* 3d ed. New York: Basic Books.

White, D.D.; Kinczkowski, L.M.; Speelman, P.; and Olijnyk, M.J. 2002. Is domestic violence about to spill into your client's workplace? *Michigan Bar Journal,* 81, 28–31.

Wu, J., and Lebreton, J.M. 2011. Reconsidering the dispositional basis of counterproductive work behavior: The role of aberrant personality. *Personnel Psychology,* 64, 593–626.

PART II

HARMFUL BEHAVIORS AND
WORK STRESS

7

THE IMPACT OF OSTRACISM ON WELL-BEING IN ORGANIZATIONS

JANE O'REILLY, SANDRA L. ROBINSON, AND KIRA F. SCHABRAM

Unethical behavior in organizations is often social in nature. Decades of research, under the guises of incivility, aggression, interpersonal injustice, revenge, harassment, social undermining, or interpersonal deviance (Robinson and Greenberg, 1998), have identified the many ways by which organizational members hurt one another. Although these dysfunctional, overt, and direct relations obviously threaten the well-being of organizational members, we propose that a more common, yet possibly more harmful, type of interaction is passive and covert in nature, namely, ignoring, excluding, or ostracizing others in the workplace.

In this chapter, we discuss the nature of ostracism in the workplace, explaining how it is a more socially acceptable and preferred mode of social interaction because it is perceived as relatively harmless and more ethical. However, as we will explicate, ostracism and social exclusion are in fact very harmful, impacting the well-being of their targets, their instigators, third-party witnesses, and organizations themselves.

OSTRACISM IN THE WORKPLACE

Familiar forms of harmful social behaviors, such as aggression, harassment, and interpersonal deviance, involve overt interactions that serve the actor at the expense of the target and/or the organization. These unethical behaviors can fill various functions, but often are intended to cause harm to another, and often succeed in doing so. Indeed, we know that being subjected to these behaviors increases stress, emotional distress, depression, and even physical ailments (e.g. Hoobler et al., 2010; LeBlanc and Kelloway, 2002). Likewise, they take a toll on organizations, increasing their legal liability and the costs associated with underproduction, absenteeism, and turnover (Barling and Phillips, 1993; Berkley and Kaplan, 2009; Dittrich and Carrell, 1979; Donovan, Drasgow, and Munsen, 1998). Given the costs, organizations enact injunctions against these behaviors, such as reinforcing norms that constrain overt expressions of hostility or conflict, crafting antiharassment policies, or conducting investigations to weed out and punish offenders who have committed the more serious violations.

For the most part, organizational members themselves tend to toe the line. Organizational members are constrained from engaging in overtly harmful behavior with one another to the extent that it violates norms, is formally prohibited, and/or increases the likelihood of punishment (Johns, 1991; Robinson, 1993; Robinson and O'Leary-Kelly, 1998). However, if organizational members tend to eschew overtly harmful behavior, how do they grapple with inevitable conflict or strong negative feelings toward each other? Research suggests that one of the most common ways that organizational members may choose to hurt one another is by engaging in ostracism, when a group or individual ignores, rejects, or socially excludes another individual or group in a given social context (Ferris et al., 2008; Williams, 1997). Examples of ostracism in organizations include having one's greetings go ignored by colleagues, being left out of an important e-mail chain, or being uninvited and unwelcomed to join one's work group for lunch and social gatherings.

Although one may engage in ostracism for many reasons and it is not always intended to cause harm, a common motive for ostracism is to punish, retaliate against, or hurt others (Williams, 1997). One may argue that such behavior can be extremely functional for individuals and groups, as a means by which to rein in problematic behavior and encourage appropriate group and organizational behavior. And rather than engaging in verbal aggression, harassment, or other overtly hostile behaviors, one can opt for the use of the "silent treatment" to achieve these goals. In line with this perspective of ostracism, many whistle-blowers are shunned, rejected, and unsupported by their colleagues and supervisors as a form of punishment for disrupting the status quo (Miceli and Near, 1992). The advantage of ignoring, excluding, and ostracizing others at work is that it appears to pose little risk to the actor. Unlike more overt acts of aggression, ignoring others is typically perceived by most as harmless and socially acceptable within their organization (O'Reilly et al., 2011). Beyond the organization, children's "time-outs" and prisoners' solitary confinement are both perceived as humane ways of curbing unwanted behavior. Moreover, giving someone the silent treatment does not require the expression of emotion, and therefore appears "more professional" and tolerable in organizations. As a result, relatively few social norms or formal policies oppose such behavior. Even if such constraints exist, ignoring, excluding, and ostracizing is subtle, often invisible to anyone but the target, and therefore easily refuted by the actor if he or she is called out. Individuals or groups can often engage in such behavior with relative impunity. Not surprisingly, in our research we find that ostracizing behaviors are somewhat more common in the workplace than more overt or obviously harmful forms of social mistreatment (O'Reilly et al., 2011).

Despite the frequency and social acceptability of ostracism, and its perceived lack of harm, we contend that ostracism is far from innocuous. Thus, although one can argue that it is functional for regulating and encouraging others' organizational behavior, we contend that it may be unethical because of the undue harm it can cause. Indeed, in the next sections of this chapter, we present arguments and empirical evidence to show that ostracism is as harmful as more obvious, direct or overt forms of aggression and other interpersonal mistreatment. Moreover, we explain how ostracism impacts not only the targets but also the perpetrators, witnesses, and organizations as a whole.

THE IMPACT OF OSTRACISM ON THE TARGET'S WELL-BEING

When an individual first experiences ostracism it can lead to a reflexive reaction characterized by negative emotions and pain, which are often unmitigated by individual and contextual factors (Williams, 2001, 2007). In other words, ostracism results in immediate and direct negative emotional and physical consequences. Following this immediate reaction, these initial negative emotions are often accompanied by other negative experiences such as strong feelings of loneliness and low self-esteem. Finally, negative actions by the victim can further perpetuate feelings of social exclusion beyond the initial event. We proceed with a more in-depth discussion of each of these consequences.

Immediate Consequences

Being excluded or ignored by other individuals or groups, regardless of the reason, has been linked to a long list of immediate negative emotional reactions. Research indicates that victims feel sad (Buckley, Winkel, and Leary, 2004; Chow, Tiedens, and Govan, 2008), hurt (Leary et al., 1998), angry (Chow, Tiedens, and Govan, 2008; Zadro, Williams, and Richardson, 2004), ashamed (Chow, Tiedens, and Govan, 2008), lonely (Jones, 1990), ill (Schneider, Hitlan, and Radhakrishnan, 2000), and even violent under certain circumstances (Williams, 2007), following an ostracism event. It is important to note that research investigating the potential individual moderators of these negative effects of ostracism has found that for the most part ostracism is an equally painful experience for everyone. Tests of individual differences including individualism, social anxiety, introversion, agreeableness, secure attachment, self-esteem, and preexisting loneliness have suggested that individual differences have a relatively small impact on how one responds to ostracism (see Williams, 2007, for a review). Gender and rejection sensitivity are two factors that have been shown to affect one's perception of and reaction to exclusion (Downey et al., 2004; Hitlan, Cliffton, and DeSoto, 2006; Mor Barak, Cherin, and Berkman, 1998; Williams and Sommer, 1997).

Even when targets do not experience an immediate negative emotional response to an experience of ostracism, Baumeister and colleagues (Baumeister, Twenge, and Nuss, 2002; Twenge, Catanese, and Baumeister, 2003) have argued that it can lead to a negative, "deconstructed state" better characterized by lethargy, or a lack of strong emotions altogether. Baumeister and colleagues argue that because ostracism can be such a painful experience that threatens one's self-worth, targets can often react by cognitively and emotionally avoiding the situation in an attempt to escape the otherwise negative effects of ostracism. Ostracism provoked by acts of severe perceived transgression such as whistle-blowing, can induce a state of learned helplessness (Andersen, 1990; Faulkner and Williams, 1999) in which the victim reverses course from action and advocacy toward passivity and acquiescence. Such escape can have further negative effects, as research has linked a deconstructed state to problems with self-regulation (Twenge, Catanese, and Baumeister, 2003). In line with this theory, a recent meta-analysis found that while in general the negative impact of social rejection is more salient than the positive impact of social acceptance, and that rejected people feel worse than neutral controls, rejected individuals "have typically reported emotional states that are almost precisely neutral or indicating slightly more positive than negative emotion" (Blackhart et al., 2009, p. 300). They concluded that "the emotional impact of rejection appears to involve a significant move toward a state of affective neutrality, involving neither much positive nor negative emotion" (ibid.), which supports the notion of a deconstructed state. As it stands, we need more empirical research to examine the link between ostracism and emotional reactions. It may be that these differential findings are explained by differences between episodic rejection and more global and longer-term ostracism, as well as differences between those emotions immediately following experiences and emotions that emerge over time.

Interestingly, neuroscience research has drawn a link between the social pain inflicted by ostracism and the physical pain one experiences with a physical injury (Eisenberger, Lieberman, and Williams, 2003; MacDonald and Leary, 2005). Eisenberger and Lieberman (2004) explain that the neural circuitry in the anterior cingulated cortex that alerts the brain of physical pain overlaps with the sensors indicating social pain. In other words, the pain associated with a "broken heart" is neurologically similar to the pain one experiences with a "broken bone." This interconnection of social and physical pain may be an evolutionary adaptive response, alerting victims to the potential danger of being isolated from their protective group (Williams, 2007). In fact, an important theoretical explanation for ostracism's detrimental effects may be that it challenges an individual's sense of membership. Needing to belong has been identified as a core human need in the psychology literature (Baumeister and Leary, 1995; Pickett, Gardner, and Knowles, 2004; Stevens and Fiske, 1995).

Subsequent Consequences

In order to fully understand the ostracized employee's reduction in happiness, health, and holistic well-being, we must consider its influence on the victim's psychological and emotional state beyond the actual event. For one, ostracism can produce feelings of social isolation that are strongly related to various patterns of unhappiness (Argyle, 2001; Baumeister, 1991). Baumeister and Tice (1990) also propose that social exclusion is one of the most salient and common causes of anxiety. Furthermore, ostracism can accompany a reduction in self-esteem. In addition, intentional and unintentional social exclusion lead to similar reductions in self-esteem. Self-esteem has been conceptualized as a psychological indicator of one's level of social inclusion and thus serves as a proxy for the more fundamental underlying need for belongingness (Ashforth and Mael, 1989; Leary and Baumeister, 2000). These psychological effects may be especially strong when one is ostracized not just by an individual but by many or all of one's colleagues.

Perhaps the best-studied potential companion of ostracism is loneliness. A lack of social ties is accompanied by an increased risk of morbidity and mortality (Seeman and Crimmins, 2006). The lonely individual not only experiences a decrease in immune competence (Kiecolt-Glaser et al., 1984) but also perceives the stressors accompanying feelings of exclusion more intensely and in a greater diversity of situations (Cacioppo, Hawkley, and Berntson, 2003). Enhanced awareness of social exclusion thus produces a cycle of "wear and tear" on the victim's nervous system.

Behavioral Consequences

The initial experience of ostracism can motivate a target to engage in behaviors that can precipitate additional experiences of ostracism. An explanation for this perpetuating cycle of ostracism is that victims of ostracism are more likely to engage in self-defeating behavior. In a series of experiments, Twenge, Catanese, and Baumeister (2002) found that participants ostracized by a group were more likely to engage in irrational, self-defeating, risky, and unhealthy behaviors, compared to the control participants. For example, in one study, participants were given the option to study for a test that was seemingly part of a different study or to procrastinate on other tasks. Participants in the ostracism condition were more likely to choose to procrastinate. Social exclusion has also been shown to lead to a reduced interest in caring about one's wellness, fluctuating personal care, and a lack of responsibility in seeking medical attention or tending to one's health (Seeman and Crimmins, 2006).

An explanation for these self-defeating behaviors is that ostracism signals that one is no longer deserving of others' attention (Bastian and Haslam, 2010), undermines one's sense of self-worth, and invokes a sense of "social death" (Sommer et al., 2001). Indeed, Baumeister et al. (2005) found that ostracized participants believed that those who excluded them perceived them as less "human." It comes as no surprise that when one's fundamental need to belong is attacked, maladaptive behaviors that further deteriorate the target's socioemotional and physical well-being follow.

THE IMPACT OF OSTRACISM ON PERPETRATORS' WELL-BEING

Although the reader may be readily persuaded of the negative impact of ostracism on the target's well-being, a less obvious way by which ostracism is harmful is through the toll it takes on the actor engaging in it. Behaviors such as ignoring, exclusion, and ostracism appear, at first glance, to be largely beneficial to the actor. As already noted, ostracism can be a means by which employees can express their strong negative feelings and hurt one another, and thus it may seem to be a functional behavior for the actors. However, examining the social dynamics involved in ostracism and social exclusion yields a different picture: mounting theoretical and empirical evidence suggests that ostracizing others also hurts actors as much as it may help them. We contend that engaging in ostracism can hurt the well-being of actors in four distinct ways: cognitive, emotional, physical, and relational. We will discuss each of these in turn.

Cognitive Consequences

Engaging in avoidance or ignoring behavior appears, on the surface, to be relatively effortless, compared to more overt aggressive behavior; after all, it is the absence of behavior. A closer examination of ostracizing behavior, however, suggests that it is actually mentally effortful and cognitively taxing (Ciarocco, Sommer, and Baumeister, 2001). Individuals are socialized to follow scripts in everyday interactions (Goffman, 1959), and it is relatively effortless to automatically engage in well-worn social scripts throughout one's workday. Likewise, each social context is replete with taken-for-granted norms governing acceptable social behavior. Thus, most of us will reflexively acknowledge people we know when we encounter them, respond when someone speaks to us, reciprocate a smile, or swap banter about the weather to fill dead air space. In contrast, it takes considerable concentration and self-regulation to violate social norms, stay cognizant of, and avoid following the routine of social scripts most familiar to us (Ciarocco, Sommer, and Baumeister, 2001) for the purpose of "giving someone the silent treatment." It is cognitively far less taxing to follow norms, exchange pleasantries, smile, and engage in the same social routines than it is to remember one cannot do this with particular others, and must instead withhold the automated script, violate norms, and inhibit one's responses.

The above logic is consistent with the findings of the "Scarlet Letter" study of Williams et al. (2000). Over the course of five days, the authors recorded their thoughts and feelings when they took turns being ostracized or ostracizing one another. Those in the role of ostracizer reported that ignoring and avoiding the colleague with the "Scarlet Letter" for the day took significant mental effort, especially if they were close to the target. Similarly, Ciarocco, Sommer, and Baumeister (2001) reported that subjects who were required to ignore a confederate for three minutes suffered from declines in cognitive capacity on a variety of subsequent tasks. Their two experiments demonstrated that engaging in ostracism drew significantly upon one's cognitive resources because it required substantial self-regulation.

Emotional Consequences

Engaging in social exclusion and ostracism also hurts the actor in emotional ways. Although it may feel good to ignore or exclude others, especially if one is doing so for the sake of revenge or retaliation, it appears that ostracism also comes with a host of accompanying negative emotions. Williams and Sommer (1997), in a set of experiments designed to study the impact of ostracism on targets, reported that their experimental confederates, paid to engage with one another but ostracize a subject, fully carried out their task as required, but reported finding it both difficult and uncomfortable. Likewise, Baumeister, Wotman, and Stillwell (1993) reported that those who had to reject another's affections were left with feelings of stress and unpleasantness. Finally, Ciarocco, Sommer, and Baumeister (2001) found that when subjects were required to socially ignore a confederate, compared to being required to converse with them, they reported higher negative affect and more guilt. Although one may be engaging in ostracism for the express purpose of hurting or punishing another, because ostracizers, like most people, have likely experienced ostracism at some point in their life (Faulkner et al., 1997), they may readily imagine the pain they are inflicting. Thus, they may experience satisfaction in hurting another, but also empathy for their target's pain, and guilt about causing it.

Relational Consequences

Given that ostracism leads to a *relational* loss, it should impact not just the target but also the actors. Those engaging in ostracism no longer possess the same sense of attachment to the one they are ignoring, excluding, or avoiding. The ostracizers, like the target, lose the psychological value of the relationship as well as any extrinsic or instrumental gains that come with it, be it advice, support in doing one's job, or having an ally on the political front.

Williams, Wheeler, and Harvey (2001), using an event-sampling method whereby subjects recorded details when they ostracized someone during a two-week period, found that when a participant engaged in ostracism, he or she also reported a lost sense of belonging. In another study, Williams, Shore, and Grahe (1998) asked undergraduates to recall specific behaviors that occurred when they received or gave another the "silent treatment." They found that giving the "silent treatment" fortified one's sense of control, but at the expense of a lesser sense of belonging and sense of meaningful existence. So while ostracizers may gain a sense of control by giving others the "silent treatment," they lose companionship and relationship security and can experience a violation of belongingness similar to the targets of ostracism.

Physical Consequences

Although we are not aware of any studies that have examined the impact of ostracizing behavior on physical well-being, some related research provides indirect evidence of this possibility. A number of empirical studies have shown that "holding grudges" is correlated with heart attacks, high blood pressure, ulcers, and a host of other physical ailments (Cottington et al., 1985; Johnson, Schork, and Spielberger, 1987; Messias et al., 2010). More generally, emotional repression has been found to be linked to cancer and other diseases (Fox et al., 1994; Greer and Morris, 1975; Jansen and Muenz, 1984). Taken together, these results suggest that those who are prone to using ostracism or giving others the "silent treatment" are perhaps more likely to suffer detrimental physical consequences.

THE IMPACT OF OSTRACISM ON THIRD PARTIES

To date, we know little about how third parties are impacted by ostracism. We define third parties, in the context of ostracism, as any party who is aware that another is ostracized, but who is not responsible for it (O'Reilly and Aquino, 2011; Skarlicki and Kulik, 2005). For example, one might notice a colleague's anguished, perplexed frown as her comments go ignored by her supervisor at a morning meeting, or see one's coworker left to eat alone at his desk while the rest of the group heads out for lunch.

Research has found that witnessing mistreatment, in general, can lead to greater dissatisfaction with one's job and work relationships (e.g., Low et al., 2007), withdrawal (e.g., Miner-Rubino and Cortina, 2004), poorer performance reduced citizenship behaviors (e.g., Porath and Erez, 2009), and greater interpersonal deviance (e.g., Ferguson and Barry, 2011).

Wesselmann, Bagg, and Williams (2009) specifically looked at the effects of ostracism on third parties. The authors found that those who witnessed a player being ostracized by multiple others in a computer game reported more negative affect and a greater threat to their needs of belonging, control, esteem, and meaningful existence than those in the control condition. They argued that because ostracism is associated with one of the most fundamental human needs (i.e., being included and protected in a group), humans are equipped with a crude evolutionary-based social detection system that helps them to recognize ostracism extremely readily (Spoor and Williams, 2007), even when it is directed toward someone else. The study of Wesselman, Bagg, and Williams (2009) is important as it is the first to directly and specifically demonstrate the negative impact of ostracism on third parties. What remains to be learned is why third parties may be impacted by ostracism. To answer this question, we offer two theoretical perspectives: the empathy perspective and the deontic perspective.

The Empathy Perspective

Empathy refers to an affective response characterized by emotions that are more appropriate for another person's state than for one's one (Hoffman, 2000). It can range from an automatic and reflexive process, to a more thoughtful and reflective one, such as imagining how one would feel if one were similarly treated or taking on the perspective of others and imagining their feelings (Batson et al., 2003; Hoffman, 2000). Empathy is a powerful determinant of how people react when witnessing harmed, disenfranchised, or vulnerable others (Batson, 2011; Hoffman, 2000). Given that ostracism is such a painful experience that human beings are naturally disposed to detect, it is likely that third parties will recognize this pain in others (Spoor and Williams, 2007; Wesselman, Bagg, and Williams 2009). Scholars have documented that empathy can turn into either *sympathy,* an other-focused emotion that involves concern for others' welfare, or *personal distress,* a self-focused emotion that is characterized by anxiety toward one's own state of being (Batson, 1998; Eisenberg, 2000; Hoffman, 2000). Sympathy is generally associated with prosocial and altruistic responses directed toward victims of harm and misfortune (Eisenberg, 2000); however, such responses can have detrimental effects on those who provide compassion and support to others in need. Work on *secondary traumatic stress* describes how people who are exposed to stressful information when they provide support to victims of traumatic events can experience threats to their own emotional and psychological needs (Aguilera, 1995; Salston and Figley, 2003). In other words, people who provide sympathy and support may experience burnout and emotional exhaustion as a result.

Empathetic reactions can create stress for bystanders who witness mistreatment. As such, some have conceptualized workplace mistreatment as an ambient social stressor in the environment that can cause psychological and emotional problems for those who are not the direct target of such acts (e.g., Barling, 1996; Glomb et al., 1997; Miner-Rubino and Cortina, 2004). Witnessing or learning about such events can lead to a variety of negative emotions. For example, Barling (1996) postulated that witnessing or learning about others' mistreatment can lead to fear that one will be a future victim of the abuser. Fear may be particularly salient in the case of third-party ostracism because ostracism is so strongly linked to the fundamental need to belong and be accepted by others (Spoor and Williams, 2007). Witnessing others' ostracism can also lead to negative affect (Truss, 2005; Wesselman, Bagg, and Williams, 2009). In fact, some researchers have noted that it can be extremely uncomfortable and unnerving to watch participants experience ostracism in an experimental context (Williams and Sommer, 1997).

Third parties can also become distressed and frustrated when situational constraints prevent them from providing help to those suffering mistreatment (Neuman and Baron, 1998; Rogers and Kelloway, 1997). Situational constraints such as social norms and pressures can prevent third parties from providing help to an ostracism victim. A third party might worry that helping a victim of ostracism will spark their own future mistreatment or cause a falling out between themselves and the rest of their work group. Third parties can sometimes lack the social skills and resources required to provide adequate help and support to a victim of ostracism. In other words a third party may *want* to help but not know how best to provide aid. Frustration caused by the inability to help those in need can affect not only third parties' personal well-being but also how they treat victims of ostracism. In a related line of research, Fine (1982) found that social workers who felt powerless to help the troubled youth they served due to resource constraints were more likely to blame these youths and attribute their problems to unfixable causes. Third-party witnesses to ostracism who feel powerless to prevent mistreatment or to support the victims may compensate by blaming the victims for their own predicament and treating them accordingly.

The Deontic Perspective

Based on the deontic perspective, third parties may be impacted by ostracism directed toward others because they feel that it represents unfair interpersonal treatment that violates significant moral norms concerning social conduct (Folger, 2001; Folger, Cropanzano, and Goldman, 2005; O'Reilly and Aquino, 2011). Given that ostracism has been shown to have such harmful effects on its targets, it is likely that at least some bystanders will acknowledge acts of ostracism as considerably unfair and morally wrong. In a sense, ostracism is a form of *interpersonal injustice,* which is defined as treating people with a lack of dignity and respect (Colquitt, 2001).

The deontic perspective suggests that ostracism can be harmful because of its negative consequences for the relationship between the third party and the perpetrator(s) of ostracism. According to Folger and colleagues' model of deontic justice (Folger, 2001; Folger, Cropanzano, and Goldman, 2005), when third parties learn about or witness an event that they feel violates a significant moral norm concerning how people ought to be treated, it provokes the emotional response of *moral indignation,* characterized by anger and hostility toward the norm violator and the recognition that a significant social standard of conduct has been violated. These emotions motivate third parties to punish the harm-doer in order to restore justice, or to "right the wrong" that they feel has occurred.

On the one hand, such reactions have the potential to have positive effects for a target of mistreatment as they can prevent future mistreatment (Bies and Tripp, 1995). On the other hand, such responses run the risk of creating conflict between a third party and those perpetrating the ostracism. Past research has established that vengeful acts of punishment for wrongdoing can lead to conflict spirals. Conflict spirals follow a "tit-for-tat" pattern and can be particularly salient when punishment comes in a seemingly ambiguous or subtle form (e.g., Andersson and Pearson, 1999; Bies and Tripp, 1995). Punishment from a third party rather than a direct victim has even more potential to create conflict spirals, as ostracizers may be unclear about why they are suddenly being mistreated by an individual with whom they did not formally have a preexisting conflict. Even when overt conflict spirals do not occur, the anger one feels toward an ostracizer can strain their relationship and create tense interpersonal interactions.

Finally, in addition to the anger one feels toward the ostracizer for mistreating a colleague, a third party can develop a sense of indignation directed toward his or her organization. When people witness their colleagues being mistreated by another member of the organization they can become outraged at their organization for not preventing the mistreatment in the first place and failing to punish harm-doers once it has occurred (Neuman and Baron, 1998; Rogers and Kelloway, 1997). Thus, in addition to feeling empathetic stress and negative affect, witnessing or learning about ostracism toward others also has the potential to generate negative emotions that ultimately strain the relationship between a third party and the ostracizer, and/or a third party and his or her organization.

THE IMPACT OF OSTRACISM ON THE ORGANIZATION'S WELL-BEING

Research overwhelmingly indicates that the well-being of employees is not the only reason that companies should take ostracism seriously. First and foremost, studies demonstrate a variety of antisocial behaviors perpetrated by the target of social exclusion. Experimental research demonstrates that ostracism can quickly denigrate social relations for both parties: the targets of ostracism report increased dislike (Pepitone and Wilpizeski, 1960) and prejudice (Hitlan et al., 2006) toward group members and can demonstrate an overall increase in aggression (Twenge et al., 2001). For example, when individuals were excluded from a simulated ball-toss game between other people, they laced an innocent stranger's food with four times as much hot sauce as their counterparts who were not ostracized. Ostracized individuals, compared to controls, also perform more counterproductive behaviors, engage in less helping behavior (e.g., Hitlan, Cliffton, and DeSoto, 2006; Hitlan and Noel, 2009; Thau, Aquino, and Poortvliet, 2007), and report a general impairment in empathy (Twenge et al., 2007). Further, ostracized individuals show lower commitment to the organization as a whole (Hitlan et al., 2006). One explanation may be that ostracism attacks one's feelings of control over a situation (Williams, 1997; Zadro, Williams, and Richardson, 2004), and the individual's deviance is an attempt to restore control. Aggressive responses to ostracism may thus depend on the degree to which ostracism threatens the control needs of the target.

Ostracism can also evoke a number of performance-related destructive organizational behaviors. Conservation of resources theory (COR) posits that individuals stock up resources (e.g., buffers against stress) and that "resource loss is disproportionately more salient than resource gain" (Hobfoll, 2001, p. 343). COR can explain much of the reactive behavior by targets of ostracism that hinders their organizational performance. Ostracized individuals redirect much of their mental energy to refute or reduce the source of their ostracism. For example, Baumeister, Stillwell, and Heatherton (2001) and Vangelisti, Daly, and Rudnick (1991) demonstrated that individuals who felt excluded exerted energy to induce guilt when their attachment was threatened. Twenge, Catanese, and Baumeister (2003) suggest that victims of ostracism demonstrate decreased self-awareness and a lack of concern for long-term goals. In addition, victims show impaired logical reasoning, (Baumeister Twenge, and Nuss, 2002), a lack of self-regulation (Baumeister et al., 2005), and reduced efforts in contributing to their work group (Kerr et al., 2008). In an experimental study by Baumeister et al. (2005) in which subjects were told that no one else wanted to work with them, participants quit a frustrating task sooner and showed impaired attention in a listening activity. In summary, ostracism can result in decreased performance or productivity (Baba, Jamal, and Tourigny, 1998; Cartwright and Cooper, 1997), misdirection of mental resources to understanding the reasons for exclusion (Baumeister et al., 2005; Thau, Aquino, and Poortvliet, 2007), and thus decreased effort in accomplishing work tasks (Blackhart, Baumeister, and Twenge, 2006; Thau, Aquino, and Poortvliet, 2007).

Ostracism can impact the organization in financial ways as well. Ostracism can lead to increased sick days and related insurance costs (Hart and Cooper, 2001; Lofland, Pizzi, and Frick, 2004.) Increased stress, anxiety, and loneliness of ostracism targets can, in turn, contribute to a reduced interest in remaining with the organization (Cropanzano, Rupp, and Byrne, 2003; Maslach, 1982). While at first negative emotions only occasionally undermine one's willingness to go to work, in the long-run they lead to increased turnover intention and a search for work elsewhere (Lee and Ashforth, 1996; Wright and Cropanzano, 1998).

MANAGERIAL ADVICE

Ostracism presents unique practical and ethical challenges for managers. Ostracism, compared to other forms of more obvious and overt mistreatment, is a relatively concealed phenomenon where only the direct target, the actors, and third-party witnesses may realize it is occurring. Even if managers do recognize ostracism when it occurs, they often perceive it to be accidental. This is compounded by the fact that ostracism is not always intentional and not always meant to cause harm. It can also be difficult for managers to oblige employees to involve one another on social gatherings and to follow proper informal norms of inclusion. Despite these challenges, ensuring the well-being and healthy functioning of one's work group is an important responsibility of managers. Thus, learning how to properly address and prevent ostracism at work is a significant endeavor. Managers can consider several specific strategies to curtail and manage its effects.

The first step to reducing ostracism in organizations is for those in power to recognize its frequency and potential for harm. Until managers appreciate the fact that ostracism poses a risk to the well-being of their employees, and thus costs the organization, there will be little motivation to enact change to eliminate it. Thus, before all else, managers and supervisors need to be educated about the nature, form, and frequency of ostracism in their organization, and to be made aware of the direct negative implications of ostracism for the workforce and the bottom line.

Second, management has to reduce the social acceptability of ostracism. Organizations can more formally undermine its social acceptability by policy. Where organizations have policies and regulations against harassment and bullying, they should similarly add policies regarding ostracism. These policies should highlight what constitutes inappropriate behavior and clarify its consequences. Such communication may also happen informally, as would any change in norms and values. Management should openly address its occurrence, pointing out its nature and inappropriateness, and, at the same time, directing employees to more constructive alternative behaviors. With time, these actions may send the necessary message that ostracism is no more socially appropriate, harmless, or condoned than any more obviously harmful social mistreatment, be it racial slurs, verbal abuse, or sexual harassment.

Third, organizations may seek to invest in training their workforce in more effective and constructive responses to conflict, problematic behavior, and tension. We contend that providing information about alternative ways of coping with everyday frustrations and problems, and arming employees with the necessary skills to enact them, may reduce not only ostracism but, possibly, other destructive interpersonal behaviors as well. For example, offering training in conflict resolution and negotiation may provide employees with a better way to work with one another. Likewise, providing training in effective communication, how to cope with stress, or how to provide constructive feedback, may give employees the sense of competence, and confidence, to directly resolve issues with other employees instead of resorting to ignoring, avoiding, and excluding them.

Finally, even if organizations cannot entirely eliminate ostracism, they may be able to buffer against negative effects.

RESEARCH IMPLICATIONS

Much research has established that ostracism is a painful experience and has a significant impact on one's well-being and happiness. Despite this research, a number of research questions remain unanswered, and the workplace provides a particularly salient and relevant social context in which to extend our understanding of this form of mistreatment. Of particular interest are the potential different effects of being ostracized by a specific individual at work versus an entire work group. As noted above, ostracism can stem from both individuals and groups, and past investigations have tended to focus on the experience of ostracism itself rather than delineating between ostracism from different sources. No doubt ostracism from a specific individual strains the relationship between the ostracism target and the actor, but future research could also explore the spillover effects of this conflict on work group well-being and functioning as a whole. Being shunned and excluded by the majority of one's workgroup is also likely to have a greater impact on one's social well-being (Keyes, 1998), the extent to which one positively appraises his or her role in the functioning of the group, trust in the group, and the effectiveness of the group.

We would also suggest that a fruitful avenue for future research on the impact of ostracism on well-being is to examine it with a more fine-grained approach. To date, this issue has been examined as a singular experience in the lab, or in a general sense of one's experience over time in field surveys. We believe that it would be very useful to drill down and examine how one's well-being is impacted by who is doing the ostracism, how often, and when. It is possible that being somewhat ostracized by a lot of individuals is worse than, say, being strongly ostracized by one powerful person; or that being ostracized by those upon whom you usually depend for social support is more impactful than being ostracized by those with whom one has never had a positive relationship. Methodological approaches such as social network analysis may be particularly useful here.

Another research question to be addressed is this: What are the long- versus short-term effects of ostracism on the well-being of targets, perpetrators, and third parties? As alluded to previously, there are inconsistencies in the literature concerning the emotional impact of ostracism. Some research has found that ostracism has a consistent negative impact whereas other research has found that the impact of ostracism is best described as a deconstructed state. Future research could explore the relevance of time on the impact of ostracism. It is possible that as one becomes accustomed to being excluded on a regular basis at work he or she becomes seemingly apathetic toward the mistreatment and acts in ways that further provoke being ignored. Such a question could perhaps be best addressed using a diary approach or event-sampling methodology.

Finally, future research should explore the effects of ostracism on the actors and third-party witnesses to this mistreatment more completely and systematically. We are only beginning to appreciate the importance of third parties in organizational research, and, in particular, how they are impacted by organizational events in which they are neither actor nor target. The phenomenon of ostracism seems to be a particularly valuable place in which to examine the role of third parties.

CONCLUSION

Organizational researchers and managers have long understood the unethical and harmful nature of overt forms of mistreatment at work, such as acts of aggression, bullying, social undermining, sexual harassment, and the like. Emerging research, however, suggests that more subtle and passive forms of mistreatment, in the form of ostracism, can also pose a significant social risk in organizations. Research has shown that behaviors such as ignoring, excluding, or "giving the silent treatment" to others at work can have a severe impact on targets' overall emotional and psychological well-being. Furthermore, recent research has provided mounting evidence to suggest that ostracism can be just as painful to inflict as it is to receive. Finally, given that ostracism is a painful experience, it is likely to have stressful consequences for those who witness or learn about such behavior against others. We also highlight the important fact that ostracism's significant negative impact has real, significant implications for the smooth functioning of organizations and poses a cost to an organization's bottom line. As such, managers need to take ostracism seriously as a potential form of social mistreatment at work.

REFERENCES

Aguilera, D. 1995. *Crisis Intervention: Theory and Methodology*. St. Louis, MO: Mosby.

Andersen, S.L. 1990. Patient advocacy and whistle-blowing in nursing: Help for the helpers. *Nursing Forum*, 25, 3, 5–13.

Andersson, L.M., and Pearson, C.M. 1999. Tit for tat? The spiraling effect of incivility in the workplace. *Academy of Management Review,* 24, 3, 452–471.

Argyle, M. 2001. *The Psychology of Happiness.* London: Routledge.

Ashforth, B.E., and Mael, F. 1989. Social identity theory and the organization. *Academy of Management Review,* 14, 1, 20–39.

Baba, V.V.; Jamal, M.; and Tourigny, L. 1998. Work and mental health: A decade in Canadian research. *Canadian Psychology/Psychologie Canadienne*, 39, 1–2, 94–107.

Barling, J. 1996. The prediction, experience, and consequences of workplace violence. In *Violence on the Job: Identifying Risks and Developing Solutions,* ed. G. VandenBos and E.G. Bulatao, 29–49. Washington, DC: American Psychological Association.

Barling, J., and Phillips, M. 1993. Interactional, formal, and distributive justice in the workplace: An exploratory study. *Journal of Psychology,* 127, 6, 649–656.

Bastian, B., and Haslam, N. 2010. Excluded from humanity: The dehumanizing effects of social ostracism. *Journal of Experimental Social Psychology,* 46, 1, 107–113.

Batson C.D. 1998. Altruism and prosocial behavior. In *The Handbook of Social Psychology,* vol. 2, ed. D.T. Gilbert, S.T. Fiske, and G. Lindzey, 282–316. Boston: McGraw-Hill.

———. 2011. *Altruism in Humans.* New York: Oxford University Press.

Batson, C.D.; Lishner, D.A.; Carpenter, A.; Dulin, L.; Harjusola-Webb, S.; Stocks, E.L.; Gale, S.; et al. 2003. " . . . As you would have them do unto you": Does imagining yourself in the other's place stimulate moral action? *Personality and Social Psychology Bulletin,* 29, 9, 1190–1201.

Baumeister, R.F. 1991. *Meanings of Life.* New York: Guilford Press.

Baumeister, R.F., and Leary, M.R. 1995. The need to belong: Desire for interpersonal attachments as a fundamental human motivation. *Psychological Bulletin,* 117, 497–529.

Baumeister, R. F., Stillwell, A. M., & Heatherton, T. F. (1994). Guilt: An interpersonal approach. *Psychological Bulletin*, 115(2), 243-267.

Baumeister, R.F., and Tice, D.M. 1990. Point-counterpoints: Anxiety and social exclusion. *Journal of Social and Clinical Psychology,* 9, 2, 165–195.

Baumeister, R.F.; Twenge, J.M.; and Nuss, C.K. 2002. Effects of social exclusion on cognitive processes: Anticipated aloneness reduces intelligent thought. *Journal of Personality and Social Psychology,* 83, 817–827.

Baumeister, R.F.; Wotman, S.R.; and Stillwell, A.M. 1993. Unrequited love: On heartbreak, anger, guilt, scriptlessness, and humiliation. *Journal of Personality and Social Psychology,* 64, 3, 377–394.

Baumeister, R.F.; DeWall, C.N.; Ciarocco, N.J.; and Twenge, J.M. 2005. Social exclusion impairs self-regulation. *Journal of Personality and Social Psychology,* 88, 4, 589–604.

Berkley, R.A., and Kaplan, D.M. 2009. Assessing liability for sexual harassment: Reactions of potential jurors to email versus face-to-face incidents. *Employee Responsibilities and Rights Journal,* 21, 3, 195–211.

Bies, R., and Tripp, T.M. 1995. Beyond distrust: "Getting even" and the need for revenge. In *Trust in Organizations,* ed. R.M. Kramer and T. Tyler, 246–260. Newbury Park, CA: Sage.

Blackhart, G.C.; Baumeister, R.F.; and Twenge, J.M. 2006. Rejection's impact on self-defeating, prosocial, antisocial, and self-regulatory behaviors. In *Self and Relationships,* ed. K. Vohs and E. Finkel. New York: Guilford Press.

Blackhart, G.C.; Nelson, B.C.; Knowles, M.L.; and Baumeister, R.F. 2009. Rejection elicits emotional reactions but neither causes immediate distress nor lowers self-esteem: A meta-analytic review of 192 studies on social exclusion. *Personality and Social Psychology Review,* 13, 4, 269–309.

Buckley, K.E.; Winkel, R.E.; and Leary, M.R. 2004. Reactions to acceptance and rejection: Effects of level and sequence of relational evaluation. *Journal of Experimental Social Psychology,* 40, 1, 14–28.

Cacioppo, J.T.; Hawkley, L.C.; and Berntson, G.G. 2003. The anatomy of loneliness. *Current Directions in Psychological Science,* 12, 3, 71–74.

Cartwright, S., and Cooper, C.L. 1997. *Managing Workplace Stress.* Thousand Oaks, CA: Sage.

Chow, R.M.; Tiedens, L.Z.; and Govan, C.L. 2008. Excluded emotions: The role of anger in antisocial responses to ostracism. *Journal of Experimental Social Psychology,* 44, 3, 896–903.

Ciarocco, N.J.; Sommer, K.L.; and Baumeister, R.F. 2001. Ostracism and ego depletion: The strains of silence. *Personality and Social Psychology Bulletin,* 27, 9, 1156–1163.

Colquitt, J.A. 2001. On the dimensionality of organizational justice: A construct validation of a measure. *Journal of Applied Psychology,* 86, 3, 386–400.

Cottington, E.M.; Brock, B.M.; House, J.S.; and Hawthorne, V.M. 1985. Psychosocial factors and blood pressure in the Michigan statewide blood pressure survey. *American Journal of Epidemiology,* 121, 4, 515–552.

Cropanzano, R.; Rupp, D.E.; and Byrne, Z.S. 2003. The relationship of emotional exhaustion to work attitudes, job performance, and organizational citizenship behaviors. *Journal of Applied Psychology,* 88, 1, 160–169.

Dittrich, J.E., and Carrell, M.R. 1979. Organizational equity perceptions, employee job satisfaction, and departmental absence and turnover rates. *Organizational Behavior and Human Performance,* 24, 1, 29–40.

Donovan, M.A.; Drasgow, F.; and Munson, L.J. 1998. The perceptions of fair interpersonal treatment scale: Development and validation of a measure of interpersonal treatment in the workplace. *Journal of Applied Psychology,* 83, 5, 683–692.

Downey, G.; Mougios, V.; Ayduk, O.; London, B.; Shoda, Y. 2004. Rejection sensitivity and the defensive motivational system: Insights from the startle response to rejection cues. *Psychological Science,* 15, 668–673.

Eisenberg, N. 2000. Emotion, regulation, and moral development. *Annual Review of Psychology,* 51, 1, 665–697.

Eisenberger, N.I., and Lieberman, M.D. 2004. Why rejection hurts: A common neural alarm system for physical and social pain. *Trends in Cognitive Sciences,* 8, 7, 294–300.

Eisenberger, N.I.; Lieberman, M.D.; and Williams, K.D. 2003. Does rejection hurt? An fMRI study of social exclusion. *Science,* 302, 5643, 290–292.

Faulkner, S.J.; and Williams, K.D. April 1999. *After the whistle is blown: The aversive impact of ostracism.* Paper presented at the seventy-first Annual Meeting of the Midwestern Psychological Association, Chicago, IL.

Faulkner, S.; Williams, K.; Sherman, B.; and Williams, E. May 1997. The "silent treatment": Its incidence and impact. Paper presented at the sixty-ninth Annual Midwestern Psychological Association, Chicago, IL.

Ferguson, M., and Barry, B. 2011. I know what you did: The effects of interpersonal deviance on bystanders. *Journal of Occupational Health Psychology,* 16, 1, 80–94.

Ferris, D.L.; Brown, D.J.; Berry, J.W.; and Lian, H. 2008. The development and validation of the workplace ostracism scale. *Journal of Applied Psychology,* 93, 6, 1348–1366.

Fine, M. 1982. When nonvictims derogate: Powerlessness in the helping professions. *Personality and Social Psychology Bulletin,* 8, 637–643.

Folger, R. 2001. Fairness as deonance. In *Research in Social Issues in Management,* vol. 1, ed. S.W. Gilliland, D.D. Steinger, and D.P. Skarlicki, 3–33. New York: Information Age.

Folger, R.; Cropanzano, R.; and Goldman, B. 2005. What is the relationship between justice and morality? In *Handbook of Organizational Justice,* ed. J. Greenberg and J.A. Colquitt, 215–246. Mahwah, NJ: Erlbaum.

Fox, C.M.; Harper, A.P.; Hyner, G.C.; and Lyle, R.M. 1994. Loneliness, emotional repression, marital quality, and major life events in women who develop breast cancer. *Journal of Community Health,* 19, 6, 467–482.

Glomb, T.M.; Richman, W.L.; Hulin, C.L.; Drasgow, F.; Schneider, K.T.; and Fitzgerald, L.F. 1997. Ambient sexual harassment: An integrated model of antecedents and consequences. *Organizational Behavior and Human Decision Processes,* 71, 3, 309–328.

Goffman, E. 1959. *The Presentation of Self in Everyday Life.* Garden City, NY: Anchor Doubleday.

Greer, S., and Morris, T. 1975. Psychological attributes of women who develop breast cancer: A controlled study. *Journal of Psychosomatic Research,* 19, 2, 147–153.

Hart, P.M., and Cooper, C.L. 2001. Occupational stress: Toward a more integrated framework. In *Handbook of Industrial, Work, and Organizational Psychology,* vol. 2, ed. N. Anderson, D.S. Ones, H.K. Sinangil, and C. Viswesvaran, 93–114. Thousand Oaks, CA: Sage.

Hitlan, R.T., and Noel, J. 2009. The influence of workplace exclusion and personality on counterproductive work behaviours: An interactionist perspective. *European Journal of Work and Organizational Psychology*, 18, 4, 477–502.

Hitlan, R.T.; Cliffton, R.J.; and DeSoto, M.C. 2006. Perceived exclusion in the workplace: The moderating effects of gender on work-related attitudes and psychological health. *North American Journal of Psychology*, 8, 2, 217–236.

Hitlan, R.T.; Kelly, K.M.; Schepman, S.; Schneider, K.T.; and Zárate, M.A. 2006. Language exclusion and the consequences of perceived ostracism in the workplace. *Group Dynamics*, 10, 1, 56–70.

Hobfoll, S.E. 2001. The influence of culture, community, and the nested-self in the stress process: Advancing conservation of resources theory. *Applied Psychology: An International Review*, 50, 3, 337–370.

Hoffman, M.L. 2000. *Empathy and Moral Development*. Cambridge: Cambridge University Press.

Hoobler, J.M.; Rospenda, K.M.; Lemmon, G.; and Rosa, J.A. 2010. A within-subject longitudinal study of the effects of positive job experiences and generalized workplace harassment on well-being. *Journal of Occupational Health Psychology*, 15, 4, 434–451.

Jansen, M.A.; and Muenz, L.R. 1984. A retrospective study of personality variables associated with fibrocystic disease and breast cancer. *Journal of Psychosomatic Research*, 28, 1, 35–42.

Johns, G. 1991. Substantive and methodological constraints on behavior and attitudes in organizational research. *Organizational Behavior and Human Decision Processes*, 49, 1, 80–104.

Johnson, E.H.; Schork, N.J.; and Spielberger, C.D. 1987. Emotional and familial determinants of elevated blood pressure in black and white adolescent females. *Journal of Psychosomatic Research*, 31, 6, 731–741.

Jones, W.H. 1990. Loneliness and social exclusion. *Journal of Social and Clinical Psychology*, 9, 2, 214–220.

Kerr, N.L.; Seok, D-H.; Poulsen, J.R.; Harris, D.W.; and Messe, L.A. 2008. Social ostracism and group motivation. *European Journal of Social Psychology*, 38, 736–746.

Keyes, C.L.M. 1998. Social well-being. *Social Psychology Quarterly*, 61, 121–140.

Kiecolt-Glaser, J.; Ricker, D.; George, J.; Messick, G.; Speicher, C.; Garner, W.; and Glaser, R. 1984. Urinary cortisol levels, cellular immunocompetency, and loneliness in psychiatric inpatients. *Psychosomatic Medicine*, 46, 1, 15–23.

Leary, M.R., and Baumeister, R.F. 2000. The nature and function of self-esteem: Sociometer theory. *Advances in Experimental Social Psychology*, 32, 1–62.

Leary, M.R.; Springer, C.; Negel, L.; Ansell, E.; and Evans, K. 1998. The causes, phenomenology, and consequences of hurt feelings. *Journal of Personality and Social Psychology*, 74, 5, 1225–1237.

LeBlanc, M.M., and Kelloway, E.K. 2002. Predictors and outcomes of workplace violence and aggression. *Journal of Applied Psychology*, 87, 3, 444–453.

Lee, R.T., and Ashforth, B.E. 1996. A meta-analytic examination of the correlates of the three dimensions of job burnout. *Journal of Applied Psychology*, 81, 123–133.

Lofland, J.H.; Pizzi, L; and Frick, K.D. 2004. A review of health-related workplace productivity loss instruments. *PharmacoEconomics*, 22, 3, 165–184.

Low, K.S.; Radhakrishnan, P.; Schneider, K.T.; and Rounds, J. 2007. The experiences of bystanders of workplace ethnic harassment. *Journal of Applied Social Psychology*, 37, 10, 2261–2297.

MacDonald, G., and Leary, M.R. 2005. Why does social exclusion hurt? The relationship between social and physical pain. *Psychological Bulletin*, 131, 2, 202–223.

Maslach, A. 1982. *Burnout: The Cost of Caring*. Englewood Cliffs, NJ: Prentice Hall.

Messias, E.; Saini, A.; Sinato, P.; and Welch, S. 2010. Bearing grudges and physical health: Relationship to smoking, cardiovascular health and ulcers. *Social Psychiatry and Psychiatric Epidemiology*, 45, 2, 183–187.

Miceli, M.P., and Near, J.P. 1992. *Blowing the Whistle: The Organizational and Legal Implications for Companies and Their Employees*. New York: Lexington.

Miner-Rubino, K., and Cortina, L.M. 2004. Working in a context of hostility toward women: implications for employees' well-being. *Journal of Occupational Health Psychology*, 9, 2, 107–122.

Mor Barak, M.E.; Cherin, D.A.; and Berkman, S. 1998. Organizational and personal dimensions in diversity climate. *Journal of Applied Behavioral Science*, 34, 1, 82–104.

Neuman, J.H., and Baron, R.A. 1998. Workplace violence and workplace aggression: Evidence concerning specific forms, potential causes, and preferred targets. *Journal of Management*, 24, 3, 391–419.

O'Reilly, J., and Aquino, K. 2011. A model of third parties' morally motivated responses to injustice. *Academy of Management Review*, 36, 3, 526–543.

O'Reilly, J.; Robinson, S.L.; Banki, S.; and Berdahl, J. 2011. Frozen out or burned by fire: The comparative effects of ostracism and aggression at work. Unpublished manuscript.

Pepitone, A., and Wilpizeski, C. 1960. Some consequences of experimental rejection. *Journal of Abnormal and Social Psychology*, 60, 359–364.

Pickett, C.L.; Gardner, W.L.; and Knowles, M. 2004. Getting a cue: The need to belong and enhanced sensitivity to social cues. *Personality and Social Psychology Bulletin*, 30, 9, 1095–1107.

Porath, C.L., and Erez, A. 2009. Overlooked but not untouched: How rudeness reduces onlookers' performance on routine and creative tasks. *Organizational Behavior and Human Decision Processes*, 109, 1, 29–44.

Robinson, S.L. 1993. Retreat, voice, silence and destruction: A typology and behavioral responses to organizational dissatisfaction and an examination of their contextual predictors. PhD diss. Northwestern University.

Robinson, S.L., and Greenberg, J. 1998. Employees behaving badly: Dimensions, determinants and dilemmas in the study of workplace deviance. In *Trends in Organizational Behavior*, vol. 5, ed. C.L. Cooper, and D.M. Rousseau. New York: Wiley.

Robinson, S.L., and O'Leary-Kelly, A.M. 1998. Monkey see, monkey do: The influence of work groups on the antisocial behavior of employees. *Academy of Management Journal*, 41, 6, 658–672.

Rogers, K.A., and Kelloway, E.K. 1997. Violence at work: Personal and organizational outcomes. *Journal of Occupational Health Psychology*, 2, 1, 63–71.

Salston, M., and Figley, C.R. 2003. Secondary traumatic stress effects of working with survivors of criminal victimization. *Journal of Traumatic Stress*, 16, 167–174.

Schneider, K.T.; Hitlan, R.T.; and Radhakrishnan, P. 2000. An examination of the nature and correlates of ethnic harassment experiences in multiple contexts. *Journal of Applied Psychology*, 85, 1, 3–12.

Seeman, T.E., and Crimmins, E. 2006. Social environment effects on health and aging. *Annals of the New York Academy of Sciences*, 954, 1, 88–117.

Skarlicki, D.P., and Kulik, C.T. 2005. Third party reactions to employee (mis)treatment: A justice perspective. *Research in Organizational Behavior: An Annual Series of Analytical Essays and Critical Reviews*, 26, 183–229.

Sommer, K.L.; Williams, K.D.; Ciarocco, N.J.; and Baumeister, R.F. 2001. When silence speaks louder than words: Explorations into the intrapsychic and interpersonal consequences of social ostracism. *Basic and Applied Social Psychology*, 23, 225–243.

Spoor, J., and Williams, K. 2007. The evolution of an ostracism detection system. In *The Evolution of the Social Mind: Evolutionary Psychology and Social Cognition*, ed. J.P. Forgas, M. Haselton, and W. von Hippel, 279–292. New York: Psychology Press.

Stevens, L.E., and Fiske, S.T. 1995. Motivation and cognition in social life: A social survival perspective. *Social Cognition*, 13, 3, 189–214.

Thau, S.; Aquino, K.; and Poortvliet, P.M. 2007. Self-defeating behaviors in organizations: The relationship between thwarted belonging and interpersonal work behaviors. *Journal of Applied Psychology*, 92, 3, 840–847.

Truss, L. 2005. *Talk to the Hand: The Utter Bloody Rudeness of the World Today, or Six Good Reasons to Stay Home and Bolt the Door*. New York: Gotham Books.

Twenge, J.M.; Catanese, K.R.; and Baumeister, R.F. 2002. Social exclusion causes self-defeating behavior. *Journal of Personality and Social Psychology*, 83, 3, 606–615.

———. 2003. Social exclusion and the deconstructed state: Time perception, meaninglessness, lethargy, lack of emotion, and self-awareness. *Journal of Personality and Social Psychology*, 85, 409–423.

Twenge, J.M.; Baumeister, R.F.; Tice, D.M.; and Stucke, T.S. 2001. If you can't join them, beat them: Effects of social exclusion on aggressive behavior. *Journal of Personality and Social Psychology*, 81, 1058–1069.

Twenge, J.M.; Baumeister, R.F.; DeWall, C.N.; Ciarocco, N.J.; and Bartels, J.M. 2007. Social exclusion decreases prosocial behavior. *Journal of Personality and Social Psychology*, 92, 1, 56–66.

Vangelisti, A.; Daly, J.A.; and Rudnick, J.R. 1991. Making people feel guilty in conversation. *Human Communication Research* 18, 1, 3–39.

Wesselmann, E.D.; Bagg, D.; and Williams, K.D. 2009. "I feel your pain": The effects of observing ostracism on the ostracism detection system. *Journal of Experimental Social Psychology*, 45, 6, 1308–1311.

Williams, K.D. 1997. Social ostracism. In *Aversive Interpersonal Behaviors*, ed. R.M. Kowalski, 133–170. New York: Plenum.

———. 2001. *Ostracism: The Power of Silence*. New York: Guilford Press.

———. 2007. Ostracism. *Annual Review of Psychology*, 58, 425–452.

Williams, K.D., and Sommer, K.L. 1997. Social ostracism by coworkers: Does rejection lead to loafing or compensation? *Personality and Social Psychology Bulletin,* 23, 7, 693–706.
Williams, K.D.; Shore, W.J.; and Grahe, J.E. 1998. The silent treatment: Perceptions of its behaviors and associated feelings. *Group Processes and Intergroup Relations,* 1, 2, 117–141.
Williams, K.D.; Wheeler, L.; and Harvey, L. 2001. Inside the social mind of the ostracizer. In *The Social Mind: Cognitive and Motivational Aspects of Interpersonal Behavior*, ed. J. Forgas, K. Williams, and L. Wheeler, 294–320. New York: Cambridge University Press.
Williams, K.D.; Bernieri, F.J.; Faulkner, S.L.; Gada-Jain, N.; and Grahe, J.E. 2000. The Scarlet Letter study: Five days of social ostracism. *Journal of Loss and Trauma,* 5, 1, 19–63.
Wright, T.A., and Cropanzano, R. 1998. Emotional exhaustion as a predictor of job performance and voluntary turnover. *Journal of Applied Psychology,* 83, 486–493.
Zadro, L.; Williams, K.D.; and Richardson, R. 2004. How low can you go? Ostracism by a computer is sufficient to lower self-reported levels of belonging, control, self-esteem, and meaningful existence. *Journal of Experimental Social Psychology,* 40, 4, 560–567.

8

CRAFTING AN IMAGE AT ANOTHER'S EXPENSE

Understanding Unethical Impression Management in Organizations

WILLIAM H. TURNLEY, ANTHONY C. KLOTZ, AND
MARK C. BOLINO

Since Goffman's (1959) seminal exploration of self-presentation in everyday life, researchers have made great strides in understanding the ways that individuals use impression management (IM) to achieve their personal goals (see Bolino et al., 2008, for a review). Much of this work has been conducted in organizational settings, and for good reason. IM influences most of the important aspects of an employee's working life, including preemployment interviews (Barrick, Shaffer, and DeGrassi, 2009; Higgins and Judge, 2004; Stevens and Kristof, 1995), performance appraisals (Bolino and Turnley, 2003a; Gordon, 1996; Wayne and Kacmar, 1991; Wayne and Liden, 1995), career success (Judge and Bretz, 1994), and supervisor–subordinate relations (Wayne and Ferris, 1990; Yukl and Tracey, 1992).

IM refers to attempts by individuals to develop, maintain, defend, or in any other way influence the image that others have of them (Bozeman and Kacmar, 1997). In organizational settings, employees use a wide array of IM tactics (Bolino et al., 2008). Almost all prior research has focused on how IM affects the target of the IM attempt or how it influences the outcomes that the actor receives. However, coworkers and others not directly involved in the IM process can also be affected by these actions, which raises important questions about the ethics of such behavior (e.g., Bolino and Turnley, 2003b; Turnley and Bolino, 2001; Wayne, Kacmar, and Ferris, 1995). Furthermore, limiting the study of IM tactics to the actor and target constrains our understanding of the full impact that these behaviors have in the workplace.

Specifically, there are likely a number of circumstances in which the use of IM by one employee negatively affects not only the attitudes but also the well-being of that individual's coworkers (Rosenfeld, Giacalone, and Riordan, 1995). For instance, an employee who works extra hard when the boss is around in order to look good can increase the supervisor's performance expectations for all employees. Or, an employee who uses self-promotion or ingratiation to curry favor with a supervisor may be promoted over an equally (or more) deserving colleague. By increasing the workload of coworkers or causing them anxiety over a missed promotion opportunity, the IM behavior of one employee can negatively influence the psychological and physiological well-being of other organizational members (Giacalone and Promislo, 2010).

In this chapter, we explore the ethics of IM behavior. Whereas prior IM research has focused on how such behavior can have organizational costs by politicizing the workplace, we use an ethics lens to understand how IM can harm other individuals. Our chapter has three principal goals. First, we draw upon three moral theories to clarify when IM may be unethical or harmful. Second, using Jones and Pittman's (1982) taxonomy of IM tactics, we discuss specific ways in which five different types of IM behavior—ingratiation, self-promotion, exemplification, intimidation, and supplication—may damage the well-being of others in organizations. Finally, we address the practical implications of our analysis by explaining why understanding unethical and harmful IM is important for managers and administrators.

UNETHICAL AND HARMFUL IMPRESSION MANAGEMENT

Prior research has sometimes suggested that engaging in IM is inherently deceptive and unethical (e.g., Fletcher, 1989; Leary, 1995; Rosenfeld, Giacalone, and Riordan, 1995). In particular, early discussions of the topic tended to take a negative view of IM and generally portrayed such behaviors in a less than desirable light. However, over time, research on IM in organizations has taken on a more balanced tone. Today, the prevailing idea seems to be that "there is nothing intrinsically ethical or unethical about impression management" (Schlenker, 1980, p. 304).

It is generally acknowledged that individuals regularly engage in IM, and that some degree of IM is functional for both individuals and organizations. Indeed, Goffman (1959) proposed that the ability to manage different images plays a vital role in the facilitation of social interaction among individuals. As such, common types of IM often go unquestioned on ethical grounds. For instance, it is generally expected that graduating college students who are applying for a job will dress more professionally for an interview than they do on a day-to-day basis. In addition, it is also expected that they will attempt to portray themselves in the most positive light during interviews. Thus, in general, few would suggest that using IM to try to appear competent to a potential employer would be unethical (Provis, 2010). On the other hand, distortions of one's GPA (grade point average) or work history in an effort to land a job would commonly be perceived as unethical (Levashina and Campion, 2007).

Beyond blatant ethical transgressions such as manipulating one's résumé, there are times when engaging in IM might be considered harmful or unethical because of the negative impact that it has on coworker well-being. For example, employees are often told to maintain a wide network of connections with individuals who might be able to help facilitate their career success. Clearly, not all individuals have equal access to such networks, so employees who engage in IM while following this advice may be operating in a way that helps to make them appear more promotable in comparison to their peers from less privileged and, thus, less well-connected backgrounds. In addition, when individuals use ingratiation to broaden their network, the targets of such IM attempts often end up feeling used because they thought the individual was interested in a genuine friendship when, in reality, the individual was only concerned with making a potentially career-beneficial contact. In instances such as these, the line between ethical and unethical IM is often ambiguous.

Several approaches have been taken to examine the ethics of IM and other forms of political behavior in organizations, with most of these focusing on instances when individuals engage in such behaviors in an effort to gain a political advantage within the organization (Bolino et al., 2008; Ferris and Treadway, 2012). In this vein, three general types of moral theories can be used to examine whether IM behaviors are ethical or unethical—theories focused on deontological ethics (such as Kant's categorical imperative), utilitarian theories, and theories focused on concepts of justice (Cavanagh, Moberg, and Velasquez, 1981). Each of these approaches will be discussed briefly, and collectively they provide useful frameworks for examining the ethics of IM behaviors that might benefit employees while potentially causing harm to colleagues.

Deontological Approach to Ethics

Deontological approaches focus on one's ethical duties or obligations when confronted with moral issues. Specifically, such approaches propose universal ethical principles that should be applied in all situations (Trevino and Nelson, 2011). From this perspective, moral principles are binding, regardless of their consequences or outcomes. One example of a deontological approach is Kant's categorical imperative (Kant, 1964). Kant argues that individuals should act only in ways that they would be willing to see made into universal rules that everyone should follow and that actions are not moral if they treat others as a means to accomplish some end. Thus, it is generally accepted that Kant's categorical imperative suggests that any forms of lying and deception are wrong (Boatright, 2007). With regard to IM, this framework implies that any form of IM that is deceptive or that attempts to influence or manipulate the perceptions of others for one's own benefit would be unethical. While the ethicality of some forms of IM could be debated within this framework, a deontological approach would generally lead to a less nuanced assessment of IM than would utilitarian or justice frameworks, which tend to examine the ethicality of actions based on their outcomes.

Utilitarian Approach to Ethics

Within the utilitarian framework, actions are judged on their consequences. Specifically, behaviors are judged to be moral to the extent that they do more good than harm. According to this approach, ethical behaviors are those that maximize overall utility by producing the greatest amount of good for the greatest number of individuals (Mill, 1863). Thus, from a utilitarian perspective, specific IM behaviors would likely be judged to be unethical to the extent that they focused on the attainment of the individual's personal goals at the expense of what was best for the organization overall (Cavanagh, Moberg, and Velasquez, 1981).

Naturally, not all instances of IM would be seen as unethical by this standard. People who use IM to portray themselves accurately, or those who use IM to get a job or promotion that they truly deserve, would generally be acting in ways that are consistent with a utilitarian perspective. In contrast, those who use IM to achieve personal goals that do more harm than good for the organization or those who engage in IM that ends up creating harm for their colleagues would be judged to be acting unethically. As is true in all utilitarian analyses, one limitation is that considering the interests of all parties who might be either directly or indirectly affected by specific instances of IM becomes a "calculative nightmare" (Cavanagh, Moberg, and Velasquez, 1981, p. 365) and, thus, such analyses are almost always simplified.

Justice Approaches to Ethics

Theories working from a justice perspective tend to characterize actions as ethical or unethical to the extent that they create fairness. Multiple types of fairness have been identified (e.g., distributive justice versus procedural justice), but, on the whole, the basic consideration in the context of IM would be whether such actions lead to the unfair treatment of other employees. For instance, the success of certain types of IM tends to be dependent on what would generally be considered irrelevant characteristics like gender or race. As an example, prior studies suggest that men and women who engage in exactly the same types of IM are often treated and evaluated very differently (Bolino and Turnley, 2003a; Rudman, 1998; Singh, Kumra, and Vinnicombe, 2002). Likewise, according to this perspective, the ethicality of IM behaviors can be brought into question to the extent that engaging in IM focuses attention on factors that should be less relevant to the decision at hand (e.g., who is most outgoing versus who is most technically competent).

Authentic, Deceptive, and Exclusionary Forms of IM

Beyond these three ethical frameworks, people are often characterized as engaging in either "authentic" or "deceptive" forms of IM (Leary, 1995). Specifically, individuals who use IM in an effort to portray themselves as consistent with their own self-image are described as engaging in authentic IM. Such instances typically involve people sharing information or behaving in ways that allow others to see them as they truly are (or at least as they perceive themselves to be). In contrast, deceptive IM involves actions designed to create an image of oneself that, while inconsistent with one's true self, reflects an image believed to be valued by an important other (Leary, 1995). This manipulative form of IM is often associated with Machiavellianism (Christie and Geis, 1970), and the ethicality of such IM is often called into question.

In addition to authentic and deceptive types of IM, Leary (1995) also notes that individuals sometimes engage in "exclusionary" (or evasive) forms of IM. Specifically, when people do not perceive that an accurate self-presentation will be well received, they often try to withhold as much information as they can. Indeed, almost everyone attempts to withhold certain unflattering information about themselves at one time or another. The significance of the information and the extent to which such information is relevant to the situation at hand helps to determine whether such instances of IM would generally be perceived as ethical or not. For instance, choosing not to disclose which political causes one supports or the fact that one is part of a nonmainstream religion, for fear of alienating potential employers, would not typically generate ethical concerns if those activities did not have any bearing on one's work qualifications or ability to carry out the responsibilities of one's job. However, failing to report prior actions that would disqualify one from employment or that have the potential to create significant harm to one's employer would be considered unethical.

Overall, then, determining whether a particular instance of IM is ethical or unethical is a complex process. While instances of deceptive IM are much more likely to be perceived as unethical than instances of authentic IM, not all instances of deceptive IM would be considered unethical, and not all forms of deceptive IM are harmful to others. For instance, engaging in harmless flattery (e.g., telling others they look nice even if one does not find their outfit particularly attractive) may be seen as kinder than creating hurt feelings by revealing one's true thoughts. Likewise, social norms dictate that applicants are expected to portray themselves in the best possible light during an interview or that marketers are expected to portray their products in the best possible light in advertisements.

In the next section of this chapter, we examine instances in which five specific forms of IM have harmful (though sometimes unintended) consequences for coworkers. Some of the instances are based on deceptive and manipulative forms of IM. In such cases, it is most likely that the IM would be judged to be unethical based on justice principles because the behaviors give one employee an undeserved advantage over another employee (e.g., in the context of promotions). In other cases, the ethicality of IM can be questioned from a utilitarian perspective because the overall harm done to others who are affected by the behavior exceeds the benefits that accrue to the individual who engages in the impression management.

THE HARMFUL EFFECTS OF IM ON COWORKER WELL-BEING

Jones and Pittman (1982) identified five types of IM that employees use to shape their images at work (Bolino and Turnley, 1999; Harris et al., 2007; Turnley and Bolino, 2001). In this section, we first focus on how IM tactics that are generally associated with positive image outcomes—ingratiation, self-promotion, and exemplification—can damage coworker well-being. Then, the effects of two IM tactics commonly associated with negative image outcomes—intimidation and supplication—are explored. Table 8.1 presents an overview of the potential damage to the professional and personal well-being of coworkers that can result from these acts of IM.

Ingratiation

Ingratiation consists of flattery, favor-doing, and other behaviors aimed at getting others to like the actor. The effective use of ingratiation is associated with a number of positive outcomes, including increased liking (Gordon, 1996; Wayne and Liden, 1995), higher evaluations of performance (Gordon, 1996; Higgins, Judge, and Ferris, 2003), enhanced ratings of citizenship behavior (Bolino et al., 2006), and greater career success (Judge and Bretz, 1994). Accordingly, many workers recognize the benefits associated with ingratiatory behavior and are often motivated to engage in this form of IM. However, Pandey (1986) noted that observers often evaluate the ingratiator far less favorably than does the target of the ingratiation. Indeed, coworkers who observe their fellow employees using ingratiation to earn the favor of their shared supervisor may become resentful, and such actions could result in more distrustful and self-interested behavior between colleagues.

Employees who observe a colleague's ingratiatory behavior may also feel pressured to mimic the actor's behavior in order to maintain the same relative amount of liking from their supervisor. However, such behaviors are not without risks or costs. In particular, targets of ingratiation are less inclined to respond favorably when they feel as if they are being manipulated (Allen and Rush, 1998; Eastman, 1994). Thus, employees who engage in supervisor-focused ingratiation to "keep up" with their coworkers can end up hurting their relationship with their boss, especially if their motives are more transparent as a result. Employees with low-quality relationships with their bosses experience higher levels of stress at work than those with good relationships with superiors (Harris and Kacmar, 2006); as such, employee ingratiation may harm coworker well-being when it motivates coworkers to ingratiate in an insincere manner.

In addition, most organizations have a finite amount of compensational resources, thereby making salaries, raises, and bonuses a zero-sum matter (Bloom, 1999). So, it is often the case that one employee's success will invariably result in at least an incrementally worse result for his or her colleagues. In such environments, then, colleagues become especially resentful of those who they feel are succeeding via ingratiation rather than actual performance. Moreover, employees who are high in equity sensitivity, a personality trait describing individuals' preferences for equity (Huseman, Hatfield, and Miles, 1987), may feel particularly distressed when the ingratiatory tactics of their peers are rewarded.

Related to the above, the process of being passed over for a promotion often elicits strong feelings of inequity in the rejected employee (Schwarzwald, Koslowsky, and Shalit, 1992). Further, these feelings of inequity are associated with attitudinal and behavioral changes that can be detrimental to employees' jobs such as reduced commitment (ibid.), increased absenteeism (Lam and Schaubroeck, 2000), lower job satisfaction, decreased levels of trust, and fewer acts of organizational citizenship (Colquitt et al., 2001). Employee physical well-being is also negatively affected by feelings of injustice, as perceptions of injustice can lead to increased cardiovascular stress (Vermunt and Steensma, 2003), sickness (Taris, Kalimo, and Schaufeli, 2002), insomnia (Greenberg, 2006), and lower back pain (de Jonge et al., 2000). Therefore, when employees observe a coworker with whom they are competing for a promotion engage in ingratiation, their psychological and physiological well-being may be damaged due to concerns regarding potential inequities.

Table 8.1

How Impression Management (IM) Helps Employees at the Expense of Coworker Well-Being

IM tactic	Positive outcomes for employee	Negative consequences for coworker	Damage to coworker well-being
Ingratiation	Increased performance evaluations	Relatively lower performance evaluations	Increased stress levels
	Career success	Decreased opportunity for promotions	Increased cardiovascular stress
	Supervisor liking	Pressure to engage in ingratiation in a nontransparent manner	Sickness
	Greater perceived fit and higher recommendations in interviews	Reduced salaries, raises, and bonuses in zero-sum reward systems	Insomnia
	Increased supervisor ratings of organizational citizenship behavior	Experience feelings of inequity	Lower back pain
Self-promotion	Greater success in interviews	May be perceived as less competent	Increased risk taking
	More likely to gain job offer from internships	Passed over for promotions or job opportunities that they "deserve"	Aggression
	Appear more competent in ambiguous situations	Experience negative emotions such as jealousy or resentment	Procrastination
	Higher supervisor ratings for those politically skilled	Deepen positive stereotypes associated with majority group	Higher blood pressure
		Causes female employees to copy IM, making them appear less likable	Unhealthy eating

Strategy			
Exemplification	Higher supervisor ratings for those politically skilled	Escalating citizenship expectations	Burnout
	Appearance of dedication to the job and organization	Increased stress and role overload	Emotional exhaustion
		Those with outside-of-work commitments may be especially taxed	Increased cynicism
		Leads to the development of "job creep"	Lower ability to accomplish work
Intimidation	Gain power over supervisors	Decreased job satisfaction, particularly for those high in equity-sensitivity	Reduced cognitive resources
	Increased performance evaluations in males	Social anxiety of having to manage impressions with intimidating coworker	Increased stress levels
	Higher supervisor ratings for those politically skilled	Discourages coworkers to blow whistle	Sweating and twitching
		Causes female employees to copy IM, making them appear less likable	
Supplication	Higher performance ratings for males	Increased workload and job strain	Cardiovascular mortality
	Higher supervisor ratings for those politically skilled	Less supervisor resources dedicated to coworkers	
		Reinforces the negative stereotypes if supplicator is minority	

Self-Promotion

Self-promotion involves highlighting one's abilities and accomplishments with the goal of appearing competent. Prior work has shown that people who use self-promotion often come across as more competent in shorter-term interactions such as internships (Zhao and Liden, 2011) and interviews (Stevens and Kristof, 1995), and in ambiguous situations in which such claims are not easy to verify (Sedikides et al., 2002). Because it is often difficult to fully assess the extent to which an individual's performance claims are truthful, coworkers who do not promote themselves tend to be perceived as less competent than those who do, even if their actual level of performance is similar. As a result, when self-promotion is used effectively, others experience several negative repercussions. In particular, these coworkers are at risk of being passed over for promotions or job opportunities that they "deserve." In addition, employees may experience emotions such as jealousy or resentment, which could also have a negative effect on working relationships (Rosenfeld, Giacalone, and Riordan, 1995).

Furthermore, coworkers of self-promoting employees can feel compelled to start promoting themselves, too, particularly when they have a relatively small window of time to impress someone important. For example, workers may have few opportunities to interact with a member of their firm's top management team, and these interactions often take place in the context of a group meeting. In such a situation, coworkers often feel compelled to engage in self-promotion in order to be seen as equally competent in comparison with their self-promoting peers. However, self-promotion is often risky; in particular, unsuccessful self-promoters can appear conceited (Turnley and Bolino, 2001) and unlikable (Giacalone, 1985), which can ultimately negatively impact career success (Judge and Bretz, 1994). In sum, self-promotion can cause resentment from coworkers toward the self-promoter and compel coworkers to also engage in self-promotion, which can harm coworker likability. Thus, self-promotion can cause considerable damage to the social connections among coworkers, which is related to the psychological well-being of employees (Rook, 1984). In this way, self-promotion can be seen as unethical.

When the self-promoting employee is a member of a majority group (e.g., a white male), supervisors may deepen their positive stereotypes associated with that group, thereby damaging the relative status of coworkers in minority or disadvantaged groups. Further, the self-promoting behavior of employees in the majority creates a stereotype threat among minority coworkers. Put another way, when an employee in a majority group self-promotes and succeeds in achieving an image of competence, minority coworkers' worries of being judged and treated according to a negative stereotype associated with their group may be activated (Roberson and Kulik, 2007; Steele, Spencer, and Aronson, 2002). When a stereotype threat is created in this way, the well-being of minority employees is impaired in at least two ways. First, stereotype threats negatively affect the perceived job performance of minorities, leading to lower performance evaluations and reduced job satisfaction (Gonzales, Blanton, and Williams, 2002; Steele and Aronson, 1995). Second, because stereotype threat elicits higher blood pressure levels (Blascovich et al., 2001), the physical well-being of minority employees may also be harmed. In sum, employee self-promotion can activate or deepen the effects of stereotype threat in the workplace, thereby harming the well-being of minority coworkers.

Finally, self-promotion is especially risky for women. Because self-promotion is a counterstereotypical IM tactic for women, prior research indicates that such behaviors can harm the employee's image in unintended ways. Rudman (1998) found that women who used self-promotion tactics were seen as more capable, but they were also seen as less likable. Thus, a self-promoting male coworker may end up being especially harmful for female colleagues. Not only does he accrue a relative advantage by appearing more competent, but women who feel compelled to mirror the IM behavior may end up being perceived negatively and, therefore, socially excluded as a result. Feelings of social exclusion can be quite detrimental to individual well-being. Indeed, social exclusion has been linked to a number of self-defeating behaviors, such as unhealthy eating, procrastination, increased risk taking, and aggression toward others (Twenge, 2008). To the extent that IM ostracizes coworkers, thereby endangering their well-being, it can be considered unethical.

Exemplification

Exemplification refers to engaging in organizational behavior that is perceived to be virtuous, such as staying late, coming in early, and trying to appear busy in order to be seen as a dedicated employee (Bolino and Turnley, 1999; Jones and Pittman, 1982). When the boss asks for someone to stay late, volunteer for a new task force, or train a new employee, exemplifiers are motivated to take on these visible tasks to reinforce their image of superiority in the boss's eyes. However, going beyond the call of duty in this way can also have ramifications for one's peers. In particular, by engaging in high levels of organizational citizenship behaviors (Organ, 1988), exemplifiers can raise the bar for what is considered "excellent" performance in the workplace. In doing so, they make the contributions of their coworkers seem less impressive. This may contribute to "escalating citizenship" where, in order to stand out, employees must either perform more novel acts of citizenship to catch their supervisor's attention or go to greater and greater lengths to demonstrate their dedication (e.g., stay even later at work to stand out) (Bolino and Turnley, 2003c).

Further, the exemplification behaviors of one employee can add to the in-role expectations of coworkers via "job creep." Job creep refers to "the slow and subtle expansion of employee job duties that is not officially recognized by the organization" (Van Dyne and Ellis, 2004, p. 181). For example, if one employee eats lunch at his or her desk to appear dedicated, the supervisor's productivity-related expectations may change for all of his or her employees. Increased supervisor expectations due to the IM efforts of one employee, then, ultimately lead other employees to feel pressured to go the extra mile and to experience higher levels of job stress and role overload (Bolino et al., 2010). This issue is often of particular concern to employees who have heavy obligations outside of work. For instance, whereas staying late may have little impact on the work–life balance of a newly graduated unmarried employee, it may be extremely difficult for a working mother who has to pick up her children from school after work. And, if those who stay late are doing so for IM reasons, then employees who complete nearly the same amount of work during the normal workweek are likely to be especially resentful of colleagues who have the flexibility to spend more hours in the workplace (even if it does not result in higher performance).

If left unchecked, the job creep and escalating citizenship that result from exemplifying employees can lead to burnout in their coworkers. When employees enter a state of burnout, they are emotionally unable to put any further effort into their jobs, they develop cynical attitudes toward their work and reduce their estimations of what they can accomplish in their role (Halbesleben and Buckley, 2004). Clearly, this state of overload will negatively affect the employee's psychological well-being on the job (Bolino et al., 2010) and outside of work as well (Ilies et al., 2007).

Intimidation

Intimidation refers to threatening or bullying behaviors that employees use to instill fear in their target (Bolino and Turnley, 1999). As such, intimidation almost always has a negative effect on the target of the action. Specifically, intimidators tend to create a stressful work environment for the targets of their actions (Jones and Pittman, 1982), which, clearly, can have a deleterious effect on employee well-being. While fear and stress are the most obvious negative consequences of intimidation, such behaviors can have less obvious, but equally damaging effects, in a variety of ways (Sutton, 2007). Moreover, the harmful effects of intimidation are not limited to the targets of such behavior. Other colleagues and even the intimidator himself or herself may be the victim of this type of IM.

In contrast to other forms of IM, which typically involve subordinates trying to be perceived more positively by supervisors, intimidation most often occurs downward (from supervisor to subordinate) or laterally (from coworker to coworker). Naturally, when intimidation is used in a downward fashion, the power dynamic between the intimidator and the target of the intimidation can make this a particularly threatening form of IM. However, there are also situations in which subordinates successfully intimidate their supervisors (Rosenfeld, Giacalone, and Riordan, 1995). For instance, Bartol and Martin (1990) demonstrated that when supervisors were dependent on employees, they gave them larger raises than other employees. Factors such as expertise, protected status, political connections, and access to resources can give subordinates power over supervisors (French and Raven, 1959).

When powerful employees choose to intimidate their supervisors, there may be negative consequences for other subordinates. Because the supervisor cannot control one employee, two sets of standards can emerge. In other words, "regular" employees may be forced to follow the rules, while the intimidator is free to bend these same rules. In such situations, coworkers feel compelled to manage impressions with respect to two powerful others who hold different expectations. That is, the intimidator may create an IM dilemma for coworkers, as they feel pressured to make a positive impression not only on their formal supervisor but also on their intimidating coworker. If they fail to keep the intimidating coworker happy, he or she could punish them or coerce the supervisor to do the same.

Managing multiple impressions in such situations is likely to be particularly stressful and may cause social anxiety for the employee (Schlenker and Leary, 1982). When coworkers experience this intimidation-induced social anxiety, they are likely to shift cognitive resources toward the distressing situation, experience higher levels of negative affect, attempt to avoid situations involving the intimidating coworkers, and experience physiological responses such as sweating and twitching (Rapee and Heimberg, 1997). This combination of psychological and behavioral reactions to an intimidating coworker is likely to be quite detrimental to an employee's well-being.

Finally, and similar to the outcomes that sometimes occur from self-promotion, the use of intimidation can create situations that are especially unfair for women. In general, women tend to be less assertive and aggressive than men (Eagly and Steffen, 1986), and, as a result, women sometimes come across as being less decisive and competent than their male colleagues. Thus, women are sometimes advised to "play like a man" and be more forceful and aggressive within their organizations (Wentling, 1995). However, prior research suggests that when women use intimidation it is not received in the same way as when men use intimidation. In fact, in one study, women who used intimidation did not see the same increase in performance ratings that their male colleagues did; however, they were perceived as less likable than their male colleagues who used intimidation (Bolino and Turnley, 2003a). As we have described, when employee IM leads to the reduced likability of coworkers, it therefore also harms the coworkers' overall well-being.

Supplication

Supplication involves advertising one's weakness or dependence with the goal of obtaining help or avoiding unpleasant tasks (Jones and Pittman, 1982). Like intimidation, supplication is an IM strategy that can be especially likely to have harmful effects on those who use it (Turnley and Bolino, 2001). For example, this tactic is particularly risky when aimed at supervisors, because, if not managed correctly, supplicators may appear lazy, uncooperative, or incompetent. Thus, even if a supplicator manages to avoid an undesirable work assignment by playing dumb, he or she may be judged negatively and thus miss out on future opportunities.

Although risky, when supervisor-focused supplication is successful, it leads to the supervisor recognizing the employee's need for help and often results in some type of assistance being offered. But, in an environment where some or all of the work tasks are shared among coworkers, successful supplication by one employee can have negative consequences for coworkers. For instance, the supervisor might assign some of the supplicator's work to another colleague, thereby increasing his or her workload. Or, the supervisor could assign a coworker to work with and train the supplicator in order to get him or her up to speed, which is also likely to increase the strain on the coworker. Even if the supervisor steps in to directly help the supplicator, this may decrease the supervisor's ability and time to help other coworkers. Finally, if the supervisor provides additional resources (e.g., training, new equipment, an assistant) to help the supplicator with his or her job, then this can have negative ramifications by reducing the resources available to other employees who need them.

In addition, supplication can lead to increased job strain on other employees even if the supervisor does not provide the supplicator with additional resources. Many forms of supplication, such as decreasing one's work effort, not working to one's potential, or broadcasting one's limitations, represent forms of social loafing (Becker and Martin, 1995). When fellow employees have a high degree of task interdependence or have a high degree of intrinsic motivation, colleagues may actually increase their work effort in the presence of a social loafer (Liden et al., 2004). In particular, according to the social compensation hypothesis, individuals who view their group's work as very important will tend to work harder when they perceive that a coworker is not able or motivated to do a good job (Williams and Karau, 1991). Clearly, then, supplication by one employee can often cause coworkers to experience job strain, characterized by increased psychological demands coupled with low control over the source of the demands. Job strain can be especially harmful to coworker well-being, as it has been linked to cardiovascular mortality and reduced quality of life (Johnson et al., 1996; Lerner et al., 1994). Thus, while supplicators may view the damage that they cause to their own image worth the help that they receive, they may not consider that their IM tactics inflict harm on the wellness of their coworkers.

Supplication can also result in feelings of resentment from other employees in the presence of a particularly needy or incompetent colleague. Such instances can reduce employee well-being by decreasing trust and commitment within the group. Moreover, peers may react with anger to underperforming colleagues who seem to be taking advantage of others (LePine and Van Dyne, 2001). Indeed, peers sometimes ostracize, retaliate against, or direct counterproductive work behaviors toward the employee who is slacking off (Hung, Chi, and Lu, 2009; LePine and Van Dyne, 2001).

In other circumstances, supplication has a more indirect influence on coworkers. In particular, if the supplicator is a member of a group that is stereotyped as being weaker or needier in the workplace (e.g., women, older workers, new employees), supplicating tactics reinforce the negative stereotypes held by the supervisor and other coworkers who are not members of that group. For example, if a woman uses supplication to avoid having to work overtime, then the supervisor may assume that women in general are less dedicated to their jobs and less willing to work overtime than men. In this way, the well-being of coworkers who share a group membership with a supplicator can suffer damage.

IMPLICATIONS FOR RESEARCH

Whereas prior research on IM has generally focused on how the use of such tactics enables employees to cultivate images that contribute to achieving important outcomes (e.g., promotions, higher performance evaluations), in this chapter we have sought to understand how a variety of IM behaviors could be unethical because of the damage they inflict on the well-being of others. In doing so, we have contributed to the IM literature in at least three important ways. First, we illustrated how different lenses can be useful for understanding the ethical implications of IM. Second, we clarified that IM behavior does not necessarily have to be deceptive in order to harm others. Third, we explained how various types of IM can negatively affect the well-being of fellow organizational members.

Beyond these contributions, our work also has implications for future research at the intersection of IM, ethics, and employee well-being. In this chapter, we have described how IM can, at times, be unethical because of the harm it causes to the well-being of other employees. However, it could be that IM is one mechanism through which employee individual differences in morally relevant traits cause diminished well-being of organizational members. For instance, employees who are high in Machiavellianism (i.e., manipulative, cynical, and immoral; Christie and Geis, 1970) may view unethical IM as especially useful because it not only achieves their desired image goals but also injures the well-being of their coworkers at the same time. Similarly, workers with weak moral identities (Aquino and Reed, 2002), low moral attentiveness (Reynolds, 2008), or personal moral philosophies that are low in idealism and/or high in relativism (Forsyth, 1992) may have a particularly elevated tendency to engage in IM that ends up harming coworker well-being. Hence, future research should examine the association between these traits and IM use that negatively influences coworker well-being.

Clearly, an additional avenue for future research is to empirically investigate some of the ideas discussed in this chapter. In doing so, researchers could use the IM scale developed by Bolino and Turnley (1999) to measure the five IM tactics described by Jones and Pittman (1982). In addition, Giacalone and Promislo (2010) outlined a model of unethical behavior and well-being, which could serve as an organizing framework for research along these lines. Most relevant to the issues raised in this chapter are the aspects of their model concerned with the people affected and how unethical behavior causes stress, trauma, and poor health behavior which, in turn, contribute to lower levels of subjective well-being (e.g., how satisfied one is with his/her life) and physical health (ibid.). It would be useful for future studies to determine how using IM in unethical ways or how using morally questionable IM tactics (e.g., intimidation) might be associated with self-reported psychological disorders (e.g., anxiety, depression) or adverse physiological reactions (e.g., higher blood pressure). Further, Bolino and Turnley (2003b) found that some people tend to use all five IM tactics in an aggressive fashion, while others are either passive in their use of IM or emphasize the positive tactics of ingratiation, self-promotion, and exemplification. It would be interesting to determine whether there is a meaningful relationship between these patterns of IM and indicators of well-being among their coworkers.

A similar approach is also needed to further examine the harm done to the targets or victims of unethical IM. Previous research has found that the attributions targets and observers make about IM behavior are important in determining how they respond to such behavior (Bolino et al., 2008). Similarly, Giacalone and Promislo (2010) indicate that the perceptions and appraisal of victims will influence the negative impact of unethical acts on victims. It would be useful, therefore, to develop empirical studies that integrate these two perspectives to understand how victims interpret the use of unethical IM by others and how this influences both their impressions of the offender and their own well-being.

IMPLICATIONS FOR MANAGERS

In discussing the practical implications of IM, researchers generally emphasize two overarching points. First, they tend to note that individuals can benefit from the use of IM tactics, but only to the extent that they are used appropriately and skillfully within a given context (e.g., Bolino and Turnley, 2003a, 2003b; Gardner, 1992; Turnley and Bolino, 2001). Second, they tend to caution practicing managers not to be deceived or unduly influenced by the use of IM by job applicants or their subordinates (e.g., Bolino et al., 2006; Gardner, 1992). While these recommendations are clearly important, our analysis of unethical IM yields some additional considerations for practicing managers.

In particular, managers should contemplate how functional or dysfunctional it is for their employees to use IM in the workplace. For instance, if IM is used to facilitate peer interactions or improve customer service, high levels of IM can be considered quite functional, even if such behavior is not always sincere. However, if IM is rampant and has the effect of politicizing the workplace, then managers should take actions that reduce the degree to which their employees play politics and manage impressions. At the same time, managers should also be honest with themselves about the degree to which they themselves may directly or indirectly encourage IM in the workplace by rewarding such behavior or punishing those who are less concerned with managing impressions.

Managers who believe that IM is healthy and functional should consider the possibility that IM can indirectly harm the psychological and physiological well-being of subordinates. For example, consider situations where the results of an employee survey show that workers are experiencing high levels of stress, or where the results of an annual health-insurance physical that show that employees in a work group have particularly high levels of blood pressure. Rather than simply attributing these symptoms of reduced employee well-being to work overload, managers should consider the degree to which the work climate encourages IM. Put another way, managers should recognize the different ways that IM can cause a ripple effect and negatively impact the physical and psychological health of other members of the organization.

Alternatively, managers could try to find ways to enable employees to better cope with this source of stress. For instance, managers could offer training opportunities for employees who want to learn how to present themselves more effectively or offer more traditional stress-relief practices. However, making employees more equally adept at IM is still unlikely to reduce the feelings of injustice that might be felt by employees who perceive that they have lost out on promotions, raises, and other opportunities owing to the IM tactics of their colleagues. Moreover, when employees widely engage in IM, they are expending mental and physical resources that might be better directed toward organizational goals rather than image goals. Overall, then, managers need to give greater thought to the costs of IM in their organization.

Finally, managers and organizations that seek to manage diversity more effectively need to be especially attentive to the outcomes of unethical IM. Indeed, as described in this chapter, some IM behaviors can activate positive stereotypes associated with majority groups and reinforce negative stereotypes held about minority groups. Likewise, if minority members use IM, such behavior may be poorly received. Accordingly, managers should ask themselves if they are able to react in an unbiased manner to the IM behaviors used by male and female employees. Put simply, IM could potentially lead to instances of discrimination in organizations, which makes this a particularly important issue for managers and organizations.

REFERENCES

Allen, T.D., and Rush, M.C. 1998. The effects of organizational citizenship behavior on performance judgments: A field study and a laboratory experiment. *Journal of Applied Psychology,* 83, 2, 247–260.

Aquino, K., and Reed, A. 2002. The self-importance of moral identity. *Journal of Personality and Social Psychology,* 83, 6, 1423–1440.

Barrick, M.R.; Shaffer, J.A.; and DeGrassi, S.W. 2009. What you see may not be what you get: Relationships among self-presentation tactics and ratings of interview and job performance. *Journal of Applied Psychology,* 94, 6, 1394–1411.

Bartol, K.M., and Martin, D.C. 1990. When politics pays: Factors influencing managerial compensation decisions. *Personnel Psychology,* 43, 3, 599–614.

Becker, T.E., and Martin, S.L. 1995. Trying to look bad at work: Methods and motives for managing poor impressions in organizations. *Academy of Management Journal,* 38, 1, 174–199.

Blascovich, J.; Spencer, S.J.; Quinn, D.; and Steele, C. 2001. African Americans and high blood pressure: The role of stereotype threat. *Psychological Science,* 12, 3, 225–229.

Bloom, M. 1999. The performance effects of pay dispersion on individuals and organizations. *Academy of Management Journal,* 42, 1, 25–40.

Boatright, J.R. 2007. *Ethics and the Conduct of Business.* 5th ed. Upper Saddle River, NJ: Pearson/Prentice Hall.

Bolino, M.C., and Turnley, W.H. 1999. Measuring impression management in organizations: A scale development based on the Jones and Pittman taxonomy. *Organizational Research Methods,* 2, 2, 187–206.

———. 2003a. Counternormative impression management, likeability, and performance ratings: The use of intimidation in an organizational setting. *Journal of Organizational Behavior,* 24, 2, 237–250.

———. 2003b. More than one way to make an impression: Exploring profiles of impression management. *Journal of Management,* 29, 2, 141–160.

———. 2003c. Going the extra mile: Cultivating and managing employee citizenship behavior. *Academy of Management Executive,* 17, 3, 60–71.

Bolino, M.C.; Kacmar, K.M.; Turnley, W.H.; and Gilstrap, J.B. 2008. A multi-level review of impression management motives and behaviors. *Journal of Management,* 34, 6, 1080–1109.

Bolino, M.C.; Turnley, W.H.; Gilstrap, J.B.; and Suazo, M.M. 2010. Citizenship under pressure: What's a "good soldier" to do? *Journal of Organizational Behavior,* 31, 6, 835–855.

Bolino, M.C.; Varela, J.A.; Bande, B.; and Turnley, W.H. 2006. The impact of impression-management tactics on supervisor ratings of organizational citizenship behavior. *Journal of Organizational Behavior,* 27, 3, 281–297.

Bozeman, D.P., and Kacmar, K.M. 1997. A cybernetic model of impression management processes in organizations. *Organizational Behavior and Human Decision Processes,* 69, 1, 9–30.

Cavanagh, G.F.; Moberg, D.J.; and Velasquez, M. 1981. The ethics of organizational politics. *Academy of Management Review,* 6, 3, 363–374.

Christie, R., and Geis, F.L. 1970. *Studies in Machiavellianism.* New York: Academic Press.

Colquitt, J.A.; Conlon, D.E.; Wesson, M.J.; Porter, C.O.; and Ng, K.Y. 2001. Justice at the millennium: A meta-analytic review of 25 years of organizational justice research. *Journal of Applied Psychology,* 86, 3, 425–445.

de Jonge, J.; Bosma, H.; Peter, R.; and Siegrist, J. 2000. Job strain, effort-reward imbalance and employee well-being: A large-scale cross-sectional study. *Social Science and Medicine,* 50, 9, 1317–1327.

Eagly, A.H., and Steffen, V.J. 1986. Gender and aggressive behavior: A meta-analytic review of the social psychological literature. *Psychological Bulletin,* 100, 3, 309–330.

Eastman, K.K. 1994. In the eyes of the beholder: An attributional approach to ingratiation and organizational citizenship behavior. *Academy of Management Journal,* 37, 5, 1379–1391.

Ferris, G.R., and Treadway, D.C. 2012. *Politics in Organizations: Theory and Research Considerations.* New York: Routledge/Taylor and Francis.

Fletcher, C. 1989. Impression management in the selection interview. In *Impression Management in the Organization,* ed. R.A. Giacalone and P.R. Rosenfeld, 269–281. Hillsdale, NJ: Erlbaum.

Forsyth, D.R. 1992. Judging the morality of business practices: The influence of personal moral philosophies. *Journal of Business Ethics,* 11, 5–6, 461–470.

French, J.R.P., and Raven, B. 1959. The bases of social power. In *Group Dynamics,* ed. D. Cartwright and A. Zander, 150–167. Evanston: Row, Peterson.

Gardner, W.L. 1992. Lessons in organizational dramaturgy: The art of impression management. *Organizational Dynamics,* 21, 1, 33–46.

Giacalone, R.A. 1985. On slipping when you thought you had put your best forward: Self-promotion, self-destruction, and entitlements. *Group and Organization Studies,* 10, 1, 61–80.

Giacalone, R.A., and Promislo, M.D. 2010. Unethical and unwell: Decrements in well-being and unethical activity at work. *Journal of Business Ethics,* 91, 2, 275–297.

Goffman, E. 1959. *The Presentation of Self in Everyday Life.* New York: Doubleday.

Gonzales, P.M.; Blanton, H.; and Williams, K.J. 2002. The effects of stereotype threat and double-minority status on the test performance of Latino women. *Personality and Social Psychology Bulletin,* 28, 5, 659–670.

Gordon, R.A. 1996. Impact of ingratiation on judgments and evaluations: A meta-analytic investigation. *Journal of Personality and Social Psychology,* 71, 1, 54–70.

Greenberg, J. 2006. Losing sleep over organizational injustice: Attenuating insomniac reactions to underpayment inequity with supervisory training in interactional justice. *Journal of Applied Psychology,* 91, 1, 58–69.

Halbesleben, J.R.B., and Buckley, M.R. 2004. Burnout in organizational life. *Journal of Management,* 30, 6, 859–879.

Harris, K.J., and Kacmar, K.M. 2006. Too much of a good thing: The curvilinear effect of leader-member exchange on stress. *Journal of Social Psychology,* 146, 1, 65–84.

Harris, K.J.; Kacmar, K.M.; Zivnuska, S.; and Shaw, J.D. 2007. The impact of political skill on impression management effectiveness. *Journal of Applied Psychology,* 92, 1, 278–285.

Higgins, C.A., and Judge, T.A. 2004. The effect of applicant influence tactics on recruiter perceptions of fit and hiring recommendations: A field study. *Journal of Applied Psychology,* 89, 4, 622–632.

Higgins, C.A.; Judge, T.A.; and Ferris, G.R. 2003. Influence tactics and work outcomes: A meta-analysis. *Journal of Organizational Behavior,* 24, 1, 89–106.

Hung, T.K.; Chi, N.W.; and Lu, W.L. 2009. Exploring the relationships between perceived coworker loafing and counterproductive work behaviors: The mediating role of a revenge motive. *Journal of Business and Psychology,* 24, 3, 257–270.

Huseman, R.C.; Hatfield, J.D.; and Miles, E.W. 1987. A new perspective on equity theory: The equity sensitivity construct. *Academy of Management Review,* 12, 2, 222–234.

Ilies, R.; Schwind, K.M.; Wagner, D.T.; Johnson, M.D.; DeRue, D.S.; and Ilgen, D.R. 2007. When can employees have a family life? The effects of daily workload and affect on work-family conflict and social behaviors at home. *Journal of Applied Psychology,* 92, 5, 1368–1379.

Johnson, J.V.; Stewart, W.; Hall, E.M.; Fredlund, P.; and Theorell, T. 1996. Long-term psychosocial work environment and cardiovascular mortality among Swedish men. *American Journal of Public Health,* 86, 3, 324–331.

Jones, E.E., and Pittman, T.S. 1982. Toward a general theory of strategic self-presentation. In *Psychological Perspectives on the Self,* ed. J. Suls, 231–261. Hillsdale, NJ: Erlbaum.

Judge, T.A., and Bretz, R.D. 1994. Political influence behavior and career success. *Journal of Management,* 20, 1, 43–65.

Kant, I. 1964. *Groundwork of the Metaphysics of Morals,* trans. H.J. Paton. New York: Harper and Row. Original published in 1785.

Lam, S.S.K., and Schaubroeck, J. 2000. The role of locus of control in reactions to being promoted and to being passed over: A quasi experiment. *Academy of Management Journal,* 43, 1, 66–78.

Leary, M.R. 1995. *Self-Presentation: Impression Management and Interpersonal Behavior.* Boulder, CO: Westview Press.

LePine, J.A., and Van Dyne, L. 2001. Peer responses to low performers: An attributional model of helping in the context of groups. *Academy of Management Review,* 26, 1, 67–84.

Lerner, D.J.; Levine, S.; Malspeis, S.; and D'Agostino, R.B. 1994. Job strain and health-related quality of life in a national sample. *American Journal of Public Health,* 84, 10, 1580–1585.

Levashina, J., and Campion, M.A. 2007. Measuring faking in the employment interview: Development and validation of an interview faking behavior scale. *Journal of Applied Psychology,* 92, 6, 1638–1656.

Liden, R.C.; Wayne, S.J.; Jaworski, R.A.; and Bennett, N. 2004. Social loafing: A field investigation. *Journal of Management,* 30, 2, 285–304.

Mill, J.S. 1863 [1957]. *Utilitarianism.* Indianapolis, IN: Bobbs-Merrill.

Organ, D.W. 1988. *Organizational Citizenship Behavior: The Good Soldier Syndrome.* Lexington, MA: Lexington Books.

Pandey, J. 1986. Sociocultural perspectives on ingratiation. In *Progress in Experimental Personality Research,* vol. 14, ed. B. Maher, 205–229. New York: Academic Press.

Provis, C. 2010. The ethics of impression management. *Business Ethics: A European Review,* 19, 2, 199–212.

Rapee, R.M., and Heimberg, R.G. 1997. A cognitive-behavioral model of anxiety in social phobia. *Behaviour Research and Therapy,* 35, 8, 741–756.

Reynolds, S.J. 2008. Moral attentiveness: Who pays attention to the moral aspects of life? *Journal of Applied Psychology,* 93, 5, 1027–1041.

Roberson, L., and Kulik, C.T. 2007. Stereotype threat at work. *Academy of Management Perspectives,* 21, 2, 24–40.

Rook, K.S. 1984. The negative side of social interaction: Impact on psychological well-being. *Journal of Personality and Social Psychology,* 46, 5, 1097–1108.

Rosenfeld, P.R.; Giacalone, R.A.; and Riordan, C.A. 1995. *Impression Management in Organizations: Theory, Measurement, and Practice.* New York: Routledge.

Rudman, L.A. 1998. Self-promotion as a risk factor for women: The costs and benefits of counterstereotypical impression management. *Journal of Personality and Social Psychology,* 74, 3, 629–645.

Schlenker, B.R. 1980. *Impression Management: The Self-Concept, Social Identity, and Interpersonal Relations.* Monterey, CA: Brooks/Cole.

Schlenker, B.R., and Leary, M.R. 1982. Social anxiety and self-presentation: A conceptualization model. *Psychological Bulletin,* 92, 3, 641–669.

Schwarzwald, J.; Koslowsky, M.; and Shalit, B. 1992. A field study of employees' attitudes and behaviors after promotion decisions. *Journal of Applied Psychology,* 77, 4, 511–514.

Sedikides, C.; Herbst, K.C.; Hardin, D.P.; and Dardis, G.J. 2002. Accountability as a deterrent to self-enhancement: The search for mechanisms. *Journal of Personality and Social Psychology,* 83, 3, 592–605.

Singh, V.; Kumra, S.; and Vinnicombe, S. 2002. Gender and impression management: Playing the promotion game. *Journal of Business Ethics,* 37, 1, 77–89.

Steele, C.M., and Aronson, J. 1995. Stereotype threat and the intellectual test performance of African Americans. *Journal of Personality and Social Psychology,* 69, 5, 797–811.

Steele, C.M.; Spencer, S.J.; and Aronson, J. 2002. Contending with group image: The psychology of stereotype and social identity threat. In *Advances in Experimental Social Psychology,* vol. 34., ed. M.P. Zanna, 379–440. San Diego, CA: Academic Press.

Stevens, C.K., and Kristof, A.L. 1995. Making the right impression: A field study of applicant impression management during job interviews. *Journal of Applied Psychology,* 80, 5, 587–606.

Sutton, R.I. 2007. *The No Asshole Rule: Building a Civilized Workplace and Surviving One That Isn't.* New York: Warner Business Books.

Taris, T.W.; Kalimo, R.; and Schaufeli, W.B. 2002. Inequity at work: Its measurement and association with worker health. *Work and Stress,* 16, 4, 287–301.

Turnley, W.H., and Bolino, M.C. 2001. Achieving desired images while avoiding undesired images: Exploring the role of self-monitoring in impression management. *Journal of Applied Psychology,* 86, 2, 351–360.

Trevino, L.K., and Nelson, K.A. 2011. *Managing Business Ethics: Straight Talk About How To Do It Right.* 5th ed. Hoboken, NJ: Wiley.

Twenge, J.M. 2008. Why breakups lead to drunkenness and ice cream. In *Handbook of Motivational Science,* ed. J.Y. Shah and W.L. Gardner, 508–532. New York: Guilford Press.

Van Dyne, L., and Ellis, J.B. 2004. Job creep: A reactance theory perspective on organizational citizenship behavior as over-fulfillment of obligations. In *The Employment Relationship: Examining Psychological and Contextual Perspectives,* ed. J.A.-M. Coyle-Shapiro, L.M. Shore, M.S. Taylor, and L.E. Tetrick, 181–205. Oxford: Oxford University Press.

Vermunt, R., and Steensma, H. 2003. Physiological relaxation: Stress reduction through fair treatment. *Social Justice Research,* 16, 2, 135–149.

Wayne, S.J., and Ferris, G.R. 1990. Influence tactics, affect, and exchange quality in supervisor-subordinate interactions: A laboratory experiment and field study. *Journal of Applied Psychology,* 75, 5, 487–499.

Wayne, S.J., and Kacmar, K.M. 1991. The effects of impression management on the performance appraisal process. *Organizational Behavior and Human Decision Processes,* 48, 1, 70–88.

Wayne, S.J., and Liden, R.C. 1995. Effects of impression management on performance ratings: A longitudinal study. *Academy of Management Journal,* 38, 1, 232–260.

Wayne, S.J.; Kacmar, M.; and Ferris, G.R. 1995. Coworker responses to others' ingratiation attempts. *Journal of Managerial Issues,* 7, 3, 277–289.

Wentling, R.M. 1995. Breaking down barriers to women's success. *Human Resource Magazine,* 40, 5, 79.

Williams, K.D., and Karau, S.J. 1991. Social loafing and social compensation: The effects of expectations of co-worker performance. *Journal of Personality and Social Psychology,* 61, 4, 570–581.

Yukl, G., and Tracey, J.B. 1992. Consequences of influence tactics used with subordinates, peers, and the boss. *Journal of Applied Psychology,* 77, 4, 525–535.

Zhao, H., and Liden, R.C. 2011. Internship: A recruitment and selection perspective. *Journal of Applied Psychology,* 96, 1, 221–229.

9

ETHICAL AND UNETHICAL LEADER BEHAVIORS AND THEIR IMPACT ON INDIVIDUAL WELL-BEING AND DEVIANCE

KARIANNE KALSHOVEN AND DEANNE N. DEN HARTOG

Over the past decade, both ethical and unethical leadership have attracted a lot of research attention, while remaining separate literatures with little integration. Recent work focuses either on the positive side of ethical and authentic leader behavior (Brown, Trevino, and Harrison, 2005; Walumbwa et al., 2008) or on the "dark side" of leadership, including unethical leadership, abusive supervision, leader bullying, and pseudo-transformational leadership or personalized charisma (see, e.g., Ashforth, 1994; Bass and Steidlmeier, 1999; Bies, 2000; Tepper, 2000, 2007). In this chapter, we focus on both ethical and unethical forms of leadership at all hierarchical levels of the organization. Both forms have a strong impact on followers as (un)ethical leadership involves a mind-set that leads to certain types of decision making, attitudes, and behaviors. We focus on both forms of leadership in relation to employee well-being and work behavior and, specifically, employee deviance.

Ethical leadership can be defined as "the demonstration of normatively appropriate conduct through personal actions and interpersonal relationships, and the promotion of such conduct to followers through two-way communication, reinforcement, and decision-making" (Brown, Treviño, and Harrison, 2005, p. 120). Examples of ethical leader behaviors include modeling ethical behavior, sharing power and allowing voice, discussing ethics at work, and showing fairness and concern (e.g., Brown, Treviño, and Harrison, 2005; De Hoogh and Den Hartog, 2008; Kalshoven, Den Hartog, and De Hoogh, 2011). Unethical leadership can be defined as "the systematic and repeated behavior by a leader, supervisor or manager that violates the legitimate interest of the organization by undermining and/or sabotaging the organization's goals, tasks, resources and effectiveness and/or motivation, well-being or job satisfaction of subordinates" (Einarsen, Aasland, and Skogstad, 2007, p. 208). Examples of unethical leader behaviors include social isolation, silent treatment, overly harsh criticism, and excessive monitoring of subordinates, as well as withholding information from them or depriving them of responsibility (Ferris et al., 2007; Salin, 2003; Tepper, 2007).

The relationship between supervisors and subordinates is a common source of stress and decreased well-being at work (Van Dierendonck et al., 2004), and in this chapter we outline how both ethical and unethical forms of leadership are likely to affect well-being, albeit in different ways. In addition, leaders at all levels are seen as role models of appropriate or inappropriate behavior (e.g., Yaffe and Kark, 2011), and followers are likely to copy their leader's ethical or unethical behaviors. We argue that one especially relevant behavioral consequence of (un)ethical forms of leadership is likely to be employee deviance. Thus, we focus specifically on the consequences of (un)ethical leader behavior for deviance.

Despite the proclaimed relevance of both ethical and unethical leader behaviors for subordinate outcomes such as well-being and deviance, integration of these emerging literatures has lagged and, so far, most research has focused either on ethical leadership (e.g., Brown and Treviño, 2006a; Brown, Treviño, and Harrison, 2005) or unethical (leader) behavior (Kish-Gephart, Harrision, and Treviño, 2010; Tepper, 2007) rather than both. Many of the described behaviors and effects of unethical leaders seem polar opposites of those described for ethical leaders, begging the question whether these forms of leadership are separate constructs or mostly form opposite poles of a continuum. Thus, in this chapter, we review the available empirical evidence that relates (un)ethical leadership to employee well-being and deviance (e.g., Avey, Palanski, and Walumbwa 2011; Brown and Treviño, 2006b). We map out the underlying processes by which such leaders affect these outcomes and propose well-being as a mediator in the relationship between leadership and deviance (see Figure 9.1).

Below, we first present an overview of the ethical and unethical leadership types and behaviors and the theories used most often to explain why these leaders have an impact on followers. Next, we link (un)ethical leadership to well-being and deviance and develop our proposed mediational model. Finally, we argue that in this relationship behavior foci, time issues, and bystander effects are highly important, and we highlight these as prominent areas for future research.

THE CONSTRUCTS OF ETHICAL AND UNETHICAL
LEADER BEHAVIOR

As mentioned, so far, most studies have focused on either ethical or unethical leadership. Based on the definition given in the introduction, ethical leaders are described as honest, transparent, trustworthy, fair, and caring. Ethical leaders also act as role models, set ethical standards, and hold others and themselves accountable (Brown, Treviño, and Harrison, 2005; Treviño, Brown, and Hartman, 2003). Since the crux of ethical leadership concerns the way leaders use their social power, De Hoogh and Den Hartog (2009) describe ethical leadership as a process of influencing in a socially responsible way the activities of an organized group toward goal achievement. They distinguish between forms of ethical leader behavior through their link to different connotations of social responsibility. For example, they distinguish integrity, fairness, role clarification, caring, and power sharing as components of the social responsible use of power and ethical leadership at work (cf. Kalshoven, Den Hartog, and De Hoogh, 2011; Resick et al., 2006).

Similarly, research on unethical aspects of leadership clearly documents that unethical leadership includes a variety of different behaviors and definitions, such as intimidation, abusiveness, belittling, manipulation, and bullying (e.g., Einarsen, Aasland, and Skogstad, 2007; Tepper, 2000). Many of the behaviors described in the growing literature on unethical leadership show overlap or are in direct contrast with those described in the work on ethical leadership. For example, a lack of consideration reflects being unapproachable or unfriendly, which is in contrast to the people orientation of ethical leadership (cf., Treviño, Brown, and Hartman, 2003). Howell and Avolio (1992) describe unethical leadership as self-absorbing and manipulative—that is, leaders who wield power to serve their self-interests, who are insensitive to followers' needs, and have little regard for behaving in socially constructive ways. This contrasts with the socially responsible use of power described as important for ethical leaders (e.g., De Hoogh and Den Hartog, 2009). Similarly, Aronson (2001) identifies despotic leadership, which is based on personal dominance and authoritarian behavior that serves the self-interest of the leader, is self-aggrandizing and exploitative of others. Such despotic leaders are domineering, controlling, and vengeful (House and Howell, 1992; McClelland, 1975).

Leader bullying behavior is conceptualized as strategically influencing and achieving personal and organizational objectives (Ferris et al., 2007). Bullying behaviors are viewed on the one hand

142

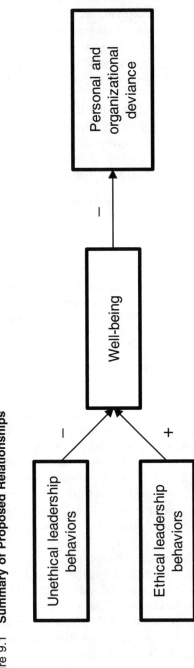

Figure 9.1   **Summary of Proposed Relationships**

as negative and dysfunctional and on the other hand as a potential mask that calculating leaders can use in order to effectively arrange outcomes (ibid.). However, both the dysfunctional and calculative bullying behaviors seem to involve unfair treatment of others. In this regard, it is all about the leader successfully influencing the employees to act in some preconceived direction or manner and subordinate employees to a position of weakness or helplessness, which reinforces the leader's power and increases the achievement of objectives (e.g., Harris, Kacmar, and Zivnuska, 2007). Nevertheless, employees could develop admiration for the leader who is powerful and uses bullying behaviors tactfully (Ferris et al., 2007).

Another form of unethical leadership that has received much attention in the literature is abusive supervision (Tepper, 2000, 2007). Tepper (2000, p. 178) conceptualizes abusive supervision as the extent to which supervisors engage in the sustained display of hostile verbal and nonverbal behaviors, excluding physical behaviors. Only repeated hierarchical mistreatment is labeled as abusive supervision (Tepper, 2007). However, abusive supervision does not include the intended consequences of the leader's actions (Tepper, 2000). A similar form of nonphysical yet destructive leader behaviors is petty tyranny, which reflects leaders' use of power and authority oppressively, capriciously, and vindictively (Ashforth, 1994, 1997). Both tyrannical and abusive leadership are elements of autocratic leadership (Hoel et al., 2010). Autocratic leaders make decisions without considering the opinions of employees. They give orders and foster dependency. Employees have no influence in decision making, reflecting a lack of employee empowerment (Yukl, 2006). In direct contrast, ethical leaders are concerned about their followers and are likely to accept and encourage their employees' participation. Kalshoven, Den Hartog, and De Hoogh (2011) show that these leadership styles are negatively correlated ($r = -.26$).

Next, supervisor undermining is leader behavior intended to hinder over time the ability to establish and maintain positive interpersonal work-related success and favorable reputation (Duffy, Ganster and Pagon, 2002, p. 332). Supervisor undermining focuses on interpersonal relationships and has three key aspects, namely, the perception of intentional hindering of an employee, surreptitiously causing harm, and taking a form of action or withholding (Duffy, Ganster, and Pagon, 2002). An example of intentional hindering of an employee given by Duffy and colleagues is the failure to do promised work or to provide needed information. Keeping promises and providing employees with information are parts of ethical leadership (Kalshoven, Den Hartog, and De Hoogh, 2011). It seems that supervisor undermining only touches part of (un)ethical leadership.

Finally, Einarsen, Aasland, and Skogstad (2007) hold that passive leaders violate legitimate involvement in the organization, as they waste time, are unmotivated, and fail to support or guide their followers. The authors conclude that passive leadership is a form of destructive leadership. In a study of Kalshoven, Den Hartog, and De Hoogh (2011), passive leadership (i.e., laissez faire and management by exception; Bass, 1985) and ethical leadership are negatively related ($r = -.40$). Because passive leaders put in a minimal amount of effort to get required work done, avoid problems and involvement, come into action when problems are already urgent, and do not meet their responsibilities or duties (Bass, 1985; Den Hartog, Van Muijen, and Koopman, 1997), followers experience such leaders as less ethical.

Ethical and unethical leadership are sometimes framed as polar opposites. For example, some of the researchers interested in the ethical potential of leadership have portrayed it as a basic tension between altruism and egoism (e.g., Turner et al., 2002). Kanungo (2001) holds that the leader, in order to be ethical, must engage in virtuous behaviors that benefit others, and must refrain from evil behaviors that harm others. Such acts must stem from altruistic rather than egoistic motives. Thus, these authors implicitly place ethical and unethical leadership on a continuum where leaders are either one or the other. Similarly, Craig and Gustafson (1998) focus on the absence of unethical leadership as an indicator of leaders' ethical behavior. Furthermore, in the transformational and charismatic leadership field, researchers differentiate between an ethical and an unethical behavioral component (cf., personalized versus socialized charismatic leadership, e.g., House and Howell, 1992; authentic versus pseudo-transformational leadership, e.g., Bass and Steidlmeier, 1999; Howell and Avolio, 1992).

However, there are also other views. Brown and Treviño (2006a) point out in their review that being low on ethical leadership is not equivalent to being high on unethical leadership and vice versa. They argue that the absence of ethical leadership can either imply unethical leadership or simply the lack of a proactive ethics-related agenda (ibid). Duffy, Ganster, and Pagon (2002) found that inconsistent leader behaviors, namely, being both unethical and supportive, have a more negative effect than unethical behavior by itself on levels of insecurity, diminishing control, and low levels of trust. This implies that low levels of ethical leadership do not always reflect high levels of unethical leadership and vice versa.

Thus, we argue that ethical and unethical leadership are conceptually different and negatively related rather than polar opposites. So far, however, empirical evidence on this matter is scarce. Kalshoven, Den Hartog, and De Hoogh (2011) found that passive leadership and ethical leadership are negatively related ($r = -.40$). Followers experience passive leaders who avoid responsibilities as less ethical (e.g., Bass, 1985; Den Hartog, Van Muijen, and Koopman, 1997). Similarly, De Hoogh and Den Hartog (2008) found a negative correlation between despotic leadership and ethical leadership ($r = -.56$). Finally, Detert and colleagues (2007) showed that ethical leadership and abusive supervision were negatively related ($r = -.51$). These correlations are sizable and suggest that ethical and unethical forms are strongly negatively related, yet they are not high enough to conclude that such styles are polar opposites. Dalal (2005) argues that constructs that are very strongly negatively related to each other (approaching -1.00) and that exhibit very similar patterns of relationships with external variables may be considered opposite poles of the same latent factor. Thus, the few studies that have included both ethical and unethical leader behaviors also suggest that these constructs should not be considered as complete polar opposites at the dyadic (supervisor–subordinate) level, but rather as negatively related, yet different constructs. Conceptually, this is important as it leaves room for the possibility that leaders at times could show both ethical and unethical behaviors, and it is thus of interest to study whether this occurs and how it affects subordinates.

THEORIES OF (UN)ETHICAL LEADER BEHAVIOR

It is typically suggested that ethical leaders have mostly positive effects on subordinate well-being, behavior, organizational behaviors, and performance, whereas unethical leaders have mostly negative effects. Several underlying mechanisms have been used to explain the influence of ethical and unethical leader behaviors on subordinates based on social learning, social exchange, and justice theory. Some of these mechanisms such as positive and negative social exchange are found respectively in both the ethical and unethical leadership literature, which again suggests some overlap and a negative relationship between these two different leadership styles. However, several proposed mechanisms are different, especially some of those focusing on how and why unethical leadership affects on followers.

Social learning can play a role in both ethical and unethical leadership. Subordinates learn what forms appropriate behavior in a given context by watching relevant role models such as leaders. Brown, Treviño, and Harrison (2005) approach ethical leadership from a social learning perspective and suggest that followers will come to behave in an ethical and responsible manner similar to that of their leader through imitation and observational learning (cf., Bandura, 1986). However, this also holds when the modeled behavior is unethical. Leaders are particularly influential as role models if they authorize unethical behavior through their own acts, sanctioning abilities, and legitimate power (Brief, Buttram, and Dukerich, 2001).

Researchers using social exchange theory in the ethical leadership field demonstrate that followers are willing to reciprocate when treated fairly, open-mindedly, and with concern, resulting in positive work outcomes (e.g., Kalshoven, Den Hartog, and De Hoogh, in press; Mayer et al., 2009). Reciprocity is also used to explain unethical leadership processes (e.g., Mitchell and Ambrose, 2007). Employees react with negative responses to being treated unfairly by the leader. When leaders treat subordinates unethically, employees see the exchange relationship as imbalanced or feel exploited, which affects subordinates' well-being or behaviors (Tepper, 2000).

In addition, in the unethical leadership literature, justice and fairness, reactance theory, and the political leadership perspective are also used to explain the relation between leadership and follower outcomes (e.g., Ferris et al., 2007; Mitchell and Ambrose, 2007; Tepper, 2000). In his research on abusive supervision, Tepper (2000) focuses on justice and argues that when employees feel treated unfairly, positive attitudes and behaviors diminish. Similarly, the fairness perspective is based on equity considerations (Folger and Cropanzano, 1998). Employees cognitively compare what actually happened with what could, should, and would have happened (e.g., Duffy et al., 2006).

Reactance theory focuses on the maintenance of personal control. Followers who experience their leader as unethical will feel little or no control and consequently will try to reestablish their control (Zellars, Tepper, and Duffy, 2002). This can yield negative reactions. The political perspective focuses on selecting situation-appropriate tactics of influence to exercise influence and to perform such tactics in a successful manner (e.g., Ammeter et al., 2002). From this perspective, researchers suggest that political and bullying behaviors are not always necessarily bad and leaders showing such behaviors do not exclusively act in a selfish manner or against organizational goals (Ferris et al., 2007). For example, Treadway et al. (2004) found that leader political skill positively predicted trust and job satisfaction and negatively predicted organizational cynicism through its positive relationship with perceived organizational support. Using these theoretical frameworks, we now focus on why and how unethical and ethical leaders are likely to affect well-being and deviance.

(UN)ETHICAL LEADER BEHAVIOR AND EMPLOYEE WELL-BEING

Available research links both ethical and unethical leader behaviors to well-being–related outcomes. Table 9.1 presents an overview of relationships found between (un)ethical leadership and various forms of employee well-being (and deviance, discussed later on in this chapter). Well-being is a broad construct that includes indicators of employees' physical and psychological health. Studies investigating subjective well-being have focused on both affective (hedonic balance or the balance between pleasant and unpleasant affect) and cognitive (life satisfaction) components of well-being (e.g., Schimmack et al., 2002). Studies investigating psychological well-being draw on various conceptualizaions of mental health (Keyes, Shmotkin, and Ryff, 2002). A common distinction is also made between context-free and context-specific well-being (Grebner, Semmer, and Elfering, 2005). Context-free or general well-being includes general health, life satisfaction, and happiness, whereas context-specific or job-related well-being focuses on the work context, and includes job-related affective well-being (ibid.). Here, we will focus on and differentiate between employees' satisfaction-related and health-related well-being in a work context. We relate these to (un)ethical leadership.

Table 9.1

Overview of Previous Studies: (Un)Ethical Leadership, Well-Being, and Deviance

	Attitudes well-being	Deviant work behaviors	Health well-being
Ethical leadership	Normative and affective commitment[2, 9] Follower optimism[1] Job satisfaction[5, 9] Satisfaction with leader[3] Cynicism[5]	Counterproductive work behavior[7] Organizational deviance[4] Workgroup deviance[6, 9]	Affective well-being[8]
Unethical leadership	Job tension[17] Organizational commitment[12, 14, 22] Family undermining[13] Psychological distress[21] Job satisfaction[22, 23]	Workplace deviance[16, 18, 27] Counterproductive behavior[14, 15] Supervisor-directed deviance[16, 27, 28] Interpersonal deviance[16, 27] Supervisor–target aggression[19] Dysfunctional resistance[20] Organizational deviance[14, 24, 26]	Problem drinking[25] Emotional exhaustion[10, 11, 17]

Note: Numbers in the table correspond to these references:

1. De Hoogh and Den Hartog (2008)
2. Den Hartog and De Hoogh (2009)
3. Brown, Treviño, and Harrison (2005)
4. Brown and Treviño (2006a)
5. Kalshoven, Den Hartog, and De Hoogh (2011)
6. Mayer et al. (2012)
7. Avey, Palanski, and Walumbwa (2011)
8. Kalshoven and Boon (2012)
9. Neubert et al. (2009)
10. Aryee et al. (2008)
11. Wu and Hu (2009)
12. Aryee et al. (2007)
13. Hoobler and Brass (2006)
14. Duffy, Ganster, and Pagon (2002)

15. Detert et al. (2007)
16. Mitchell and Ambrose (2007)
17. Harvey et al. (2007)
18. Thau et al. (2009)
19. Inness, Barling, and Turner (2005)
20. Tepper, Duffy, and Shaw (2001)
21. Tepper et al. (2007)
22. Tepper (2000)
23. Tepper et al. (2004)
24. Tepper, Henle, Lambert, Giacalone, and Duffy (2008)
25. Bamberger and Bacharach (2006)
26. Brown and Treviño (2006b)
27. Tepper et al. (2009)
28. Thau and Mitchell (2010)

First, unethical leadership is related to employees' being less satisfied with their jobs, less committed to their organizations, and more psychologically distressed (Ashforth, 1997; Duffy, Ganster, and Pagon, 2002; Tepper, 2000; Tepper et al., 2004, 2007; Tepper, Duffy, and Shaw, 2001; Zellars, Tepper, and Duffy, 2002). Other consequences of such leadership include heightened levels of emotional exhaustion (Aryee et al., 2008; Harvey et al., 2007; Wu and Hu, 2009). Overall, the available studies thus far show that unethical leadership diminishes both satisfaction and health-related well-being. These relationships may reflect that unethical leadership can lead employees to feel that they are unfairly treated and can cause them to feel unhappy (e.g., Burton and Hoobler, 2006; Tepper, 2000). The research suggests that this relationship likely stems from the heightened interpersonal conflict and the chronic assault on subordinates' feelings, self-worth, and abilities that are associated with many unethical forms of supervision.

Next, research shows a positive relationship of ethical leadership with satisfaction, optimism, and commitment and a negative relationship with cynicism (Brown, Treviño, and Harrison, 2005; De Hoogh and Den Hartog, 2008; Den Hartog and De Hoogh, 2009; Kalshoven, Den Hartog, and De Hoogh, 2011). Thus, the available studies show that ethical leadership is positively related to satisfaction-related well-being. However, studies have not yet extensively investigated ethical leadership and health-related well-being (e.g., Ilies, Morgeson, and Nahrgang, 2005), with one exception, showing that ethical leadership is related to job-related affective well-being (Kalshoven and Boon, 2012). On the basis of social exchange theory, we expect a positive relationship with affective well-being. When employees observe that they receive support, trust, and fair treatment from their ethical leader, they are likely to feel more positive about their work (i.e., high well-being). Research on related forms of leadership such as transformational leadership supports this idea (e.g., Van Dierendonck et al., 2004). Furthermore, social learning theory would suggest that employees actively engage in their work environment in order to increase the chances of obtaining positive reinforcement (Bandura, 1986). Employees act to enhance the likelihood of reinforcement from the ethical leader (Brown, Treviño, and Harrison, 2005), which results in feelings of pleasure for receiving such reinforcement. Thus, we expect that ethical leadership is likely to affect subordinates health-related well-being.

Overall, research shows negative relationships with both satisfaction and health-related well-being for unethical forms of leadership. A positive relationship of ethical leadership with satisfaction-based well-being has been established and is expected for health-related well-being as well, although research is needed. As stated, we propose a central role for well-being in the relationship between (un)ethical leadership and work deviance, adding to the literature on how these leaders affect follower deviance.

(UN)ETHICAL LEADER BEHAVIOR, WELL-BEING, AND DEVIANCE

Workplace deviance is defined as behavior that violates significant organizational norms and harms organizations and its members (Robinson and Bennett, 1995). Deviance can thus be seen as unethical behavior of employees and is thus likely to relate to (un)ethical leadership. Forms of deviance described in the literature include workplace deviance (ibid.), aggression (Neuman and Baron, 1998), counterproductive work behavior (Fox and Spector, 1999), social undermining (Duffy, Ganster, and Pagon, 2002), and retaliation (Skarlicki and Folger, 1997). Various studies show that unethical leadership is positively related to undesirable behaviors at the follower, leader, and organizational levels (Mitchell and Ambrose, 2007; Tepper et al., 2008, 2009; Thau et al., 2009) (see Table 9.1). In contrast, recent studies show that ethical leadership is negatively related to follower, work-group, and organizational deviance (Avey, Palanski, and Walumbwa, 2011; Brown and Treviño, 2006b; Mayer et al., 2012).

Deviant behaviors can be directed at colleagues, the leader, or the organization. Even if employees are reacting to the leader's unethical actions, they are not very likely to react with unethical behaviors openly directed at the leader, who is in a more powerful position (Tepper, Duffy, and Shaw, 2001). Subordinates may be afraid that retaliation would follow and that a direct and open act toward the leader may provoke further unethical treatment by the supervisor. Thus, Mitchell and Ambrose (2007) argue that subordinates will typically react aggressively toward the organizations when treated unethically by their leaders. In line with this, research shows that unethical leadership is positively related to organizational deviance (Mitchell and Ambrose, 2007; Tepper et al., 2008, 2009; Thau et al., 2009). Social exchange theory suggests that subordinates do not have to repay the original exchange giver due to the indirect and ambiguous nature of the exchange (whether it is good or bad), and for unethical leader behavior it seems that subordinates are likely to repay the organization.

For subordinates working for an ethical leader the positive feelings about their work (i.e., high well-being) are likely to result in positive or collaborative work behaviors rather than deviant work behavior. Subordinates are not likely to see deviant behavior directed at colleagues, the leader, or the organization as appropriate exchange behavior to offer in return for the ethical treatment they receive from their leader. Additionally, ethical leaders are likely to emphasize both the individual and the collective as they care about their direct reports, the work group, and organization and are able to take the interests and requirements of the organization into account when making decisions (Kalshoven, Den Hartog, and De Hoogh, 2011). This is likely to minimize deviant behavior. Thus, ethical leadership is likely to relate negatively to deviant behavior targeted at different levels, whereas unethical leadership is positively related to deviant behavior, mostly deviance targeted at the organization.

Subordinates who are happy with their work seem to "translate" their resources into positive work behaviors rather than deviant behavior. This supports the happy-productive worker thesis, which states that happy workers generally perform better (Zelenski, Murphy, and Jenkins, 2008). Over time, unethical leadership has a negative effect on performance and other outcomes. However, some forms of unethical leadership can sometimes have short-term, immediate, positive effects on followers' performance or efficiency (Ferris et al., 2007; Zapf and Gross, 2001), which is probably not due to feeling happy at work. In the study of Zapf and Gross, employees react with compliance when faced with leader bullying. This suggests that unethical leadership that is mostly task related could have some positive effects on task-related outcomes even though well-being might suffer, especially in the longer term. This is also in line with the conflict literature, showing that task conflict can increase performance under certain circumstances; however, affective and relationship conflicts do not have any positive effects (Jehn, 1995). Leadership is seldom only task-oriented and tends to have an affective and relational component, suggesting that unethical forms of leadership will hurt well-being and likely also effectiveness in the longer term, even if short-term performance does not suffer. So far, studies focus mainly on performance and are often not longitudinal. Future research on both ethical and unethical leadership is thus needed, and should include how such leaders affect performance, well-being, and deviance over time

Social learning theory suggests observer effects of (un)ethical leadership (Bandura, 1986). In other words, (un)ethical leadership behaviors affect not only the target subordinate but also the other subordinates who observe (un)ethical leadership. Studies show that subordinates witnessing unethical leader behavior in the form of bullying experience higher levels of stress, less job satisfaction, and higher turnover rates than those subordinates who have not observed bullying

(Hoel, Faragher, and Cooper, 2004; Rayner, Hoel, and Cooper, 2002). The observing subordinates will work harder to perform better to avoid being targeted with unethical behaviors themselves by the leader. Duffy et al. (2006) argue that if a supervisor treats all employees unethically, the impact of these unethical leader behaviors is likely to be attenuated, especially in comparison with a leader who treats a single employee differently.

Hoel et al. (2010) studied the connection between leadership style and both employees' perceived exposure to bullying at work and observations of others being bullied at work. A "noncontingent punishment" leadership style emerged as the strongest predictor of self-perceived exposure to bullying, while autocratic leadership was the strongest predictor of observed bullying. Thus, while observers particularly associate bullying with highly autocratic or tyrannical leader behavior, targets themselves relate bullying more to receiving noncontingent punishment—in other words an unpredictable style of leadership, where punishment is meted out or delivered on leaders' own terms, independent of the behavior of subordinates. Finally, laissez-faire leadership also emerged as a predictor of both self-reported and observed bullying. Thus, unequal treatment has a major impact on deviant behavior for the targeted subordinates and colleagues. While similar research on ethical leadership is lacking, equal treatment is also important for ethical leadership and thus for the influence of such leadership on outcomes.

OUTLINE FOR FUTURE RESEARCH

Figure 9.1 (see page 142) summarizes how (un)ethical leadership affects follower well-being and deviance. The effects of (un)ethical leadership on these outcomes are likely to be dependent on the context (e.g., Brass, Butterfield, and Skaggs, 1998; Kalshoven, Den Hartog, and De Hoogh, in press; Treviño, Butterfield, and McCabe, 1998). Thus, we expect that (un)ethical leadership has a greater impact on well-being and deviance behavior under certain conditions. However, research that examines situational factors influencing (un)ethical leadership in relation to these outcomes is still lacking and future research is thus needed to shed light on potential situational differences in these relationships. For example, one important area is bystander or observer effects, as our review of the evidence from unethical leadership research suggests that observing how others are treated has a strong impact. This suggests that incorporating different perspectives into the (un)ethical leadership research is needed. For instance leader, subordinate, work group, consumers, and/or other third parties are relevant in the relationship between unethical and ethical leadership and well-being.

Studying the wider organizational context in relation to (un)ethical leadership is also of interest. Certain combinations of human resource management (HRM) practices such as training, teamwork, performance appraisal, and rewards (e.g., Sun, Aryee, and Law, 2007) can potentially play an important role in buffering the effects of leadership. Substitutes for leadership theory (Kerr and Jermier, 1978) suggest that certain HRM practices may act as a substitute for leadership. Substitutes for leadership affect mainly employee outcomes, and they replace the effect of leadership. For example, Podsakoff, MacKenzie, and Bommer (1996) studied substitute variables for transformational leadership and found that organizational rewards act as a substitute for the effect of such leadership on satisfaction, such that transformational leadership seems less important for employees' valuing of organizational rewards. Such effects may also occur for (un) ethical leadership. Facing low levels of ethical leadership, employees receiving organizational resources from HRM are likely to maintain their well-being (Kalshoven and Boon, 2012). HRM provides resources on which to draw and produces in the organization and its members a feeling of obligation to reciprocate, and thus HRM may function as a substitute for ethical leadership.

For example, Kalshoven and Boon (2012) show that ethical leadership is more strongly related to well-being when employees perceive low levels of HRM.

A key question also remains for future research: How can behaviors that harm the organization or its employees not be in quantitative opposition to behaviors that benefit the organization or its employees? One answer requires researchers to focus not on the target of the behaviors (the organization or other employees in the organization) but on their source: the leader. Could it be that both unethical and ethical leader behavior are geared toward the same goal: achieving a good mood or a high level of satisfaction or performance in the future? Furthermore, an ethical leader is not a "saint" and will probably at times make unethical decisions in the eyes of followers (and vice versa: people are also unlikely to always act unethically). To learn more about combinations of unethical and ethical actions of leaders, different leader behaviors need to be studied simultaneously. Specifically related to this chapter, future research is needed that studies both ethical and unethical forms of leadership and their effects on subordinate well-being and deviant behavior over time. A longitudinal design is also needed to show the causal directions of proposed relationships.

PRACTICAL IMPLICATIONS: A BALANCED PERSPECTIVE

Understanding sustained success in today's business world requires increased attention to the multiple conceptualizations of ethical and unethical leader behavior. After reviewing the literature, we suggested that ethical and unethical leadership are negatively related but different constructs. Our chapter showed that leaders may use both unethical and ethical leadership at the same time, as these may be overlapping but also partly different constructs. This has consequences in practice as well. For instance, an organizational intervention designed to facilitate ethical leadership may not simultaneously deter every form of unethical leadership. Different strategies seem appropriate to stimulate specific behaviors and deter others. Measuring these forms of leadership in appraisals might help in making it easier to discuss desired forms of leadership in the organization. In this vein, ethical and unethical leadership may then need to be evaluated separately during performance appraisals. For example, rather than evaluating leaders along a continuum ranging from unethical to ethical leadership, it may be necessary to evaluate the frequency of these separately. In this way, one could assess whether the leader is (a) perceived to act ethically as well as unethically, (b) not perceived as ethical but only as unethical, (c) perceived as only ethical, not unethical, or (d) not perceived as either. Such profiles can be linked to training and mentoring programs.

Management needs to be aware of the signaling function of leadership even when directed toward others. Also, leaders should pay close attention to aligning messages communicated to employees to send a consistent signal about fair behavior, expectations, and results. A leader who shows only unethical or both ethical and unethical leadership, and especially one who is unpredictable, is likely to lower well-being and increase deviance, thus helping leaders to develop more consistency is likely to be beneficial for the organization.

Management should focus on training leaders to treat their employees ethically and to build strong social relationships with their followers. Previous research has shown that ethical leadership is only partly based on leader personality (cf., Walumbwa and Schaubroeck, 2009), which suggests that training leaders to show more ethical behaviors and fewer unethical ones may be a realistic option for enhancing well-being and desired work behavior and decreasing deviance. In doing so, organizations can make leaders aware of their important position as role models of appropriate behavior and emphasize that followers are likely to react to ethical leader behavior with higher well-being and lower deviance.

REFERENCES

Ammeter, C. Douglas; Gardner, W.L.; Hochwarter, W.A.; and Ferris, G.R. 2002. Toward a political theory of leadership. *Leadership Quarterly,* 13, 751–796.

Aronson, E. 2001. Integrating leadership styles and ethical perspectives. *Canadian Journal of Administrative Sciences,* 18, 244–256.

Aryee, S.; Chen, Z.X.; Sun, L.; and Debrah, Y.A. 2007. Antecedents and outcomes of abusive supervision: Test of a trickle-down model. *Journal of Applied Psychology,* 92, 191–201.

Aryee, S.; Sun, L.Y.; Chen, Z.X.; and Debrah, Y.A. 2008. Abusive supervision and contextual performance: The mediating role of emotional exhaustion and the moderating role of work unit structure. *Management and Organization Review,* 4, 393–411.

Ashforth, B. 1994. Petty tyranny in organizations. *Human Relations,* 47, 755–778.

———. 1997. Petty tyranny in organizations: A preliminary examination of antecedents and consequences. *Canadian Journal of Administrative Sciences,* 14, 126–140.

Avey, J.B.; Palanski, M.E.; and Walumbwa, F.O. 2011. When leadership goes unnoticed: The moderating role of follower self-esteem on the relationship between ethical leadership and follower behavior. *Journal of Business Ethics,* 98, 573–582.

Bamberger, P.A., and Bacharach, S.B. 2006. Abusive supervision and subordinate problem drinking: Taking resistance, stress, and subordinate personality into account. *Human Relations,* 59, 1–30.

Bandura, A. 1986. *Social Foundation of Thought and Action.* Englewood Cliffs, NJ: Prentice Hall.

Bass, B.M. 1985. *Leadership and Performance Beyond Expectations.* New York: Free Press.

Bass, B.M., and Steidlmeier, P. 1999. Ethics, character and authentic transformational leadership behavior. *Leadership Quarterly,* 10, 181–217.

Bies, R.J. 2000. Interactional (in)justice: The sacred and the profane. In *Advances in Organizational Behavior,* ed. J. Greenberg and R. Cropanzano. Stanford, CA: Stanford University Press.

Brass, D.; Butterfield, K.; and Skaggs, B. 1998. Relationships and unethical behavior: A social network perspective. *Academy of Management Review,* 23, 14–31.

Brief, A.P.; Buttram, R.T.; and Dukerich, J.M. 2001. Collective corruption in the corporate world: Toward a process model. In *Groups at Work: Theory and Research,* ed. M.E. Turner, 471–499. Mahwah, NJ: Erlbaum.

Brown, M.E., and Treviño, L.K. 2006a. Ethical leadership: A review and future directions. *Leadership Quarterly,* 17, 595–616.

———. 2006b. Socialized charismatic leadership, values congruence and deviance in work groups. *Journal of Applied Psychology,* 91, 954–962.

Brown, M.E.; Treviño, L.K.; and Harrison, D.A. 2005. Ethical leadership: A social learning perspective for construct development and testing. *Organizational Behavior and Human Decision Processes,* 97, 117–134.

Burton, J., and Hoobler, J. 2006. Subordinate self-esteem and abusive supervision. *Journal of Managerial Issues,* 18, 340–355.

Craig, B.S., and Gustafson, S.B. 1998. Perceived leader integrity scale: An instrument for assessing employee perceptions of leader integrity. *Leadership Quarterly,* 9, 127–145.

Dalal, R.S. 2005. A meta-analysis of the relationship between organizational citizenship behavior and counterproductive work behavior. *Journal of Applied Psychology,* 90, 1241–1255.

De Hoogh, A.H.B., and Den Hartog, D.N. 2008. Ethical and despotic leadership, relationships with leader's social responsibility, top management team effectiveness and subordinates' optimism: A multi-method study. *Leadership Quarterly,* 19, 297–311.

———. 2009. Ethical leadership: The socially responsible use of power. In *Power and Interdependence in Organizations,* ed. D. Tjosvold and B.M. Van Knippenberg, 338–354. Cambridge: University Press.

Den Hartog, D.N., and De Hoogh, A. 2009. Empowering behaviour and leader fairness and integrity: Studying perceptions of ethical leader behaviour from a levels-of-analysis perspective. *European Journal of Work and Organizational Psychology,* 18, 2, 199–230.

Den Hartog, D.N.; Van Muijen, J.J.; and Koopman, P.L. 1997. Transactional versus transformational leadership: An analysis of the MLQ. *Journal of Occupational and Organizational Psychology,* 70, 19–34.

Detert, J.R.; Treviño, L.K.; Burris, E.R.; and Andiappan, M. 2007. Managerial modes of influence and counterproductivity in organizations: A longitudinal business-unit-level investigation. *Journal of Applied Psychology,* 94, 993–1005.

Duffy, M.K.; Ganster, D.C.; and Pagon, M. 2002. Social undermining in the workplace. *Academy of Management Journal*, 45, 331–351.

Duffy, M.K.; Ganster, D.C.; Shaw, J.D.; Johnson, J.L.; and Pagon, M. 2006. The social context of undermining behavior at work. *Organizational Behavior and Human Decision Processes*, 101, 105–126.

Einarsen, S.; Aasland, M.S.; and Skogstad, A. 2007. Destructive leadership behavior: A definition and conceptual model. *Leadership Quarterly*, 18, 207–216.

Ferris, G.R.; Zinko, R.; Brouer, R.L.; Buckley, M.R.; and Harvey, M.G. 2007. Strategic bullying as a supplementary balanced perspective on destructive leadership. *Leadership Quarterly*, 18, 195–206.

Folger, R., and Cropanzano, R. 1998. *Organizational Justice and Human Resource Management*. Thousand Oaks, CA: Sage.

Fox, S., and Spector, P.E. 1999. A model of work frustration-aggression. *Journal of Organizational Behavior*, 20, 6, 915–931.

Grebner, S.; Semmer, N.K.; and Elfering, A. 2005. Working conditions and three types of well-being: A longitudinal study with self-report and rating data. *Journal of Occupational Health Psychology*, 10, 1, 31–43.

Harris, K.J.; Kacmar, K.M.; and Zivnuska, S. 2007. An investigation of abusive supervision as a predictor of performance and the meaning of work as a moderator of the relationship. *Leadership Quarterly*, 18, 252–263.

Harvey, P.; Stoner, J.; Hochwarter, W.; and Kacmar, C. 2007. Coping with abusive supervision: The neutralizing effects of ingratiation and positive affect on negative employee outcomes. *Leadership Quarterly*, 18, 264–280.

Hoel, H.; Faragher, B.; and Cooper, C.L. 2004. Bullying is detrimental to health, but all bullying behaviours are not equally damaging. *British Journal of Guidance and Counselling*, 32, 367–387.

Hoel, H.B.; Glaso, L.; Hetland, J.; Cooper, C.L.; and Einarsen, S. 2010. Leadership styles as predictors of self-reported and observed workplace bullying. *British Journal of Management*, 21, 453–468.

Hoobler, J.M.; and Brass, D.J. 2006. Abusive supervision and family undermining as displaced aggression. *Journal of Applied Psychology*, 91, 1125–1133.

House, R.J., and Howell, J.M. 1992. Personality and charismatic leadership. *Leadership Quarterly*, 3, 81–108.

Howell, J.M., and Avolio, B.J. 1992. The ethics of charismatic leadership: Submission or liberation? *Academy of Management Executive*, 6, 43–54.

Ilies, R.; Morgeson, F.P.; and Nahrgang, J.D. 2005. Authentic leadership and eudemonic well-being: Understanding leader-follower outcomes. *Leadership Quarterly*, 16, 373–394.

Inness, M.; Barling, J.; and Turner, N. 2005. Understanding supervisor-targeted aggression: A within-person between-jobs design. *Journal of Applied Psychology*, 90, 731–739.

Jehn, K.A. 1995. A multimethod examination of the benefits and detriments of intragroup conflict. *Administrative Science Quarterly*, 40, 256–82.

Kalshoven, K.; and Boon, C.T. 2012. Ethical leadership, employee well-being and helping: The moderating role of HRM. *Journal of Personnel Psychology*, 11, 60–68.

Kalshoven, K.; Den Hartog, D.N.; and De Hoogh, A.H.B. 2011. Ethical leadership at work questionnaire (ELW): Development and validation of a multidimensional measure. *Leadership Quarterly*, 22, 51–69.

Kalshoven, K.; Den Hartog, D.N.; and De Hoogh, A.H.B. Ethical Leadership and Followers' Helping and Initiative: The Role of Demonstrated Responsibility and Job Autonomy. *European Journal of Work and Organizational Psychology*, in press.

Kanungo, R.N. 2001. Ethical values of transactional and transformational leaders. *Canadian Journal of Administrative Sciences*, 18, 257–265.

Kerr, S., and Jermier, J.M. 1978. Substitutes for leadership: Their meaning and measurement. *Organizational Behavior and Human Performance*, 22, 375–403.

Keyes, C.L.M.; Shmotkin, D.; and Ryff, C.D. 2002. Optimizing well-being: The empirical encounter of two traditions. *Journal of Personality and Social Psychology*, 82, 1007–1022.

Kish-Gephart, J.J.; Harrison, D.A.; and Treviño, L.K. 2010. Bad apples, bad cases, and bad barrels: Meta-analytic evidence about sources of unethical decisions at work. *Journal of Applied Psychology*, 95, 1–31.

Mayer, D.M.; Aquino, K.; Greenbaum, R.L.; and Kuenzi, M. 2012. Who displays ethical leadership and why does it matter? An examination of antecedents and consequences of ethical leadership. *Academy of Management Journal*, 55, 151–171.

Mayer, D.M.; Kuenzi, M.; Greenbaum, R.; Bardes, M.; and Salvador, R. 2009. How low does ethical leadership flow? How low does ethical leadership flow? Test of a trickle-down model. *Organizational Behavior and Human Decision Processes,* 108, 1–13.

McClelland, D.C. 1975. *Power the Inner Experience.* New York: Irvington.

Mitchell, M.S., and Ambrose, M.L. 2007. Abusive supervision and workplace deviance and the moderating effects of negative reciprocity beliefs. *Journal of Applied Psychology,* 92, 1159–1168.

Neubert, M.J.; Carlson, D.S.; Kacmar, K.M.; Roberts, J.A.; and Chonko, L.B. 2009. The virtuous influence of ethical leadership behavior: Evidence from the field. *Journal of Business Ethics,* 90, 157–170.

Neuman, J.H., and Baron, R.A. 1998. Workplace violence and workplace aggression: Evidence concerning specific forms, potential causes, and preferred targets. *Journal of Management,* 24, 391–419.

Podsakoff, P.M.; MacKenzie, S.B.; and Bommer, W.H. 1996. Transformational leader behaviors and substitutes for leadership as determinants of employee satisfaction, commitment, trust, and organizational citizenship behaviors. *Journal of Management,* 22, 259–298.

Rayner, C.; Hoel, H; and Cooper, C.L. 2002. *Workplace Bullying. What We Know, Who Is to Blame, and What Can We Do?* London: Taylor and Francis.

Resick, C.J.; Hanges, P.J.; Dickson, M.W.; and Mitchelson, J.K. 2006. A cross-cultural examination of the endorsement of ethical leadership. *Journal of Business Ethics,* 63, 345–359.

Robinson, S.L., and Bennett, R.J. 1995. A typology of deviant workplace behaviors: A multidimensional scaling study. *Academy of Management Journal,* 38, 555–572.

Salin, D. 2003. Ways of explaining workplace bullying: A review of enabling, motivating and precipitating structures and processes in the work environment. *Human Relations,* 56, 1213–1232.

Schimmack, U.; Radhakrishnan, P.; Oishi, S.; and Dzokoto, V. 2002. Culture, personality, and subjective well-being: Integrating process models of life satisfaction. *Journal of Personality and Social Psychology,* 82, 582–593.

Skarlicki, D.P.; and Folger, R. 1997. Retaliation in the workplace: The roles of distributive, procedural, and interactional justice. *Journal of Applied Psychology,* 82, 434–443.

Sun, L.Y.; Aryee, S.; and Law, K.S. 2007. High performance human resources practices, citizenship behavior and organizational performance: A relational perspective. *Academy of Management Journal,* 50, 558–577.

Tepper, B.J. 2000. Consequences of abusive supervision. *Academy of Management Journal,* 43, 178–191.

———. 2007. Abusive supervision in work organizations: review, synthesis, and research agenda. *Journal of Management,* 33, 261–289.

Tepper, B.J.; Duffy, M.K.; and Shaw, J.D. 2001. Personality moderates the relationship between abusive supervision and subordinates' resistance. *Journal of Applied Psychology,* 86, 974–983.

Tepper, B.J.; Duffy, M.K.; Hoobler, J.M.; and Ensley, M.D. 2004. Moderators of the relationship between coworkers' organizational citizenship behavior and fellow employees' attitudes. *Journal of Applied Psychology,* 89, 455–465.

Tepper, B.J.; Moss, S.M.; Lockhart, D.E.; Carr, J.C. 2007. Abusive supervision, upward maintenance communication, and subordinates' psychological distress. *Academy of Management Journal,* 50, 5, 1169–1180.

Tepper, B.J.; Henle, C.A.; Lambert, L.S.; Giacalone, R.A.; Duffy, M.K. 2008. Abusive supervision and subordinates' organization deviance. *Journal of Applied Psychology,* 93, 721–732.

Tepper, B.J.; Carr, J.C.; Breaux, D.M.; Geider, S.; Hu, C.; and Hua, W. 2009. Abusive supervision, intentions to quit and employees' workplace deviance: A power/dependence analysis. *Organizational Behavior and Human Decision Processes,* 109, 156–167.

Thau, S.; and Mitchell, M.S. 2010. Self-gain or self-regulation impairment? Examining two explanations of the supervisor abuse—employee deviance relationship through distributive justice perceptions. *Journal of Applied Psychology,* 95, 1009–1031.

Thau, S.; Bennett, R.J.; Mitchell, M.S.; and Marrs, M.B. 2009. How management style moderates the relationship between abusive supervision and workplace deviance: An uncertainty management theory perspective. *Organizational Behavior and Human Decision Processes,* 108, 79–92.

Treadway, D.C.; Hochwarter, W.A.; Ferris, G.R.; Kacmar, C.J.; Douglas, C.; Ammeter, A.P.; and Buckley, M.R. 2004. Leader political skill and employee reactions. *Leadership Quarterly,* 15, 493–513.

Treviño, L.K.; Brown, M.; and Hartman, L.P. 2003. A qualitative investigation of perceived executive ethical leadership: Perceptions from inside and outside the executive suite. *Human Relations,* 56, 5–37.

Treviño, L.K.; Butterfield, K.D.; and McCabe, D.L. 1998. The ethical context in organizations: Influences on employee attitudes and behaviors. *Leadership Quarterly,* 8, 447–476.

Turner, N.; Barling, J.; Epitropaki, O.; Butcher, V.; and Milner, C. 2002. Transformational leadership and moral reasoning. *Journal of Applied Psychology, 87,* 304–311.

Van Dierendonck, D.; Haynes, C.; Borrill, C.; and Stride, C. 2004. Leadership behavior and subordinate well-being. *Journal of Occupational Health Psychology, 9, 2,* 165–175.

Walumbwa, F.O.; Avolio, B.J.; Gardner, W.L.; Wernsing, T.S.; and Peterson, S.J. 2008. Authentic leadership: Development and validation of a theory-based measure. *Journal of Management, 34,* 89–126.

Walumbwa, F.O.; and Schaubroeck, J. 2009. Leader personality traits and employee voice behavior: Mediating roles of ethical leadership and workgroup psychological safety. *Journal of Applied Psychology, 94,* 1275–1286.

Wu, T.-Y., and Hu, C. 2009. Abusive supervision and employee emotional exhaustion. *Group and Organization Management, 34,* 143–169.

Yaffe, T., and Kark, R. 2011. Leading by example: The case of leader OCB. *Journal of Applied Psychology, 96,* 806–826.

Yukl, G. 2006. *Leadership in Organizations.* 6th ed. Englewood Cliffs, NJ: Prentice Hall.

Zapf, D.; and Gross, C. 2001. Conflict Escalation and Coping with Workplace Bullying: A Replication and Extension. *European Journal of Work and Organizational Psychology, 10,* 497–522.

Zelenski, J.M.; Murphy, S.A.; and Jenkins, D.A. 2008. The happy-productive worker thesis revisited. *Journal of Happiness Studies, 9, 4,* 521–537.

Zellars, K.L.; Tepper, B.J.; and Duffy, M.K. 2002. Abusive supervision and subordinates' organizational citizenship behavior. *Journal of Applied Psychology, 86,* 1068–1076.

10

AGE DISCRIMINATION IN THE WORKPLACE AND WELL-BEING

ANASTASIA S. VOGT YUAN

By 2030, 19 percent of the population of the United States is projected to be age sixty-five and older (Jacobsen et al., 2011). This changing age structure has implications for the age composition of the workplace. Currently, 20.6 percent of the U.S. workforce is made up of workers over age fifty-five with only 4.7 percent age sixty-five and older (U.S. Bureau of Labor Statistics, 2011). By 2030, the United States is projected to have 23 percent of its workforce older than age fifty-five (Lee and Mather, 2008).

With increasing age diversity in the workplace, age discrimination in the workplace could potentially become more pervasive. Although some age discrimination occurs among twenty-year-olds (Gee, Pavalko, and Long, 2007), most age discrimination in the workplace tends to occur between the ages of thirty-nine and sixty-nine (Roscigno et al., 2007). Increasing the amount of age discrimination not only influences the victims of discrimination but also creates an ethical problem. Moreover, it is in the best interests of both government and industry to decrease age discrimination. The government needs an increased number of older workers to decrease the dependency ratio (i.e., the ratio of the population not in the labor force and thus dependent upon government subsidies or working-age individuals to the population in the labor force) in order to sustain both the tax base and the Social Security program. Industry will need an increase in the percentage of older workers to support pension and retirement programs and other employment benefits (Taqi, 2002; Walker, 2002). Age discrimination discourages older workers from continuing and seeking employment and thus constitutes a barrier to increasing the older age workforce.

Age discrimination was outlawed in the United States by the Age Discrimination in Employment Act (ADEA) in 1967. This act originally outlawed discrimination against workers between ages forty and sixty-five, but has been extended to all workers older than age forty. However, despite these laws, it is still difficult to determine when age discrimination occurs, partially because its definition is somewhat ambiguous and is influenced by an individual's perceptions and judgment of ethical behaviors. Ageism is considered to be the "systematic stereotyping of and discrimination against people because they are old just as racism and sexism accomplish this for skin color and gender" (Butler, 1969, p. 243). However, this definition itself is often unclear when considered in particular situations. Economists generally consider age discrimination to occur "when factors unrelated to productivity affect the employment relationship" (Johnson and Neumark, 1997, p. 780). This definition is inclusive of both interpersonal and institutional age discrimination in the workplace. Interpersonal discrimination occurs when a person treats someone unfairly due to her/his group membership, whereas institutional discrimination occurs when institutions have policies that systematically disadvantage members of a particular group.

Both interpersonal and institutional age discrimination detrimentally impact the job opportunities of older workers, thereby damaging their economic well-being. Interpersonal age discrimination in the workplace may be overt but often occurs covertly through internalized ageist beliefs that influence managerial decisions and/or evaluations. For instance, older workers have a harder time finding and keeping a job, due to ageist beliefs that they have lower job performance and productivity than younger workers (McCann and Giles, 2002). Ageist stereotypes particularly have a detrimental impact on the probability of older workers being hired, as equally qualified older workers are less likely to get hired over younger workers (Bendick, Brown, and Wall, 1999; Dennis and Thomas, 2007). Additionally, due to employers' age bias, older workers are less likely than younger workers to participate in employer training programs (Taylor and Urwin, 2001). Older men and women reported similar amounts of old age discrimination in terms of fewer opportunities for training (Duncan and Lovetto, 2004).

Older people also suffer more from economic dislocations, including layoffs, which may be due to either interpersonal or institutional age discrimination. Older workers are often targeted for layoffs not only due to these workers having higher pay scales and being near retirement, but also due to perceptions of older people as less productive and with lower potential to learn and utilize new skills and technologies (e.g., Dennis and Thomas, 2007). Whatever the reason, employers forced to reduce employment often concentrate on older workers (Walker, 2002). For instance, Henry and Jennings (2004) illustrated how, as a cost-saving measure, companies often laid off workers who were higher-paid, highly skilled, and near retirement. Moreover, McMullin and Marshall (2001) explicated how older people were especially likely to become and remain unemployed when companies closed down and reopened under a new company name with nonunionized workers. While these policies often do not constitute a form of interpersonal age discrimination, they indicate a way that institutional age discrimination takes place due to economic strategies that systematically disadvantage older workers. These types of policies are extremely detrimental to older workers not only in the short term but also in the long term, as older workers are more likely than younger workers to face long-term unemployment (Walker, 2002) or an involuntary retirement when they cannot find employment (Berger, 2006).

ETHICAL CONSIDERATIONS OF AGE DISCRIMINATION

Carroll (1979) indicates that there are four domains of corporate social responsibility—economic, legal, ethical, and discretionary (i.e., philanthropic) responsibilities. Thus, businesses have social responsibilities to society beyond being an economic unit that abides by officially mandated laws and regulations. Schwartz and Carroll (2003) designated three ethical standards—conventional, consequential, and deontological standards. Conventional standards are the accepted norms of an organization, industry, profession, or society for a business to function. However, this standard is highly relativistic and thus should also comply with the minimum criteria of the two following standards. Consequential standards are determined by the consequences of an action or policy for promoting the greater benefit (or lowest cost) to society compared to other actions or policies. Deontological standards consider duty and obligations, especially in terms of moral rights and justice. Justice can include distributive (i.e., equitably distributed), compensatory (i.e., proportionate to loss), and retributive (i.e., punishments fit the crime) justice. Age discrimination in the workplace often violates consequential and deontological standards by having adverse social consequences and/or violating rights and justice norms.

Consequential standards are important to consider, since some corporate policies and actions may violate the social contract—that is, management has obligations not only to stockholders of the corporation but also to society (Henry and Jennings, 2004). A common age discriminatory measure adopted by corporations is to lay off older workers, especially those who earn higher wages and are nearing retirement. Although laying off highly paid workers may provide a cost-cutting measure consistent with stockholder objectives, it has numerous negative consequences for society, thereby violating the corporation's societal obligations. For example, management is responsible for corporate behavior that negatively impacts the economic well-being of the local labor force, discriminates against workers based upon age, race, or gender, and jeopardizes the livelihoods (including retirement incomes) of those unable to find alternative employment (Henry and Jennings, 2004, p. 220). Thus, corporations and management should uphold societal obligations in their business practices and consider the social consequences of their actions for fulfilling these responsibilities.

Age discrimination also violates deontological standards by violating several U.S. principles regarding rights and justice. Age discrimination in the workplace violates the democratic principles of equal opportunity, since employment opportunities for hiring and promotion are not equal but determined by age (Taqi, 2002). In addition, it violates the ideal that employment should be based upon merit including skills and experiences rather than based upon social characteristics such as age, race, or gender, since discriminatory policies and actions having disparate impacts on people, depending upon their group membership rather than their merit (Kurland, 2001). Age discrimination in the workplace violates basic assumptions of justice and fairness, if employment rewards (e.g., positions and promotions) and punishments (e.g., demotions and firings) are not based upon merit (Gilbert, 2000). For example, Ferris and King (1992) find that older workers unfairly received lower performance evaluations due to having higher interpersonal distance from supervisors and engaging in less subordinate behavior. Thus, evaluations need to be determined by fair and just standards rather than being based on the politics of the organization (Ferris and King, 1992).

HOW COMMON IS AGE DISCRIMINATION?

It is difficult to determine how common age discrimination is, not only in general but also within the workplace. Percentages from the 2004–2006 Midlife Development in the United States survey indicate that roughly 10.8 percent of respondents in the sample reported that they had experienced age discrimination in their lifetime (based upon author calculations). Although these are lifetime percentages, these numbers may underreport discrimination, as they are reported retrospectively. Gee, Pavalko, and Long (2007) indicated proportions as high as 8 percent reporting age discrimination in the past five years, depending upon age and cohort. Moreover, Johnson and Neumark (1997) found that on average, 7 percent of older men (over forty-five years old) reported experiencing age discrimination within the workplace in the past five years and 3 percent reported experiencing age discrimination with their current employer. However, these numbers are self-reported and are thus based upon perceptions, which may or may not be accurate. Although this is potentially problematic, it is likely that old age discrimination is under-rather than overreported, because older people are less likely to report having experienced any type of discrimination (Kessler, Mickelson, and Williams, 1999; Yuan, 2007). Thus, age discrimination in the workplace appears to be reported by a substantial minority of respondents.

Additionally, it is difficult to determine the situations under which age discrimination occurs. The 2004–2006 Midlife Development in the United States survey provides data regarding whether respondents reported certain types of work-related discrimination as well as potential reasons for this discrimination (e.g., age, race, and gender) across a lifetime. Although incidences and reasons are not directly linked, they provide some context for whether a person reporting age discrimination also indicated that s/he had experienced various types of work discrimination. Figure 10.1 shows the percentages reporting three types of work discrimination over a lifetime depending on

Figure 10.1   **Percentage Experiencing Work Discrimination Based upon Discrimination Status**

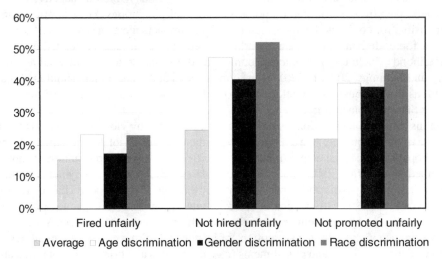

Source: 2004–2006 Midlife Development in the United States—MIDUS2.

discrimination status (i.e., on average and for those who experienced age, gender, or race discrimination). Respondents who reported experiencing age discrimination were most likely to indicate that they were not hired (47.4 percent) or not promoted unfairly (39.4 percent) in their lifetimes. These differences reflected that, on average, people were most likely to report being unfairly not hired (24.7 percent), followed by unfairly not promoted (21.7 percent), and lastly unfairly fired (15.4 percent). However, being unfairly fired was the only work situation where proportions for age discrimination (23.3 percent) were higher than for race (23.1 percent) or gender (17.3 percent) discrimination. For both not hired and not promoted unfairly, percentages for age discrimination fell between race (the highest) and gender (the lowest) discrimination.

These self-reported perceptions of discriminatory experiences both differ and match results from other studies. For instance, Yuan (2007) found that those who reported age discrimination were more likely to report discrimination due to being fired from a job or not being given a promotion. Moreover, Johnson and Neumark (1997) using self-reported data found that not being promoted is experienced the most, followed by general company discrimination and not being hired or interviewed. Age discrimination was least likely to be reported as occurring for cases of being demoted or laid off (ibid.). Differences here could occur due to time period, since the data were collected between 1966 and 1980. Furthermore, Roscigno et al. (2007) found expulsion (e.g., firing) to compose the majority of verified age discrimination litigation cases, but they were using litigation data. Similarly, Neumark (2009) also found that hiring and promotion age discrimination litigation cases were much less common than discharge and layoff cases. Roscigno et al. (2007) and Neumark (2009) could differ from Johnson and Neumark (1997) because age discrimination may be easier to prove in instances of firing. Alternatively, people may feel that the consequences of expulsion are more extensive, making them more willing to pursue litigation despite its emotional and economic costs. It is also possible that being laid off was justified by employees as due to market forces rather than age discrimination (e.g., McMullin and Marshall, 2001). Future research should further explore the situations under which age discrimination in the workplace occurs as well as when workers perceive that it occurs.

Who reports age discrimination in the workplace? As previously mentioned, age discrimination is higher in the early twenties age group, decreases with age, and peaks even higher in the fifties (Gee, Pavalko, and Long, 2007). Gender by itself is not related to age discrimination, but gender interacts with age so that old age discrimination occurs at a younger age for women (Duncan and Lovetto, 2004). For example, Duncan and Lovetto (2004) found that women in their thirties reported discrimination due to gender, young age, and old age (that is, women in their thirties received negative treatment because they were viewed by older colleagues as "too young" and by younger colleagues as "too old" to perform their job well), but men in their thirties reported discrimination only for young age. Age discrimination tended to be reported more by white workers, probably because nonwhite workers often attribute discrimination to race rather than age (Roscigno et al., 2007), although some research found no significant racial differences (e.g., Johnson and Neumark, 1997).

There is some question as to whether the employment sector influences age discrimination. Skilled and semiskilled workers represented the majority of litigation cases for age discrimination (Roscigno et al., 2007). Alternatively, Walker et al. (2007) indicated that women in professional jobs were more likely to have experienced or observed age discrimination in the workplace, although women in these occupations may simply be more aware that such discrimination is occurring. There is disagreement as to whether public sector jobs have fewer instances of age discrimination. Byron (2010) found that employment discrimination litigation cases vary little between public and private sectors, although there were more promotion discrimination cases from the public section and more firing discrimination cases from the private sector. However, Johnson and Neumark (1997) found that self-reported age discrimination in the workplace was lower among workers in the public sector.

REASONS FOR AGE DISCRIMINATION IN THE WORKPLACE

There are several reasons why age discrimination occurs. Age discrimination against older people can serve an ego-protective function for the perpetrator of ageism (Snyder and Meine, 1994). Snyder and Meine (1994) posited that ageist stereotypes help younger people to deny the aspects of aging (e.g., becoming sick and weak and eventually dying) that they find threatening. Thus, perpetrators may engage in age discrimination as a way to alleviate their own anxiety about aging by distancing themselves from this potential future in-group. That is, ageism is a "prejudice against our feared future self" (Nelson, 2005, p. 207).

An alternative explanation is that ageism occurs due to competition between generations over institutional resources. As the population ages, older age groups become larger and are thereby viewed as a potential threat in competing for scarce resources. Preston (1984) posited that two categories of dependents—children and the elderly—compete over governmental resources, which were more likely to be spent on the elderly, as all age groups hope to someday benefit from the allocation of resources to the elderly. On the other hand, as the older population grows, this age group could become more normative. Uhlenberg (1988) explored whether an older age structure led to a gerontocracy and concluded that it did not, as older people from 1940 to the 1980s were less likely to be in leadership positions.

Moreover, cultural perceptions of age, including ageist stereotypes, are internalized through socialization processes and contribute to ageism both inside and outside the workplace. However, ageist stereotypes are not universally negative but are both positive and negative, including perceptions of the elderly as warm but incompetent (Cuddy, Norton, and Fiske, 2005; Fiske et al., 2002; Kite et al., 2005). Similarly, ageist stereotypes of workers are both positive and negative. For example, older workers are valued for their experience, knowledge, work habits, and loyalty, but they are also perceived as inflexible, unwilling to adapt to technology, and resistant to new ways (Dennis and Thomas, 2007). Furthermore, Van Dalen, Henkens, and Schippers (2010) found that older workers in the Netherlands were perceived to have higher and lower productivity, depending upon the underlying dimension of productivity. Older workers were perceived to have higher reliability, commitment to the organization, social skills, customer-oriented skills, and accuracy, whereas younger workers were perceived to have higher creativity, flexibility, physical capacity, new technology skills, and willingness to learn (ibid.).

AGE DISCRIMINATION IN THE WORKPLACE AND WELL-BEING

Perceived discrimination in general influences multiple aspects of well-being. For example, age discrimination is associated with higher psychological distress (Kessler, Mickelson, and Williams, 1999; Pavalko, Mossakoski, and Hamilton, 2003; Yuan, 2007), more depressive symptoms (Borrell et al., 2006; Kessler, Mickelson, and Williams, 1999), anxiety disorder (Kessler, Mickelson, and Williams, 1999), alcohol abuse (Martin, Tuch, and Roman, 2003), lower positive well-being (Yuan, 2007), worse physical health (Borrell et al., 2006), and more functional limitations (Pavalko, Mossakoski, and Hamilton, 2003). Age discrimination also influences numerous aspects of well-being for both the victims and the perpetrators on the micro and macro levels. Table 10.1 summarizes the possible consequences of age discrimination for well-being.

Age discrimination has negative *consequences for the victims* of age discrimination. On the micro level, it influences workplace, economic, psychological, and physical well-being. Age discrimination in the workplace detrimentally influences victims' work experiences and satisfaction. Snape and Redman (2003) found that old age discrimination decreased affective commitment to the organization, although it increased continuance commitment (possibly due to perceived low employability elsewhere). Duncan and Lovetto (2004) asked respondents to indicate the age for their peak earnings and found that, controlling for age, the lowest average age was reported by women who had experienced age discrimination. This finding suggests that women's perceived age for the peak of their career is inversely influenced by perceived age discrimination. Future research should explore whether older women workers who perceived their career to have peaked at a young age are less likely to seek promotions or retire earlier.

Age discrimination in the workplace impacts victims' economic well-being because it makes it harder for older workers to find and keep jobs (McCann and Giles, 2002) compared to younger workers (Bendick, Brown, and Wall, 1999; Dennis and Thomas, 2007). It also makes it more likely that older workers will be laid off (Henry and Jennings, 2004; McMullin and Marshall, 2001; Walker, 2002), involuntarily retire (Berger, 2006), and remain unemployed for longer periods of time (Johnson and Neumark, 1997; Walker, 2002). Further, age discrimination decreases job training opportunities for older workers (Duncan and Lovetto, 2004; Taylor and Urwin, 2001). In addition, Johnson and Neumark (1997) found that workers who experienced age discrimination in the workplace were more likely to separate from their employers. Snape and Redman (2003) similarly found that old age discrimination increased intentions to retire early among workers age forty-five and older. Moreover, those workers who experienced job separations after age discrimination were more likely to not be employed (rather than moving to another job or becoming self-employed) and to have lower subsequent wages (Johnson and Neumark, 1997). Being laid off due to age discrimination detrimentally impacts not only a person's ability to find a job supporting a similar standard of living but also her/his retirement and medical benefits (Henry and Jennings, 2004).

Age discrimination influences victims' emotional well-being. Yuan (2007) found that perceived age discrimination increased depressive symptoms and decreased positive well-being, especially for women. Similarly, Pavalko, Mossakowski, and Hamilton (2003) found that older working women, especially white women, who experienced discrimination at work in the past five years had more emotional distress. Moreover, Berger (2006) found that older workers seeking employment who perceived their age to be a barrier for employment questioned their self-worth and had more negative emotions including feeling humiliated and degraded. In addition, Walker et al. (2007) noted that older women workers' self-esteem was particularly detrimentally influenced by age discrimination, especially regarding the necessity for women to maintain a youthful appearance in the workplace. Thus, age discrimination in the workplace is associated with worse emotional well-being in terms of higher depressive symptoms, emotional distress, and negative emotions as well as lower positive well-being and self-worth.

Age discrimination and discrimination in the workplace are also associated with physical health. Pavalko, Mossakowski, and Hamilton (2003) found that older working women who reported discrimination in the workplace when they were younger had more current functional limitations (i.e., impairment in physical movement or activities), although discrimination in the past five years had no significant association with current functional limitations. This result seems to indicate that the detrimental consequences of discrimination for health may take time to manifest. However, for older black working women, the physical detriments of discrimination in the workplace appear to take less time to manifest, as only discrimination in the past five years increased their functional limitations (ibid.). In addition, unemployment among older workers (especially, if involuntary), which often occurs due to institutional discrimination, detrimentally influences older workers' health. For example, older workers' involuntary job loss was related to worse physical functioning (Gallo et al., 2000). Higher unemployment rates among men ages fifty-five to sixty-four were associated with higher suicide rates in the United States and Japan (Taylor, 2003). Thus, not only interpersonal age discrimination in the workplace but also institutional age discrimination have detrimental health consequences for older workers.

The detrimental consequences of age discrimination for the victims have macrolevel (societal) impacts through families and the political economic structure. Age discrimination in the workplace impacts the family of workers in at least two ways. First, it may negatively impact the well-being of people in the worker's nuclear family including a spouse/partner. Older workers are less likely to have children living at home, but age discrimination against younger workers may have detrimental consequences for children as well. In particular, age discrimination may negatively impact workers' earnings through underemployment or unemployment, thereby resulting in economic hardship for the family unit, which negatively impacts the well-being of adults (Mirowsky and Ross, 2001) and children (Duncan, Brooks-Gunn, and Klebanov, 1994). Second, age discrimination could decrease the resources available to workers, thereby increasing their reliance upon their extended family and friend networks. When facing workplace barriers due to age, they may rely on family and friends for economic or emotional support (e.g., Berger, 2006; Rife, 1995). Thus, age discrimination in the workplace affects not only individuals but also their families.

Age discrimination in the workplace has negative consequences for the political economic structure. Since age discrimination makes it harder for older workers to get hired and remain employed (McCann and Giles, 2002) and increases the probability that older workers will get laid off (Henry and Jennings, 2004), age discrimination should increase unemployment rates in areas with higher percentages of older people. In addition, high unemployment rates for older people increase their reliance upon governmental assistance programs including unemployment compensation.

Table 10.1

Consequences of Age Discrimination for the Well-Being of Victims and Offenders on Both the Micro- and Macro-Level

Area of well-being	Aspect of well-being affected	Research examples
Victims		
Micro level		
Economic	Harder time finding and keeping jobs	McCann and Giles (2002)
	Older workers less likely to get hired than younger workers	Bendick, Brown, and Wall (1999); Dennis and Thomas (2007)
	More likely to be laid off	Henry and Jennings (2004); McMullin and Marshall (2001); Walker (2002)
		Berger (2006)
	Increased involuntary retirement	Johnson and Neumark (1997); Walker (2002)
	More likely to remain unemployed	Duncan and Lovetto (2004); Taylor and Urwin (2001)
	Fewer opportunities for training	Johnson and Neumark (1997)
	More likely to willingly separate from their jobs	Snape and Redman (2003)
	Increased intentions to retire early	Pavalko, Mossakowski, and Hamilton (2003)
Physiological	More functional limitations	Gallo et al. (2000)
	Involuntary job loss among older workers related to worse physical functioning	
	Higher suicide rates, especially for men (also a psychological outcome)	Taylor (2003)
Psychological	Increased depressive symptoms	Yuan (2007)
	Decreased positive well-being	Yuan (2007)
	Questioned their self-worth	Berger (2006)
	Viewed themselves as old	Berger (2006)
	Increased negative emotions including feeling humiliated and degraded	Berger (2006)
	Decreased self-esteem, especially for women	Walker et al. (2007)
Macro level		
Economic	May increase unemployment rates in areas with high percentage of older workers	Henry and Jennings (2004)
	Increased reliance on Social Security	Taqi (2002)
	Decrease in older workers' consumer spending due to uncertainty about their economic futures	Needs further research

Category	Description	References
Contextual and social	Increased reliance of older people upon their friends and family	Berger (2006)
	Increased family economic hardship, thereby detrimentally influencing the well-being of family members	Duncan, Brooks-Gunn, and Klebanov (1994); Mirowsky and Ross (2001)
	Fewer governmental resources for younger age groups	Preston (1984)
Offender		
Micro level		
Economic	Possibly beneficial for position in the organization because seen as an effective strategy as a cost-saving measure	Needs further research, but supported by McMullin and Marshall (2001)
Physiological	Increased cardiovascular disease risk factors	Needs further research, but supported by Melamed et al. (1997)
	Increased sleeping problems	Needs further research, but supported by Knudsen, Ducharme, and Roman (2007)
	More likely to have worse health overall	Needs further research, but supported by Thoits (2010)
Psychological	Potentially positive by supporting their sense of vitality and youthfulness	Snyder and Meine (1994)
	No effect, because viewed as exercising good judgment or as a cost-effective measure	Bendick, Brown, and Wall (1999); McMullin and Marshall (2001)
	Experience guilt and sorrow	Gilbert (2000); Iyer, Leach, and Crosby (2003)
	Increased fear about future prospects as one gets older	Nelson (2005)
Macro level		
Economic	Laying off older workers may be a cost-saving measure, at least initially	McMullin and Marshall (2001)
	Decreased older workers' affective commitment to the organization	Snape and Redman (2003)
	Might not have enough workers to support retirement and pension programs	Taqi (2002); Walker (2002)
Contextual and social	May be viewed negatively as a potential employer decreasing potential hiring pool	Needs further research

Since governmental resources are scarce, this situation means that less governmental assistance is available for other age groups including governmental programs supporting younger workers (Preston, 1984). Moreover, higher unemployment and early retirement rates for older workers increases the strain on Social Security (Taqi, 2002). The consumer spending of older people may also decline due to uncertainty about their economic future thereby lowering consumer spending overall. Future research needs to explore these factors in more detail especially for determining how age discrimination affects unemployment rates, demand for unemployment compensation, and consumer spending locally, statewide, and regionally.

Age discrimination also has *consequences for the perpetrators* that may be positive, neutral, or negative. First, age discrimination may positively impact perpetrators by supporting their own sense of vitality and youthfulness (Snyder and Meine, 1994). Second, perpetrators of age discrimination may not be aware that they are discriminating by age, but instead may feel that they are simply considering the relative merits of potential workers, and thus, may simply view themselves as exercising good judgment without realizing that their views are biased by perceptions of age (e.g., Bendick, Brown, and Wall, 1999). Similarly, perpetrators who lay off workers based upon age may again see this as a cost-effective measure indicating that they are performing their jobs well rather than viewing it as age-based discrimination (e.g., McMullin and Marshall, 2001). Some potential negative consequences of age discrimination for the perpetrators is that they may come to view their expendability due to age as inevitable and come to see their worth to the company as declining with age, similar to the manner that other types of older workers come to question their own worth to employers (Berger, 2006). Additionally, Gilbert (2000) indicated that perpetrators who lay off workers often feel guilt (when moral issues are involved) and sorrow in response to human suffering. Iyer, Leach, and Crosby (2003) found that those who felt white guilt—either due to being a perpetrator or belonging to a group (whites) who discriminated against African Americans—were more likely to support policies that seek to compensate for past harm done to African Americans but were no more or less likely to support policies that equalized racial opportunities.

More research is needed on the physiological consequences of age discrimination for individual offenders. Committing such offenses could result in stress for the offenders, especially regarding their future work prospects as they age. Stress has been shown to be related to several types of physiological problems, including cardiovascular disease risk factors (Melamed et al., 1997), sleeping problems (Knudsen, Ducharme, and Roman, 2007), and worse health overall (Thoits, 2010). Thus, future research should explore whether engaging in discriminatory behavior influences such outcomes, especially when the offender felt such behavior was unethical and feared for her/his future job security with increasing age.

On the macro level, age discrimination can also impact organizations. A positive outcome is that some of these age discriminatory policies or actions may be effective cost-saving measures (McMullin and Marshall, 2001). However, there are potential costs to the organization as well. Age discrimination may decrease the number of workers available to support retirement and pension programs (Taqi, 2002; Walker, 2002). Additionally, age discrimination decreases older workers' affective commitment to the organization, which may lower productivity (Snape and Redman, 2003). Furthermore, these workers may be more likely to negatively portray the company to others, thereby making it more difficult for the company to hire qualified workers of all ages. This negative image of the company may be not only disseminated by disgruntled workers but also mentioned in the press. Future research should explore the circumstances under which such negative images are disseminated within the community and how they are dispersed from person to person as well as the short- and long-term consequences of these negative images for the organization.

AGE DISCRIMINATION, STRATEGIES FOR EMPLOYERS, AND PUBLIC POLICY

Employers can use several strategies to try to decrease age discrimination in the workplace. Dennis and Thomas (2007) suggest three possible strategies. First, recognition programs (including the AARP Best Employers for Workers Over 50 Program) acknowledge companies that have policies and practices that address issues relevant to older workers. Organizations receiving such awards may garner positive press that makes it easier for them to recruit highly qualified workers. Second, diversity training programs should be used not only for diversity training in race, gender, and ethnicity but also for age. Third, the knowledge and training of older workers needs to be retained beyond retirement; therefore, knowledge-retention approaches need to be utilized by employers including rehiring retirees to train future workers or encouraging workers to postpone retirements through bonuses (Dennis and Thomas, 2007, p. 88).

Several policies are already in place to combat age discrimination in the workplace, yet these policies should be more broadly enforced and new policies should be added. First, the Age Discrimination in Employment Act needs to be more widely enforced (Taqi, 2002). To some extent, the Equal Employment Opportunity Commission is already doing this by focusing more on discrimination complaints for reasons beyond just race (Wakefield and Uggen, 2004). Second, training programs for dislocated workers should particularly target older workers. The Workforce Investment Act of 1998 targets the retraining of dislocated workers, but particular investments should be made to reach older workers with programs already in place. Older worker programs can also help in finding employment, but these programs should emphasize measures to deal with the emotional ramifications of age discrimination (Berger, 2004). Furthermore, tax incentives should be given to older workers to further their own skills through education and training programs, as older workers are less likely than younger ones to be offered employer training programs (Taylor and Urwin, 2001). Finally, Neumark (2009) suggested that employers could decrease health insurance costs by hiring workers age sixty-five and older who qualify for Medicare. However, governmental policies regard Medicare as only the secondary payer for employers with twenty or more employees; thus, a change in policy to Medicare as the primary payer regardless of number of employees could make older workers more in demand as employees for larger companies.

Most of these strategies seek to equalize opportunities by age by providing more job opportunities for older workers. However, more punitive ramifications for companies who engage in age discrimination should encourage companies to use merit-based criteria for hiring, firing, and promotion. Finally, organizations need incentives to follow the social contract, which are provided by recognition programs and decreased health insurance costs.

CONCLUSIONS

Age discrimination in the workplace is currently a problem that affects only a substantial minority of workers, but is likely to increase as the population of the United States becomes older and as the number of older workers rises. Age discrimination for younger workers tends to occur in the early twenties age group, but then age discrimination increases again for workers older than forty, reaching a peak around age fifty-four (although age discrimination for older workers appears to occur at younger ages for women than for men). The consequences of age discrimination in the workplace for social, economic, emotional, and physical well-being are great, and include negative effects on the well-being of victims, victims' families, the political economy, and even possibly perpetrators themselves. Age discrimination in the workplace violates principles of equal opportunity, justice, and fairness as well as the social contract that employers have with society. Some strategies that employers can use to combat age discrimination in the workplace include recognition programs for companies with policies supportive of older workers and diversity training programs that address ageist stereotypes and attitudes. The government can also discourage age discrimination in the workforce by more vigorously enforcing the Age Discrimination in Employment Act.

REFERENCES

Bendick, M. Jr.; Brown, L.E.; and Wall, K. 1999. No foot in the door: An experimental study of employment discrimination against older workers. *Journal of Aging and Social Policy,* 10 (4), 5–23.

Berger, E.D. 2006. "Aging" identities: Degradation and negotiation in the search for employment. *Journal of Aging Studies,* 20 (4), 303–316.

Borrell, L.N.; Kiefe, C.I.; Williams, D.R.; Diez-Roux, A.V.; and Gordon-Larsen, P. 2006. Self-reported health, perceived racial discrimination, and skin color in African Americans in the CARDIA study. *Social Science and Medicine,* 63 (6), 1415–1427.

Butler, R. 1969. Ageism: Another form of bigotry. *Gerontologist,* 9 (4), 243–246.

Byron, R.A. 2010. Discrimination, complexity, and the public/private sector question. *Work and Occupations,* 37 (4), 435–475.

Carroll, A.B. 1979. A three-dimensional conceptual model of corporate performance. *Academy of Management Review,* 4 (4), 497–505.

Cuddy, A.J.C.; Norton, M.I.; and Fiske, S.T. 2005. This old stereotype: The pervasiveness and persistence of the elderly stereotype. *Journal of Social Issues,* 61 (2), 267–285.

Dennis, H., and Thomas, K. 2007. Ageism in the workplace. *Generations,* 31 (1), 84–89.

Duncan, C., and Lovetto, W. 2004. Never the right age? Gender and age-based discrimination in employment. *Gender, Work, and Organization,* 11 (1), 95–115.

Duncan, G.J.; Brooks-Gunn, J.; and Klebanov, P.K. 1994. Economic deprivation and early childhood development. *Child Development,* 65 (2), 296–318.

Ferris, G.R., and King, T.R. 1992. The politics of age discrimination in organizations. *Journal of Business Ethics,* 11 (5–6), 341–350.

Fiske, S.T.; Cuddy, A.J.C.; Glick, R.; and Xu, J. 2002. A model of (often mixed) stereotype content: Competence and warmth respectively follow from perceived status and competition. *Journal of Personality and Social Psychology,* 82 (6), 878–902.

Gallo, W.T.; Bradley, E.H.; Siegel, M.; and Kasl, S.V. 2000. Health effects of involuntary job loss among older workers: Findings from the Health and Retirement Survey. *Journal of Gerontology: Social Sciences,* 55B (3), S131–S140.

Gee, G.C.; Pavalko, E.K.; and Long, J.S. 2007. Age, cohort and perceived age discrimination: Using the life course to assess self-reported age discrimination. *Social Forces,* 86 (1), 265–290.

Gilbert, J. 2000. Sorrow and guilt: An ethical analysis of layoffs. *S.A.M. Advanced Management Journal,* 65 (2), 4–13.

Henry, E.G., and Jennings, J.P. 2004. Age discrimination in layoffs: Factors of injustice. *Journal of Business Ethnics,* 54 (3), 217–224.

Iyer, A.; Leach, C.W.; and Crosby, F.J. 2003. White guilt and racial compensation: The benefits and limits of self-focus. *Personality and Social Psychology Bulletin,* 29 (1), 117–129.

Jacobsen, L.A.; Kent, M.; Lee, M.; and Mather, M. 2011. America's aging population. *Population Bulletin,* 66 (1), 1–16.

Johnson, R.W., and Neumark, D. 1997. Age discrimination, job separations, employment status of older workers: Evidence from self-reports. *Journal of Human Resources,* 32 (4), 779–811.

Kessler, R.C.; Mickelson, K.D.; and Williams, D.R. 1999. The prevalence, distribution, and mental health correlates of perceived discrimination in the United States. *Journal of Health and Social Behavior,* 40 (3), 208–230.

Kite, M.E.; Stockdale, G.D.; Whitley, B.E. Jr.; and Johnson, B.T. 2005. Attitudes toward younger and older adults: An updated meta-analytic review. *Journal of Social Issues,* 61 (2), 241–266.

Knudsen, H.; Ducharme, L.J.; and Roman, P.M. 2007. Job stress and poor sleep quality: Data from an American sample of full-time workers. *Social Science and Medicine,* 64 (10), 1997–2007.

Kurland, N.B. 2001. The impact of legal age discrimination on women in professional occupations. *Business Ethics Quarterly,* 11 (2), 331–348.

Lee, M.A., and Mather, M. 2008. U.S. labor force trends. *Population Bulletin,* 63 (2), 1–16.

Martin, J.K.; Tuch, S.A.; and Roman, P.M. 2003. Problem drinking patterns among African Americans: The impacts of reports of discrimination, perceptions of prejudice, and "risky" coping strategies. *Journal of Health and Social Behavior,* 44 (3), 408–425.

McCann, R., and Giles, H. 2002. Ageism in the workplace: A communication perspective. In *Ageism: Stereotyping and Prejudice Against Older Persons,* ed. T.D. Nelson, 163–199. Cambridge, MA: MIT Press.

McMullin, J.A., and Marshall, V.W. 2001. Ageism, age relations, and garment industry work in Montreal. *Gerontologist,* 41 (1), 111–122.

Melamed, S.; Kushner, T.; Strauss, E.; and Vigisur, D. 1997. Negative associations between reported life events and cardiovascular disease risk factors in employed men: The CARDIS Study. *Journal of Psychosomatic Research,* 43 (3), 247–258.

Mirowsky, J., and Ross, C.E. 2001. Age and the effect of economic hardship on depression. *Journal of Health and Social Behavior,* 42 (2), 132–150.

Nelson, T.D. 2005. Ageism: Prejudice against our feared future self. *Journal of Social Issues,* 61 (2), 207–221.

Neumark, D. 2009. The age discrimination in employment act and the challenge of population aging. *Research on Aging,* 31 (1), 41–68.

Pavalko, E.K.; Mossakowski, K.N.; and Hamilton, V.J. 2003. Does perceived discrimination affect health? Longitudinal relationships between work discrimination and women's physical and emotional health. *Journal of Health and Social Behavior,* 44 (1), 18–33.

Preston, S.H. 1984. Children and the elderly: Divergent paths for America's dependents. *Demography,* 21 (4), 435–457.

Rife, J.C. 1995. Older unemployed women and job search activity: The role of social support. *Journal of Women and Aging,* 7 (3), 55–68.

Roscigno, V.J.; Mong, S.; Byron, R.; and Tester, G. 2007. Age discrimination, social closure, and employment. *Social Forces,* 86 (1), 313–334.

Schwartz, M.S., and Carroll, A.B. 2003. Corporate social responsibility: A three-domain approach. *Business Ethics Quarterly,* 13 (4), 503–530.

Snape, E., and Redman, T. 2003. Too old or too young? The impact of perceived age discrimination. *Human Resource Management Journal,* 13 (1), 78–89.

Snyder, M., and Meine, P. 1994. Stereotyping of the elderly: A functional approach. *British Journal of Social Psychology,* 33 (1), 63–82.

Taqi, A. 2002. Older people, work and equal opportunity. *International Social Security Review,* 55 (1), 107–120.

Taylor, P. 2003. Age, labour market conditions and male suicide rates in selected countries. *Ageing and Society,* 23 (1), 25–40.

Taylor, P., and Urwin, P. 2001. Age and participation in vocational education and training. *Work, Employment and Society,* 15 (4), 763–779.

Thoits, Peggy A. 2010. Stress and health: Major findings and policy implications. *Journal of Health and Social Behavior,* 51 (1), S41–S53.

Uhlenberg, P. 1988. Does population ageing produce increasing gerontocracy? *Sociological Forum,* 3 (3), 454–463.

U.S. Bureau of Labor Statistics. 2011. Employment status of the civilian noninstitutional population by age, sex, and race. Table, December. www.bls.gov/web/empsit/cpseea13.pdf.

Van Dalen, H.P.; Henkens, K.; and Schippers, J. 2010. Productivity of older workers: Perceptions of employers and employees. *Population and Development Review,* 36 (2), 309–330.

Wakefield, S., and Uggen, C. 2004. The declining significance of race in federal civil rights law: The social structure of employment discrimination claims. *Sociological Inquiry,* 74 (1), 128–157.

Walker, A. 2002. A strategy for active ageing. *International Social Security Review,* 55 (1), 121–139.

Walker, H.; Grant, D.; Meadows, M.; and Cook, I. 2007. Women's experiences and perceptions of age discrimination in employment: Implications for research and policy. *Social Policy and Society,* 6 (1), 37–48.

Yuan, A.S.V. 2007. Perceived age discrimination and mental health. *Social Forces,* 86 (1), 291–311.

11

UNETHICAL WORK BEHAVIOR AS A STRESSOR

Laurenz L. Meier, Norbert K. Semmer, and Paul E. Spector

A large and growing body of research on occupational stress has established the existence of a variety of environmental conditions termed stressors that have detrimental physical and psychological effects on people, termed strains. Whereas some stressors are inherent in the nature of job tasks (e.g., role ambiguity and role conflict, see Katz and Kahn, 1978), social stressors involve interpersonal interactions among people and are considered as particularly stressful (e.g., Bolger et al., 1989). Social stressors have been studied under different labels, such as interpersonal conflict (Spector and Jex, 1998), bullying (Einarsen et al., 2010), injustice (Greenberg, 2004), incivility (Andersson and Pearson, 1999), emotional abuse (Keashly and Harvey, 2005), social undermining (Duffy, Ganster, and Pagon, 2002), abusive supervision (Tepper, 2007), and sexual harassment (Fitzgerald et al., 1997). A common feature of all these stressors is that they can involve instances of unethical behavior, which in many cases imply threats to self-esteem through expressions of disrespect, a lack of acceptance, and social exclusion. Such behaviors are unethical when they are intended to harm others for no legitimate purpose, or when they aim at attaining illegitimate advantages at the expense of others. In this chapter we will discuss various mechanisms regarding how social stressors arising from unethical behavior of one employee toward others lead to strains, integrating the ethics literature with the theory of stress as offense to self (for an overview, see Figure 11.1).

STRESS AS OFFENSE TO SELF

Maintaining a positive self-evaluation and receiving positive evaluations by others are strong motives for most people (Sedikides and Strube, 1997). People strive to perceive themselves and to convince others that they are worthwhile, competent, and moral individuals. Given that it is so important for people to preserve a positive self-worth, threats to self-esteem may serve as particularly salient stressors, a point emphasized by Lazarus (e.g., 1999). Surprisingly, however, threats to self-esteem as a stressor have not played a prominent role in occupational stress research. Typically, self-esteem is either investigated as a resource that attenuates the effects of stressful situations (e.g., Jex and Elacqua, 2004) or as outcome, in that stress may impede self-esteem (e.g., Frone, 2000). However, it is rarely conceptualized as a core element of the stress experience itself. To fill this gap, Semmer and colleagues (e.g., Semmer et al., 2007; Semmer, McGrath, and Beehr, 2005) have introduced the "stress as offense to self" (SOS) perspective to stress research. On a general level, this perspective suggests that many aversive work conditions are perceived as stressful because they threaten people's positive self-view. On the one hand, people's self-esteem may be threatened by internally attributed failure experiences, for instance, to a lack of competence or to a lack of moral strength ("stress as insufficiency," SIN); on the other hand, people's self-esteem

169

Figure 11.1 **Stress and Unethical Behavior: Conceptual Model**

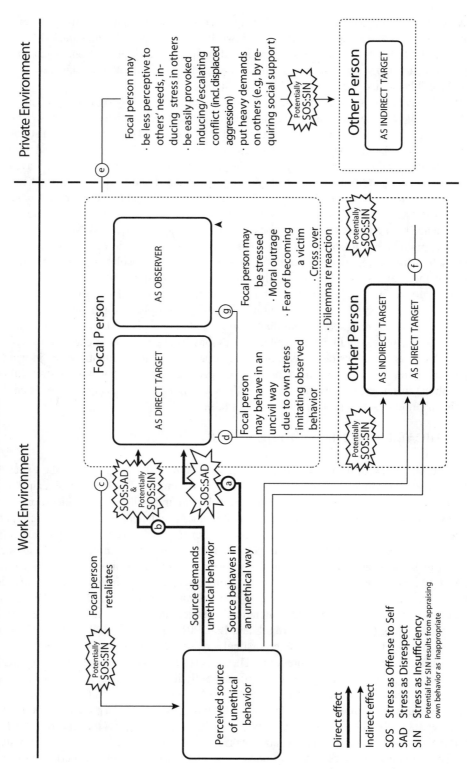

may be threatened by others' behavior that signals disrespect, such as various forms of unethical behavior ("stress as disrespect," SAD). It follows that being a target of unethical behavior is likely to create an offense to self in terms of stress as disrespect.[1] Realizing that one is reacting to such behavior in an inappropriate way (e.g., incivility against innocent others), may, however, lead to moral self-blame, and thus stress through insufficiency.

People have a strong need to be accepted and socially included by significant others, and one's self-esteem is strongly affected by the approval of others (Baumeister and Leary, 1995; Leary and Baumeister, 2000). Penhaglion, Louis, and Restubog (2009) showed that mistreatment by coworkers was related to depression and (organizational-based) self-esteem, and that this relationship was mediated by perceived rejection. We therefore assume that unethical behavior, which signals disrespect, unfairness, and social exclusion, threatens one's self-esteem and hence causes stress (path a in Figure 11.1). It is important to note that we do not assume that an unethical act necessarily has to actually diminish one's self-esteem. People use various strategies to protect and enhance their self-esteem (e.g., Crocker and Park, 2004), which may be effective at least in the short run. Unethical behavior that signals disrespect and rejection might therefore represent a threat to self-esteem, but people are often able to dismiss such isolated threats and find ways to maintain their self-esteem. In line with this, in experimental studies, rejected individuals reported more negative affect (i.e., strain) but not a lower state self-esteem than individuals in the control group; however, in studies of exclusion in field settings, people who are chronically rejected by others report lower trait self-esteem than nonrejected people (Blackhart et al., 2009). The lack of effects on self-esteem in experimental studies may be because the threat to self-esteem is too weak (due to ethical considerations), or it might be due to successful strategies in warding off the threat. In any case, according to the SOS perspective, unethical behavior is stressful because it is a threat to self-esteem, even if an actual drop in self-esteem is successfully averted. In other words, the threat itself is sufficient to induce strain.

UNETHICAL BEHAVIOR AND THE TARGET'S WELL-BEING

In the following section, we present some selected studies that suggest that the experience of unethical behavior by others is stressful and may cause impaired well-being. Because relatively few studies have focused explicitly on unethical behavior and well-being, we incorporate research about related constructs such as deviance, bullying, and injustice, which can all be regarded as instances of violating commonly agreed ethical norms. Two recent meta-analyses show that various forms of unethical behavior targeted against the employee are related to indicators of well-being such as depression, burnout, self-esteem, and physical symptoms (Bowling and Beehr, 2006; Hershcovis and Barling, 2009). Most of this research has utilized cross-sectional designs, which strongly limits insight into the direction and duration of a proposed effect. However, some studies have examined across-time associations between unethical behavior and well-being. For example, bullying (e.g., Finne, Knardahl, and Lau, 2011; Kivimäki et al., 2003), injustice (e.g., Ylipaavalniemi et al., 2005), and interpersonal stressors (e.g., Dormann and Zapf, 1999) have been prospectively linked to depression. The effects are not restricted to psychological well-being. Lack of justice (Kivimäki et al., 2006), and bullying (Kivimäki et al., 2003) have also been shown to be related to cardiovascular disease (CVD), and Berset et al. (2011) have shown that interpersonal stressors are also linked to the body-mass index, which is predictive for many health outcomes such as diabetes and CVD. Thus, previous research suggests that chronic experience of unethical behavior by others may negatively impair psychological and physical well-being in the long run. Furthermore, recent diary studies show that not only chronic experience of unethical behavior impairs well-being. In addition, even the experience of isolated unethical behavior can deteriorate well-being in the short run. For example, daily fluctuations of unfairness and conflicts have been linked to negative mood (Ilies, Johnson, and Judge, 2011; Meier et al., 2011), job satisfaction, and impaired sleep quality (Meier et al., 2011).

A special case of unethical behavior can arise when one is expected to perform immoral acts (path b in Figure 11.1). For instance, the expectation to promote selling of a product by making unrealistic promises may induce a moral dilemma. Such situations would constitute a role conflict, more specifically a person–role conflict (Kahn et al., 1964; cf. Beehr and Glazer, 2005). Unfortunately, person–role conflict has not been prominent in research on role conflict, which "is typically envisaged as disagreement between two or more role-senders" (Katz and Kahn, 1978, p. 204). Perceived pressure to perform in an unethical way is therefore a research domain that deserves more attention.

Note that pressure to perform in an unethical way can imply both facets of stress as offense to self, first, feeling pressured represents stress as disrespect, since the role sender disregards one's moral standards and, thus, one's interests as a person. Second, giving in to such pressure would lead to self-blame, as one would not be fulfilling one's moral standards; in the SOS model, this situation should lead to stress through insufficiency.

UNETHICAL BEHAVIOR EXPOSURE THAT EXTENDS BEYOND THE TARGET

So far, we have presented the theoretical background and empirical findings for negative effects of unethical behavior on the target person's well-being. In the following section, we outline that the effects of such unethical behavior can extend beyond the original target. First, we present research showing that the victim may become a perpetrator and that threatened self-esteem and hence strain play a prominent role in this transformation. Second, we illustrate that unethical behavior may also be stressful for observers or third parties who merely witness the unethical behavior directed toward others and that third parties may also imitate such acts and hence unethical behavior becomes widespread.

When the Victim Becomes a Perpetrator

Exposure to unethical behavior can be a threat to self-esteem. However, an experienced threat to self-esteem not only leads to physical and psychological strains but also can affect behavior. According to Baumeister, Smart, and Boden (1996), threatened self-esteem can cause either withdrawal or aggressive behavior, depending on whether the person accepts or rejects the negative evaluation. If the person accepts the negative evaluation, the person revises his or her self-esteem, which causes negative emotions toward the self (e.g., sadness) and withdrawal behavior. However, if the person rejects the negative evaluation and hence maintains his or her self-esteem, negative emotions toward the source of the threat (e.g., anger) are triggered, which can lead to aggressive behavior directed toward the source of the threat. Because people are highly motivated to protect and maintain their self-esteem, as mentioned above, the latter reaction is likely. Thus, aggressive behavior, as an act of self-affirmation (see also Steele, 1988), is a common reaction to threatened self-esteem. Aggression can be directed against the perpetrator (path c in Figure 11.1). With acts of revenge, people try to restore justice (Bies, Tripp, and Kramer, 1997; Jones, 2009) and to discourage further unethical behavior, whether from the perpetrator or from third parties who should learn that such behavior may not be tolerated (Tedeschi and Felson, 1994).

However, aggression against the perpetrator is an option only if no further punishment is expected (e.g., Aquino, Tripp, and Bies, 2001). The perpetrator may be too powerful or not available. Since anger is associated with a general tendency toward being aggressive (Berkowitz, 2003; Haidt, 2003), aggression may be displaced against others, such as coworkers, who were not involved in the original unethical behavior (path d in Figure 11.1) or family members (path e in Figure 11.1) (Marcus-Newhall et al., 2000; Miller et al., 2003). Previous research indicates that experienced unethical behavior by the supervisor may cause unethical behavior toward family members. For example, Hoobler and Brass (2006) showed that abusive supervision (reported by the employee) is positively related to undermining behavior against family members (reported by the spouse). In two studies Restubog, Scott, and Zagencyzk (2011) showed that this relationship might be mediated by the employee's level of distress. Thus, the experience of unethical behavior can cause strain, and particularly anger, which can trigger unethical behavior toward third parties.

However, unethical behavior against third parties does not have to be driven by a conscious decision to harm; it may also be driven by an impaired capacity to control one's impulses, including impulses to behave in an aggressive, inconsiderate, or selfish way. Unethical behavior represents behavior that breaches norms of mutual respect. Following norms often requires self-control, which depends on a limited energy resource (see Muraven and Baumeister, 2000). This resource determines how successfully one can regulate one's behavior, but also becomes depleted by self-control acts. The experience of unethical behavior is assumed to deplete self-control capacities. According to Baumeister, Vohs, and Tice (2007), dealing with difficult people, including being kind in response to others' bad behavior and managing negative emotions, requires self-control resources. If this self-control breaks down, individuals tend to act in a more selfish, impulsive, or antisocial way (see Baumeister and Exline, 1999). Consistent with these assumptions, experimental lab studies (e.g., DeBono, Shmueli, and Muraven, 2010; Gino et al., 2011) as well as a field study in the work context (Barnes et al., 2011) found that individuals show more unethical behavior when their self-control resources have been depleted.

However, the indirect effects of being treated in an unethical way are not confined to showing unethical behavior toward others; they can also induce a general reduction of the quality of social interactions. The fact that a person is stressed and in a bad mood may influence what is attended to, and it may color perceptions and appraisals of events in a negative way (Forgas, 2002; Frijda, 2009). Such a mood-congruent appraisal may instigate behaviors that are less friendly, considerate, and supportive than the person's normal behaviors; the person may not show unethical behavior, yet deprive others of prosocial behavior or positive feedback, which can still imply harm to others and to social relationships. Furthermore, the person might appraise more negatively the behavior of others that might constitute a norm violation—for instance, by being more prone to attribute intent rather than clumsiness or mindlessness; or by interpreting negative feedback as an attack on oneself; as a consequence, he or she might feel hurt, or provoked, more easily. A person may even interpret a positive behavior negatively, as when a smile is interpreted as an arrogant grin (Forgas, Bower, and Krantz, 1984), and, in line with this appraisal, react negatively.

In sum, the experience of unethical behavior may trigger further unethical behavior that is targeted against the perpetrator or against others such as coworkers or family members who were not involved in the original unethical behavior. The experience of stress—including feelings of anger and depleted self-regulatory resources—caused by a threat to self-esteem plays an important role in how the experience of unethical behavior leads to further unethical behavior. Furthermore, it may color appraisal of events and behaviors in a negative way and reduce the quality of social interactions in general.

In terms of the SOS model, such reactions are triggered by stress as disrespect. At the same time, they entail the danger of stress through insufficiency. If we realize that we are hurting innocent others by acting unethically, we are likely to blame ourselves, which is the core of the SIN facet of SOS. Such blame may be in terms of moral categories ("I am punishing an innocent"), or in terms of competence ("I am not able to show the politeness and respect toward others that I usually do").

Witnessing Unethical Behavior

Unethical behavior may affect third parties (e.g., coworkers) who merely witness it (path f in Figure 11.1). Experimental studies show that the observation of injustice against others causes negative affect (De Cremer and van Hiel, 2006). Moreover, work group (Lim, Cortina, and Magley, 2008) and organizational (Griffin, 2010) incivility is related to impaired well-being over and above personal incivility and general job stress. Furthermore, research on the so-called survivor effect has shown that downsizing associated with perceived unfairness in dismissing employees may be stressful for the "survivors," inducing insecurity, mistrust, cynicism, and guilt in them (Appelbaum et al., 1997; Appelbaum and Donia, 2000; Brockner, 1988; Brockner et al., 1994). Thus, not only unethical behavior directed against an employee him- or herself (see above) but also witnessing unethical behavior against coworkers seems to impact well-being. Several theoretical explanations for such an effect are plausible.

First, the moral virtue model assumes that people care about justice because they have a basic respect for human dignity and worth (e.g., Cropanzano et al., 2001; Folger, 1998). Proposing that justice is beyond personal interest and that it affirms people's identity and positive self-view within valued groups (relational model; Tyler and Lind, 1992), this model complements previous fairness theories assuming that people concern themselves with justice because it is in their economic interest (instrumental model; Thibaut and Walker, 1975). According to Williams (1997), human beings have at least four psychological needs, namely, control, belonging, self-esteem, and finding meaning in their lives. Moral purpose is one manifestation of the search for meaning (Becker, 1973; see also Cropanzano et al., 2001). Cropanzano et al. (2001) mapped these four needs onto the three models of justice: Control is integrated in the instrumental model, belonging and self-esteem in the relational model, and meaningful existence in the moral virtue model. Thus, experienced injustice is a threat to several basic needs, including meaningful existence, and hence stressful, even if the person only observes injustice without being directly affected by it.

Second, observers of unethical behavior may fear becoming victims as well in the future. Thus, fear of being laid off oneself is considered part of the "survivor syndrome" (Appelbaum et al., 1997; Appelbaum and Donia, 2000). Fear also plays an important role in how experienced violence causes negative outcomes in the long run (Barling, 1996). A recent study by Mueller and Tschan (2011) showed that the relationship between experienced workplace violence and well-being was mediated by the fear of future violence. More specifically, the experience of violence was related to the perceived likelihood of future violence, which, in turn, was linked to fear of future violence, and the fear of future violence was directly related to impaired well-being. Thus, observing unethical behavior in the workplace may increase the perception of the probability of becoming a victim in the future, which triggers fear and impairs well-being.

Third, a person's affective experience has an impact on the affective experience of other individuals and the work group (see Kelly and Barsade, 2001). Both laboratory (e.g., Barsade, 2000, cited in Kelly and Barsade, 2001) and field studies (Totterdell et al., 1998, 2004) indicate that the moods and emotions of one person may be transferred to nearby others (i.e., emotional contagion). One mechanism that has been proposed as an explanation of this phenomenon is that people automatically mimic and synchronize manifestations of emotional behavior such as facial expression and the postures of others (see Hatfield, Cacioppo, and Rapson, 1994), which then shapes their emotional states (e.g., Strack, Martin, and Stepper, 1988). Another possible mechanism refers to empathy with the victim (De Waal, 2008). Thus, the negative affective state of a victim of unethical behavior may spread to other employees; however, it may also spill over into private life and affect family members (cross-over; cf. Allen et al., 2000; Amstad and Semmer, 2009; Bakker and Demerouti, 2009; Bakker, Westman, and Van Emmerik, 2009; cf. also the remarks concerning the impact on the quality of social interactions above; these can also be triggered by observing unethical behavior).

Finally, those who have witnessed unethical behavior may model similar unethical behavior in their interactions with the target, the instigator, or other organizational members (Andersson and Pearson, 1999; path g in Figure 11.1). The observation may change norms for respect and negatively affect the organizational (violence) climate. It is important to note that a bad climate is related to impaired well-being (Kessler et al., 2008).

In contrast to being the target of unethical behavior, which indicates stress as disrespect, and in contrast to a victim's turning into a perpetrator, which may induce stress through insufficiency, the stress induced by witnessing unethical behavior is not readily explained by the SOS model but constitutes a path in its own right. With regard to the last mechanism mentioned, however, SOS is pertinent again: If one starts modeling unethical behavior oneself, stress through insufficiency may result if one realizes what one is doing ("How could I ever lower my standards to such an extent?"). Furthermore, someone who is witnessing unethical behavior has to decide about how to react. Not reporting a theft, for instance, may induce guilt and constitute an offense to self in terms of personal insufficiency. Guilt is even more likely if one witnesses unethical behavior toward a third person but does not intervene to support the victim (cf. the research on "bystander apathy"; Darley and Latané, 1968; Latané and Nida, 1981).

FUTURE RESEARCH

In the following section we present some avenues for future research. First, different types of unethical behavior and their relationship with well-being have already been examined. But, as outlined above, perceived pressure to perform in an unethical way has not been investigated in detail, although it is reasonable to assume that this type of person–role conflict is stressful and—at least in certain types of jobs—not uncommon. Second, individuals differ in how they interpret and react to stressful work situations (see Semmer and Meier, 2009; Spector, 2003), and future research should examine which individuals react particularly strongly to unethical behavior. One might consider the usual suspects such as neuroticism and negative affectivity; however, we suggest focusing on personality variables that are more directly linked to the core of the stressful experience of unethical behavior. For example, as we assume that unethical behavior is often a threat to self-esteem, people with fragile self-esteem may react particularly strongly to unethical behavior (e.g., Meier, Semmer, and Hupfeld, 2009). Third, specific emotional reactions to unethical behavior deserve a stronger research focus; this includes reactions such as feeling deprecated by unethical behavior, feeling guilty about overacting either toward the source of the unethical behavior or toward others, and it may include feelings of guilt after conforming to pressure to perform in an unethical way. Furthermore, feelings of guilt as a result of not supporting others who are being treated in an unethical way are worth investigating, as are emotional reactions to not having reported unethical behavior (e.g., a theft).

CONCLUSION

Exposure to unethical behavior can be considered a stressor that can negatively affect both the psychological and physical well-being of the direct target in the short and long run. Many forms of unethical behavior signal disrespect and rejection and therefore represent a threat to one's positive self-view and social standing. As people strive for a positive self-view and have a strong need to be accepted by others (Baumeister and Leary, 1995; Sedikides and Strube, 1997), being the target of unethical behavior should be particularly stressful (see also the SOS perspective by Semmer et al., 2007). Furthermore, witnessing unethical behavior can induce stress in observers, and the decisions they have to make in that situation (reporting or not; supporting a victim or not) may not only involve considerable stress during the situation but also imply the risk of regret and guilt in the aftermath.

Moreover, unethical behavior also negatively affects the well-being of third parties such as coworkers and spouses, because the victim becomes a perpetrator of unethical behavior that is displaced to more available targets, both at work and in private life (i.e., crossover). In addition, being a victim or witness of unethical behavior may lower the quality of social interactions in general. Thus, the experience of unethical behavior can start a vicious circle that causes harm beyond the original target. Organizations and supervisors are therefore urged to reduce the amount of unethical behavior at the workplace. On the one hand, they should be concerned with their own behavior (e.g., abusive supervision; inducing person–role conflict by communicating expectations to behave in an unethical way); on the other hand, they should try to prevent unethical behavior by their employees (e.g., bullying). It is important to note that unethical behavior among employees may often not be immediately visible for supervisors, as employees often hide bad news from supervisors (Tourish and Robson, 2006). In a similar way, employees may not communicate to supervisors that they perceive their behavior as unethical. Supervisors therefore have to actively seek information and feedback about possible unethical behavior by themselves and their employees. Establishing a system of protecting whistle-blowers also seems important. Accusations should be taken seriously yet not at face value, lest inaccurate accusations cause stress in the accused. By demonstrating normatively appropriate conduct and promoting such conduct to followers (i.e., ethical leadership; Brown, Treviño, and Harrison, 2005), supervisors can positively affect the work environment, which can then reduce various forms of unethical behavior (e.g., Hauge, Skogstad, and Einarsen, 2007, 2009; Stouten et al., 2010). In the end, such efforts are likely to result in less stress and better well-being.

NOTE

1. This should be true for unethical behavior that is directed against the focal person such as discrimination. Based on the notion that maintaining a positive self-evaluation and a positive evaluation by others are strong motives, we assume that this type of unethical behavior is particularly stressful. Witnessing unethical behavior toward others (e.g., bullying of coworkers), the organization (e.g., theft), or larger units (e.g., society or nature, such as in terms of environmental irresponsibility) may also be stressful but mainly for reasons other than a threat to self-esteem. As outlined in more detail later, possible reasons are moral outrage, fear of becoming a victim in the future, and emotional contagion.

REFERENCES

Allen, T.D.; Herst, D.E.L.; Bruck, C.S.; and Sutton, M. 2000. Consequences associated with work-to-family conflict: A review and agenda for future research. *Journal of Occupational Health Psychology,* 5, 278–308.

Amstad, F.T., and Semmer, N.K. 2009. Recovery and the work-family interface. In *Research in Occupational Stress and Well-Being,* vol. 7: *Current Perspectives on Job-Stress Recovery,* ed. P.L. Perrewé, D.C. Ganster, and S. Sonnentag, 125–166. Bingley, UK: Emerald Group.

Andersson, L., and Pearson, C. 1999. Tit for tat? The spiraling effect of incivility in the workplace. *Academy of Management Review,* 24, 452–471.

Aquino, K.; Tripp, T.M.; and Bies, R.J. 2001. How employees respond to personal offense: The effects of blame attribution, victim status, and offender status on revenge and reconciliation in the workplace. *Journal of Applied Psychology,* 86, 52–59.

Appelbaum, S.H., and Donia, M. 2000. The realistic downsizing preview: A management intervention in the prevention of survivor syndrome (Part I). *Career Development International,* 2, 278–286.

Appelbaum, S.H.; Delage, C.; Labib, N.; and Gault, G. 1997. The survivor syndrome: Aftermath of downsizing. *Career Development International,* 2, 333–350.

Bakker, A.B., and Demerouti, E. 2009. The crossover of work engagement between working couples: A closer look at the role of empathy. *Journal of Managerial Psychology,* 24, 220–236.

Bakker, A.B.; Westman, M.; and Van Emmerik, I.J.H. 2009. Advances in crossover theory. *Journal of Managerial Psychology,* 24, 206–219.

Barling, J. 1996. The prediction, experience, and consequences of workplace violence. In *Violence on the Job: Identifying Risks and Developing Solutions,* ed. G.R. VandenBos and E.Q. Bulatao, 29–49. Washington, DC: American Psychological Association.

Barnes, C.M.; Schaubroeck, J.; Huth, M.; and Ghumman, S. 2011. Lack of sleep and unethical conduct. *Organizational Behavior and Human Decision Processes,* 115, 169–180.

Baumeister, R.F., and Exline, J. 1999. Virtue, personality, and social relations: Self-control as the moral muscle. *Journal of Personality,* 67, 1165–1194.

Baumeister, R.F., and Leary, M.R. 1995. The need to belong: Desire for interpersonal attachments as a fundamental human motivation. *Psychological Bulletin,* 117, 497–529.

Baumeister, R.F.; Smart, L.; and Boden, J.M. 1996. Relation of threatened egotism to violence and aggression: The dark side of high self-esteem. *Psychological Review,* 103, 5–33.

Baumeister, R.F.; Vohs, K.; and Tice, D. 2007. The strength model of self-control. *Current Directions in Psychological Science,* 16, 351–355.

Becker, E. 1973. *The Denial of Death.* New York: The Free Press.

Beehr, T. A., and Glazer, S. 2005. Organizational role stress. In *Handbook of Work Stress*, ed. J. Barling, E.K. Kelloway, and M.R. Frone, 7–33. Thousand Oaks, CA: Sage.

Berkowitz, L. 2003. Affect, aggression, and antisocial behavior. In *Handbook of Affective Sciences,* ed. R.J. Davidson, K.R. Scherer, and H.H. Goldsmith, 804–823. New York: Oxford University Press.

Berset, M.; Semmer, N.K.; Elfering, A.; Jacobshagen, N.; and Meier, L. 2011. Does stress at work make you gain weight? A two-year longitudinal study. *Scandinavian Journal of Work and Environmental Health,* 37, 45–53.

Bies, R.J.; Tripp, T.M.; and Kramer, R.M. 1997. At the breaking point: Cognitive and social dynamics of revenge in organizations. In *Antisocial Behavior in Organizations,* ed. R.A. Giacalone and J. Greenberg, 18–36. Thousand Oaks, CA: Sage.

Blackhart, G.C.; Nelson, B.C.; Knowles, M.L.; and Baumeister, R.F. 2009. Rejection elicits emotional reactions but neither causes immediate distress nor lowers self-esteem: A meta-analytic review of 192 studies on social exclusion. *Personality and Social Psychology Review,* 13, 269–309.

Bolger, N.; DeLongis, A.; Kessler, R.C.; and Schilling, A. 1989. Effects of daily stress on negative mood. *Journal of Personality and Social Psychology,* 57, 808–818.

Bowling, N.A., and Beehr, T.A. 2006. Workplace harassment from the victim's perspective: A theoretical model and meta-analysis. *Journal of Applied Psychology,* 91, 998–1012.

Brockner, J. 1988. The effects of work layoffs on survivors: Research, theory and practice. In *Research in Organizational Behavior,* vol. 10, ed. B.M. Staw and L.L. Cummings, 213–255.

Brockner, J.; Konovsky, M.; Cooper-Schneider, R.; Folger, R.; Martin, C.; and Bies, R.J. 1994. Interactive effects of procedural justice and outcome negativity on victims and survivors of job loss. *Academy of Management Journal,* 37, 397–409.

Brown, M.E.; Treviño, L.K.; and Harrison, D.A. 2005. Ethical leadership: A social learning perspective for construct development and testing. *Organizational Behavior and Human Decision Processes,* 97, 117–134.

Crocker, J., and Park, L.E. 2004. The costly pursuit of self-esteem. *Psychological Bulletin,* 130, 392–414.

Cropanzano, R.; Byrne, Z.S.; Bobocel, D.R.; and Rupp, D.E. 2001. Moral virtues, fairness heuristics, social entities, and other denizens of organizational justice. *Journal of Vocational Behavior,* 58, 164–209.

Darley, J.M., and Latané, B. 1968. Bystander intervention in emergencies: Diffusion of responsibility. *Journal of Personality and Social Psychology,* 8, 377–383.

De Cremer, D., and van Hiel, A. 2006. Effects of another person's fair treatment on one's own emotions and behaviors: The moderating role of how much the other cares for you. *Organizational Behavior and Human Decision Processes,* 100, 231–249.

DeBono, A.; Shmueli, D.; and Muraven, M. 2010. Rude and inappropriate: The role of self-control in following social norms. *Personality and Social Psychology Bulletin,* 37, 136–146.

De Waal, F.B.M. 2008. Putting the altruism back into altruism: The evolution of empathy. *Annual Review of Psychology,* 59, 297–300.

Dormann, C., and Zapf, D. 1999. Social support, social stressors at work, and depressive symptoms: Testing for main and moderating effects with structural equations in a three-wave longitudinal study. *Journal of Applied Psychology,* 84, 874–884.

Duffy, M.K.; Ganster, D.C.; and Pagon, M. 2002. Social undermining in the workplace. *Academy of Management Journal,* 45, 2, 331–351.

Einarsen, S.E.; Hoel, H.; Zapf, D.; and Cooper, C.L. 2010. The concept of bullying at work: The European tradition. In *Bullying and Harassment in the Workplace: Developments in Theory, Research, and Practice,* 2d ed., ed. S. Einarsen, H. Hoel, D. Zapf, and C.L. Cooper, 3–39. London: Taylor and Francis.

Finne, L.B.; Knardahl, S.; and Lau, B. 2011. Workplace bullying and mental distress: A prospective study of Norwegian employees. *Scandinavian Journal of Work and Environmental Health,* 37, 276–286.

Fitzgerald, L.F.; Drasgow, F.; Hulin, C.L.; Gelfand, J.J.; and Magley, V.J. 1997. Antecedents and consequences of sexual harassment in organizations: A test of an integrated model. *Journal of Applied Psychology,* 82, 578–589.

Folger, R. 1998. Fairness as a moral virtue. In *Managerial Ethics: Moral Management of People and Processes,* ed. M. Schminke, 13–34. Mahwah, NJ: Erlbaum.

Forgas, J. P. 2002. Feeling and doing: Affective influences on interpersonal behavior. *Psychological Inquiry,* 13, 1–28.

Forgas, J.P.; Bower, G.H.; and Krantz, S. 1984. The influence of mood on perceptions of social interactions. *Journal of Experimental Social Psychology,* 20, 497–513.

Frijda, N.H. 2009. Mood. In *The Oxford Companion to Emotion and the Affective Sciences,* ed. D. Sander and K.R. Scherer, 258–259. Oxford: Oxford University Press.

Frone, M.R. 2000. Interpersonal conflict at work and psychological outcomes: Testing a model among young workers. *Journal of Occupational Health Psychology,* 5, 246–255.

Gino, F.; Schweitzer, M.E.; Mead, N.L.; and Ariely, D. 2011. Unable to resist temptation: How self-control depletion promotes unethical behavior. *Organizational Behavior and Human Decision Processes,* 115, 191–203.

Greenberg, J. 2004. Stress fairness to fare no stress: Managing workplace stress by promoting organizational justice. *Organizational Dynamics,* 33, 352–365.

Griffin, B. 2010. Multilevel relationships between organizational-level incivility, justice and intention to stay. *Work and Stress,* 24, 309–323.

Haidt, J. 2003. The moral emotions. In *Handbook of Affective Sciences,* ed. R.J. Davidson, K.R. Scherer, and H.H. Goldsmith, 852–870. New York: Oxford University Press.

Hatfield, E.; Cacioppo, J.; and Rapson, R.L. 1994. *Emotional Contagion.* New York: Cambridge University Press.

Hauge, L.J.; Skogstad, A.; and Einarsen, S. 2007. Relationships between stressful work environments and bullying: Results of a large representative study. *Work and Stress,* 21, 220–242.

———. 2009. Individual and situational predictors of workplace bullying: Why do perpetrators engage in the bullying of others? *Work and Stress,* 23, 349–358.

Hershcovis, M.S., and Barling, J. 2009. Towards a multi-foci approach to workplace aggression: A meta-analytic review of outcomes from different perpetrators. *Journal of Organizational Behavior,* 31, 24–44.

Hoobler, J.M., and Brass, D.J. 2006. Abusive supervision and family undermining as displaced aggression. *Journal of Applied Psychology,* 91, 1125–1133.

Ilies, R.; Johnson, M.; and Judge, T. 2011. A within-individual study of interpersonal conflict as a work stressor: Dispositional and situational moderators. *Journal of Organizational Behavior,* 32, 44–64.

Jex, S.M., and Elacqua, T.C. 2004. Self-esteem as a moderator: A comparison of global and organization-based measures. *Journal of Occupational and Organizational Psychology,* 72, 71–81.

Jones, D.A. 2009. Getting even with one's supervisor and one's organization: Relationships among types of injustice, desires for revenge, and counterproductive work behaviors. *Journal of Organizational Behavior,* 30, 525–542.

Kahn, R.L.; Wolfe, D.M.; Quinn, R.P.; Snoek, J.D.; and Rosenthal, R.A. 1964. *Organizational Stress: Studies in Role Conflict and Ambiguity.* New York: Wiley.

Katz, D., and Kahn, R.L. 1978. *The Social Psychology of Organizations.* New York: Wiley.

Keashly, L., and Harvey, S. 2005. Emotional abuse in the workplace. In *Counterproductive Work Behavior: Investigations of Actors and Targets,* ed. S. Fox and P.E. Spector, 201–236. Washington, DC: American Psychological Association.

Kelly, J.R., and Barsade, S.G. 2001. Mood and emotions in small groups and work teams. *Organizational Behavior and Human Decision Processes,* 86, 99–130.

Kessler, S.R.; Spector, P.E.; Chang, C.-H.; and Parr, A.D. 2008. Organizational violence and aggression: Development of the three-factor Violence Climate Survey. *Work and Stress,* 22, 108–124.

Kivimäki, M.; Virtanen, M.; Vartia, M.; Elovainio, M.; Vahtera, J.; and Keltikangas-Jarvinen, L. 2003. Workplace bullying and the risk of cardiovascular disease and depression. *Occupational and Environmental Medicine,* 60, 779–783.

Kivimäki, M.; Virtanen, M.; Elovainio, M.; Kuovonenm, A.; Väänänen, A.; and Vahtera, J. 2006. Work stress in the etiology of coronary heart disease: A meta-analysis. *Scandinavian Journal of Work, Environment and Health,* 32, 431–442.

Latané, B., and Nida, S. 1981. Ten years of research on group size and helping. *Psychological Bulletin,* 89, 308–324.

Lazarus, R.S. 1999. *Stress and Emotion.* London: Free Association Books.

Leary, M.R., and Baumeister R.F. 2000. The nature and function of self-esteem: Sociometer theory. *Advances in Experimental Social Psychology,* 32, 1–62.

Lim, S.; Cortina, L.M.; and Magley, V.J. 2008. Personal and workgroup incivility: Impact on work and health outcomes. *Journal of Applied Psychology,* 93, 95–107.

Marcus-Newhall, A.; Pedersen, W.C.; Carlson, M.; and Miller, N. 2000. Displaced aggression is alive and well: A meta-analytic review. *Journal of Personality and Social Psychology,* 78, 670–689.

Meier, L.L.; Semmer, N.K.; and Hupfeld, J. 2009. The impact of unfair treatment on depressive mood: The moderating role of self-esteem level and self-esteem instability. *Personality and Social Psychology Bulletin,* 35, 643–655.

Meier, L.L.; Gross, S.; Spector, P.E.; and Semmer, N.K. 2011. Conflicts at work and well-being: Reciprocal short-term effects. Manuscript submitted for publication.

Miller, N.; Pedersen, W.; Earleywine, M.; and Pollock, V.E. 2003. A theoretical model of triggered displaced aggression. *Personality and Social Psychology Review,* 7, 75–97.

Mueller, S., and Tschan, F. 2011. Consequences of client-initiated workplace violence: The role of fear and perceived prevention. *Journal of Occupational Health Psychology,* 16, 217–229.

Muraven, M., and Baumeister, R.F. 2000. Self-regulation and depletion of limited resources: Does self-control resemble a muscle? *Psychological Bulletin,* 126, 247–259.

Penhaligon, N.L.; Louis, W.R.; and Restubog, S.L.D. 2009. Emotional anguish at work: The mediating role of perceived rejection on workgroup mistreatment and affective outcomes. *Journal of Occupational Health Psychology,* 14, 34–45.

Restubog, S.L.D.; Scott, K.L.; and Zagenczyk, T.J. 2011. When distress hits home: The role of contextual factors and psychological distress in predicting employees' responses to abusive supervision. *Journal of Applied Psychology,* 96, 4, 713–729.

Sedikides, C., and Strube, M.J. 1997. Self-evaluation: To thine own self be good, to thine own self be sure, to thine own self be true, and to thine own self be better. In *Advances in Experimental Social Psychology,* vol. 29, ed. M.P. Zanna, 209–269. New York: Academic Press.

Semmer, N.K., and Meier, L.L. 2009. Individual differences, work stress and health. In *Handbook of Work and Health Psychology,* 3d ed., ed. M.J. Schabracq, J.A. Winnubst, and C.L. Cooper, 99–122. Chichester: Wiley.

Semmer, N.K.; McGrath, J.E.; and Beehr, T.A. 2005. Conceptual issues in research on stress and health. In *Handbook of Stress and Health,* 2d ed., ed. C.L. Cooper, 1–43. New York: CRC Press.

Semmer, N.K.; Jacobshagen, N.; Meier, L.L.; and Elfering, A. 2007. Occupational stress research: The "Stress-as-Offense-to-Self" perspective. In *Occupational Health Psychology: European Perspectives on Research, Education and Practice,* vol. 2, ed. J. Houdmont and S. McIntyre, 43–60. Castelo da Maia, Portugal: ISMAI.

Spector, P.E. 2003. Individual differences in health and well-being in organizations. In *Health and Safety in Organizations: A Multilevel Perspective*, ed. D.A. Hofmann, and L.E. Tetrick, 29–55. San Francisco, CA: Jossey-Bass.

Spector, P.E., and Jex, S.M. 1998. Development of four self-report measures of job stressors and strain: Interpersonal conflict at work scale, organizational constraints scale, quantitative workload inventory, and physical symptoms inventory. *Journal of Occupational Health Psychology,* 3, 356–367.

Steele, C.M. 1988. The psychology of self-affirmation: Sustaining the integrity of the self. In *Advances in Experimental Social Psychology*, vol. 21, ed. L. Berkowitz, 261–302. New York: Academic Press.

Stouten, J.; Baillien, E.; van den Broeck, A.; Camps, J.; de Witte, H.; and Euwema, M. 2010. Discouraging bullying: The role of ethical leadership and its effects on the work environment. *Journal of Business Ethics*, 95, 17–27.

Strack, F.; Martin, L.L.; and Stepper, S. 1988. Inhibiting and facilitating conditions of the human smile: A nonobtrusive test of the facial feedback hypothesis. *Journal of Personality and Social Psychology,* 54, 768–776.

Tedeschi, J.T., and Felson, R.B. 1994. *Violence, Aggression, and Coercive Actions*. Washington, DC: American Psychological Association.

Tepper, B.J. 2007. Abusive supervision in work organizations: Review, synthesis, and research agenda. *Journal of Management,* 33, 261–289.

Thibaut, J., and Walker, L. 1975. *Procedural Justice: a Psychological Analysis*. Hillsdale, NJ: Erlbaum.

Totterdell, P.; Kellett, S.; Teuchmann, K.; and Briner, R.B. 1998. Evidence of mood linkage in work groups. *Journal of Personality and Social Psychology,* 74, 1504–1515.

Totterdell, P.; Wall, T.; Holman, D.; Diamond, H.; and Epitropaki, O. 2004. Affect networks: A structural analysis of the relationship between work ties and job-related affect. *Journal of Applied Psychology,* 89, 854–867.

Tourish, D., and Robson, P. 2006. Sensemaking and the distortion of critical upward communication in organizations. *Journal of Management Studies,* 43, 711–730.

Tyler, T.R., and Lind, E.A. 1992. A relational model of authority in groups. In *Advances in Experimental Social Psychology*, vol. 25, ed. M. Zanna, 115–191. San Diego, CA: Academic Press.

Williams, K.D. 1997. Social ostracism. In *Aversive Interpersonal Behaviors*, ed. R.M. Kowalski, 133–170. New York: Plenum Press.

Ylipaavalniemi, J.; Kivimäki, M.; Elovainio, M.; Virtanen, M.; Keltikangas-Järvinen, L.; and Vahtera, J. 2005. Psychosocial work characteristics and incidence of newly diagnosed depression: A prospective cohort study of three different models. *Social Science and Medicine,* 61, 111–122.

PART III

INDIVIDUAL DIFFERENCES,
JUSTICE, AND MORAL EMOTIONS

12

MACHIAVELLIANISM, UNETHICAL BEHAVIOR AND WELL-BEING IN ORGANIZATIONAL LIFE

JASON J. DAHLING, DANIEL KUYUMCU, AND ERIKA H. LIBRIZZI

> *At this point one may note that men must be either pampered or annihilated.*
> *They avenge light offenses; they cannot avenge severe ones; hence,*
> *the harm one does to a man must be such as to obviate any fear of revenge.*
> (Machiavelli, 1513/1981, p. 16)

Machiavellianism is an individual difference that speaks to having a cynical worldview, a willingness to behave unethically, and a repertoire of manipulative tactics that can be used to secure power and gains for oneself (Christie and Geis, 1970). As the preceding quote from Niccolo Machiavelli's *The Prince* illustrates, a Machiavellian employee can be a considerable threat to the well-being of the people around him or her, and the problems created by Machiavellian employees can have far-ranging consequences. In this chapter, we will provide a brief overview of Machiavellian personality, summarize the types of unethical behaviors that highly Machiavellian people commit in the workplace, and explore how Machiavellian tactics might detract from well-being throughout the organization. Although the effects of Machiavellian tactics on targeted victims are well-established, we suggest that Machiavellian behavior can harm the broader workgroup context and, paradoxically, the Machiavellian perpetrator as well. We conclude with some practical suggestions for how Machiavellian employees might be identified and managed in the interest of preventing them from harming others and themselves.

MACHIAVELLIAN PERSONALITY: ORIGINS AND CHARACTERISTICS

The concept of Machiavellianism originated in the writing of Niccolo Machiavelli, a political figure in sixteenth-century Florence, Italy. Machiavelli's most enduring work, *The Prince*, was written during the first year of an exile from politics in 1513; Florence had been conquered by the Medici family in 1512, and in the wake of this defeat, Machiavelli was arrested for conspiracy, tortured, stripped of his office, and banished from home (de Grazia, 1989). *The Prince,* which was addressed to Lorenzo de' Medici, provided a frank body of advice on ruling others that was intended to showcase Machiavelli's experience and advocate for the restoration of his political appointments. The openly amoral counsel that Machiavelli gave in *The Prince* remains deeply influential to managers, psychologists, and political scientists nearly 500 years after its original distribution.

The concept of Machiavellianism as a personality variable was first described by Christie and Geis (1970), who used concepts from *The Prince* and a later work by Machiavelli, *The Discourses on Livy,* as a starting point for describing people with a Machiavellian disposition. As Christie (1970) explained, people high in Machiavellianism tend to have three key characteristics inferred from Machiavelli's writing. First, they adopt a cynical view of the world and other people, expecting that each person is invested solely in his or her own self-interests. Second, they are willing to utilize manipulative tactics to influence others and secure desired outcomes. Third, they are quite willing to depart from ethical standards when unethical behavior provides a necessary advantage over others. To this end, Machiavellianism entails a freedom from ethical consideration rather than a propensity to always behave unethically. More recent research on Machiavellianism has elaborated on these ideas, pointing out that Machiavellian people behave this way predominantly out of a motivation to secure extrinsic achievements, rewards, status, and power over other people (Dahling, Whitaker, and Levy, 2009; McHoskey, 1999; Stewart and Stewart, 2006).

Consistent with this research, Machiavellianism is best considered a stable motivational orientation, and it is important to clarify what Machiavellianism does *not* involve before proceeding further. First, Machiavellianism implies only a desire to manipulate, not necessarily a particular ability to exercise manipulative tactics effectively. Machiavellianism is distinct from traits like emotional intelligence, cognitive ability, and social skills (e.g., Austin et al., 2007; Dahling, Whitaker, and Levy, 2009; Jones and Paulhus, 2009) that facilitate effective manipulation, so it is important to recognize that Machiavellians are motivated to manipulate, but may not be skilled at manipulation by default. Second, Machiavellianism is related to, but distinct from, psychological disorders such as clinical psychopathy and narcissism (e.g., Paulhus and Williams, 2002). Machiavellian behavior is consequently present in the population of everyday working adults and is, unfortunately, a common experience in many organizations, which may have important consequences for employees' well-being.

MACHIAVELLIANISM AND UNETHICAL WORKPLACE BEHAVIORS

Given their propensity to behave amorally and manipulate others, it is not surprising that Machiavellian employees commit a wide variety of unethical, counterproductive behaviors at work (e.g., Granitz, 2003; Gunnthorsdottir, McCabe, and Smith, 2002; Hegarty and Sims, 1979; Tang and Chen, 2007). Machiavellians will go to great lengths to get ahead of others, and likewise, they readily engage in interpersonal deviance to achieve these ends. For example, O'Fallon and Butterfield (2005) reviewed the empirical literature on ethical decision-making from 1996 to 2003 and found that Machiavellianism was consistently and negatively linked to ethical decision making, a trend reflected in large bodies of research on stealing, lying, sabotage, and cheating committed by Machiavellian employees.

Theft

Research illustrates that Machiavellians are readily willing to steal, even within trusting relationships. Harrell and Hartnagel (1976) found, for example, that Machiavellians stole from both trusting and distrustful employers. Their study allowed both high- and low-Machiavellians to steal in simulated worker–supervisor situations. In one condition, the confederate supervisor was blatantly untrusting of the participant worker and would regularly monitor his or her behavior. In another condition, the confederate supervisor was trustful of the worker and disclosed that he or she would not be monitoring the worker's behavior. Most of the participants stole from the untrusting supervisor, but only the highly Machiavellian participants were more likely to steal from the trusting supervisor. Moreover, they also stole in greater quantities across both conditions when compared to participants with low Machiavellianism. Highly Machiavellian participants also tried to hide their theft and even denied it when interrogated by the distrustful supervisor. In a more recent study, Machiavellians were found to be unlikely to reciprocate trust when it was extended to them in a negotiation, and they generally had no qualms about using morally questionable tactics to achieve their goals and take most of the winnings for themselves (Gunnthorsdottir, McCabe, and Smith, 2002).

Machiavellians are also willing to steal intangible knowledge resources from others. Winter, Stylianou, and Giacalone (2004) found that Machiavellians were willing to ignore a wide range of intellectual property rights; highly Machiavellian employees endorsed behaviors such as taking confidential records from work and using proprietary system knowledge from one employer to re-create a product or service for another employer. They also found that Machiavellian employees were more willing to violate the privacy of coworkers by accessing personal data without permission and reading communications that were meant to be private. Thus, Machiavellian employees seem motivated to steal both tangible resources and intangible information from others.

Lying and Deceit

Lying is another unethical tactic employed by Machiavellians, who tend to make more believable liars (Geis and Moon, 1981; Janisse and Bradley, 1980). For example, Ross and Robertson (2000) found that Machiavellians were inclined to lie overtly and to take advantage of ambiguity in ethical guidelines to deceive others. McLeod and Genereux (2008) clarified that Machiavellians typically lie only in circumstances that will benefit them, and not for reasons of altruism or social acceptance (e.g., to show kindness to others with a "white lie"). They identified Machiavellianism as one of the key predictors of one's propensity to condone as well as engage in self-gain or conflict-avoidance lies.

Sabotage

Machiavellians are also known to engage in acts of sabotage in the workplace. For example, people who are high in both Machiavellianism and hostility tend to justify acts of sabotage more so than individuals who are neither hostile nor Machiavellian (Giacalone and Knouse, 1990). Similarly, McLeod and Genereux (2008) predicted that Machiavellians would be prone to justifying acts of sabotage because of their self-focused behavior. Their results indicated that Machiavellianism coupled with hostility allowed the individual to justify profit sabotage (e.g., providing misleading information about revenue), as well as information sabotage (e.g., spreading hurtful rumors). The authors explained that a hostile attitude can heighten a Machiavellian disposition and promote corrupt actions. Further, Machiavellians are most likely to engage in corrupt strategies if they are not likely to be caught and if the potential gains are to their benefit (Giacalone and Knouse, 1990; Shlenker, 1980).

Cheating

Machiavellians typically show little interest in conforming to organizational rules that are designed to promote fairness and ethical behavior. For example, in a laboratory experiment, Hegarty and Sims (1979) found that Machiavellians would be more likely to pay mock purchasing agents illicit bonuses in order to increase sales. In a role-play experiment on consumer cheating on service guarantees, Wirtz and Kum (2004) found that highly Machiavellian participants were more likely to cheat on service guarantees than participants with low Machiavellianism. Furthermore, Machiavellians are more accepting of active academic cheating (e.g., copying another student's test), as well as passive cheating (e.g., remaining silent when a bill is miscalculated in their favor; Bloodgood, Turnley, and Mudrack, 2010). These authors also examined the effect that an ethics course would have on attitudes toward these types of cheating and found that the attitudes of highly Machiavellian participants toward passive cheating were unchanged after receiving the ethics training. The implications of this finding are that Machiavellians may indeed be immune to such ethics instruction.

Bass, Barnett, and Brown (1999) identified several relationships between Machiavellianism and ethical orientations that explain why Machiavellians tend to employ these unethical tactics. For example, they found associations between Machiavellianism and relativism, which they defined as the degree to which one accepts or disregards universal moral principles when making decisions (Forsyth, 1980). They also suggested that Machiavellianism is inversely related to idealism, which refers to a tendency to seek balanced and favorable outcomes for all parties (Forsyth, 1980). Bass, Barnett, and Brown (1999) also confirmed that Machiavellians are less inclined to support social rules and follow authority.

Given all of these findings concerning theft, lying, sabotage, and cheating, it is not surprising that Machiavellianism is one of the strongest trait predictors of unethical behavior in many contexts (Jones and Kavanagh, 1996). Unfortunately, these Machiavellian behaviors can pose a considerable risk to the well-being of organizational members in many respects.

EFFECTS OF MACHIAVELLIAN BEHAVIOR ON WELL-BEING

We have given evidence that Machiavellian behaviors are characteristically unethical and manipulative; here, we suggest that the nature of these behaviors is an important determinant of well-being in the workplace. Consistent with Giacalone and Promislo (2010), we define well-being in terms of both subjective elements (e.g., satisfaction and psychological appraisals of life events) and objective elements (e.g., physiological wellness, stress, and illness). From this perspective, well-being involves being satisfied with one's work and nonwork circumstances, experiencing positive emotional states, and being healthy in the sense of freedom from psychological and physiological illnesses.

Given that the unethical acts committed by Machiavellians can include a wide range of behaviors (e.g., stealing, lying, and cheating), it seems logical that Machiavellianism has a multidimensional effect on well-being, affecting not only the targets or victims of the behaviors but also work teams and the organization in a much more general sense (ibid.). Interestingly, because Machiavellianism is a personality construct, the perpetrator (i.e., the Machiavellian) should also experience significant detrimental effects on his/her own well-being resulting from this innate, amoral orientation and the actual execution of unethical acts.

Unethical Behavior and the Well-Being of Machiavellian Employees

Although the effects of Machiavellian behaviors on others are well-established, less research has considered how the well-being of Machiavellians is impacted by their own unethical behavior. Moreover, much of the existing research on this topic shows inconsistent results, which may reflect differences in job type, organizational setting, or the level of career success among Machiavellian individuals (Jones and Paulhus, 2009). Nevertheless, some emergent trends in the literature suggest that Machiavellian employees may suffer more than they benefit from their orientation toward others with respect to lower satisfaction, higher anxiety, and compromised psychological well-being.

Job and Career Satisfaction

Research has shown that Machiavellianism is associated with higher levels of job strain and lower levels of self-reported satisfaction with both current jobs and overall career progress (Corzine, Buntzman, and Busch, 1999; Fehr, Samsom, and Paulhus, 1992; Gemmill and Heisler, 1972; Jones and Paulhus, 2009). For example, Gable and Topol (1988) found significant negative relationships between Machiavellianism and six different facets of job satisfaction (i.e., index of total job satisfaction, satisfaction with feedback and freedom, satisfaction with closure, satisfaction with variety, general job satisfaction, and satisfaction with career). Highly Machiavellian employees are thought to be less satisfied for a variety of reasons, such as their extrinsically oriented motivation system (McHoskey, 1999), their tendency to engage themselves in hostile and stressful situations (Gemmill and Heisler, 1972), or the worry that their careers have plateaued (Corzine, Buntzman, and Busch, 1999). A consequence of this perennial dissatisfaction is that Machiavellians are prone to frequent turnover from jobs in the search for more favorable employment circumstances (Wilson, Near, and Miller, 1996), which reduces their likelihood of becoming established and successful in a role.

Anxiety

In their review of the literature on Machiavellianism from 1971 to 1987, Fehr, Samson, and Paulhus (1992) found that Machiavellianism was consistently associated with anxiety. For example, Nigro and Galli (1985) illustrated that Machiavellianism was positively associated with both trait and state anxiety, which suggests that these individuals are not only inherently more anxious but are also more likely to experience anxiety when presented with psychologically stressful situations. The anxious feelings that highly Machiavellian people report may be related to their subjective reports of being envied by coworkers and their propensity to exhibit symptoms of paranoia and distrust of others (Vecchio, 2005).

Psychological Well-Being and Emotional Experiences

In terms of emotional well-being, Machiavellians tend to be less empathetic toward others and show symptoms that are broadly consistent with alexithymia, a sense of disconnectedness with respect to one's own emotions (Andrew, Cooke, and Muncer, 2008; Wastell and Booth, 2003). Research also indicates a negative relationship between Machiavellianism and self-esteem, which may be related to research showing that Machiavellianism is distinct from other traits such as emotional intelligence, cognitive, and social skills (Austin et al., 2007; Dahling, Whitaker, and Levy, 2009; Jones and Paulhus, 2009; McHoskey et al., 1999). Machiavellianism has also been linked to low guilt-proneness, suggesting that although Machiavellians are consciously aware of their unethical behaviors and actions, they do not commonly express remorse for them (Wastell and Booth, 2003). Interestingly, it seems as if Machiavellians are aware of both their unethical tendencies and the effects of these behaviors on their own well-being. For example, McHoskey et al. (1999) found that Machiavellianism was negatively associated with self-reports of subjective well-being.

An initial analysis of the relationship between Machiavellianism and the propensity to engage in unethical behaviors may lead one to believe that Machiavellianism is synonymous with other well-established personality disorders. It is important to understand that although Machiavellianism may overlap with these socially aversive personalities, such as narcissism and psychopathy, it is a distinct construct of psychopathology (Paulhus and Williams, 2002). For example, research has demonstrated that Machiavellians do not significantly differ from non-Machiavellians in their level of neuroticism, psychoticism, or occupational, home, health, and emotional adjustment (Skinner, 1982). Similarly, LaTorre and McLeoad (1978) found no clear link between Machiavellianism and depression. Together, these findings suggest that Machiavellians can be generally psychologically stable individuals who nevertheless may be dissatisfied with their accomplishments, prone to high anxiety, and oftentimes disconnected from their emotions in ways that greatly compromise their overall well-being.

Machiavellianism and Well-Being Among Dyadic Partners

As previously noted, Machiavellians behave unethically when such actions can advance their own interests (Christie and Geis, 1970). Not surprisingly, the intended targets of these unethical behaviors tend to suffer lower well-being, and the majority of Machiavellianism research has focused on documenting these consequences in studies of dyadic interactions.

For example, some of the most compelling organizational research on the effects of Machiavellian behaviors has focused on supervisor–subordinate dyads. Employee perceptions of supervisor Machiavellianism negatively correlate with employee perceptions of supervisor credibility, subordinate motivation, and subordinate job satisfaction (Teven, McCroskey, and Richmond, 2006). Research has also demonstrated that supervisor Machiavellianism is positively associated with subordinate perceptions of abusive supervision, which detracts from psychological well-being and enhances anxiety among the victims of such acts (Hobman et al., 2009; Kiazad et al., 2010). These results suggest that Machiavellian behaviors exhibited by individuals in power positions may be especially devastating to the well-being of their respective subordinates. Conversely, subordinate Machiavellianism has been associated with lower levels of supervisor satisfaction (Walter, Anderson, and Martin, 2005). Together, these findings indicate that Machiavellianism, whether exhibited upward by the subordinate or downward by the supervisor, has a detrimental influence on the well-being of the other party. Further, the detrimental effects of Machiavellianism are also seen between peers at the same hierarchical level. For example, O'Hair and Cody (1987) found that Machiavellians utilized cynical and deceitful distributive tactics in their social interactions with same-status peers to strategically build social obligations for the peers to reciprocate with favors and loyalty.

Machiavellianism and Well-Being Detriments in Work Groups

Less research has expanded beyond dyadic relationships to consider the effects of Machiavellianism in teams and social networks, and the existing research in this area is somewhat inconsistent. For example, some findings conclude that young Machiavellians are generally well-liked by peers and display social skills similar to those of their non-Machiavellian counterparts (Hawley, 2003). Other reports have found negative associations with social interest and prosocial tendencies; similarly, Machiavellianism has been positively linked to antisocial behaviors and several facets of social alienation that might compromise the ability of a Machiavellian employee to influence his or her work group (McHoskey, 1999).

The differences seen in this literature can be explained in light of the intentions that underlie the social interactions of Machiavellian employees. As previously mentioned, Machiavellians utilize manipulative tactics to influence others in order to secure a desired outcome. In some cases, Machiavellians may find it more beneficial to utilize integrative tactics, such as flattery, to achieve their goals, which results in their being judged as socially competent and well-liked by those who are targeted by such flattery (O'Hair and Cody, 1987). Machiavellian employees are also known to engage in organizational citizenship behaviors that can result in favorable social impressions, but they only express these behaviors for impression management purposes (Becker and O'Hair, 2007). Conversely, the antisocial, unethical, and disruptive behaviors exhibited by Machiavellians in circumstances when it is to their advantage to do so may explain the more negative ratings of social skill and competence given to Machiavellians in some research (McHoskey, 1999; O'Hair and Cody, 1987).

Despite this mixed literature, we can reasonably infer that any constructive social behavior exhibited by Machiavellian employees is a consequence of self-interest, and highly Machiavellian employees cannot be counted on to have genuinely prosocial motives or to demonstrate commitment when others need their help with no benefits to offer in exchange (Becker and O'Hair, 2007; Wilson, Near, and Miller, 1996). Within the context of workplace social networks, we expect that Machiavellian employees detract from social relationships in several ways. First, Machiavellian employees are unlikely to share information or resources (Liu, 2008), and they are prone to seek to maintain positions of strategic power as boundary spanners between groups that would benefit from greater social exchanges (e.g., Borgatti and Foster, 2003). Second, Machiavellian unethical behaviors should prevent the development of identification-based trust between people who can improve the quality of social relationships and work in organizations (Mayer, Davis, and Schoorman, 1995). Because Machiavellians are so prone to betray the trust shown to them by others (Harrell and Hartnagel, 1976), it is unlikely that the coworkers of Machiavellian employees can settle into stable exchange relationships without worrying that they are being deceived.

Machiavellianism and Well-Being in the Broader Organization

Thus far, we have documented that Machiavellian unethical behaviors harm the Machiavellian perpetrator, the intended target of the unethical behavior, and the social work group in which these behaviors occur. We consequently propose that the unethical acts committed by Machiavellians in the workplace may aggregate to indirectly detract from the well-being of the larger organizational system as well. The manipulative tactics employed by Machiavellians are all committed in an effort to obtain a desired outcome, usually for their own self-interest. These acts may secure them individual prestige, power, or status, but may come at the expense of the organization. Similar ideas are reflected in previous research on extreme careerism in organizations (e.g., Bratton and Kacmar, 2004; Feldman and Weitz, 1991). Extreme careerism involves the advancement of individual careers through negative impression-management tactics rather than the substantive performance that makes one qualified to move up within an organization. Bratton and Kacmar (2004) proposed that Machiavellians were especially likely to engage in extreme careerism, and allowing Machiavellians to assume positions of leadership and influence within an organization is likely to detract from the organization's success by placing self-interested and potentially underqualified people in positions of responsibility.

The detrimental effects of Machiavellian unethical behaviors throughout the organization can affect several group outcomes that undermine general organizational success. For example, both the depression experienced by victims of unethical behavior and the job stress that the Machiavellian perpetrator experiences can result in impaired group performance (Gemmill and Heisler, 1972; Penhaligon, Louis, and Restubog, 2009). Also, as previously described, supervisor Machiavellianism is positively linked to employee perceptions of abusive supervision (Kiazed et al., 2010), which can encourage retaliatory deviance, detract from relationship quality, or undermine the organization's climate for fairness or justice (Colquitt, Noe, and Jackson, 2002). For example,

Restubog, Scott, and Zagenczyk (2011) found an increase in supervisor-directed deviance among individuals who had experienced abusive supervision. Reductions in job performance and increases in workplace strife can have serious consequences for the prosperous operation and financial success of the organization. In summary, the available evidence suggests that the aggregate result of Machiavellian unethical behavior unfolding in dyadic relationships and work groups may be the compromised well-being and performance of the entire organization.

FUTURE RESEARCH DIRECTIONS ON MACHIAVELLIANISM AND WELL-BEING

Although an impressive body of evidence has documented the detrimental effects of Machiavellian unethical behaviors on well-being, additional research is needed to clarify several issues. Most important, future research should expand beyond a focus on either Machiavellian individuals or dyadic relationships to explore how Machiavellianism impacts the broader social network and organizational performance criteria. Most research to date has drawn inferences about how Machiavellian behavior might poison the broader organization, but evidence of these consequences is limited.

Social network analysis (Borgatti and Foster, 2003) offers a particularly fruitful approach for answering these questions. Social network analysis involves mapping the social relationships between people in an identifiable organization to examine how tangible and social assets (knowledge, trust, liking, etc.) are shared. In a social network, individual power is a consequence of having many connections in a relatively sparse network full of structural holes. In such a context, powerful people have access to resources and are able to broker relationships between other people who would otherwise be unconnected. We expect that Machiavellians seek to find and occupy these strategic positions that bridge structural holes to keep themselves well-informed and important in the social network. This idea is broadly consistent with some findings that show that Machiavellianism only contributes to performance as tenure increases, which suggests that Machiavellian employees need time to strategically embed themselves in the social network of an organization before they can capitalize on their motivations and become successful (Dahling, Whitaker, and Levy, 2009). Notably, such an arrangement is detrimental to the overall health of the social network, as denser networks with fewer structural holes allow for a freer exchange of resources and information where they are needed to enhance organizational productivity. Future research on social networks could compellingly demonstrate how Machiavellian employees threaten the organization by perpetuating ineffective social arrangements that best serve themselves.

Another important direction for future research concerns the Machiavellianism exhibited by top leaders who are in key positions to impact organizational success. The limited research on Machiavellian leaders has presented mixed evidence about when Machiavellian leadership will detract from organizational well-being. For example, Deluga (2001) found that Machiavellianism (as inferred from historical profiles) was positively related to ratings of charisma and performance among all past American presidents. Evidence from lab studies also suggests that Machiavellian leaders can be highly adaptive in uncertain contexts and that they adopt a task-oriented style to help clarify objectives. However, Machiavellian leaders also tend to be very inconsiderate of followers, ineffective when resolving group conflicts, and easily frustrated when faced with tasks that are unfavorable or difficult (Drory and Gluskinos, 1980). Despite these important preliminary findings, little is known about Machiavellianism and its effects among real business leaders, which is a critical shortcoming of the literature. Future research should focus on how leader Machiavellianism impacts both internal and external organizational criteria, such as the development of an ethical climate inside the organization (Schminke, Ambrose, and Neubaum, 2005) and the profitability of the organization relative to its external competitors.

RECOMMENDATIONS FOR MANAGING MACHIAVELLIANISM

The negative effects of Machiavellianism on well-being are best managed by preventing the expression of Machiavellian unethical behavior in the first place, and the literature on Machiavellianism fortunately offers several useful suggestions for managers. First, we emphasize again that Machiavellian employees are *amoral,* not *immoral.* If individual reward systems are carefully constructed to encourage rule abidance, ethical conduct, and helpful behaviors, Machiavellians will respond accordingly. Such interventions depend on a careful knowledge of how reward systems can inadvertently encourage deviant behavior (Litzky, Eddleston, and Kidder, 2006) and a thoughtful alignment of individual and organizational interests. Effective reward systems should draw on the perspectives of multiple raters and observers in the organization to minimize the impact of social manipulation, apply uniformly consistent standards for ethical conduct in the evaluation process to send a clear message about ethical expectations, and incentivize group or team performance to emphasize a collective orientation. Recent work by Kasser and colleagues (e.g., Kasser, 2011; Kasser, Vansteenkiste, and Deckop, 2006) on making organizations less materialistic could help in this respect. For example, Kasser, Vansteenkiste, and Deckop (2006) suggested that organizations can be less materialistic by providing group- or organization-level rewards, adopting gain-sharing plans, rewarding servant leadership, and eliminating pay-for-performance systems that undermine intrinsic motivation. Such contexts are extremely unlikely to attract Machiavellian candidates or elicit unethical behavior among current employees who are predominately concerned with extrinsic, material rewards.

Previous research also clearly indicates that Machiavellians are most likely to thrive when working in unstructured contexts that provide an opportunity to engage in unethical behavior without being monitored or caught. For example, Machiavellians are more successful and more satisfied in jobs that are characterized by what Sparks (1994) referred to as a high "latitude for improvisation," the opportunity for regularly independent operations with little supervision. Similarly, Shultz (1993) found that highly Machiavellian employees outperformed low Machiavellians only in organizations characterized by loose rather than tight structure. More recently, Whitaker (2011) found that autonomy moderated the link between Machiavellianism and coworker intimidation such that intimidation occurs only when autonomy is high rather than low. A clear recommendation based on these findings is that close management and monitoring with a narrow span of control may reduce unethical Machiavellian behavior. In a related finding, politically skilled managers are better able to recognize and discount the influence tactics of Machiavellian employees, and these managers consequently see Machiavellians as less worthy of promotion (ibid.). Thus, the quality of the monitoring is important as well; Machiavellian unethical behavior is most likely to be thwarted when countered with structured work and close supervision by a manager with strong social skills.

Finally, we note that several measures of Machiavellianism are available in the literature (Christie and Geis, 1970; Dahling, Whitaker, and Levy 2009; Kessler et al., 2010), and it may be possible to screen for Machiavellian personality when hiring. As suggested previously, the most dangerous profile for a potential candidate pairs high Machiavellianism with high cognitive and emotional ability. The potentially destructive consequences of this combination are reflected in recent research on counterproductive, "dark" uses of emotional intelligence in organizational settings (Kilduff, Chiaburu, and Menges, 2010). Employees with high Machiavellianism and high emotional and cognitive abilities possess both the "motive" and the "means," respectively, to significantly harm colleagues and organizations (Neuman and Keashly, 2010). When coupled with the opportunity afforded by loosely structured work, these employees pose a considerable threat to well-being that managers cannot ignore.

In conclusion, Machiavellian employees exhibit a wide range of unethical workplace behaviors that threaten the well-being of the Machiavellian perpetrator, the intended target of the behaviors, and the broader work group and organization. However, effective management in the form of structured monitoring, carefully constructed reward systems, and rigorous selection processes can thwart these undesirable outcomes. Moreover, such practices communicate to employees that ethical behavior is encouraged and in their best interests, which contributes to organizational growth and development.

REFERENCES

Andrew, J.; Cooke, M.; and Muncer, S.J. 2008. The relationship between empathy and Machiavellianism: An alternative to empathizing-systemizing theory. *Personality and Individual Differences,* 44, 1203–1211.

Austin, E.J.; Farrelly, D.; Black, C.; and Moore, H. 2007. Emotional intelligence, Machiavellianism and emotional manipulation: Does EI have a dark side? *Personality and Individual Differences,* 43, 179–189.

Bass, K.; Barnett, T.; and Brown, G. 1999. Individual difference variables, ethical judgments, and ethical behavioral intentions. *Business Ethics Quarterly,* 9, 183–205.

Becker, J.A.H., and O'Hair, H.D. 2007. Machiavellians' motives in organizational citizenship behavior. *Journal of Applied Communication Research,* 35, 246–267.

Bloodgood, J.M.; Turnley, W.H.; and Mudrack, P.E. 2010. Ethics instruction and the perceived acceptability of cheating. *Journal of Business Ethics,* 95, 23–37.

Borgatti, S.P., and Foster, P.C. 2003. The network paradigm in organizational research: A review and typology. *Journal of Management,* 29, 991–1013.

Bratton, V.K., and Kacmar, K.M. 2004. Extreme careerism: The dark side of impression management. In *The Dark Side of Organizational Behavior,* ed. R.W. Griffin and A.M. O'Leary-Kelly, 291–308. San Francisco, CA: Jossey-Bass.

Christie, R. 1970. Why Machiavelli? In *Studies in Machiavellianism,* ed. R. Christie and F. Geis, 1–9. New York: Academic Press.

Christie, R., and Geis, F. (eds.). 1970. *Studies in Machiavellianism.* New York: Academic Press.

Colquitt, J.A.; Noe, R.A.; and Jackson, C.L. 2002. Justice in teams: Antecedents and consequences of procedural justice climate. *Personnel Psychology,* 55, 83–109.

Corzine, J.B.; Buntzman, G.F.; and Busch, E.T. 1999. Machiavellianism in U.S. bankers. *International Journal of Organizational Analysis,* 7, 72–83.

Dahling, J.J., Whitaker, B.G., and Levy, P.E. 2009. The development and validation of a new Machiavellianism scale. *Journal of Management,* 35, 219–257.

de Grazia, S. 1989. *Machiavelli in Hell.* Princeton, NJ: Princeton University Press.

Deluga, R.J. 2001. American presidential Machiavellianism: Implications for charismatic leadership and rated performance. *The Leadership Quarterly,* 12, 339–363.

Drory, A., and Gluskinos, U.M. 1980. Machiavellianism and leadership. *Journal of Applied Psychology,* 65, 81–86.

Fehr, B.; Samsom, D.; and Paulhus, D.L. 1992. The construct of Machiavellianism: Twenty years later. In *Advances in Personality Assessment,* vol. 9, ed. C.D. Spielberger and J.M. Butcher, 77–116. Hillsdale, NJ: Erlbaum.

Feldman, D.C., and Weitz, B.A. 1991. From the invisible hand to the glad hand: Understanding a careerist orientation to work. *Human Resource Management,* 30, 237–257.

Forsyth, D.R. 1980. A taxonomy of ethical ideologies. *Journal of Personality and Social Psychology,* 39, 175–184.

Gable, M., and Topol, M. 1988. Machiavellianism and the department store executive. *Journal of Retailing,* 64, 68–84.

Geis, F.L., and Moon, T.H. 1981. Machiavellianism and deception. *Journal of Personality and Social Psychology,* 41, 766–775.

Gemmill, G.R., and Heisler, W.J. 1972. Machiavellianism as a factor in managerial job strain, job satisfaction, and upward mobility. *Academy of Management Journal,* 15, 51–62.

Giacalone, R.A., and Knouse, S.B. 1990. Justifying wrongful employee behavior: The role of personality in organizational sabotage. *Journal of Business Ethics,* 9, 55–61.

Giacalone, R.A., and Promislo, M.D. 2010. Unethical and unwell: Decrements in well-being and unethical activity at work. *Journal of Business Ethics,* 91, 275–297.

Granitz, N.A. 2003. Individual, social and organizational sources of sharing and variation in the ethical reasoning of managers. *Journal of Business Ethics,* 42, 101–124.

Gunnthorsdottir, A.; McCabe, K.; and Smith, V. 2002. Using the Machiavellianism instrument to predict trustworthiness in a bargaining game. *Journal of Economic Psychology,* 23, 49–66.

Harrell, W.A., and Hartnagel, T. 1976. The impact of Machiavellianism and the trustfulness of the victim on laboratory theft. *Sociometry,* 39, 157–165.

Hawley, P.H. 2003. Prosocial and coercive configurations of resources control in early adolescence: A case for the well-adapted Machiavellian. *Merrill-Palmer Quarterly,* 49, 279–309.

Hegarty, W.H. and Sims, H.P., Jr. 1979. Organizational philosophy, policies, and objective related to unethical decision behavior: A laboratory experiment. *Journal of Applied Psychology,* 64, 331–338.

Hobman, E.V.; Restubog, S.L.D.; Bordia, P.; and Tang, R.L. 2009. Abusive supervision in advising relationships: Investigating the role of social support. *Applied Psychology: An International Review,* 58, 233–256.

Janisse, M.P., and Bradley, M.T. 1980. Deception, information and the papillary response. *Perceptual and Motor Skills,* 50, 748–750.

Jones, D.N., and Paulhus, D.L. 2009. Machiavellianism. In *Handbook of Individual Differences in Social Behavior,* ed. M.R. Leary and R.H. Hoyle, 93–108. New York: Guilford Press.

Jones, G.E., and Kavanagh, M.J. 1996. An experimental examination of the effects of individual and situational factors on unethical behavioral intentions in the workplace. *Journal of Business Ethics,* 15, 511–523.

Kasser, T. 2011. Cultural values and the well-being of future generations: A cross-national study. *Journal of Cross-Cultural Psychology,* 42, 206–215.

Kasser, T.; Vansteenkiste, M.; and Deckop, J.R. 2006. The ethical problems of a materialistic value orientation for businesses (and some suggestions for alternatives). In *Human Resource Management Ethics,* ed. J.R. Deckop, 283–306. Greenwich, CT: Information Age.

Kessler, S.R.; Bandelli, A.C.; Spector, P.E.; Borman, W.C.; Nelson, C.E.; and Penney, L.M. 2010. Re-examining Machiavelli: A three-dimensional model of Machiavellianism in the workplace. *Journal of Applied Social Psychology,* 40, 1868–1896.

Kiazad, K.; Restubog, S.L.D.; Zagencyk, T.J.; Kiewitz, C.; and Tang, R.L. 2010. In pursuit of power: The role of authoritarian leadership in the relationship between supervisors' Machiavellianism and subordinates' perceptions of abusive supervisory behavior. *Journal of Research in Personality,* 44, 512–519.

Kilduff, M.; Chiaburu, D.S.; and Menges, J.I. 2010. Strategic use of emotional intelligence in organizational settings: Exploring the dark side. *Research in Organizational Behavior,* 30, 129–152.

LaTorre, R.A., and McLeoad, E. 1978. Machiavellianism and clinical depression in a geriatric sample. *Journal of Clinical Psychology,* 34, 659–660.

Litzky, B.E.; Eddleston, K.A.; and Kidder, D.L. 2006. The good, the bad, and the misguided: How managers inadvertently encourage deviant behaviors. *Academy of Management Perspectives,* 20, 91–103.

Liu, C.C. 2008. The relationship between Machiavellianism and knowledge sharing willingness. *Journal of Business and Psychology,* 22, 223–240.

Machiavelli, N. 1513/1981. *The Prince,* trans. D. Donno. New York: Bantam Books.

Mayer, R.C.; Davis, J.H.; and Schoorman, F.D. 1995. An integrative model of organizational trust. *Academy of Management Review,* 20, 709–734.

McHoskey, J.W. 1999. Machiavellianism, intrinsic versus extrinsic goals and social interest: A self-determination theory analysis. *Motivation and Emotion,* 23, 267–283.

McHoskey, J.W.; Hicks, B.; Betris, T.; Szyarto, C.; Worzel, W.; Kelly, K.; et al. 1999. Machiavellianism, adjustment, and ethics. *Psychological Reports,* 85, 138–142.

McLeod, B.A., and Genereux, R.L. 2008. Predicting the acceptability and likelihood of lying: The interaction of personality with type of lie. *Personality and Individual Differences,* 45, 591–596.

Neuman, J.H., and Keashly, L. 2010. Means, motive, opportunity, and aggressive workplace behavior. In *Insidious Workplace Behavior,* ed. J. Greenberg, 31–76. New York: Routledge.

Nigro, G., and Galli, I. 1985. On the relationship between Machiavellianism and anxiety among Italian undergraduates. *Psychological Reports,* 56, 37–38.

O'Fallon, M.J., and Butterfield, K.D. 2005. A review of the empirical ethical decision-making literature: 1996–2003. *Journal of Business Ethics,* 59, 375–413.

O'Hair, D., and Cody, M. 1987. Machiavellian beliefs and social influence. *Western Journal of Speech Communication,* 51, 279–303.

Paulhus, D.L., and Williams, K.M. 2002. The dark triad of personality: Narcissism, Machiavellianism and psychopathy. *Journal of Research in Personality,* 36, 556–563.

Penhaligon, N.L.; Louis, W.R.; and Restubog, S.L.D. 2009. Emotional anguish at work: The mediating role of perceived rejection on workgroup mistreatment and affective outcomes. *Journal of Occupational Health Psychology,* 14, 34–45.

Restubog, S.L.D.; Scott, K.L.; and Zagenczyk, T.J. 2011. When distress hits home: The role of contextual factors and psychological distress in predicting employees' responses to abusive supervision. *Journal of Applied Psychology,* 96, 4, 713–729.

Ross, W.T., and Robertson, D.C. 2000. Lying: The impact of decision context. *Business Ethics Quarterly,* 10, 409–440.

Schminke, M.; Ambrose, M.L.; and Neubaum, D.O. 2005. The effect of leader moral development on ethical climate and employee attitudes. *Organizational Behavior and Human Decision Processes,* 97, 135–151.

Shlenker, B.R. 1980. *Impression Management.* Monterey, CA: Brooks/Cole.

Shultz, C.J. 1993. Situational and dispositional predictors of performance: A test of the hypothesized Machiavellianism x structure interaction among sales persons. *Journal of Applied Social Psychology,* 23, 478–498.

Skinner, N.F. 1982. Personality correlates of Machiavellianism: IV. Machiavellianism and psychopathology. *Social Behavior and Personality,* 10, 201–203.

Sparks, J.R. 1994. Machiavellianism and personal success in marketing: The moderating role of latitude for improvisation. *Journal of the Academy of Marketing Science,* 22, 393–400.

Stewart, A.E., and Stewart, E.A. 2006. The preference to excel and its relationship to selected personality variables. *Journal of Individual Psychology,* 62, 270–284.

Tang, T.L., and Chen, Y. 2007. Intelligence vs. wisdom: The love of money, Machiavellianism, and unethical behavior across college major and gender. *Journal of Business Ethics,* 82, 1–26.

Teven, J.J.; McCroskey, J.C.; and Richmond, V.P. 2006. Communication correlates of perceived Machiavellianism of supervisors: Communication orientations and outcomes. *Communication Quarterly,* 54, 127–142.

Vecchio, R.P. 2005. Exploration in employee envy: Feeling envious and feeling envied. *Cognition and Emotion,* 19, 69–81.

Walter, H.L.; Anderson, C.M.; and Martin, M.M. 2005. How subordinates' Machiavellianism and motives relate to satisfaction with superiors. *Communication Quarterly,* 53, 57–70.

Wastell, C.A., and Booth, A. 2003. Machiavellianism: An alexithymic perspective. *Journal of Social and Clinical Psychology,* 22, 730–744.

Whitaker, B.G. 2011. Extreme careerism and supervisor reactions to peer intimidation. Paper presented at the 2011 meeting of the Academy of Management, August 15, San Antonio, TX.

Wilson, D.S.; Near, D.; and Miller, R.R. 1996. Machiavellianism: A synthesis of the evolutionary and psychological literatures. *Psychological Bulletin,* 119, 285–299.

Winter, S.J.; Stylianou, A.C.; and Giacalone, R.A. 2004. Individual differences in the acceptability of unethical information technology practices: The case of Machiavellianism and ethical ideology. *Journal of Business Ethics,* 54, 279–301.

Wirtz, J., and Kum, D. 2004. Consumer cheating on service guarantees. *Journal of the Academy of Marketing Science,* 32, 159–175.

13

ORGANIZATIONAL JUSTICE AND CARDIOVASCULAR HEALTH

Marko Elovainio and Mika Kivimäki

Research on organizational justice, that is, an individual's perception of fairness in an organization, has not generally focused on the normative nature of justice or fairness in organizations (Cohen-Charash and Spector, 2001; Colquitt, 2001; Colquitt, Greenberg, and Zapata-Phelan, 2005). The main focus has been on what individuals perceive as being fair in organizations and what the consequences of such perceptions might be. Early justice studies were interested in consequences arising from organizational functioning, such as effectiveness, work attitudes, and work performance (Heponiemi et al., 2007; McFarlin and Sweeney, 1992; Moorman, 1991; Phillips, Douthitt, and Hyland, 2001; Skarlicki and Folger, 1997). Only during the past decade has research on organizational justice and work-related psychosocial health risks been combined such that organizational justice is seen as a psychosocial determinant of health. Indeed, few studies on the association between organizational justice and health were published before 2000 (Schmitt and Dorfel, 1999; Tepper, 2001). The first large-scale epidemiological studies on this issue appeared in 2001 (Elovainio, Kivimäki, and Helkama, 2001; Elovainio, Kivimäki, and Vahtera, 2002). Since then the focus has widened to cover a range of different well-being and health outcomes, with the first study that looked at the fair treatment of employees in conjunction with objectively assessed heart disease being published in 2005 (Kivimäki et al., 2005).

In this chapter, we review this literature, compare the findings of these studies with those that deal with other psychosocial work factors, and outline directions for future research. The central theme of this chapter is that organizational justice encompasses not simply the cooperation of employees, an acceptance of decisions, and behavior that matches with organizational aims, but also as something that can enhance employee self-respect, well-being, and even physical and mental health.

There is a widespread belief in the general public and the media that adverse psychosocial work factors or "stresses at work" affect health. One health outcome that has often been studied in relation to work stress is coronary heart disease (CHD). CHD is a leading cause of mortality and an important contributing factor to disability in the industrialized world. To date, the status of psychosocial factors at work as a cause of CHD is still not recognized within most clinical guidelines (De Backer, et. al. 2003; Pearson et al., 2002), although psychosocial factors are mentioned at least in European guidelines on cardiovascular disease prevention in clinical practice (Graham et al., 2007). In this chapter, we concentrate on studies examining organizational injustice as a risk factor for CHD and also review its associations with other health outcomes that could potentially mediate the link between justice and CHD.

THE CONCEPT OF ORGANIZATIONAL JUSTICE

Organizational justice is defined as the extent to which employees are treated with justice at their workplace. According to D.T. Miller (2001), a pioneer in this field of research, injustice is experienced when people perceive that they are treated in a way that they do not deserve to be treated or that they are not treated in the way they deserve. More specifically, organizational justice is a combination of resource distribution, decision-making principles, and treatment practices that people in general may experience as being fair or unfair. High organizational justice means that people within that organization perceive that they get what they deserve (their input and what they get back from the organization are in balance), that the rules treat them fairly (the decisions made follow fair rules), and that other people, especially their supervisors, treat them fairly (supervisors can be trusted and are respectful) (for a review see Cropanzano et al., 2001). These three fundamental dimensions of organizational justice are referred to as distributive, procedural, and interactional justice.

Although justice has long attracted the interest of researchers and philosophers, justice by way of what people perceive to be fair is a relatively new research issue in the behavioral sciences (Lind and Tyler, 1988). Classic social psychology theories such as balance theory (Heider, 1958) and social exchange theory (Homans, 1958) have contributed to the development of conceptual tools for dealing with organizational and social justice. Social exchange theory proposes that all interactions between humans can be understood as a series of exchanges, and along the way people create normative expectations for future exchanges. The theory also suggests that participants in an exchange normally expect profit that is proportional to their investment, also in situations where social goods, such as respect and esteem, are exchanged.

These early theories in conjunction with equity theory as explicated by Adams (1965) came to define what is commonly called distributive justice. *Distributive justice* refers to the fair and equitable allocation of burdens and privileges, rights and responsibilities, and inputs and outputs. By definition, distributive justice is the perception of getting what one deserves. Thus, each person should receive what is due him or her, in a fair and equitable manner. Although many theories of justice, even in the field of organizational studies, define justice as a balance of inputs and outputs (effort–reward imbalance theory) (Siegrist, 1996), there is a fundamental problem in ascertaining what a person is due. Should we focus on merit and decide that people should be rewarded based on effort, or should we focus on need and decide that a distribution of resources is based on what people need? These kinds of conceptual problems have motivated researchers to further elaborate on the justice concept by extending the focus to rules that define how resources are distributed.

Procedural justice refers to clear, transparent, informative, respectful, and participatory decision-making rules and processes within organizations, or in fact, within any kind of groups. Following the principle set forth by Leventhal (1980), procedural justice defines the extent to which decision-making procedures are accurate, correctable, ethical, free of bias, applied consistently, and representative of all concerns (Lind and Tyler, 1988). Fair decisions affecting important issues in people's lives ought to follow due process, and they should be impartial. This type of justice is seen as particularly important in organizations when decisions are made to hire, promote, and fire people.

Other procedures that are generally held as fair are those used in our legal systems; in fact, procedural justice was for the first time explicated as part of a comparison of legal systems (Thibaut and Walker, 1975). According to empirical studies (ibid.), the legal system that was perceived as more fair was the one that confirmed that all parties have a fair hearing in the decision-making process.

Distributive and procedural types of justice are two—sometimes complementary—dimensions of the same process. The former relates to sharing resources and responsibilities, such as money and esteem, while the latter concerns the decision-making process that has led to these distributions. In addition to distributive and procedural justice, relational or interactional justice is an essential part of defining exchange in social relationships.

Relational or *interpersonal justice* refers to treating others with dignity and respect (Cropanzano et al., 2001; Folger and Bies, 1989) and the quality of treatments employees experience in their interpersonal interactions during the completion of organizational processes; specifically, it is employees receiving polite and considerate treatment from their supervisors (Bies and Moag, 1986). Distributive, procedural, and relational justice all reflect basic justice principles in slightly different ways. Distributive justice is about the division of outcomes contingent on one's own actions or inputs. Procedural justice incorporates this principle and the rules to execute the decision. Some procedures are to be applied to all (everybody should be heard in important issues concerning themselves) and some according to their input (anyone who exceeds the standard may have a bonus). Relational justice is about universalism: All employees are entitled to be treated with respect and dignity.

The dimensions of organizational justice include objective resources, such as salary, rewards, and job offers, as well as subjective resources, such as esteem, respect, dignity, and appreciation. It has repeatedly been found that people (and even highly developed animals, such as monkeys) are extremely sensitive to detecting violations in any of the dimensions of organizational justice. Studies have shown that perceived violations provoke negative feelings and emotions (Miller, 2001; Weiss, Suckow, and Cropanzano, 1999). According to the group-value theory of justice, unfair treatment can be a threat to self-esteem and a sense of control over the important issues in one's life and environment, as well as interfering with feelings of membership in an organization or a group (Blader and Tyler, 2003). It has been found that violations of self-esteem, the unpredictability of one's environment, and social isolation increase the risk of experiencing psychological stress (Ferrie, 2001; Sarason et al., 1985; Stansfeld, Fuhrer, and Shipley, 1998). Unfair treatment of an employee can be made worse if organizational decision-making procedures are applied by those who have the power over those who are affected by the decisions. Thus, individuals cannot easily escape or defend themselves, and if the unfair situation continues for a long time this may lead to prolonged psychological stress and be accompanied by negative physiological changes.

Experienced organizational justice has been shown to predict employee work attitudes (e.g., organizational commitment and job involvement) and behaviors (e.g., willingness to support decisions and decision makers (Greenberg and Colquitt, 2005; Lind and Tyler, 1988). A rapidly growing body of evidence also suggests that fair treatment might reduce the adverse effects of various sources of stress on health (Elovainio, Kivimäki, and Helkama, 2001a and b; Ferrie et al., 2006; Gimeno et al., 2010; Hayashi et al., 2011; Helkavaara, Saastamoinen, and Lahelma, 2011; Ybema and VandenBos, 2010).

ALTERNATIVE MODELS OF PSYCHOSOCIAL FACTORS AT WORK

As with organizational justice, other psychosocial risk factors at work refer to aspects of the work process itself, the organization and management, and the social and technical processes, all of which may potentially cause harm to employee health (Cox and Griffiths, 1996). The overarching aim is to describe those psychosocial factors that are likely to elicit harmful stress at work in a significant proportion of employees, but are still detailed and explicit enough to facilitate the planning of interventions (Kivimäki and Lindström, 2006). These factors are conceptualized at a level of generalization that allows for their identification in a wide range of occupations. It is assumed that psychosocial factors at work can affect employee health directly or be mediated though behavioral, psychological, or physiological reactions (Chandola et al., 2008). Extensive working hours, for example, can potentially have a direct effect on health (for example, through prolonged stress reaction and psychological exhaustion) or indirectly through a longer exposure to harmful substances and harmful coping behavior, such as smoking or a sedentary lifestyle. Psychosocial factors, including organizational justice, typically act through behavioral, psychological, and physiological mechanisms.

The most widely tested model of psychosocial factors at work is the two-dimensional job strain model (Theorell et al., 1998). It proposes that employees who simultaneously experience high job demands and low job control are in a high-job-strain situation. If that high-strain situation lasts for long or is especially intense, it increases the risk of stress-related morbidity. Job control refers to both socially predetermined control over detailed aspects of task performance (e.g., pace, quantity of work, policies and procedures, and scheduled hours) and skill discretion (i.e., control over the use of skills by the worker). An expanded version of the job-strain model adds social support as a third component. The highest risk of illness is assumed to relate to "iso-strain jobs" (abbreviation of isolated job strain), characterized by high demands, low job control, and low social support. The job-strain model thus defines the risk factor dimensions relating to work processes and, to some extent, social relations at work.

More recent theoretical models have broadened the view beyond work characteristics to cover aspects of organizational processes and the labor market context. An example utilizing the classic exchange theory and distributive justice concept is the effort–reward imbalance model (Siegrist, 1996). This model maintains that the experience of imbalance between high effort spent at work and a perception of low reward received is particularly stressful as this imbalance violates core expectations about reciprocity and adequate exchange at work. Furthermore, overcommitment and heavy obligations in one's private life (e.g., large debts) may contribute to a high expenditure of effort. Low rewards can be related to insufficient pay, low esteem (e.g., lack of help or acceptance by supervisors and colleagues), and poor career opportunities (no promotion prospects, poor job security, and status inconsistency).

THE INTERHEART STUDY

Evidence from the recent INTERHEART study shows that psychosocial factors were associated with acute myocardial infarction in a study of 15,000 cases and controls from fifty-two countries in basically all continents (Yusuf et al., 2004). The study found that smoking, elevated lipid levels, history of hypertension, diabetes, abdominal obesity, low consumption of fruits and vegetables, lack of physical activity, and psychosocial factors, including work stress, were all strongly related to acute myocardial infarction. Exposure to psychosocial factors added to risk even after taking into account the combined exposure to smoking, diabetes, hypertension, ApoB/ApoA1 ratio, and obesity; the odds ratio increased from 68.5 to 182.9 compared with those free of all these risk factors. These findings were tremendously robust. A similar pattern of associations was found in men and women, old and young, and on all continents of the world.

The INTERHEART study is probably the largest study of psychosocial factors and CHD. However, given that myocardial infarction is typically developed by a long subclinical phase of atherosclerosis development, a case-control study, irrespective of its size, cannot demonstrate conclusively that the perception of psychosocial stress is, in fact, a consequence of disease process rather than a cause (Figure 13.1). More specifically, people with advanced atherosclerosis may experience exhaustion more easily than others and therefore consider their environments as more demanding than those who are more physically fit. Thus, to determine causality between organizational justice and health, especially CHD, requires working out whether the association is independent, that is, not confounded by third factors, whether there are plausible mechanisms linking justice to CHD, and whether the temporal order of the association between organizational justice and CHD supports the hypothesis.

REVIEW OF EVIDENCE

Considering the robust evidence from a large number of studies, there is little doubt of an association between psychosocial factors and CHD. Evaluating the strength and causal nature of this association is, however, difficult. Systematic reviews are used to synthesize the evidence for the relationship because they provide a quantitative summary estimate across the studies. However, variations in methodological quality are recognized as a source of heterogeneity of the findings in epidemiological studies. Therefore, classifying the findings by the quality of the papers reviewed is one way of improving estimations of the true effect size. For example, the following criteria were used to construct a summary score for study quality in a recent systematic review assessing the quality of articles published up to 2008 on work-related psychosocial factors and ischemic heart disease (Eller et al., 2009): validity of exposure assessment, validity of endpoint assessment, ascertainment of CHD-free status at baseline, representativeness of working population, coverage of full age range, follow-up less than ten years, sex-specific analysis, and adjustment for potential confounding factors. The quality score could also take into account sample sizes and statistical power (i.e., the possibility to detect differences in outcome). In the following section, we utilize a recent systematic review and describe individual key papers in the field.

The Association Between Justice and CHD

Several reviews are available summarizing the evidence from prospective studies on psychosocial factors at work and CHD (Belkic et al., 2004; Eller et al., 2009; Kivimäki et al., 2006). Most of these are narrative based, with only one providing quantitative estimates based on a meta-analysis. The meta-analysis (Kivimäki et al., 2006), published in January 2006, includes papers on job strain, the effort–reward imbalance, and organizational injustice from fourteen prospective cohort studies, with follow-up periods ranging from three years to over twenty-five years. The findings show that employees exposed to high effort–reward imbalance or low organizational justice have an average 50 percent excess risk for CHD compared to those who are unexposed. Four independent studies were identified for the effort–reward imbalance model (ibid.). The summary estimate for these studies suggests an age- and sex-adjusted excess risk for employees reporting high effort and low reward (relative risk 1.6; 95 percent confidence interval [CI] 0.8 to 3.0, n.s.). This overall relative risk was slightly enhanced after multiple adjustments for other CHD risk factors; rate ratio (RR) 2.1, 95 percent CI 1.0 to 4.3 ($p < 0.05$). The two studies on organizational injustice and CHD reported an age- and sex-adjusted relative risk of 1.6 (95 percent CI 1.2 to 2.1), an estimate that remained statistically significant after additional adjustment for other risk factors, including job strain and effort–reward imbalance (1.5, 95 percent CI 1.2 to 2.0).

The two studies on organizational justice and CHD have the following strengths: ascertainment of the incident of CHD based on clinical data, ascertainment of CHD-free status at baseline, coverage of full age range, and adjustment for a range of potential confounding factors. On the other hand, neither of the studies was based on a standard measure of organizational justice. The first study (Kivimäki et al., 2005) was based on the British Whitehall II study (Marmot and Brunner, 2005), which is one of the principal studies on psychosocial factors and health. An important contribution of this study has been the use of longitudinal data from the study with the possibility

200

Figure 13.1   **Hypothesized Pathways from Psychosocial Factors to CHD and Alternative Explanations for This Association**

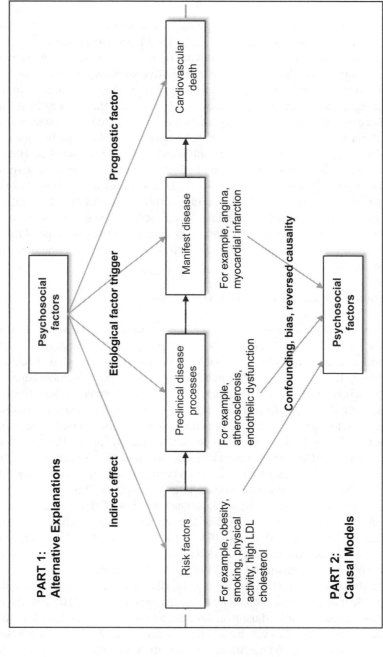

Source: Adapted from Kivimäki et al. 2006. Used by permission of the *Scandinavian Journal of Work and Environmental Health.*

to measure repeated exposure to organizational justice (Elovainio et al., 2010; Ferrie et al., 2006; Kivimäki et al., 2005). As CHD develops over a long time span, long-term rather than short-term levels of adverse psychosocial factors are assumed to influence CHD incidence. For employees with stable psychosocial stress, a single measurement may provide an accurate estimate of long-term exposure. However, this is not necessarily the case and most studies in the field are based on a single measurement of work-related psychosocial factors.

The target population in the Whitehall II study was London-based civil servants ages thirty-five to fifty-five years at baseline (Marmot and Brunner, 2005). Repeated five-yearly medical examinations and additional questionnaire surveys between these examinations at two- to three-year intervals included two measurements of organizational justice. The correlation co-efficient for the repeated measurements of organizational justice indicators between the first two examinations was moderate (Cronbach's alpha for repeated measurements 0.5). In this particular study, only men with no history of CHD at baseline were included (n = 6,400) and the outcome was a CHD death, first nonfatal myocardial infarction, or definite angina occurring after the organizational justice measures based on medical records (mean follow-up, nine years). Cox proportional hazard models adjusted for age, while employment grade showed that employees who experienced a high level of justice at work had a lower risk of incident CHD than employees with a low or an intermediate level of justice (hazard ratio, 0.7; 95 percent CI 0.5–0.9). The hazard ratio did not materially change after additional adjustment for baseline cholesterol concentration, body-mass index, hypertension, smoking, alcohol consumption, and physical activity. Although other psychosocial models such as job strain and effort–reward imbalance predicted CHD in these data, the level of justice remained an independent predictor of the incident CHD after adjustment for these factors.

The second study (Elovainio, Leino-Arjas et al., 2006) was based on the prospective data of 804 Finnish engineering industry employees (540 men and 264 women) without apparent cardiovascular disease at baseline in 1973. The perceived organizational justice was measured at baseline along with several other measures, such as sex, age, occupational, group, smoking status, physical activity, systolic blood pressure, serum total cholesterol, body-mass index, and psychosocial factors, as indicated by job strain and effort–reward imbalance. Mortality data were collected from the Finnish national mortality register using personal identification codes. The date and cause of death for all participants who died between 1973 and 2000 were obtained (thus, the follow-up exceeded ten years). The causes of death were pooled to indicate death due to cardiovascular diseases from the following categories: ischemic heart diseases (ICD-10/I20–I25), other heart diseases (I30–I52), cerebrovascular diseases (I60–I69), and other diseases of the cardiovascular system (I00–I19, I26–I29, I70–I99). All other causes of death were categorized as noncardiovascular. After adjustment for age and sex, a 45 percent reduced risk was found for those who experienced high justice as compared with others, and this finding did not materially change after further adjustment for socioeconomic, biologic, and psychosocial risk factors. Stratified analyses showed no major difference in the effect of justice by socioeconomic position.

In sum, these studies found a modestly elevated risk of CHD among individuals exposed to low organizational justice. The impact of potential confounding did not seem to explain the association. So it seems that at least limited evidence supports the association and even the expected temporal order between organizational justice and CHD. Further evidence is, however, needed before the organizational justice model as a risk factor for stress-related CHD can be considered convincing. In particular, determining a plausible mechanism that links organizational justice to CHD is crucial.

What Are the Plausible Mechanisms Linking Organizational Justice and CHD?

Plausibility is an important consideration in examining causality. Several plausible mechanisms have been proposed through which psychosocial factors may have an adverse impact on health (Theorell et al., 1991). First, they can influence CHD risk indirectly by increasing health-risk behaviors and reducing help-seeking and compliance with medical treatment. Second, in addition to indirect effects, psychosocial factors may relate to biological changes directly involved in CHD etiology and prognosis. These mechanisms include prolonged overactivation and dysregulation of the autonomic nervous system and the hypothalamus–pituitary–adrenal cortex (HPA) axis (McEwen, 1998); both are assumed to increase disease risk, accelerate existing disease processes by affecting inflammatory systems, act as triggers of acute events, such as heart attack, as well as worsen prognosis. Psychosocial risk factors are also hypothesized to increase the risk of the metabolic syndrome, insulin resistance, lipoprotein disturbances, reduced fibrolysis, and central obesity in susceptible individuals.

The Finnish Public Sector study (Vahtera, Kivimäki, and Pentti, 1997) involving over 50,000 participants—one of the largest cohort studies in the field—and the above-mentioned Whitehall II study probably constitute the most comprehensive tests of the association between organizational justice and CHD risk factors (Marmot and Brunner, 2005). In the Whitehall II study (Gimeno et al., 2010), men who experienced a high level of justice at work had a lower risk of incident metabolic syndrome than employees with a low level of justice (hazard ratio 0.75; 95 percent CI 0.63 to 0.89). In that study, organizational justice was determined by means of a questionnaire on two occasions between 1985 and 1990. Follow-up for metabolic syndrome and its components occurring from 1990 to 2004 was based on clinical assessments on three occasions over more than eighteen years. Another report from this study (Elovainio et al., 2010) showed that low organizational justice was associated with increased circulating inflammatory marker, C-reactive protein (CRP), during a ten-year follow-up and an increased inflammatory market, interleukin-6 (IL-6), during a five-year follow-up. The long-term associations were largely independent of covariates, such as age, employment grade, body-mass index, and depressive symptoms. Positive findings in both of these studies were observed only in men.

Studies using the data from the 10-Town occupational cohort study of 15,300 Finnish public sector local government employees nested in 2,400 work units found that participants who reported low procedural justice at baseline were approximately 1.2 times more likely to be heavy drinkers at follow-up compared with their counterparts reporting high justice (Kouvonen et al., 2008). Similarly, after adjustment for age, education, socioeconomic position, marital status, job contract, and negative affectivity, smokers who reported low procedural justice were about 1.4 times more likely to smoke twenty cigarettes or more per day compared with smokers who reported high levels of justice (Kouvonen et al., 2007). In a similar way, low levels of justice in interpersonal treatment were significantly associated with an increased prevalence of heavy smoking (odds ratio 1.4, 95 percent CI 1.0 to 1.8 for men and odds ratio 1.4, 95 percent CI 1.1 to 1.8 for women). Further adjustment for job strain and effort–reward imbalance had little effect on these results.

A small-scale Finnish study looked at cardiac dysregulation, which is a potential physiological mechanism or marker underlying the development of CHD (Elovainio, Kivimäki et al., 2006). The participants were fifty-seven women working in long-term care homes. Heart rate variability and systolic arterial pressure variability were used as markers of autonomic function. The results from logistic regression models showed that the risk for increased low frequency band systolic arterial pressure variability was 3.8–5.8 times higher in employees with low justice than in employees with high justice. Low perceived justice was also related to an 80 percent excess risk of reduced high frequency heart rate variability compared to high perceived justice, though this association was not statistically significant.

These studies suggest that organizational justice is associated with several plausible pathways, which may link justice to CHD. However, only one study to date has explicitly tested the mediating role of a physiological mechanism between justice and CHD by comparing the extent to which this association attenuates after adjustment. Among the Whitehall II study participants without CHD and hypertension at study entry, the association between higher organizational justice and lower CHD incidence was not attenuated after further adjustment for measures of blood pressure (BP) and hypertension, although these measures were associated with increased CHD risk. Thus, this analysis suggests that sustained lower levels of BP do not represent a key mechanism for explaining lower CHD risk among employees with high organizational justice.

CONCLUSIONS AND FUTURE CHALLENGES

The idea that organizational justice represents a work-related psychosocial health risk is relatively new, and more evidence is needed to support its role as a potentially important risk marker. Prospective studies with valid and reliable exposure measures are particularly needed. We have sought to provide a review of the evidence on organizational justice at work and CHD highlighting the strengths and potential drawbacks of the evidence. The following arguments can be made to support the status of organizational justice as a causal risk factor for CHD:

- There is evidence of cross-sectional associations between organizational justice and CHD across different populations.
- Prospective cohort studies showing that organizational justice at work predicts future CHD in employees free from CHD at the study inception have established that the temporal order fits a causal association.
- Studies show that organizational justice is associated with physiological and behavioral factors that support the plausibility of the justice–CHD association.

However, we also found that the current evidence is not strong enough to exclude the possibility of confounding and bias as an explanation for the observed associations. Studies are prone to information biases, with multiple instruments used to determine exposure to organizational justice at work and the absence of a widely agreed standardized instrument. There is no evidence of reversibility, that is, that reducing or enhancing organizational justice at work would lead to a corresponding change in CHD risk among employees. In order to construct conventional tests to determine causality, standard intervention studies to affect organizational justice are needed.

In addition, more studies are needed on the potential effects of different dimensions of organizational justice and CHD risk and the potential theoretical explanations for the differences. This may be important in order to find the "toxic" component of organizational justice and the psychological appraisal processes linking unfair experiences to health problems or health-related behaviors.

REFERENCES

Adams, J.S. 1965. Inequity in social exchange. In *Advances in Experimental Social Psychology,* vol. 2, ed. L. Berkowitz, 267–299. New York: Academic Press.

Belkic, K.; Landsbergis, P.; Schnall, P.; and Baker, D. 2004. Is job strain a major source of cardiovascular disease risk? *Scandinavian Journal of Work Environment and Health,* 30, 85–128.

Bies, R.J., and Moag, J.S. 1986. Interactional justice: Communication criteria of fairness. In *Research on*

Negotiations in Organizations, ed. R.J. Lewicki, B.H. Sheppard, and M.Z. Bazerman, 43–55. Greenwich: JAI Press.

Blader, S.L., and Tyler, T. 2003. What constitutes fairness in work settings? A four component model of procedural justice. *Human Resource Management Review,* 13, 107–126.

Chandola, T.; Britton, A.; Brunner, E.; Hemingway, H.; Malik, M.; Kumari, M.; Badrick, E.; Kivimäki, M.; and Marmot, M. 2008. Work stress and coronary heart disease: What are the mechanisms? *European Heart Journal,* 29, 5, 640–648. doi: 10.1093/eurheartj/ehm584.

Cohen-Charash, Y., and Spector, P.E. 2001. The role of justice in organizations: A meta-analysis. *Organizational Behavior and Human Decision Processes,* 86, 2, 278–321.

Colquitt, J.A. 2001. On the dimensionality of organizational justice: A construct validation of a measure. *Journal of Applied Psychology,* 86, 3, 386–400.

Colquitt, J.A.; Greenberg, J.; and Zapata-Phelan, C.P. 2005. What is organizational justice? A historical overview. In *Handbook of Organizational Justice,* ed. J. Greenberg and J.A. Colquitt, 3–56. Mahwah, NJ: Erlbaum.

Cox, T., and Griffiths, A. (eds.). 1996. *Assessment of Psychosocial Hazards at Work.* Chichester, West Sussex, UK: Wiley.

Cropanzano, R.; Byrne, Z.S.; Bobocel, R.D.; and Rupp, D.E. 2001. Moral virtues, fairness heuristics, social entities and denizens of organizational justice. *Journal of Vocational Behavior,* 91, 164–209.

De Backer, G.; Ambrosioni, E.; Borch-Johnsen, K.; et al. 2003. European guidelines on cardiovascular disease prevention in clinical practice. Third Joint Task Force of European and Other Societies on Cardiovascular Disease Prevention in Clinical Practice. *European Heart Journal,* 24, 1601–1610.

Eller, N.; Netterstrom, B.; Gyntelberg, F.; Kristensen, T.; Nielsen, F.; Steptoe, A.; and Theorell, T. 2009. Work-related psychosocial factors and the development of ischemic heart disease: A systematic review. *Cardiological Review,* 17, 83–97.

Elovainio, M.; Kivimäki, M.; and Helkama, K. 2001a. Organization justice evaluations, job control, and occupational strain. *Journal of Applied Psychology,* 86, 3, 418–424.

———. 2001b. Procedural justice, job control and occupational strain. *Journal of Applied Psychology,* 86, 418–424.

Elovainio, M.; Kivimäki, M.; and Vahtera, J. 2002. Organizational justice: Evidence of a new psychosocial predictor of health. *American Journal of Public Health,* 92, 1, 105–108.

Elovainio, M.; Leino-Arjas, P.; Vahtera, J.; and Kivimäki, M. 2006. Justice at work and cardiovascular mortality: A prospective cohort study. *Journal of Psychosomatic Research,* 61, 2, 271–274. doi: 10.1016/j.jpsychores.2006.02.018.

Elovainio, M.; Kivimäki, M.; Puttonen, S.; Lindholm, H.; Pohjonen, T.; and Sinervo, T. 2006. Organisational injustice and impaired cardiovascular regulation among female employees. *Occupational and Environmental Medicine,* 63, 2, 141–144. doi: 10.1136/oem.2005.019737.

Elovainio, M.; Ferrie, J.E.; Singh-Manoux, A.; Gimeno, D.; De Vogli, R.; et al. 2010. Organisational justice and markers of inflammation: The Whitehall II study. *Occupational and Environmental Medicine,* 67, 2, 78–83.

Ferrie, J.E. 2001. Is job insecurity harmful to health? *Journal of the Royal Society of Medicine,* 94, 2, 71–76.

Ferrie, J.E.; Head, J.; Shipley, M.; Vahtera, J.; Marmot, M.; and Kivimäki, M. 2006. Injustice at work and incidence of psychiatric morbidity: The Whitehall II study. *Occupational and Environmental Medicine,* 63, 442–350.

Folger, R., and Bies, R.J. 1989. Managerial responsibilities and procedural justice. *Employee Responsibilities and Rights Journal,* 2, 2, 79–90.

Gimeno, D.; Tabak, A.G.; Ferrie, J.E.; Shipley, M.J.; De Vogli, R.; Elovainio, M.; Vahtera, J.; Marmot, M.G.; and Kivimäki, M. 2010. Justice at work and metabolic syndrome: The Whitehall II study. *Occupational and Environmental Medicine,* 67, 4, 256–262.

Graham, I.; Atar, D.; Borch-Johnsen, K.; Boysen, G.; et al. 2007. European guidelines on cardiovascular disease prevention in clinical practice. Fourth Joint Task Force of the European Society of Cardiology and Other Societies on Cardiovascular Disease Prevention in Clinical Practice (constituted by representatives of nine societies and by invited experts). *European Heart Journal,* 28, 19, 2375–2414.

Greenberg, J., and Colquitt, J.A. 2005. *Handbook of Organizational Justice.* Mahwah, NJ: Erlbaum.

Hayashi, T.; Odagiri, Y.; Ohya, Y.; Tanaka, K.; and Shimomitsu, T. 2011. Organizational justice, willingness to work, and psychological distress: Results from a private Japanese company. *Journal of Occupational and Environmental Medicine,* 53, 2, 174–181. doi: 10.1097/JOM.0b013e31820665cd.

Heider, F. 1958. *The Psychology of Interpersonal Relations.* New York: Wiley.

Helkavaara, M.; Saastamoinen, P.; and Lahelma, E. 2011. Psychosocial work environment and emotional exhaustion among middle-aged employees. *BMC Research Notes,* 4, 101. doi: 10.1186/1756-0500-4-101.

Heponiemi, T.; Elovainio, M.; Laine, J.; Pekkarinen, L.; Eccles, M.; Noro, A.; Finne-Soveri, H.; and Sinervo, T. 2007. Productivity and employees' organizational justice perceptions in long term care for the elderly. *Research in Nursing and Health,* 30, 5, 498–507.

Homans, G.C. 1958. Social behavior as exchange. *American Journal of Sociology,* 63, 597–606.

Kivimäki, M., and Lindström, K. 2006. Psychosocial approach to occupational health. In *Handbook of Human Factors and Ergonomics,* 3d ed., ed. G. Salvendy, 801–817. New York: Wiley.

Kivimäki, M.; Virtanen, M.; Elovainio, M.; Kouvonen, A.; Vaananen, A.; and Vahtera, J. 2006. Work stress in the etiology of coronary heart disease: A meta-analysis. *Scandinavian Journal of Work and Environmental Health,* 32, 6, 431–442. doi: 10.5271/sjweh.1049.

Kivimäki, M.; Ferrie, J.; Brunner, E.; Head, J.; Shipley, M.; Vahtera, J.; and Marmot, M. 2005. Justice at work and reduced risk of coronary heart disease among employees: The Whitehall II study. *Archives of Internal Medicine,* 24, 2245–2251.

Kouvonen, A.; Vahtera, J.; Elovainio, M.; Cox, S.J.; Cox, T.; Linna, A.; Virtanen, M.; and Kivimäki, M. 2007. Organisational justice and smoking: The Finnish Public Sector Study. *Journal of Epidemiology and Community Health,* 61, 5, 427–433.

Kouvonen, A.; Kivimäki, M.; Elovainio, M.; Vaananen, A.; De Vogli, R.; Heponiemi, T.; Linna, A.; Pentti, J.; and Vahtera, J. 2008. Low organisational justice and heavy drinking: A prospective cohort study. *Occupational and Environmental Medicine,* 65, 1, 44–50.

Leventhal, G.S. 1980. What should be done with equity theory? New approaches to the study of fairness in social relationships. In *Social Exchange: Advances in Theory and Research,* ed. K.J. Gergen, M.S. Greenberg, and R.H. Willis, 27–55. New York: Plenum.

Lind, E.A., and Tyler, T.R. 1988. *The Social Psychology of Procedural Justice.* New York: Plenum.

Marmot, M., and Brunner, E. 2005. Cohort profile: The Whitehall II study. *International Journal of Epidemiology,* 34, 2, 251–256.

McEwen, B.S. 1998. Protective and damaging effects of stress mediators. *New England Journal of Medicine,* 338, 3, 171–179.

McFarlin, D.B., and Sweeney, P.D. 1992. Distributive and procedural justice as predictors of satisfaction with personal and organizational outcomes. *Academy of Management Journal,* 36, 626–637.

Miller, D.T. 2001. Disrespect and the experience of injustice. *Annual Review of Psychology,* 52, 527–553.

Moorman, R.H. 1991. Relationship between organizational justice and organizational citizenship behaviors: Do fairness perceptions influence employee citizenship? *Journal of Applied Psychology,* 76, 6, 845–855.

Pearson, T.A.; Blair, S.N.; Daniels, S.R.; et al. 2002. AHA Guidelines for Primary Prevention of Cardiovascular Disease and Stroke: 2002 Update. Consensus Panel Guide to Comprehensive Risk Reduction for Adult Patients Without Coronary or Other Atherosclerotic Vascular Diseases. *Circulation,* 106, 388–391.

Phillips, J.M.; Douthitt, E.A.; and Hyland, M.M. 2001. The role of justice in team member satisfaction with the leader and attachment to the team. *Journal of Applied Psychology,* 86, 2, 316–325.

Sarason, I.G.; Sarason, B.R.; Potter, E.H. III; and Antoni, M.H. 1985. Life events, social support, and illness. *Psychosomatic Medicine,* 47, 2, 156–163.

Schmitt, M., and Dorfel, M. 1999. Procedural injustice at work, justice sensitivity, job satisfaction and psychosomatic wellbeing. *European Journal of Social Psychology,* 29, 443–453.

Siegrist, J. 1996. Adverse health effects of high-effort/low-reward conditions. *Journal of Occupational Health Psychology,* 1, 1, 27–41.

Skarlicki, D.P., and Folger, R. 1997. Retaliation in the workplace: the roles of distributive, procedural, and interactional justice. *Journal of Applied Psychology,* 82, 3, 434–443.

Stansfeld, S.A.; Fuhrer, R.; and Shipley, M.J. 1998. Types of social support as predictors of psychiatric morbidity in a cohort of British civil servants (Whitehall II Study). *Psychological Medicine,* 28, 4, 881–892.

Tepper, B.J. 2001. Health consequences of organizational injustice: Tests of main and interactive effects. *Organizational Behavior and Human Decision Processes,* 86, 2, 197–215.

Theorell, T.; Perski, A.; Orth-Gomer, K.; Hamsten, A.; and de Faire, U. 1991. The effects of the strain of returning to work on the risk of cardiac death after a first myocardial infarction before the age of 45. *International Journal of Cardiology,* 30, 61–67.

Theorell, T.; Tsutsumi, A.; Hallquist, J.; Reuterwall, C.; Hogstedt, C.; Fredlund, P.; Emlund, N.; and Johnson, J.V. 1998. Decision latitude, job strain, and myocardial infarction: A study of working men in Stockholm.

The SHEEP Study Group. Stockholm Heart Epidemiology Program. *American Journal of Public Health,* 88, 3, 382–388.

Thibaut, J., and Walker, L. 1975. *Procedural Justice: A Psychological Analysis.* Hillsdale, NJ: Erlbaum.

Vahtera, J.; Kivimäki, M.; and Pentti, J. 1997. Effect of organisational downsizing on health of employees. *Lancet,* 350, 9085, 1124–1128.

Weiss, H.M.; Suckow, K.; and Cropanzano, R.S. 1999. Effects of justice conditions on discrete emotions. *Journal of Applied Psychology,* 84, 786–794.

Ybema, J.F., and VandenBos, K. 2010. Effects of organizational justice on depressive symptoms and sickness absence: A longitudinal perspective. *Social Science and Medicine,* 70, 10, 1609–1617. doi: 10.1016/j.socscimed.2010.01.027.

Yusuf, S.; Hawken, S.; Ounpuu, S.; et al. 2004. Effect of potentially modifiable risk factors associated with myocardial infarction in 52 countries (the INTERHEART study): Case-control study. *Lancet,* 364, 937–952.

14

MORAL EMOTIONS AND UNETHICAL BEHAVIOR

The Case of Shame and Guilt

ILONA E. DE HOOGE

Moral emotions may be the most important emotions in interpersonal situations. They motivate group behaviors such as cooperation and competition (De Hooge, Breugelmans, and Zeelenberg, 2008; Fessler and Haley, 2003), provoke interpersonal behaviors such as gift-giving, advice-taking, and prosocial behavior (De Hooge, 2012a; De Hooge, Verlegh, and Tzioti, 2012; Keltner and Buswell, 1996; Smith, 1759), and encourage intrapersonal aspects such as feelings of empathy and distress (Hoffman, 1982). As the two most prevalent moral emotions, shame and guilt motivate people to act in line with group norms in order to avoid such negative feelings beforehand (Tangney, Stuewig, and Mashek, 2007) and to eliminate these negative feelings when people do experience them (Baumeister, Stillwell, and Heatherton, 1994; De Hooge, Zeelenberg, and Breugelmans, 2010). It may thus not come as a surprise that shame and guilt also play a vital role in unethical behavior and well-being in the workplace (Giacalone and Promislo, 2010).

However, while recent research suggests that shame and guilt are emotions that occur often in the workplace, a general overview of the different influences of shame and guilt on unethical behavior and well-being is lacking. This chapter aims to give a clear picture of shame and guilt. Unethical behaviors in the workplace appear on a daily basis. These behaviors can include abusive supervision, theft, bullying, unsafe working conditions, discrimination, drug use and drug testing, and organizational injustice (ibid.), and these unethical and socially irresponsible activities can be carried out by different parties such as supervisors, employees, and direct or indirect colleagues. Accordingly, multiple parties might be involved and affected by the unethical behavior: the perpetrator (the cause) of the unethical behavior, the victim of the unethical behavior, witnesses of the unethical behavior, and people associated (e.g., by group membership) with the perpetrator or with the victim (Evans et al., 2007; Giacalone and Promislo, 2010). In all of these different parties, shame and guilt feelings can occur and may influence people's well-being. Therefore, this chapter begins with an overview of the research on shame and guilt to reveal what we know about the influences of those emotions on behavior in general and to offer thoughts about how these two moral emotions can also stimulate unethical behaviors. Next, I concentrate on shame and guilt feelings that arise after unethical behavior in the workplace, showing how shame and guilt feelings can arise in the perpetrator, the victim, and possible witnesses or associated parties. Together, these two lines of thought can generate new research ideas concerning moral emotions such as shame and guilt in workplace behaviors and well-being, and assist managers and practitioners in dealing with the negative consequences of such emotions.

EXISTING KNOWLEDGE ON THE EMOTIONS OF SHAME AND GUILT

Both shame and guilt belong in the category of moral emotions (Emde and Oppenheim, 1995; Izard, 1977). Moral emotions such as elevation, compassion, and gratitude are linked to the well-being of others and society as a whole (Haidt, 2003). In many situations a direct conflict exists between self-interest and others' interests (i.e., a social dilemma) (Camerer, 2003). While people may have the natural tendency to behave in a self-interested way, moral emotions motivate people to take into account other people's interests (Smith, 1759). In other words, these emotions motivate people to act in a morally appropriate way (to do good and to avoid doing bad), even though this might be contrary to their immediate economic self-interest (Kroll and Egan, 2004; Tangney, Stuewig, and Mashek, 2007). In that sense, moral emotions can be thought of as commitment devices: they commit people to a prosocial, long-term strategy, when selfishness might seduce them into choosing immediate rewards at the expense of others. When choosing the immediate reward elicits unpleasant moral emotions such as shame or guilt, this behavioral alternative becomes less attractive. Thus, moral emotions have an interpersonal function in that they stimulate prosocial behaviors in the short run, committing people to long-term prosocial strategies (Frank, 1988, 2004).

Not only do shame and guilt belong to the category of moral emotions, they are often also perceived to be self-conscious emotions (Lindsay-Hartz, 1984; Tangney, 1991). Self-conscious emotions such as pride, embarrassment, and guilt focus mostly upon self-evaluation (Tangney, 1999). This means that people experience such self-conscious emotions when they are aware of their self-image (they have a "sense of self"), and compare their self-image and their behaviors with their own or with social standards. It is important to note that self-conscious emotions contain an interpersonal element: not only are people's goals and standards often shaped by others, but self-conscious emotions also often arise in interpersonal settings, and their prime function is to adjust interpersonal relationships (Caplovitz Barrett, 1995; De Rivera, 1984). Due to this interpersonal focus, self-conscious emotions thus seem essential for the current focus on unethical behaviors in interpersonal settings such as the workplace.

Shame

Most emotion researchers perceive shame to be "one of the most powerful, painful, and potentially destructive experiences known to humans" (Gilbert, 1997, p. 113). This moral emotion arises after a moral transgression or incompetence, in which people perceive themselves to have violated a moral or social standard (Fessler, 2004; Keltner and Buswell, 1996). Because this behavior generalizes to the whole self-image, people have a heightened degree of self-awareness or self-consciousness and think that the whole self is fundamentally flawed (Izard, 1977; Lewis, 1971; Sabini and Silver, 1997). People not only are consciously focused on their self-image, but also are aware of others around them, and they focus on others' actual or imagined negative evaluations (Fessler, 2004; Haidt, 2003; Tangney and Dearing, 2002). As a consequence, people feel small, alone, powerless, helpless, and inferior to others (Breugelmans and Poortinga, 2006; Fontaine et al., 2006; Nathanson, 1992). This feeling of shame also expresses itself in the bodily posture: when experiencing shame, the body is often collapsed with the shoulders falling in, a downward lip, and lowered eyes with the gaze downward (Keltner and Buswell, 1996; Lewis, 2003).

Most shame theories assume that shame has negative influences on behavior. Shame is thought to make speech, movement, and action more difficult and less likely (Gilbert, 1997). It would relate to submission and motivate social avoidance, withdrawal, rejection, and disengagement from others (Dickerson and Gruenewald, 2004; Lewis, 2003; Probyn, 2004; Tangney, 1991; Tangney, Stuewig, and Mashek, 2007). For example, if Robert feels ashamed after being a victim of bullying at the workplace, he might, according to these shame theories, hide in his office, not join lunches, or work at home more often to avoid contact with colleagues. Tangney (1999, p. 545) even states that shame motivates behaviors that "are likely to sever or interfere with interpersonal relationships." These submissive and withdrawal behaviors function as a form of appeasement, signaling to others that people are aware of their norm-violating behavior and will not fight back but will conform to the group standards (Gilbert, 1997; Mills, 2005; Nathanson, 1987). As a consequence, shame is thought to have negative consequences for well-being. For example, chronic experiences of shame have been linked to a higher likelihood of depression, eating disorders, sociopathology, and chronic low self-esteem (e.g., Gibert, Pehl, and Allan, 1994; Harder, Cutler, and Rockart, 1992). This negative view of shame contrasts with the view of shame as a moral emotion that stimulates prosocial behaviors. How can shame motivate such negative, avoidant behaviors on the one hand and such prosocial, moral behaviors on the other hand?

Recently, my colleagues and I have explained these contrasting views. The central theme of shame appears to be a negative or hurt self-image (Lewis, 1971). One of the most important fundamental human motives is the desire to have a positive self-image (e.g., Alexander and Knight, 1971; Schlenker and Leary, 1982; Taylor and Brown, 1988). People compare themselves to others, make self-serving attributions, and react protectively or act assertively to achieve and maintain such a positive self-image (Gibbons, 1990). Exactly this positive self-image is threatened during a shame experience (Lewis, 1971), and this generates feelings of inferiority and worthlessness and negative thoughts about oneself and about what others will think about oneself. Thus, the goal of shame would be to deal with this threatened self-image. Shame motivates two different ways of dealing with this threatened self-image (De Hooge, Zeelenberg, and Breugelmans, 2010, 2011).

First, shame motivates approach behaviors to restore the negative self-image. Because having a positive self-image is a fundamental motive, people experiencing shame are motivated to restore that positive self-image. This restore motive elicits approach behaviors such as entering achievement situations, performing new challenges, and acting prosocially toward others. As these examples show, approach behaviors can be expressed as many different behaviors, depending on the situation. In all these behaviors, ashamed people actively engage in attempts to improve their self-image and their social position within their group. Indeed, in multiple different studies we found that ashamed people were motivated, for example, to engage in new performance situations and to act prosocially (De Hooge, Breugelmans, and Zeelenberg, 2008; De Hooge, Zeelenberg, and Breugelmans, 2010, 2011). Thus, according to this theory, Robert might accept more work projects, socialize with colleagues, and put more effort into his tasks to show his colleagues that he is a good and capable person.

Precisely because approach behaviors can be expressed as many different behaviors, shame can also motivate antisocial or unethical behaviors. What exactly is defined as restoring one's self-image and the image that others have of oneself depends on people's own norms and values, and on their group norms and values. This means that restoring one's self-image can involve prosocial behavior if people's norms include, for example, being a friendly and social person, but restoring one's self-image can also involve unethical behavior if, for example, people's norms include outperforming others or reaching a top executive position. When perpetrators behave unethically following a shame experience, they are likely to justify this behavior or not be fully aware of the negative consequences for others. They are simply focused upon fulfilling their own requirements for a positive self-image. As an extreme and very recent example, a Dutch full professor was recently found to have purposely falsified data in order to publish many interesting articles. While his unethical behavior is forbidden in the scientific community and it damaged many of his colleagues and employees, he justified his behavior based on wanting to fulfill his standards and those of the science community on being a high-performing professor. When confronted with their unethical behaviors, some perpetrators have the feeling that they have done nothing wrong and do not experience guilt feelings afterward.

Shame feelings can also motivate unethical behavior when people try to restore the image that others have of them. The way in which this social image is restored depends mostly on the norms and values of the group to which people want to belong. For instance, group norms may include being sociable and cooperative, in which case shame motivates prosocial behavior. However, when the group norms include placing the in-group above other groups, shame can actually motivate unethical behaviors such as bullying, lying, and discrimination against out-group members. For instance, when Lydia starts working in her new job at the personnel department and finds out that discriminating against colleagues from a different department is part of her colleagues' in-group behavior, she may start discriminating as well. This effect of shame is also frequently seen in gangs, where gang members have to show their capacities and avoid or recover from shame experiences by stealing and bullying (and sometimes even murdering) members of different gangs (Gini, 2006). In these shame situations, perpetrators may actually be fully aware of their unethical behavior or internally struggle with the contrast between following the societal norms and the controversial group norms. Perpetrators are then more likely to do penance and show guilt feelings when confronted with their unethical behaviors. For example, even though Lydia engages in discriminatory behaviors, she might be bothered by her behavior and decide to apologize to the colleagues against whom she discriminated, and quit her job.

Besides all of these situations in which shame motivates approach behaviors, there are some instances where engaging in new performance situations or acting prosocially might be too risky or simply not possible. For example, if Robert is bullied in a small company where only he and his bully work, he has no opportunities to show others that he is a good and capable employee. In situations where it is impossible or too risky to restore the self-image, shame motivates withdrawal behaviors instead of approach behaviors to protect the threatened self-image from more possible harm. Thus, shame "can prompt behaviors to protect the self from additional scrutiny or self-threatening exposure" (Ferguson, 2005, p. 378). In fact, our findings revealed that shame activated not only a restore motive but also a protect motive, which together motivated approach behaviors (De Hooge, Zeelenberg, and Breugelmans, 2010). In addition, follow-up studies showed that when repair after a shame event is risky, the restore motive lessens and the protect motive stimulates avoidance behavior (De Hooge, Zeelenberg, and Breugelmans, 2011). Thus, after extensive bullying and shame feelings, Robert might decide to protect himself from further bullying and leave the company. On a more general level, in the workplace, such avoidance behaviors can translate to bullying, denigrating, or discriminating against out-group members. These types of avoidance behaviors can occur not only when perpetrators try to protect their self-image after a shame experience but also when they try to avoid any situations in which they might experience shame feelings.

In conclusion, shame can motivate both approach and avoidance behaviors in the workplace, and these approach and avoidance behaviors can translate into prosocial behaviors or unethical behaviors. What are the effects of shame on well-being? In the short term, shame feelings can make people feel less satisfied with their lives by making them feel they have failed in one or more important aspects of their lives. Moreover, if the situation continues for a longer time, for example, if it is impossible or risky to restore one's self-image or if the person chronically experiences shame, it can also have a negative effect on people's living conditions. For example, victims or perpetrators of discrimination or bullying might experience insomnia, lower self-esteem, or even depression. However, when ashamed people are able to restore their self-image and overcome the shame experience, the consequences for well-being can be more positive. For example, if Robert is able perform his job tasks well and thus receives a promotion, in the end, he might feel more satisfied with his life because he succeeded despite having been bullied. One might even wonder whether shame feelings increase well-being in such a way that people have higher subjective well-being if they succeed after having overcome shameful experiences compared to having been successful without experiencing any shame beforehand.

Guilt

The picture that emotion literature sketches for guilt is much more positive than that for shame. Guilt arises primarily after a moral transgression in which people have hurt another person, intentionally or unintentionally (Fessler and Haley, 2003; Izard, 1977; Tangney, 1991). They are then completely focused on the harm and distress that they have caused to the other person (the victim) (Baumeister, Stillwell, and Heatherton, 1994; Lewis, 1987). After the transgression, people often feel tense, remorseful, worried, and preoccupied with the transgression (Ferguson, Stegge, and Damhuis, 1991; Lewis, 1971; Tangney, 1999). The function of guilt is thought to be a preservation and strengthening of the hurt relationship by making amends for the past transgression and by stimulating more appropriate behavior in the future (Amodio, Devine, and Harmon-Jones, 2007; Baumeister, Stillwell, and Heatherton, 1994). There is no known bodily expression for guilt.

Guilt is thought to have many positive consequences for interpersonal behavior. It has been found to motivate a heightened sense of personal responsibility, compliance, and forgiveness, and to generate more constructive strategies for coping with anger (Freedman, Wallington, and Bless, 1967; McCullough, Worthington, and Rachal, 1997; Strelan, 2007; Tangney et al., 1992). Guilt is related to taking a better perspective and greater feelings of empathy (Leith and Baumeister, 1998; Tangney and Dearing, 2002). Experiences of guilt are thought to motivate a desire to compensate the victim and to undertake reparative actions such as confessions, apologies, and attempts to undo the harm (Caplovitz Barrett, 1995; Lindsay-Hartz, 1984; Thrane, 1979). Indeed, several studies have shown that guilt is strongly related to reparative intentions (Schmader and Lickel, 2006; Tangney, 1993). A recent series of studies on prosocial behavior in dyadic relationships has found that guilt motivates prosocial behavior in social dilemma games (De Hooge, Zeelenberg, and Breugelmans, 2007; Ketelaar and Au, 2003; Nelissen, Dijker, and De Vries, 2007). An important finding of cross-cultural studies is that these characteristics of guilt are quite similar across a wide array of cultures (Breugelmans and Poortinga, 2006; Fontaine et al., 2006), which is testimony to the universal moral character of guilt.

However, while guilt appears to be a good, moral emotion that produces beneficial consequences for people in one's social milieu, my colleagues and I suggest otherwise (De Hooge, 2012b in press; De Hooge et al., 2011). The summary of guilt literature above shows that the central theme in guilt is a hurt relationship that needs to be dealt with. People are focused on what they have done wrong and on the victim of their actions (Lewis, 1971). It follows that guilt mostly motivates prosocial behavior aimed at restoring that hurt relationship. But in daily life people interact with multiple others at the same time. Accordingly, the dyadic preoccupation that is central to experiences of guilt can lead to behavior that is negative for the outcomes of others in one's social milieu. When focusing on repairing the hurt relationship, people temporarily pay less attention to other social partners and generally compensate at the expense of the resources allocated to others rather than to themselves. In other words, guilt can lead to an extra investment in the relationship with the victim but someone else will have to pay the bill. Our findings support these claims, revealing that in three-person situations, guilt motivates prosocial behavior toward the victim at the expense of a third person (in terms of giving less, taking away money, or canceling appointments) and not at the expense of oneself (De Hooge et al., 2011).

These findings have important consequences for guilt in the workplace. For example, suppose Michel experiences guilt feelings for having stated multiple times that his employee Nadine is not able to fulfill her job properly because she is a woman. He then makes up with her by helping her with difficult tasks and taking a lot of time to provide her with feedback. This reparative behavior, however, might then come at the expense of other employees, who receive less help and feedback. Thus, by improving the situation for the colleague hurt by guilty people earlier, they may act unethically toward other colleagues. These unethical behaviors are expressed in unjust treatments, discrimination, or abusive supervision, and so on. The duration of these unethical behaviors depends on the judgments of the perpetrators and on approvals of the victims: only when all damage from the original transgression is perceived (by both transgressors and victims) as being fully repaired, will the prosocial behaviors toward the victims and thus unethical behaviors toward third parties stop.

In summary, while it is a moral emotion, guilt can have very negative interpersonal consequences and stimulate unethical behaviors in the workplace. One question that remains is how these guilt feelings affect well-being. Research on the relationship between chronic experiences of guilt and psychopathology does not show a clear picture. On the one hand, the traditional view of guilt states that it is a very negative feeling and contributes significantly to distress and psychopathology symptoms such as melancholia, obsessional neuroses, and masochism (e.g., Freud, 1917/1957, 1923/1961; Harder, 1995; Harder, Cutler, and Rockart, 1992). On the other hand, chronic experiences of guilt have sometimes been found to be unrelated to psychological symptoms (e.g., Tangney, 1993; Tangney, Wagner, and Gramzow, 1992). Taking a broader perspective on well-being, beyond psychopathology, one could argue that guilt improves well-being as long as people can repair the negative feelings. After having made up for their transgressions, people feel relief for having solved the problem and have better interpersonal relationships, which in turn can stimulate higher satisfaction with life and better living conditions. Future research is needed to answer the question of how guilt relates to well-being.

SHAME AND GUILT AFTER UNETHICAL BEHAVIOR IN THE WORKPLACE

As stated at the beginning of this chapter, unethical behaviors in the workplace can have an effect on multiple different parties. For example, Michel, discriminating against his female employees might have an influence on himself, his female employees, witnesses such as his other employees, and associated parties such as employers from different departments in Michel's organization. In all of these different parties, shame and guilt feelings can occur after such unethical behaviors and thus influence well-being.

The Perpetrators

People who engage in unethical behavior in the workplace might experience shame or guilt later. For example, soldiers who have committed crimes of violence in wartime have been shown to experience guilt and shame feelings afterward (McNally, 2003). Also, employees engaging in theft or work failure due to drug use or alcohol addiction might experience shame and guilt feelings when they are caught. The development of shame and guilt feelings in perpetrators depends on two factors: whether the perpetrator perceives the unethical behavior as a transgression, and whether the perpetrator takes personal responsibility for the act. Following the definition of shame and guilt, these emotions occur only when people perceive their own behavior as a (moral) transgression. Thus, before perpetrators experience shame or guilt, they have to perceive that they have done something wrong (Byrne, 2003). This interpretation is subjective, and may depend on the person (people differ in norms and values and thus differ in what they perceive as unethical) and on the situation (people have different motives based on the situation to enact such behavior). For example, the drug-using employee might not feel any shame or guilt when he interprets the drug use as a necessary stimulant to be more creative in his work. Additionally, according to some emotion theories, perpetrators have to take personal responsibility for the unethical behavior (Baumeister, Stillwell, and Heatherton, 1994). For example, when perpetrators perceive that they were obliged to act in such a fashion (e.g., the manager suggested that the drug-using employee use alternative approaches to improve creativity), they might not experience shame or guilt.

Experiences of shame or guilt after unethical behavior in the workplace can motivate different behaviors in perpetrators. When experiencing shame, perpetrators will be mostly focused on their self-image, which they are motivated to restore (De Hooge, Zeelenberg, and Breugelmans, 2010, 2011). For example, they can do so by engaging in ethical behavior in the future or acting prosocially toward victims and witnesses of their original unethical behavior. The drug-using employee can work longer hours without being paid or take up tasks that others do not want to fulfill. When such restorative actions are not possible or too risky, the perpetrator mostly avoids victims and witnesses or, in extreme circumstances, avoids the workplace altogether.

Feelings of guilt concentrate perpetrators' focus mainly on repairing the damage done to the victims (De Hooge, Zeelenberg, and Breugelmans, 2007). This has three potential consequences. First, perpetrators may engage in reparative, prosocial actions to improve the situation for the victims. This can be expressed in many different ways, such as offering apologies, giving victims the next promotion, or setting up an organization that will actively deal with unethical behavior in the workplace. Second, while restoring the damage done to victims, perpetrators might forget or harm the well-being of others in their social milieu (De Hooge et al., 2011), for example, by paying less attention to other employees who were not the victims of their original unethical behavior, or even using the resources (such as money or time) of other employees for the victims. While perpetrators may not notice such developments, it can generate dangerous situations within an organization if such third parties do notice and are dissatisfied with these developments. Third, if perpetrators do not have a chance to repair the damage caused to the victims, they may engage in self-punitive behaviors. For instance, perpetrators have been shown to become distressed and self-punitive when there is a large discrepancy between their ideal self and their actual self (Carver and Ganellen, 1983). Recent research has called this self-punishment tendency the Dobby effect, following the tendency of Dobby in Harry Potter movies and books to punish himself each time he opposes the will of his masters (Nelissen and Zeelenberg, 2009). Clearly, these self-punitive behaviors are not beneficial for subjective well-being in the long run: perpetrators engaging repeatedly in self-punitive behaviors might experience lower life satisfaction, lower self-esteem, a higher likelihood of depression, and even damage to their physical health.

The Victims

While it might seem contradictory, the victims of unethical behaviors can experience feelings of shame as well (Weiss, 2010). As an example outside the workplace context, the mistreatment of children such as abuse, neglect, or harsh parenting have been shown to play a role in the development of shame proneness (the general tendency to experience shame) (Alessandri and Lewis, 1996; Ferguson and Stegge, 1995). Consequently, such children can be prone to shame, guilt, depression, and delinquency behaviors in adolescence (Stuewig and McCloskey, 2005). Furthermore, victims of sexual harassment have been shown to experience feelings of shame (Weiss, 2010). The consequences of such shame behaviors can be severe. Overall, after mistreatment, victims have few possibilities to restore their self-image. When restoring the self-image after experiencing shame is too difficult or too risky, the protect motive and related avoidance behaviors follow feelings of shame (De Hooge, Zeelenberg, and Breugelmans, 2010, 2011). Indeed, victims of sexual harassment who experience shame have a tendency not to report the sexual assault (Weiss, 2010). In the workplace this protect tendency can translate into avoidance of perpetrators and witnesses of the unethical behavior, absenteeism, or, in extreme cases, even resignation. Research has shown that in situations where leaving is impossible and shame is ever present, subjective well-being is badly damaged (e.g., leading to a higher likelihood of depression, eating disorders, sociopathology, and chronic low self-esteem) (e.g., Gilbert, Pehl, and Allan, 1994; Harder, Cutler, and Rockart, 1992).

Witnesses and Associated Parties

Surprisingly, even witnesses or associated parties can experience shame or guilt feelings after unethical behavior in the workplace. Associated parties can be anyone who feels connected to the event, such as family and friends of the perpetrator or victim, as well as fellow colleagues, employees, bosses, or even people who have the same job position as the perpetrator or the victim (e.g., as a Dutch marketing professor, I might feel associated with all marketing professors working in the Netherlands). These emotions, caused by another person's behavior, are often called vicarious or collective emotions, and they can occur even with regard to actions of others whom people do not know at all or have never seen (Tangney, Stuewig, and Mashek, 2007). For example, people may experience guilt for historical wrongdoings of group members in the past (Doosje et al., 1998). The consequences of these vicarious emotions for the behavior and well-being of witnesses and associated parties depend on whether the experienced emotion is vicarious shame or vicarious guilt.

Witnesses and associated parties sometimes experience feelings of vicarious shame (Pollock, 1999). On the one hand, they experience vicarious feelings of shame for the actions of perpetrators when they feel associated with the perpetrators and when they perceive the actions of the perpetrators as unethical. On the other hand, people experience vicarious feelings of shame for the victims of unethical behavior when they feel associated with the victims. In either case, the feelings of vicarious shame can be based on two processes: social identity threat and cognitive empathy (Welten, Zeelenberg, and Breugelmans, 2012b). The social identity threat process suggests that people's social identity (their group identity) is threatened when the actions of an in-group member confirm or reveal flawed aspects of the social identity (Lickel et al., 2005). In this process, the shame felt for another person's actions is often called group-based shame (Welten Zeelenberg, and Breugelmans, 2012b). For this process to occur, the perpetrators or the victims of the unethical behavior have to be familiar to the associated parties or be perceived as in-group members (Welten, Breugelmans, and Zeelenberg, 2012). For example, as a personnel manager at Philips, Linda may experience group-based shame for the unfair treatment of a black employee by a personnel manager of Shell when she perceives both herself and the Shell personnel manager to be in-group members of the "personnel manager" category. However, Linda will probably not experience group-based shame if she perceives that the Shell personnel manager belongs to a group different from hers (e.g., the Shell group instead of her Philips group). It is important to note recent research suggesting that group-based shame motivates people to punish their in-group members for unethical behaviors or to undertake actions to improve the image of the group (Schmader and Lickel, 2006; Welten, Breugelmans, and Zeelenberg, 2012; Welten, Zeelenberg, and Breugelmans, 2012b). Linda might complain about the behavior of the Shell personnel manager to his supervisor or even file a lawsuit against the Shell personnel manager. Group-based shame can thus motivate associated parties to improve the well-being of both perpetrators and victims by punishing the perpetrators or by improving the situation of the victims. Additionally, group-based shame can function as an in-group correction device that prevents group members and especially perpetrators from acting immorally.

Vicarious feelings of shame can be based on a second process: the cognitive empathy process. This process is founded upon the assumption that people can take another's perspective and experience emotions as if they were in that situation themselves (Miller, 1987). In this process, vicarious shame is the feeling that arises when people's selves are affected by the shameful behaviors of others because through taking another's perspective they experience an imagined self-threat (Welten, Zeelenberg, and Breugelmans, 2012b). In this case, the vicarious shame is often called empathic shame, and the perpetrators or the victims need not be familiar to or in-group members of the associated parties (ibid.). For example, imagining herself as behaving in the way that the Shell personnel manager did, Linda might experience empathic shame. The goal of these empathic shame feelings is to provide a learning function (Welten, Zeelenberg, and Breugelmans, 2012a). In other words, witnesses and associated parties may not actively engage in punitive or reparative behaviors as with group-based shame, but they can learn from the unethical behavior and its consequences and avoid such shameful behaviors themselves. In the example, Linda might learn from the Shell personnel manager that she should not behave in such discriminatory ways or she will feel remorseful.

Vicarious guilt, also called collective guilt, arises mostly when people associate themselves with perpetrators of unethical behaviors. As with group-based shame, in order to experience collective guilt, the associated parties have to acknowledge their own membership and the perpetrator's membership in a group (Doosje et al., 1998). Furthermore, associated parties have to perceive the behavior of the perpetrator-group member as inconsistent with their own values or inconsistent with the norms or values of the group (Branscombe and Doosje, 2004). Collective guilt feelings can occur both when one's own group has gained a high-status (advantaged) position in the workplace (e.g., due to an unjust promotion) or when an out-group has been cast in a low-status or disadvantaged position in the workplace (e.g., due to discrimination or bullying) (Iyer, Leach, and Crosby, 2003; Powell, Branscombe, and Schmitt, 2005). As a consequence of these collective guilt feelings, research has shown that group members experience tendencies to compensate the victims of the perpetrator's actions and to support reparative actions toward out-groups (Branscombe and Doosje, 2004). For example, if Linda sees that one of her direct colleagues treats a black employee unfairly, she might then interpret this as inconsistent with the norms of her group of colleagues, and might try to improve the situation by giving the black employee a salary increase or a bonus. The goal of these actions is to create or restore an equitable relationship with the harmed out-group (member). Thus, collective guilt can benefit the well-being of both associated parties and victims by motivating prosocial actions in associated parties and by improving the relationships between associated parties and victims.

MANAGERIAL IMPLICATIONS

Apparently, shame and guilt can have both positive and negative consequences for the well-being of perpetrators, victims, and associated parties. Feelings of shame and guilt after unethical behavior can motivate perpetrators toward penance and prosocial behavior in the future. In addition, witnesses and associated parties can learn from the unethical behavior by means of vicarious shame and guilt, and thus be motivated to punish perpetrators, improve the situation for victims, and avoid unethical behaviors themselves. In that sense, experiences of shame and guilt can improve the well-being of multiple involved parties by increasing self-esteem and life satisfaction. However, feelings of shame in victims may actually work against them, by stimulating them to avoid shameful situations in the workplace and to avoid reporting perpetrators. Moreover, perpetrators may engage in avoidant behavior when they experience shame but do not perceive ways to restore their self-image, and they may even hurt others in their social milieu when trying to make up with the victims. In these situations, shame and guilt can have negative effects on well-being by reducing self-esteem and life satisfaction and increasing the likelihood of depression.

These findings have important implications for managers and practitioners. While feelings of shame and guilt in perpetrators after unethical behavior are often interpreted as a good sign and a first step toward improving the situation for all parties involved, these feelings can in fact also have negative consequences. Practitioners and managers should be aware of the dangers of these emotions when trying to restore balance in the workplace and should make sure that only the positive effects of shame and guilt occur. We now know that the negative effects of shame most often occur in situations where there is no clear solution: feelings of shame have negative effects on victims who cannot find a way out of the victimization and on perpetrators who do not perceive ways to restore their self-image. This suggests that practitioners and managers should try to generate situations in which victims and perpetrators are able to overcome their damaged self-image and feelings of shame by undertaking reparative actions. For example, Robert, the target of bullying mentioned at the beginning of this chapter, might be given new work projects with new team members in where he can reveal his abilities.

The two moral emotions not only play a role after unethical behavior in the workplace has occurred. Shame and guilt can stimulate unethical behavior in the first place. Restoring one's self-image from shame experiences, protecting the self-image from more possible damage after shame experiences, and actions to make up with victims of guilt transgressions can all yield unethical behaviors. The degree to which these unethical behaviors ensue depends on the possibilities that employees receive for expressing and dealing with their emotions in the workplace. Managers and practitioners should be aware of the possible effects of moral emotion and guide employees toward positive behaviors when they notice that employees experience such emotions.

RESEARCH IMPLICATIONS

This chapter shows us that much research on shame, guilt, and well-being is still needed. The effects of shame and guilt on all aspects of subjective well-being for all involved parties are unclear. While this chapter contains some hypotheses about the effects of shame and guilt on the well-being of perpetrators, victims, witnesses, and associated parties, empirical research has studied the effects of chronic experiences of shame and guilt only on depression, self-esteem, and psychopathology (e.g., Tangney, 1993; Tangney and Dearing, 2002). One possible line of research would be to study the effects of shame and guilt on social well-being. According to Keyes (1998), well-being should also include a social dimension that focuses on people's functioning in society. One could think of aspects such as social integration (feeling a part of society), social acceptance (believing others to be trustworthy, kind, and industrious), social contribution (feeling a vital member of society), social actualization (believing that society has potential), and social coherence (understanding the world). Both shame and guilt focus on people's position in relation to groups and society, and therefore it is possible that shame and guilt exert influences on different aspects of social well-being. For example, shame could be related to social integration (people feel less a part of society when experiencing shame because the feelings of shame indicate that one's status as an in-group member might be at risk), while guilt would be more related to social contribution (people feel less useful as members of society when experiencing guilt because the guilt feelings signal that one's previous actions were not useful for society).

This chapter has focused mainly upon the moral emotions of shame and guilt, but these are not the only moral emotions. Moral emotions such as gratitude, compassion, elevation, or disgust have been found to influence interpersonal behaviors such as avoiding contact with others (in the case of moral disgust) or helping behavior (Haidt, 2003), and they might give rise to or be the consequences of unethical behaviors in the workplace. One area of research would be to study how these moral emotions influence unethical behaviors, and how they affect all parties involved. In addition, some of these moral emotions have been found to exert a distinct influence on subjective well-being: for example, feelings of gratitude have been shown to contribute to personal well-being, civic engagement, and spiritual satisfaction (Emmons and Crumpler, 2000). Regarding the moral emotions for which the effects on well-being have not yet been studied, an important next step would be to focus on their long-term effects for both subjective and social well-being.

CONCLUSION

The effects of shame and guilt may not be as predictable as they seem. Perceiving shame and guilt as moral emotions has stimulated researchers to predict positive interpersonal, ethical effects, while emotion researchers have suggested that shame motivates avoidance behaviors and guilt motivates reparative behaviors. It now appears that they can do both: shame and guilt can generate ethical and unethical behaviors in the workplace, with important consequences for the well-being of perpetrators, victims, witnesses, and associated parties. Only with a full understanding of these specific emotions will one be able to predict their effects and manage them successfully.

REFERENCES

Alessandri, S., and Lewis, M. 1996. Differences in pride and shame in maltreated and nonmaltreated pre-schoolers. *Child Development,* 67, 1857–1869.

Alexander, C.N., and Knight, G.W. 1971. Situated identities and social psychological experimentation. *Sociometry,* 34, 65–82.

Amodio, D.M.; Devine, P.G.; and Harmon-Jones, E. 2007. A dynamic model of guilt: Implications for motivation and self-regulation in the context of prejudice. *Psychological Science,* 18, 524–530.

Baumeister, R.F.; Stillwell, A.M.; and Heatherton, T.F. 1994. Guilt: An interpersonal approach. *Psychological Bulletin,* 115, 243–267.

Branscombe, N.R., and Doosje, B. 2004. *Collective Guilt: International Perspectives.* New York: Cambridge University Press.

Breugelmans, S.M., and Poortinga, Y.H. 2006. Emotion without a word: Shame and guilt with Rarámuri Indians and rural Javanese. *Journal of Personality and Social Psychology,* 91, 1111–1122.

Byrne, M.K. 2003. Traumatic reactions in the offender. *International Journal of Forensic Psychology,* 1, 59–70.

Camerer, C.F. 2003. *Behavioral Game Theory: Experiments in Strategic Interaction.* Princeton, NJ: Princeton University Press.

Caplovitz Barrett, K. 1995. A functionalist approach to shame and guilt. In *Self-Conscious Emotions: The Psychology of Shame, Guilt, Embarrassment, and Pride,* ed. J.P. Tangney and K.W. Fischer, 25–63. New York: Guilford Press.

Carver, C.S., and Ganellen, R.J. 1983. Depression and components of self-punitiveness: High standards, self-criticism, and overgeneralization. *Journal of Abnormal Psychology*, 92, 330–337.

de Hooge, I.E. 2012a. Emotion dimensions in gift-giving: Your emotions may decide what gift to buy. Manuscript submitted for publication.

———. In press. 2012b. The exemplary social emotion guilt: Not so relationship-oriented when another person repairs for you. *Cognition & Emotion*.

de Hooge, I.E.; Breugelmans, S.M.; and Zeelenberg, M. 2008. Not so ugly after all: When shame acts as a commitment device. *Journal of Personality and Social Psychology*, 95, 933–943.

de Hooge, I.E.; Verlegh, P.; and Tzioti, S.C. 2012. Self-focused and other-focused emotions in advice taking. Manuscript submitted for publication.

de Hooge, I.E.; Zeelenberg, M.; and Breugelmans, S.M. 2007. Moral sentiments and cooperation: Differential influences of shame and guilt. *Cognition and Emotion*, 21, 1025–1042.

———. 2010. Restore and protect motivations following shame. *Cognition and Emotion*, 24, 111–127.

———. 2011. A functionalist account of shame induced behaviour. *Cognition and Emotion*, 25, 939–946.

de Hooge, I.E.; Nelissen, R.M.A.; Breugelmans, S.M.; and Zeelenberg, M. 2011. What is moral about guilt? Acting "prosocially" at the disadvantage of others. *Journal of Personality and Social Psychology*, 100, 462–473.

De Rivera, J. 1984. The structure of emotional relationships. In *Review of Personality and Social Psychology*. Vol. 5: *Emotions, Relationships, and Health*, ed. P. Shaver, 116–145. Beverly Hills, CA: Sage.

Dickerson, S.S., and Gruenewald, T.L. 2004. When the social self is threatened: Shame, physiology, and health. *Journal of Personality*, 72, 1191–1216.

Doosje, B.; Branscombe, N.R.; Spears, R.; and Manstead, A.S.R. 1998. Guilty by association: When one's group has a negative history. *Journal of Personality and Social Psychology*, 75, 872–886.

Emde, R.N., and Oppenheim, D. 1995. Shame, guilt, and the oedipal drama: Developmental considerations concerning morality and the referencing of critical others. In *Self-Conscious Emotions: The Psychology of Shame, Guilt, Embarrassment, and Pride*, ed. J. P. Tangney and K.W. Fischer, 413–438. New York: Guilford Press.

Emmons, R.A., and Crumpler, C.A. 2000. Gratitude as a human strength: Appraising the evidence. *Journal of Social and Clinical Psychology*, 19, 56–69.

Evans, C.; Ehlers, A.; Mezey, G.; and Clark, D.M. 2007. Intrusive memories in perpetrators of violent crime: Emotions and cognitions. *Journal of Consulting and Clinical Psychology*, 75, 134–144.

Ferguson, T.J. 2005. Mapping shame and its functions in relationships. *Child Maltreatment*, 10, 377–386.

Ferguson, T.J., and Stegge, H. 1995. Emotional states and traits in children: The case of guilt and shame. In *Self-Conscious Emotions*, ed. J.P. Tangney and A.H. Fischer, 174–197. New York: Guilford Press.

Ferguson, T.J.; Stegge, H.; and Damhuis, I. 1991. Children's understanding of guilt and shame. *Child Development*, 62, 827–839.

Fessler, D.M.T. 2004. Shame in two cultures: Implications for evolutionary approaches. *Journal of Cognition and Culture*, 4, 207–262.

Fessler, D.M.T., and Haley, K.J. 2003. The strategy of affect: Emotions in human cooperation. In *The Genetic and Cultural Evolution of Cooperation*, ed. P. Hammerstein, 7–36. Cambridge, MA: MIT Press.

Fontaine, J.R.J.; Luyten, P.; De Boeck, P.; Corveleyn, J.; Fernandez, M.; Herrera, D.; et al. 2006. Untying the Gordian knot of guilt and shame: The structure of guilt and shame reactions based on situation and person variation in Belgium, Hungary, and Peru. *Journal of Cross-Cultural Psychology*, 37, 273–292.

Frank, R.H. 1988. *Passions Within Reason: The Strategic Role of the Emotions*. New York: Norton.

———. 2004. Introducing moral emotions into models of rational choice. In *Feelings and Emotions: The Amsterdam Symposium*, ed. A.S.R. Manstead, N. Frijda, and A. Fischer, 422–440. Cambridge: Cambridge University Press.

Freedman, J.L.; Wallington, S.A.; and Bless, E. 1967. Compliance without pressure: The effects of guilt. *Journal of Personality and Social Psychology*, 7, 117–124.

Freud, S. 1917/1957. Mourning and melancholia. In *The Standard Edition of the Complete Psychological Works of Sigmund Freud*, vol. 14, ed. J. Strachey, 237–260. London: Hogarth Press.

———. 1923/1961. The ego and the id. In *The Standard Edition of the Complete Psychological Works of Sigmund Freud*, vol. 19, ed. J. Strachey, 3–66. London: Hogarth Press.

Giacalone, R.A., and Promislo, M.D. 2010. Unethical and unwell: Decrements in well-being and unethical activity at work. *Journal of Business Ethics*, 91, 275–297.

Gibbons, F.X. 1990. The impact of focus of attention and affect on social behaviour. In *Shyness and Embarrassment: Perspectives from Social Psychology,* ed. W.R. Crozier, 119–143. Cambridge: Cambridge University Press.

Gilbert, P. 1997. The evolution of social attractiveness and its role in shame, humiliation, guilt, and therapy. *British Journal of Medical Psychology,* 70, 113–147.

Gilbert, P.; Pehl, J.; and Allan, S. 1994. The phenomenology of shame and guilt: An empirical investigation. *British Journal of Medical Psychology,* 67, 23–36.

Gini, G. 2006. Social cognition and moral cognition in bullying: What's wrong? *Aggressive Behavior,* 32, 528–539.

Haidt, J. 2003. The moral emotions. In *Handbook of Affective Sciences,* ed. R.J. Davidson, K.R. Scherer, and H.H. Goldsmith, 852–870. Oxford: Oxford University Press.

Harder, D.W. 1995. Shame and guilt assessment, and relationships of shame- and guilt-proneness to psychopathology. In *Self-Conscious Emotions: The Psychology of Shame, Guilt, Embarrassment, and Pride,* ed. J.P. Tangney and K.W. Fischer, 368–392. New York: Guilford Press.

Harder, D.W.; Cutler, L.; and Rockart, L. 1992. Assessment of shame and guilt and their relationships to psychopathology. *Journal of Personality Assessment,* 59, 584–604.

Hoffman, M.L. 1982. Development of prosocial motivation: Empathy and guilt. In *The Development of Prosocial Behavior,* ed. N. Eisenberg, 281–313. New York: Academic Press.

Iyer, A.; Leach, C.W.; and Crosby, F.J. 2003. White guilt and racial compensation: The benefits and limits of self-focus. *Personality and Social Psychology Bulletin,* 29, 117–129.

Izard, C.E. 1977. *Human Emotions.* New York: Plenum Press.

Keltner, D., and Buswell, B.N. 1996. Evidence for the distinctness of embarrassment, shame and guilt: A study of recalled antecedents and facial expressions of emotion. *Cognition and Emotion,* 10, 155–171.

Ketelaar, T., and Au, W.T. 2003. The effects of guilt on the behaviour of uncooperative individuals in repeated social bargaining games: An affect-as-information interpretation of the role of emotion in social interaction. *Cognition and Emotion,* 17, 429–453.

Keyes, C.L.M. 1998. Social well-being. *Social Psychology Quarterly,* 61, 121–140.

Kroll, J., and Egan, E. 2004. Psychiatry, moral worry, and moral emotions. *Journal of Psychiatric Practice,* 10, 352–360.

Leith, K.P., and Baumeister, R.F. 1998. Empathy, shame, guilt, and narratives of interpersonal conflicts: Guilt-prone people are better at perspective taking. *Journal of Personality,* 66, 1–38.

Lewis, H.B. 1971. *Shame and Guilt in Neurosis.* New York: International Universities Press.

———. 1987. Shame and the narcissistic personality. In *The Many Faces of Shame*, ed. D.L. Nathanson, 93–124. New York: Guilford Press.

Lewis, M. 2003. The role of the self in shame. *Social Research,* 70, 1181–1204.

Lickel, B.; Schmader, T.; Curtis, M.; Scarnier, M.; and Ames, D.R. 2005. Vicarious shame and guilt. *Group Processes and Intergroup Relations,* 8, 145–157.

Lindsay-Hartz, J. 1984. Contrasting experiences of shame and guilt. *American Behavioral Scientist,* 27, 689–704.

McCullough, M.E.; Worthington, E.L.J.; and Rachal, K.C. 1997. Interpersonal forgiving in close relationships. *Journal of Personality and Social Psychology,* 73, 321–336.

McNally, R.J. 2003. Progress and controversy in the study of posttraumatic stress disorder. *Annual Review of Psychology,* 54, 229–252.

Miller, R.S. 1987. Empathic embarrassment: Situational and personal determinants of reactions to the embarrassment of another. *Journal of Personality and Social Psychology,* 53, 1061–1069.

Mills, R.S.L. 2005. Taking stock of the developmental literature on shame. *Developmental Review,* 25, 26–63.

Nathanson, D.L. (ed.). 1987. *The Many Faces of Shame.* New York: Guilford Press.

———. 1992. *Shame and Pride.* New York: Norton.

Nelissen, R.M.A., and Zeelenberg, M. 2009. When guilt evokes self-punishment: Evidence for the existence of a Dobby-effect. *Emotion,* 9, 118–122.

Nelissen, R.M.A.; Dijker, A.J.; and De Vries, N.K. 2007. How to turn a hawk into a dove and vice versa: Interactions between emotions and goals in a give-some dilemma game. *Journal of Experimental Social Psychology,* 43, 280–286.

Pollock, P.H. 1999. When the killer suffers: Posttraumatic stress reactions following homicide. *Legal and Criminological Psychology,* 4, 185–202.

Powell, A.A.; Branscombe, N.R.; and Schmitt, M.T. 2005. Inequality as ingroup privilege or outgroup dis-advantage: The impact of group focus on collective guilt and interracial attitudes. *Personality and Social Psychology Bulletin,* 31, 508–521.

Probyn, E. 2004. Everyday shame. *Cultural Studies,* 18, 328–349.

Sabini, J., and Silver, M. 1997. In defense of shame: Shame in the context of guilt and embarrassment. *Journal for the Theory of Social Behaviour,* 27, 1–15.

Schlenker, B.R., and Leary, M.R. 1982. Social anxiety and self-presentation: A conceptualization and model. *Psychological Bulletin,* 92, 641–669.

Schmader, T., and Lickel, B. 2006. The approach and avoidance function of guilt and shame emotions: Comparing reactions to self-caused and other-caused wrongdoing. *Motivation and Emotion,* 30, 43–56.

Smith, A. 1759. *The Theory of Moral Sentiments.* London: Miller.

Strelan, P. 2007. Who forgives others, themselves, and situations? The roles of narcissism, guilt, self-esteem, and agreeableness. *Personality and Individual Differences,* 42, 259–269.

Stuewig, J., and McCloskey, L. 2005. The impact of maltreatment on adolescent shame and guilt: Psychological routes to depression and delinquency. *Child Maltreatment,* 10, 324–336.

Tangney, J.P. 1991. Moral affect: The good, the bad, and the ugly. *Journal of Personality and Social Psychology,* 61, 598–607.

———. 1993. Shame and guilt. In *Symptoms of Depression,* ed. C.G. Costello, 161–180. New York: Wiley.

———. 1999. The self-conscious emotions: Shame, guilt, embarrassment, and pride. In *Handbook of Cognition and Emotion,* ed. T. Dalgleish and M. Power, 541–568. Chichester, UK: Wiley.

Tangney, J.P., and Dearing, R.L. 2002. *Shame and Guilt.* New York: Guilford Press.

Tangney, J.P.; Stuewig, J.; and Mashek, D.J. 2007. Moral emotions and moral behavior. *Annual Review of Psychology,* 58, 345–372.

Tangney, J.P.; Wagner, P.E.; and Gramzow, R. 1992. Proneness to shame, proneness to guilt, and psychopathology. *Journal of Abnormal Psychology,* 103, 469–478.

Tangney, J.P.; Wagner, P.E.; Fletcher, C.; and Gramzow, R. 1992. Shamed into anger? The relation of shame and guilt to anger and self-reported aggression. *Journal of Personality and Social Psychology,* 62, 669–675.

Taylor, S.E., and Brown, J.D. 1988. Illusion and well-being: A social psychological perspective on mental health. *Psychological Bulletin,* 103, 193–210.

Thrane, G. 1979. Shame. *Journal for the Theory of Social Behaviour,* 9, 139–166.

Weiss, K.G. 2010. Too ashamed to report: Deconstructing the shame of sexual victimization. *Feminist Criminology,* 5, 286–310.

Welten, S.C.M.; Breugelmans, S.M.; and Zeelenberg, M. 2012. The self in shame. Manuscript submitted for publication.

Welten, S.C.M.; Zeelenberg, M.; and Breugelmans, S.M. 2012a. Empathic shame promotes vicarious learning. Manuscript submitted for publication.

———. 2012b. Vicarious shame. Manuscript submitted for publication.

15

ETHICS POSITION THEORY AND UNETHICAL WORK BEHAVIOR

DONELSON R. FORSYTH AND ERNEST H. O'BOYLE JR.

No one can dispute the negative impact of unethical work behavior on productivity and profit. The Center for Retail Research's study of retailers in forty-two countries estimated the loss due to shoplifting, fraud, and employee theft to be $107.3 billion in 2010, which is more than 1 percent of all retail sales in those countries (Mannes, 2010). A 2010 workplace survey conducted by the International Labour Office identified worldwide increases in workplace violence, which can include bullying, mobbing, threats, sexual assault, and homicide, with an estimated cost to employers in the billions (Chappell and Di Martino, 2006). Harris and Ogbonna's (2002) study of workers in the hospitality industry found that 85 percent regularly engaged in some form of sabotage against their employer and customers, in part to retaliate for mistreatment by other coworkers.

But unethical work behaviors harm more than just the bottom line, for they yield a range of negative psychological and interpersonal consequences for both those who act immorally and those who are party to or targets of those actions. Giacalone and Promislo (2010), in their trauma model of the impact of unethical behavior on well-being, suggest that the well-being and adjustment of victims, witnesses, associates, and even the perpetrators themselves are undermined when moral turpitude intrudes into the workplace. In many cases individuals commit unethical actions because they succumb to pressures that they should resist—social pressure, stress, anger, or financial exigencies—and in consequence they experience debilitating anxiety, remorse, sadness, depression, and vulnerability when they reflect on their actions (Canter and Ioannou, 2004). Those who are bullied, discriminated against, and treated unjustly by others in the workplace display a range of negative reactions to these untoward actions, including lowered self-esteem, demoralization, depression, job-induced stress, insomnia, and general mental health problems (Hansen, Hogh, and Persson, 2011). Others, even if not directly victimized, may experience considerable distress when they find themselves bystanders to the contemptible actions of others or even unwitting collaborators who are drawn into the sordid experience (Vartia, 2001). Giacalone and Promislo (2010) suggest that the vicarious reactions of friends, associates, and family of those who are victimized by others can be as negative as the original target's reaction.

This chapter explores these psychological and interpersonal consequences of unethical work behavior, but focuses on who reacts most negatively to such indiscretions and why. We base our analysis on ethics positions theory (EPT), which suggests that people's reactions in morally toned situations can be traced to variations in their intuitive, personal moral philosophies (Forsyth, 1980). After summarizing the theory and its basic assumptions, we examine the relationship between these variations in moral philosophies and well-being, focusing on the way people respond, psychologically and emotionally, when they act in morally evaluable ways. We then shift the analysis up to the group level to consider the impact of diversity in moral outlook on the workplace relationships, for when individuals who adopt differing moral philosophies must work together, the result may be moral anomie, interpersonal conflict, and distrust. We then conclude by considering some managerial and leadership implications of the ethics position theory perspective for promoting workplace adjustment and well-being.

ETHICS POSITION THEORY

An individual's personal philosophy about fairness, justice, and ethics will likely contain a number of unique, idiosyncratic elements produced by a lifetime of experience in confronting and resolving moral issues. Ethics position theory assumes that these unique, idiographic characteristics are sustained by two nomothetic regularities that appear consistently across most people's moral values and beliefs (Forsyth, 1980, 1992). First, most individuals take a position with regard to the usefulness of moral absolutes as guides to action and judgment. At one end of the continuum, highly relativistic individuals are so skeptical about the possibility of formulating universal moral principles that they eschew moral rules or principles when deciding between what is right and what is wrong. Other people, in contrast, make use of principles that define morality. They believe that moral principles, such as "Tell the truth to others" and "Do unto others as you would have them do unto you," provide a clear yardstick for judging and guiding actions. Second, most people explicitly consider the relative importance of minimizing harmful, injurious consequences, but they vary from idealistic to the completely pragmatic. Those who are more idealistic stress the welfare of others more than those who are more pragmatic, for they assume that people should avoid harming others and reject the idea that harm will sometimes be necessary to produce good.

These two dimensions, relativism and idealism, parallel the distinction between moral theories based on principles (deontological models) and models that stress the consequences of actions (teleological models) in moral philosophy. These dimensions are also consistent with psychological analyses of morality, such as the work of Piaget (1953), Kohlberg (1983), and Gilligan (1982). Kohlberg (1983), for example, maintained that morally mature individuals tend to rely on principles when thinking about ethics, but that they also accept the sanctity of human life as a core value. Similarly Gilligan's (1982, p. 65) analyses of sex differences in moral thought suggest that women tend to accept an ethic of care that requires finding "a way of solving conflicts so that no one will be hurt" (concern for positive consequences) whereas men tend to stress the rational application of principles.

EPT, rather than assuming individuals are either rule-oriented or consequence-oriented, argues that individuals can range from high to low in their emphasis on principles and in their emphasis on consequences. The model thus identifies the four ethics positions or ideologies summarized in Table 15.1: absolutism, situationism, exceptionism, and subjectivism.

Absolutists

Absolutists are idealistic and principled: they believe that one should strive to produce positive consequences (high idealism) but at the same time maintain strict adherence to general moral principles (low relativism). They condemn actions that harm people, particularly if these actions are inconsistent with fundamental moral absolutes. Such an outlook is, in general, deontological, for it prescribes adherence to duty and exceptionless universal moral rules.

Situationists

Situationists are idealistic contextualists; they feel that people should strive to produce positive consequences and avoid negative consequences, but they also believe that morality so depends on the particulars of a given situation that cross-situational rules concerning morality cannot be

Table 15.1

Four Ethics Positions

		Relativism	
		Low	High
Idealism	High	**Absolutists:** Principled idealists who believe people should act in ways that are consistent with moral rules, for doing so will in most cases yield the best outcomes for all concerned.	**Situationists:** Idealistic contextualists who urge acting in ways that will secure the best possible consequences for all concerned even if doing so will violate traditional rules that define what is right and what is wrong.
	Low	**Exceptionists:** Principled pragmatists who endorse moral rules as guides for action, but do not believe that following rules will necessarily generate the best consequences for all concerned.	**Subjectivists:** Pragmatic relativists who base their ethical choices on personal considerations, such as individualized values, moral emotions, or idiosyncratic moral philosophy.

Source: Adapted from Forsyth (1980).

formulated (high relativism). Situationism corresponds to skeptical philosophies of ethics such as situation ethics or value pluralism.

Exceptionists

Exceptionists are principled realists; they rely on moral principles as guidelines for action (low relativism) but they do not believe that harm can always be avoided or that innocent people can always be protected (low idealism). In consequence, they are utilitarian in that they pragmatically admit that judgments should be made by balancing the positive consequences of an action against the negative consequences of an action.

Subjectivists

Subjectivists are realistic contextualists; they reject moral rules (high relativism) but they are not particularly optimistic about the possibility of achieving positive outcomes for everyone concerned (low idealism). Because such individuals describe their moral decisions as subjective, individualistic judgments that cannot be made on the basis of moral absolutes or the extent to which the action benefits others, their viewpoint parallels an egoistic moral philosophy. This position maintains that no moral judgments can be considered valid except in reference to one's own behavior. Some subjectivists may conclude that all people should act to promote their own self-interest, rather than focus on producing positive outcomes for others in general.

PERSONAL ETHICS AND WELL-BEING

Nearly all perspectives on psychological development suggest that moral socialization provides the foundation for the healthy, happy adult. Plato, for example, wrote that virtue is "the health and beauty and well-being of the soul," and those who fail morally will likely end up unhappy, unfulfilled, and physically unwell (Plato, 1973, p. 136). In psychoanalytic theory, the individual's personality and eventual adjustment as an adult hinges upon the development of a moral outlook or conscience. In the clinical realm, psychological health is often defined as the ability to discriminate between right and wrong, to avoid infractions of societal rules and principles, and to become capable of fairly judging the behaviors of others. Positive psychologists, such as Peterson and Seligman (2004), suggest that virtues and character strengths are the markers of psychological well-being, just as the symptoms identified in the diagnostic handbook of psychiatric disorders are the markers of dysfunction.

The strength of the relationship between morality and well-being may depend, however, on the individual's personal moral philosophy. Ethics position theory describes four basic approaches to morality, which are distinguished by acceptance of moral principles (relativism) and concern for helping, or at least not harming, others (idealism), but do these variations have consequences for individuals' subjective well-being, happiness, or self-appraisals in ethical contexts? Does, for example, the absolutist's emphasis on principles and making choices that consider others' outcomes ensure that they act with moral integrity even in challenging, morally turbulent situations? Does the exceptionist, in contrast, experience little shame when acting in ways that harm others, so long as the action is consistent with standard practices? Do individual differences in idealism and relativism moderate the relationship between moral quality of one's actions and the psychological and interpersonal consequences of those actions?

Ethics and Moral Integrity

Peterson and Seligman, in their analysis of the character strengths that people need to reach their highest potential, include integrity, which they define as "moral probity and self-unity" (2004, p. 250). Of the four moral types described by EPT, which type is likely to display moral integrity? Do the situationists live up to their emphasis on achieving positive consequences even if they must act against commonly accepted standards of right and wrong? Do the absolutists, who believe that it is wrong to lie, that moral imperatives guide action, and that one must act to protect the dignity and welfare of others, act on these principles at all times? Do the exceptionists and subjectivists, with their emphasis on pragmatic acceptance of expediency, tend to make choices that others condemn as immoral?

The evidence pertaining to the unique moral integrity of any one of these four types is checkered, at best. A number of investigators have found differences in each moral position's intention to act ethically (e.g., Singhapakdi et al., 2000) and attitudes about specific types of immoral actions (e.g., Etter, Cramer, and Finn, 2006; Rawwas, Al-Khatib, and Vitell, 2004), but individuals who endorse any one of the types have yet to emerge as consistently more morally commendable than the others. Forsyth and Berger (1982), for example, tested students from all four categories by tempting them to cheat on a test of social intelligence. Many did (36 percent), but the cheaters included subjects from all four moral categories. In their second study, they tested resistance to moral temptation by using an accomplice who himself cheated before urging other students to do likewise. Eighty-three percent complied by cheating, but again ethical ideology failed to predict who would succumb to the temptation. Henle, Giacalone, and Jurkiewicz (2005) report that idealistic individuals were less likely to engage in various forms of interpersonal deviance at work (e.g., acting rudely) and that situationists were less likely to engage in organizational deviance (e.g., employee theft) compared to exceptionists and absolutists, but that subjectivists were the most likely to admit to organizational deviance. Douglas and Wier (2000) and Greenfield,

Norman, and Wier (2008) found that idealism was negatively related to questionable budgetary practices (e.g., slack creation behavior and earnings management accounting), but relativism was positively correlated with such practices. However, ethics ideology was unrelated to willingness to get involved in a prosocial protest against animal rights abuses (Nickell and Herzog, 1996).

These findings highlight the importance of considering the nature of the situation before making predictions about individual differences in moral conduct. Absolutists and exceptionists stress the importance of moral rules, so they should be less likely to act in ways that are widely recognized as immoral. They should lie, steal, or cheat less frequently. But if they are not aware that their actions will violate moral rules, or the press of the situation is so great that they are not able to consider their personal values before they act, then the relationship between their ethics position and their actions will be nil. As Schwartz explains, "if a person construes a decision he faces to be a moral choice, relevant moral norms he holds are likely to be activated and to affect his behavior. When he fails to perceive that a moral decision is at stake, however, particular moral norms are unlikely to be activated" (1968, p. 355). Conversely, since the idealistic ideologies—situationism and absolutism—stress the need to achieve positive, humanitarian consequences, then individuals who accept these ideals might be tempted to engage in immoral action if such actions are the means to help others—especially if they are relativistic (the situationists).

Forsyth and Nye (1990) tested this "person X situation" approach by tempting their subjects to tell a lie to another person. For some subjects this false information was described only as feedback, but in other conditions it was explicitly labeled a lie. In addition, half of the subjects were told that they would receive a bonus of $3 for giving the information (either lie or feedback), but others were told the person who would be told the lie would benefit from getting the information. As anticipated, the two situational variables—the salience of moral norms and the consequences of action—had a strong impact on moral action. While only 50 percent of the subjects lied when they were offered $3 and were told that they would be lying rather than giving feedback, this proportion averaged 76.2 percent across the other three conditions. In addition, idealism influenced moral behavior. Although high idealists espouse a philosophy that condemns harming others, they were more likely to lie than the low idealists: 78.6 percent of the situationists and absolutists (high idealists) agreed to tell the lie, while only 62.5 percent of the subjectivists and exceptionists (low idealists) complied with the experimenter's request. In fact, situationists and absolutists usually lied no matter what the consequences or salience of moral norms. Exceptionists, in contrast, were less likely to lie if offered money to lie, and subjectivists were less likely to lie if they stood to gain from the lie and the action was labeled a lie.

This study supports the commonsense notion that people who espouse lofty moral values may tend to behave the most immorally. Although both situationists and absolutists endorse such beliefs as "One should never psychologically or physically harm another person" and "It is never necessary to sacrifice the welfare of others," both groups were willing to tell a total stranger a hurtful lie. While these findings are not too damaging for situationists since these individuals believe that lying is permissible in some settings, absolutists staunchly maintain that lying violates fundamental moral principles and are quite harsh when judging others who have broken this moral absolute. Yet, when they themselves were tempted to lie, they were more likely to succumb. These findings attest to a "hypocrisy effect" that may be obscuring the link between moral values and moral behaviors: People who say they are the most morally upright may be most likely to fall prey to temptation.

This inconsistency between moral intentions and moral actions may also be due, in part, to the tension between absolutists' concern for principles and their concern for securing benefits for others. Many of the absolutists and situationists, when asked why they agreed to lie, said that they did as they were told to help the experimenter. They did not consider their behavior to be an antisocial act that harmed another person, but rather a prosocial act that helped someone. Moreover, the impact of high idealists' moral values on their moral actions may have been overwhelmed by the powerful social situation in which they found themselves. A number of theorists now believe that individuals with different personalities seek out, create, or evoke different interpersonal situations (Diener, Larsen, and Emmons, 1984). Applied to moral choices, individuals who are idealistic may generally avoid situations that will force them to choose between failing to meet a commitment and harming another person. When forced into this ordinarily avoided situation, the high idealists responded by following the orders of the experimenter.

Ethics and Self-Flagellation

Nietzsche notwithstanding, most philosophers have maintained that acting morally is a sure path to happiness (Wienand, 2009). There is, however, another way in which morality and well-being are linked, and that is by the emotional and psychological reactions people experience as a result of acting morally or immorally. This connection between morality and a sense of well-being may be relatively unsubstantial, or altogether absent, for some people. The cynical Machiavellian who puts expediency before principle, the narcissist who feels entitled to far more than a fair share, and the psychopath who is devoid of concern for other people and moral principles are likely not plagued by feelings of guilt or remorse when they act immorally, nor do they swell with happiness when they act in ways that earn them moral praise (O'Boyle et al., forthcoming). Most people, however, experience guilt over their moral failings, and if these feelings become pronounced, they may lead to a range of problems in psychological and social adjustment.

Ethics position may not be a strong predictor of who will behave morally and who will not, but it does predict who is more likely to suffer negative psychological reactions following an indiscretion. Klass, after reviewing a number of previous studies of individuals' feelings of guilt, shame, and self-esteem after breaking moral norms, concludes that "the same overt action seems to make some people feel better and others feel worse, and for still others, has no effects" (1978, p. 766). EPT accounts for these divergences by suggesting that individuals who emphasize obedience to moral norms (low relativists) but nonetheless find themselves acting contrary to a salient moral norm should display more negative post-transgression reactions than relativists. In contrast, idealistic individuals who achieve positive consequences for others should display more positive affective reactions following their transgression.

Forsyth and Berger (1982) partially confirmed these predictions in their studies of academic cheating. Students worked on extremely difficult anagrams, but they could copy the solutions to the problems from the master key, which was left behind by the examiner. After they completed the test, respondents rated themselves on a series of adjective pairs, including sad/happy, upset/at ease, weak/strong, and nervous/calm. Only the absolutists' self-ratings were consistently correlated with these self-evaluations, for the more they cheated, the more negatively they evaluated themselves. Subjectivists also rated themselves more negatively when they cheated, but their ratings reflected anxiety over being found out (e.g., nervous/calm) more so than self-condemnation. In a second study, Forsyth and Berger (1982) found that absolutists who were prodded into cheating on a test rated themselves as more negative, weak, unlikable, and dirty than individuals in all the other individual moral philosophy categories. Forsyth and Nye (1990) documented a similar reaction in absolutists in their study of lying. They found that when subjects were paid to lie, the representatives of the various ethical types responded similarly in terms of self-rated morality and anxiety. When no money changed hands, absolutists rated themselves as less moral, honest, friendly, good, and so on, particularly compared to situationists.

Ethics and Self-Approbation

Just as individuals who differ in ethics position respond differently when they act immorally, they also respond differently when they act in morally commendable ways.

Forsyth (1993) examined the relationship between ethics positions, moral action, and emotions to answer a centuries-old philosophical issue: Do honorable intentions make an action praiseworthy or is the best action one that generates the greatest good for the greatest number? Immanuel Kant (1785/1973, p. 63) argued that the answer lies in the inherent goodness of one's intentions, for a "good will is good not because of what it performs or effects, not by its aptness for the attainment of some proposed end, but simply by virtue of the volition, that is, it is good in itself." Other ethicists—notably, consequentialists—maintained that few actions can be judged a priori, for an action that generates the greatest good for the greatest number of people is far more praiseworthy than an action that matches accepted canons of morality but yields little in the way of positive consequences.

To examine the impact of consequences on moral emotions Forsyth arranged for individuals who differed in ethics positions to work on tasks that would yield a monetary payoff if completed successfully. Egoistically motivated participants were told they could keep whatever money they earned. Others, in contrast, were charitably motivated: they were told that their earnings would be donated to a charity. After the task was completed, subjects were given bogus information about their level of performance. If successful, those who were working for themselves received their pay, but if they were working for a charity, their pay was donated to a worthy cause. Those given failure feedback were told that they did not meet the minimum standards needed for payment. After receiving their feedback they rated their affect, their level of morality, and their self-esteem.

Overall, subjects' self-ratings were more positive when they succeeded rather than failed. Differences due to individual moral philosophy, however, were obtained after failure.

Absolutists put intentions before consequences. Although they reported feeling more upset in comparison to other subjects, absolutists felt the most positive about their own morality when they were working for a charity rather than themselves. Working for a good cause was sufficient to garner moral approbation, irrespective of the overall success or failure of the effort. Their virtue lay in their volition, rather than its successful fruition.

Situationists did not rate themselves as positively when working for a charity, but otherwise they responded similarly to the absolutists. All subjects reported more positive self-esteem when they succeeded rather than failed, but this asymmetry was particularly pronounced for the high idealists. Absolutists' and situationists' thoughts were also more negative in content when they failed rather than succeeded, reflecting their greater concern for achieving positive outcomes. Low idealists did not show such a negative preoccupation after failure. The idealists, when working for a charity, were also more likely to report thoughts pertaining to the charity—either remorse over failing it or happiness over helping it—and when working for their own benefit they reported more self-reflective thoughts. Low idealists rarely mentioned the charity and reported few self-reflective thoughts.

Exceptionists, however, responded unexpectedly. Like subjects in all ethical categories, their global self-ratings, including overall affect, attractiveness, and self-esteem, were influenced more by performance than motive: When they succeeded they rated themselves more positively than when they failed. Exceptionists, however, reported feeling distressed when laboring for a charity rather than themselves, and they also felt more morally virtuous when working for themselves rather than the charity. Exceptionists also reported more positive thoughts in the self-motivated conditions rather than the charitable conditions. At least two explanations can be offered for their reactions. First, these individuals may have felt anxiety about failing to live up to the demands of working for a good cause and failing. Second, they may be less supportive of charitable actions, in general, or the specific charity that would be receiving their donation (a state-sponsored fund).

Ethics and Well-Being

Because people judge themselves in moral terms, unethical actions are, in general, antithetical to well-being and happiness. Very few studies, however, have directly assessed the causal chain leading from moral misstep to posttransgression self-condemnation to reduction in well-being, so the link between variations in ethics position and well-being is an uncertain one. Kernes and Kinnier (2005) found that the professional psychologists they studied tended to be either absolutists or situationists, but they found no significant relationship between idealism, relativism, and their measures of happiness, life-satisfaction, and well-being. Forsyth, Iyer, and Haidt (2012), in contrast, reported a significant correlation between relativism and levels of well-being, anxiety, and depression. Exceptionists claimed the highest levels of well-being, followed by absolutists, subjectivists, and situationists.

These findings with regard to the high level of well-being reported by exceptionists are consistent with cross-cultural differences in overall happiness. Forsyth, O'Boyle, and McDaniel (2008), using meta-analytic methods, identified patterned variations in EPT across countries, with an exceptionist ethic more common in Western countries, subjectivism and situationism in Eastern countries, and absolutism and situationism in Middle Eastern countries. These patterns were systematically related to variations in levels of happiness, as indexed by the Marks et al. (2006) ratings of global happiness levels. Happiness scores were highest in the countries where more of the citizens reportedly endorsed an exceptionistic ethic (e.g., Canada, Austria, Belgium), but lowest in countries whose mean idealism and relativism scores suggested an absolutist ethic (e.g., Egypt, South Africa, Poland). The two clusters of relativistic countries fell intermediate; see (Figure 15.1).

COLLECTIVE ETHICS AND WELL-BEING

Moral behavior tends to be social behavior, for it occurs in an interpersonal context. In the preceding sections we examined the relationships among individuals' morally evaluable actions, their ethics position, and their well-being, but well-being is as much a group-level process as an individual-level one (O'Boyle, Forsyth, and O'Boyle, 2011). When one works with others who conduct themselves in morally commendable ways in challenging circumstances, job and life satisfaction are amplified, but even the observation of morally offensive actions in the workplace is likely to lower satisfaction and increase stress (Ferguson and Barry, 2011). Here we consider the possibility that differences in ethics positions, within an organizational setting, can contribute to conflict, moral misunderstandings, and declines in social welfare (Keyes, 1998).

Well-Being and Moral Diversity

Evolutionary models of morality suggest that norms that define what is right and wrong serve an indispensable function in collective enterprises (e.g., Ridley, 1996). Moral norms are a fundamental element of social structure; they are the "cement of society" (Elster, 1989, p. 251). They simplify behavioral choices, provide direction and motivation, organize social interactions, and make other people's responses predictable and meaningful. Unlike common social norms, which

Figure 15.1   Differences in Mean Levels of Happiness in Twenty-Four Countries with Varying Ethics Positions

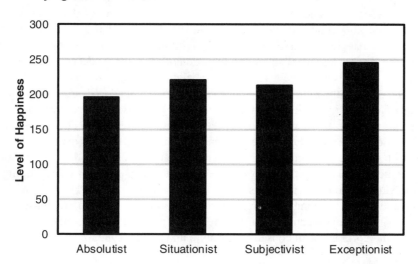

describe degree of consensus on relatively inconsequential aspects of social life, moral norms define which behaviors are praiseworthy, laudable, and aspirational, and which ones are corrupt, contemptible, and shameful. Each person in society is restrained to a degree by moral norms, but each person also benefits from the order that norms provide.

In many cases people agree about right and wrong. It is wrong to embezzle from an employer; to knowingly sell faulty products that cause severe injury to uninformed consumers; to fire employees because of their race, or creed, or color; and to misrepresent the value of the company's stock to shareholders. This consensus is lost, however, when the discussion turns to less clear-cut issues and when individuals differ in their ethics position: what is considered morally contemptible by an absolutist may be viewed as the expedient, and appropriate, choice by the exceptionist. At the bivariate level, the model predicts that absolutists and exceptionists (low relativists) will more strongly condemn actions that break rules, whereas absolutists and situationists (high idealists) will respond more negatively to actions that yield negative consequences. At the multivariate level, the model maintains that absolutists' emphasis on conformity to moral principles and sensitivity to negative consequences will prompt them to respond the most negatively to rule violations that harm others, whereas subjectivists will be the most lenient in their appraisals of such actions.

Researchers have confirmed that, in general, absolutists are the most likely to consider an issue to be a moral one, and that they also tend to be harsher when judging those who have violated moral norms. Forsyth (1980), for example, reported relationships between the ethics positions and a number of contemporary moral issues, particularly for men. More than respondents within each of the other ethical categories, male absolutists felt that cloning was immoral, that mercy killing should not be tolerated, and that marijuana use, homosexuality, and abortion were wrong. Singh and Forsyth (1989) reported this same negativity in their study of sexuality. The significant interaction of idealism and relativism on ratings of the morality of premarital sex, extramarital sex, and homosexuality occurred because evaluators became more negative as their individual moral philosophies became more idealistic and less relativistic. Forsyth (1981) found that absolutists judged those who produced negative consequences as less moral than did exceptionist judges, provided the individuals in question were somewhat responsible for their actions. Individuals who adopt differing ethics positions also tend to diverge in their judgments of the ethics of psychological research. Absolutists tend to be more heavily influenced by the perceived costs of research and the potential for harm, and this emphasis led them to evaluate research more negatively than those who adopted other ethical ideologies (Forsyth, 1985). Idealists, in general, are more likely to consider an action that yields negative consequences for others to be one that must be evaluated on moral grounds, whereas less idealistic individuals do not consider the act one that requires moral scrutiny (Bowes-Sperry and Powell, 1999; Singhapakdi, Vitell, and Kraft, 1996).

These differences in the moral thought and evaluation may lead to dysfunctional processes in the workplace. Although variation in opinions on political issues, sports, or even business strategies may be common in most work settings, differences with regard to ethical issues are more discomfiting. Most individuals take moral consensus for granted, and thus expect that other people will agree with their moral conclusions. Evidence suggests, however, that an absolutist and a subjectivist, when working together, may reach very different conclusions when judging the same action or individual. Such disagreements about what is morally right and what is morally wrong create a fundamental, unsettling, paradox: "in making a moral reproach one must first act as if the other's behavior were objectively a violation; yet the proof of the correctness of the particular application of the norm is social consensus" (Sabini and Silver, 1982, p. 46).

Moral Fit

Workplaces, perhaps to deal with moral ambiguities, tend to establish their own moral norms and use these norms to govern the judgment of right and wrong and the consequences of violating the norms. But because moral norms are socially constructed, behaviors that are judged to be acceptable or even praiseworthy in one setting may be only tolerated or even condemned in another (Feldman, 1984). Furthermore, larger organizations likely possess multiple sets of moral norms that vary widely depending on location. Thus, when individuals join an organization, they enter a morally ambiguous workplace where ethical position can conflict with the established moral norms. Diversity may enhance organizational performance, but *moral* diversity can create ethical schisms within the group, leaving some members feeling isolated and ostracized, and trigger increases in counternormative work behavior (CWB) such as sabotage, malicious gossip, and theft (Liao, Joshi, and Chuang, 2004).

Moral Misfits and Moral Conformity

Upon entering an organization, individuals seek out others who share similar views, interests, and backgrounds. This process integrates the person into the organization, promotes identity and cohesion, and reduces conflict. Fitting in by accepting norms that define what is right and wrong differs substantially, however, from adopting the group's standards pertaining to more mundane activities, such as dress, punctuality, and work habits—particularly for those who take their moral principles more seriously and personally. Low relativists (absolutists and exceptionists), for example, may feel their moral outlook is challenged when working in a firm of mostly situationists and subjectivists, and they may exhibit withdrawal behaviors as this dissimilarity causes them to feel disconnected from the organization (Wheeler et al., 2007).

Norms are very powerful shapers of behavior, and no EPT is impervious to their influence, but EPT groups likely differ in their ability to rationalize conformity to norms inconsistent with their own moral philosophy. For example, those high in idealism may adjust to the moral norms of an organization by assuming that these norms promote, in general, positive outcomes for those inside and outside of the organization. Thus, even if the rules are not unusual ones or ones that differ from one's personal standards, they may nonetheless be considered acceptable since they yield positive consequences. Relativism, in contrast, suggests a more mercurial moral outlook and so may lead to one of two outcomes: more moral deviance or a relatively unperturbed shift in morality to match the organization's views.

When examining the moral misfit and the interaction of idealism and relativism, absolutists are perhaps the most interesting as their individual moral philosophy would suggest that in the face of moral diversity they would be likely to conform to the organizational norms and therefore also be more likely to become moral misfits. However, if absolutists can reconcile their beliefs with the moral norms of the organization, then these individuals may be able to embrace the organization's norms, and even become advocates. Absolutists can embrace moral norms so long as they promote positive outcomes and are considered situationally robust, and organizational norms that are widely shared may meet this requirement (Van Kenhove, Vermeir, and Verniers, 2001).

Moral Misfit and Conflict

Differences in moral outlook will likely also create conflict within the workplace, and that conflict will likely be more personal rather than procedural. Morrill's (1995) study of high-level corporate executives, for example, found that many of the most intense conflicts in the organizations he studied occurred because disputants questioned each other's moral values. Unfortunately, whereas work-groups can often successfully manage task-related conflicts, when problems stem from personal conflicts, including differences in values and moral outlook, attempts at conflict management tend to exacerbate the group conflict more than mollify it (e.g., De Dreu and Weingart, 2003). Klein et al. (2011) found that conflict increased when members of a work team differed in their emphasis on traditional moral principles, particularly when their leader adopted a relationship- rather than task-oriented management style.

Conflicts rooted in moral disparities may be particularly likely when absolutists must cope with the moral flexibilities of relativists. Absolutists, with their belief in moral rules and idealistic outcomes, are more attuned to the violation of these rules by themselves or coworkers. Relativists, in contrast, should be more likely to overlook differences in moral appraisals, since their ethical philosophy explicitly eschews certitude in moral pronouncements. Absolutists, then, are more likely to display a range of negative psychological and physical reactions, including burnout, stress, negative emotions, and absenteeism (Robbins, Ford, and Tetrick, 2012). Also, drawing from the organizational retribution literature (e.g., Skarlicki and Folger, 1997; Skarlicki, van Jaarsveld, and Walker, 2008), when an absolutist observes that rule violations go unpunished because the moral norms of the organization tolerate it, they may seek vengeance or retribution. Ironically, if the conflict becomes so intense that it generates counterproductive work behaviors such as bullying, spreading rumors, and speaking derogatively about the organization, absolutists are more likely than all other ethical types to experience stress and the loss of well-being.

Moral Misfit and Well-Being

Just as a lack of moral integrity may lower overall well-being, a lack of connectedness to cowork-ers, inability to conform to organizational norms that define what is right and what is wrong, and engagement in CWB may also undermine happiness, life-satisfaction, and well-being deficits. A lack of fit results in lowered job satisfaction and increased strain (Kristof-Brown, Zimmerman, and Johnson, 2005), and moral misfit is perhaps more poignant than other forms of misfit due to the implications of having a different set of morals from coworkers. Whereas other nonnormative behavior may be viewed by others as the action of an eccentric, moral deviance is judged harshly—particularly by absolutists. Violation of descriptive social norms may result in mild social ridicule or reduced inclusion, but violation of injunctive norms results in far more serious social consequences that may, in time, reduce well-being. The individual and group distrust each other and this hampers organizational effectiveness (Kramer, 1999; McAllister, 1995) and reduces well-being (Ward and Meyer, 2009). There is some evidence that an individual zealot does have the power to alter norms either through persuasion (Mobilia, 2003) or through the introduction of external forces such as whistle-blowing (Dozier and Miceli, 1985), but norms typically overcome individual dissent and the individual either conforms reluctantly or leaves the organization. In either case, well-being is likely to suffer.

IMPLICATIONS

Ethics position theory, with its roots in personality theory and social psychology, assumes that morality is both a personal and an interpersonal process. The theory suggests that people differ in their moral outlooks, with some stressing the importance of principles and others suggesting that the most moral action is the one that causes the least harm to others. These variations have implications for understanding how people act in morally challenging situations and their reactions to others' morally questionable actions, but they may also be linked in fundamental ways to health, happiness, and well-being. Plato (1973) was certain that moral virtue is healthy whereas wickedness brings disease and grief, but virtue lies in the eye—and the ethics position—of the beholder.

Well-being is, however, determined not only by one's personal ethics position but also by social context. The lone absolutist teamed with exceptionists, the situationist working for a company that pledges corporate philanthropy but privately gives little back to the community, the subjectivist who must pledge allegiance to a corporate credo, and the exceptionist who passes up risky, but potentially quite lucrative, ventures must find ways to cope with life in a morally diverse workplace. As the concept of moral fit suggests, it is not enough to be virtuous, but one must be virtuous in ways that are defined as morally correct in the given situation (Kakabadse, Kakabadse, and Lee-Davis, 2007).

Researchers and practitioners alike can benefit from an integrated perspective of immoral behavior in the workplace. EPT suggests that one's personal moral philosophy affects moral thought, emotion, action, and judgments of others' actions, but the complex of associations linking ethics position and well-being remains uninvestigated. Whereas absolutists are more likely to lay claim to virtues such as honesty, compassion, and duty, more research is needed to determine if and when these principles translate into well-being. Given that strong moral convictions provide only partial protection against moral temptations combined with absolutists' tendency toward self-flagellation, virtuousness in the principled sense may lead to unhappiness rather than well-being. Idealism, too, may also be negatively associated with happiness, given that in an uncertain world harm can rarely be avoided entirely. As a result, those who are virtuous, but expediently so, may be the happiest of all.

More research is also needed to examine the social side of morality. It is not yet known how individuals respond when they discover that their moral judgments are unshared by others in the group, when they join an organization that expresses values that conflict with their own, when they are confronted by someone in the workplace who challenges their moral beliefs, and when they witness actions that run counter to their personal moral code. The extant literature tends to be myopic in that it views the consequences of moral judgments and behaviors from a single source and direction. For example, studies of workplace deviance (Robinson and Bennett, 1995) rarely recognize the perpetrator's perspective, abusive supervision (Tepper, 2000) is primarily indexed through reports by the victim, and workplace incivility (Andersson and Pearson, 1999) is often used to capture bystanders' perception of immoral behavior within the organization. The well-being of all three (perpetrator, target, and bystander) is affected by immoral behavior, and the ripple effects of immorality require closer study.

EPT's most fundamental implication for improving work conditions is based on its most central assumption: that people differ in their thoughts, actions, and feelings about moral matters. These differences, because they are linked to variations in ethics positions, may be inevitable, but the negative consequences of moral disunity need not be. Employees, managers, and leaders, recognizing that variation in moral outlook is normal, should not assume that their own moral outlook (a) is the only legitimate position to take on the issue or (b) will be widely shared by others. EPT suggests that morality often requires the close consideration of principles and consequences when making decisions, but the perspective remains a descriptive approach to ethics rather than a prescriptive one. Kohlberg (1983), for example, deliberately accepted a deontological model as the most mature approach to making moral judgments, and ranked other views as inferior. EPT, in contrast, merely describes individual differences in moral thought, and does not argue that any one philosophy is more morally advanced than another. Absolutists, given their emphasis on principles, are more likely to assume that their moral decisions are ethically righteous, particularly as compared to the more relativistic positions, but all individuals must resist false consensus: assuming that their moral perspective is widely shared with others.

This diversity in moral outlook also suggests that groups and organizations may need to put into place programs that clarify the collective's ethics orientation so as to reach shared understanding of issues with moral undertones or complications. If a company expects its employees to adhere closely to a code of ethics, then considerable normative work will be needed to make certain that employees understand the link between moral codes, moral judgments, and moral actions. Clearly, codifying ethics will prove more difficult in organizations with substantial numbers of relativists, as well in those organizations that are located in areas of the world where relativistic views dominate more rule-based approaches to ethics. Evidence suggests that companies that operate in countries whose residents tend to be more relativistic generally adopt codes of ethics that are less principle-focused than companies that operate in countries that stress adherence to rules and principles (Forsyth and O'Boyle, 2011). However, because morality is ultimately a social process, the relative importance of the many factors that influence moral judgments can and should be enumerated, clarified, and weighed through informed discussion.

REFERENCES

Andersson, L.M., and Pearson, C.M. 1999. Tit for tat? The spiraling effect of incivility in the workplace. *Academy of Management Review,* 24, 452–471.

Bowes-Sperry, L., and Powell, G.N. 1999. Observers' reactions to social-sexual behavior at work: An ethical decision-making perspective. *Journal of Management,* 25, 779–802.

Canter, D.V., and Ioannou, M. 2004. Criminals' emotional experiences during crimes. *International Journal of Forensic Psychology,* 1, 71–81.

Chappell, D., and Di Martino, V. 2006. *Violence at Work.* 3d ed. Geneva: International Labour Office.

De Dreu, C.K.W., and Weingart, L.R. 2003. Task versus relationship conflict, team performance, and team member satisfaction: A meta-analysis. *Journal of Applied Psychology,* 88, 741–749.

Diener, E.; Larsen, R.J.; and Emmons, R.A. 1984. Person X situation interactions: Choice of situations and congruence response models. *Journal of Personality and Social Psychology,* 47, 580–592.

Douglas, P., and Wier, B. 2000. Integrating ethical dimensions into a model of budgetary slack creation. *Journal of Business Ethics,* 28, 267–277.

Dozier, J.B., and Miceli, M.P. 1985. Potential predictors of whistle-blowing: A prosocial behavior perspective. *Academy of Management Review,* 10, 823–836.

Elster, J. 1989. *The Cement of Society: A Study of Social Order.* Cambridge: Cambridge University Press.

Etter, S.; Cramer, J.J.; and Finn, S. 2006. Origins of academic dishonesty: Ethical orientations and personality factors associated with attitudes about cheating with information technology. *Journal of Research on Technology in Education,* 39, 133–155.

Feldman, D.C. 1984. The development and enforcement of group norms. *Academy of Management Review,* 9, 47–53.

Ferguson, M., and Barry, B. 2011. I know what you did: The effects of interpersonal deviance on bystanders. *Journal of Occupational Health Psychology,* 16, 80–94.

Forsyth, D.R. 1980. A taxonomy of ethical ideologies. *Journal of Personality and Social Psychology,* 39, 175–184.

———. 1981. Moral judgment: The influence of ethical ideology. *Personality and Social Psychology Bulletin,* 7, 218–223.

———. 1985. Individual differences in information integration during moral judgment. *Journal of Personality and Social Psychology,* 49, 264–272.

———. 1992. Judging the morality of business practices: The influence of personal moral philosophies. *Journal of Business Ethics,* 11, 461–470.

———. 1993. Honorable intentions versus praiseworthy accomplishments: The impact of motives and outcomes on the moral self. *Current Psychology,* 12, 298–311.

Forsyth, D.R., and Berger, R.E. 1982. The effects of ethical ideology on moral behavior. *The Journal of Social Psychology,* 117, 53–56.

Forsyth, D.R., and Nye, J.L. 1990. Personal moral philosophies and moral choice. *Journal of Research in Personality,* 24, 398–414.

Forsyth, D.R., and O'Boyle, E.H. Jr. 2011. Rules, standards, and ethics: Relativism predicts cross-national differences in the codification of moral standards. *International Business Review,* 20, 353–361.

Forsyth, D.R.; Iyer, R.; and Haidt, J. 2012. Idealism, relativism, and ethics: The moral foundations of individual differences in political orientation. Paper presented at the Annual Meeting of the Society for Personality and Social Psychology, San Diego, CA, January 26–28.

Forsyth, D.R.; O'Boyle, E.H. Jr.; and McDaniel, M.A. 2008. East meets west: A meta-analytic investigation of cultural variations in idealism and relativism. *Journal of Business Ethics,* 83, 813–833.

Giacalone, R.A., and Promislo, M.D. 2010. Unethical and unwell: Decrements in well-being and unethical activity at work. *Journal of Business Ethics,* 91, 275–297.

Gilligan, C. 1982. *In a Different Voice: Psychological Theory and Women's Development.* Cambridge, MA: Harvard University Press.

Greenfield, A.C. Jr.; Norman, C.S.; and Wier, B. 2008. The effect of ethical orientation and professional commitment on earnings management behavior. *Journal of Business Ethics,* 83, 419–434.

Hansen, Å.M.; Hogh, A.; and Persson, R. 2011. Frequency of bullying at work, physiological response, and mental health. *Journal of Psychosomatic Research,* 70, 19–27.

Harris, L.C., and Ogbonna, E. 2002. Exploring service sabotage: The antecedents, types and consequences of frontline, deviant, antiservice behaviors. *Journal of Service Research,* 4, 163–183.

Henle, C.; Giacalone, R.; and Jurkiewicz, C. 2005. The role of ethical ideology in workplace deviance. *Journal of Business Ethics,* 56, 219–230.

Kakabadse, A.P.; Kakabadse, N.K.; and Lee-Davis, L. 2007. Three temptations of leaders. *Leadership and Organization Development Journal,* 28, 196–208.

Kant, I. 1873/1973. Critique of pure reason and other works on the theory of ethics. T.K. Abbott (trans). In *Introduction to Moral Philosophy*, ed. P.E. Davis, 62–94. Columbus, OH: Merrill.

Kernes, J.L., and Kinnier, R.T. 2005. Psychologists' search for the good life. *Journal of Humanistic Psychology,* 45, 82–105.

Keyes, C.L.M. 1998. Social well-being. *Social Psychology Quarterly,* 61, 121–140.

Klass, E.T. 1978. Psychological effects of immoral actions: The experimental evidence. *Psychological Bulletin,* 85, 756–771.

Klein, K.J.; Knight, A.P.; Ziegert, J.C.; Lim, B.C.; and Saltz, J.L. 2011. When team members' values differ: The moderating role of team leadership. *Organizational Behavior and Human Decision Processes,* 114, 25–36.

Kohlberg, L. 1983. *Essays in Moral Development.* New York: Harper and Row.

Kramer, R.M. 1999. Trust and distrust in organizations: Emerging perspectives, enduring questions. *Annual Review of Psychology,* 50, 569–598.

Kristof-Brown, A.L.; Zimmerman, R.D.; and Johnson, E.C. 2005. Consequences of individuals' fit at work: A meta-analysis of person-job, person-organization, person-group, and person-supervisor fit. *Personnel Psychology,* 58, 281–342.

Liao, H.; Joshi, A.; and Chuang, A. 2004. Sticking out like a sore thumb: Employee dissimilarity and deviance at work. *Personnel Psychology,* 57, 969–1000.

Mannes, T. 2010. Shoplifting down around the world. *San Diego Union Tribune*, October 24. www.utsandiego.com/news/2010/oct/24/shoplifting-down-around-world/?print&page=all/.

Marks, N.; Abdallah, S.; Simms, A.; Thompson, S. 2006. *The Happy Planet Index.* London: New Economics Foundation.

McAllister D.J. 1995. Affect- and cognition-based trust as foundations for interpersonal cooperation in organizations. *Academy of Management Journal,* 38, 24–59.

Mobilia, M. 2003. Does a single zealot affect an infinite group of voters? *Physical Review Letters,* July 11, 91 (2) 028701, 1–4.

Morrill, C. 1995. *The Executive Way.* Chicago: University of Chicago Press.

Nickell, D., and Herzog, H.A. Jr. 1996. Ethical ideology and moral persuasion: Personal moral philosophy, gender, and judgments of pro- and anti-animal research propaganda. *Society and Animals,* 4, 1, 53–64.

O'Boyle, E.H. Jr.; Forsyth, D.R.; and O'Boyle, A.S. 2011. Bad apples or bad barrels: An examination of group- and organizational-level effects in the study of counterproductive work behavior. *Group and Organization Management,* 36, 39–69.

O'Boyle, E.H. Jr.; Forsyth, D.R.; Banks, G.; and McDaniel, M. Forthcoming. A meta-analysis of the dark triad and work outcomes: A social exchange perspective. *Journal of Applied Psychology.*

Ogbonna, E., and Harris, L.C. 2001. The performance implications of the work-oriented cognitions of shopfloor workers: A study of British retailing. *International Journal of Human Resource Management,* 12, 1005–1028.

Peterson, C., and Seligman, M.E.P. 2004. *Character Strengths and Virtues: A Handbook and Classification.* Washington, DC: American Psychological Association.

Piaget, J. 1953. *The Origins of Intelligence in Children.* London: Routledge and Kegan Paul.

Plato. 1973. *The Republic and Other Works*, trans. B. Jowett. New York: Anchor.

Rawwas, M.Y.A.; Al-Khatib, J.; and Vitell, S.J. 2004. Academic dishonesty: A cross-cultural comparison of U.S. and Chinese marketing students. *Journal of Marketing Education,* 26, 89–100.

Ridley, M. 1996. *The Origins of Virtue.* London: Penguin.

Robbins, J.M.; Ford, M.T.; and Tetrick, L.E. (2012). Perceived unfairness and employee health: A meta-analytic integration. *Journal of Applied Psychology,* 97, 235–272.

Robinson, S.L., and Bennett, R.J. 1995. A typology of deviant workplace behaviors: A multidimensional scaling study. *Academy of Management Journal,* 38, 555–572.

Sabini, J., and Silver, P. 1982. *Moralities of Everyday Life.* New York: Oxford University Press.

Schwartz, S.H. 1968. Awareness of consequences and the influence of moral norms on interpersonal behavior. *Sociometry,* 31, 355–369.

Singh, B., and Forsyth, D.R. 1989. Sexual attitudes and moral values: The importance of idealism and relativism. *Bulletin of the Psychonomic Society,* 27, 160–162.

Singhapakdi, A.; Vitell, S.J.; and Kraft, K.L. 1996. Moral intensity and ethical decision-making of marketing professionals. *Journal of Business Research,* 36, 245–55.

Singhapakdi, A.; Salyachivin, S.; Virakul, B.; and Veerayangkur, V. 2000. Some important factors underlying ethical decision making of managers in Thailand. *Journal of Business Ethics,* 25, 271–84.

Skarlicki, D.P., and Folger, R. 1997. Retaliation in the workplace: The roles of distributive, procedural, and interactional justice. *Journal of Applied Psychology,* 82, 434–443.

Skarlicki, D.P.; van Jaarsveld, D.D.; and Walker, D.D. 2008. Getting even for customer mistreatment: The role of moral identity in the relationship between customer interpersonal injustice and employee sabotage. *Journal of Applied Psychology,* 93, 1335–1347.

Tepper, B.J. 2000. Consequences of abusive supervision. *Academy of Management Journal,* 43, 178–190.

Van Kenhove, P.; Vermeir, I.; and Verniers, S. 2001. An empirical investigation of the relationships between ethical beliefs, ethical ideology, political preference, and need for closure. *Journal of Business Ethics,* 32, 347–361.

Vartia, M. A-L. 2001. Consequences of workplace bullying with respect to the well-being of its targets and the observers of bullying. *Scandinavian Journal of Work, Environment and Health,* 27, 63–69.

Ward, P., and Meyer, S. 2009. Trust, social quality and well-being: A sociological exegesis. *Development and Society,* 38, 339–363.

Wheeler, A.; Gallagher, V.; Brouer, R.; and Sablynski, C. 2007. When person-organization (mis)fit and (dis)satisfaction lead to turnover: The moderating role of perceived job mobility. *Journal of Managerial Psychology,* 22, 203–219.

Wienand, I. 2009. Discourses on happiness: A reading of Descartes and Nietzsche. *Ethical Perspectives,* 16, 103–128.

16

PERCEIVED JUSTICE AND WELL-BEING AT WORK

How and for Whom Do Unethical Practices Matter?

TODD LUCAS AND CRAIG A. WENDORF

Justice is a defining characteristic of social relationships that is implicated in many aspects of the work environment (cf. Brockner, 2010; Greenberg, 2011). Moreover, an impressive body of research supports the idea that a belief in justice may be essential to work effectiveness and satisfaction. For example, perceived justice at work has been shown to predict diminished job burnout, less absenteeism, and reduced work–family conflict (for reviews, see Cropanzano and Wright, 2011; Fujishiro and Heaney, 2009). In recent times, perceptions of justice are increasingly implicated in health aspects of work well-being, including links to workers' physical and mental health (e.g., Kivimäki et al., 2005; Tepper, 2001). Thus, it is increasingly clear that beliefs about justice are an especially important element of one's work because of their ties to significant and costly work-related psychological disorders and physical illnesses.

Given that justice perceptions are implicated in both the psychological structure and resulting health consequences of the workplace, there would seem to be considerable potential in exploring connections between justice and well-being within the context of unethical work practices. However, the justice and workplace ethics literatures have thus far existed largely parallel to one another, such that linking justice to well-being at work via unethical work practices remains largely unexplored. The purpose of the current chapter is thus to consider possible interconnections among perceptions of justice, unethical work behavior, and worker well-being. To begin, we introduce a psychological approach to justice, and we briefly review research linking perceived justice to health and well-being. We then describe state and trait conceptualizations of justice, and we suggest ways that both sources might interface with unethical work practices to affect worker health. Finally, we propose and evaluate an initial conceptual framework for integrating justice perceptions with unethical work practices, and for organizing initial research on resultant health effects. Throughout, we emphasize that justice perceptions are multidimensional, and we consider the potential for precise, unique, and complex links to unethical work practices and workplace health based on specific sources and operationalizations of justice. In addition, we attempt throughout to give examples suggesting that justice perceptions can affect victims, perpetrators, and witnesses of unethical work practices (cf. Giacalone and Promislo, 2010).

OVERVIEW OF PSYCHOLOGICAL JUSTICE AND LINKS TO
WELL-BEING

Justice is a fundamental consideration of many disciplines that range from psychology, philosophy, and theology to economics, law, and public health (for a review, see Tyler and Smith, 1998). Of present concern, the concept of social justice has been used to describe how individuals and groups *should* behave toward one another in order to ensure that societies are ethical and moral. A common thread in many prior considerations of social justice is the idea that power and resource advantage should not singularly determine how individuals and groups govern one another. As described by Jost and Kay (2010), social justice may be defined according to three principles. First, justice describes the disbursement of benefits and burdens across individuals according to a preordained allocative principle. Second, justice describes the procedures, rules, and norms that govern decisions about the rights, liberties, and entitlements of individuals and groups. Finally, principles of justice ensure that individuals are treated with dignity and respect by authorities and each other.

In psychology, justice and fairness are largely synonymous terms that encompass theory and research on the causes and consequences of perceived fairness. In contrast to the broader approaches taken by many disciplines, a psychological approach tends to be evaluative rather than prescriptive of justice. For example, rather than suggest whether or when a workplace policy is morally appropriate or objectively fair, or what policies ought to be adopted by organizations to achieve impartiality in the workplace, psychological research instead focuses on *how* individual workers arrive at their view of specific policies or workplace occurrences as fair or unfair, or else on thoughts, feelings, and actions that *result from* workers' subjective judgments of justice. Thus, a psychological approach to justice may be largely understood as an empirical attempt to identify inputs that affect individuals' perceptions of fairness, and also attitudes, behaviors, and other consequences that result from perceived fairness.

Of current relevance, one especially important consequence of perceived fairness is personal well-being. That is, perceptions of justice and injustice are of interest to many because of their potential to affect the psychological and physical health of individuals (for recent reviews, see Elovainio, Kivimäki, and Vahtera, 2002; Jackson, Kubzansky, and Wright, 2006). Most clearly evident are associations between perceived fairness and mental health, especially including an inverse relationship between fairness and negative emotion (e.g., Lucas, 2009; Otto et al., 2006; Ritter, Benson, and Snyder, 1990). Moreover, organizational studies have shown that justice perceptions are linked to work-related anxiety and depression (e.g., Judge and Colquitt, 2004; Tepper, 2001; Ybema and VandenBos, 2010). In addition to mental well-being, justice perceptions are increasingly implicated in physical health, and this especially includes cardiovascular illness (Siegrist, 1996). Recent research supports that perceived unfairness is a unique causal determinant of coronary artery disease and myocardial infarction, and that perceived justice and fairness at work may protect cardiovascular health (De Vogli et al., 2007; Elovainio et al., 2006a, 2006b; Kivimäki et al., 2005; Kivimäki et al., 2006).

From a mechanistic standpoint, the health effects of justice are thought to occur predominantly through links to stress (e.g., Vermunt and Steensma, 2005). Stress pathways are empirically supported through studies linking perceived fairness to biological indices of stress reactivity, including activation of the sympathetic adrenal-medullary axis (Tomaka and Blascovich, 1994) and the hypothalamic-pituitary-adrenal axis (Vermunt, Peeters, and Berggren, 2007). Accordingly, it is suggested that perceived injustice acts as a stressor, and this has led some to proffer that a justice-based approach to stress in the workplace may be useful (e.g., Vermunt and Steensma,

2001). Similar to other well-known approaches (e.g., Lazarus and Folkman, 1984), a justice approach to stress implicates cognitive appraisals of stressors. This includes evaluations of the threat value of an unfair event (i.e., primary appraisal), and also whether personal resources are adequate to cope with unfairness (i.e., secondary appraisal). Links to cognitive appraisals and biological reactivity are consistent with research suggesting that justice is especially important to heart health and depression, which have also been strongly linked to stress. More recently, research has identified health behaviors such as smoking, diet, and exercise, and other forms of health detection and prevention as additional pathways through which justice beliefs may affect health (e.g., Lucas et al., 2008).

While links to health and well-being underscore that there are important consequences associated with fairness, another prominent direction involves theory and research on the underlying causes (i.e., the function) of justice perceptions. Accordingly, much of the psychological literature has focused on the proposed *justice motive*—a latent and universal desire among individuals to view the world as a fair and just place, and to subsequently defend a *belief in a just world* (Lerner, 1980). Of current interest, the justice motive suggests that fairness may be fundamentally important to individuals, even at the occasional expense of self-interest (Jost and Kay, 2010). For example, individuals may avoid behaving unethically in the workplace—even if doing so would be personally advantageous—precisely because a fundamental desire for justice outweighs the need for personal gain. Furthermore, theory and research on justice motivations have emphasized that exposure to injustice may threaten one's view of the world as fair and just. This, in turn, may lead individuals to adopt attitudes and actions aimed at protecting or restoring a belief in justice. One often-used defense strategy involves derogating victims of injustice in order to maintain one's view of the world as fair and just, especially through believing that victims "get what they deserve." However, many other beliefs and behaviors also aid in preserving justice beliefs, such as opting to help rather than blame victims of injustice (for a comprehensive review, see Hafer and Bègue, 2005). In general, the belief in a just world is thought to serve a palliative function, making the world seem orderly and predictable, and thus more manageable to individuals. In this way, the belief in a just world may act as a coping resource (Dalbert, 2001), implicating personal well-being in motivations to protect and endorse a belief in justice. This health-protective function of justice has ultimately led to descriptions of justice motivations as a double-edged sword, inasmuch as defending a belief in justice may protect individual well-being while simultaneously encouraging individuals to either endorse or engage in callous treatment of others.

Given the apparent ethical connotations of many just world preservation strategies, such as opting to help or blame victims of injustice, and also parallels to psychological research on stress and coping, there would seem to be considerable potential in applying a justice motive approach to the study of workplace ethics and worker well-being. In general, we encourage readers of this chapter to consider that work-related health and wellness might ultimately stem from a desire to protect one's view of the world or workplace as fair and just, and that there are likely to be ethical implications of associated attitudes and behaviors for the victims, perpetrators, and witnesses of unethical work practices. For example, deciding whether to report a coworker for a perceived unethical behavior such as bullying poses a dilemma that could simultaneously reflect one's need to maintain a belief in justice and desire to diminish anger or anxiety. Moreover, one's motivation to maintain a belief in a just world could provide psychological justification to engage in, or even personally endure workplace bullying. Although defense of justice possibly underlies links between workplace ethics and worker well-being, the current chapter does not intend to exhaustively consider links to a broad justice motive. Rather, our primary goal is to illuminate the potential of *specific kinds* of justice judgments to link unethical work behavior to health and well-being. We thus focus on two kinds of justice judgments. First, we consider the potential of unethical work practices to transmit links between situational or *state judgments of justice* in the workplace and worker illness. Second, we consider a probable role of dispositional tendencies or *trait justice beliefs.*

STATE JUSTICE JUDGMENTS, ETHICS AT WORK, AND WORKER WELL-BEING

In general, situational or state justice refers to perceptions of fairness that are associated with specific places and social interactions, or other precise occurrences. Compared to trait justice beliefs, situational justice judgments are context specific and adaptable to evaluations of particular situations or social settings. Of current interest is the *organizational justice* framework, which encompasses perceptions of fairness that are specifically associated with workplace situations and contexts (e.g., Colquitt, Greenberg, and Zapata-Phelan, 2005). Three long-standing and well-recognized kinds of justice are encased within the organizational justice framework. *Distributive justice* refers to perceptions of fairness associated with decision outcomes and resource allocations (Adams, 1965; Walster, Walster, and Berscheid, 1978). *Procedural justice* refers to perceived fairness that is associated with the decision processes used to determine outcomes and distributions (Greenberg, 1993; Lind and Tyler, 1988; Thibaut and Walker, 1975). Finally, *interactional justice* refers to fairness that is associated with treatment accorded to people during the implementation of allocation procedures (Bies and Moag, 1986).

One prospect suggested by an organizational justice framework is that evaluations of workplace ethics might *reflect* perceptions of distributive, procedural, and interactional justice in the workplace. In turn, perceived workplace ethics might act as a mechanism linking workers' organizational justice judgments to workplace health and well-being. As such, we propose an *ethics mediation framework* as a potentially useful starting point for linking situational justice judgments to well-being at work. In doing so, we propose that perceptions of justice at work may affect worker health through perceptions of workplace practices as ethical or unethical. Currently, we suggest use of the organizational justice framework to catalogue and compare the health effects of antecedent justice perceptions that, in turn, are transmitted by perceptions of workplace ethics. Specifically, we briefly consider possibilities associated with each of the three sources of organizational justice, including a potential for ethics to mediate conjoint effects of organizational justice judgments on worker health.

Distributive Justice

Distributive justice suggests that evaluations of workplace outcomes and allocations as fair or unfair may be reflected in workers' perceptions of their workplace as ethical or unethical. In terms of ethics and well-being, initial questions could involve the specific distributive justice criteria that are implicated in perceived ethics violations. For example, equity theory emphasizes that workers evaluate fairness according to a ratio of outcomes to inputs, and that social comparison is used by workers to assess whether ratios are proportionally balanced (Adams, 1965; Walster, Walster, and Berscheid, 1978). It could be that deviations from perceived equity especially lead to a judgment that one's workplace is unethical, and that equity-based ethics violations ultimately produce poor workplace health. Beyond equity, workers may use other allocation criteria such as equality, merit, seniority, or need to assess distributive justice in the workplace and, in turn, to consider whether ethics violations have taken place (for a review, see Reis, 1987). Thus, questions such as whether or when uses of different distributive principles result in greater perceived ethical breaches seem especially noteworthy.

Another possibility highlighted by distributive justice concerns whether particular outcome domains result in the kinds of perceived ethics violations that affect worker health. That is, although emphasis is usually placed on the psychological evaluation of financial exchanges that occur within the workplace (e.g., Walster, Walster, and Berscheid 1978), distributive justice principles may be used to consider whether fairness exists in other workplace allocation domains. For example, Foa and Foa (1974) catalogued six different types of resources that may be exchanged by individuals, including money, goods, status, love, information, and services. It could be that ethics violations associated with some of these resource domains affect health more acutely than others. For example, perceived ethics violations stemming from a perceived unethical promotion (i.e., misallocation of workplace status) might affect worker depression more or differently than violations involving wages. Another possibility is that resource domains are uniquely linked to *specific* physical or psychological illnesses. For example, while perceived ethics violations involving financial allocations could result in anger, violations involving status allocations might affect depression. Whether, when, and how specific workplace outcomes result in perceived greater ethics violations may be important for linking distributive justice to workplace ethics and worker well-being.

Procedural Justice

Another possibility is that workplace ethics serve to link procedural justice judgments to work-related health and illness. Procedural justice focuses not on the outcome per se, but rather on rules and procedures that are used to make allocation decisions (cf. Tyler and Smith, 1998). Like distributive justice, one possibility for ethics and well-being research concerns comparison of various known determinants of procedural justice. For example, Thibaut and Walker (1975) specified two antecedent criteria of procedural justice: *decision control* to address whether an individual has a direct say in a final outcome or decision, and *process control* or *voice* to address whether individuals feel they can contribute to the decision-making processes that lead up to a decision. Theory and research suggest that process control is often superior to decision control in terms of affecting a perception of justice, especially to the extent that having a voice may promote a feeling of control over an outcome (i.e., the instrumental functions of procedural justice). In the work context, it could be that a perceived lack of voice is especially stressful to workers in part because a lack of control over one's work may be viewed as unethical. For example, an employee who perceives discrimination or incivility from a supervisor could also feel a resulting lack of control over his or her work, and this in turn could result in stress and poor health (cf. Karasek and Theorell, 1990).

Another framework for considering procedural justice is suggested by Leventhal (1980), who identified six procedural justice principles, three of which are consistency, bias suppression, and accuracy. Questions about whether, when, or how much each of Leventhal's procedural justice principles contribute to perceived ethics violations in the workplace may also be of interest, especially in terms of the capacity of each input to ultimately affect worker health. For example, in understanding how unethical work practices relate procedural justice to worker well-being, it may be fundamentally important to first grasp whether workplace procedures seem more unethical when they lack consistency versus accuracy.

A related framework posed by Tyler (1994) has highlighted the importance of three factors in assessing the fairness of a procedure or set of procedures: neutrality, trust in the benevolence of the decision maker, and standing (i.e., respect and politeness). Similar to the above discussion about Leventhal's principles, side-by-side comparisons involving trust, neutrality, and standing could be undertaken. One additional direction suggested by Tyler's procedural justice framework might be to explore the relational foundations of links between procedural justice and perceived unethical workplaces. According to Tyler, a primary function of procedural justice is to communicate to individuals that they are valued and worthwhile members of a social group, inasmuch as fair rules and processes convey that one is valued by others (Lind, and Tyler, 1988; Tyler and Blader, 2003). It could be that social belongingness functions of procedural justice are intertwined with ethics perceptions, such that a lack of procedural justice in the workplace is conducive to poor worker health specifically because it communicates to workers that they are not socially valued by coworkers, supervisors, or organizations. In turn, a lack of social identity at work might lead to a perception that one's workplace is unethical, thereby placing workplace ethics as an intermediary between the social belongingness functions of procedural justice and worker health.

Interactional Justice

Interactional justice is thought to encompass two specific subtypes of justice: *interpersonal justice,* referring to employees' perceptions of fair and respectful treatment by a supervisor or authority, and *informational justice,* reflecting workers' views that allocations or procedures are adequately explained to them (see Colquitt, 2001). Not unlike distributive and procedural justice, interactional justice suggests that interpersonal and informational treatment may be connected to worker health through links to workplace ethics. For example, elements of interpersonal justice such as courteousness, honesty, and timeliness of feedback from a supervisor may be fundamental to creating a view of one's workplace as fair and ethical. Similarly, Bies and Shapiro (1987) have shown that adequate causal accounts—reasonable explanations for why a specific decision was made—contribute to perceptions of fairness through their effect on informational justice perceptions; it could be that providing employees with satisfying accounts for specific workplace decisions is necessary in order to foster a view of one's workplace as ethical. In parallel to distributive and procedural justice, the interactional component of organizational justice easily accommodates relative importance kinds of questions. For example, whether or when timeliness versus causal accounts are more important to a view of one's workplace as ethical may lead to important insights concerning the potential of workplace ethics to link interactional justice to worker health. Moreover, interactional justice seems easily amenable to considering the psychological underpinnings of justice health effects. Specifically, and similar to procedural justice, it may be that a lack interactional justice is conducive to an unethical workplace specifically because of perceived social support functions that are served by interpersonal and informational justice (see Fujishiro and Heaney, 2009).

Additional Considerations for Organizational Justice

In general, the preceding review illustrates that an organizational justice framework may be useful in permitting researchers to consider, simultaneously specify, and compare multiple sources of workplace justice, and to observe whether or when workplace ethics differentially link specific kinds of justice judgments to particular aspects of health and well-being. Thus far, our overview has highlighted that comparisons of antecedent justice criteria may be undertaken *within* organizational justice subtypes. Another direction might be to gauge relative importance *across* organizational justice types. Namely, distributive, procedural, and interactional justice might be overall compared with one another in terms of their potential to affect worker health via workplace ethics.

In parallel, it also may be fruitful to consider synergistic or combined effects of distributive, procedural, and interactional justice judgments, and whether workplace ethics mediate conjoint effects of organizational justice on worker health. For example, fair process effects are well recognized by justice researchers as describing the potential of procedural justice to alleviate negative consequences associated with unfair allocations (Folger et al., 1979). It could be that health effects of a perceived unfair work outcome might be lessened if workers at least perceive that they were allotted a high level of procedural, interpersonal, or informational justice; such interactive effects may also be transmitted through unethical work practices (for related examples, see Hui, Au, and Zhao, 2007; Tepper, 2001). Thus, researchers may wish to consider interactive effects of organizational justice criteria that reveal especially potent links between justice at work, perceived ethics, and worker health (see also Giacalone and Promislo, 2010).

TRAIT JUSTICE BELIEFS, UNETHICAL WORK BEHAVIOR, AND WORKER WELL-BEING

Although state justice judgments are one likely avenue through which unethical work behavior affects individual well-being, another important source involves individual differences characteristics or "trait" justice beliefs. A sizable literature supports not only the idea that justice judgments describe evaluations of specific situations or social encounters, but also that individuals may be characterized by their stable and enduring tendencies to perceive justice in the world (for reviews, see Dalbert, 2009; Furnham, 2003). Moreover, similar to state justice judgments, trait justice beliefs are thought to be multidimensional. Thus, a potential for nuanced connections to workplace ethics and well-being is again highlighted.

One initial possibility suggested by an individual differences approach is that justice and ethics conjointly influence worker health. In other words, the effects of workplace ethics on worker well-being may depend on the trait justice beliefs of individual workers. We thus propose an *ethics moderation framework* as one additional approach for connecting justice perceptions and workplace ethics to worker well-being, and we suggest that a moderator structure may be particularly suited to examining trait or individual difference conceptualizations of justice. Currently, we review and integrate two individual difference distinctions that seem especially promising in revealing ethics-moderated health effects of dispositional justice tendencies. For both distinctions, we highlight that dispositional tendencies to believe in justice might either prevent or promote negative health consequences that are associated with unethical work practices. These possibilities are aligned with research suggesting that strong justice beliefs often promote personal health (see Dalbert, 2001, for a review), but that violations of justice beliefs also may be stressful to individuals (Vermunt and Steensma, 2001).

Personal and General Justice Beliefs

One important and often-used individual difference partition is the distinction between personal and general justice beliefs (Bègue and Bastounis, 2003; Dalbert, 1999; Lipkus, Dalbert, and Siegler, 1996; Sutton and Douglas, 2005). *Personal justice beliefs* describe a stable propensity to view the world as fair to oneself, whereas *general justice beliefs* refer to the tendency to view the world in broad terms as fair and to believe in justice for others. Within the justice literature, there is strong support for conceptualizing and measuring personal and general justice beliefs as unique dispositional tendencies. Moreover, personal and general justice are known for divergent and mutually exclusive links to health and social attitudes; whereas beliefs that the world is fair to oneself tend to predict measures of personal well-being, beliefs about justice for others are typically linked to the endorsement of harsh social attitudes. Thus, the distinction between personal and general justice illustrates the double-edged nature of justice by showing that tendencies to perceive fairness can promote both personal well-being and also intolerant views of others.

Conjoint effects of workplace ethics and dispositional justice tendencies on workplace health could readily encompass personal justice beliefs. One specific possibility is that unethical workplace practices are especially stressful and ultimately compromise the health of workers who believe that the world is personally fair and just. In other words, because unethical work practices could violate a core dispositional tendency about justice for oneself, strong personal justice beliefs could connote an increased susceptibility to negative health effects that are associated with unethical work practices. An alternative and perhaps more likely possibility is that personal justice beliefs *protect* workers from the negative health effects of unethical workplace practices, such that workplace ethics violations are less compromising to individuals who possess a strong sense of personal justice. This latter possibility is supported by numerous studies showing that justice beliefs are negatively associated with stress, and that justice beliefs are fundamental to personal well-being through their capacity to deflect health consequences associated with stress (cf. Dalbert, 2001). Thus, while future research might recognize and explore a potential for personal justice beliefs to connote susceptibility to negative health consequences of unethical work practices, an initial hypothesis might implicate resiliency or health protective functions of personal justice beliefs, wherein a belief in justice for oneself reduces negative health effects associated with unethical work practices.

While competing possibilities suggested by personal justice beliefs seem relatively straight-forward, the potential for general justice beliefs to affect personal health via workplace ethics is less obvious. Nevertheless, it also may be that general justice beliefs affect workplace health through interactive relationships with unethical workplace practices. As such, justice researchers may wish to consider workplace ethics as a unique context for reexamining the hitherto exclusive link between personal justice beliefs and well-being. One specific and novel possibility is that general justice beliefs help to *sustain* unethical work practices, and that general justice beliefs affect *vicarious* rather than personal health consequences in the workplace. In other words, while personal justice beliefs may be implicated in personal workplace health, general justice beliefs may be implicated in general workplace health, possibly through encouraging unethical workplace practices that affect the health of others. This possibility dovetails especially well with workplace ethics theoretical frameworks, which recognize that unethical work practices can affect not only the health of victims, but also perpetrators and witnesses (e.g., Giacalone and Promislo, 2010). Moreover, recognizing a potential to affect health vicariously seems appropriate given that general justice beliefs are especially implicated in harsh or dismissive (i.e., unethical) attitudes toward others. For example, a strong belief in justice for others might lead a witness to view an instance of workplace incivility not as unethical, but rather as an occasion where a coworker has "earned" harsh or disrespectful treatment. In turn, a view of workplace incivility as fair and deserved could perpetuate an uncivil workplace to the extent that the health of others is ultimately compromised. However, like personal justice beliefs, another possibility is that general justice beliefs *protect* rather than impede vicarious workplace health. For example, individuals who possess a strong belief in justice for others may be inclined to confront rather than psychologically justify unethical work practices. Thus, future research may wish to recognize and explore the boundaries of the competing susceptibility and resiliency possibilities that are associated with general justice beliefs and vicarious workplace health.

Procedural and Distributive Justice Beliefs

Beyond the distinction between personal and general justice beliefs, another recent individual difference partition suggests that people also may be characterized by tendencies to perceive distributive and procedural justice. That is, procedural and distributive justice beliefs also encompass stable dispositional tendencies to perceive outcomes and allocations (i.e., *distributive justice beliefs)* versus rules and processes (i.e., *procedural justice beliefs)* as fair and deserved (Lucas et al., 2007). Of current interest, and similar to personal and general justice, we suggest that procedural and distributive justice beliefs may be linked to well-being at work through conjoint relationships with unethical work practices. However, whereas general and personal justice beliefs may be linked to personal and vicarious well-being at work in mutually exclusive ways, we suggest that procedural and distributive justice beliefs may be simultaneously implicated in *both* personal and vicarious workplace health. That is, distributive and procedural justice each may link to *specific kinds* of personal and vicarious health, such that their conjoint effects with workplace ethics are graduated rather than mutually exclusive. For example, whereas personal justice beliefs are exclusively linked to emotional health, prior research has shown that distributive justice is especially associated with enhanced positive affect, while procedural justice plays an especially prominent role in reducing negative affect (Lucas, 2009; Weiss, Suckow, and Cropanzano, 1999). In parallel, while general justice beliefs are thought to better link to all forms of social attitudes, distributive justice beliefs may be particularly linked to *harsh* views or treatment of others, while procedural justice beliefs may connote *inclusive, prosocial,* or *benevolent* social attitudes (e.g., Lucas et al., 2011).

A Four-Factor Approach

One additional approach to connecting justice beliefs to workplace ethics and health comes from very recent work in which the distributive and procedural justice distinction is integrated with the personal and general justice beliefs to specify four unique dispositional justice tendencies (Lucas, Zhdanova, and Alexander, 2011). In this approach, individuals may be described by tendencies to believe in distributive and procedural justice for self, and also distributive and procedural justice for others. Initial research suggests that using a four-factor measurement approach could be useful in refining links between dispositional justice beliefs, health, and social attitudes. For example, Lucas and colleagues (2011) showed that while distributive justice beliefs for self exclusively predict measures of *personal health,* such as self-rated health, procedural justice beliefs for self exclusively predicted *interpersonal health,* such as conflict at work. We foresee similar capabilities for distilling connections to workplace health in applying a four-factor measurement approach to unethical work practices. For example, the aforementioned potential for personal and general justice beliefs to either enhance or lessen the health effects of unethical work practices could depend on distributive and procedural justice tendencies, with each benchmarking a specific health susceptibility or resiliency moderator influence.

In Figure 16.1, we suggest initial possibilities for connecting ethics and workplace health to four-factor measurement of distributive and procedural justice beliefs for self and others. As previously suggested, we propose that personal justice beliefs best predict personal workplace health, while general justice beliefs best predict vicarious workplace health. Moreover, we suggest that distributive and procedural justice tendencies may distill links to specific forms of personal and vicarious health. Specifically, we suggest that beliefs about distributive justice for self encompass links to *personal* health measures, while beliefs about procedural justice for self predict *interpersonal* health measures. In similar fashion, Figure 16.1 outlines possibilities for

Figure 16.1   **A Four-Factor Model of Trait Justice Beliefs, Workplace Ethics, and Work Well-Being**

SOCIAL IDENTITY

	Justice beliefs for self	Justice beliefs for others
Distributive justice beliefs	**Distributive Justice for Self** Personal identity and proself values (Interactions with unethical work practices link to personal health measures, such as self-reported health)	**Distributive Justice for Others** Social identity and proself values (Interactions with unethical practices link to vicarious workplace illness through encouraging harsh workplace attitudes)
Procedural justice beliefs	**Procedural Justice for Self** Personal identity and prosocial values (Interactions with unethical work practices link to interpersonal health measures, such as conflict at work)	**Procedural Justice for Others** Social identity and prosocial values (Interactions with unethical practices link to vicarious workplace health through encouraging benevolent workplace attitudes)

SOCIAL VALUE ORIENTATION

vicarious workplace health; whereas beliefs about distributive justice for others are hypothesized to predict harsh (i.e., unethical) attitudes that negatively affect vicarious workplace health, beliefs about procedural justice for others are hypothesized to predict benevolent workplace attitudes, and to positively affect or protect vicarious workplace health from unethical work practices. For all four individual differences, we underscore that potential effects on workplace health encompass conjoint associations with unethical work practices. For example, we would expect a strong belief in distributive justice for others to strengthen the negative and vicarious health consequences of unethical work practices.

Figure 16.1 also incorporates social identity and social value orientation theoretical frameworks that have been previously suggested as supporting four-factor measurement of dispositional justice beliefs. Social identity theory (Tajfel and Turner, 1979) suggests that individuals possess multiple identities that include both a "personal self" and "social selves." A personal identity defines the individual in terms of his or her self-knowledge of perceived unique attributes, while social identities define the individual in terms of perceived membership in a particular social group or culture. In specifying a four-factor measurement model, Lucas and colleagues (2011) have suggested that measuring personal justice beliefs may implicate tendencies toward personal identity, while measurement of general justice beliefs may implicate social identification tendencies. In parallel, social value orientation (McClintock, 1978) refers to a relatively stable pattern of preferences for allotments between self and others. Proself individuals prefer to maximize personal outcomes, whereas prosocial individuals prefer to maximize shared or joint outcomes. Similar to links between social identity theory and measurement of personal and general justice beliefs, Lucas and colleagues (2011) have suggested that a proself value orientation may underlie measurement of distributive justice tendencies, while prosocial tendencies are benchmarked by the measurement of procedural justice beliefs. One potential benefit of using a four-factor measurement approach to connect justice tendencies to unethical workplace practices and worker health thus may be its potential to bridge social identity theory and social value orientation, such that justice beliefs act as a conduit for linking workplace ethics and work well-being to these fundamental social psychological theories. For example, one's beliefs about procedural justice for self may be associated with reduced interpersonal conflict at work specifically because of links to both personal identity and prosocial values.

AN INTEGRATIVE CONCEPTUAL FRAMEWORK

In this chapter, we have suggested that unethical work practices may act as a mechanism linking organizational justice judgments to workplace health, and that dispositional differences in these justice judgments influence workplace health by moderating the health and illness effects of unethical work practices. Moreover, we have suggested that health consequences of justice can include effects of justice on both personal and vicarious workplace health, and that these effects are produced by stress and health behavior effects of unethical work practices. To integrate and summarize these assertions, we propose the theoretical framework presented in Figure 16.2. At its core, this framework emphasizes that the impact of unethical work practices on workplace health is fundamentally driven by effects of justice perceptions on worker stress and (un)healthy behavior. Organizational justice judgments, including workers' perceptions of distributive, procedural, and interactional justice, precede individual perceptions of unethical workplaces, while employees' dispositional justice beliefs—including tendencies to believe in distributive and procedural justice for selves and others—are implicated for their potential to moderate relationships between unethical work practices and stress.

Although this framework may be useful for guiding initial research, we do not wish to exclude numerous other possibilities for linking trait and state justice to workplace ethics and health. For example, it is entirely conceivable that workplace ethics also mediate the health effects of trait justice beliefs, or that state justice beliefs moderate the health consequences of unethical work practices. Moreover, state and trait justice perceptions presumably work together as both antecedents and moderators of ethics-related health effects. Thus, the currently proposed conceptual framework should not be taken as an attempt to exclude other possibilities for linking trait and state justice judgments to ethics and health. Rather, we assert only that initial research may benefit from first conceptualizing state justice beliefs as components of mediated effects, and trait justice beliefs as useful as moderator influences on the links between unethical work practices and worker well-being.

LIMITATIONS AND OTHER DIRECTIONS

The current chapter has suggested several components of psychological justice that may be relevant to unethical work practices, and also directions for initially considering how justice perceptions may interface with unethical work practices to affect worker health. Specifically, we introduced theory and research on justice motivations, organizational justice, and individual differences tendencies to suggest numerous possibilities for future research. Managers, practitioners, and scholars who are interested in the health effects of unethical work practices would do well to consider both state and trait justice criteria by incorporating formal measurements into investigations of the linkages between workplace ethics and health. Measurement of justice concepts may be easily attained by administering self-report individual differences measures to workers during initial assessment periods (e.g., Lucas et al., 2011), or by embedding well-known organizational justice measures (e.g., Colquitt, 2001) into

Figure 16.2   A Proposed Conceptual Framework for Linking State and Trait Justice to Unethical Work Practices and Work Well-Being

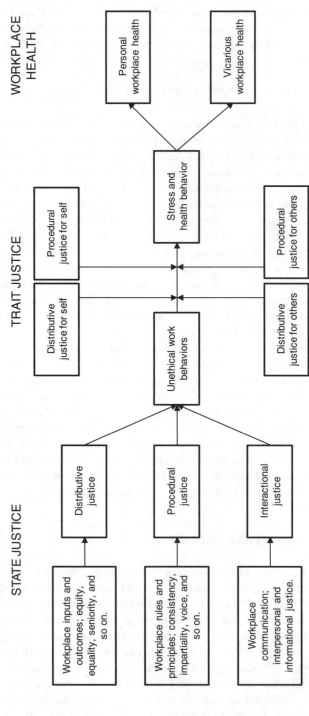

assessments of psychological climate or other workplace characteristics that are often administered in attempts to ascertain health effects of psychological workplace influences. We further encourage the formal examination of hypotheses involving the capacity of workplace ethics perceptions to mediate the health effects of workplace justice perceptions, and also the possibilities encompassing the conjoint influences of trait justice and workplace ethics on worker health. Both approaches are easily amenable to many health measurement strategies, and this includes both self-report and biological measurement of health and wellness in the workplace. While the currently reviewed justice concepts should offer researchers a number of useful directions, it is beyond the scope of the current chapter to introduce all of the possibilities associated with linking the health effects of unethical work practices to research on justice and fairness. Many additional justice concepts such as morality, climate, and culture, may nonetheless be useful in pursuing links between justice and ethics at work. To conclude, we briefly entertain two specific possibilities.

One possibility encompasses what might generally be termed "reverse pathways" between justice, ethics, and health. Specifically, and somewhat in contrast to the current review, recent research has highlighted that perceived organizational injustice may reflect rather than produce depressive symptoms in the workplace (Lang, et al. 2011). While the current chapter has largely proposed that justice and ethics are antecedents of workplace health and illness, it is possible that they additionally or instead function as consequences. For example, while we suggest that perceived injustice may lead to poor workplace health through links to perceived unethical work practices, poor health might instead lead workers to view their workplace as unethical, and this in turn could manifest as diminished perceptions of organizational justice. Accordingly, researchers might recognize the potential for justice to reflect rather than precede links between unethical work practices and workplace health. The use of prospective or experimental studies to disentangle the causal nature of these relationships thus appears to be one important future direction. However, we believe that unethical work practices could potentially mediate or moderate links between justice and well-being irrespective of their causal direction and, as such, the proposed conceptual framework might still prove useful in pursuit of a longitudinal research program.

A second possibility concerns the potential to incorporate other forms of both state and trait conceptualizations of justice into the currently proposed framework. In terms of state conceptualizations, one specific possibility concerns a potential for retributive or restorative forms of justice to contribute to links between workplace ethics and well-being. Specifically, it is possible that one's desire to restore justice after being victimized, or to punish the perpetrators of unethical work practices, may produce health and wellness consequences for workers. One related and promising direction could encompass recent research on the links between justice and forgiveness (e.g., Lucas, et. al. 2010; Strelan and Sutton, 2011). To the extents that forgiveness has been shown to both reflect justice concerns and protect personal well-being and that forgiveness may be utilized by individuals to cope with unethical workplace behavior, it may be fruitful to consider issues of restorative justice and unethical workplace practices by examining revenge and forgiveness as possible justice-based and health-affecting social responses. Regarding trait conceptualizations of justice, we suggest that other distinctions not reviewed herein may prove useful. For example, Maes (1998) suggested a distinction between the tendency to believe that justice has already occurred (imminent justice) or rather that justice will eventually occur (ultimate justice); it could be that this distinction also provides a useful pathway for exploring the connections between justice, workplace ethics, and worker health. Another intriguing but hitherto unexplored possibility may involve trait conceptualizations of interactional justice that would describe enduring tendencies to perceive informational and interpersonal justice in the world or workplace, which could also possibly moderate the health effects of unethical work practices.

REFERENCES

Adams, J.S. 1965. Inequity in social exchange. In *Advances in Experimental Social Psychology,* ed. L. Berkowitz, Vol. 2, 267–299. New York: Academic Press.

Bègue, L., and Bastounis, M. 2003. Two spheres of belief in justice: Extensive support for the bidimensional model of belief in a just world. *Journal of Personality,* 71, 435–463.

Bies, R.J., and Moag, J.F. 1986. Interactional justice: Communication criteria of fairness. *Research on Negotiations in Organizations,* 1, 43–55.

Bies, R.J., and Shapiro, D.L. 1987. Interactional justice: The influence of causal accounts. *Social Justice Research,* 1, 199–218.

Brockner, J. 2010. *A Contemporary Look at Organizational Justice: Multiplying Insult Times Injury.* New York: Routledge.

Colquitt, J.A. 2001. On the dimensionality of organizational justice: A construct validation of a measure. *Journal of Applied Psychology,* 86, 386–400.

Colquitt, J.A., Greenberg, J., and Zapata-Phelan, C.P. 2005. What is organizational justice? A historical overview. In *The Handbook of Organizational Justice,* ed. J. Greenberg and J.A. Colquitt, 3–56. Mahwah, NJ: Erlbaum.

Cropanzano, R., and Wright, T.A. 2011. The impact of organizational justice on occupational health. In *Handbook of Occupational Health Psychology,* 2nd ed., ed. J.C. Quick and L.E. Tetrick, 205–219. Washington, DC: American Psychological Association.

Dalbert, C. 1999. The world is more just for me than generally: About the personal belief in a just world scale validity. *Social Justice Research,* 12, 79–98.

———. 2001. *The Justice Motive as a Personal Resource: Dealing with Challenges and Critical Life Events.* New York: Plenum.

———. 2009. Belief in a just world. In *Handbook of Individual Differences in Social Behavior,* ed. M.R. Leary and R.H. Hoyle, 288–297. New York: Guilford.

De Vogli, R., Ferrie, J.E., Chandola, T., Kivimäki. M., and Marmot, M.G. 2007. Unfairness and health: Evidence from the Whitehall II study. *Journal of Epidemiology and Community Health,* 61, 513–518.

Elovainio M., Kivimäki, M., and Vahtera J. 2002. Organizational justice: Evidence of a new psychosocial predictor of health. *American Journal of Public Health,* 92, 105–108.

Elovainio, M., Kivimäki, M., Puttonen, S., Lindholm, H., Pohjonen, T., and Sinervo, T. 2006a. Organizational injustice and impaired cardiovascular regulation among female employees. *Occupational and Environmental Medicine,* 63, 141–144.

Elovainio, M., Leino-Arjas, P., Vahtera, J., and Kivimäki, M. 2006b. Justice at work and cardiovascular mortality: A prospective cohort study. *Journal of Psychosomatic Research,* 61, 271–274.

Foa, U.G., and Foa, E.B. 1974. *Societal Structures of the Mind.* Springfield, IL: Thomas.

Folger, R., Rosenfield, D., Grove, J., and Corkran, L. 1979. Effects of "voice" and peer opinions on responses to inequity. *Journal of Personality and Social Psychology,* 37, 2243–2261.

Fujishiro, K., and Heaney, C.A. 2009. Justice at work, job stress, and employee health. *Health Education and Behavior,* 36, 487–504.

Furnham, A. 2003. Belief in a just world: Research progress over the past decade. *Personality and Individual Differences,* 34, 795–817.

Giacalone, R.A., and Promislo, M.D. 2010. Unethical and unwell: Decrements in well-being and unethical activity at work. *Journal of Business Ethics,* 9, 275–297.

Greenberg, J. 1993. The social side of fairness: Interpersonal and informational classes of organizational justice. In *Justice in the Workplace: Approaching Fairness in Human Resource Management,* ed. R. Cropanzano, 79–103. Hillsdale, NJ: Erlbaum.

———. 2011. Organizational justice: The dynamics of fairness in the workplace. In *Handbook of Industrial and Organizational Psychology,* ed. S. Zedeck, 227–327. Washington, DC: American Psychological Association.

Hafer, C.L., and Bègue, L. 2005. Experimental research on just-world theory: Problems, developments, and future challenges. *Psychological Bulletin,* 131, 128–167.

Hui, M.K., Au, K.Y., and Zhao, X. 2007. Interactional justice and the fair process effect: The role of outcome uncertainty. *Journal of Experimental Social Psychology,* 43, 210–220.

Jackson, B., Kubzansky, L.D., and Wright, R.J. 2006. Linking perceived unfairness to physical health: The perceived unfairness model. *Review of General Psychology,* 10, 21–40.

Jost, J.T., and Kay, A.C. 2010. Social justice: History, theory, and research. In *Handbook of Social Psychology,* 5th ed., vol. 2, ed. S.T. Fiske, D. Gilbert, and G. Lindzey, 1122–1165. Hoboken, NJ: Wiley.

Judge, T.J., and Colquitt, J.A. 2004. Organizational justice and stress: The mediating role of work-family conflict. *Journal of Applied Psychology,* 89, 395–404.

Karasek, R.A., and Theorell, T. 1990. *Healthy Work: Stress, Productivity, and the Reconstruction of Working Life.* New York: Basic Books.

Kivimäki, M., Virtanen, M., Elovainio, M., Kouvonen, A., Väänanen, A., and Vahtera, J. 2006. Work stress in the etiology of coronary heart disease: A meta-analysis. *Scandinavian Journal of Work and Environmental Health,* 32, 431–442.

Kivimäki, M., Ferrie, J.E., Brunner, E., Head, J., Shipley, M.J., Vahtera, J., and Marmot, M.G. 2005. Justice at work and reduced risk of coronary heart disease among employees. *Archives of Internal Medicine,* 165, 2245–2251.

Lang, J., Bliese, P.D., Lang, J.W.B., and Adler, A.B. 2011. Work gets unfair for the depressed: Cross-lagged relations between organizational justice perceptions and depressive symptoms. *Journal of Applied Psychology,* 96, 602–618.

Lazarus, R.S., and Folkman, S. 1984. *Stress, Appraisal and Coping.* New York: Springer-Verlag.

Lerner, M.J. 1980. *The Belief in a Just World: A Fundamental Delusion.* New York: Plenum.

Leventhal, G.S. 1980. What should be done with equity theory? New approaches to the study of fairness in social relationships. In *Social Exchanges: Advances in Theory and Research,* ed. K. Gergen, M. Greenberg, and R. Willis, 27–55. New York: Plenum.

Lind, E.A., and Tyler, T.R. 1988. *The Social Psychology of Procedural Justice.* New York: Plenum.

Lipkus, I.M., Dalbert, C., and Siegler, I.C. 1996. The importance of distinguishing the belief in a just world for self versus others. *Personality and Social Psychology Bulletin,* 22, 666–677.

Lucas, T. 2009. Justifying outcomes versus processes: Procedural and distributive justice beliefs as predictors of positive and negative affectivity. *Current Psychology,* 4, 249–265.

Lucas, T.; Zhdanova, L.; and Alexander, S. 2011. Procedural and distributive justice beliefs for self and others: Assessment of a four-factor individual differences model. *Journal of Individual Differences,* 32, 14–25.

Lucas, T., Alexander, S., Firestone, I.J., and LeBreton, J.M. 2007. Development and initial validation of a procedural and distributive just world measure. *Personality and Individual Differences,* 43, 71–82.

Lucas, T., Alexander S., Firestone, I.J., and LeBreton, J.M. 2008. Just world beliefs, perceived stress, and health behavior: The impact of a procedurally just world. *Psychology and Health,* 23, 849–866.

Lucas, T., Young, J.D., Zhdanova, L., and Alexander, S. 2010. Self and other justice beliefs, impulsivity, rumination, and forgiveness: Justice beliefs can both prevent and promote forgiveness. *Personality and Individual Differences,* 49, 851–856.

Lucas, T., Rudolph, C.W., Barkho, E., Zhdanova, L., and Casper, C. 2011. Procedural justice for others and inclusive treatment of immigrants. Unpublished manuscript.

Maes, J. 1998. Immanent justice and ultimate justice: Two ways of believing in justice. In *Responses to Victimizations and Belief in the Just World,* ed. L. Montada, and M. Lerner, 43–53. New York: Plenum.

McClintock, C.G. 1978. Social values: Their definition, measurement and development. *Journal of Research and Development in Education,* 12, 121–137.

Otto, K., Boos, A., Dalbert, C., Schöps, D., and Hoyer, J. 2006. Posttraumatic symptoms, depression, and anxiety of flood victims: The impact of the belief in a just world. *Personality and Individual Differences,* 40, 1075–1084.

Reis, H.T. 1987. The nature of the justice motive: Some thoughts on operation, internalization, and justification. In *Social Comparison, Social Justice, and Relative Deprivation: Theoretical, Empirical, and Policy Perspectives,* ed. J.C. Masters and W.P. Smith, 131–150. Hillsdale, NJ: Erlbaum.

Ritter, C., Benson, D.E., and Snyder, C. 1990. Belief in a just world and depression. *Sociological Perspectives,* 33, 235–252.

Siegrist, J. 1996. Adverse health effects of high-effort/low-reward conditions. *Journal of Occupational Health Psychology,* 1, 27–41.

Strelan, P., and Sutton, R.M. 2011. When just world beliefs promote and when they inhibit forgiveness. *Personality and Individual Differences,* 50, 163–168.

Sutton, R.M., and Douglas, K.M. 2005. Justice for all, or just for me? More support for self-other differences in just world beliefs. *Personality and Individual Differences,* 39, 637–645.

Tajfel, H., and Turner, J.C. 1979. An integrative theory of intergroup conflict. In *The Social Psychology of Intergroup Relations,* ed. W.G. Austin and S. Worchel, 33–47. Monterey, CA: Brooks-Cole.

Tepper, B.E. 2001. Health consequences of organizational injustice: Tests of main and interactive effects. *Organizational Behavior and Human Decision Processes,* 86, 197–215.

Thibaut, J., and Walker, L. 1975. *Procedural Justice: A Psychological Analysis.* Hillsdale, NJ: Erlbaum.

Tomaka, J., and Blascovich, J. 1994. Effects of justice beliefs on cognitive appraisal of and subjective physiological and behavioral responses to potential stress. *Journal of Personality and Social Psychology,* 67, 732–740.

Tyler, T.R. 1994. Psychological models of the justice motive: antecedents of distributive and procedural justice. *Journal of Personality and Social Psychology,* 67, 850–863.

Tyler, T.R., and Blader, S.L. 2003. The group engagement model: Procedural justice, social identity, and cooperative behavior. *Personality and Social Psychology Review,* 7, 349–361.

Tyler, T.R., and Smith, H.J. 1998. Social justice and social movements. In *The Handbook of Social Psychology,* 4th ed., vol. 2, ed. D.T. Gilbert, S.T. Fiske, and G. Lindzey, 595–629. Boston: McGraw-Hill.

Vermunt, R., and Steensma, H. 2001. Stress and justice in organizations: An exploration into justice processes with the aim to find mechanisms to reduce stress. In *Justice in the Workplace,* vol. 2, ed. R. Cropanzano, 27–48. Mahwah, NJ: Erlbaum.

———. 2005. How can justice be used to manage stress in organizations. In *Handbook of Organizational Justice,* ed. J. Greenberg and J.A. Colquitt, 383–410. Mahwah, NJ: Erlbaum.

Vermunt, R., Peeters, Y., and Berggren, K. 2007. How fair treatment affects saliva cortisol release in stressed low and high type-A behavior individuals. *Scandinavian Journal of Psychology,* 48, 547–555.

Walster, E., Walster, G.W., and Berscheid, E. 1978. *Equity: Theory and Research.* Boston: Allyn and Bacon.

Weiss, H.M., Suckow, K., and Cropanzano, R. 1999. Effects of justice conditions on discrete emotions. *Journal of Applied Psychology,* 84, 786–794.

Ybema, J.F., and VandenBos, K. 2010. Effects of organizational justice on depressive symptoms and sickness absence: A longitudinal perspective. *Social Science and Medicine,* 70, 1609–1617.

17

ETHICS, EMPATHY, AND EMPLOYMENT

Seeking a Compassionate Workplace

NOREEN TEHRANI

Human beings are by nature social animals and reliant upon creating and maintaining positive relationships within their family, group, and community to protect their safety and emotional well-being. This ethical, compassionate, and altruistic attitude is not a recent development (Boehm, 2008) but one that has been present for at least 45,000 years. The evolution of the human species has favored altruistic individuals capable of supportive relationships, starting at birth (Bowlby, 1979) and continuing throughout life (Spinelli, 2007). These reciprocal relationships are central to the effective and healthy functioning of individuals, groups, and society (Keltner, Haidt, and Shiota, 2006). The ability to empathize is fundamental to building successful human relationships and has been described at two levels: first, cognitive empathy, in which an observer assesses the behavior or appearance of another person, and thus is able to infer the person's mental state (Baron-Cohen and Wheelwright, 2004); and second, emotional empathy, in which an observer identifies with and responds to another person's emotional state (Eisenberg and Miller, 1987). While the presence of empathy is generally regarded positively, growing evidence indicates that people with high levels of empathy are prone to developing burnout, compassion fatigue, and secondary traumatic stress due to their ability to accurately pick up and empathize with other people's distress (Adams, Boscarino, and Figley, 2006; Figley, 1995; Saakvitne and Pearlman, 1996). Research using brain imaging has discovered the neurological processes involved in the creation and maintenance of empathy (Baron-Cohen, 2011; Damasio, 2003; Gilbert, 2005).

Despite our evolved tendency to show empathy and behave in a prosocial manner, some people behave in ways that are harmful to themselves and others. While some writers and researchers regard evil and human cruelty as an integral or unavoidable part of human nature (e.g., Daniels, 2005; Frey-Rohn, 1967; Hare, 1993), a view frequently presented by the media when reporting distressing crimes, this is not a position held by all psychologists, researchers, and theologians (Baron-Cohen, 2011; Esslemont, 1970) who regard that the concept of evil as unhelpful in explaining and dealing with antisocial or unethical behaviors. The position taken in this chapter is that in order to understand and address the harm caused by cruel and callous acts, it is necessary to look beyond a simple naming and blaming of individuals identified as wrongdoers or perpetrators and to identify reasons for their behavior and seek solutions.

However, regardless of the reason for unethical and damaging behaviors, it is clear that in the workplace these behaviors can have a detrimental impact on the health and well-being of the victims, witnesses, and unwilling perpetrators as well as on the organization itself. However, people do not need to have a direct experience of bad behaviors to be harmed; families, friends, and counselors of the victims along with investigators of illegal, unethical, or callous behaviors can find that their secondary exposure to unethical behaviors affects their health and well-being.

This chapter examines workplace ethics and well-being from a psychological perspective and is in four sections. The first section looks at the development of empathy and its importance in maintaining and supporting ethical behaviors. The second section explores the effects of unethical acts on organizations and individuals, using case studies to illustrate a range of unethical behaviors and how these have affected targets, observers, families, and friends. The third section concentrates on the harm experienced by witnesses, colleagues, investigators, and supporters exposed to unethical and other damaging behaviors. Finally, the fourth section offers suggestions on how organizations can become more empathetic and how individuals may grow following exposure to unethical exposure.

THE EVOLUTION OF EMPATHY

The evolution of empathy has been identified as an essential precursor to the development of compassionate behaviors in many animal species. Research undertaken by Baron-Cohen (2011) increases our understanding of unethical and antisocial behaviors. Grounded in his work on autism, Baron-Cohen examined extreme cruelty and discovered that these behaviors become possible when individuals develop an intense focus on their immediate interests, goals, wishes, or plans paying little attention to the thoughts, needs, or feelings of others. At times, most people engage in goal-focused thinking, particularly when trying to achieve a highly valued objective or financial inducement; however, a few dysfunctional people exist in a constant state of zero empathy. Empathy is created within the brain's "empathy circuit," which was recently discovered in brain imaging (Damasio, 2003; Preston and de Waal, 2002). The circuit is made up of a set of interconnected pathways that are highly flexible and responsive to changing circumstances and emotional states. While the empathy circuit is hardwired in the brain, its functioning is modified for good or ill by life experiences, particularly the emotional attachments created with a parent or caregiver. Early experiences of sympathy, compassion, love, and other positive emotions have been shown to be essential in the development of morality (Skoe, 2010). As with most capacities, the presence of empathy in the population follows a normal distribution curve with most people falling within the middle range and small numbers being either hyper-empathetic or having little or zero empathy. Although low levels of empathy may be permanent in a few people, it is usually transient in people who are under extreme pressure to achieve targets and find the threat of failure so great that they are unable to sustain any meaningful attention to the needs or feelings of others. While cognitive and emotional empathy tend to produce prosocial behaviors, very high levels of emotional empathy can be harmful, in that highly empathetic individuals find themselves constantly battered by the emotional stress of having to deal with their emotional responses to people and situations. Excessive emotional empathetic attunement also makes it more difficult to take measured or rational approaches to problem solving, a situation that is less likely in cognitively empathetic individuals.

COST OF BREACHING VALUES, BELIEFS, AND EMPATHETIC BONDS

When individuals are faced with a situation that abuses their values, beliefs, or the well-being of their colleagues or when they fail to act or defend their beliefs, they are likely to experience feelings of intense psychological discomfort and physiological arousal. This dissonant state (Festinger, 1957) can be observed when employees who regard themselves as fundamentally honest are confronted with the unethical behaviors of their organization or colleagues. A number of studies have revealed the emotional and physical pain experienced by people who breach their empathetic bond with others by lying or deceiving (Christ et al., 2009), faking emotions (Grebner et al., 2003), or being hypocritical (Fointiat, Somat, and Grosbras, 2011). The discomfort accompanying dissonance causes some people to change their attitudes and perceptions to their behavior through rationalizing, "I only behaved badly because I was provoked," or discounting, "it was not that bad, other people do the same thing." Where the deviant behavior relates to another person, similar discounting applies, "he was only doing his job" or "she deserved it." While it is possible for employees to resolve these dissonant states by changing their attitudes, behaviors, or beliefs, this defensive action can cause a state of free-floating guilt, shame, and grief, which Damasio (2003) describes as being similar to unhealthy sorrow or bereavement.

While the brain is important in determining ethical behavior, evidence gained from victims of trauma has shown that the body also stores memories that influence responses whenever the memories are triggered (van der Kolk, 1996). Sensory stimuli can activate physiological responses or dispositions to behave in particular ways, which are often outside conscious awareness. For example, when a university manager who had been bullied by a subordinate returned to work, she found that there were times when she became upset for no apparent reason. She later discovered that it was exposure to subtle physical and environmental stimuli or reminders of her "persecutor" that triggered the major stress responses and panic attacks, which led her to avoid places and activities associated with the bullying (Tehrani, 2009). The somatic marker hypothesis (Damasio, Tranel, and Damasio, 1991) proposes that the autonomic nervous system with its pathways to and from the amygdala plays a critical role in decision making. Selective attention is paid to situations or events that are attached to negative outcomes, and without any conscious awareness the body responds, creating a mildly aversive sensation that results in increased caution or avoidant behavior. Somatic markers do not determine whether an individual will make an ethical or unethical decision but rather inform the process by creating the emotions, feelings, and physical sensations of disgust, fear, distress, or shame when unethical actions are contemplated or there is a possibility of being seen by others as behaving badly, and a risk of breaking the empathetic bonds.

FEELING THE PAIN

Organizations are naturally interested in the way unethical behaviors affect their financial status or corporate image, but they spend much less time considering how individual or corporate behaviors can affect the health and well-being of employees and other stakeholders (Jain, Leka, and Zwetsloot, 2011). Much of the research on the health and safety in organizations has focused on measuring the incidence of psychological stress and stress-related illness and identifying those factors or stressors most implicated in these negative outcomes. If unethical behavior includes placing employees in situations where they face unreasonable pressures, physical risks, violence, harassment, tedious, boring, or demeaning work, with a lack of support and poor communication, it is clear that many organizations are unethical places in which to work. A recent survey in Europe showed that 5 percent of workers had been subjected to physical violence, 5 percent to bullying/harassment, and 2 percent to sexual harassment. Forty percent of people who had experienced violence, bullying, or harassment were found to be affected by physical and psychological ailments (European Foundation for the Improvement of Living and Working Conditions, 2007).

Unethical Behaviors in the Workplace

It has been suggested that human beings have a number of basic needs that must be met if they are to achieve well-being. These include safety, trust, self-esteem, control, and intimacy (McCann and Pearlman, 1990). While a disruption of these basic needs can be distressing for the individual involved, observing that others are deprived of one or more of these needs can have an impact on colleagues, associates, and families. The following anonymous case studies have been taken from the author's casework and illustrate how targets, witnesses, and families respond when these needs are violated.

Safety/Security

Employees have a need to feel safe and secure in their employment, which includes personal, physical, financial, and job security. One of the common risks to security occurs when an employee's job is put in jeopardy. Outsourcing, restructuring, layoffs, and redundancy can affect those who lose their jobs as well as those who are left behind, who are expected to take on extra responsibilities and face dealing with disruptions in their normal working patterns. Many survivors experience feelings of guilt, upset that they have retained their jobs while many of their ex-colleagues are unemployed. Poorly handled layoffs of employees can have a major negative effect on the psychological well-being of the displaced workers and their families, which contributes to marital problems and problems with children, while for the survivors there is a decrease in productivity and morale (Feldman and Leana, 1989).

Case Example. Mike worked as a supervisor in a manufacturing organization and was exposed to a period of sustained victimization and bullying by his team of subordinate workers. The victimization included threats of physical violence, personal verbal abuse, humiliation, and other negative acts. Mike sought help from the company to deal with the ringleaders, but nothing was done to protect him. He became physically and emotionally unwell, suffering nightmares, flashbacks, and panic attacks, and was signed out sick from work. After a period of six months' absence from work, his pay was cut, and a few months later, despite the failure of the organization to address the victimization, his employment terminated. During this time, other workers and supervisors at the plant were aware of what was happening but felt afraid to do anything for fear of becoming the next target. The ringleaders became bolder in their abusive behaviors, believing that they had the freedom to do whatever they wanted as neither union nor management had taken action against them. Several people resigned from the organization rather than put up with the situation, believing that reporting the bullying would be useless. While most of the team had been involved in the victimization to some extent, it was orchestrated by two or three powerful leaders. The dissonance created in the "team followers" was immense and initially resolved by these team members regarding Mike as weak and deserving of the personal attacks; however, the dissonance reappeared when the abuse began to be targeted at other supervisors and any team member who failed to conform to the views of the ringleaders.

Commentary. While Mike recognized that his initial problems had been caused by bullies in his team, the real distress was caused by the inaction of the organization, which allowed the victimization to continue, and their decision to terminate his employment despite many years of loyal service. The termination of his employment was justified by his inability to return to work, but Mike believed that his illness had been caused by the organization's having failed in its duty to protect him from the behavior of the bullies in his team. At home Mike became a shadow of his former self, his body and mind sensitized to such an extent that a letter or telephone call from the organization triggered a major physical and psychological response, which could take days to subside. Family, colleagues, and friends were empathetic but unable to do anything to influence the situation. Colleagues would contact him and talk about what had happened, expressing their anger and disappointment. Close family members found Mike's continual focus on the past and inability to move on upsetting, but felt helpless and frustrated at their inability to do anything to help.

Trust/Honesty

Many cases of dishonesty have been reported in the media that involve organizational and institutional malpractice, including the use of bribery, tax evasion, dishonest advertising, phone tapping, and insider share dealing (Miller, Delves, and Harris, 2010). Employees become unhappy and embarrassed when they feel that they are working for an organization that fails to meet their personal codes or standards. The cost of this mismatch leads to stress, illness, and absenteeism (Dewe, 1993). A review of the hidden costs of organizational dishonesty (Cialdini, Petrova, and Goldstein, 2004) revealed that while unethical business practices can lead to a short-term profit, in the longer term, there tended to be a greater loss due to the demoralization of employees and leading to reduced productivity, absenteeism, ill health, a loss of trust and team spirit, which leads employees to cheat and bypass company systems whenever possible.

Case Example. Louise was a part-time employee at an academic institution. Soon after she joined, she discovered that one of the tutors had been charging students for organizing their work placements, and he also had been known to accept bribes from a company providing services. The tutor was a brash and forceful individual and made no secret of what he was doing. Louise felt angry and upset when she thought of students helping to fund the tutor's lavish holidays. A couple of colleagues listened to Louise's concerns and were supportive toward her. She discussed the possibility of whistle-blowing with them but they identified a different solution that would block the opportunities for the tutor to continue gathering the illicit funds. Reflecting on these events some years later, Louise said, "I became very good friends with these two chaps, I think it was watching a nasty situation unfold and then seeing it be dealt with that bonded us. When we discussed the matter a couple of years later I was surprised to find that all of us still held feelings of distaste about what had happened. Looking back now I wonder whether being taken under their wings contributed to me not having done anything. I know that at the time whistle-blowing would have been dangerous to my career; I think that they may have been protecting me as well as educating me on how things are done around here."

Commentary. This account has a number of roles, including the unaware victims (students), the witnesses/supporters who protected the female, and the offender who abused his position to defraud the students. The female appears to have wanted to play the role of an avenger but was persuaded not to take this role by the two supportive witnesses. The Organizational Drama Model (Tehrani, 2011) offers a means of looking at the dynamics between these four players (Figure 17.1). The model recognizes how victims, offenders, supporters, and avengers interact with each other and may change roles as a means of maintaining the stability of the dysfunctional system. In Louise's story, the offender (tutor) was able to continue his offending only as long as he was not identified as an offender by the naive victims (students) and was supported by the passive witnesses (colleagues and organization).

The entry of Louise as a potential avenger created a major risk to the stability of the system and the organization. The witnesses, who had previously tolerated or tacitly supported the tutor now moved to openly support Louise. This created an imbalance in which the previously

Figure 17.1   **The Organizational Drama Model**

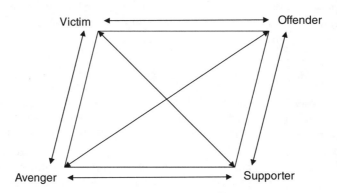

passive organization had no alternative but to take an offensive role, relieving the tutor first of his responsibilities and then of his job. The tutor, having started as an offender, became a victim of the changed situation and was forced to leave the organization.

Self-Esteem/Respect

Bullying, harassment, and victimization are tools used to attack targeted employees and undermine their self-esteem and self-confidence. Studies have found that exposure to bullying is associated with chronic fatigue, insomnia, anxiety, depression, posttraumatic stress, and suicide (Hogh, Gemzøe-Mikkelsen, and Hansen, 2011), and in workplaces, higher levels of bullying are associated with an increase in absenteeism, turnover of staff, and reduced productivity and increased stress in observers and bystanders (Hoel et al., 2011).

Case Example. Tony was a senior executive in a news-gathering organization. He was suspended from work following an anonymous complaint accusing him of dishonesty. This came as a shock to Tony, but within a few weeks he was cleared of all allegations. During the period of suspension Tony was subjected to surveillance of his home and the illegal investigation of his financial circumstances. He returned to work, but the surveillance continued, causing him and his family great distress. At work, Tony's role was taken from him and he was placed in a number of other roles, in all of which he had less authority and prestige than he had in his previous role. Despite his best efforts, Tony never regained his former position and was made to work for a manager who continually undermined his authority and subjected him to victimization and bullying. The bullying was so intense that Tony began to have panic attacks, palpitations, and intense distress. Tony said that he never felt happy, one minute he would be coping with his life and the next he was in deep despair. He described waking in the early morning feeling very low and tearful, with thoughts that he could not get out of his mind. He experienced nightmares in which he saw people laughing at him or he was in situations where he was unable to protect himself or his family. During the day, Tony avoided visiting anywhere he might meet people he knew. He became isolated and irritable and found that his children no longer came to him to discuss their problems or even to talk about the events of the day. He said that he felt as if he were on automatic pilot, cut off from the real world. His wife and children were badly affected, as he had become moody and difficult, and his behavior and mood changes alienated his children.

Commentary. While the impact of bullying on an individual is significant, within the family the presence of a bullied family member can breach or undermine the normal empathetic bonds. Tony had not told his children about the suspension, demotion, and bullying. Consequently, the children had no way of understanding why his behavior toward them had changed. Interpreting that the depressed atmosphere in the family was caused by their father, they were unsympathetic and avoidant. His wife, on the other hand, was aware of what had been happened and was empathetic and supportive, but her empathetic attunement and wish to help caused her to suffer from headaches and depression brought about by her extreme anger toward the organization.

Control/Independence

The need for employees to have some control and independence in the way that they carry out their work has long been recognized as an important risk factor in the occupational stress literature (e.g., Karasek, 1979). Being given opportunities to achieve independence and control are important to employee well-being (Troup and Dewe, 2002). Employees who feel they are being micromanaged, have their responsibilities taken away, and are able to exert little control or influence over their work often describe themselves as being the victims of bullying (Varta, 1996).

Case Example. Jenny and the rest of her team of employee counselors had a difficult relationship with their manager. The manager was highly controlling and constantly checking minor details of their work, challenging team members, and placing major restrictions and constraints on how they carried out their duties. There was no trust within the team, and the manager would frequently complain to senior management about team members' incompetence. One day Jenny reported that a confidential records cabinet had been left open overnight. Later it became obvious that it was the manager who had failed to lock the cabinet. Instead of acknowledging her error the manager blamed Jenny and then began a process of checking and identifying minor errors in Jenny's work. Most of the complaints were unfounded, but the manager would not listen to anything that did not confirm her view of Jenny as incompetent and not able to be trusted to do her job. Jenny said that this constant battering was extremely distressing. "I was very unwell; I had to take ten days off from work and was sick with a range of ailments. I had one infection after another. I was continually shaky, had palpitations, and was in a constant state of anxiety and high alert. I was irritable at home, tearful, and guilt ridden when I shouted at my husband and children. The children became upset as they could not understand what they had done to make me so cross with them all the time. I felt angry and fearful that no one would believe what had been happening." There was also a big impact on the other members of the team who felt unable to support Jenny for fear of being subjected to similar treatment. Everyone in the team constantly watched their backs, unable to make decisions for fear of what might happen if anything went wrong. Eventually, the manager's boss became involved and, while there appeared to be some acknowledgment of issues with the manager, nothing changed. Jenny said, "Whenever I see my manager, read her name, or think about what happened, I feel tense, angry, and physically sick. However, most of my anger is directed toward the managers above her who have allowed the team to be constantly exposed to this behavior."

Commentary. It would be easy to see the manager as vindictive, punishing, and cruel, and to punish her for her bad behavior. However, if bad behaviors are to be changed, it is important to understand why they occur. From an early age children become aware of their internal emotional states and begin to create theories about what other people are thinking or feeling (Rutherford, 2004). They use these theories to predict the behavior and reactions of others (Wimmer and Perner, 1983). In life, negotiating social interactions and relationships is an essential skill, because without the ability to predict the responses of others the world would be uncertain and unpredictable (Nickerson, 1999). However, these theories can cause difficulties, particularly if a child discovers that the expression of strong emotions such as anger, fear, or distress is not acceptable to their caregivers who require the child to modify, deny, or control these strong emotions. In order to be loved and avoid being punished, the child learns to hide "unacceptable" emotions, a process that occurs outside conscious awareness. The internal conflicts formed within the child develop into a shadowy world in which they hide those aspects of themselves that they have learned are unacceptable to others (Page, 1999). The hiding of these emotions leaves the child in a state of unresolved distress, which can be released only by projecting the unacknowledged emotions onto other people by open or passive aggression, engaging in hyperactivity, or striving obsessively for recognition as a means of avoiding feelings of incompetence and failure. These defensive behaviors that originated in childhood continue into adulthood and are played out in workplaces. Jenny's manager found it impossible to accept that she might have made a mistake. In order to avoid feelings of guilt, shame, and failure, she projected her responsibility for not locking the cabinet onto Jenny. Her unconscious fear of making a mistake was also projected onto members of her team, with the result that she felt she could not trust them unless she continually checked their work.

Intimacy/Relationship

The workplace provides workers with opportunities to meet and share time, ideas, feelings, interests, and values. Working on shared goals that require close cooperation and support can forge close relationships and be rewarding for those involved and for the organization. Increasingly, the workplace is the place to make friends and form relationships. The incidence of office romances is high: 40 percent of employees surveyed have engaged in a workplace romance at least once during their careers (Cole, 2009). However, not all romances have positive endings, and many romances end in disappointment, conflict, and occasionally the firing of one or both parties (Parks, 2006). Workplace romances between employees of equal or similar status (lateral romance) tend to be less problematic than those involving employees of a different status (hierarchical romance). Hierarchical romances are more likely to lead to allegations of sexual harassment when the relationship breaks down (Pierce and Aguinis, 1997). In a study of sexual harassment, it was found that the affected women experienced threats to their physical, financial, and personal safety and security, which led to symptoms of traumatic stress (Avina and O'Donohue, 2002). Sexual harassment, like bullying, causes injury to the targets and observers. In a study of academics (McDermut, Haaga, and Kirk, 2000), it was found that sexual harassment led to an increase in negative self-beliefs, distress, and symptoms of posttraumatic stress.

Case Study. Christine had ended a stormy relationship and was offered support by James, her line manager, whom she found to be understanding and attentive. Fairly quickly the couple moved in together. Everyone knew about the relationship, but when Christine got an unexpected promotion, some comments were made about favoritism. Initially, Christine was flattered by the attention James gave her, but after six months she began to recognize that James was trying to control her life, demanding that she dress in clothes he had chosen for her, and preventing her from seeing her family and friends. Over time she became isolated from colleagues at work and other social contacts. When she complained, he became violent and abusive. After a year, Christine decided to leave James. Christine's colleagues were unaware of what was happening, as James was careful in the way he behaved toward her in public. After the separation, James began to identify errors in Christine's work and openly criticized her. He told everyone how she had cheated on him and that he had asked her to leave. Christine said that she felt helpless, upset, and unwell, and developed an irritable bowel condition. She moved to a new department, but the harassment continued, with James constantly contacting her on the telephone. He then began to stalk her, driving past her home or sitting outside the house in his car. Christine called the police. After a police warning, James left the organization, but when Christine formed a new relationship, the harassment started again, with James causing damage to her car and threatening her new partner. Christine was frightened of James and what he might do; she blamed herself for what had happened. She became withdrawn and was given a diagnosis of anxiety, depression, and symptoms of traumatic stress. Initially, Christine did not ask for help, because she was afraid of how James might react. As soon as the police became involved in following James's more extreme behavior, Christine gained support from her female colleagues after she began talking about what had been happening; however, many of her male colleagues were unsympathetic and suggested that she had brought the problems on herself by treating James badly.

Commentary. The ability to empathize with a target is a strong predictor of whether an observer will take action. Observers are unlikely to intervene when the behavior is ambiguous. In Christine's case, James behaved relatively normally at work, despite his controlling behavior toward her at home. After the relationship broke up, Christine felt able to talk to some of her female colleagues, many of whom recognized the situation and empathized with her. When James's behavior became extreme, her colleagues encouraged and supported her in contacting the police. The male colleagues on the other hand did not empathize with Christine until the police placed a restraining order on James that prevented him from approaching Christine or her home. A study of responses to sexual discrimination (Iyer and Ryan, 2009) found that women who empathized with the target tended to become angry and supportive. Less empathetic female observers became angry and involved only when there was clear evidence of discrimination. Empathetic men tended show anger and sympathy toward targets of discrimination, while less empathetic men did not become angry and only took action where they had evidence that the discrimination was both inappropriate and pervasive.

WITNESSES AND WHISTLE-BLOWERS

Witnesses of unethical behaviors are never neutral, as their responses support, block, or challenge the unethical acts. A study of the effects of unethical behaviors on witnesses (Bloch, 2012) has shown how witnesses of bullying face moral and ethical dilemmas (dissonance) caused by challenges to their values and beliefs when witnessing acts that they believed to be wrong or unfair. These problems were reduced when the witness had the power to change or influence the situation, but where this was not possible, the witness began to suffer similar symptoms to those experienced by the target. Bloch found that even when witnesses were not directly involved as a bully or a target, they never played a passive role, as their actions and inactions influenced the interactions between the players and often determined the fate of the victim and/or the offender. An important finding in Bloch's research was the evidence for the identification of worthy and unworthy victims. Witnesses would initially empathize with worthy victims, but their sympathy could wear thin if the victim did little to help resolve his or her difficulties. Witnesses tire of trying to support an overdemanding, incompetent, or socially deviant victim, the discomfort or dissonance brought about by a change in belief in which the victim was seen as worthy; to one where the victim is regarded as the author of his or her misfortune. In the changed perception of the witness the abrasive approach of the manager is viewed as legitimate.

> There are some people who always seem to be losers; you cannot help them no matter how you try. . . . I know that she had a difficult time and she had not been trained properly, but most of us just get on with it. . . . She just seemed to become more and more needy and helpless. . . . In the end I just wanted her to go away. . . . I still feel guilty about not doing enough, but I was pleased when she got the sack. (Witness)

Witnesses were found to play an important role in "merry-go-round" bullying (Tehrani, 2005), in which the manager attempts to maintain abusive power by sequentially bullying members of their team. In a bullying investigation undertaken by the author, a senior nurse was accused of merry-go-round bullying by several of her subordinates, some of whom reported that it was more distressing being a witness than being bullied, because witnesses could do nothing to help their colleague and were in constant fear of when it would be their time to be bullied.

> At least when I was being picked on I knew what to expect, when it happened to others I felt guilty for not doing anything to help them and ashamed of feeling relieved that it wasn't my turn. (Nurse, merry-go-round victim)

An assessment of the physical and psychological well-being of four of the nurses was undertaken as part of the investigation. All of the nurses assessed were found to have symptoms consistent with a diagnosis of post-traumatic stress disorder (PTSD); they also had high levels of anxiety and depression, and most were suffering from panic attacks and phobias. Their physical well-being had also been affected with symptoms of migraine, irritable bowel, skin conditions, and sleep problems. Personal relationships can also suffer when partners and children become deeply affected.

> Life at home is difficult. Nothing in my life is normal; I am constantly upset or angry for no particular reason. My husband has been supportive but even he is beginning to lose patience with the situation. I started to avoid talking about what was happening at work because he would get angry. It seemed to me that while he was angry with my supervisor it was me that he shouted at. I think that he felt he should have been able to protect me and because there was nothing he could do he became upset and frustrated. (Nurse, merry-go-round victim)

Compassion Fatigue and Secondary Trauma

For many years, it has been recognized that doctors, nurses, and counselors witness unethical and other distressing events through the experiences of their patients or clients and as a result may come to suffer burnout, compassion fatigue, or secondary trauma (Figley, 1995). Recently, similar symptoms have been found in crime analysts (Burns et al., 2008), lawyers (Vrklevski and Franklin, 2008), insurance workers (Ludick, Alexander, and Carmichael 2007), social workers (Richardson, 2011), and teachers (Lowe, 2011), where the exposure to a traumatic incident or victim is experienced indirectly through stories, artifacts, images, auditory records, and written testimony. It has been found that individuals with the greatest capacity for feeling and expressing empathy are most likely to develop burnout, compassion fatigue, or secondary trauma (Figley, 1995) and to experience symptoms similar to those of the victims with whom they have direct or indirect contact (Pearlman and Saakvitne, 1995).

> I had been used to working with difficult cases and thought I could cope with most things, but this case was different. The victim was a similar age to me and she had been jogging in a park that I actually know quite well. She was grabbed from behind and pulled into the bushes where she was raped. I started analyzing the data but then I burst into tears. It was as if for all these years I had a shield protecting me from the reality of the work—knowing the place and thinking that it could have been me—I just went to pieces. (Crime analyst)

When dealing with difficult or distressing cases, workers may unconsciously activate their physiological responses through the activation of somatic markers caused by the heightened emotions of anger, fear, grief, or despair (Damasio, 2003). Danieli (1996) found that workers involved with victims defend themselves by becoming dissociated (emotionally detached), questioning the reliability of the victim's story, or minimizing the victim's experience. Failing to deal with the emotional cost of working with victims can cause a range of physical, psychological, and relationship issues, such as feeling overwhelmed, distressed, or helpless, overworking, neglecting one's own needs and those of their families, and not engaging in previously valued leisure activities. A number of studies have investigated the effect of working with distressed and traumatized clients (Figley, 1995; McCann and Pearlman, 1990; Stamm, 1995), and have shown that up to 50 percent of care workers were vulnerable to experiencing secondary trauma or compassion fatigue (Steed and Bicknell, 2001). It is suggested (Wilson and Thomas, 2004) that workers are more likely to develop secondary traumatic stress if they are empathetically attuned to the experiences of a trauma victim or if some aspect of the traumatic material takes on a special meaning or resonance with the workers' own life and experiences. For example, when the name or appearance of a trauma victim is similar to that of a close friend, a link may be formed and the worker begins to experience distressing emotions as if the trauma victim were a friend. This phenomenon is even more prevalent when the worker reads traumatic testimony such as a witness's statements describing a distressing event. Here, the worker automatically creates images or pictures of the event he or she is reading about in order to make sense of the narrative. When working with investigators, it is common for individuals to become secondarily traumatized to objects that they have inadvertently included in their construction of the event described. For example, the author has had the experience of supporting a worker whose role involved analyzing transcripts describing child abuse; the worker had unconsciously included aspects of her own bathroom when reading about a child being abused in a bath.

> I kept seeing these images of me abusing my own children in our bathroom. It was so bad that I could not bathe the children and would not go into the bathroom. I don't understand why it happened; I have done this work for three years with no problems. I began to wonder if the work had damaged me or if I was really capable of child abuse. I am thinking about changing my job. (Child abuse investigator)

The secondary trauma process makes it difficult for these workers to separate personal life, experiences, and responses from those experienced by the child or parent who is directly affected by these shocking crimes. It is essential that workers in such roles have the support of a psychologist capable of dealing with these "empathy constructed" traumas.

Whistle-Blowing

Witnesses to unethical behavior may come to find the situation so morally untenable that they decide to inform the organization. This is often the case when the whistle-blower has experienced similar situations in the past that make him or her more sensitive to the issue and determined to see it addressed. At this stage, whistle-blowers believe that because they have taken a moral position, the organization will be grateful and will take action. While whistle-blowers may regard their action as justified, their complaints can come to be seen as unfair, unwarranted, unfounded, malicious, or as overreactions. Reprisals against whistle-blowers are common, and up to 38 percent of whistle-blowers experience some form of reprisal (Public Concern at Work, 2011). This is particularly true when the whistle-blower is female and has little or no support from her manager (Rehg et al., 2008). While some organizations respond appropriately to whistle-blowing, in many cases it is ignored and whistle-blowers become the targets of victimization or dismissal. It is not surprising, therefore, that many people do not take action in support of victims or against wrongdoing, not because they lack values but rather because they have been able to regard whistle-blowing as the responsibility of others and not part of their job. In a survey of managers (Samuelson and Gentile, 2005), it was found that managers would typically avoid facing moral dilemmas by distracting themselves with their work or, when asked to do something unethical, finding ways out of the situation by lying or using other avoidance techniques.

EMPATHY IN RELATIONSHIPS AND ORGANIZATIONS

In this chapter, we have looked at the impact of unethical behaviors on primary victims, who respond directly to the punishing behaviors directed toward them. When one is bullied, harassed, or discriminated against it is easy to see how the victim becomes emotionally and physically distressed. It is perhaps less easy to see how observers and witnesses can come to suffer the same kind of distress as colleagues or feel the impact of a foolhardy or careless act on customers, stakeholders, or members of the public. This chapter proposes that empathizing with those affected by negative acts can lead to physical, emotional, and psychological symptoms in observers and witnesses similar to those experienced by the primary victims. In this final section, we look at empathy as an organizational tool for reducing the incidence of unethical behaviors and show how the harmful aspects of empathy can be transformed into action with the creation of new learning and resilience.

Organizations can provide a social environment in which empathy and other prosocial behaviors can grow and develop. To achieve this, organizations should provide opportunities for workers to create a state of empathy with colleagues and customers. Empathy requires contact and two-way communication to establish and maintain respectful relationships. Unfortunately, many organizations create zero-empathy cultures that are highly driven by competition, performance, and reward, and in which there is little time or opportunity for social engagement and relationship building. Under pressure to achieve targets, the individual and organizational empathy circuits are switched off and become totally performance focused with little thought of the impact of their actions on others.

Organizations have needs similar to those required by individuals in order to be empathetic and healthy. Healthy organizations live by a strong set of values and beliefs that help to inform their decision making as well as those of their workers. The organization needs to be in contact with and engage its members in solving problems, making decisions, and resolving conflicts if it is to function effectively. There is a need for emotional intelligence and sensitivity, and organizations engaged in more emotionally demanding work have a greater requirement to recognize that the organization itself can become traumatized and begin to exhibit the three major symptoms of traumatic stress: avoidance in dealing with distressing issues, hyperactivity in responding to events, and reexperience of issues through constant reference to problems from the past (Bloom, 2012). Healthy organizations are not afraid to admit errors, feel comfortable in responding to the emotional needs of workers and customers, can apologize, and feel proud of what they produce or provide as a service.

While exposure to unethical behaviors may not be inevitable, when it occurs it is distressing and harmful to physical and mental health. However, it is possible to use the experience of dealing with unethical behavior as a stimulus to the growth of self-knowledge and experience. A growing body of research shows how victims of distressing and demanding circumstances can find positive outcomes emerging from their misfortune (Linley and Joseph, 2004). This is particularly true where people are able to learn something about themselves following their exposure to unethical behaviors, which enables them to emerge from the experience with a sense of positive self-worth, improved interpersonal relationships, and an enriched philosophy of life. "Posttrauma growth" is the term often used to describe the positive changes that occur after a highly distressing or traumatic exposure such as the abuse of ethical standards. It has been suggested (Janoff-Bulman, 1989) that the more extreme the traumatic exposure the greater the potential for growth. A study that looked at workers in occupational health, human resources, counseling, and the police (Tehrani, 2010) found that the changes brought about by exposure to distressing or demanding events initially caused negative physical and psychological consequences, but, through reflection, these negative outcomes were transformed into positive learning and growth.

The ability to empathize and show compassion toward others is a strong deterrent to unethical behavior. Where people see themselves as part of a supportive team or group, developing altruistic attitudes toward their colleagues, managers, customers, and other stakeholders, they are unlikely to choose to behave in a way that disrupts these important and rewarding relationships.

REFERENCES

Adams, R.; Boscarino, J.A.; and Figley, C.R. 2006. Compassion fatigue and psychological distress among social workers: A validation study. *American Journal of Orthopsychiatry, 76*, 1, 103–108.

Avina, C., and O'Donohue, W. 2002. Sexual harassment and PTSD: Is sexual harassment diagnosable trauma? *Journal of Traumatic Stress, 15*, 1, 69–75.

Baron-Cohen, S. 2011. *Zero Degrees of Empathy: A New Theory of Human Cruelty.* London: Allen Lane.

Baron-Cohen, S., and Wheelwright, S. 2004. The empathy quotient: An investigation of adults with Asperger syndrome or high functioning autism and normal sex differences. *Journal of Autism and Development Disorders, 34*, 163–175.

Bloch, C. 2012. How witnesses contribute to bullying in the workplace. In *Managing Bullying in the Workplace: Symptoms and Solutions,* ed. N. Tehrani, 81–96. London: Routledge.

Bloom, S. 2012. Building resilient workers and organization: The sanctuary model of organisational change. In *Managing Bullying in the Workplace: Symptoms and Solutions,* ed. N. Tehrani, 260–277. London: Routledge.

Boehm, C. 2008. Purposive social selection and the evolution of human altruism. *Cross Cultural Research, 42*, 4, 319–352.

Bowlby, J. 1979. *The Making and Breaking of Affectional Bonds.* London: Tavistock.

Burns, C.M.; Morley, J.; Bradshaw, R.; and Domene, J. 2008. The emotional impact on and coping strategies employed by police teams investigating Internet child exploitation. *Traumatology, 14*, 20–31.

Christ, S.E.; von Essen, D.C.; Watson, J.M.; Brubaker, L.E.; and McDermott, K.B. 2009. The contributions of prefrontal cortex and executive control to deception: Evidence for activation likelihood estimate meta-analyses. *Cerebral Cortex, 19*, 7, 1557–1566.

Cialdini, R. B.; Petrova, P.K.; and Goldstein, N. J. (2004). The hidden costs of organizational dishonesty. *MIT Sloan Management Review*, 45, 67–73.

Cole, N. 2009. Workplace romance: A justice analysis. *Journal of Business Psychology, 24*, 363–372.

Damasio, A. 2003. *Looking for Spinoza: Joy, Sorrow and the Feeling Brain.* London: Heinemann.

Damasio, A.R.; Tranel, D.; and Damasio, H. 1991. Somatic markers and the guidance of behavior: Theory and preliminary testing. In *Frontal Lobe Function and Dysfunction*, ed. H.S. Levin, H.M. Eisenberg, and A.L. Benton, 217–229. New York: Oxford University Press.

Danieli, Y. 1996. Who takes care of the caretakers? The emotional life of those working with children in situations of violence. In *Minefields in Their Hearts: The Mental Health of Children in War and Communal Violence,* ed. R.J. Appel and B. Simon, 189–205. New Haven, CT: Yale University Press.

Daniels, M. 2005. Towards a transpersonal psychology of evil. In *Shadow, Self, Spirit: Essays in Transpersonal Psychology,* 95–114. Charlottesville, VA: Imprint Academic.

Dewe, P. 1993. Measuring primary appraisal: Scale construction and directions for future research. *Journal of Social Behavior and Personality,* 8, 673–685.

Eisenberg, N., and Miller, P.A. 1987. The relation of empathy to prosocial and related behaviors. *Psychological Bulletin,* 101, 1, 91–119.

Esslemont, J.E. 1980. *Bahá'u'lláh and the New Era.* Wilmette, IL: Baha'i Publishing Trust.

European Foundation for the Improvement of Living and Working Conditions. 2007. Description. January 3. www.eubusiness.com/topics/social/european-foundation-for-the-improvement-of-living-and-working-conditions/ (accessed September 19, 2011).

Feldman, D.C., and Leana, C.R. 1989. Managing layoffs: Experiences at the Challenger disaster site and the Pittsburgh steel mills. *Organizational Dynamics,* 18, 1, 52–64.

Festinger, L.A. 1957. *A Theory of Cognitive Dissonance.* Stanford, CA: Stanford University Press.

Figley, C.R. (ed.). 1995. *Compassion Fatigue: Coping with Secondary Traumatic Stress Disorder in Those Who Treat the Traumatized.* New York: Brunner/Mazel.

Fointiat, V.; Somat, A.; and Grosbras, J.-M. 2011. Saying, but not doing: Induced hypocrisy, trivialisation and misattribution. *Social Behavior and Personality,* 39, 4, 465–476.

Frey-Rohn, L. 1967. Evil from a psychological point of view. In *Evil: Studies in Jungian Thought,* ed. Curatorium of the C.G. Jung Institute and trans. R. Manheim and H. Nagel, 151–200. Evanston, IL: Northwestern University Press.

Gilbert, P. 2005. *Compassion: Conceptualisation, Research and Use in Psychotherapy.* London, Routledge.

Grebner, S.; Semmer, N.K.; Lo Faso, L.; Gut, S.; Kälin, W.; and Ekfering, A. 2003. Working conditions, well-being, and job-related attitudes among call centre agents. *European Journal of Work and Organizational Psychology,* 12, 4, 341–365.

Hare, R.D. 1993. *Without Conscience: The Disturbing World of the Psychopaths Among Us.* New York: Guilford Press.

Hoel, H.; Sheehan, M.J.; Cooper, C.L.; and Einarsen, S. 2011. Organisational effects of workplace bullying. In *Bullying and Harassment in the Workplace: Developments in Theory, Research, and Practice,* 2d ed., ed. S. Einarsen, H. Hoel, D. Zapf, and C.L. Cooper, 129–158. Boca Raton, FL: CRC Press.

Hogh, A.; Gemzøe-Mikkelsen, E.; and Hansen, A.M. 2011. Individual consequences of workplace bullying/mobbing. In *Bullying and Harassment in the Workplace: Developments in Theory, Research, and Practice,* 2d ed., ed. S. Einarsen, H. Hoel, D. Zapf, and C.L. Cooper, 107–128. Boca Raton, FL: CRC Press.

Iyer, A., and Ryan, M.K. 2009. Why do men and women challenge gender discrimination? The role of group status and in-group identification in predicting pathways to collective action. *Journal of Social Issues,* 65, 791–814.

Jain, A.; Leka, S.; and Zwetsloot, G. 2011. Corporate social responsibility and psychosocial risk management in Europe. *Journal of Business Ethics,* 101, 4, 619–633.

Janoff-Bulman, R. 1989. Assumptive worlds and the stress of traumatic events: Applications of the schema construct. *Social Cognition,* 7, 2, 113–136.

Karasek, R.A. Jr. 1979. Job demands, job decision latitude and mental strain: Implications for job redesign. *Administration Science Quarterly,* 24, 2, 285–308.

Keltner, D.; Haidt, J.; and Shiota, M.N. 2006. Social functionalism and the evolution of emotions. In *Evolution and Social Psychology,* ed. M. Schaller, J.A. Simpson, and D.T. Kenrick. New York: Psychology Press.

Linley P.A., and Joseph, S. 2004. Positive change following trauma and adversity: A review. *Journal of Traumatic Stress,* 17, 1, 11–21.

Lowe, T. 2011. The impact of disasters on schools and the school community. In *Managing Trauma in the Workplace: Supporting Workers and Organisations,* ed. N. Tehrani, 81–99. London: Routledge.

Ludick, M.; Alexander, D.; and Carmichael, T. 2007. Vicarious traumatisation: Secondary traumatic stress levels in claims workers in the short-term insurance industry in South Africa. *Problems and Perspectives in Management,* 5, 3, 99–109.

McCann, I.L., and Pearlman, L.A. 1990. *Psychological Trauma and the Adult Survivor: Theory, Therapy, and Transformation.* New York: Brunner/Mazel.

McDermut, J.F.; Haaga, D.A.F.; and Kirk, L. 2000. An evaluation of stress symptoms associated with academic sexual harassment. *Journal of Traumatic Stress,* 13, 3, 397–411.

Miller, C.C.J.M.; Delves, R.; and Harris, P. 2010. Ethical and unethical leadership: Double vision? *Journal of Public Affairs,* 10, 3, 109–120.

Nickerson, R.S. 1999. How we know—and sometimes misjudge—what others know: Inputting one's own knowledge into others. *Psychological Bulletin,* 125, 737–759.

Page, S. 1999. *The Shadow and the Counsellor: Working with the Darker Aspects of the Person, Role and Profession.* London: Routledge.

Parks, M. 2006. *2006 Workplace Romance: Poll Findings.* SHRM Report, January. Alexandria, VA: Society for Human Resource Management.

Pearlman, L.A., and Saakvitne, K.W. 1995. *Trauma and the Therapist: Countertransference and Vicarious Traumatization in Psychotherapy with Incest Survivors.* New York: Norton.

Pierce, C.A., and Aguinis, H. 1997. Bridging the gap between romantic relationships and sexual harassment in organisations. *Journal of Organizational Behavior,* 18, 197–200.

Preston, S.D., and de Waal, B.M. 2002. Empathy: its ultimate and proximate basis. *Behavioral and Brain Sciences,* 25, 1, 1–71.

Public Concern at Work. 2011. *Speaking up for Vulnerable Adults: What Whistleblowers Say.* Report, April. www.pcaw.org.uk/policy/care/ (accessed July 16, 2011).

Rehg, M.T.; Miceli, M.P.; Near, J.P.; and Van Scotter, J.R. 2008. Antecedents and outcomes of retaliation against whistleblowers: Gender differences and power relationships. *Organization Science,* 19, 2, 221–240.

Richardson, K. 2011. Child protection, social work and secondary trauma. In *Managing Trauma in the Workplace: Supporting Workers and Organisations,* ed. N. Tehrani, 3–16. London: Routledge.

Rutherford, M.D. 2004. The effect of social role on the theory of mind reasoning. *British Journal of Psychology,* 95, 1, 91–103.

Saakvitne, K.W., and Pearlman, L.A. 1996. *Transforming the Pain: A Workbook on Vicarious Traumatization.* New York: Norton.

Samuelson, J., and Gentile, M. 2005. Get aggressive about passivity. *Harvard Business Review,* 83, 11, 18–20.

Skoe, E.E.A. 2010. The relationship between empathy-related constructs and care-based moral development in young adults. *Journal of Moral Development,* 39, 2, 191–211.

Spinelli, E. 2007. *Practising Existential Psychotherapy: The Relational World.* London: Sage.

Stamm, B.H. 1995. *Secondary Traumatic Stress: Self-care Issues for Clinicians, Researchers, and Educators.* Lutherville, MD: Sidran Press.

Steed, L., and Bicknell, J. 2001. Trauma and the therapist: The experience of therapists working with perpetrators of sexual abuse. *Australasian Journal of Disaster and Trauma Studies,* 1, 1–9.

Tehrani, N. 2005. *Bullying at Work: Beyond Policies to a Culture of Respect.* London: Chartered Institute of Personnel and Development.

———. 2009. Lost in translation: Using bilingual difference to increase emotional mastery following bullying. *Counselling and Psychotherapy Research,* 9, 1, 11–17.

———. 2010. Compassion fatigue: Experiences in occupational health, human resources, counselling and police. *Occupational Medicine,* 60, 2, 133–138.

———. 2011. Workplace bullying: The role for counselling. In *Bullying and Harassment in the Workplace: Developments in Theory, Research and Practice,* ed. S. Einarsen, H. Hoel, D. Zapf, and C.L. Cooper, 381–396. London: CRC Press.

Troup, C., and Dewe, P. 2002. Exploring the nature of control and its role in the appraisal of workplace stress. *Work and Stress,* 16, 4, 335–355.

Van der Kolk, B.A. 1996. The body keeps score: Approaches to the psychobiology of posttraumatic stress disorder. In *Traumatic Stress: The Effects of Overwhelming Experience on Mind, Body and Society,* ed. B.A Van der Kolk, A.C. McFarlane, and L. Weisaeth. 214–278. New York: Guilford Press.

Varta, M. 1996. The sources of bullying: Psychological work environment and organisational climate. *European Journal of Work and Organisational Psychology,* 5, 203–214.

Vrklevski, L.P., and Franklin, J. 2008. Vicarious trauma: The impact on solicitors of exposure to traumatic material. *Traumatology,* 14, 106–118.

Wilson, J.P., and Thomas, R.B. 2004. *Empathy in the Treatment of Trauma and PTSD.* London: Routledge.

Wimmer, H., and Perner, J. 1983. Beliefs about beliefs: Representation and constraining function of wrong beliefs in young children's understanding of deception. *Cognition,* 13, 103–128.

PART IV

ORGANIZATIONAL AND
SOCIETAL PERSPECTIVES

18

ETHICAL CLIMATE

Causes, Consequences, and
Implications for Improving Well-Being

CHARLES H. SCHWEPKER JR.

Several ethical decision-making models have been developed to describe individual ethical decision making in the organization (Bommer et al., 1987; Ferrell and Gresham, 1985; Ferrell, Gresham, and Fraedrich, 1989; Hunt and Vitell, 1986; Jones, 1991; Trevino, 1986). These models suggest that an organization's environment plays a key role in shaping ethical decisions. One important element of an organization's environment that influences ethical behavior is its climate.

Climate refers to the ways that organizations operationalize routine behaviors and the actions that are expected, supported, and rewarded (Schneider and Rentsch, 1988). Due to the various positions and work groups within the organization, and subsequently differing employment histories, perceptions of organizational climate may vary within the firm (Victor and Cullen, 1988). In addition, the opportunity exists for an assortment of climates—including an ethical climate (Schneider, 1975).

An organization's ethical climate has the potential to play a significant role in the well-being of the organization and its members due to its influence on various job-related outcomes. An unethical climate can result in deviant workplace behaviors such as vandalism, sabotage, violence, and bullying, as well as work-related injuries, all of which can result in harm to individuals in the organization. Moreover, workplace climates that are unethical lead to role stress, or to the committing of acts such as fraud and lying, all of which can lead to stress, and ultimately damaging distress. Distress has negative behavioral (e.g., alcohol and drug abuse), psychological (e.g., sleep disturbances, depression), and medical (e.g., heart disease and stroke, ulcer disease) consequences (Quick and Quick, 1984). Although the external environment can help shape an organization's internal environment, this chapter focuses on describing internal organizational drivers of ethical climate, the consequences of ethical climate, means for improving the organization's ethical climate and subsequently improving individual well-being, and directions for future research.

ETHICAL CLIMATE DEFINED

Ethical climate has been defined as "the prevailing perceptions of typical organizational practices and procedures that have ethical content" (Victor and Cullen, 1988, p. 101). Subsequently, it may be viewed as a composite of organizational perceptions of the ethical values and behaviors supported and practiced by organizational members. It reflects the ethical character of the organization and serves as a basis for what is considered "right" behavior in the organization (Cullen, Parboteeah, and Victor, 2003; Martin and Cullen, 2006). As such, it influences the ethical decision making and behavior of organizational members (Martin and Cullen, 2006).

The view of ethical climate's dimensionality and subsequent measurement has varied across research studies. Using ethical philosophy and sociological theory of reference groups, Victor and Cullen (1988) developed a typology of ethical work climates. The typology consists of five empirically distilled dimensions of ethical climate: "caring," "rules," "law and code," "independence," and "instrumental." In a *caring* climate, organizational members' concern for the well-being of others drives their decisions and behaviors, as members perceive that the organization's policies, practices, and strategies support such concern. A caring climate has often been found to be employees' most preferred ethical work climate (Martin and Cullen, 2006). In a *rules* climate, ethical decisions are perceived to be guided by a set of organizational rules or standards, such as a code of ethics. The *law and code* climate is characterized by perceptions that the organization supports ethical decision making based on external codes such as the Bible, law, or professional codes. Those who perceive an *independence* climate view decisions and behaviors with ethical content as being based on deeply held personal moral convictions, with minimal external influence driving ethical decisions. Finally, an *instrumental* climate is believed to exist when organizational members perceive that individual and/or organizational self-interest drives moral reasoning, even to the detriment of others. Studies find this to be the least preferred form of ethical climate (cf. Martin and Cullen, 2006). There is evidence linking ethical behavior with the caring, law and code, rules, and independence dimensions of ethical climate, while the instrumental dimension is associated with unethical behavior (Wimbush, Shepard, and Markham, 1997).

While the Victor and Cullen (1988) typology and their ensuing ethical climate questionnaire have been used quite often in research on ethical climate, a significant amount of research has been conducted focusing on climate from the perspective of factors that delineate acceptable and unacceptable behavior, with the focus being on the presence and enforcement of ethical codes, ethical policies, and punishment as a means to define and measure ethical climate (e.g., Ferrell, LeClair, and Ferrell, 1997; Mulki, Jaramillo, and Locander, 2006; Schwepker, 2001; Schwepker, Ferrell, and Ingram, 1997; Weeks et al., 2004). Ingram, LaForge, and Schwepker (2007) refer to this as the structural dimension of ethical climate. The particular emphasis placed on this aspect of ethical climate is likely due to the finding of Victor and Cullen (1988) that the *rules* and *law and code* dimensions of ethical climate are dominant in for-profit contexts. Moreover, this emphasis has likely occurred because the rules climate is arguably the type of ethical climate upon which management can exert the strongest degree of influence.

DETERMINING ETHICAL CLIMATE

An organization's structure can influence its climate (Schneider and Reichers, 1983). One aspect of a firm's structure, a written code of ethics—a formal, management-initiated control that provides guidelines regarding expected moral behavior (Brothers, 1991; Weaver, 1993), may be one of the most significant influences on the firm's ethical climate. Although the effectiveness of ethical codes in shaping behavior has been questioned (cf. Grundstein-Amado, 2001; Tsalikis and Fritzsche, 1989), evidence suggests that they positively affect the ethical climate and ethical decision making within an organization (Barnett and Vaicys, 2000; Hegarty and Sims, 1978; McCabe, Trevino, and Butterfield, 1996), particularly when they are enforced (Ferrell and Skinner, 1988) and internalized (Schwepker and Hartline, 2005). Additionally, similar to codes of ethics, corporate goals and policies concerning ethical behavior serve as formal control mechanisms that influence members' ethical decision making (Bommer et al., 1987; Hegarty and Sims, 1979) and subsequently influence their perceptions of ethical climate.

Another important influence on the firm's ethical climate is the organization's utilization of punishment for unethical behavior (Posner and Schmidt, 1987). According to control theory, punishment, or the threat of punishment, serves as a formal control intended to shape employee behavior (Jaworski, 1988; Nielsen, 2000). Discipline that is suitably distributed can correct problem behavior (Podsakoff, 1982). On the other hand, the opportunity for unethical behavior increases in the absence of punishment or its threat. Imposing punishment helps to establish expectations regarding acceptable behavior, thus diminishing the perceived opportunity to engage in unethical actions (Hegarty and Sims, 1978; Schwepker and Hartline, 2005; Trevino, 1986; Trevino and Ball, 1992). Subsequently, less unethical behavior is anticipated as punishment clearly articulates normative values regarding ethical behavior (Sims, 1994; Wimbush and Shepard, 1994). Research shows that punishment of unethical behavior leads to organizational members' perceptions of a more ethical climate (Schwepker and Hartline, 2005). In summary, when ethical codes, ethical policies, and punishment for ethical behavior are perceived to exist and be enforced, the organization's structural dimension of climate is perceived as more ethical.

While structural dimensions can influence climate perceptions, so can individuals and their histories in the organization (Victor and Cullen, 1988). Ingram, LaForge, and Schwepker (2007) suggest that firms also have an *interpersonal* dimension of ethical climate that is created by perceptions of the ethical (unethical) behaviors of organizational members (while these authors do not point this out, this dimension would seem to encompass Victor and Cullen's [1988] caring, instrumental, and independence dimensions of climate). People's ethical values (Ferrell and Gresham, 1985) and moral reasoning (Kohlberg, 1969) influence their ethical decision making and subsequent behavior. As such, perceptions of the organization's ethicalness (i.e., perceptions of ethical climate) are believed to be formed in part by the ethical (unethical) behaviors of individuals in the organization. The extent to which organizational members are intrinsically concerned about doing what is appropriate for internal and external organizational stakeholders and thus act accordingly (i.e., doing what is "right" is internalized), the more ethical the climate is expected to be perceived. Conversely, the more organizational members are perceived as being unethical, and thus practice immoral behavior, the less ethical the climate will be perceived. Such positive and negative perceptions are likely to be stimulated by the frequency of communication in the organization. Verbeke, Ouwerkerk, and Peelen (1996) found that communication provides a mechanism for employees to learn about and take others' needs and perspectives into account, thus influencing their ethical perceptions and decisions. A rules and procedures ethical climate tends to promote greater communication, while an instrumental climate leads to less communication among employees (Ruppel and Harrington, 2000).

Leadership behavior likewise appears to play a vital role in the formation of ethical climate perceptions in organizations (Dickson et al., 2001). Through their words and actions, leaders have the ability to convey values deemed important to the organization. When managers hold themselves to high ethical values and behaviors, they create a more ethical climate (Grojean et al., 2004). Further, leaders who develop professionalism, team spirit, and social responsibility will produce a more ethical climate (Elci and Alpkan, 2009). Not only do leaders serve as role models for organizational members, they play an important role in determining the types of individuals who are selected into the organization. Through attraction–selection–attrition processes, similar types of individuals are attracted to, selected, and retained by organizations (Schneider and Reichers, 1983). Thus, ethical leadership breeds ethical followers, which results in ethical hiring. Such actions tend to shape and reinforce the ethical climate of the organization (cf. Schminke, Ambrose, and Neubaum, 2005).

Interestingly, two different types of leadership style have been found to be associated with ethical climate. Instrumental leadership is positively related to ethical climate (Mulki, Jaramillo, and Locander, 2008). Instrumental leaders clearly describe employee roles, establish clear task guidelines, and provide direction and guidance for completing tasks (Evans, 1970). This type of leader clearly spells out the boundaries of ethical behavior and would appear to be relying on factors used to create the structural dimension of ethical climate. Likewise, transformational leaders appear to have the ability to create a more ethical climate (Engelbrecht, van Aswegen, and Theron, 2005; Ingram, LaForge, and Schwepker, 2007). Transformational leaders accomplish organizational goals by openly and frequently interacting with followers (Bass, 1985, 1995; Burns, 1978). They clearly articulate a vision, serve as role models, provide individual support and consideration, stimulate the intellect of employees, and encourage the acceptance of high performance standards and group goals (Podsakoff et al., 1990). Through these behaviors, transformational leaders are able to influence organizational members to identify with both the leader and the organization, and consequently internalize the norms and values of the organization. Such leadership is likely to improve the interpersonal dimension of ethical climate.

CONSEQUENCES OF ETHICAL CLIMATE

Ethical climate is related to various job outcomes that can affect an individual's subjective, psychological, physical, and social well-being. Subjective well-being conceptualizes well-being in terms of overall life satisfaction and happiness. Psychological well-being, however, has been conceptualized as consisting of six dimensions that individuals strive to achieve: self-acceptance, environmental mastery, positive relations, personal growth, purpose in life (i.e., finding meaning in one's efforts and challenges), and autonomy (i.e., seeking a sense of self-determination and personal authority) (Keyes, Shmotkin, and Ryff, 2002). Presumably, the more one excels at each, the greater the psychological well-being. Physical well-being deals with an individual's anatomical well-being (e.g., one who is physically well-off does not have heart disease or an ulcer). Finally, social well-being is made up of social integration (i.e., feelings of belonging to society), social acceptance (i.e., viewing human nature favorably and being comfortable with others), social contribution (i.e., feeling as if one adds value to society), social actualization (i.e., recognizing society's potential), and social coherence (i.e., understanding and caring about the world) (Keyes 1998). A positive relationship is believed to exist between each of these elements and social well-being.

Ethical climate significantly influences role stress, in the form of role conflict and role ambiguity. Role conflict occurs when two or more role expectations occur simultaneously, such that completing one would make completing the other difficult or impossible (Kahn et al., 1964). Role ambiguity is the degree to which one is unsure regarding expectations about a role, the most suitable ways to accomplish these expectations, and the consequences of role performance (Behrman and Perreault, 1984). When employees perceive their climate to be more ethical, they experience lower levels of role conflict and role ambiguity (Babin, Boles, and Robin, 2000; Jaramillo, Mulki, and Solomon, 2006; Mulki, Jaramillo, and Locander, 2008; Schwepker and Hartline, 2005), with the research having focused primarily on the structural dimension of climate. Further, an ethical climate is likely to result in less ethical conflict (i.e., greater values congruence between employees and the manager and/or organization), and subsequently less role conflict (Schwepker, Ferrell, and Ingram, 1997). Jaramillo, Mulki, and Solomon (2006) believe that ethical climate can help workers deal with ambiguous and conflicting expectations from stakeholders by clarifying ethical expectations. This was demonstrated in a study that found the structural dimension of ethical climate to positively influence sales managers' understanding of what is considered an ethical violation, which increased the likelihood of their considering ethics when evaluating salespeople to hire and devoting more time to ethics in sales training, and decreased their willingness to allow their salespeople to behave unethically (Schwepker and Good, 2009).

Ethical climate may play a significant role in affecting one's well-being through its impact on role stress. Role stress is a major contributor to job stress, which can lead to lower levels of motivation, job satisfaction, and performance as well as increased work alienation (Ingram, LaForge, and Schwepker, 2011), all of which can affect one's subjective and psychological well-being, in part due to their impact on overall happiness and life satisfaction. In addition, job stress can result in individual distress, which can have negative behavioral (e.g., appetite disorders, drug abuse, accident proneness), psychological (e.g., burnout, depression), and physical (e.g., heart disease, liver disease, backache) consequences (Quick and Quick, 1984). Further, some evidence suggests that conflict at work, regardless of the source, is associated with psychosomatic complaints, feelings of burnout, and stress-related indicators such as chronic fatigue (De Dreu, Van Dierendonck, and De Best-Waldhober, 2002; Spector and Jex, 1998). However, conflict is more likely to negatively affect well-being when individuals are low in agreeableness, extraversion, or emotional stability (Dijkstra et al., 2005). By fostering a more ethical climate, role stress and its ensuing negative impact on well-being may be reduced.

Ethical climate has the ability to affect deviant workplace behavior, which can take a toll on one's well-being. Workplace deviance involves voluntary behavior that runs counter to organizational norms and threatens the well-being of organizational members (Robinson and Bennett, 1995). Large numbers of employees have participated in deviant workplace behaviors such as theft, fraud, vandalism, sabotage, violence, lying, spreading rumors, withholding effort, and absenteeism, resulting in revenue loss and damage to the workplace environment (cf. Appelbaum, Deguire, and Lay, 2005). Some of these behaviors are illegal, while many are likewise unethical. Such deviant behaviors, however, may harm the well-being of the victim, witnesses, and the perpetrator. Acts of workplace deviance committed against organizational members can harm their physical well-being (e.g., stress-related problems; harm from physical violence), psychological well-being (e.g., a feeling of less control over their environment), and subjective well-being (e.g., unhappiness resulting from lost work time; leaving the company due to a poor work environment) (Henle, Giacalone, and Jurkiewicz, 2005). Victims and witnesses of sustained deviant behavior may begin to have less favorable views about human nature and subsequently experience diminished social well-being. Moreover, the perpetrator, such as an individual pressured into committing fraud on behalf of the company, may experience a great deal of stress and suffer both physically and emotionally.

In general, research shows that rules/law and caring ethical climates can reduce deviant workplace behavior (Martin and Cullen, 2006; Peterson, 2002; Schminke, Ambrose, and Neubaum, 2005; Vardi, 2001). More specifically, a caring ethical climate reduces a firm's incidence of political deviance (i.e., gossip, blaming, showing favoritism) and rules/law and code climates reduce property deviance (i.e., kickbacks, lying about hours worked, stealing from the company, sabotaging equipment) (Peterson, 2002). When an instrumental climate exists, production deviance (i.e., using company time for personal matters, taking extended breaks, intentionally working slowly) is more likely to occur (ibid.).

A specific type of workplace deviant behavior, bullying, has received attention as it relates to ethical climate. Bullying is repetitive, hostile, and unethical communication that is systematically aimed at a helpless individual over a sustained period (cf. Bulutlar and Oz, 2009). It may involve personal attacks, physical threats, and underestimating or undervaluing the person being bullied (ibid.). Take, for instance, the case of Paula (who asked that her real name not be used), a foreign-language middle school teacher with twelve years of experience, whose lesson plans and teaching style were repeatedly criticized by an older colleague. According to Paula, her colleague would get in her face in front of students and scream that she was not professional and did not have the ability to get along well with others. "She makes me feel like the worst person in the world," says Paula (Rowley, 2011). Paula is not alone, with research suggesting that roughly 70 percent of employees are bullied (Mattice, 2009).

Bullying has several negative consequences including increased absenteeism, greater turnover, reduced organizational commitment and job satisfaction, lower productivity and efficiency, diminished psychological and physical health, greater anxiety and depression (cf. Bulutlar and Oz, 2009). A survey on workplace bullying found that it affects the physical well-being of targets, with 45 percent of those bullied suffering stress-related health problems such as debilitating anxiety, panic attacks, clinical depression, and posttraumatic stress (Workplace Bullying Institute, 2007). Moreover, targets of bullying have experienced headaches, stomach pain, loss of appetite, inability to sleep, an increased sense of vulnerability, feelings of frustration and/or helplessness, anger and shock (Oppermann, 2008). Subjective well-being appears to be affected as well, as reductions in both productivity and job satisfaction, coupled with increases in turnover point toward diminished life satisfaction (at least temporarily). The effects of bullying are also likely to take a toll on one's psychological well-being, as feelings of self-acceptance and autonomy (i.e., feelings of self-determination) are reduced from repeated bullying attacks. Moreover, victims of bullying may feel less socially accepted, thus experiencing reduced social well-being. As such, it is evident that bullying affects the physical, subjective, psychological, and possibly social well-being of organization members. While codes, caring, and independence climates reduce the incidence of bullying, instrumental climates promote such behavior (Bulutlar and Oz, 2009).

Injuries in the workplace are a serious concern that costs organizations hundreds of billions of dollars (cf. Parboteeah and Kapp, 2008). In 2009, there were more than 3.1 million nonfatal occupational injuries and 4,551 workplace deaths (U.S. Bureau of Labor Statistics, 2010, 2011). The experiences at large pipe manufacturer McWane Inc., where 4,600 injuries (e.g., maimed, burned, sickened) and 9 deaths have occurred due to safety (i.e., 400 violations) and health violations since 1995 (Barstow and Bergman, 2003a, 2003b), suggest that ethical climate impacts workplace injury. Management at McWane calculated regulatory fines to be less costly than full compliance with safety and environmental rules. When faced with OSHA safety inspections, they lied and covered up violations to deceive investigators (Barstow and Bergman, 2003a). Management at McWane created an unethical climate by putting cost savings above the health and safety of its employees. Research suggests that a caring ethical climate is associated with fewer incidences of workplace injuries (Parboteeah and Kapp, 2008). Additionally, when independence, rules and law/ code dimensions of ethical climate exist, organization members are more motivated to participate in and comply with work-related safety behaviors (ibid.).

It is important to note that when the firm's climate is more ethical, the ethical behavior of employees improves (Cohen, 1995; Schminke, Arnaud, and Kuenzi, 2007; Schneider, 1975; Verbeke, Ouwerkerk, and Peelen, 1996; Victor and Cullen, 1988; Wimbush and Shepard, 1994). This is critical, given strong support for a relationship between unethical behavior and diminished well-being (Giacalone and Promislo, 2010). Improving ethical behavior is also important, given evidence suggesting a positive relationship between ethical behavior and individual performance (Schminke, Arnaud, and Kuenzi, 2007; cf. Schwepker and Good, 2010). Some evidence suggests that ethical climate itself is positively related to individual effort (Mulki, Jaramillo, and Locander, 2009) and performance (Mulki, Jaramillo, and Locander, 2008; Weeks et al., 2004). Moreover, managers perceive a stronger link between ethics and success when the firm's climate is high on the caring dimension of ethical climate and low on instrumentalism (Deshpande, 1996a). Positive individual performance and success on the job is likely to contribute to an individual's well-being, as it may foster feelings of job security, enhance one's self-esteem, evoke feelings of satisfaction, and possibly lead to increased pay, which could be used to improve one's quality of life. In fact, research finds a positive relationship between subjective well-being and success on the job (cf. Pavot and Diener, 2004). Conversely, an unethical climate can diminish employee morale (cf. Mulki, Jaramillo, and Locander, 2008; Thomas, Schermerhorn, and Dienhardt, 2004), potentially resulting in negative affect, and reduced life satisfaction, subsequently harming one's well-being.

Considerable research has examined the relationship between ethical climate and employee job satisfaction. In general, a more ethical climate leads to more satisfied employees (Babin, Boles, and Robin, 2000; Cullen, Parboteeah, and Victor, 2003; DeConinck, 2010; Jaramillo, Mulki, and Solomon, 2006; Koh and Boo, 2001; Mulki, Jaramillo, and Locander, 2006, 2008, 2009; Schwepker, 2001). The relationship between facets of job satisfaction and dimensions of ethical climate have likewise been examined, with the caring and rules dimensions being positively related to overall job satisfaction, satisfaction with pay, and satisfaction with supervisors, and the satisfaction with promotion dimension being related only to the rules dimension (Joseph and Deshpande, 1997). Similarly, the law and professional codes dimension of climate has been shown to positively affect job satisfaction (Elci and Alpkan, 2009; Martin and Cullen, 2006). The instrumental dimension of climate, however, has been found to be negatively related to overall job satisfaction, as well as to satisfaction with promotion, coworkers, and supervisors (Deshpande, 1996b). Studies have similarly found the structural dimension of ethical climate to positively impact overall job satisfaction (Schwepker and Hartline, 2005), satisfaction with supervisor (Mulki, Jaramillo, and Locander, 2008), as well as various facets of job satisfaction (pay, promotion, supervisor, policy, workers, job, overall) (Schwepker, 2001). According to Parboteeah and Cullen (2003), an ethical climate that offers ethical rules makes individuals feel good about their job and stimulates important work that is believed to be more than satisfying.

One's job is an important part of one's life. Thus, satisfaction with one's job is likely to positively influence one's assessment of their life satisfaction, an important component of subjective well-being. In fact, Judge and Locke (1993) found job satisfaction to positively affect subjective well-being. As such, an ethical climate should foster greater job satisfaction and subsequently greater well-being.

DEVELOPING AN ETHICAL CLIMATE

As illustrated, ethical climate plays an important role in the well-being of organizational members. By fostering a more ethical climate, positive job-related outcomes may be achieved, resulting in improved physical, subjective, psychological, and social well-being. However, when the organization's climate is viewed as unethical, members' job-related outcomes may be negatively impacted, which in turn poses serious negative consequences to one's well-being. Fortunately, ethical climate may be the most manageable factor management can use to influence ethical behavior in an organization (Schwepker, Ferrell, and Ingram, 1997). As such, several steps can and should be taken to improve an organization's ethical climate, and consequently the well-being of its members.

Assessing the Ethical Climate

The first step is to assess the current state of the firm's ethical climate. Doing so will allow the organization to determine the current strengths and weaknesses of the ethical climate and which areas need attention. At least two widely used assessment instruments can be utilized to determine members' ethical climate perceptions. One of these, Victor and Cullen's (1988) Ethical Climate Questionnaire (twenty-six items) discussed earlier, can be administered to employees. As pointed out, it can provide the organization with its members' perceptions of five ethical climate dimensions. Another alternative is to use a seven-item ethical climate measure developed to assess the presence and enforcement of codes of ethics, corporate policies on ethics, and top-management actions related to ethics (Schwepker, Ferrell, and Ingram, 1997). However, this tool focuses on assessing the structural dimension of ethical climate and it may best be used in conjunction with an alternative assessment tool. Assessment should be conducted periodically so that action can be taken as necessary to ensure a healthy ethical climate.

Although we know that improving the firm's ethical climate should increase the well-being of its employees, it might be constructive to determine which dimensions of climate have the greatest impact on the different types of well-being. For instance, does having a strong structural ethical climate created via ethical codes, ethical policies, and punishment reduce employee ambiguity regarding expected ethical behavior thus leading to less physical stress? Perhaps a strong caring ethical climate will have a bigger impact on the subjective well-being of organizational members. The social satisfaction derived from the feeling that others care about one is likely to lead to enhanced feelings of life satisfaction.

Setting Ethical Parameters

In general, several actions can be taken to create or improve a firm's ethical climate. These are likely to be dictated by the findings from the ethical climate assessment. For starters, the organization must establish clear expectations of ethical behavior. The primary mechanisms for accomplishing this are ethical codes, policies related to ethical behavior and the company's disciplinary system. The organization should develop a code of ethics that embraces the ethical values and behaviors desired of organizational members as well as ethical policies that clearly outline members' expected behaviors. The Ethics Resource Center, a private nonprofit organization, offers useful guidelines for creating a code of ethics. Ethical policies should be developed based on ethical principles, the law, and industry standards. To be effective, however, codes and policies must be successfully communicated (both orally and in writing) to organizational members, be understood, and become an active part of an employee's working knowledge (Hegarty and Sims, 1979; Weeks and Nantel, 1992). This can be accomplished in part through the organization's socialization process, the process by which members acquire the organizational values, job skills, social knowledge, attitudes, and expected behaviors necessary to effectively perform organizational tasks (cf. Grant and Bush, 1996). As individuals experience others in the organization living by and/or discussing the company's codes and policies, they are likely to internalize these over time (Schwepker and Hartline, 2005). In addition, training, to be discussed later, is a significant tool for socializing individuals into the organization.

Codes and policies must also be enforced. Actual discipline, or even the threat of punishment, may indirectly influence the decision to behave ethically through its effects on one's perceptions of likely consequences and the desirability of those consequences. In other words, if an employee believes that he or she will be punished for an unethical act then the employee is less likely to act unethically. However, the absence of punishment provides an opportunity for unethical behavior. Most firms expect ethical behavior and therefore do not go out of their way to reward it. Nevertheless, it is important to ensure that unethical behavior is not being rewarded. For instance, letting an employee get away with padding an expense account is, in essence, rewarding him or her for unethical behavior. It is important therefore to punish or even eliminate the "bad apples" as their behavior will significantly influence the behavior of others in the organization (Ferrell and Gresham, 1985).

Although, as suggested above, improving the structural dimension of ethical climate may provide boundaries, thus reducing stress for those who desire clarification for practicing ethical behavior, it may increase the stress for those who are not ethically inclined. These individuals may feel the pressure from such parameters as they attempt to circumvent appropriately sanctioned behavior. However, this may not be bad, because the result of such stress could be that these individuals leave the organization, thus improving the overall ethical climate.

To facilitate enforcement of ethical codes and policies, it is useful to set up mechanisms for reporting and correcting unethical behavior. Ideally, it would be helpful to construct some type of ethics "hotline" to enable employees to give anonymous feedback on abuses, and to have someone responsible for overseeing it. Employees must be made to feel comfortable in reporting unethical transgressions, otherwise their well-being may be negatively impacted. For instance, if an individual is concerned that word may get out that he or she blew the whistle on someone, this could cause undue stress resulting in consequences such as sleeplessness, headaches, and nausea. Moreover, the employee may fear being ostracized, or worse yet actually be ostracized, leading to both diminished psychological and social well-being.

Developing an Ethical Fit

Having determined the ethical foundation for the organization, steps can be taken to ensure a fit between the ethical values espoused by the organization and those of its members. As alluded to earlier, a good ethical fit leads to less role conflict (Schwepker, Ferrell, and Ingram, 1997). This should diminish job stress, thus improving well-being. Shared person–organization values are directly related to positive work attitudes (Posner, Kouzes, and Schmidt, 1985), which presumably should lead to greater subjective well-being. However, when an individual believes that his or her values are not compatible with those of the organization, psychological, physiological, and behavior strains result (French, Caplan, and Harrison, 1982).

The recruitment and selection process presents one opportunity to ensure an ethical fit. The organization should institutionalize into its selection and hiring process mechanisms for identifying and hiring candidates whose ethical values are consistent with those advocated by the organization. This requires identifying key ethical characteristics (e.g., honesty, integrity) that the organization is looking for in employees and then making those part of the stated job qualifications for each position. Subsequently, individuals must be evaluated against such criteria during the selection process. Byham (2004), for example, developed a series of questions that could be used (or serve as an example) when interviewing job candidates to help determine their ethical values. Additionally, the company may wish to have candidates complete a multidimensional ethics scale intended to measure various individual moral value frameworks (Reidenbach and Robin, 1988, 1990). Using this scale, candidates would be asked to respond to different unethical scenarios by reacting to eight, seven-point semantic differential statements anchored by bipolar adjectives (e.g., fair/unfair; morally right/not morally right) after reading each scenario. The statements capture three ethical dimensions: (1) a broad-based moral equity dimension; (2) a relativistic dimension; and (3) a contractualism dimension consisting of three different ethical philosophies including justice, relativism, and deontology. Numerous studies have examined and confirmed the psychometric properties of this scale (cf. McMahon and Harvey, 2007). Information gleaned from this assessment can offer insights regarding the candidate's moral judgment and be used in conjunction with other assessment tools in determining the candidate's overall fit with the organization.

Training provides an important mechanism for aligning individual and organizational values. An ethical climate assessment may be useful in dictating specific training objectives. Certainly, for new hires, training on the company's ethical codes and policies is vital. Members should not only be provided with codes and policies, but also taught how they apply to their work setting. Also, employees must be made aware of ethical issues in the workplace so that they are able to identify them as they arise. They need to be sensitized to issues with ethical content that they may face and instructed on appropriate responses to such issues. Moreover, training can be conducted to develop improved moral judgment and reasoning skills. Four- to twelve-week programs that involve interactive discussions of moral dilemmas, role-playing, and scenario analyses, allow employees to develop their moral decision-making skills by questioning their own and others' moral reasoning (Schminke, Arnaud, and Kuonzi 2007). Role-plays, in particular, are useful for allowing employees to act out ethical dilemmas and model appropriate behavior demonstrated by the instructor. To promote higher-level moral reasoning, it may be beneficial to administer the defining issues test (Rest, 1986) to assess employees' cognitive moral development (CMD). CMD theory focuses on the reasons one uses to justify a moral choice (Trevino, 1986) and postulates that an individual's moral decision making becomes more complex and sophisticated with development (Kohlberg, 1969). When an individual is exposed to moral reasoning at a level higher than what he or she is accustomed to, cognitive disequilibrium occurs, the individual questions the adequacy of his/her own level of reasoning, and considers the merits of the other (Trevino, 1986). Thus, it is possible to raise one's level of moral reasoning. As a supplement to organized training sessions, internal newsletters, for example, can be used to provide information that reinforces organizational values such as honesty, fairness, and integrity.

Influencing Through Leadership

Although managers are ultimately responsible for the actions previously described for influencing ethical climate, they play an additional, significant role more directly through the words and behaviors they exhibit as leaders. Through the direction given by management, employees can be influenced to make more ethical decisions (Ferrell and Gresham, 1985), thus creating a more ethical climate. Such guidance is likely to confirm the values of ethically inclined individuals, resulting in less conflict and subsequently improved well-being (or at least not diminished well-being). It may likewise diminish ambiguity for those who are unsure regarding the appropriate course of action to take when it comes to ethical issues. However, this may create conflict and tension for less ethically inclined individuals, who view such direction as counter to their desired behavior, thus diminishing their well-being.

Differential association theory (Sutherland and Cressey, 1970) suggests that we learn behaviors from those with whom we interact. Similarly, social learning theory (Bandura, 1977) claims that we learn by observing the behavior of others and its consequences. Therefore, managers can influence the ethical values and behaviors of subordinates by setting a good example—adhering to and living by the ethical values espoused by the organization. A potentially useful leadership style for developing more ethical individuals and subsequently a more ethical climate is transformational leadership.

Managers should consider supplementing transactional leadership, which relies on contingent reward and punishment, with transformational leadership. Transformational leadership behaviors (i.e., expressing a vision, providing a suitable role model, nurturing the acceptance of group goals, offering individualized support and intellectual stimulation, and communicating significant performance expectations) can transform both followers and leader by elevating their ethical aspirations and moral conduct (Burns, 1978; Podsakoff et al., 1990). By exhibiting a strong conviction in the moral righteousness of his or her beliefs, the transformational leader can increase influence (Bass, 1985). Leaders are believed to be truly transformational when they build awareness about what is and what is not acceptable behavior and inspire employees to place a higher priority on what is good for the organization than on their own self-interests (Bass and Steidlmeier, 1999). Thus, by conveying their high ethical values, transformational leaders are able to change followers' goals and beliefs, as they internalize the beliefs of their leader (Carlson and Perrewe, 1995).

Coaching and mentoring interventions offer managers an effective means for getting their message across regarding appropriate ethical conduct. As a coach, the manager focuses on continuous development of employees through supervisory feedback and role modeling. In terms of role modeling, the manager should live by the company's ethical codes and policies, thus demonstrating the type of behavior to be modeled. Managers should also provide feedback to employees on the handling of work-related activities that give information about how and why a desired outcome is achieved. Guidance and feedback should come as close as possible to the occurrence of an appropriate event related to developing employees' ethical attitudes or behaviors (Ingram et al., 2009).

DIRECTIONS FOR FUTURE RESEARCH

The research suggests that ethical climate primarily indirectly influences an individual's well-being via its effect on various job-related outcomes. It could certainly be instructive to more carefully examine the manner in which each outcome affects well-being (e.g., which type of well-being is affected and how). Likewise, it might be useful to determine whether ethical climate has direct effects on well-being, which types of well-being are most affected, and which dimensions of ethical climate have the greatest effects. Workplace norms (Hammer et al., 2004) and cultural values and beliefs (Peterson and Wilson, 2004) that are unhealthy can lead to stress. Such characteristics describe an unethical climate. What are the most common obstacles to well-being likely to be derived from such stress—headaches, ulcers, anxiety, drug or alcohol abuse, sleep disturbances, and so on? Moreover, improvements in which dimensions of ethical climate are likely to eliminate the results of stress and improve one's well-being? For instance, is physical well-being more likely to be diminished as a result of stress caused by ambiguity when the organization does not have a strong structural ethical climate created via ethical codes, ethical policies, and punishment? Could it be that a robust caring ethical climate is more likely than any other dimension to affect the subjective and or psychological well-being of organizational members?

We also know little about the influence of ethical climate on the well-being of perpetrators, witnesses, and associated parties. As suggested earlier, an individual who happens to be unethically inclined may not feel at ease in an ethical climate. How does this conflict affect the well-being of this employee who may desire to partake in unethical acts but sees roadblocks in his or her way as evidenced by an ethical climate? Also, what about the perpetrator whose unethical climate "pressures" him or her to commit unethical acts that he or she would not otherwise commit? In what manner is the well-being of this individual affected? Is the well-being of witnesses to unethical acts likely to be affected more in an ethical than unethical climate, perhaps due to the trauma resulting from witnessing acts that are not typically witnessed? Such trauma is likely to result from unethical behavior challenging employees' key values and beliefs underlying their assumptions regarding the world and how it works (Koltko-Rivera, 2004). Additionally, betrayal trauma may result when those we depend upon violate our trust (Freyd, 1996), such as could occur when an individual commits an act that runs counter to organizationally accepted values and beliefs. Finally, does ethical climate affect the well-being of people associated with those operating within that environment? Take, for instance, an employee operating in an unethical climate who feels pressure to commit unethical acts for fear of losing his or her job. How does the fear and tension felt by this individual affect those with whom he or she interacts outside of the workplace, for instance, a spouse?

Additional research could be conducted on variables affected by ethical climate that could subsequently affect well-being. For instance, the more ethical the climate, the greater the trust in one's supervisor (DeConinck, 2011; Mulki, Jaramillo, and Locander, 2006, 2008; Ruppel and Harrington, 2000). It seems that greater trust is likely to lead to a stronger employee–supervisor relationship given that trust forms the foundation of relationships. However, an unethical climate is likely to diminish trust, resulting in a weaker relationship, and subsequently diminished psychological well-being due to negative relations.

Two other variables that deserve further consideration as they pertain to ethical climate are organizational commitment and turnover. When the organization's climate is perceived as being ethical, employees are more committed (Babin, Boles, and Robin, 2000; Cullen, Parboteeah, and Victor, 2003; DeConinck, 2010; Kelley and Dorsch, 1991; Koh and Boo, 2001; Martin and Cullen, 2006; Mulki, Jaramillo, and Locander, 2009; Schwepker, 2001; Weeks et al., 2004) and turnover is lower (Cullen, Parboteeah, and Victor, 2003; DeConinck, 2011; Koh and Boo, 2001; Mulki, Jaramillo, and Locander, 2006, 2008). This is because employees are more likely to perceive that there is a mutual commitment to shared values and the welfare of the other party in a relationship (Barnett and Schubert, 2002). How does the well-being of more committed employees who are less likely to leave the organization as a result of these shared values compare with those who do not experience the shared values brought about by an ethical climate? Which types of well-being, if any, are most likely to be affected as a result? Furthermore, does the turnover resulting from those who leave an unethical climate that does not correspond with their values improve their well-being (e.g., perhaps individuals are happy to depart from an organization that operates unethically and thus feel more at peace in doing so)?

CONCLUSION

An organizational climate perceived as unethical can have serious consequences for both its members and the organization as a whole. Climate perceptions result from actions and behaviors undertaken by the organization and its members. Fortunately, the organization has an opportunity to mold these perceptions by taking steps to create an ethical climate within the organization. Doing so is likely to result in many positive job outcomes that affect individual well-being. Employees in an ethical climate tend to behave more ethically, exhibit less deviant work behavior, experience less role stress, encounter fewer injuries on the job, and be more satisfied with their job. Such outcomes are associated with improved well-being. However, an unethical climate will negatively affect these job outcomes and subsequently diminish individual well-being in various ways.

REFERENCES

Appelbaum, S.H.; Deguire, K.J.; and Lay, M. 2005. The relationship of ethical climate to deviant workplace behaviour. *Corporate Governance,* 5, 43–55.
Babin, B.J.; Boles, J.S.; and Robin, D.P. 2000. Representing the perceived ethical work climate among marketing employees. *Journal of the Academy of Marketing Science,* 28, 345–358.
Bandura, A. 1977. *Social Learning Theory.* Englewood, NJ: Prentice Hall.
Barnett, T., and Schubert, E. 2002. Perceptions of the ethical work climate and covenantal relationships. *Journal of Business Ethics,* 36, 279–290.

Barnett, T., and Vaicys, C. 2000. The moderating effect of individuals' perceptions of ethical work climate on ethical judgments and behavioral intentions. *Journal of Business Ethics,* 27, 351–362.

Barstow, D., and Bergman, L. 2003a. Deaths on the job, slaps on the wrists. *New York Times,* January 10, A1.

———. 2003b. Criminal Inquiry Under Way at Large Pipe Manufacturer. *New York Times,* May 15, A1.

Bass, B.M. 1985. Leadership: Good, better, best. *Organizational Dynamics,* 13, 26–40.

———. 1995. *Transformational Leadership: Industry, Military, and Educational Impact.* Mahwah, NJ: Erlbaum.

Bass, B.M., and Steidlmeier, P. 1999. Ethics, character, and authentic transformational leadership behavior. *Leadership Quarterly,* 10, 181–216.

Behrman, D.N., and Perreault, W.D. 1984. A role stress model of the performance and satisfaction of industrial salespersons. *Journal of Marketing,* 48, 9–21.

Bommer, M.; Gratto, C.; Gravander, J.; and Tuttle, M. 1987. A behavioral model of ethical and unethical decision making. *Journal of Business Ethics,* 6, 265–280.

Brothers, T. 1991. *Corporate Ethics: Developing New Standards of Accountability.* New York: Conference Board.

Bulutlar, F., and Oz, E.U. 2009. The effects of ethical climates on bullying behavior in the workplace. *Journal of Business Ethics,* 86, 273–295. doi: 10.1007/s10551–008–9847–4.

Burns, J.M. 1978. *Leadership.* New York: Harper and Row.

Byham, W.C. 2004. Can you interview for integrity? *Across the Board Magazine,* 41, 34–38.

Carlson, D.S., and Perrewe, P.L. 1995. Institutionalization of organizational ethics through transformational leadership. *Journal of Business Ethics,* 14, 829–838.

Cohen, D.V. 1995. Creating ethical work climates: A socioeconomic perspective. *Journal of Socio-Economics,* 24, 317–343.

Cullen, J.B.; Parboteeah, K.P.; Victor, B. 2003. The effects of ethical climates on organizational commitment: A two-study analysis. *Journal of Business Ethics,* 46, 127–141.

DeConinck, J.B. 2010. The influence of ethical climate on marketing employees' job attitudes and behaviors. *Journal of Business Research,* 63, 384–391. doi: 10.106/j.jbusres.2008.11.009.

———. 2011. The effects of ethical climate on organizational identification, supervisory trust, and turnover among salespeople. *Journal of Business Research,* 64, 617–624. doi: 10.1016/j.jbusres.2010.06.014.

De Dreu, C.K.W.; Van Dierendonck, D.; and De Best-Waldhober, M. 2002. Conflict at work and individual well-being. In *The Handbook of Work and Health Psychology*, ed. M.J. Schabracq, C.L. Cooper, C.L. and K.A.M. Winnubst, 495–515. Chichester, UK: Wiley.

Deshpande, S.P. 1996a. Ethical climate and the link between success and ethical behavior: An empirical investigation of a non-profit organization. *Journal of Business Ethics,* 15, 315–320.

———. 1996b. The impact of ethical climate types on facets of job satisfaction: An empirical investigation. *Journal of Business Ethics,* 15, 655–660.

Dickson, M.W.; Smith, D.B.; Grojean, M.W.; and Ehrhart, M. 2001. An organizational climate regarding ethics: The outcome of leader values and the practices that reflect them. *Leadership Quarterly,* 12, 197–217.

Dijkstra, M.T.; van Dierendonck, D.; Evers, A.; and De Dreu, C.K.W. 2005. Conflict and well-being at work: The moderating role of personality. *Journal of Managerial Psychology,* 20, 87–104.

Elci, M., and Alpkan, L. 2009. The impact of perceived organizational ethical climate on work satisfaction. *Journal of Business Ethics,* 84, 297–311.

Engelbrecht, A.S.; van Aswegen, A.S.; and Theron, C.C. 2005. The effect of ethical values on transformational leadership and ethical climate in organisations. *South African Journal of Business Management,* 36, 19–26.

Evans, M.G. 1970. The effects of supervisory behavior on the path-goal relationship. *Organizational Behavior and Human Performance,* 5, 277–298. doi: 10.1016/0030–5073(70)90021–8.

Ferrell, O.C., and Gresham, L.G. 1985. A contingency framework for understanding ethical decision making. *Journal of Marketing,* 49, 87–96.

Ferrell, O.C., and Skinner, S.J. 1988. Ethical behavior and bureaucratic structure in marketing research organizations. *Journal of Marketing Research,* 25, 103–109.

Ferrell, O.C.; Gresham, L.G.; and Fraedrich, J. 1989. A synthesis of ethical decision models for marketing. *Journal of Macromarketing,* 9, 55–64.

Ferrell, O.C.; LeClair, D.T.; and Ferrell, L. 1997. Environmental activities related to social responsibility and ethical climate. *Journal of Marketing Management,* 7, 1–13.

French, J.R.P. Jr.; Caplan, R.D.; and Harrison, R.V. 1982. *The Mechanisms of Job Stress and Strain.* London: Wiley.

Freyd, J.J. 1996. *Betrayal Trauma: The Logic of Forgetting Childhood Abuse.* Cambridge, MA: Harvard University Press.

Giacalone, R.A., and Promislo, M.D. 2010. Unethical and unwell: Decrements in well-being and unethical activity at work. *Journal of Business Ethics,* 91, 275–297.

Grant, E.S., and Bush, A.J. 1996. Salesforce socialization tactics: Building organizational value congruence. *Journal of Personal Selling and Sales Management,* 16, 17–32.

Grojean, M.W.; Resick, C.J.; Dickson, M.W.; and Smith, D.B. 2004. Leaders, values, and organizational climate: Examining leadership strategies for establishing an organizational climate regarding ethics. *Journal of Business Ethics,* 55, 223–241.

Grundstein-Amado, R. 2001. A strategy for formulation and implementation of codes of ethics in public service organizations. *International Journal of Public Administration,* 24, 461–478.

Hammer, T.H.; Saksvik, P.O.; Nytro, K.; Torvatn, H.; and Bayazit, M. 2004. Expanding the psychosocial work environment: Workplace norms and work–family conflict as correlates of stress and health. *Journal of Occupational Health Psychology,* 9, 83–97.

Hegarty, W.H., and Sims, H.P. Jr. 1978. Some determinants of unethical decision behavior: An experiment. *Journal of Applied Psychology,* 63, 451–457.

———. 1979. Organizational philosophy, policies, and objectives related to unethical decision behavior: A laboratory experiment. *Journal of Applied Psychology,* 64, 331–338.

Henle, C.A.; Giacalone, R.A.; and Jurkiewicz, C.L. 2005. The role of ethical ideology in workplace deviance. *Journal of Business Ethics,* 56, 219–230.

Hunt, S.D., and Vitell, S. 1986. A general theory of marketing ethics. *Journal of Macromarketing,* 6, 5–16.

Ingram, T.N.; LaForge, R.W.; and Schwepker, C.H. Jr. 2007. Salesperson ethical decision making: The impact of sales leadership and sales management control strategy. *Journal of Personal Selling and Sales Management,* 27, 301–315.

———. 2011. Addressing job stress in the salesforce. In *The Oxford Handbook of Sales Management and Sales Strategy,* ed. K. Le Meunier-Fitzhugh, N. Piercy, and D. Cravens, 253–276. Oxford: Oxford University Press.

Ingram, T.N.; LaForge, R.W.; Avila, R.; Schwepker, C.H. Jr.; and Williams, M. 2009. *Sales Management: Analysis and Decision Making.* 7th ed. Armonk, NY: M.E. Sharpe.

Jaramillo, F.; Mulki, J.P.; and Solomon, P. 2006. The role of ethical climate on salesperson's role stress, job attitudes, turnover intention, and job performance. *Journal of Personal Selling and Sales Management,* 26, 271–282.

Jaworski, B. 1988. Toward a theory of marketing control: Environmental context, control types, and consequences. *Journal of Marketing,* 52, 23–39.

Jones, T.M. 1991. Ethical decision making by individuals in organizations: An issue-contingent model. *Academy of Management Review,* 16, 366–395.

Joseph, J., and Deshpande, S.P. 1997. The impact of ethical climate on job satisfaction of nurses. *Healthcare Management Review,* 22, 76–81.

Judge, T.A. and Locke, E.A. 1993. Effect of dysfunctional thought processes on subjective well-being and job satisfaction. *Journal of Applied Psychology,* 78, 475–490.

Kahn, R.L.; Wolfe, D.M.; Quinn, R.P.; Snoek, J.D.; and Rosenthal, R.A. 1964. *Organizational Stress: Studies in Role Conflict and Ambiguity.* New York: Wiley.

Kelley, S.W.; and Dorsch, M.J. 1991. Ethical climate, organizational commitment, and indebtedness among purchasing executives. *Journal of Personal Selling and Sales Management,* 11, 55–66.

Keyes, C.L.M. 1998. Social well-being. *Social Psychology Quarterly,* 61, 121–140.

Keyes, C.L.M.; Shmotkin, D.; and Ryff, C.D. 2002. Optimizing well-being: The empirical encounter of two traditions. *Journal of Personality and Social Psychology,* 82, 1007–1022.

Koh, H.C.; and Boo, E.H.Y. 2001. The link between organizational ethics and job satisfaction: A study of managers in Singapore. *Journal of Business Ethics,* 29, 309–324.

Kohlberg, L. 1969. Stage and sequence: The cognitive-developmental approach to socialization. In *Handbook of Socialization Theory and Research,* ed. D.A. Goslin, 347–480. Chicago: Rand McNally.

Koltko-Rivera, M.E. 2004. The psychology of worldviews. *Review of General Psychology,* 8, 3–58.

Martin, K.D., and Cullen, J.B. 2006. Continuities and extensions of ethical climate theory: A meta-analytic review. *Journal of Business Ethics,* 69, 175–194. doi: 10.1007/s10551–006–9084–7.

Mattice, C. 2009. Successful learning organizations understand the power of positive workplaces. http://noworkplacebullies.com/yahoo_site_admin/assets/docs/Kirkpatrick_Article.36120227.pdf (accessed June 13, 2011).

McCabe, D.L.; Trevino, L.K.; and Butterfield, K.D. 1996. The influence of collegiate and corporate codes of conduct on ethics-related behavior in the workplace. *Business Ethics Quarterly,* 6, 461–476.

McMahon, J.M.; and Harvey, R.J. 2007. Psychometric properties of the Reidenbach-Robin multidimensional ethics scale. *Journal of Business Ethics,* 72, 27–39.

Mulki, J.P.; Jaramillo, F.; and Locander, W.B. 2006. Effects of ethical climate and supervisory trust on salesperson's job attitudes and intentions to quit. *Journal of Personal Selling and Sales Management,* 26, 19–26. doi: 10.2753/PSS0885–313426102.

———. 2008. Effect of ethical climate on turnover intention: Linking attitudinal- and stress theory. *Journal of Business Ethics,* 78, 559–574. doi: 10.1007/s10551–007–9368–6.

———. 2009. Critical role of leadership on ethical climate and salesperson behaviors. *Journal of Business Ethics,* 86, 125–141. doi: 10.1007/s10551–008–9839–4.

Nielsen, R.P. 2000. Do internal due process system permit adequate political and moral space for ethics voice, praxis, and community? *Journal of Business Ethics,* 24, 1–27.

Oppermann, S. 2008. Workplace bullying: Psychological violence? FedSmith.com, December 3. www.workplacebullying.org/2009/05/04/workplace-bullying-psychological-violence/ (accessed June 13, 2011).

Parboteeah, K.P., and Cullen, J.B. 2003. Ethical climates and spirituality: An exploratory examination of theoretical links. In *Handbook of Workplace Spirituality and Organizational Performance,* ed. R.A. Giacalone and C.L. Jurkiewicz, 137–151. Armonk, NY: M.E. Sharpe.

Parboteeah, K.P., and Kapp, E.A. 2008. Ethical climates and workplace safety behaviors: An empirical Investigation. *Journal of Business Ethics,* 80, 515–529. doi: 10.1007/s10551–007–9452-y.

Pavot, W., and Diener, E. 2004. The subjective evaluation of well-being in adulthood: Findings and implications. *Ageing International,* 29, 113–135.

Peterson, D.K. 2002. Deviant workplace behavior and the organization's ethical climate. *Journal of Business and Psychology,* 17, 47–61.

Peterson, M., and Wilson, J.F. 2004. Work stress in America. *International Journal of Stress Management,* 11, 91–113.

Podsakoff, P.M. 1982. Determinants of a supervisor's use of rewards and punishments: A literature review and suggestions for further research. *Organizational Behavior and Human Performance,* 29, 58–83.

Podsakoff, P.; MacKenzie, S.B.; Moorman, R.H.; and Fetter, R. 1990. Transformational leader behaviors and their effects on followers' trust in leader, satisfaction and organizational citizenship behaviors. *Leadership Quarterly,* 1, 107–142.

Posner, B.Z., and Schmidt, W.H. 1987. Ethics in American companies: A managerial perspective. *Journal of Business Ethics,* 6, 383–391.

Posner, B.; Kouzes, J.M.; and Schmidt, W.H. 1985. Shared values make a difference: An empirical test of corporate culture. *Human Resource Management,* 24, 293–310.

Quick, J.C., and Quick, J.D. 1984. *Organizational Stress and Preventive Management.* New York: McGraw-Hill.

Reidenbach, R.E., and Robin, D.P. 1988. Some initial steps toward improving the measurement of ethical evaluations of marketing activities. *Journal of Business Ethics,* 7, 871–879.

———. 1990. Toward the development of a multidimensional scale for improving evaluations of business ethics. *Journal of Business Ethics,* 9, 639–653.

Rest, J.R. 1986. *Moral Development: Advances in Research and Theory.* New York: Praeger.

Robinson, S., and Bennett, R. 1995. A typology of deviant workplace behaviors: A multi-dimensional scaling study. *Academy of Management,* 38, 555–572.

Rowley, Laura. 2011. The financial toll of workplace bullies. Yahoo Finance, May 5. www.workplacebullying.org/2011/05/06/yahoo/#more-4273 (accessed June 13, 2011).

Ruppel, C.P., and Harrington, S.J. 2000. The relationship of communication, ethical work climate, and trust to commitment and innovation. *Journal of Business Ethics,* 25, 313–328.

Schminke, M.; Ambrose, M.L.; and Neubaum, D.O. 2005. The effect of leader moral development on ethical climate and employee attitudes. *Organizational Behavior and Human Decision Process,* 97, 135–151. doi: 10.1016/j.obhdp.2005.03.006.

Schminke, M., Arnaud, A., and Kuenzi, M. (2007). The power of ethical work climates. *Organizational Dynamics*, 36, 171–186. Doi: 10.1016/j.orgdyn.2007.03.005

Schneider, B. 1975. Organizational climate: An essay. *Personnel Psychology,* 28, 447–479.

Schneider, B., and Reichers, A. 1983. On the etiology of climates. *Personnel Psychology,* 36, 19–39.

Schneider, B., and Rentsch, J. 1988. Managing climates and cultures: A futures perspective. In *Futures of Organizations,* ed. J. Hage, 181–200. Lexington, MA: Lexington Books.

Schwepker, C.H. Jr. 2001. Ethical climate's relationship to job satisfaction, organizational commitment and turnover intention in the salesforce. *Journal of Business Research,* 54, 39–52.

Schwepker, C.H. Jr., and Good, D.J. 2009. Ethical climate's influence on sales management practices. *Journal of Selling and Major Account Management,* 9, 8–24.

———. 2010. Transformational leadership and its impact on moral judgment. *Journal of Personal Selling and Sales Management,* 30, 299–317.

Schwepker, C.H. Jr., and Hartline, M. 2005. Managing the ethical climate of customer-contact service employees. *Journal of Service Research,* 7, 377–397.

Schwepker, C.H. Jr.; Ferrell, O.C.; and Ingram, T.N. 1997. The influence of ethical climate and ethical conflict on role stress in the sales force. *Journal of the Academy of Marketing Science,* 25, 99–108.

Sims, R.R. 1994. *Ethics and Organizational Decision Making: A Call for Renewal.* Westport, CT: Quorum Books.

Spector, P.E., and Jex, S.M. 1998. Development of four self-report measures of job stressors and strain: Interpersonal Conflict at Work Scale, Organizational Constraints Scale, Quantitative Workload Inventory, and Physical Symptoms Inventory. *Journal of Occupational Health Psychology,* 3, 356–367.

Sutherland, E., and Cressey, D.R. 1970. *Principles of Criminology.* Chicago: Lippincott.

Thomas, T., Schermerhorn, J.R. Jr., and Dienhart, J.W. 2004. Strategic leadership of ethical behavior in business. *Academy of Management Executive*, 18, 56–66.

Trevino, L.K. 1986. Ethical decision making in organizations: A person–situation interactionist model. *Academy of Management Review,* 11, 601–617.

Trevino, L.K., and Ball, G.A. 1992. The social implications of punishing unethical behavior: Observers' cognitive and affective reactions. *Journal of Management,* 18, 751–768.

Tsalikis, J., and Fritzsche, D.J. 1989. Business ethics: A literature review with a focus on marketing ethics. *Journal of Business Ethics,* 8, 695–743.

U.S. Bureau of Labor Statistics. 2010. Workplace injuries and illnesses—2009. News release, October 21. www.bls.gov/news.release/archives/osh_10212010.pdf (accessed June 15, 2011).

———. 2011. Revisions to the 2009 census of fatal occupational injuries (CFOI) counts. May 4. www.bls.gov/iif/oshwc/cfoi/cfoi_revised09.pdf (accessed June 15, 2011).

Vardi, Y. 2001. The effects of organizational and ethical climates on misconduct at work. *Journal of Business Ethics,* 29, 325–337.

Verbeke, W.; Ouwerkerk, C.; and Peelen, E. 1996. Exploring the contextual and individual factors on ethical decision making of salespeople. *Journal of Business Ethics,* 15, 1175–1187.

Victor, B., and Cullen, J.B. 1988. The organizational bases of ethical work climates. *Administrative Science Quarterly,* 33, 101–125.

Weaver, G.R. 1993. Corporate codes of ethics: Purpose, process and content issues. *Business and Society,* 32, 44–58.

Weeks, W.A., and Nantel, J. 1992. Corporate codes of ethics and sales force behavior: A case study. *Journal of Business Ethics,* 11, 753–760.

Weeks, W.A.; Loe, T.W.; Chonko, L.B.; and Wakefield, K. 2004. The effect of perceived ethical climate on the search for salesforce excellence. *Journal of Personal Selling and Sales Management,* 24, 199–214.

Wimbush, J.C., and Shepard, J.M. 1994. Toward an understanding of ethical climate: Its relationship to ethical behavior and supervisory influence. *Journal of Business Ethics,* 13, 637–647.

Wimbush, J.C., Shepard, J.M.; and Markham, S.E. 1997. An empirical examination of the multi-dimensionality of ethical climate in organizations. *Journal of Business Ethics,* 16, 67–77.

Workplace Bullying Institute. 2007. Results of the 2007 WBI U.S. Workplace Bullying Survey. www.workplacebullying.org/wbiresearch/wbi-2007/ (accessed June 13, 2011).

19

THE VIRTUOUS BUSINESS CYCLE MODEL

A Proposal

CHARLOTTE MCDANIEL AND COREY L.M. KEYES

To succeed, most business leaders believe they should focus on the alleviation of liabilities, inefficiencies, and sources of strain and discontent among workers and customers. However, to increase the level and range of overall success, organizations ought to cultivate a virtuous orientation toward business. We define a virtuous organization as a productive and profitable business over time that also addresses its stated values for workers, customers, and product(s). What sets a virtuous organization apart from businesses that merely turn profits and increase shareholder value, however, is that it seeks to promote and sustain high levels of employee well-being and does so by providing its leadership with legitimate authority sustained by an ethics environment.

The nature of well-being, as well as how and why organizations would seek to develop and sustain ethics—or decrease unethical activities—is the focus of this chapter. We argue that organizations with ethics environments are desirable organizations, and as such are more efficient and constructive producers of profits because, in part, legitimation of managers' leadership and authority and the maintenance of an ethics environment aids in enhancing employee well-being. In turn, businesses in which employees report higher levels of well-being not only tend to report high profits but also have been found to reflect greater customer loyalty and work satisfaction, higher rates of employee retention and attendance, and higher levels of productivity and cooperation among coworkers (Harter, Schmidt, and Keyes, 2003; McDaniel, 2011; McDaniel, Schoeps, and Lincourt, 2001; Spector, 1997; Warr, 1999).

FROM SUBJECTIVE WELL-BEING TO WORKPLACE OUTCOMES

The study of subjective well-being has been divided into two streams of research, one that equates well-being with happiness as feeling good and the other with happiness as human potential that, when pursued and developed, results in positive functioning in life. The streams of subjective well-being research grew from two distinct philosophical viewpoints on happiness—one reflecting the Epicurean view that believed happiness was about feeling positive emotions (i.e., hedonic), and another reflecting the Aristotelian (and Socratic) view that happiness was about striving toward excellence and positive functioning (i.e., eudaimonia).

The Hedonic Tradition: Feeling Good

The hedonic tradition, the first viewpoint regarding subjective well-being, embodies human concerns with maximizing the amount or duration of positive, pleasant feelings while minimizing the amount or duration of negative, unpleasant feelings. Briefly summarized here, it is reflected in the stream of research on subjective *emotional* well-being (i.e., happiness, satisfaction, and affect balance). Emotional well-being is a specific dimension of subjective well-being that consists of perceptions of avowed happiness and satisfaction with life, and the balancing of positive and negative emotions. Whereas happiness is based upon spontaneous reflections of pleasant and unpleasant affects in one's immediate experience, life satisfaction represents a long-term assessment of one's life.

The Eudaimonic Tradition: Functioning Well

The second subjective viewpoint on well-being is the tradition of eudaimonia, which animates human concerns with developing nascent abilities and capacities toward becoming a more fully functioning person and citizen. This tradition is reflected in the stream of research on subjective *psychological* (Ryff, 1989) and *social* (Keyes, 1998) well-being that reflects how well individuals see themselves functioning in life, striving to achieve secular standards of excellence such as purpose, contribution, integration, intimacy, acceptance, and mastery.

A variety of concepts from personality, developmental, and clinical psychology have been synthesized by Ryff (1989) to operationalize psychological well-being. In contrast to hedonic measures of subjective well-being, psychological well-being requires individuals to self-report about the quality with which they are functioning in their lives. Each of the six dimensions of psychological well-being has indicated the challenges that individuals encounter as they strive to function fully and realize their unique talents (Ryff, 1989; Ryff and Keyes, 1995). The six dimensions encompass a breadth of well-being: Positive evaluation of oneself and one's past life, a sense of continued growth and development as a person, the belief that one's life is purposeful and meaningful, the possession of quality relations with others, the capacity to manage effectively one's life and surrounding world, and a sense of self-determination (Ryff and Keyes, 1995).

Self-acceptance is the criterion toward which individuals must strive in order to feel good about themselves. Such self-acceptance is characterized by a positive attitude toward the self, acknowledging and accepting multiple aspects of self, including unpleasant personal aspects. In addition, self-acceptance includes positive feelings about one's past life. The scale, *positive relations with others,* measures the possession of, or the ability to cultivate, warm, trusting, intimate relationships with others. A concern for the welfare of others and the ability to empathize, to cooperate, and to compromise are all implied aspects of the ability to develop warm and trusting interpersonal relationships. *Autonomy* reflects the seeking of self-determination and personal authority or independence in a society that sometimes compels obedience and compliance. The abilities to resist social pressures so as to think or behave in certain ways, and to guide and evaluate behavior based on internalized standards and values, are crucial in this domain. Individuals with high autonomy feel confident about thinking and expressing their own ideas and opinions.

Environmental mastery includes the ability to manage everyday affairs, to control a complex array of external activities, to make effective use of surrounding opportunities, and to choose or create contexts suitable to personal needs. A sense of mastery results when individuals recognize personal needs and desires and also feel capable of taking an active role in getting what they need from their environments, and feel they are permitted to do so. *Purpose in life* consists of one's aims and objectives for living, including the presence of life goals and a sense of directedness. Those with high purpose in life see their daily lives as fulfilling a direction and purpose and therefore view their present and past life as meaningful. Finally, *personal growth* reflects the continuous pursuit of existing skills, talents, and opportunities for personal development and for realizing one's potential. In addition, personal growth includes the capacity to remain open to experience and to identify challenges in a variety of circumstances.

Whereas psychological well-being is conceptualized as a primarily private phenomenon that is focused on the challenges encountered by individuals in their personal lives, social well-being represents a more public experience that is focused on the social tasks encountered by individuals in their social structures and communities. Social well-being consists of five elements that indicate whether and to what degree individuals are functioning well in their social world (e.g., as neighbors, as coworkers, or as citizens) (Keyes, 1998). Social well-being originates in the sociological interest in individuals' anomie and alienation in society, which were classic themes in the writings of Emile Durkheim and Karl Marx. Drawing on these theoretical roots, Keyes (1998) developed multiple operational dimensions of social well-being that have been reported to represent the challenges individuals face as members of society, groups, institutions, and communities.

Social integration is the evaluation of the quality of one's relationship to society and community. Integration is therefore the extent to which people feel they have something in common with others who constitute their social reality (e.g., their neighborhood), as well as the degree to which they feel that they belong to their communities and society. *Social contribution* is the evaluation of one's value to society. It includes the belief that one is a vital member of society, with something of value to give to the world. Social coherence is the perception of the quality, organization, and operation of the social world, and it includes a concern for knowing about the world. *Social coherence* is analogous to meaningfulness in life involving appraisals that society is discernable, sensible, and predictable.

Social actualization is the evaluation of the potential and trajectory of society. This is the belief in the evolution of society and the sense that society has potential that is being realized through its institutions and citizens. *Social acceptance* is the construal of society through the character and qualities of other people as a generalized category. Individuals must function in a public arena that consists primarily of strangers. Individuals who illustrate social acceptance trust others, think that others are capable of kindness, and believe that people can be industrious. Socially accepting people hold favorable views of human nature and feel comfortable with others.

What is the utility of employee well-being for organizations? As employees' well-being increases, the productivity and profitability of the organization also has a tendency to increase (Spector, 1997). While studies have yet to show whether employee well-being is a cause or effect of positive business outcomes such as productivity, chances are that the causal arrows operate in both directions. That is, it is likely that productivity promotes an employee's feelings of well-being (e.g., by making them feel competent and useful), and that subjective well-being is likely to increase productivity. In regard to the latter, studies have shown that individuals in positive affective states think more efficiently and creatively, and are more likely to engage in prosocial behaviors (Isen, 1987).

Research also reveals that employees who are more satisfied with life and aspects of work are more cooperative, more helpful to their colleagues, more punctual, report fewer sick days, and remain employed for longer periods than do dissatisfied employees (Spector, 1997; Warr, 1999). Moreover, employees who report a greater balance of positive to negative feelings receive higher performance ratings from supervisors than employees who report lower levels of emotional well-being (Wright and Bonett, 1997; Wright and Cropanzano, 2000; Wright and Staw, 1999).

Studies have revealed a pervasive and positive relationship of employee well-being to better business-unit outcomes (Harter, Schmidt, and Keyes, 2003). Businesses in which employees report greater workplace satisfaction, personal development through work, and friendships at work, for example, have been found to report higher levels of customer satisfaction and loyalty, profitability, productivity, and retention of employees. Utility analyses conservatively estimate that companies with the most employees with high levels of well-being report dramatically higher monetary returns than companies in the lowest quartile of employee well-being.

THE NATURE AND ROLE OF ETHICS ENVIRONMENTS IN THE WORKPLACE

If a CEO (chief executive officer)—as a legitimated leader—were asked whether his/her organization was an ethical one, it would be difficult to imagine a valid leader responding with either a firm "no" or "don't know." The ability to develop and to sustain an ethical organization, highlighted through knowledge of the ethics environment, has been central to the work of most innovative leaders (McDaniel, 2004). This assertion has been corroborated by descriptions found in *A Great Place to Work* (Levering, 2000), reports on corporate success (Bennis, 1984), as well as studies on employees and ethics environments (McDaniel, 1995; McDaniel, Schoeps, and Lincourt, 2001). Retaining a high quality workplace, whether referring here to the organization as a whole or to the units and sections within that organization, is a close cousin to the desire for a place of employment that also exhibits ethics. Qualities that characterize a desirable place to work, one representing fewer *un*ethical behaviors, have been found across various types of organizations, including health care, business, and education, for example (McDaniel, 2005; McDaniel et al., 2006; McDaniel, Roche, and Veledar, 2011; McDaniel, Schoeps, and Lincourt, 2001). These findings have also held true for large or small organizations. Indeed, while studies have addressed issues arising from ethics environments, the countervailing approach regarding *un*ethical ramifications is frequently ignored. We turn now to those *unethical* behaviors and acts to ascertain what we might learn from them and how they influence employees.

Most of the reports detailing the outright costs of unethical behaviors reference the monetary losses. Those losses are further detailed in reductions revealed in profit losses, as well as expenses due to difficult and complicated legal matters, including litigation and lawsuits. Executives at Enron knew this all too well. However, what is less well examined, but equally compelling, is the loss to the organization in terms of its unethical behaviors. Those losses include, among others, inability to retain valued employees or increases in turnover, adverse effects on teamwork and thus productivity, loss of morale, decreased ability to trust, and concerns for supervisory support. All of these may also adversely influence the work processes as well as the psychosocial and emotional well-being and satisfaction exhibited among the employees. It is to these that we now turn in order to examine them in more detail, pertaining also to their separate, yet adverse influences. We assume here that all organizations have both unethical and ethical behaviors, since they employ human beings. What quality leaders who are legitimated desire, however, are *under*representations of *un*ethical behaviors, especially among their valued employees.

Ethics Environments

History has affirmed the concerned attention paid to the actions and behaviors of individuals, as well as those in a proposed "community" (Aristotle, 350 BCE/2009). Examination of one's moral life as well as attention to the many thoughtful and complex decisions with their resulting actions and influences on others, especially in a collectivity, provide a foundation for the development of the ethics environment. As a system of analysis and an endeavor, ethics pertains to the analytical phenomenon that poses the question: all things considered, what should one do (Baier, 1958)? What is the moral point of view? Which is the preferred or best action? How decisions are made, the considerations that influence those decisions, and the ensuing outcomes of those decisions continue to challenge contemporary society. Never has this been more important than in the complex and compelling decisions made by employees in contemporary organizations. While ethics has typically highlighted the decisions of individuals or decisions engaged by one-on-one exchanges, it has also been found, for example, that the organizational environment in which employees function—whether it addresses ethics or not—is fundamental to supporting and sustaining organizational environments with ethics (McDaniel, 2004). It is this setting of ethics that informs and influences employee decisions and their resulting actions. Empirical evidence compels continuing examination of such environments and their influences on workers.

The ethics environment reflects the perception that employees, for example, have of their current work setting. As measured empirically on the Ethics Environment Questionnaire (EEQ), it has been found to represent a unidimensional assessment of the organization based on twenty statements with factor loadings above the preset criterion of 0.50 (see, e.g., McDaniel, 2004). As a measure that reflects the perception of moral concerns present in the setting, it also parallels the concern for behaviors that reflect ethics. Multiple studies among a variety of settings, for example, representing a cross-section of employees in business, health care, or education, have revealed that where an ethics environment is robust, one also finds attractive features of work processes among those employees (McDaniel, 2011). Among these features are employee retention, productivity, morale and work satisfaction, cooperation and trust, and constructive supervisory support. These aspects of work processes that have been measured and reported are similar to several features of subjective employee well-being, and are projected to be related to it.

Employee Turnover

Employees have been found to prefer work in environments that are perceived to represent ethics (McDaniel, 2004). In contrast, when they perceive their work environment to be less than ethical, even frankly *un*ethical in nature, they may tend to look elsewhere for work. It is impossible to calculate precisely what the lag time is before an employee begins searching elsewhere for another job once he or she discovers less desirable behaviors. Likewise, the ability to tolerate the old situation varies among employees; it is also influenced by the personal—as well as the financial—situation of the employee. Clearly, an employee who supports a family has differing responsibilities and thus constraints than one who does not. Nevertheless, it has been found, for example, that when corporate employees think that their work environment presents a less than desirable ethics or is less than ethically desirable in their perception, they also tend to leave or anticipate turnover (McDaniel, Schoeps, and Lincourt, 2001). Their anticipatory turnover has been found to be higher in lower rated ethics environments, whereas in settings with a perceived robust or higher ethics the employees remain for longer periods of time.

While some employee loss is anticipated and inevitable in contemporary work, the loss of good employees is expensive. Most analyses calculate the cost of employee loss in terms of the annual salary, whereas more nuanced analyses will include the link to outcomes. Other costs may also occur. For example, not only does a leader need to replace the departing employee, itself a calculated loss, but also involved are the effort, time, and monetary investment in the interview and rehire of a new employee. Where an employee works within a team, those team members are typically included in aspects of the hire, thus multiplying exponentially the amount of personnel investment for replacement processes.

Indeed, when one or several employees leave a place of employment, it may be that others wish that they, too, could find alternative work. The intensity of this desire may, variously, depend on the severity or prevalence of the unethical behavior, compounded by the position and the "affinity" for the employee who leaves. When truly "good" or desirable employees leave a work setting, the ripple effect across the work site may be profound. The overall influence on the system may be close to disastrous, especially for the work processes.

Desirable corporate workplaces are also those in which valued employees not only remain but also find support for important work issues such as the ability to be creative or to be attentive to diversity; they have been found to report a greater competitive edge (Gilbert, Stead, and Ivancevich1999). Similarly, when corporate employees have been found to affirm an ethics environment, they, too, remain in their positions longer and reflect the diversity of the population, especially as it pertains to gender (McDaniel, Schoeps, and Lincourt, 2001).

In health-care settings where professionals attest to unethical behaviors—a business, albeit one typically claimed as nonprofit—registered nurses, for example, have been reported to have "one foot in the door and one out" while they may continue to seek employment in other settings (McDaniel, 1995, 1998). In contrast, nurses have been reported to "love their jobs" when ethics is perceived as high.

When unethical actions occur and workers are seeking alternative work, whether among health-care professionals or corporate employees, it is obvious that their full attention may not be on the work at hand. This can have an "osmotic effect" on other employees; it is rare for an employee to leave a work setting while other employees, especially those working in a team format, remain unaware of the departing employee's negative attitudes. Unethical behaviors as reasons for turnover may commonly be telescoped throughout the organization. Thus, one significant dimension of a robust ethics environment is reduction in anticipated turnover, or increase in job retention among employees in health care and business.

REDUCED WORK PROCESSES AND PRODUCTIVITY

In addition to actual turnover, another negative influence of sites where employees rate the ethics environment as low, with higher unethical behaviors and anticipated departure, is the decrease in productivity (McDaniel, 2004; McDaniel, Schoeps, and Lincourt, 2001). Productivity is explored as a separate concern, since not all employees are able to depart from an undesirable work site. Thus, when processes are affected, there are two forms of reduction in employee productivity. One, as explored above, pertains to employee turnover and its resulting extant loss. The second, explored here, occurs when employees perceive unethical behaviors, but cannot depart. However, when this latter situation emerges—employees dislike the workplace, but remain and feel "trapped"—the productivity level, typically, will be negatively influenced. While all work sites have both desirable and undesirable aspects—we claim there is no perfect workplace and/or it varies with the perception of employees—places that demonstrate frank unethical behaviors create situations in which productivity is directly and adversely related to it.

The resulting influences on employees when they remain in undesirable (un)ethical settings are myriad and may be illustrated in decreased work processes, fragmented or reduced teamwork, lessened morale, creativity, and energy, which characterize today's less-than-desirable workplaces. The obverse of these characteristics, or positive dimensions, is also linked with well-being. While the interaction between work processes and outcomes is complex, as noted above, we differentiate between financial loss and influence on work processes, because the latter have such negative and lingering influences on employees. These latter downturns are also more subtle, complex, and difficult to enumerate. Decreases in work processes also delimit the potential for future work, work that is not measured in monetary aspects. Where workers would usually be creative and energetic, looking forward to a new workday, in unethical environments, the dread of work and its daily interactions may cast a telling gloom on the workplace. Thus, a second outcome of a compromised ethics environment is the potential reduction or slowdown in overall work processes found in such unattractive employment.

Among employees in a large corporation, for example, who reported that their workplace represented a less-than-desirable ethics environment, differences between males and females pertaining to perceptions of that ethics environment have also been found (McDaniel, Schoeps, and Lincourt, 2001). In addition, lack of attention to diversity, of which gender is an example, is one instance that has been reported as limiting the full potential of employees, especially for employee advancement (Gilbert, Stead, and Ivancevich, 1999).

Even more compelling is the fact that many employees who perceive their work environment as unethical and, yet, cannot leave, generate a level of dissatisfaction with work that borders on unhealthy—heightened anger and frustration—and, if continued, leads to psychosocial and physical concerns; inability to work within a team and conduct constructive work; and sabotage on the job, attitudes that have also been noted as having potential negative influences on others (Robin and Babin, 1997; Sims and Keenan, 1998). These unethical aspects of employment potentially and adversely affect well-being.

It is in the settings discussed above, with reported perceptions of a reduced ethics environment and highly unsatisfactory workplaces, that employees may potentially move toward work sabotage. It is not necessary to detail the results of such attitudes and behaviors here. A classic case used to illustrate this point is the anecdotal, yet, well-known report of assembly-line workers in a former car production plant in Detroit. Very dissatisfied with the way they were being treated by their supervisors, in retaliation, line workers "shoved" soda bottles into the gas tanks of cars as they proceeded down the assembly line, thereby ruining the products for customers, and ultimately for the company. The expression "going postal" also refers to similar situations. Unethical behaviors when perceived by employees—and especially if perceived as directed *toward* them—are costly and may adversely affect work productivity and, potentially, their well-being.

Reduction in Morale

Among the issues related to *un*ethical behaviors, especially when such actions result in turnover, is the reduction in employee morale. Attitudes toward work have been found to be interrelated with the psychosocial dimensions of workers, and are essential components of employees' makeup (Eagly and Chaiken, 1993). One important attitude relates to employee morale. Depending on how the situation is managed by the leader, the influence on coworkers in the area from which an employee resigns due to stated unethical behaviors may leave a wake of issues for the remaining employees. Among those issues is loss of morale. Gossip, "water-cooler" conversations, and comments by the departing staff member may exacerbate any concerns other employees already have. These assertions potentially decrease investment in the organization, raise questions about continuation, and even heighten concerns about the product itself.

If the unethical behavior is shared—participated in—by other employees, they, too, may have concerns for job continuation. In contrast, if different—noninvolved—employees share the attitudes of the person leaving, there may be parallel concern for continuation, but for entirely different reasons. Either way, unethical behaviors can lead to reduction in morale.

Additionally, the implications for employees who remain in a "known quantity" where unethical acts occur also may be tantamount to future job constraint. An employee may find it increasingly difficult to change employment when moving from a place where the reputation of a team or organization is less than satisfactory. Loss of morale itself can then translate into loss of investment in a team, reduction in work processes, or abject work reduction while remaining on the job. Indeed, the overall loss of morale may be difficult to measure or even identify; it may be exhibited in features such as inattention on the job or lessened investment in one's team. It has been reported to negatively influence the ability to manage conflicts, or cooperation, in the work itself (McDaniel, 1995). Reduced satisfaction in one's job has also been found to be related to a lower perceived ethics environment. Thus, one aspect of unethical actions creating a poor ethics work environment may be overall reduction in the workforce morale.

Loss of Trust

Related to reduction in retention and work processes, and the potential decrease in morale, is the parallel loss of trust in the organization when unethical behaviors are prevalent in an organization. Trust is a central attitude regarding relationships generally and is important for any employee in an organization (Eagly and Chaiken, 1993). Needless to say, loss of trust can also negatively influence other aspects of work. These aspects can include, but are not limited to the inability to invest strongly in the work, or lack of enthusiasm for the job itself, much less one's coworkers. In contrast, it can also lead to the sharing of important—otherwise confidential—information pertinent to the success of the company or its valued product. Never has this been of more concern than in contemporary organizations where technological advances are so prevalent. Sharing secrets, for example, can be the "end" of a robust organization.

Because we know that unethical acts on the job, particularly those that directly bear on an employee, are of both direct and indirect concern for those employees, it is critical to address them before they continue too long or become too pervasive in a firm (McDaniel, 2004). An overall lack of trust may itself become a problem. Once trust is lost, it is extremely difficult to regain. Employees may even mistrust the efforts to regain trust, an ironic downturn in the workplace. Thus, explicit efforts to address unethical behaviors may be important as a way to retain trust in contemporary organizations. Unethical acts need to be addressed in a timely manner.

Supervisory Support

Among other issues of concern to today's employees is the perception—or the seeming lack—of support and concern on the part of supervisors when employees are either confronted with or otherwise discover unethical behaviors (McDaniel, 2004). Here, the supervisor is reported as the direct supervisor; however, most of the results can be applied to leaders in general: administrators, team leaders, directors, and other similar supervisory positions. Support, however, does not imply agreement; rather, it denotes a shared concern, attention to the issue, and willingness to listen to the employee on the part of the immediate supervisor. These realizations of unethical actions at work pose troubling situations for employees. Workers want to know that their immediate supervisors—those to whom they take their cares and concerns directly—share their interests and concerns about appropriate behaviors in the workplace. Important to employees is the sense that supervisors will create and sustain a positive work site.

Indeed, employees have reported that they want a supervisor who "supports" them when confronted with known unethical behaviors (McDaniel, 2004; McDaniel, Schoeps, and Lincourt, 2001). This desire is especially prevalent among professional employees who also influence the outcomes of human lives such as physicians and registered nurses. Thus, another adverse concern in the workplace pertaining to unethical behavior is dissatisfaction and loss when supervisors either do not support or they ignore the concerns of their subordinate employees, those who express and identify unethical actions at work. Unethical behaviors at work may require both immediate and detailed attention from supervisors in order to show support and concern for their employees.

Among issues that may be of concern to employees in any workplace is attention to ethical issues such as honesty, justice, diversity or lack of discrimination, and attention to harassment. This begs the question of leaders as legitimate and positive role models, which is another reason employees often turn to their supervisors when faced with problematic issues. Therefore, the manner in which the supervisor addresses the unethical concern may create a lasting impression on an employee as well as on the team members in the unit. It may be the difference between retaining valued employees and averting sabotage of the work site.

However, when employees perceive that their supervisors—whether managers, team leaders, administrators, or others—ignore blatant unethical behaviors, the result for employees may be a continuing erosion in trust and unwillingness to "take orders," including unwillingness to implement the work goals. Supervisors who do not express even minimal concern when employees report unethical actions occurring in the workplace may face the risk of losing valued employees. At a minimum, superiors may risk losing their employees' innovative contributions if unethical acts are not addressed. Unethical behavior may be related to important human resource concerns, such as the retention of valued and creative workers, employees with positive work processes, and higher levels of trust and morale. Quality leaders with legitimate power who occupy a designated position, including especially the employees' supervisors, are those who attend to unethical acts and do so in a constructive and timely manner.

ETHICS ENVIRONMENTS AND DESIRABLE OUTCOMES

The above discussion has presented both the anticipated and proposed links plus examination of work aspects in which the extant research results connect a less-than-positive ethics environment with both work processes and outcomes, for example, exploring the more or less negative manifestations of such environments among employees and their work processes. These are the decidedly negative dimensions of work—atmospheres in which few quality employees would find it desirable to work as evidenced in their negative work processes. However, we now turn to the obverse, or to the research that presents the positive dimensions examining the links and outcomes when ethics environments are rated highly, or at least represent a setting in which the ethics environment is perceived to be positive. As noted earlier, among those organizational settings in which the ethics environment has been rated as positive, or has been found to be robust and dense (McDaniel, 2004), such work sites have also been found not only to be more desirable but also to create the possibility of a virtuous domain in which to work.

Several research reports exploring work sites among business employees, registered nurses, physicians, long-term care employees, and even social workers and clergy in health-care settings, have obtained similar findings, both nationally (i.e., the United States) and internationally (McDaniel, 2004; McDaniel, 2011). Likewise, these findings have also been revealed in educational settings among professional students in their learning situations (McDaniel, 2005). Presented here in a generic manner, the summary findings are striking because, indeed, regardless of location, whether national or international, whether business, education, or health care, regardless of worker type, whether business employees, professionals, or students, workers and their colleagues uniformly have been reported to prefer a place of work that is deemed to have an ethics environment. Thus, as revealed in several reports, the ethics environment is a significant consideration for contemporary employees.

Where the ethics environment has been found to be rated or perceived as high, here ranging above the average of three or higher on a scale of one to five, employees have also been found to demonstrate a robust correlation with work retention as well as their anticipation of remaining at work (McDaniel, 2004, 2011). This was found to hold true for business and health-care workers, the latter especially prone to high turnover, even among practicing physicians. The ethics environment has also been reported to be linked with work satisfaction, which is also related to retention. Among registered nurses, the organizational culture has been positively linked with ethics work satisfaction (McDaniel, 1995). Additionally, the ethics environment itself has been reported as robustly (i.e., $r \geq 0.75$) linked with productivity, defined as the ability to attain the stated goals or mission of the work unit and the ability to manage disagreements among colleagues and between worker groupings. Finally, a strong ethics environment has been found to be associated with employees' positive opinions regarding their work. This latter finding has been especially noteworthy, as these results were reported among several employee populations. However, for this discussion it is highlighted among workers in long-term care facilities, sites also garnering attention for reporting a long-standing history of employee difficulty (McDaniel, Roche and Veledar, 2011. Thus, identifying, developing and sustaining an ethics environment hold promise for links with a number of central employee concerns based on the extant research noted above (McDaniel, 2004). If these findings continue to hold for an expanded, diverse, and wide-ranging employee base, they garner attention, especially for the link of ethics environment, among others, with work satisfaction, productivity, and retention, which potentially represent several important characteristics of employee well-being. Since it is possible to alter the ethics environment, the significance for CEOs and managers—the important leaders of business sites—is evident.

CONCLUSION

We propose that businesses that prioritize an ethics environment are more likely to invest in practices that promote the well-being of employees. As seen in Figure 19.1, this creates what we would call a "virtuous cycle" in which the ethics environment promotes better business outcomes by promoting employee well-being and desirable business outcomes that reinforce the importance of an ethics environment. In an ethics environment, leaders and managers may be more open to influence from employees (e.g., innovations and suggestions), who are able to exert influence on the direction of work without negative consequences from management. Without an ethics environment, leaders may exercise power and authority in ways (e.g., controlling and territorial) that generate negative feelings (e.g., uncertainty, anxiety, fear, anger) among employees and undermine employees' psychological (e.g., personal growth and environmental mastery) and social well-being (e.g., social integration, social acceptance). In turn, we expect that employees who work for leaders who are more open will have high levels of subjective well-being. To the extent that employees feel happier and more satisfied, report higher levels of psychological well-being (e.g., personal growth), and social well-being (i.e., social contribution), subordinates are likely to continue to endorse the authority of their managers and the way things are done in that business unit.

To the extent that employees with higher well-being are more effective, less likely to resign, and more able to develop positive relationships with customers, we should expect legitimated leadership units to enhance business outcomes. In the model of positive organizations with ethics environments, it is anticipated that effective leaders will create sustainable businesses by promoting and sustaining their employees' well-being. Organizations that are productive, profitable, and able to retain employees are likely to sustain, if not promote, employees' well-being and they, in turn, also influence the organizational atmosphere. Such organizations will also attend to—via their managers or leaders—the desirable behaviors that are revealed in the firm. That is, an employee's sense of personal growth, purpose in life, and sense of social contribution, for example,

Figure 19.1   **The Virtuous Business Cycle Model**

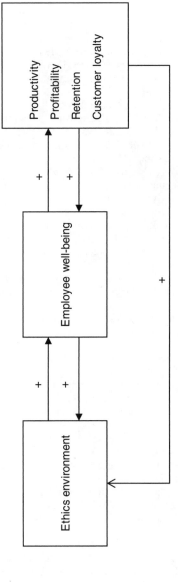

Source: McDaniel and Keyes (2011). Copyright © by McDaniel and Keyes.

should be bolstered by organizational outcomes, provided their ideas and effort are attributed to the company's success (i.e., rather than solely the leadership or the marketplace).

REFERENCES

Andrews, F.M., and Withey, S.B. 1976. *Social Indicators of Well-Being: Americans' Perceptions of Life Quality.* New York: Plenum.

Aristotle. 350 BCE/2009. *Nicomachean Ethics,* trans. David Ross and Lesley Brown. Oxford and New York: Oxford University Press.

Baier, K. 1958. *The Moral Point of View.* London: Oxford University Press.

Bennis, W. 1984. The four competencies of leadership. *Training and Development Journal,* 8, 1519.

Eagly, A., and Chaiken, S. 1993. *Psychology of Attitudes.* Fort Worth, TX: Harcourt, Brace, and Jovanovich.

Gilbert, J.; Stead, B.; and Ivancevich, J. 1999. Diversity management: A new organizational paradigm. *Journal of Business Ethics,* 21, 61–67.

Harter, J.K.; Schmidt, F.L.; and Keyes, C.L.M. 2003. Well-being in the workplace and its relationship to business outcomes: A review of the Gallup studies. In *Flourishing: The Positive Person and the Good Life,* ed. C.L.M. Keyes and J. Haidt, 205–224. Washington, DC: American Psychological Association.

Isen, A.M. 1987. Positive affect, cognitive processes, and social behavior. In *Advances in Experimental Social Psychology,* vol. 20, ed. L. Berkowitz, 203–253. San Diego, CA: Academic Press.

Jahoda, M. 1958. *Current Concepts of Positive Mental Health.* New York: Basic Books.

Keyes, C.L.M. 1998. Social well-being. *Social Psychology Quarterly,* 61, 121–140.

Levering, R. 2000. *A Great Place to Work: What Makes Some Employers So Good, and Most So Bad?* San Francisco, CA: Great Places to Work Institute.

McDaniel, C. 1995. Organizational culture and ethics work satisfaction. *Journal of Nursing Administration,* 25, 11, 15–21.

———. 1998. Ethical environment: Reports of practicing nurses. *Nursing Clinics of North America,* 33, 2, 363–372. Special issue: Ethics in Practice.

———. 2004. *Organizational Ethics: Research and Ethics Environments.* Aldershot, UK: Ashgate.

———. 2005. Reflection seminars as loci for critical thinking. *Theological Education Journal,* 30, Supplement, 15–25.

———. 2011. *Empirical Ethics: Best Practices.* Charlottesville, VA: KNK.

McDaniel, C.; Roche, J.; and Veledar, E. 2011. Ethics environment and long-term care. *Journal of Applied Gerontology,* 30, 1, 67–84.

McDaniel, C.; Schoeps, N.; and Lincourt, J. 2001. Organizational ethics: Employee perceptions by gender. *Journal of Business Ethics,* 33, 3, 245–265.

McDaniel, C.; Veledar, E.; LaConte, S.; Peltier, S.; and Maciubu, A. 2006. Ethics environment, healthcare work, and patient outcomes. *American Journal of Bioethics,* 6, 5, W17–W29.

Robin, D., and Babin, L. 1997. Making sense of the research on gender and ethics in business: A critical analysis and extension. *Business Ethics Quarterly,* 7, 4, 61–90.

Ryff, C.D. 1989. Happiness is everything, or is it? Explorations on the meaning of psychological well-being. *Journal of Personality and Social Psychology,* 57, 1069–1081.

Ryff, C.D., and Keyes, C.L.M. 1995. The structure of psychological well-being revisited. *Journal of Personality and Social Psychology,* 69, 719–727.

Sims, R., and Keenan, J. 1998. Predictors of external whistle blowing: Organizational and intra-personal variables. *Journal of Business Ethics,* 17, 4, 411–421.

Spector, P.E. 1997. *Job Satisfaction: Application, Assessment, Cause, and Consequences.* Thousand Oaks, CA: Sage.

Warr, P. 1999. Well-being and the workplace. In *Well-being: The Foundations of Hedonic Psychology,* ed. D. Kahneman, E. Diener, and N. Schwarz, 392–412. New York: Russell Sage Foundation.

Wright, T.A., and Bonett, D.G. 1997. The role of pleasantness and activation-based well-being in performance prediction. *Journal of Occupational Health Psychology,* 2, 212–219.

Wright, T.A., and Cropanzano, R. 2000. Psychological well-being and job satisfaction as predictors of job performance. *Journal of Occupational Health Psychology,* 5, 84–94.

Wright, T.A., and Staw, B.M. 1999. Affect and favorable work outcomes: Two longitudinal tests of the happy-productive worker thesis. *Journal Organizational Behavior,* 20, 1–23.

20

MACRO-ETHINOMICS

The Long-Term Costs of Short-Term Thinking

CAROLE L. JURKIEWICZ AND BORIS MOROZOV

The objective analysis of the detrimental effects of governmental distrust, first credited to Machiavelli (1515), is a concept arguably more essential in this century than at any point in history (Gillespie and Mann, 2004). While trust is a key organizational factor related to employee well-being (Gilbert and Tang, 1998), trust at the governmental level is ultimately crucial for citizen well-being. Those in the public sector have power over us that those in other sectors do not, including control of our freedoms, lifestyles, imprisonment, legalized killing, whom we can wed, whether we procreate, and whether we live or die. Yet trust in the U.S. government has been eroding since Watergate, declining by half over the past year alone (Pew Research Center, 2010), and calling into question the competency of all government functions (Burke et al., 2007). The public is increasingly dissatisfied with the lack of accountability and ethicality exhibited by our public officials, as articulated in the calls for restoring confidence in government, reassurance that taxes are spent for the good of the whole, and that government representatives act for the greater good (Pew Research Center, 2010). The Occupy Wall Street and general Occupy movement across the United States attests to the growing dissatisfaction and disillusionment of the general populace regarding government performance (Occupy Wall Street, 2011). As this distrust increases, a reduction in general well-being can be expected to result.

PUBLIC CORRUPTION

At the core of public sector efficacy is ethical competency. It is a commonly held belief that those employed in the public sector should embody a discrete set of moral standards referred to as "public service values." While the definition of public service values varies, and research indicates that they are no longer values predominant in or unique to the public sector (Bürgi, 2010; Jurkiewicz and Massey, 1997; Jurkiewicz and Massey, 1998 Sanders, 2008; Ulrich, 2008; Wheeler and Brady, 1998), the concept remains a cornerstone of our most fundamental societal beliefs. Citizens want public administrators and politicians to be motivated by service, equality, fairness, and altruism, and also to be above seeking personal over public good, to set aside politics and personal preference, and to operate with the goal of serving the public. Because the behavior of public sector employees is linked to the foundation of what it means to be an American, unethical actions on their part shake our basic beliefs and values, ultimately challenging how we view our world (Koltko-Rivera, 2004).

The growth of "other-oriented" values in society in general have deepened the belief that one's personal goals and others' goals are interconnected, and have led to high and salient expectations that mutually beneficial outcomes should be achieved through cooperative relationships as opposed to manipulative ones (Caldwell et al., 2011; Eisler, 1987; Greenleaf, 1977; Maynard and Mehrtens, 1993). These other-oriented values influence public conceptions of what is expected from leaders: inclusive decision-making processes that will benefit society overall (Block, 1993; Greenleaf, 1977; Jaworski, 1996). When these basic values are violated, the experience can be traumatic (Freyd, 1996; Janoff-Bulman, 1989), resulting in negative psychological and physical health impacts (Evans et al., 2007) and concomitant declines in well-being (e.g., Lev-Wiesel and Amir, 2001).

The key cause of dissatisfaction and distrust of government is the perception that government officials are seeking personal gain through public office rather than working on behalf of the public good. Nye's seminal definition of public corruption as "behavior which deviates from the formal duties of a public role because of private-regarding (personal, close family, private clique) pecuniary or status gains; or violates rules against the exercise of certain types of private-regarding influence" (1967, p. 419) embodies the source of this dissatisfaction. Thus, the short-term focus of public administrators in seeking self-advantage over public advantage is corruptive. This can take many forms, including bribery, embezzlement, nepotism, preferential contracting, intentional inaction in the face of injustice, and using public funds for campaigning.

Inglehart and Welzel (2005) found in their longitudinal, cross-cultural values study that societies that emphasize freedom of individual choice and democracy tend to be less permissive of corruption and experience more distress when values of trust, national pride, and human choice are violated. Certainly, there are individual differences in the degree of dissatisfaction experienced as a result of government corruption, due to variations among citizens as well as the type of corruption to which they are exposed. Accordingly, the degree to which citizens reach the point that they feel powerless to address the corruption and assume some individual guilt over their inability to correct the problem varies as well. The consequence of this powerlessness leads to an exacerbation of the level of corruption, given that collective citizen action is the only impediment to its spread (Catterberg and Moreno, 2005), and arguably can be expected to lead to a concomitant decline in well-being. Giacalone and Promislo (2010) cite a wide-ranging literature indicating that when institutions violate citizens' pivotal values and beliefs, the individuals affected both directly and indirectly by the violations experience trauma, stress, and significant declines in well-being (Meichenbaum, 1996; Pollock, 1999). It seems logical that this pattern would exist at the governmental level as well.

The degree to which corruption is tolerated, termed "corruption permissiveness," has been correlated with various demographic and cultural characteristics, and citizens with high levels of permissiveness experience less dissatisfaction with corrupt behavior. Research indicates, for instance, that women (e.g., Swamy et al., 2001); older individuals (e.g, Seligson, 2002); those with higher levels of education (e.g., Melgar, Rossi, and Smith, 2010); and disenfranchised minorities (e.g., You and Khagram, 2005) tend to have a lower level of corruption permissiveness than do their counterparts. Socioeconomic status is also correlated with corruption permissiveness in that the wealthy tend to accept that corruption is a normalized method of preserving and advancing their position in society, as it is rarely punished and has become embedded in the general methods of conducting business (ibid.).

THE EFFECTS OF PUBLIC CORRUPTION ON WELL-BEING

Research on the negative effects of public sector corruption have focused thus far on depressed economic development (e.g., Blackburn, Bose, and Haque, 2006), harm to the environment (e.g.,

Cole, 2007), its geographical contagion (Bardhan, 2006), and facilitation of lapses in judicial oversight (Cordis, 2009). However, the increased attention being paid in the scholarly, policy, and public arenas to measures of citizen well-being indicates to many (e.g., Helliwell and Barrington-Leigh, 2010) a trend toward psychological outcomes and enhanced realism in the study of economic behavior. For instance, Dearman and Grier (2009) have demonstrated that trust in government is a significant factor in economic development. Partisan concerns, wherein having one's favored party in the political majority could intuitively be thought to enhance those citizens' well-being, have been disavowed by Tavits (2008) and Anderson and Tverdova (2003), who separately assert that this is true except when the government is corrupt, and that corruption trumps the positive rewards of partisan fulfillment.

CORRELATION OF CORRUPTION WITH WELL-BEING

Prior to this point, the relationship between public corruption and public well-being has been conjectural, yet, given extant research extending the negative well-being impacts to those not only immediately subject to the unethical behavior but to those who witness, hear reports of, or seek to mitigate the effects of these acts, it can be expected that increases in public corruption can be correlated with well-being.

While there is debate on the various measures of corruption and well-being, the two sets of data employed here, reported separately, have the most substantive and well-grounded bases for facilitating the consideration of public corruption effects on public well-being. The Department of Justice Census Bureau's *Report to Congress on the Activities and Operations of the Public Integrity Section for 2006* (USDOJ, 2008) was the source of our data on public corruption, an inherently difficult measure. The report itemizes public corruption cases at the federal, state, and local levels; the state levels are utilized in this analysis (since states vary in population, we report the number of convictions per capita). Table 20.1 reports the scores for each of the fifty states on this measure as well as the District of Columbia, which is clearly an outlier due to the concentration of public sector jobs in that location. As can be noted, there is wide variation in the incidence of corruption across the fifty states.

The Well-Being Index (WBI) is the source of the well-being measure in our analysis. Reported for the first time in 2010, the joint effort between Gallup, Healthways, and America's Health Insurance Plans represents an annual live survey of 1,000 English- and Spanish-speaking households conducted daily on an ongoing basis. The sample represents 98 percent of the U.S. adult population employing both landline and cell phone random-selected respondents, weighted to compensate for disproportionate probabilities and nonresponses, as well as to match demographic targets established by the U.S. Census Bureau (see www.well-beingindex.com/methodology.asp for a detailed methodology). The survey reports an overall WBI score as well as scores for the six domain factors that constitute it (Gallup-Healthways, 2010): Life Evaluation (a comparison of one's present life situation with one's anticipated life situation five years hence); Emotional Health (a composite of ten daily emotional experiences); Physical Health (a composite of nine daily health experiences and history of disease); Healthy Behavior (made up of four lifestyle habits related to smoking, exercise, and diet); Work Environment (which includes one's feelings and perceptions about one's work environment, ranging from positive, wherein employees express satisfaction with their work, ability to use their strengths, and a culture of trust and partnership, to negative environments, characterized by lack of satisfying work and poor supervision); and Basic Access (a composite of thirteen measures of citizens' access to food, shelter, health care, and safe and satisfying places to live).

Table 20.1

U.S. Department of Justice Census Bureau Report of Public Corruption per Capita by State and District of Columbia

Rank	Convictions	State
1	66.9	Washington, DC
2	8.3	North Dakota
3	7.9	Alaska
4	7.5	Louisiana
5	7.4	Mississippi
6	6.4	Montana
7	5.9	Kentucky
8	5.6	Alabama
9	5.4	Delaware
10	5.4	South Dakota
11	4.9	Florida
12	4.9	New Jersey
13	4.8	Ohio
14	4.5	Pennsylvania
15	4.2	Tennessee
16	4.2	Virginia
17	4.1	Hawaii
18	4.1	West Virginia
19	4.0	Illinois
20	3.7	New York
21	3.2	Connecticut
22	3.1	Oklahoma
23	3.0	Arkansas
24	3.0	Massachusetts
25	2.8	Wyoming
26	2.8	Idaho
27	2.8	Missouri
28	2.7	Maryland
29	2.6	Texas
30	2.5	Arizona
31	2.5	Rhode Island
32	2.2	Wisconsin
33	2.1	North Carolina
34	2.1	Michigan
35	2.1	Vermont
36	2.1	Nevada
37	2.0	Indiana
38	1.9	Maine
39	1.9	Georgia
40	1.8	South Carolina
41	1.7	Colorado
42	1.6	Washington
43	1.6	New Mexico
44	1.6	Utah
45	1.6	California
46	1.4	Kansas
47	1.3	Minnesota
48	1.2	Iowa
49	1.1	New Hampshire
50	1.0	Oregon
51	0.7	Nebraska

Source: USDOJ (2008).
Note: Convictions are per million residents per year.

The scores for each of the fifty states, which can range from 0 to 100 (with a reliability of .83 at the aggregate state level) are reported in Table 20.2 (Gallup-Healthways, 2010). Higher scores represent higher levels of well-being.

A Spearman's rho rank order correlation was conducted on the two sets of data (public corruption and well-being), and the results are illustrated in Figure 20.1. States' corruption rankings and WBI rankings are negatively correlated (rho = –0.38), which is significant at the .01 level. As corruption increases, the well-being of citizens decreases (the District of Columbia was excluded from the analysis because it is not reported as a separate location in the WBI).

The relationship between increased public corruption and decreased well-being appears clear. While certainly other measures of corruption and well-being have been proposed in the literature, the data reported by the U.S. Department of Justice and the Gallup-Healthways studies are substantiated and widely accepted measures of these two variables. In addition, researchers have collected broad-based data suggesting that corruption tends to be contagious (Attila, 2008; Becker, Eggar, and Seidel, 2009; Goel and Nelson, 2007) and to embed itself into government functions rather swiftly, and be perpetuated through institutionalization and socialization (Ashforth and Anand, 2003; Mishra, 2006). Such scholars conclude that because corruption becomes an aspect of organizational life and not the isolated behavior of individuals, its negative impacts on society are more pervasive as a result (Nieuwenboer and Kaptein, 2008). As the literature indicates, corruption appears to be increasing in the United States, becoming embedded in the business of government, and citizens are increasingly distrustful of the public sector as a result. Such a pattern suggests an ever-widening downward spiral leading to a logical end point of systemic corruption, public distrust, and reduced well-being. Without intervention, this may well be the case, but there are ways to slow or stop the progression of corruption and to mitigate its impacts.

MOVING FORWARD

Customarily, the success of a society is attested to by objective indicators such as economic and social measures. Yet, in most developed nations, these do not prove accurate; increases in income have not produced comparable increases in happiness or life satisfaction (D'Acci, 2011). Thus subjective measures of well-being figure prominently in recent studies (Huppert et al., 2009), refocusing societal change efforts toward enhancing these elements. This shift toward nonfinancial measures of well-being is supported by research on life satisfaction, which demonstrates that characteristics such as trust are more essential than incremental changes in income (Fischer and Boer, 2011; Helliwell and Huang, 2010). Such results suggest that there are opportunities to improve public sector environments in order to increase both well-being and workplace efficiency. Collectively, this body of research is accumulating in the direction of enhancing societal outcomes by enhancing individual well-being.

In addition to the shift from solely financial-based measures of government performance to those incorporating well-being, other research emphasizes the importance of education in combating the spread and acceptance of corruption (Glaeser and Saks, 2006). States with higher overall measures of education tend to exhibit less corruption, as do those with greater income equality and lower levels of racial fractionalization. These factors have also been correlated with enhanced measures of well-being (Binder and Coad, 2011). Ethics education of public administrators and politicians, in particular, has demonstrated a significant impact on their ability to maintain ethicality in the face of pressures to do otherwise (Jurkiewicz, 2002), whereas lack of ethics education leaves decision makers unaware of the ethical dimensions of their choices (Kennedy and Malatesta, 2010). In the majority of cases, public sector employees report wanting to uphold higher ethical standards in the

Table 20.2

Well-Being Index for Fifty U.S. States

Rank	WBI Score	State
1	71.0	Hawaii
2	69.2	Wyoming
3	68.4	North Dakota
4	68.3	Alaska
5	68.0	Colorado
6	68.0	Minnesota
7	68.0	South Dakota
8	67.9	Utah
9	67.9	Connecticut
10	67.8	Nebraska
11	67.8	Massachusetts
12	67.5	Washington
13	67.5	Maryland
14	67.3	Montana
15	67.2	New Hampshire
16	67.2	Kansas
17	67.1	Vermont
18	67.0	California
19	66.9	Iowa
20	66.9	Idaho
21	66.7	Virginia
22	66.7	Wisconsin
23	66.7	New Mexico
24	66.6	New Jersey
25	66.4	Maine
26	66.3	Illinois
27	66.3	Texas
28	66.3	Oregon
29	66.2	Arizona
30	66.1	Pennsylvania
31	66.1	Georgia
32	65.9	New York
33	65.7	Rhode Island
34	65.6	Missouri
35	65.3	South Carolina
36	65.1	North Carolina
37	65.1	Florida
38	64.9	Oklahoma
39	64.8	Indiana
40	64.8	Tennessee
41	64.6	Michigan
42	64.3	Louisiana
43	64.2	Nevada
44	64.2	Delaware
45	63.8	Ohio
46	63.7	Alabama
47	63.7	Arkansas
48	63.0	Mississippi
49	61.9	Kentucky
50	61.7	West Virginia

Source: Gallup-Healthways (2010).

Note: The District of Columbia scores are subsumed under Virginia and Maryland in accord with the metropolitan statistical area and thus are not reported separately here.

Figure 20.1 **Comparison of WBI and Corruption Rankings**

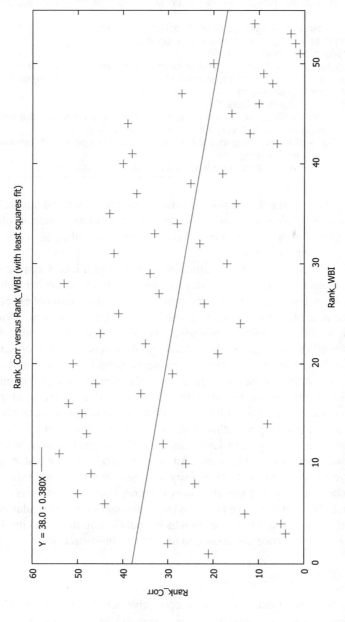

Spearman's rho = −0.38; *t* = −2.97; two-tailed *p*-value = 0.0046.

Figure 20.2   **Assessment Factors for Effective Public Sector Administration**

- Addresses ethical dilemmas on a regular basis in meetings and correspondence
- All employees are held to the same standards of moral conduct, no favoritism
- Citizen and employee feedback states they are treated respectfully and valued
- Communication is straightforward, employees/citizens feel honestly informed, gossip and rumor are minimal
- Demonstrates organizational values through policies and programs
- Employees express feeling empowered and supported
- Exhibits the values of trust and commitment
- Implements systems and policies to prevent or minimize harmful behaviors
- Low employee turnover/absenteeism, surplus of qualified applicants for open positions
- Meets/exceeds legal requirements
- Openly transparent policies and practices
- Resources and opportunities are equitably distributed inside and outside the organization
- Respects and encourages both diverse opinions and viewpoints
- Responds to claims of wrongdoing in a timely manner, with respect and transparency
- Rewards ethical behavior publicly
- Training, promotions, and awards are clearly tied to ethical performance

workplace but often find that the biggest impediment to this are the policies and politics to which they are subject, and the organizational culture in which they must participate (Jurkiewicz, 2000). Through education of both the citizenry and those employed in the public sector, a reduction in corruptive behavior appears possible.

The ethical competence of public administrators and politicians can be evidenced in the managerial decisions and organizational factors that they directly influence (Bürgi, 2011). At one end of an ethical continuum are satisficing decisions made on the basis of expediency, short-term gain, and on the other end, by decisions focused on long-term outcomes, taking into account a broad spectrum of affected parties, considering possible consequences, and seeking the best possible solution for all (Kohlberg, 1976). Tolerance of divergent opinions, emotional intelligence, adaptability, and the extent to which political gamesmanship is absent from decision making are additional measures of this competency. The amount of transparency in the organization, the degree of organizational commitment on behalf of the leaders' subordinates, the organization's reputation for trustworthiness, the objective resolution of complaints, and the confidence demonstrated in the organization and its leadership are other clear factors. As a measure of citizen oversight, certain leadership factors can be assessed in determining whether to elect, reelect, or appoint individuals to positions of influence in the public sector. An assessment of these leadership factors can provide a more objective assessment of their propensity to engage in self-serving behavior at the expense of the public good, which is the foundation of corruption. Using those factors listed in Figure 20.2 as a performance checklist can serve both to educate the public on a particular individual's ethical capabilities and to serve as a set of goals to which a public administrator could aspire in order to reduce corruption and enhance confidence in his or her administration.

CONCLUSION

Many studies demonstrate that unethical or corruptive acts by public administrators do confer short-term advantages on the perpetrator (e.g., Rose-Ackerman, 1999), yet the negative consequences for society are profound. Corruption damages the public realm and reduces the credibility of public institutions in getting the job of government done, makes collecting the necessary taxes to accomplish societal goals more difficult, and tarnishes the public ethic (Philip, 1997). As the incidence of narcissism has increased at a rapid rate in society (Twenge et al., 2008), modes of ethical reasoning that rationalize self-serving behaviors at the expense of citizen welfare are increasingly witnessed in the public sector. Such an explosion of corruptive acts reduces citizen trust and, in turn, the ability of the sector to function effectively, reduces individual well-being and affects the economic solidity of the nation. Recent studies suggest that shifting the assessment of government effectiveness from measures of income growth to measures of citizen well-being increases both the efficiency and effectiveness of organizational systems. To achieve these ends requires education of both the citizenry and those who are employed in the public sector. Without interventions such as these, the downward spiral of corruption and diminished well-being is likely to continue.

REFERENCES

Anderson, C.J., and Tverdova, Y.V. 2003. Corruption, political allegiances, and attitudes toward government in contemporary democracies. *American Journal of Political Science,* 47, 1, 91–109.

Ashforth, B.E., and Anand, V. 2003. The normalization of corruption in organizations. *Research in Organizational Behavior,* 25, 1–52.

Attila, G. 2008. Is corruption contagious? An econometric analysis. Norwegian Institute of International Affairs (NUPI) Working Paper no. 742, September. http://ssrn.com/abstract=1275804/.

Bardhan, P. 2006. The economist approach to the problem of corruption. *World Development*, 34(2), 341–348.

Becker, S.O.; Eggar, P.H.; and Seidel, T. 2009. Common political culture: Evidence on regional corruption contagion. *European Journal of Political Economy,* 25, 300–310.

Binder, M., and Coad, A. 2011. From average Joe's happiness to miserable Jane and cheerful John: Using quantile regressions to analyze the full subjective well-being distribution. *Journal of Economic Behavior and Organization,* 79, 275–290.

Blackburn, K.; Bose, N.; and Haque, E. 2006. The incidence and persistence of corruption in economic development. *Journal of Economic Development and Control,* 30, 2447–2467.

Block, P. 1993. *Stewardship: Choosing Service over Self-interest.* San Francisco, CA: Berrett-Koehler.

Bürgi, J. 2010. A comprehensive model for SMEs: Monitoring the dynamic interplay of morality, environment and management systems—towards continuous improvement. In *Ethics in Small and Medium Sized Enterprises: A Global Commentary,* ed. L. Spence and M. Painter-Morland, 147–171. Dordrecht: Springer.

Burke, S.C.; Sims, D.E.; Lazzara, E.H.; and Salas, E. 2007. Trust in leadership: A multi-level review and integration. *Leadership Quarterly,* 18, 606–632.

Caldwell, C.; Truong, D.; Linh, P.; and Tuan, A. 2011. Strategic human resource management as ethical stewardship. *Journal of Business Ethics,* 98, 1, 171–182.

Catterberg, G., and Moreno, A. 2005. The individual bases of political trust: Trends in new and established democracies. *International Journal of Public Opinion Research,* 18, 31–48.

Cole, M.A. 2007. Corruption, income, and the environment: An empirical analysis. *Ecological Economics,* 62, 637–647.

Cordis, A.S. 2009. Judicial checks on corruption in the United States. *Economics of Governance,* 10, 375–401.

D'Acci, L. 2011. Measuring well-being and progress. *Social Indicators Research,* 104, 47–65.

Dearman, J., and Grier, K. (2009). Trust and development. *Journal of Economic Behavior & Organization,* 71, 210–220.

Eisler, R. 1987. *The Chalice and the Blade: Our History, Our Future.* San Francisco: Harper and Row.

Evans, C.; Ehlers, A.; Mezey, G.; and Clark, D.M. 2007. Intrusive memories in perpetrators of violent crime: Emotions and cognitions. *Journal of Consulting and Clinical Psychology,* 75, 134–144.

Fischer, R., and Boer, D. 2011. What is more important for national well-being: Money or autonomy? A meta-analysis of well-being, burnout, and anxiety across 63 societies. *Journal of Personality and Social Psychology,* 101, 1, 164–184.

Freyd, J.J. 1996. *Betrayal Trauma: The Logic of Forgetting Childhood Abuse.* Cambridge, MA: Harvard University Press.

Gallup-Healthways Well-Being Index. 2010. www.well-beingindex.com/default.asp.

Giacalone, R.A., and Promislo, M.D. 2010. Unethical and unwell: Decrements in well-being and unethical activity at work. *Journal of Business Ethics,* 91, 275–297.

Gilbert, J.A., and Tang, T.L. 1998. An examination of organizational trust antecedents. *Public Personnel Management,* 27, 321–338.

Gillespie, N.A., and Mann, L. 2004. Transformational leadership and shared values: The building blocks of trust. *Journal of Managerial Psychology,* 19, 588–607.

Glaeser, E.L., and Saks, R.E. 2006. Corruption in America. *Journal of Public Economics,* 90, 1053–1072.

Goel, R.K., and Nelson, M.A. 2007. Are corrupt acts contagious? Evidence from the United States. *Journal of Policy Modeling,* 29, 839–850.

Greenleaf, R.K. 1977. *Servant Leadership.* New York: Paulist Press.

Helliwell, J.F., and Barrington-Leigh, C.P. 2010. Viewpoint: Measuring and understanding subjective well-being. *Canadian Journal of Economics,* 43, 3, 729–753.

Helliwell, J.F., and Huang, H. 2010. How's the job? Well-being and social capital in the workplace. *Industrial and Labor Relations Review,* 63, 2, 205–227.

Huppert, F.A.; Marks, N.; Clark, A.; Siegrist, J.; Stutzer, A.; Vittersø, J.; and Wahrendorf, M. 2009. Measuring well-being across Europe: Description of the ESS well-being module and preliminary findings. *Social Indicators Research,* 91, 301–315.

Inglehart, R.F., and Welzel, C. 2005. *Modernization, Cultural Change, and Democracy: The Human Development Sequence.* New York: Cambridge University Press.

Janoff-Bulman, R. 1989. Assumptive worlds and the stress of traumatic events: Applications of the schema construct. *Social Cognition,* 7, 113–136.

Jaworski, J. 1996. *Synchronicity: The Inner Path of Leadership.* San Francisco, CA: Berrett-Koehler.

Jurkiewicz, C.L. 2000. The trouble with ethics: Results from a national survey of healthcare executives. *HEC Forum,* 12, 2, 101–123.

———. 2002. The influence of pedagogical style on students' level of ethical reasoning. *Journal of Public Affairs Education,* 8, 4, 263–274.

Jurkiewicz, C.L., and Massey, T.K. Jr. 1997. What motivates municipal employees: A comparison study of supervisory vs. non-supervisory personnel. *Public Personnel Management,* 26, 3, 367–377.

———. 1998. The influence of ethical reasoning on leader effectiveness: An empirical study of nonprofit executives. *Nonprofit Management and Leadership,* 9, 2, 173–186.

Kennedy, S.S., and Malatesta, D. 2010. Safeguarding the public trust: Can administrative ethics be taught? *Journal of Public Affairs Education,* 16, 2, 161–180.

Kohlberg, L. 1976. Moral stages and moralization: The cognitive-developmental approach. In *Moral Development and Behavior,* ed. T. Lickona, 31–53. New York: Holt, Rinehart and Winston.

Koltko-Rivera, M.E. 2004. The psychology of worldviews. *Review of General Psychology,* 8, 3–58.

Lev-Wiesel, R., and Amir, M. 2001. Secondary traumatic stress, psychological distress, sharing of traumatic reminisces, and marital quality among spouses of holocaust child survivors. *Journal of Marital and Family Therapy,* 27, 4, 433–444.

Machiavelli, N. 1515/1984. *The Prince,* trans. D. Donno. New York: Bantam Classics.

Maynard, H.B., and Mehrtens, S.E. 1993. *The Fourth Wave: Business in the Twenty-first Century.* San Francisco, CA: Berrett-Koehler.

Meichenbaum, D. 1996. Cognitive-behavioural treatment of post-traumatic stress disorder from a narrative constructivist perspective: A conversation with Donald Meichenbaum. In *Constructive Therapies 2,* ed. M. F. Hoyt. New York: Guilford.

Melgar, N.; Rossi, M.; and Smith, T.W. 2010. The perceptions of corruption. *International Journal of Public Opinion Research,* 22, 120–131.

Mishra, A. 2006. Persistence of corruption: Some theoretical perspectives. *World Development,* 34, 2, 349–358.

Nieuwenboer, N.A., and Kaptein, M. 2008. Spiraling down into corruption: A dynamic analysis of the social identity processes that cause corruption in organizations to grow. *Journal of Business Ethics,* 83, 2, 133–146.

Nye, J. 1967. Corruption and political development: A cost-benefit analysis. *American Political Science Review,* 61, 2, 417–427.

Occupy Wall Street. 2011. http://occupywallst.org (accessed October 29, 2011).

Pew Research Center. 2010. Distrust, discontent, anger and partisan rancor. Survey, April 18. http://pewresearch.org/pubs/1569/trust%20in%20government%20distrust%20discontent%20anger%20partisanrancor/.

Philip, M. 1997. Defining political corruption. In *Political Corruption*, ed. P. Heywood, 20–46. Oxford: Blackwell.

Pollock, P. H. (1999). When the killer suffers: Post-traumatic stress reactions following homicide. *Legal and Criminological Psychology*, 4, 185–202.

Rose-Ackerman, S. 1999. *Corruption and Government: Causes, Consequences, and Reform.* Cambridge: Cambridge University Press.

Sanders, S. 2008. Defining social responsibility: Standard helps clarify a nebulous term. Quality Progress, March. http://asq.org/quality-progress/2008/03/social-responsibility/up-front-march-2008.html.

Seligson, M.A. 2002. The impact of corruption on regime legitimacy: A comparative study of four Latin American countries. *Journal of Politics,* 64, 408–433.

Swamy, A.; Knack, S.; Lee, Y.; and Azfar, O. 2001. Gender and corruption. *Journal of Development Economics,* 64, 25–55.

Tavits, M. 2008. Representation, corruption, and subjective well-being. *Comparative Political Studies,* 41, 12, 1607–1630.

Twenge, J.M.; Konrath, S.; Foster, J.D.; Campbell, W.K.; and Bushman, B.J. 2008. Egos inflating over time: A cross-temporal meta-analysis of the narcissistic personality inventory. *Journal of Personality,* 76, 875–901.

Ulrich, P. 2008. *Integrative Economic Ethics: Foundations of a Civilized Market Economy.* Cambridge: Cambridge University Press.

U.S. Department of Justice (USDOJ). 2008. *Report to Congress on the Activities and Operations of the Public Integrity Section for 2006.* www.justice.gov/criminal/pin/docs/arpt-2006.pdf.

Wheeler, G.F., and Brady, F.N. 1998. Do public-sector and private-sector personnel have different ethical dispositions? A study of two sites. *Journal of Public Administration Research and Theory,* 8, 1, 93–115.

You, J.S., and Khagram, S. 2005. A comparative study of inequality and corruption. *American Sociological Review,* 70, 136–157.

Name Index

Subject Index

ABOUT THE EDITORS AND CONTRIBUTORS

Rebecca J. Bennett is a professor of management at Louisiana Tech University in Ruston, Louisiana. She has taught courses in human resource management, conflict resolution, organizational behavior, management principles, team building, and the dynamics of family business. Her research on employee deviance and responses to offenses in the workplace has been published in academic journals and books and has been presented across the United States and internationally. She has been a visiting scholar at the National University of Singapore and at the University of Groningen, the Netherlands. She received her BA in psychology, cum laude, at Washington University and her MS and PhD degrees in organizational behavior from Northwestern University.

Mark C. Bolino is an associate professor and the Michael F. Price Chair in International Business at the University of Oklahoma. He received his PhD from the University of South Carolina. His research interests include impression management, organizational citizenship behavior, global careers, and psychological contracts. His research has appeared in journals such as the *Academy of Management Review, Journal of Applied Psychology,* and *Personnel Psychology.* He currently serves on the editorial boards of the *Academy of Management Journal, Journal of Applied Psychology, Journal of Management, Journal of Organizational Behavior,* and *Organizational Behavior and Human Decision Processes.*

Susie S. Cox is an assistant professor of management and human resources at McNeese State University and received her doctorate in business administration from Louisiana Tech University. Her research focuses on forgiveness in the workplace, communication, the use of positive touch in the workplace, and assessment practices. Her work has been published in *Human Relations, Journal of Managerial Issues, Performance Improvement Quarterly,* and *Journal of Academic Administration in Higher Education.*

Jason J. Dahling is an associate professor and coordinator of the industrial/organizational psychology specialization at The College of New Jersey (TCNJ). His research, teaching, and consulting focuses on problems with self-regulation at work, particularly with respect to deviant behavior and the management of emotions in organizational settings. He has written more than twenty refereed journal articles and book chapters on these topics in outlets such as *Journal of Management, Journal of Organizational Behavior,* and *Journal of Vocational Behavior.* He has also consulted with many educational and corporate clients concerning effective human resource management, particularly in the areas of feedback and performance appraisal. He is a member of the Society for Industrial and Organizational Psychology, the Academy of Management, and the Society for Vocational Psychology. He received his PhD in industrial/organizational psychology from the University of Akron in 2007.

Ilona E. de Hooge is an assistant professor of marketing management at Rotterdam School of Management, Erasmus University (the Netherlands). She holds an MSc (2004) in work and organizational psychology and in methodology, and a PhD in social psychology (2008) from Tilburg University. While earning her PhD, she conducted many studies on the effects of shame and guilt. More specifically, she focused on motivations and behaviors such as approach behaviors, prosocial behavior, cooperation, and situational preferences. After her move to marketing management, her research interests expanded to social and moral emotions (such as anger, envy, and gratitude), gift giving, advice giving and taking, and shame and guilt appeals in marketing. She has published multiple articles in *Journal of Personality and Social Psychology* and *Cognition and Emotion.*

Deanne N. Den Hartog is professor of organizational behavior and head of the HRM-OB section at the University of Amsterdam Business School in the Netherlands. She teaches leadership and organizational behavior. She holds a PhD from the Free University in Amsterdam, the Netherlands. Her research interests focus on inspirational, ethical, and cross-cultural leadership, trust as well as proactive employee behavior, team effectiveness, trust, and well-being. She publishes her work on these topics in the internationally recognized scientific journals in these areas such as *Journal of Applied Psychology, Journal of Organizational Behavior*, and *Leadership Quarterly.* She is action editor for *Applied Psychology: An International Review,* and serves on the editorial board of several journals. She is part of the GLOBE research project network, which is a network of international scholars that spans sixty-two countries and collectively studies leadership across cultures. She is representative at large of the Academy of Management Organizational Behavior division and serves on the board of directors of the International Association of Applied Psychology.

Marko Elovainio is a research professor (social epidemiology) at the Finnish Institute for Health and Welfare (Health Services Research unit), and visiting senior researcher (psychology/personality and well-being) at the University of Helsinki (Department of Behavioral Sciences). He collaborates with other groups globally including research groups at the University of Newcastle, UK; INSERM France; Karolinska Institute and University of Stockholm, Sweden; University of Utrecht, Netherlands; Finnish Institute of Occupational Health, and Universities of Helsinki and Turku, Finland. He has published extensively from Whitehall II and Public Sector data, including on organizational justice and health.

Robert Folger is the Distinguished Alumni Professor of Business Ethics in the Management Department of the College of Business at the University of Central Florida. He is a fellow of the Academy of Management, the American Psychological Association, the Society for Personality and Social Psychology, and the Society of Industrial and Organizational Psychology (from which he received a Distinguished Scientific Contributions Award). His honors and awards include the New Concept Award and the Best Paper Award from the Organizational Behavior Division of the Academy of Management. He has more than 100 publications, including articles in the *Academy of Management Journal, Academy of Management Review, Organizational Behavior and Human Decision Processes, Journal of Applied Psychology, Psychological Bulletin*, and *Psychological Review.* He has been on the editorial boards of the *Journal of Management, Journal of Organizational Behavior, Academy of Management Review, Organizational Behavior and Human Decision Processes*, and *Social Justice Research.* He edited *The Sense of Injustice* (1984) and coauthored *Controversial Issues in Social Research Methods* (1988). The International Association for Conflict Management named his coauthored *Organizational Justice and Human Resources Management* as its 1998 "Book of the Year."

Donelson R. Forsyth holds the Colonel Leo K. and Gaylee Thorsness Endowed Chair in Ethical Leadership in the Jepson School of Leadership Studies at the University of Richmond. Previously, he was a professor and associate department chairman at Virginia Commonwealth University. A social and personality psychologist, he studies groups, leadership, ethical thought, and moral judgment. His general analyses of group development, structure, performance, and change are complemented by his in-depth analyses of individual differences in morality. He has authored more than 150 books, chapters, and articles on groups and related topics, and his work has appeared in the *Journal of Applied Psychology, Journal of Personality and Social Psychology,* and the *American Psychologist.* His books include *Introduction to Group Dynamics* (1983), *Social Psychology* (1987), *Psychotherapy and Behavior Change* (1988), *Group Dynamics* (5th ed., 2010), and *Our Social World* (1995). He has served on the editorial boards of the *Journal of Personality and Social Psychology, Group Processes and Intergroup Relations, Journal of Social and Clinical Psychology* (as associate editor), and *Group Dynamics* (as editor). His work has been funded by grants from the National Institute of Health and the National Science Foundation.

Robert A. Giacalone (PhD) is professor of human resource management at the Fox School of Business and Management, Temple University, in Philadelphia, Pennsylvania. He is a recognized expert on behavioral business ethics, exit interviewing and surveying, workplace spirituality, impression management, employee deviance, and the role of changing values in organizational life. He is coeditor of five books and coauthor of two books, *Impression Management in Organizations: Theory, Measurement, Practice* (Routledge, 1995) and *Impression Management: Building and Enhancing Reputations at Work* (Thompson, 2002). He has also authored more than 100 articles on ethics and values, impression management and exit interviewing, published in journals such as the *Academy of Management Learning and Education, Journal of Applied Psychology, Human Relations, Business and Society Review, Journal of Business Ethics, Journal of Organizational Behavior,* and *Journal of Social Psychology.* He has served on several journal editorial boards and as editor of several special issues on business ethics. He is currently editor in chief of the *Journal of Management, Spirituality, and Religion.* He was the series editor for the Sage Series in Business Ethics and is currently coeditor of the Ethics in Practice book series.

David A. Jones is associate professor of management at the School of Business Administration, University of Vermont. He obtained his PhD in industrial and organizational psychology in 2004 from the University of Calgary. His research focuses on workplace revenge, organizational justice, and the reasons why job seekers and employees tend to respond positively to environmentally and socially responsible business practices. He has published his research in journals that include the *Journal of Applied Psychology, Journal of Management, Journal of Vocational Behavior, Journal of Occupational and Organizational Psychology,* and *Journal of Organizational Behavior,* where he is also a member of the editorial board. In his work with organizations, he regularly conducts training in the principles of organizational justice, and in leadership and management, to executive and managerial audiences. Most recently, he has worked with several organizations to develop corporate volunteerism programs and evaluate their effects on employee attitudes and behavior.

Carole L. Jurkiewicz (PhD) is the Woman's Hospital Distinguished Professor of Healthcare Management and the John W. Dupuy Endowed Professor at the E.J. Ourso College of Business at Louisiana State University. Her work focuses upon organizational performance as a function of employee ethicality and organizational culture. She has published more than 100 books, scholarly articles, and chapters in the areas of organizational and individual performance, ethics, power, and leadership, bringing to her academic career many years as an executive in private and nonprofit organizations and a government consultant.

Karianne Kalshoven is a specialist in ethical leadership and has several international publications on this topic—for example, in the *Leadership Quarterly, Journal of Business Ethics, European Journal of Work and Organizational Psychology,* and *Applied Psychology: An International Review*. She has developed a tool for measuring ethical leadership within organizations as part of her PhD thesis, the so-called Ethical Leadership at Work (ELW) questionnaire, which has been used by organizations and researchers around the world. Furthermore, she is the founder of the Amsterdam Center for Integrity and Leadership. She has been active as coach, inspirator, teacher, and scientific researcher in the field of ethics and leadership for several years. She is also a committee member in ethics at the Dutch Association of Registered Controllers. Her expertise is creating connections between people, ethics within context, and between science and practice.

Corey L.M. Keyes is professor of sociology at Emory University. He was a member of a Mac-Arthur Foundation Research Network on Successful Midlife Development, a co-chair of the first Summit of Positive Psychology held in 1999, and a member of the 2007 National Academies of Science Keck Future's Initiative on the Future of Human Healthspan: Demography, Evolution, Medicine and Bioengineering. He is in his second decade as a faculty member and has published more than seventy articles, edited six books, edited three special journal issues, and has given more than ninety national and international presentations and keynote addresses. His 2002 article, "The Mental Health Continuum," introduced scientifically the concept of flourishing, and this article was the most recent addition to the history of psychology in the *Foundations of Psychological Thought: A History of Psychology,* edited by B.F. Gentile and B.O. Miller (Sage, 2008).

Mika Kivimäki is professor of social epidemiology in the Department of Epidemiology and Public Health at the University College London in the United Kingdom. He is codirector of the ongoing Whitehall II study of British civil servants, UK, and principal investigator of the IPD-Work consortium of seventeen European cohort studies. He also leads major occupational cohort studies in Finland. In 2005, he published a paper on organizational justice and heart disease and one year later conducted the first meta-analysis of prospective cohort studies on work stress as a risk factor for incident coronary heart disease. He is interested in understanding risk and protective factors for adult-onset diseases, such as cardiovascular diseases, diabetes, and depression, and how they and other factors shape physical and cognitive functioning in later life. He was elected to the Academy of Europe in 2009.

Anthony C. Klotz is a PhD candidate in organizational behavior in the Price College of Business, University of Oklahoma. He earned his MBA at Creighton University. His research interests include impression management, organizational citizenship behavior, and team conflict. His research has appeared in the *Journal of Applied Psychology* and *Business Horizons.*

Daniel Kuyumcu is currently a doctoral candidate in industrial/organizational psychology at Pennsylvania State University. His research interests include workplace deviance, Machiavellianism, and emotional labor. He completed his BA in psychology at The College of New Jersey in 2011.

Erika H. Librizzi is currently pursuing an MS in Occupational Therapy at The Richard Stockton College of New Jersey. She completed her BA in psychology at The College of New Jersey in 2011.

Todd Lucas is assistant professor in the Department of Family Medicine and Public Health Sciences at Wayne State University (Detroit, Michigan). He received his doctorate in social psychology from Wayne State University. He completed a postdoctoral fellowship in behavioral and decision sciences at the University of Michigan, Ann Arbor. His research examines psychological and social determinants of health and well-being. His research is especially focused on relationships between perceived fairness and individual stress and health behavior, including how psychological fairness may contribute to ethnic and socioeconomic health disparities in work and other contexts. He also conducts cross-cultural and applied health communication research.

Charlotte McDaniel (PhD) began her career with faculty appointments at Yale University, followed by the University of Pittsburgh Medical Center as clinical professor of medicine, associate, Center for Ethics. She retired from Emory University, having developed extensive research and scholarly work in the emerging field of empirical ethics, including more than seventy-five publications in scholarly journals and five books. As one among few focusing on ethics and research, her attention has been mainly, but not exclusively, on health care and business concerns. She continues as a faculty associate in the Center for the Study of Law and Religion, Emory University. Additionally, she has held three Fulbright appointments with attention to assessment or research from an international perspective.

Laurenz L. Meier received his PhD in psychology at the University of Bern, Switzerland, in 2008. Afterward, he was a lecturer and postdoctoral researcher at the University of Bern, University of Neuchâtel, and at the University of Basel. Since 2011, he has been a visiting scholar at the University of South Florida, Tampa, funded by the Swiss National Science Foundation. His research focuses on the intersection of organizational and personality psychology, specifically in the fields of organizational behavior and stress. In a first current line of research, he is investigating antecedents of counterproductive work behavior. In a second current line of research, he is studying the interplay of work characteristics, personality, and stress. A methodological focus of his research is the analysis of quantitative diary and longitudinal data.

Marie S. Mitchell is assistant professor of management in the Terry College of Business, University of Georgia. She received her PhD in business administration from the University of Central Florida, specializing in management. Her expertise focuses on social and ethical issues in organizational behavior and human resource management. In general, her research examines "dark" or destructive behavior, with a specific focus on three related areas: (1) workplace deviance and abusive behavior, (2) exchange relationships, and (3) behavioral ethics. Her work has appeared in journals such as the *Journal of Applied Psychology, Organizational Behavior and Human Decision Processes, Journal of Management, Business Ethics Quarterly,* and *Journal of Business Ethics.* She also serves on the editorial boards of the *Academy of Management Journal, Journal of Applied Psychology, Journal of Management,* and *Business Ethics Quarterly.*

Boris Morozov (PhD) is assistant professor at the Public Administration Institute, Louisiana State University. His teaching and research interests are in public financial management, public budgeting and ethics, strategic management of public and private organizations, and economic development policy.

Joel H. Neuman is associate professor of management and organizational behavior and director of the Center for Applied Management in the School of Business at the State University of New

York at New Paltz. His research and consulting activities focus on workplace aggression and violence, workplace bullying, and related forms of counterproductive work behavior. His work has appeared in numerous academic journal articles and edited volumes, and interviews with him have appeared in the *New York Times, Washington Post, USA Today, Boston Globe, New York Post, San Francisco Chronicle, Fortune Magazine, Essence Magazine,* and the *Chronicle of Higher Education.* In recognition of his seminal research on workplace aggression, he was among the first recipients of the Chancellor's Award for Excellence in Research from the Research Foundation of the State University of New York. He currently serves on the Advisory Board of the New Workplace Institute at Suffolk University Law School, a not-for-profit research and education center promoting healthy, productive, and socially responsible workplaces.

Ernest H. O'Boyle Jr. is an assistant professor at the Tippie School of Management and Organizations at the University of Iowa. He completed his PhD at Virginia Commonwealth University. His research interests include counterproductive work behavior, ethical decision making, research methodology, and dark personality traits such as narcissism and Machiavellianism. His work has appeared in outlets such as *Journal of Applied Psychology, Personnel Psychology,* and *Organizational Research Methods.*

Jane O'Reilly is a PhD student in organizational behavior and human resources at the Sauder School of Business, University of British Columbia. Her research is directed at understanding how to constructively address and prevent mistreatment in organizations. Specifically, she is interested in understanding how third parties' reactions toward others' mistreatment can provide direct and indirect benefits to the victims and help punish the perpetrators of mistreatment in organizations. She is also interested in understanding the unique effects of social exclusion at work.

Mark D. Promislo is assistant professor of management at Rider University's College of Business Administration. He graduated with a PhD from Temple University in organization and human resources. His work has appeared in publications such as *Journal of Business Ethics, Journal of Organizational and Occupational Psychology,* and *Business Ethics: A European Review.* His main areas of research involve ethics and well-being, the work–family interface, and values in organizations. He received a Best Paper award from the Academy of Management in 2008 for a coauthored paper titled "Valuing Money More Than People: The Effects of Materialism on Work–Family Conflict." Prior to completing his PhD, he worked for Merck and Co. for seven years in market research and sales.

Sandra L. Robinson is a professor in the Sauder School of Business at the University of British Columbia. She obtained her PhD from Northwestern University. Over the past two decades, Sandra's research has sought to address the "dark side" of organizational behavior, with a special interest in behavior within relationships and individuals' perceptions of how they are treated by others. Her prior publications, which have appeared in various journals such as *Administrative Science Quarterly, Journal of Applied Psychology, Harvard Business Review,* and *Academy of Management Review,* have focused upon topics such as psychological contract breach, trust betrayal, workplace deviance, aggression, territorial behavior, and infringement. She has won various awards for her work, including the Cummings Award for early career achievement, the Western Academy Ascendant Scholar Award, and a Killam Research Prize. Her current research program continues her focus on the dark side of organizational relationships by addressing the effects of ostracism and social exclusion.

Denise Salin is associate professor of management and organization at Hanken School of Economics, Finland, and an adjunct professor of social psychology at Helsinki University, Finland. Her research interests include workplace bullying, organizational justice, and gender. She has carried out research projects on bullying for more than ten years, published a number of articles, and given several conference presentations on the topic. She has also been active in the International Association on Workplace Bullying and Harassment. Her work has appeared in, among other journals, *Human Relations, European Journal of Work and Organizational Psychology, Journal of Personnel Psychology,* and *Gender, Work, and Organization.*

Kira F. Schabram, a PhD student at the University of British Columbia, studies meaningfulness and morality in the workplace. Her research focuses on those individuals who have identified a societal and/or moral duty as a guiding principle in their lives and whose identity is shaped through their interaction with and understanding of this purpose; individuals for whom work is not what they do, but who they are. Currently, she is examining the expression of deeply meaningful work in environments that feature significant social or situational constraints, for example, stigmatized "dirty work" environments. She is interested in understanding how individuals react, emotionally and behaviorally, under such conditions and how these reactions shape social relations—for example, interpersonal trust or perceptions of infringement at work.

Charles H. Schwepker Jr. is the Mike and Patti Davidson Distinguished Marketing Professor at the University of Central Missouri. He has experience in wholesale and retail sales, and conducts research in sales ethics, sales management, and personal selling. His articles have appeared in the *Journal of the Academy of Marketing Science, Journal of Business Research, Journal of Public Policy and Marketing, Journal of Personal Selling and Sales Management, Journal of Service Research,* and *Journal of Business Ethics,* among other journals; various national and regional proceedings; and books including *The Oxford Handbook of Strategic Sales and Sales Management, Marketing Communications Classics*, and *Environmental Marketing.* He has received both teaching and research awards, the James Comer Award for best contribution to selling and sales management theory awarded by the *Journal of Personal Selling and Sales Management*, and three "Outstanding Paper" awards at the National Conference in Sales Management, among others. He is a member of six editorial review boards and one journal advisory board and has won five awards for outstanding reviewer. He is a coauthor of *Sales Management: Analysis and Decision Making,* 8th ed. (M.E. Sharpe, 2012) and *SELL,* 3d ed. (South-Western Cengage Learning, 2012).

Norbert K. Semmer (PhD) is a professor of the psychology of work and organizations at the University of Bern, Switzerland. He studied psychology in Regensburg (Germany), Groningen (the Netherlands), and Berlin (Germany), and he received his PhD from the Technical University of Berlin in 1983. His major areas of interest refer to (1) stress at work and its implications for health and productivity, (2) efficiency in work behavior: its characteristics and its training, and (3) human error and its implications for quality and safety. He and his coworkers have recently developed a concept that focuses on "Stress as Offense to Self"; he studies the implications of this approach in terms of, for instance, illegitimate tasks, illegitimate stressors, success and failure, and appreciation at work. He is also involved in studies on the performance of medical teams and its relationship to leadership, team coordination, and stress. He is involved in teaching at the university, doing research, and teaching/consulting outside of the university.

Paul E. Spector is a distinguished university professor of industrial/organizational (I/O) psychology and I/O doctoral program director at the University of South Florida. He is also director of the NIOSH-funded Sunshine Education and Research Center's Occupational Health Psychology doctoral program. He is the associate editor for "Point/Counterpoint" for the *Journal of Organizational Behavior* and associate editor for *Work and Stress*, and is on the editorial boards of *Journal of Applied Psychology* and *Human Resources Management Review*. His main research interests are in occupational health psychology, including injuries, stress and workplace violence, and research methodology. His work has appeared often in many of the field's journals, including *Journal of Applied Psychology, Journal of Occupational Health Psychology, Journal of Organizational Behavior, Journal of Occupational and Organizational Psychology, Journal of Vocational Behavior, Organizational Research Methods, Personnel Psychology,* and *Work and Stress.*

Noreen Tehrani (PhD) is a chartered occupational, counseling, coaching, and health psychologist. She formed her own company in 1997 to assist organizations and employees in maximizing their effectiveness and efficiency through the identification of blocks to achievement and developing support tailored to the needs of the organization and the individual. She has a special interest in working with organizations to reduce the incidence of workplace conflict and bullying. Her work has involved dealing with the causes and impact of bullying behaviors on individual workers. She has developed counseling and behavioral modification programs to address the causes and the effects of bullying. She is internationally recognized for her work and has presented papers at conferences in Europe, the United States, and Australia, and has published a number of books and guides on workplace bullying and organizational culture, including editing *Workplace Bullying: Symptoms and Solutions* (2012); *Building a Culture of Respect: Managing Bullying at Work* (2001); and *Building a Culture of Respect: Managing Bullying at Work* (2001).

William H. Turnley is professor of organizational behavior and human resource management, the Sam and Karen Forrer Chair of Business Ethics, and the director of the ConocoPhillips Excellence in Business Ethics Initiative in the College of Business Administration, Kansas State University. He received his PhD from the University of South Carolina. His research interests include psychological contracts, organizational citizenship behavior, impression management, and business ethics. His research has appeared in journals such as the *Academy of Management Review, Journal of Applied Psychology, Journal of Management,* and *Journal of Organizational Behavior.* He has served on the editorial boards of *Organizational Behavior and Human Decision Processes, Journal of Management, Journal of Organizational Behavior,* and *Human Relations.*

Ryan M. Vogel is visiting assistant professor of management and organizations in the Edwin L. Cox School of Business at Southern Methodist University. He received his PhD in organizational behavior from the University of Georgia. His research focuses on person–environment fit and supervisor–subordinate relationships, with an emphasis on dynamism and change. His work has appeared in several edited volumes and in the *Journal of Vocational Behavior.* He serves as an ad hoc reviewer for several journals, including the *Academy of Management Review.*

Anastasia S. Vogt Yuan is associate professor of sociology at Virginia Polytechnic Institute and State University. She received her BA in sociology from Grinnell College, her MA in sociology from the University of Iowa, and her PhD in sociology from The Ohio State University. Her research focuses on health and well-being across the life course and social inequalities and health and well-being, including the influence of age discrimination, racism, and sexism upon health and well-being. She has published articles in *Social Forces, Advances in Life Course Research, Journal of Youth and Adolescence, Journal of Family Issues, Sex Roles*, and *Sociological Spectrum*.

Craig A. Wendorf is professor and chair of the Department of Psychology at the University of Wisconsin–Stevens Point. He received his PhD in social psychology from Wayne State University. He is primarily interested in issues of justice, fairness, and morality in various contexts, including workplace, classroom, and social settings. He is also interested in the application of statistical methods to cross-cultural and hierarchical data sets.